ıge

Calor

Weight Control Tips

Eat Sensibly

- Avoid fad diets. Eat 3 sensible meals daily.
- Limit fats and fatty foods, sugar, soda and alcohol.

(Sample Diet Plan, Page 11)

Exercise Daily

- Get active and exercise every day!
- Include muscle-strengthening exercises. You'll lose more fat and keep it off. You'll also feel and look better, and you can eat a little more food. *(Exercise Guide, Page 12)*

Reshape Eating Behaviors

- Be aware of eating and shopping behaviors that lead to overeating.
- Also focus on social and emotional situations that make you snack compulsively.

(Extra notes - Page 14)

Keep a Food & Exercise Diary

- A diary helps you see exactly what you eat and drink, and how much you really exercise.
- An excellent motivator.
- Keeps you honest! *(Page 15)*

Arrange Moral Support

Gain the support of family and friends. Get extra professional help if required, from your doctor, dietitian, psychologist, exercise trainer, or slimming group. Beware of family saboteurs who discourage you from adopting a healthier lifestyle!

DOCTOR CHECK-UP

Ask your doctor to check you for high blood pressure, diabetes, and high blood cholesterol.

HEALTHY WEIGHTS for Men & Women (Over 18 years)

Based on weights with least risk of disease or death from heart disease, diabetes, stroke and cancer.

Based on Body Mass Index - range 20-25.

BMI calculated as: $\frac{\text{Weight (kg)}}{\text{Height (m)}^2}$

Height (No Shoes) Ft Ins	Healthy Weight Range Pounds
4'7"	86-108
4'8"	88-110
4'9"	92-114
4'10"	97-121
4'11"	99-123
5'0"	101-127
5'1"	105-132
5'2"	110-136
5'3"	112-140
5'4"	114-145
5'5"	119-149
5'6"	123-156
5'7"	127-158
5'8"	129-162
5'9"	134-167
5'10"	138-173
5'11"	143-178
6'0"	145-182
6'1"	149-187
6"2"	156-193
6'3"	158-198
6'4"	162-202
6'5'	170-211
6'6"	172-215
6'7"	175-220

Body Fat Distribution & Health

Fat above the hips carries a far greater health risk than fat on or below the hips - better to be a '**pear-shape**' than an '**apple-shape**'.

Abdominal obesity greatly increases the risk of developing diabetes, heart disease, high blood fats, hypertension, stroke and some cancers. So-called '**cellulite**' carries no extra health risk.

Waist Measurement (High Health Risk)

Men: Over 39 inches **Women:** Over 34 inches

Women who become obsessed with dieting away their thighs and buttocks on an otherwise lean body, are fighting mother nature and may well be inviting health problems.

If you are within a healthy weight range, it is better to exercise regularly to maintain body shape, rather than to be constantly dieting and lacking in energy. Accept your body shape and focus on other pursuits and enjoying life!

Abdominal obesity greatly increases the risk of ill-health and earlier death.

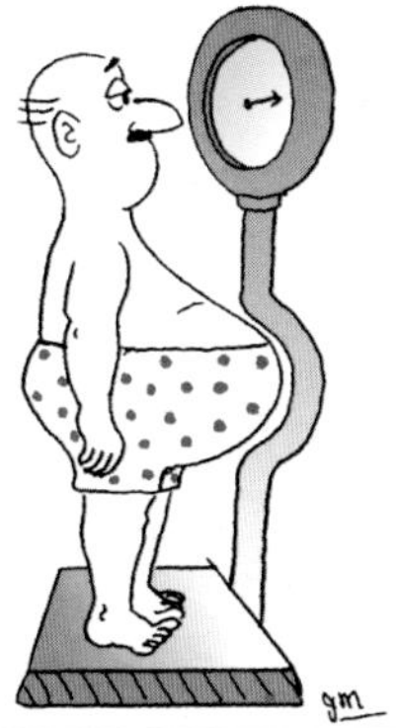

Estimating Body Fat Percentage

Body fat percentage is a better indicator of health than total weight.

Bioelectric impedance analysis (BIA) is gaining support as a practical and economical method for estimating body fat in both clinical and home settings.

BIA measures the resistance of a weak electrical current that is passed through the body. A computer within the body fat analyzer calculates the amount of body water, fat and muscle.

More Information: www.calorieking.com

HEALTHY BODY FAT RANGES

Men:	Under 30 years	~	14 - 20%
	Over 30 years	~	17 - 23%
Women:	Under 30 years	~	17 - 24%
	Over 30 years	~	20 - 27%

Note: Less than 13% body fat in women can be unhealthy.

BODY FAT & OBESITY

Men:	Above 25% body fat
Women:	Above 32% body fat

TANITA

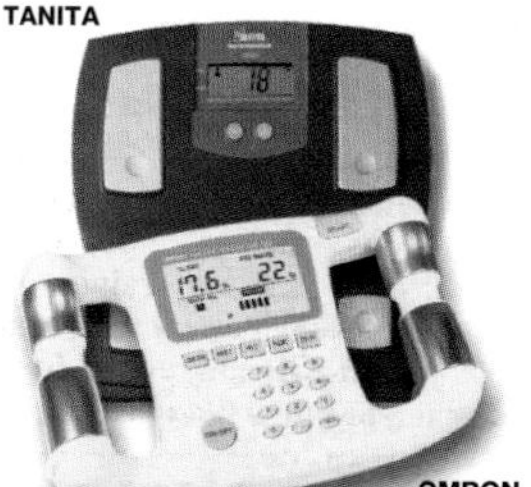

OMRON
Body Logic Pro

Examples of easy-to-use body fat monitors for home and professional use.

Scales do not distinguish between fat, muscle and fluids.

Body Fluid Changes

Body weight fluctuates from day to day. This is mainly due to changes in body fluids which make up around 70% of total body weight. It can be affected by changes in hormone levels, dietary factors such as salt and carbohydrate, and even exercise.

Weight change over several weeks is more likely to reflect changes in levels of fat and muscle rather than fluid. Unfortunately, the scales do not distinguish between weight changes due to water, fat or muscle. This is why **we shouldn't allow every fluctuation in weight to rule our lives.**

To limit fluid retention, avoid salty foods and go easy on the salt shaker. Eating sufficient fruit and vegetables supplies extra potassium which counteracts sodium and encourages fluid loss. However, **do not limit water intake.** Be sure to drink at least 6-8 glasses of water and other fluids per day.

When dining out, be aware that the extra pound or two that might show on the scales the next morning is not the result of a small dietary indiscretion. It is more likely due to fluid retention resulting from more highly seasoned and salty food.

Monthly hormonal changes in women can also account for a build-up of fluids of several pounds prior to menstruation.

Menopausal Weight Gains

Most women gain an average of 4-5 pounds in the years leading up to the menopause - usually in their middle to late 40's. This can occur even when exercise and eating habits have not changed significantly.

With hormonal changes occurring at that time, body fat also tends to be redistributed from thighs, buttocks and hips to the breast and stomach areas (a greater health risk).

Be sure to eat wisely and continue daily physical activity including strength-training to maintain or build muscles - and to boost metabolism and self-esteem.

Underactive Thyroid

Thyroid hormone is secreted into the bloodstream by the thyroid gland in the neck. When insufficient thyroid hormone is made, metabolism and body processes slow down and weight gain can occur.

Symptoms of hypothyroidism can be subtle and easily overlooked as signs of normal aging. **Early symptoms** may include fatigue, muscle weakness, sluggishness, a swollen tongue that you keep biting, and a puffy face.

As metabolism continues to slow, **further signs can include** chronically cold hands and feet, slow reflexes, constipation, dry skin and coarse hair, brittle nails, heavy menstrual periods, slower pulse, and a husky voice.

Depression-like symptoms may also develop such as forgetfulness, loss of interest, mood swings and irritability.

Weight gains of as much as 10-20 pounds (mainly fluid) can occur, as well as a **raised blood cholesterol level.**

The condition is more common in women, especially following pregnancy, around menopause, or after age 60.

A simple blood test through your doctor can detect hypothyroidism. It is easily treated in most cases with thyroid hormone pills.

Adults 35 and older should have a TSH (thyroid stimulating hormone) test every 5 years. Testing when pregnant is also wise.

Calories in Food

Calories in food are derived from protein, fat and carbohydrate. Alcohol also provides calories. Vitamins, minerals and water provide no calories.

Calorie Values Per Gram

Fat/Oil	~	9 Calories
Carbohydrate	~	4 Calories
Protein	~	4 Calories
Alcohol	~	7 Calories

Note that fats have over double the calories of protein and carbohydrate. The higher the fat content of food, the higher the calories.

Sample Calculation

QUARTER POUNDER® WITH CHEESE has 534 calories derived from:

30g Fat (x 9 cals/gram)	= 270
38g Carbohyd.(x 4 cals/gram)	= 152
28g Protein (x 4 cals/gram)	= 112
Total Calories	= 534

Calorie Levels for Weight Loss

Commence with a calorie-controlled diet that allows a moderate weight loss of 1/2 - 1 pound per week. Weight loss is usually much larger in the first few weeks due to extra fluid losses.

Note: It is better to increase exercise rather than lessen food calories too drastically.

Suggested Calories for Weight Loss

Women:	Non-active	1000 - 1200
	Active	1200 - 1500
Men:	Non-active	1200 - 1500
	Active	1500 - 1800
Teenagers:		1200 - 1800

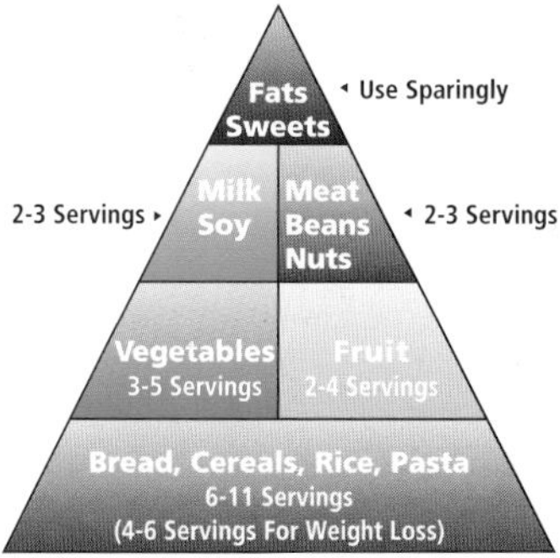

The Food Guide Pyramid emphasizes eating a wide variety of foods from the 5 major food groups. For weight loss, make lowfat choices and eat the lower number of servings.

Examples of Serving Size

Bread & Cereal Group:
- 1 slice bread
- 1/2 bun, bagel or English muffin
- 4 small crackers or 1 tortilla
- 1 oz ready-to-eat cereal
- 1/2 cup cooked cereal, rice, pasta

Fruit Group:
- 1 medium apple, orange, banana
- 1/2 cup canned fruit
- 1/4 cup dried fruit
- 3/4 cup fruit juice
- 1/4 medium avocado

Vegetable Group:
- 1 cup raw leafy vegetables
- 1 1/2 oz raw chopped vegetables
- 1/2 cup cooked vegetables
- 1/2 - 3/4 cup vegetable juice

Meat & Alternatives Group:
- 2-3oz (cooked) lean meat/poultry/fish
- 2 eggs **or** 7oz tofu **or** 1/2 cup nuts
- 1 cup (cooked) dried beans or chickpeas
- 4 Tbsp peanut butter

Milk & Alternatives Group:
- 1 cup (8 fl.oz) milk, soy drink, yogurt
- 1 1/2 oz cheese or 1/2 cup cottage cheese

Recommended Fat Intake

Americans consume too much fat with many having over 40% of total calories from fat - either as fat or oil, or as fat in foods and drinks. A range of 20-30% is healthier.

Fat Intake - Healthy Ranges	
Children	30-60g
Teenagers (Active)	40-80g
Women	30-60g
Men: Active	40-80g
Heavy Activity/Athlete	80-120g

The chart below recommends maximum fat intake for different calorie levels.

MAXIMUM DESIRABLE FAT INTAKE (Daily)

Calories	Fat	% Fat Cals
1200 cals	30g fat	23%
1500 cals	40g fat	24%
1800 cals	50g fat	25%
2000 cals	60g fat	27%
2200 cals	70g fat	28%
2500 cals	80g fat	29%
2800 cals	90g fat	29%
3000 cals	100g fat	30%
3500 cals	117g fat	30%
4000 cals	135g fat	30%

Infants Fat Intake

Infants and toddlers under 3 years should not be restricted in their fat intake because much larger volumes of food would be required to guarantee adequate calorie intake and growth. Whole milk should be used rather than light milk(1%) or nonfat milk.

Similarly, a high fiber diet is also not suitable for infants.

Calories Versus Fats

For successful weight control it is important to be aware of both fats and calories in foods. It widens your choices at the supermarket and when eating out.

While choosing more lowfat foods is wise, it does not guarantee that total calories will be reduced, particularly if portion size is not limited.

It is a mistake to think that eating lowfat or fat-free foods allows you to eat double the quantity.

Be aware that lowfat and fat-free cakes, cookies and ice cream are **not calorie-free.** Nor are soda drinks, fruit juices, beer, alcoholic spirits, sugar and sugar candy which are also fat-free. Bread, rice and pasta also have negligble fat.

Carbohydrate Calories Count

It is also a fallacy that carbohydrate calories don't count. Carbohydrates in excess of body needs can still be converted to and stored as body fat - particularly in women in their child-bearing years.

Total Calories Count!

Ultimately, **it is food portion size and total calories that count** whether from fat, carbohydrate or protein. Remember, cows get fat on grass!

FOOD LABEL MEANINGS

FDA Nutrition Claim Definitions

(All are on a Per Serving Basis.)

Low Calorie: 40 calories or less
Light or Lite: One third fewer calories or, 50% or less fat than regular product
Fat-Free: Less than half a gram of fat
Low-Fat: 3 grams or less of fat
Reduced-Fat: 25% less fat than regular product
Fewer or Less Calories: At least 25% fewer calories than regular product

Percent Fat Calories

(Percentage of Calories from Fat)

While health authorities recommend that not more than 30% of our total food calories should come from fat, it is not implied nor even recommended that you eat only those foods with less than 30% calories from fat.

Our normal diet is made up of foods that are either well above or below 30%. Only on average should the total diet be less than 30% calories from fat.

Some higher fat foods such as avocados, nuts and seeds, are highly nutritious and favor lower blood cholesterol levels. **Moderation is the aim . . . not elimination.**

Nevertheless, knowing the percentage of calories from fat can be useful in spotting high-fat foods and drinks.

FORMULA FOR CALCULATING PERCENTAGE CALORIES FROM FAT

$$\frac{\text{Grams of Fat/Serve x 9}}{\text{Total Calories/Serve}} \times \frac{100}{1}$$

EXAMPLE:

Mars Bar (11g fat, 240 cals)

Percentage Calories from Fat

$$= \frac{11 \times 9}{265} \times \frac{100}{1} = 37\%$$

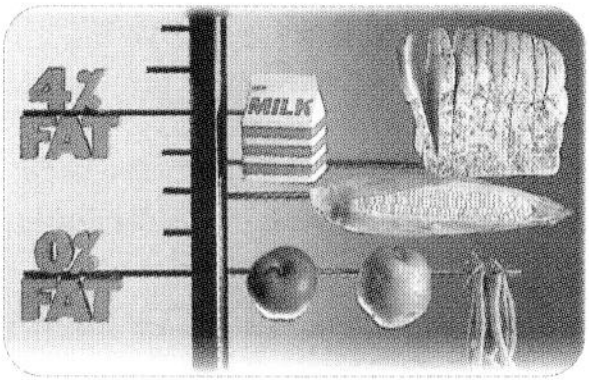

Fat Percentage Content

(Percentage of Fat in Food)

Don't be fooled by promotion of foods claiming to have a low percentage of fat. It's **serving size and total grams of fat that count.**

For example, whole milk with 3.5% fat sounds low (3.5g fat/100ml) but an 8fl.oz cup contains 8g fat (and 2 cups contain 16g fat).

Icecream with 10% fat seems high, yet a large scoop (3fl.oz) has only 5g fat. (Low-fat icecream has less than 2g fat/serve.)

❖ ❖ ❖

Also note that the percentage of fat in a food is not the same as the percentage of calories derived from fat.

Foods with a low percentage of fat can still have a high percentage of calories derived from fat - as shown below.

For example, around 50% of total calories in whole milk comes from fat - yet whole milk has less than 4% fat. Low fat/light milk with less than 1% fat has only 18% of total calories from fat - a much better choice.

FAT CONTENT & PERCENTAGES OF MILK

	Whole Milk	Reduced Fat	Low-Fat (light)	Non-Fat Skim
Percentage Fat ►	3.5%	2%	1%	0%
Fat (Grams) in 8 fl.oz Cup ►	8g	5g	2g	0g
Calories ►	150	120	100	95
Percent Calories From Fat ►	48%	38%	18%	0%

Hints to Reduce Fat

Meats & Poultry

- **Choose lean cuts** of meat with little marbling. Choose the white meat of chicken and turkey, and extra lean ground beef.
- **Trim all visible fat** from meat and remove the skin from poultry. Removal of fat after cooking is okay (to prevent dryness).
- **Eat modest portions** (3-4 oz cooked weight) of meat, poultry or fish. **Add extra** beans, lentils, tofu, tempeh, vegetables, potatoes, rice, pasta, bread, or tortillas.
- **Avoid high-fat meat products** such as salami, bacon, sausage and franks. Choose lowfat and fat-free brands. Choose lean luncheon meats (90% or more fat-free).
- **Broil or bake. Avoid frying.** Allow casseroles to cool and skim off surface fat.

Fish & Seafood

- **Choose fresh or frozen fillets**, and canned fish (in water pack).
- **Avoid fried fish**, frozen fish in batter, canned fish in oil.

Fats & Oils

- **Use minimal amounts** of all types of fat and oil. All are high in calories.
- **Choose** 'light' and 'reduced fat' spreads but still use sparingly. Check the Fats and Spreads section of this book for lower fat brands.
- Use minimal amounts of oil when stir-frying. Use no-stick sprays like *Pam*.

Salad Dressings & Sauces

- **Avoid regular mayonnaise and oil dressings.** Choose 'light', 'reduced fat' or 'fat-free' brands (Check salad dressings section of this book).
- **Choose** lowfat or fat-free sauces. Most tomato-based pasta sauces are low fat but avoid 'pesto', 'alfredo', cheese and 'creamy' sauces.

Milk, Dairy, Soy Drinks

- **Choose** lowfat or skim milks and yogurts. **Avoid** full-cream milk, cream, *Half & Half* coffee creamers.
- **Soy Drinks:** Choose lowfat brands.
- **Cheese:** Choose fat-free, lowfat and fat-reduced (e.g. cottage, part-skim ricotta). Cheese substitutes can still be high in fat.
- **Icecream:** Choose lowfat and fat-free brands, frozen yogurt, sorbet, sherbet and ices. Limit regular icecream to a small serving. Avoid rich high-fat icecreams.

Frozen Meals & Entrees

- **Choose low fat varieties** such as *Lean Cuisine, Healthy Choice* and *Weight Watchers.* Add extra vegetables.

Soups

- **Choose low fat brands.** Avoid high-fat ramen noodle blocks/soup.

FRYING ADDS FAT

The greater the surface area of potato exposed to fat or oil, the higher the fat content.

Whole Potato (3 oz)
Nil Fat, 65 Cals

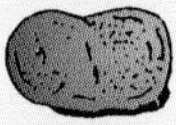

Roast Potato (3 oz)
5g Fat, 155 Cals

Fries (Large, 3 oz)
12g Fat, 220 Cals

Fries (Small, 3 oz)
15g Fat, 265 Cals

Potato Chips (3 oz)
30g Fat, 450 Cals

Bread, Bagels, Crackers

- **All breads are suitable** as well as pita, bagels, English muffins and rice cakes. Avoid croissants, sweet rolls, danish pastry and doughnuts. **Avoid** fat-soaked toast and garlic bread.
- **Choose lowfat crackers** such as graham, saltines, matzo, bread sticks, crispbreads. **Avoid** regular cheese or butter crackers.

Cereals, Pasta, Noodles, Rice

- **Most cold and hot cereals** are low in fat and nil in cholesterol. Avoid granola made with hydrogenated oils.
- **Choose** plain pasta or rice. Avoid dishes made with cream, butter or cheese sauces. **Avoid** high-fat ramen noodle blocks/soups.

Fruits & Vegetables

- **Choose all types.** (Note: Avocados contain no cholesterol. Their fat and fiber can help lower blood cholesterol.) Use mashed avocado on bread in place of fat.
- **Choose** dried beans, lentils, chick peas, baked beans.
- **Avoid** french-fried potatoes and regular potato salad. Avoid vegetables made in butter, cream or sauce.
- **Avoid** deli-style salads made with high fat dressings. Choose low-fat brands. Use low fat and fat-free salad dressings.

Snacks, Cookies, Candy

- **Avoid** high-fat snacks such as potato chips, corn/tortilla chips, cheesy balls, buttered popcorn, chocolate and carob bars.
- **Choose** fat-free potato chips andtortilla chips made with *olestra* (such as *Wow!* brand) but still limit quantity.
- **Choose** plain popcorn, lowfat cookies and muffins, hard candy, jelly beans, fruit rolls and frozen fruit bars and popsicles.
- **Choose** fresh and dried fruits, vegetables. Limit nuts and seeds if overweight.

Desserts/Sweets

- **Avoid high-fat desserts**, such as fruit pies, pastries, cheesecake, cheese board.
- **Choose** fresh fruits, fresh fruit salad, low fat custard and low fat yogurt. Use yogurt in place of cream or ice cream.
- **Avoid** regular icecream. *Choose* low fat brands but still limit quantity.
- **Choose** sugar-free gelatin desserts such as *Jell-O* (sugar-free package).

Fast-Foods & Take-Out

(Check the Fast-Foods Section of this book for actual fat counts and wise selections.)

- **Delis:** Choose sandwiches/bread rolls, pitas with lowfat fillings and plain salad. Limit meat/cheese to small portions. Request half quantities.
- **Avoid high-fat deli salads.** Choose plain salads and add your own lowfat dressing. Eat more fruit.
- **Chicken & Fish:** Avoid deep-fried chicken or fish, BBQ chicken with fat or skin, chicken nuggets. Choose broiled or baked chicken breast without fat or skin.
- **Hamburgers:** Choose medium size, lower fat burgers. Avoid bacon. Have a side salad (without dressing).
- **Pizzas:** Avoid sausage/pepperoni. Choose vegetarian topping and modest quantity of cheese. Eat a moderate serving. Eat extra salad and fruit.
- **Desserts:** Avoid apple pie, danish, choc chip cookies. Choose low fat muffins (e.g. *McDonald's*), fresh fruit or fruit salad.
- **Avoid regular shakes and sundaes.** Choose lowfat milk, lower fat shakes (such as *McDonald's*), and orange juice, but choose smaller sizes.

Hints to Reduce Sugar

• While reducing the amount of fat is an important dietary focus for weight control, sugar intake also needs to be watched.

• Many overweight, inactive persons consume over 500 calories of refined sugars per day (equivalent to over 30 level teaspoons) - a significant amount in weight control terms. Halving this amount would be reasonable and worthwhile.

Note: Naturally occurring sugars in fruits, vegetables and milk are fine when consumed in normal recommended amounts.

• Most sugar in our diet is 'hidden' in processed foods such as soft drinks, fruit drinks, candy, cookies, cake, jam, sauces, icecream, desserts, canned foods, and breakfast cereals.

Certainly enjoy moderate quantities of these foods, but for serious weight control, look for 'low calorie', 'diet' or sugar-free alternatives. Be careful not to substitute sugar-rich foods with high-fat foods which might boost calories even more!

• Sweeteners such as *Equal, NutraSweet, Sweet'n Low* and *Stevia* make it easy to cut back or eliminate sugar in drinks and recipes. (Most recipes can be adapted to contain less sugar with little effect on taste or quality.)

• The body can obtain sufficient sugar for its needs from carbohydrate-rich foods such as bread, rice, spaghetti and other pasta, potatoes, corn, fruit, vegetables, beans, nuts, seeds and lactose in milk.

These foods are also rich in other nutrients. Refined sugar is referred to as 'empty calorie' because it supplies calories but negligible nutrients and no fiber.

DIFFERENT FORMS OF SUGAR

Be aware that sugar comes in different forms. Check the label.

- Sugar
- Brown Sugar
- Dextrose
- Fructose
- Corn Syrup
- Honey
- Maple Syrup
- Sucrose
- Confectioners' Sugar
- Glucose
- Malt, Maltose
- High-Fructose Corn Syrup
- Molasses
- Turbinado Sugar

SUGAR CONTENT OF SOME COMMON FOODS

	Teaspoons of Sugar
Coca Cola or *Pepsi*, 12 oz	10
20 oz size	17
Iced tea, sweetened, 12 oz	8
Choc malted Milk, 12 oz	4.5
Honey Smacks Cereal, 1 oz	4
Popcorn, caramel, 1 cup	3.5
Chocolate Bar, 1.5 oz	6
M&M's, 1.7 oz pkg	7
Cake, sponge, jam-filled	8
Choc Chip Cookie, 1 oz	2
Donut, iced	6
Apple Pie, 1 piece	7
Jell-O, 1/2 cup	4.5
Jam, 1 Tbsp, 20g	2.5
Syrup, maple, 1 Tbsp	3

Reach for fresh fruit when you want to snack instead of candy or snack products rich in sugar and fat.

Sample Diet Plan - 1200 Calories

For Overweight Persons. Please Check With Your Doctor.
(Menu contains approximately 30-35 Grams Fat)

Breakfast (approx. 250 cal)

1 Small Fruit or 1/2 oz Dried Fruit

Plus Cereal: 1 1/2 oz Dry (high fiber)
or 1 cup cooked Oatmeal

Plus Milk (from daily allowance)

Milk Allowance (160 calories)

2 cups Skim Milk or 1 1/2 cups Low Fat Milk
or equivalent Soy Drink, Yoghurt, Cheese, Tofu

Fat Allowance (140 calories; 15g Fat)

4 tsp Fat or 6-8 tsp Diet Margarine or 3 tsp Oil
or 1 1/2 Tbsp Mayonnaise or 1/2 medium Avocado
or 1 1/2 Tbsp Peanut Butter or 30g Nuts/Seeds

Breakfast ~ Choice 2

1 Small Fruit

Plus 1 Toast (no added fat)
or 3/4 oz Cheese
or 2 oz Cottage Cheese
or 1/4 cup Baked Beans

Plus 1 Toast or 1/2 Muffin (English)

Lunch (approx. 440 calories)

2 slices Bread (2 oz) or 1 medium Roll or Bagel
or 4 Crispbreads/Crackers or 6" Pita

Plus 2 oz lean Meat, Chicken or Turkey
or 3 1/2 oz Tuna (in water) or 2 1/2 oz Salmon
or 1 oz Cheese or 3 oz Cottage Cheese
or 2 1/2 oz Ricotta Cheese
or 1/2 cup, 4 oz Fruit Yoghurt (lowfat)
or 1/2 cup (4 oz) Baked Beans or Bean Salad

Plus Large Salad (Oil-free dressing)
Plus 1 small Fruit or 1/2 oz Dried Fruit

Dinner (approx. 360 Calories)

Soup (fat-free)

Plus 3 oz lean Meat (cooked weight)
or 4 oz Chicken Breast (no skin)
or 3 oz Chicken Thigh/Leg (no skin)
or 5 oz Fish (grilled, no fat)
or 3/4 cup (6 oz) Beans (Soy, Baked, Haricot etc)/Lentils
or Low Fat Recipe Dish (e.g. Lean Cuisine)

Plus 1 small Potato or 1/2 cup Rice/Pasta or 1 slice Bread
Plus 2-3 servings Vegetables/Salad
Plus 1 small Fruit + Diet Gelatin Dessert

Between Meals: *Water, Coffee, Tea, Diet drinks, Fruit from main meals; Raw vegetable pieces, Milk from Allowance*

Note: Take a multivitamin/mineral supplement daily while dieting.

- Persons who exercise regularly **lose more weight** and keep it off longer than non-exercisers.
- Exercise also improves general health and well-being. **Mood, confidence and self-esteem** are enhanced by a sense of control and accomplishment.
- **Exercise increases the metabolic rate** of the body even for hours after exercise - a good way to 'wake up' a sluggish metabolism and burn extra fat.

  Exercise compensates for any decrease in metabolic rate with increasing age and also in some heavy smokers who stop smoking.
- **Strength training** further builds muscle and aids body reshaping. You can also eat more food!

Note: It is muscle which burns fat. Each extra pound of muscle burns an extra 100 calories daily ~ even while you sleep! Weight from exercised muscles is okay. It is surplus fat that is potentially harmful.

- **Avoid injury** by beginning with walking, low impact aerobics, or weight-supported exercise (e.g. swimming, cycling). Avoid competitive sports.
- How Much? Start with 10 - 20 minutes/day and progress to 30-45minutes/day - even if broken into 5-10 minute lots. It all adds up! **Aim to achieve 250-500 calories of exercise daily.**

  Also walk up stairs instead of using lifts. Take a brisk walk at lunch. Use an exercise bike, treadmill or stair machine while watching TV.
- How Often? While aerobic fitness requires only 3 - 4 sessions weekly, **weight control is a daily event which requires daily exercise.**

TV CAN BE FATTENING!

Many adults and children watch over 20 hours of television per week and indulge in high-fat snacks at the same time - potent contributors to obesity.

Are you a TV couch potato? Limit your TV hours and plan healthy physical activities. At least use an exercise bike or treadmill while watching TV!

Brisk walking each day is a safe and effective way to keep trim and fit. Try it - you'll like it!"

Strength-training with light weights helps to retain or rebuild muscle tissue and enhances weight control.

Middle-age spread has little to do with getting older. Too little exercise is the main culprit.

Daily exercise and sensible eating can minimize middle-age spread.

LIGHT
4 Calories/Minute

Walking, slow
Cycling, light
Gardening light
Golf, social
Tennis, doubles
Housework, cleaning
Callisthenics, Yoga
Ten Pin Bowls
Ping-pong, social
Ice Skating
Aquarobics
Skate Boarding
Line/Square Dancing

MODERATE
7 Calories/Minute

Walking, brisk
Cycling, moderate
Swimming, crawl
Weight-training, light
Tennis, singles
Racquetball, beginners
Aerobics, light
Football, Grid Iron
Basketball, Baseball
Walking Downstairs
Snow Skiing (downhill)
Shoveling snow
Dancing (vigorous)

HEAVY
10 Calories/Minute

Walking (power), Jogging
Cycling (vigorous), Spinning
Swimming, strenuous
Weight-training, heavy
Wrestling/Judo, advanced
Racquetball, advanced
Tae Bo, Kick Boxing
Football, training
Basketball (Pro)
Climbing Stairs, Skipping
Skiing (cross country)
Aquarobics, advanced
Dancing (strenuous)

Note: Only those sports or activities that are sustained over a period of time (e.g running) qualify for heavy exercise. Stop-start sports such as tennis are considered 'moderate'.

BE A GROOVY GRANNY!

You are never too old to start a fitness and strength-training program. See your local fitness center or personal trainer.

June McClean (87 y.o) is America's fittest granny - also known as the 'Groovy Granny'.

Check out her video: 'Low Impact Aerobics For Seniors'.

(Order Details ~ Page 287)

10,000 STEPS PER DAY

A pedometer can motivate you to be more active everyday.

It counts steps, miles and even calories used (some models). It clips to your belt or waist band.

Aim for 10,000 steps per day, instead of an average 3,000-4,000 steps.

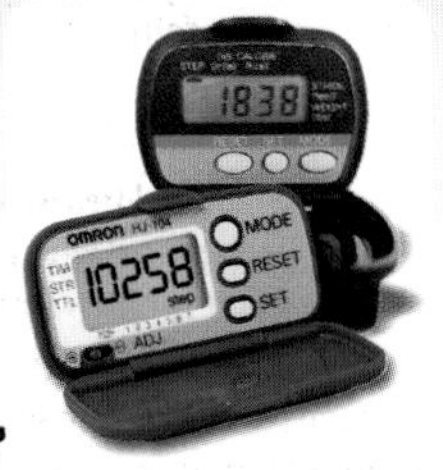

Reshape Eating Behaviors

- Eating is a behavior that is largely controlled by people with whom we live or socialize, places in which we carry out our lives, and our emotions. Become aware of those situations that commonly lead to extra food being eaten.
- We may also be unaware of 'bad' eating habits that can lead to excess calorie intake; e.g. eating quickly, large mouthsful, eating when tense or bored, finishing a large serving of food when not hungry.

Hints to help uncover and correct those 'bad' eating habits include:

- **Don't eat while engaged in other activities;** e.g. watching TV, reading. Eat only at the table, not at the fridge or while standing.
- **Don't eat quickly.** Chewing slowly allows time to register a feeling of fullness. Don't use fingers, only utensils. Cut food into smaller pieces. Don't load your fork until the previous mouthful is finished.
- **Don't purchase problem high calorie foods.** Shop from a set list to prevent impulse buying. Avoid shopping with children.
- **Buy snack foods** in the smallest package. The larger the serving size or package, the more you are likely to eat or drink.
- **Plan meals in advance. Stick to a set menu.**
- **Plan a strategy to avoid uncontrolled eating** and drinking at social events, or when your emotions urge you to binge.

  Rehearse repeatedly in your mind exactly what you will do in such situations. Remind yourself several times each day that you are in charge of your actions and that you can be strong-willed. Seek counseling or coaching on various strategies.
- **Promise yourself** that when you feel the urge to snack, you will engage in some activity that will distract you away from food (e.g. go for a walk, brush your teeth, phone a friend.)

  If you eat out of boredom, find some new hobby or interest that gets you out of the house. Even enrol in an adult education class.

Practise saying 'NO' politely but assertively.

Do you use food as an emotional crutch? If so, professional counseling may be helpful.

The food diary is the most powerful proven aid for dieters. Persons who keep a food and exercise diary not only lose more weight they also keep it off. Here are some of the reasons:

- Recording your eating and exercise habits jolts you into realizing just what you do eat and drink each day; and also whether you exercise sufficiently.
- **Helps you identify problem foods** and drinks with excessive calories and fat.
- **Helps identify moods,** situations and events that lead to excessive eating of unwanted calories. You can then plan to overcome or avoid them.
- **Prevents 'calorie amnesia'**, the forgetfulness that leads to rebound weight gain after successful weight loss. Recording puts you back on the right track.
- **Helps you develop greater self- discipline.** You will think twice about over indulging if you have to record it - especially if someone checks your diary regularly. It certainly keeps you honest!
- **Motivates you** to carefully plan your meals and to exercise each day.
- **Serves as a check system** for your doctor, dietitian or counselor to assess your progress and make recommendations.

"Keeping a diary gives me feedback on exactly what I eat each day. It helps prevent 'calorie amnesia' and reminds me to exercise each day. It's a must for successful weight control!"

SAMPLE RECORDING

		Calories: Food	Calories: Exercise	Fat Grams
Breakfast/Exercise	1 cup Bran Flakes	110		1
	1 Tbsp Wheat Germ	30		1
	1 Tbsp Sunflower Seeds	45		4
	1 small Banana, sliced	60		0
	¾ cup Milk (1% fat)	80		2
Snack/Exercise	Brisk Walk, 20 mins		140	
Lunch	2 slices Wholewheat Bread	150		2
	3 teasp Diet Margarine	40		4
	½ small Avocado	90		9
	2 Tbsp Ricotta Cheese	50		3
	1 medium Tomato	30		0
	Lettuce; Bean Sprouts	10		0
Snack/Exercise	Exercise Bike, 10 min		70	
	1 medium Apple	90		0
Dinner	Vegetable Soup (fat-free)	40		0
	Broiled Fish, 5 oz	160		2
	1 small Potato, 3 oz	60		0
	1 teasp Diet Margarine	20		2
	½ cup Broccoli	30		0
	½ cup Carrots	35		0
	1 medium Orange	80		0
Snack/Exercise	Diet Gelatin + Fruit Salad	50		0
	1 cup Popcorn	50		0
	Diet Drink	0		0
	CALORIE TOTALS	1290	210	30g
	NET CALORIES (Food Minus Exercise)	1080		
	TOTAL FAT (Grams) ►			
	FAT CALORIES (Fat x 9)			270
	PERCENTAGE FAT CALORIES (Divide Fat Calories by Total Food Calories) x 100			21%

WATER/FLUIDS (CUPS) Includes Juice/Milk/Soup ✓✓✓✓✓

Comments & Resolutions: 'A reasonable day - felt in control'

PAGE 4

Sample page from The Pocket Food & Exercise Diary, a 10-week diary to record food and exercise.

At day's end, exercise calories are deducted from food calories.

Includes Weekly Summary Page & Progress Checklist.

EXTRA DETAILS ~ SEE PAGE 288

What is Diabetes?

Diabetes is a disorder in which the body cannot make proper use of carbohydrates (sugar and starches).

- After digestion, sugar and starches are changed into **glucose** - the simplest form of sugar that is vital to body cells for energy and growth.
- **Insulin** is the hormone which acts like a key that opens the door to body cells and allows glucose to enter.
- **Without sufficient insulin**, unused glucose builds up in the blood and passes into the urine. This produces symptoms of frequent urination, continual thirst and tiredness.
- **Untreated diabetes** increases the risk of damage to nerves and blood vessels. This, in turn, increases the risk of heart disease, stroke, blindness, kidney damage, foot ulcers and gangrene, impotence and other complications.

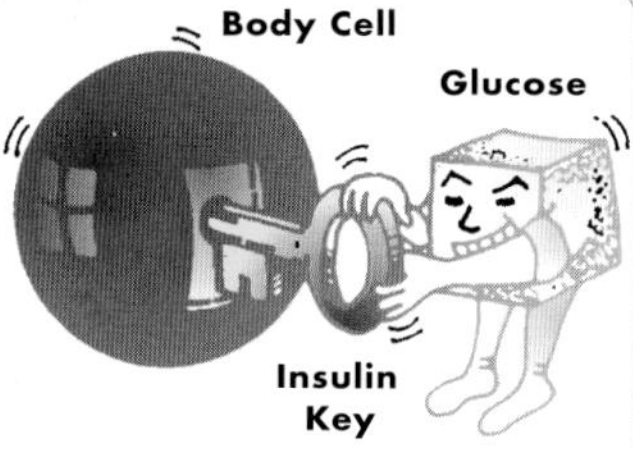

Insulin acts like a key.
It opens the door to body cells
and allows glucose to enter.

Some persons with diabetes (Type 1) have too few or no keys and require insulin injections.

Others (Type 2) have ample keys but 'mis-shapen' key holes (insulin resistant) - particularly if obese and inactive.

TYPE-1 DIABETES

Insulin-Dependent Diabetes

- Occurs in 10% of diabetes cases.
- Usually children and young adults.
- Pancreas gland produces little or no insulin. Daily insulin injections are necessary, plus:
- Regular meals with even carbohydrate distribution to match insulin dosage. Regular exercise and weight control are also important.

WARNING SIGNALS

- Frequent urination
- Continual thirst
- Rapid weight loss
- Unusual hunger
- Extreme weakness/fatigue
- Nausea, vomiting, irritability

TYPE-2 DIABETES

Non-Insulin Dependent

- Occurs in 90% of diabetes cases.
- Occurs mainly in adults - particularly in overweight and inactive persons.
- Insulin is produced but body cells resist its action and glucose cannot enter cells.
- Usually treated with diet and exercise. Sometimes requires medication (pills or insulin injections).

WARNING SIGNALS

- Any Type-1 symptom
- Blurred vision
- Excessive itching
- Skin infections with slow healing
- Tingling/numbness in feet

Importance of Weight Control

- **Type-2 diabetes** occurs 2-3 times more often in overweight persons - particularly if inactive.
- Such persons do not usually lack insulin. Rather, their insulin is less effective. As obesity develops, muscle and other body cells may resist insulin in varying degrees. The resultant build-up of blood glucose may lead to diabetic symptoms.
- **Weight loss alone** often corrects this condition in Type-2 diabetes. If overweight, try a moderate diet of 1200-1500 calories **plus daily exercise.**

  Within several weeks, body cells can lose their resistance and become sensitive once again to the effects of insulin. Insulin and blood glucose levels may normalise, and symptoms may disappear.

  Further, the need for oral antidiabetic drugs might be prevented or much lessened in dosage. **So, give diet and exercise a fair go** - and maintain them to keep symptoms under control.

Modest weight loss and daily exercise can greatly improve control of Type-2 diabetes.

Get Moving! Everyday, do at least 30 minutes of moderate intensity exercise. It's the key to improving insulin sensitivity.

Add strength-training 3-4 times a week to double the benefits.

Managing Diabetes

Don't battle diabetes alone. Establish a partnership with your doctor, dietitian, nurse educator and pharmacist. For extra support, contact the *American Diabetes Association* 1-800-342-2383.

Hints to keep blood glucose within safe limits:

- **Control your diet.** Know what and when you will eat. Seek referral to a dietitian for expert advice.
- **Exercise regularly.** It assists weight control and can improve sensitivity of body cells to insulin. Plan exercise into your daily routine.
- **Monitor your blood glucose** at home and work - ideally with a portable blood glucose meter. It will help you become familiar with your blood glucose patterns, and the effects of diet, exercise and medication. **Insulin pumps** can also help control blood glucose levels around the clock.
- **Don't skip prescribed insulin or oral medication.** If on insulin, know what action to take if hypoglycaemia (low blood glucose) occurs. Also educate family and friends.

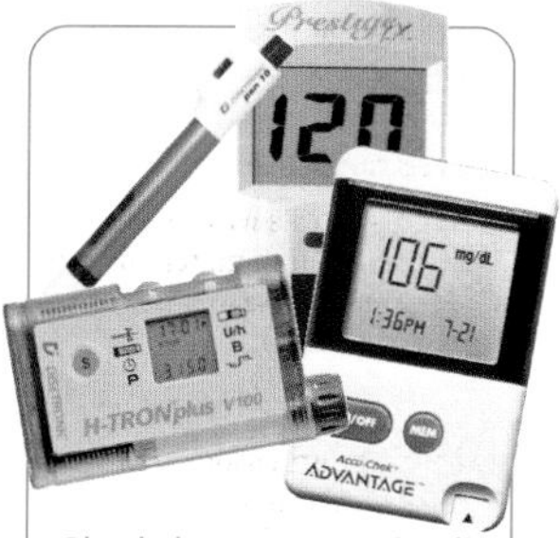

Blood glucose meters, insulin pumps and pens can greatly improve control of diabetes and lifestyle choices.

Diabetes ~ Diet Hints

Guidelines for choosing a healthy diet apply equally to persons with or without diabetes. Eating a wide variety of foods with the emphasis on low-fat, high fiber and low in refined sugars, is recommended.

However, actual food quantities, as well as when you eat, will also influence control of blood glucose. Your dietitian will individualize a diet plan to suit your food preferences, lifestyle and medical status. Here are a few hints:

- **Maintain a healthy weight.** If overweight, even a modest weight loss plus daily exercise can help to normalise blood glucose in Type-2 diabetes.
- **Don't skip meals.** If you take insulin or an oral hypoglycemic agent, regular meals are important.
- **If on insulin**, eat meals at the same time each day. Eat a similar amount of food at each meal. An even distribution of carbohydrate over the day will make best use of the available insulin and prevent wide fluctuations in blood glucose levels. Leave an interval of about 30 minutes between insulin injection and breakfast.
- **Avoid sugars and foods high in added sugar** particularly if overweight. Small amounts of sugar as part of a meal may occasionally be okay. Check with your dietitian. Use *Equal, Splenda* and *NutraSweet*-sweetened foods and drinks.
- **Choose wholegrain breads, cereals and pasta.** Eat fresh fruits, vegetables and legumes. These foods contain more fiber and slow the release of glucose into your blood after a meal.
- **Limit foods high in saturated fat and cholesterol.** Enjoy fish, soy foods, and other foods rich in omega-3 fats. *(See Fats & Cholesterol Guide, Pages 246-252)*
- **Foods (and supplements) rich in antioxidant vitamins C, E and beta-carotene**, as well as omega-3 fats, magnesium, zinc and chromium may help prevent long-term complications of diabetes (such as damage to small blood vessels and nerves). Be sure to check with your doctor.

Eat a well-balanced diet, high in fiber-containing foods and low in fat.

NEW BLOOD SUGAR LEVEL FOR DIAGNOSING DIABETES
(Adopted by American Diabetes Assoc.)

Blood Sugar Levels
Previously: 140 mg/dL
New: 126 mg/dL

Everyone 45 and older should have a blood test every 3 years.

Excess Alcohol contributes to obesity, diabetes, and high blood pressure.

The risk of hypoglycemia (low blood sugar) and drug interactions with alcohol is also increased.

- **Carbohydrate foods** in their more natural forms are an important part of a healthy diet. They provide energy, fiber, vitamins, minerals, protein and water.

  Carbohydrates are found mainly in cereal grains, fruit, vegetables and milk. Animal flesh foods contain negligible amounts.

  A healthy diet of at least 2000 calories is based around carbohydrate foods and should provide over 50% of total calories - whether or not we have diabetes. Lower calorie diets for weight control will have as little as 40% carbohydrate calories.

- **Carbohydrates include** sugars, starches and fibers. Sugars and starch provide energy to body cells. Even though fiber is not digested, it benefits the body - more so in diabetes. *(See Fiber Guide ~ Page 262)*

  The **various forms of carbohydrate** affect blood glucose levels in different ways; and it is difficult to predict the effect of particular foods, sugars or meals, simply by their actual carbohydrate content.

  Thus, the **same amount** of carbohydrate from different foods may affect blood sugar differently. It depends on many factors.

  For example, fiber can slow digestion and absorption of sugars by acting as a physical barrier or by forming a gel. Both fiber and fat also slow the emptying rate of the stomach into the intestines where further digestion and absorption takes place. The physical form of food (solid, puree, liquid) also matters - the more natural the better.

  Generally, raw foods rather than cooked foods, and whole-foods rather than ground-up foods, are more slowly absorbed.

- **Sugar: Small amounts** eaten as part of a meal, may not adversely affect blood glucose in persons with good blood glucose control. Nevertheless, minimal amounts of sugar are encouraged for nutritional and weight control reasons.

Glycemic Index

- Glycemic index (GI) indicates how fast a carbohydrate containing food is digested and how much it causes blood glucose to rise (glycemic response).

LOWER GLYCEMIC FOODS

Slower Acting Carbohydrates

These foods are more slowly digested and absorbed. They help maintain more even blood glucose levels. Use these foods regularly. Examples:

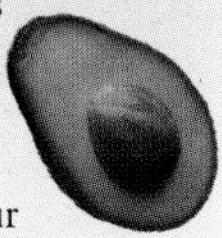

- Dried beans, peas, lentils
- Nuts and seeds
- Wholegrain breads, pita
- Bran cereals, oats
- Barley, buckwheat, bulgur
- Spaghetti, pasta, Basmati Rice
- Fresh fruit: apples, avocados, bananas (firm), cherries, grapefruit, grapes, olives, oranges, peaches, pears, plums
- Vegetables: sweet corn, yam
- Milk, yogurt, soy drinks

HIGHER GLYCEMIC FOODS

Quicker Acting Carbohydrates

These foods more rapidly raise blood glucose levels. Eat in moderation.

- White bread, rice cakes, bagels, croissants, doughnuts
- Low fiber cereals: Cornflakes, *Rice Krispies, Froot Loops*
- White potato, white rice
- Watermelon, ripe bananas, cantaloupe, pineapple
- Glucose drinks and candy

(See Carbohydrate Distribution next page)

- **For people with diabetes,** regular meals with even distribution of carbohydrate over the day are important for good control of blood sugar levels.
- **Smaller amounts of food** eaten more frequently result in steadier, more even blood glucose levels. (Be sure to control your weight.)

Recommended daily eating patterns for good blood glucose control:

1. **Three Meals & Three Snacks ~**
 Best for persons on insulin (Type-1 diabetes) with normal blood glucose variations.
2. **Three Meals ~**
 Best for Type-2 diabetes (especially if overweight).

Note: If blood sugar levels show excessive variations see doctor and dietitian.

- **Your doctor or dietitian** will select the level of calories and carbohydrate most appropriate to your weight, medication and activity. (Regular blood glucose checks will provide feedback on the level of control.)
- **Amounts of carbohydrate** in the guide below provide an average of 50% of total calories. A **rough rule of thumb is:** 13 grams of carbohydrate per 100 calories.

At calorie levels above 2000, carbohydrates approach 50-60% of total calories.

At lower calorie levels used for weight loss (1200-1500 calories), carbohydrates account for as little as 40% of total calories. This is because protein has nutritional priority.

These carbohydrate quantities (and percentages) apply equally to persons with or without diabetes.

IDEAL CARBOHYDRATE DISTRIBUTION
For Type-1 Diabetes (Insulin Dependent)
3 MEALS & 3 SNACKS
Balanced Blood Sugar Levels

GUIDE TO CARBOHYDRATE DISTRIBUTION

Daily Total Calories		Daily Total Carbohyd.	Percent Carbohyd. Cals	Each Main Meal (3)	Between Meals (3)
1200 Cals	~	120g	40%	30g	10g
1500 Cals	~	170g	45%	40g	15g
2000 Cals	~	250g	50%	60g	25g
2500 Cals	~	345g	55%	70g	45g
3000 Cals	~	450g	60%	90g	60g

Notes, Abbreviations, Measures

- Calorie and fat values have been rounded off.
  Calories - to the nearest 5 or 10 calories.
  Fat - to the nearest half gram.
  Note: Trace amounts of fat (less than 0.3 grams per serving) have been treated as zero.
- Because manufacturer's figures on labels are rounded off, figures in this book may differ slightly from the label. Serving sizes may also vary.
- Food product formulations change from time to time, and hence the need to regularly update this type of publication. Many products also come and go. Check the food label for any changes.
- **Seek Professional Advice:** This book is intended for educational purposes only. It is not a substitute for professional advice.
- **Feedback Welcome:** Please contact the author directly with your queries, and suggestions for foods to be included in future editions. (Ideally, enclose the label with the manufacturer's details.)
  Write to: Allan Borushek,
  PO Box 1616, Costa Mesa CA 92628
- **Free Information Service:** Check the author's website for new food product updates.

www.calorieking.com

C ~ Calories
F ~ Fat (grams)
Cb ~ Carbohydrate (grams)

Abbreviations

tsp	=	teaspoon
Tbsp	=	Tablespoon
oz	=	ounce(s)
c	=	cup
fl.oz	=	fluid ounce(s)
g	=	gram(s)
<1	=	less than 1

Volume Measures

3 tsp	=	1 Tbsp
2 Tbsp	=	1 fl.oz
1/2 cup	=	4 fl.oz
1 cup	=	8 fl.oz or 16 Tbsp
2 cups	=	1 Pint
2 Pints	=	1 Quart

(All measures are level)

Note: 8 oz weight is not the same as 8 fl.oz volume (space occupied). Dense foods weigh more per set volume. Examples:
1 cup popcorn weighs 1/2 oz
1 cup milk weighs 8 1/2 oz
1 cup pudding weighs 10 oz

Metric Conversion

1/2 oz	=	14 grams
1 oz	=	28.4 grams
2 oz	=	57 grams
3 1/2 oz	=	100 grams
1 fl.oz	=	30 mls
1 cup (8 fl.oz)	=	240 mls
33 fl.oz	=	1 liter (volume)

SOURCES OF INFORMATION

- U.S. Dept. of Agriculture
- Food Manufacturers
- Food Industry Boards & Councils
- Independent laboratory analysis
- Scientific publications
- Overseas food composition tables
- Author extrapolations

Quick Guide

Cow's Milk

Average All Brands

	C	F	Cb
Whole (3.5% fat):			
2 Tbsp, 1 fl.oz	20	1	1.5
1 Glass, 6 fl.oz	110	6	8.5
1 Cup, 8 fl.oz	150	8	12
1 Pint, 16 fl.oz	300	16	23
1 Quart, 946 ml	600	32	46
Reduced-fat (2% fat):			
2 Tbsp, 1 fl.oz	15	0.5	1.5
1 Glass, 6 fl.oz	90	4	8.5
1 Cup, 8 fl.oz	120	5	12
1 Pint, 16 fl.oz	240	10	23
1 Quart, 946 ml	480	20	46
Light/Lowfat (1% fat):			
2 Tbsp, 1 fl.oz	12	0.3	1.5
1 Glass, 6 fl.oz	75	2	8.5
1 Cup, 8 fl.oz	100	2.5	12
1 Pint, 16 fl.oz	200	5	23
1 Quart, 946 ml	400	10	46
Fat Free/Skim:			
2 Tbsp, 1 fl.oz	10	0	1.5
1 Cup, 8 fl.oz	90	0.5	12
1 Pint, 16 fl.oz	180	1	24
w. Replace (Oatrim Fiber): 1 cup	85	0	12
Protein-Fortified:			
2% fat, 1 cup	140	5	14
1% fat, 1 cup	120	3	14
Skim, 1 cup	100	0.5	14
Acidophilus: Average All Brands			
Reduced Fat (2%), 1 cup	130	5	13
Lowfat (1%), 1 cup	100	2	13
Buttermilk: Average All Brands			
Reduced Fat (2%), 1 cup	120	5	10
Low Fat (1%), 1 cup	100	2.5	12
Oak Farms (1%), 1 cup	100	2.5	12
Lactose-Reduced:			
Reduced Fat: *Lactaid*, 1 cup	130	5	12
Dairy Ease 100, 1 cup	130	5	12
Lowfat fat, *Lactaid*, 1 cup	110	2.5	13
Fat Free *Lactaid/Lucerne*, 1 cup	80	0	13

Soy & Non-Dairy Drinks

~ See Page 24 ~

Goat & Sheep Milk

	C	F	Cb
Goat's Milk *(Meyenberg):*			
Whole, 1 cup, 8 fl.oz	140	7	11
Light/Lowfat (1%), 8 fl.oz	90	2.5	9
Evaporated, reconst., 8 fl.oz	145	8	11
Kefir: *Alta Dena*, 1 cup	240	4.5	41
Steve's Kefir Peach, 1 cup	220	9	25
Sheep's Milk: Whole, 1 cup	265	17	13

Canned & Dried Milk

Average All Brands

	C	F	Cb
Condensed: Reg. 2 Tbsp, 1 fl.oz	130	3	22
Lowfat (*Eagle*), 2 Tbsp	120	1.5	23
Fat Free (*Eagle*), 2 Tbsp	110	0	24
Evaporated: Whole, 2 Tbsp	40	3	3
Whole, 1/2 cup	170	10	13
Lowfat (*Carnation*), 2 Tbsp	25	1	3
1/2 cup	110	3	12
Light/Skim, 1/2 cup	100	0.5	14
Dried: Whole, 1/4 cup, 1 oz	150	8	11
Skim/Nonfat, 1/3 cup	80	0	12
Made-up, 1 cup, 8 fl.oz	80	0	12
Buttermilk, sweetcream, 1 oz	110	2	3
Nonfat, 1 Tbsp	25	0	3

Whey Drink

	C	F	Cb
Acid: Dry, 1 Tbsp, 3g	10	0	2
Fluid, 1 cup, 8 fl.oz	60	0	13
Sweet: Dry, 1 Tbsp, 8g	25	0	6
Fluid, 1 cup, 8 fl.oz	65	1	13
Nutri Mil: Original, 8 fl.oz	80	3	11
Fat Free (Calcium Enriched)	60	0	11

Quick Guide

Chocolate Milk

Average All Brands: Per Cup, 8 fl.oz

	C	F	Cb
Whole Milk (3.3%): 1 cup	225	9	26
1 Pint	450	18	52
Reduced Fat (2%), 1 cup	190	5	26
Lowfat (1%), 1 cup	160	3	26

Brands ~ Chocolate Milk

Ready-To-Drink: *Per 8 fl.oz Cup*			
Albertson's, lowfat	170	2.5	30
Bodywise, nonfat	180	0	35
Borden: Dutch Choc., 1 cup	220	8	28
Bosco	230	8	33
Brown Cow Farm, 1 cup	250	8	39
Deans'Chug': Regular	220	9	26
Lowfat, 1 cup	160	2.5	27
Dominick's Lowfat, 1 cup	170	2.5	28
Golden Guernsey, 1 cup	130	2.5	15
Grocers Pride Choc D'Lite, 1 cup	120	3	22
Hershey's: Lowfat (2%) Choc Milk	190	5	25
Whole Choc., 1 cup, 240ml	230	9	28
Hood, Lowfat (1%)	150	2	27
Horizon Organic	160	2.5	27
Knudsen	200	3	32
Kroger (3.25% milk)	220	9	28
Lactaid (1%)	160	3	26
Land O'Lakes, lowfat (0.5%)	150	1.5	35
Meadow Gold (3.5%)	210	8	25
Oak Farms , 1 cup	210	8	26
Parmalat (2%)	180	5	28
Quik: (*Nestle*) Chocolate Milk	230	8	30
Strawberry Milk	220	9	31
Ralph's	240	3	34
Yoo Hoo Choc Drink, 9 fl.oz	150	1	33

Bottled Coffee (Chilled)

Ready-To-Drink: *Per bottle*			
Blue Luna: Per 12 1/2 fl.oz			
Cafe Latte	195	3	36
Lite Cafe Mocha	114	3	15
Main St Cafe:			
French Van. Ice Latte, 12 fl.oz	190	33	31
Nescafe: Caffe Latte	140	3.5	23
Mocha	140	3	26
Starbucks: Coffee; Mocha	190	3	40

Shakes & Smoothies

Smoothies	C	F	Cb
Made Up Ready-To-Drink			
(8 fl. oz Milk/Soy + Fruit): *Per 12 fl.oz*			
Average all types: w. Whole Milk	300	8	50
+ Icecream, 1 scoop	400	13	62
with Nonfat Milk	240	0	50
Langers: 8 fl.oz, all flavors	135	0	34
Shakes			
Regular: Chocolate, 10 fl.oz	360	11	58
Vanilla/Strawberrry, 10 fl.oz	320	9	53
McDonald's Reduced Fat,			
Small (14 fl.oz), all flavors	360	9	59
Burger King: Vanilla, medium	430	9	73
Chocolate w. Syrup, medium	560	10	105
Killer Shake (14oz): Choc./Van., 1 c.	210	5	36

Cocoa-Chocolate Mixes

Add extra cals/fat/carbohydrate for milk			
Alba '66 Milk Choc, 1 pkt	60	0	14
Carnation **Cocoa Mixes:**			
Chocolate Rich, 3 Tbsp/1 pkt	110	1	24
Milk Chocolate, 3 Tbsp	110	1	24
w.mini Marshmallows, 1 oz pkt	110	1	24
Malted Milk Original, 3 Tbsp	90	2	15
70 Calorie Cocoa Mix, 3 tsp	70	0.5	15
Fat-Free, 2 Tbsp/1 pkt	25	0	4
No Sugar, 1 pkt	50	0.5	8
Land O' Lakes: *Per 1 1/4 oz pkt*			
Choc.Mint/Raspb./Supreme	160	5	25
Nestle **Hot Cocoa Mix,** 1 oz	110	1	23
w. Marshmallows, 1 oz	120	1	23
French Vanilla	120	3	22
Ghirardelli: *Per 2 heaping tsp*			
Choc. Mocha/Hazelnut/Dble Choc	80	1.5	21
Pralines & Creme, 2 Tbsp	90	0	23
Ovaltine Cocoa Mixes, 4 tsp	80	0	20
Swiss Miss **Cocoa Mixes:**			
Milk Chocolate, 1 oz pkt	110	1.5	22
w. Marshmallows, 1.2 oz pkt	140	3	22
Choc. Sensation, 1.25 oz pkt	150	4	27
Lite, 1 pkt	70	0	18
Diet Cocoa Mix, 1 pkt	20	0	4
Sugar Free	60	0	10
Fat Free, 0.53 oz	50	0	9
Vending Machine, 1.34 oz pkt	145	2	24
Weight Watchers: Hot Cocoa Mix	70	0	10

Soy & Non-Dairy Drinks

Soy Non-Dairy Drinks

Per 1 Cup Serving (8 fl.oz)	C	F	Cb
American Soy: Berry	120	1.5	24
Matcha Green Tea	110	2	19
Eden Blend: 1 cup	120	3	18
***Edensoy* (Organic):** Extra Orig.	130	4	13
Carob; Vanilla; Extra Vanilla	150	3	23
Hain Soy Supreme: Original	80	3	9
Vanilla, 1 cup	100	3	12
Harmony Farms: Regular, 1 cup	80	3	10
Enriched; Vanilla, 1 cup	100	3	14
Health Source: All flavors	150	1.5	23
Health Source Plus	160	1	17
Health Valley: Soy Moo	110	0	21
Lifeway: Soy Treat, Apple	160	4	23
Pacific: Original unsweetened	100	5	5
Enriched (Soy Isoflavin): Plain	90	2.5	14
Vanilla	110	2.5	16
Fat Free: Plain	70	0	14
Vanilla	90	0	17
Select (Soy Isoflavin), Plain	100	2.5	13
Ultra: Plain/Vanilla	150	5	20
SoyDream: Original, 8 fl.oz	140	5	14
Carob/Chocolate Enriched	210	4	37
Vanilla	160	5	21
Soy-Um (*Trader Joe's*): Original	100	3	13
Chocolate	160	3	27
Vanilla	110	3	15
SunSoy: Chocolate	140	3	23
Creamy Original	80	3	8
Val/Shake: Regular	380	12	56
Vitasoy: Creamy, 1 cup	130	5	12
Carob	210	6	32
Light Original	90	2	15
Light Cocoa/Vanilla	110	2	20
Rich Cocoa: 8 fl.oz box	190	6	25
32 fl.oz size, 1 cup	210	6	32
Vanilla Delite	190	6	27
WestSoy: *Plus*, Plain	130	4	18
100% Organic: Original (2% fat)	140	5	18
Unsweetened	90	4.5	5
Nonfat: Plain; Vanilla, average	85	0	16
Lite: Plain	100	2	15
Cocoa	120	1.5	23
Vanilla	120	2.5	21
Lowfat: Plain	90	1.5	14
Vanilla	110	1.5	20
Café: Coffee; Mocha; Fr. Vanilla	130	2.5	24

WestSoy (Cont):	C	F	Cb
Vigor Aid: Chocolate Mocha	240	6	38
French Vanilla	260	6	44

Soy Powder Mix

(1 oz mix makes 1 cup, 8 fl.oz)			
Better Than Milk: Original	100	2.5	16
Light	80	0.5	13
Soyagen, 1 oz	130	7	12
Soy Protein Isolate, 1 oz	95	1	0
Soy Quik (Ener-g), 1 oz	100	4.5	8

Rice & Cereal Drinks

Almond Breeze: Original, 8 fl.oz	60	3	8
Vanilla, 8 fl.oz	90	3	16
Amazake: Almond Light, 8 fl.oz	110	2	20
Eden Blend: Rice & Soy, 1 cup	120	3	18
Eden Rice: 1 cup, 8 fl.oz	110	3	21
Hain Rice Supreme: Lowfat Orig.	100	3	16
Lowfat Cinnamon	130	3	22
Pacific Foods: Multigrain, 8 fl.oz	140	2	25
Naturally Oat: Original, 1 cup	110	1.5	21
Vanilla, 1 cup	130	1.5	24
Naturally Almond: 1 cup	70	2.5	10
Vanilla, 1 cup	90	2.5	15
Pacific Rice: Lowfat, Plain, 1 cup	90	2	17
Fat Free: Plain	70	0	17
Cocoa	90	0	20
Vanilla	110	0	24
Rice Dream: Carob, 1 cup	150	2.5	32
Chocolate; Choc. Enriched, 1 c.	170	3	36
Vanilla; Vanilla Enriched, 1 cup	130	2	28
Organic; Organic Enriched, 1 c.	120	2	25
Westbrae: Oat Plus, 1 cup	150	3	26
Original Vanilla, 1 cup	150	3	20
Rice: Plain, 1 cup	100	2.5	18
Vanilla, 1 cup	120	2.5	22

Rice/Nut Drink Mixes

Better Than Milk: *Per 2 Tbsp Powder*			
Original, 23g	100	2.5	16
Light, 19g	70	0.5	14
Vanilla, 19g	90	5	10
Nut Quik, 2 Tbsp powder, 18g	110	9	3
Solait, 3 Tbsp powder, 22g	80	1.5	13
Sun's Up, 2 scoops, 40g powder	160	2	36
Rice Moo, 2 Tbsp powder, 19g	72	0	17

Quick Guide

Yogurt

Average All Brands: Per 8 oz

	C	F	Cb
Plain Yogurt: Whole, 8 oz	180	7	11
Lowfat	140	4	16
Nonfat	110	0	18
Fruit Flavored: Whole, 8 oz	250	6	38
Lowfat	230	3	32
Nonfat, regular	150	0	32
Nonfat, no sugar added	120	0	32
Goat's Milk Yogurt-Same as Regular			

Yogurt ~ Brands

	C	F	Cb
Alex Rod: **Fat Free,** all flav., 8 oz	70	0	12
Albertson's: **Plain,** lowfat, 8 oz	140	2.5	17
Fruit on the Bottom (lowfat):			
Average all flavors, 8 oz	220	2	42
Swiss (Nonfat), average, 6 oz	90	0	14
Indulgents (Lowfat), 6 oz	180	2	35
Alta Dena: **Lowfat:** Plain, 8 oz	170	4.5	20
Vanilla, 8 oz	260	3.5	44
Nonfat: Plain, 8 oz	110	0	17
Flavors, average	190	0	39
America's Choice: **Swiss Style**	210	2.5	41
Fruit on the Bottom: Cherry Van.	270	2.5	55
Other flavors, average	220	2.5	40
Nonfat, all flavors, 8 oz	100	0	15
Berkeley Farms (8 oz Cup)			
Lowfat: Boysenberry/Cherry	230	2.5	46
Raspberry	220	2.5	43
Strawberry, Lemon, Vanilla	270	2.5	52
Nonfat: Average all flavors	100	0	16
Breyers: **Light n' Lively:** 125g	130	1	25
Lowfat: 1% fat, all flavors, 8 oz	250	2.5	48
1.5% fat, plain	130	3	15
Flavors, average	220	3	38
Smooth & Creamy: 125g	130	1	25
Brown Cow Farm (Fat Free): Plain	80	0	11
Cappuccino/Maple Alm./Vanilla	170	0	33
Cherry Vanilla/Strawberry, 8 oz	190	0	39
Chocolate, 8 oz	220	0	45
Whole Milk, 8 oz	210	8	30
Plain, 8 oz	170	10	12
Cabot: Plain, 8 oz	140	4	16
Flavors, 8 oz	220	3	42

	C	F	Cb
Cascade Fresh			
Lowfat, 6 oz	140	2	23
Fat Free, all flavors, 6 oz	110	0	20
Colombo: **Light,** all flavors, 8 oz	100	0	17
Classic (Fruit on the Bottom), 8 oz	200	4	43
Non Fat: Plain, 8 oz	110	0	17
Continental: **Nonfat,** 8 oz	200	0	38
Dannon			
Plain (Natural), 8 oz	170	8	14
Light: All flavors, 8 oz	100	0	16
w. Crunchy Toppings, aver. 8 oz	170	0	33
Nonfat: Snackpack, 4 oz	60	0	11
Fruit on the Bottom (99% FF):8 oz	230	2.5	40
Minipack, 4 oz	110	1	20
Nonfat: Plain, 8 oz	130	0	19
Blended, 4 oz	100	0	21
Chunky Fruit (Nonfat), aver., 6 oz	160	0	32
Low Fat: All types, 8 oz	220	3.5	36
Double Delights Lowfat:			
w. Fruit Topping, aver., 6 oz	170	1	34
w. Choc. Topping, 6 oz	220	1	46
Light Duets: w. fruit topping, 6 oz	90	0	34
Danimals (lowfat), 4 oz	120	1.5	20
Sprinkl'ins: All types, 4 oz	125	1	23
Dominick's: **Lowfat,** 8 oz	230	2	40
Fruit on the Bottom, aver., 8 oz	230	2	40
Fat Free 80 Calories, 8 oz	80	0	13
Plain: Lowfat, 8 oz	130	2.5	15
Nonfat, 8 oz	120	0	17
Friendship: **Fruit Flavors,** 6 oz	190	5	31
Grocer's Pride: **Lowfat,** 4.4 oz	140	1.5	28
Hood: **Fat Free,** Plain, 8 oz	130	0	18
Average all flavors, 8 oz	190	0	40
Horizon Organic			
Nonfat: Cherry, 6 oz	140	0	28
Other fruit flavors, aver., 6 oz	130	0	26
Plain: 1 cup, 8 oz	170	0	32
Fat Free, 6 oz	80	0	11
Vanilla, 1 cup, 8 oz	110	0	15
Imperial Supreme: **Lowfat,** 6 oz	140	1.5	26
Jerseymaid (Vons)			
Fruit on the Bottom, 8 oz	240	2.5	46
Prestirred (lowfat), average	240	2.5	46
Plain, lowfat, 8 oz	140	3.5	18

Jell-O	C	F	Cb
Kid Pack, all flav., 125g	130	1	25
Jewel: **Lowfat,** average, 8 oz	250	2.5	48
Knudsen: **70 Calories,** 6 oz	70	0	11
Free, average, 6 oz	170	0	33
Cottage Doubles, 5.5 oz	140	2.5	18
Kroger: **Lite,** aver. all flav., 8 oz	100	0	14
Lowfat, average all flavors, 8 oz	210	1.5	40
Health Indulgence (Nonfat):			
Fruit on the Bottom, aver.	170	0	35
Fat Free: Plain, 8 oz	120	0	18
Vanilla, 8 oz	190	0	36
98% Fat Free: Plain, 8 oz	140	4	16
Vanilla, 8 oz	240	4	42
Lactaid: **Lowfat Vanilla,** 8 oz	240	2.5	45
La Yogurt			
Fruit Flavors, average, 6 oz	170	2	32
Light, average all flavors, 6 oz	70	0	12
Fruit La More, average, 6 oz	160	0	32
Light n'Lively			
Free 50 Calories, 4 oz	50	0	8
Free 70 Calories, 6 oz	70	0	11
Free (Regular) 6 oz: Vanilla	160	0	32
Strawb. Fruit/Peach/Lem./Berry	170	0	34
Strawberry/Raspberry	180	0	36
Kidpack/Multipack, aver. 4.4 oz	140	1	28
Meadow Gold: **Plain,** 8 oz	160	5	16
Flavors, average, 8 oz	250	4	42
Mountain High			
Original: Plain, 8 oz	190	8	18
Fat Free Plain, 8 oz	120	0	20
Fat Free: all flavors, 8 oz	170	0	33
Mystic Lake Dairy (Goat Milk Yogurt)			
Plain, 1 cup, 8 oz	120	6	9
Pavel's: Orig. Russian, 8 oz	140	8	10
Lowfat Vanilla, 8 oz	120	4	12
Nonfat Russian, 8 oz	110	0	15
Private Selection (Ralph's)			
Lowfat, average all flavors, 8 oz	220	2	43
Fat Free: Coconut Cream Pie, 6 oz	130	0	23
Other flavors, average, 6 oz	100	0	16
Mountain Dairy, 6 oz	150	1.5	27

Publix	C	F	Cb
Light, average, 8 oz	130	0	21
Fruit on the Bottom, aver., 8 oz	250	2.5	43
Fat Free: Plain, 8 oz	140	0	23
Swiss Style (lowfat), 8 oz	240	2.5	41
Redwood Hill Farm (Goat Milk Yogurt)			
Fruit flavors, average, 8 oz	180	5	28
Vanilla, 8 oz	190	6	28
Plain, 8 oz	120	6	9
Snackwell's: **Nonfat,** 6 oz	160	0	36
Stonyfield Farm: **Lowfat,** 8 oz	120	1.5	22
Nonfat, aver. all flavors, 8 oz	160	0	31
"TCBY" Fat Free (Fantasies):			
Banana Creme Pie, 6 oz	110	0	18
White Chocolate, 6 oz	90	0	12
Trader Joe's: **Nonfat,** 8 oz	190	0	40
Lowfat, average, 8 oz	230	2.5	44
Yofarm: All flavors, aver., 8 oz	220	6	37
Yo Crunch, 6.5 oz (185g)	210	2	41
Yoplait: **Light:** All flavors, 6 oz	90	0	16
Original Lowfat: C'nut Creme, 6oz	200	3	35
99% Fat Free, all flavors, 6 oz	180	1.5	34
Multipack, 4 oz	120	1	22
Go-Gurt: 64g tube	80	2	12
Custard Style: All flavors, 6 oz	190	3.5	32
Trix: Multipack, 4 oz	130	1.5	24
Yumsters, 4 oz	120	2	21

Soy/Non-Dairy Yogurt

Health Source: Soy Nonfat, 6 oz	150	0	32
Nancy's Soy: Aver. all flav., 8 oz	210	4	37
Soy Nonfat, 6 oz	150	0	32
White Wave: *Per 6 oz*			
Silk Dairyless: Plain; Vanilla	105	2	16
Keylime; Lemon/Kiwi	160	2	17
Average other flavors	140	2	24

Yogurt Drinks

Alta Dena: Drinkables, 1 cup	220	0	46
Dannon: Danimals, 6 oz	180	3	32
Glen Oaks: All flav., aver., 1 cup	250	4	46
Yonique, 6 fl.oz: Pina Colada	190	4	30
Peach; Banana; Guava	170	2	30
Yo Soy, 8 fl.oz	80	4	4

Quick Guide

Icecream

Vanilla: *Average All Brands*

Other flavors ~ See Brand Listings.

	C	F	Cb
Regular Icecream (10% fat): (Examples: *Borden/Breyers/Hood*)			
3 fl.oz scoop	100	5	12
1/2 cup, 4 fl.oz	130	7	16
1 Pint, 16 fl.oz	520	28	62
1/2 Gallon (4 Pints)	2100	112	248
Rich (16% fat): *(Baskin-Robbins)*			
3 fl.oz scoop	130	8	12
1/2 cup, 4 fl.oz	170	10	17
1 Pint	690	40	68
Super-Rich (20% fat): *(Haagen-Dazs/Ben & Jerry's)*			
3 fl.oz scoop	200	14	16
1/2 cup, 4 fl.oz	270	18	21
1 Pint	1100	72	84
Reduced Fat/Light (6% fat): *(Breyer's Light/Hood Light)*			
3 fl.oz scoop	100	3	14
1/2 cup, 4 fl.oz	140	4	18
1 Pint	560	16	72
Low Fat (less than 4% fat): *(Healthy Choice/Weight Watchers/Snackwell's)*			
3 fl.oz scoop	90	2	17
1/2 cup, 4 fl.oz	120	2.5	22
1 Pint	480	10	88
Fat Free: *(Baskin-Robbins FF/Borden FF/ Breyers FF/Dreyers FF/Hood FF))*			
3 fl.oz scoop	75	0	17
1/2 cup, 4 fl.oz	100	0	22
1 Pint	400	0	88
Soft Serve: Regular, 1/2 cup	140	5	20
1 cup	280	10	40
Nonfat, 1/2 cup	90	0	23
1 cup	180	0	46

Quick Guide

Frozen Yogurt

Average All Brands

	C	F	Cb
Hard: Lowfat, 1/2 cup	140	3	26
Nonfat, 1/2 cup	110	0	29
Soft: Lowfat, 1/2 cup	120	2.5	28
Nonfat, 1/2 cup	100	0	30

Brands ~ See Icecream & Ices Section

Quick Guide

Gelato/Ices

	C	F	Cb
Gelato: *Per 1/2 Cup*			
Milk base: Vanilla	200	15	18
Choc. Hazelnut	370	29	26
Water base: 1/2 cup	100	0	25
Ice (Milk base): Average all flavors			
Hard (4% fat), 1/2 cup	100	3	15
Soft Serve (3% fat), 1/2 cup	110	2	19
Shaved Ice: Average, 12 fl. oz	160	0	40
Sherbet: Average, 1/2 cup	120	2	28
Sorbet: Fruit (no fat), 1/2 cup	120	0	30
Fruit Ice Pops	80	0	20

Tofu Frozen Desserts ~ Page 30

Sundaes

	C	F	Cb
Denny's Sundaes:			
Single Scoop, no topping	190	14	14
Double Scoop, no topping	375	27	29
Banana Split	895	43	112
Butterfinger® Hot Fudge	780	38	106
Toppings:			
Blueberry, 2 oz	70	0	17
Chocolate, 2 oz	320	25	27
Fudge, 2 oz	200	10	30
Strawberry, 2 oz	80	1	17
McDonald's Sundaes:			
Hot Fudge Sundae, 6.3 oz	340	12	52
Oreo® Cookie McFlurry™	570	20	82
Toppings: Nut/Sundae, 1/4 oz	40	3.5	2

~ Full Analysis: See Fast-Foods Section ~

Icecream Bars & Pops

See Pages 31 & 32

Icecream Cones & Cups

	C	F	Cb
Wafer Cone/Cup, average	20	0	4
Sugar Cone, average	40	0	9
Waffle Cone:			
Small	60	0	11
Large	100	1	22
Brands:			
Oreo Chocolate Cone	50	1	10
Comet Sugar Cone	50	0	11
Keebler Sugar Cone	45	0	11

Brands	C	F	Cb
Alta Dena: *Per 1/2 Cup*			
Honey Chocolate	160	9	19
Golden Honey Vanilla	160	10	17
Baskin-Robbins			
See Fast-Foods Section ~ Page 168			
Ben & Jerry's: *Per 1/2 Cup*			
Butter Pecan	330	25	22
Bovinity Divinity	160	18	30
Cherry Garcia; Vanilla	260	16	23
Choc. Chip Cookie Dough	300	17	34
Choc. Fudge Brownie	280	15	32
Chubby Hubby	350	21	33
Chunky Monkey; Coffee Heath	310	19	32
Dilbert's World Totally Nuts	310	21	27
Mint Choc. Cookie	280	17	28
New York Super Fudge Chunk	320	21	28
Nutty Waffle Cone	310	19	32
Peanut Butter Cup	380	25	32
Phish Food	300	14	41
Vanilla Caramel Fudge	300	17	33
Vanilla Heath Bar Crunch	310	19	30
Wavy Gravy	340	20	32
Lowfat: Coconut Cream Pie	160	2.5	29
Blondies; S'mores	200	2	38
Frozen Yogurt: Vanilla Heath	210	6	34
Choc. Cherry/Chip	190	4	35
Choc. Fudge Brownie	190	2.5	36
Cherry Garcia	170	3	32
Sorbet: Devil's Food Chocolate	170	2.5	36
Average other flavors	130	0	30
Pops: See Page 31			
Bon Bon's			
Vanilla w. choc. coating, 5 pieces	200	14	17
8 pieces	330	23	27
Bresler's: *Per 1/2 Cup*			
All Flavors Icecream: average	230	12	23
Royal Cremes, average	260	16	24
Royal Lites, average	220	0	49
Breyer's: *Per 1/2 Cup*			
Dulche de Leche	160	7	21
Homemade: Dble Choc Fudge	180	9	23
Butter Pecan; Van.; Neopolitan	150	8	16
Breyers Light: Average, 1/2 c.	140	4	19
Fat Free: Average	110	0	21
Reduced Fat: Average	160	6	19
Breyer's (Cont): *Per 1/2 Cup*			
All Natural: Butter Pecan	180	12	15
Cherry Vanilla; Coffee	150	7	17
Chocolate; French Vanilla	160	10	15
Choc. Chip; Mint Choc. Chip	170	10	18
Cookies 'n Cream	170	9	19
Peach; Strawberry	130	6	18
Vanilla; Van./Choc./Strawberry	150	8	16
Van. & Choc.; Van. Fudge Twirl	160	8	18
Ice Cream Parlor: Chips Ahoy	160	8	18
Candy Bar Sundae	170	8	21
Double Choc Malt	160	7	21
English Toffee	180	8	23
Hershey's Choc. w. Almonds	170	8	21
Icecream Sandwich	160	7	21
Oreo	160	8	19
Reese's P'nut Butter Cup	180	9	22
Vienetta: All flavors, 1 slice	190	11	17
No Sugar Added: Vanilla	80	4	11
Vanilla Fudge Twirl	90	3.5	14
Vanilla Chocolate Strawberry	90	4	11
Mint Chocolate Chip	100	5	21
Sorbet: Average, 1/2 cup	160	7	26
Frozen Yogurt: Average, 1/2 cup	150	4	25
Colombo: *Per 1/2 Cup*			
Frozen, Soft Serve: Nonfat var.	100	0	22
Slender Sensations varieties	65	0	11
Lowfat: Old Worlde; P'nut Butter	120	2.5	20
Vanilla varieties	110	1.5	21
Dairy Queen/Brazier			
See Fast-Foods Section ~ Page 179-180			
Dannon Frozen Yogurt: *Per 1/2 cup (4 fl.oz)*			
Light Soft, all flavors, average	90	1	21
Light 'N Crunchy, all flavors, aver.	110	1	23
Pure Indulgence, all flavors, aver.	150	3	25
Dolewhip (Soft Serve): *Per 4 fl.oz, 1/2 Cup*			
Chocolate; Vanilla	100	3	18
Fruit flavors, average	80	0.5	16
Dreyers: *Per 1/2 Cup*			
No Sugar Added: Aver. all flavors	90	3	12
Fat Free: Average all flavors	110	0	25
Fat Free - No Sugar Added	95	0	20
Candy Bar: Twix	190	9	23
Snickers; M&M's Vanilla	180	9	22
M&M's Chocolate	170	8	22
Milky Way; 3 Musketeers	160	7	22

Brands (Cont)

	C	F	Cb
Dreyers (Cont): *Per 1/2 Cup*			
Grand Light: Vanilla	100	3	15
Cookie Dough; P'nut Butter Cups	130	5	17
Other varieties, average	120	4	18
Homemade: Butter Pecan, 71g	160	9	16
Banana Crunch; Strawb. & Crm	130	6	17
Chocolate Peanut Butter, 71g	200	12	18
Cracker Jack	170	9	20
Orbit City Swirl	160	8	19
Peaches & Cream, 65g	120	5	16
Scooby Snack	170	9	19
Vanilla, 1/2 cup, 71g	140	7	16
Dreamery: Banana Boogie	290	17	27
Black Raspberry Avalanche	250	14	27
Caramel Toffee Bar: Heaven	270	14	32
Vanilla	260	15	25
Cashew Praline Parfait	260	13	30
Choc P'nut Butter Chunk	310	18	29
Choc Truffle Explosion	280	15	30
Cool Mint	280	14	34
Coney Island Waffle	300	18	31
Galactic Choc Swirl	280	12	37
Grandma's Cookie Jar	270	14	32
Harvest Peach; Strawb. Fields	220	11	25
New York Strawb. Cheesecake	250	13	27
Nuts About Malt	280	15	29
Raspberry Brownie a la Mode	270	14	33
Edys: *Per 1/2 Cup*			
Banana Split; Choc. Fudge Mousse	160	8	19
Cherry Choc; Van./Choc.; Espresso	150	8	17
Choc. Fudge Sundae; Dble Fudge	170	9	19
Ice Cream Sandwich	140	8	14
Grand Light: Vanilla	100	3	15
Butter Pecan; Choc. Almond	120	5	16
Chiquita 'N Chocolate	110	5	13
Choc. Fudge Mousse	110	3	17
Cookie Dough; P'nut Butter Cups	130	5	18
Cookies 'n Cream; Rocky Road	110	4	16
French Silk	120	4	18
Fat Free: Average all flavors	115	0	25
Eskimo Pie: *Per 1/2 Cup*			
Reduced Fat: Butter Pecan	140	7	16
Choc. Marshmallow	130	4	23
Neopolitan; Vanilla	110	4	18
Fudge Ripple	120	4	19

Bars ~ See Page 31

	C	F	Cb
Friendly's: *Per 1/2 Cup*			
Icecream: Chocolate Almond Chip	170	10	18
Forbidden Chocolate	150	9	14
Fudge Nut Brownie	200	11	23
Vanilla Choc. Strawb.; Vanilla	150	8	16
Vienna Mocha Chunk	180	11	19
Frozen Yogurt: *Per 1/2 Cup (2.6oz)*			
Lowfat flavors, average	120	3	20
Regular flavors, average	150	4	24
Frostline (Soft Serve): Choc.	90	2	20
Vanilla, 1/2 Cup	90	3	18
Frusen Gladje: *Per 1/2 Cup*			
Butter Pecan	280	21	16
Chocolate	240	17	17
Chocolate Choc. Chip	270	18	21
Mocha Chip; Praline & Cream	280	18	22
Strawberry	230	15	20
Swiss Choc. Candy Almond	270	19	18
Vanilla	230	17	16
Vanilla Swiss Almond	270	19	18
Good Humor: *Per 1/2 Cup*			
Light: Coffee	110	3	18
Choc. Chip, Toffee Bar Crunch	130	4	20
Cookies n' Crm; Praline Alm. Crnch	130	3	21
Vanilla, Vanilla Choc. Strawb.	110	3	19
Haagen-Dazs: *Per 1/2 Cup*			
Brownies a la Mode	280	18	25
Butter Pecan; Macadamia Nut	320	24	20
Cappuccino; Caramel Cone	310	21	27
Chocolate; Coffee; Vanilla	270	18	22
Choc. Choc. Chip; Cookie Dough	300	20	26
Cookies & Cream; Rum Raisin	270	17	23
Deep Choc Peanut Butter	370	25	27
Strawberry	250	16	23
Strawb. Cheesecake; Vanilla Fudge	290	18	28
Triple Brownie Overload	300	20	26
Vanilla Chocolate Chip	290	20	24
Vanilla Swiss Almond	310	21	23
Icecream Bars ~ See Page 31 & 32			
Soft Serve: Nonfat Coffee	140	4	20
Chocolate Mousse	80	0	24
Sorbets ~ See Fast Foods Section			
Frozen Yogurt: Vanilla Fudge	160	0	34
Vanilla Raspberry Swirl	130	0	28
Other flavors	140	0	30

See Full Listings - Fast-Foods Section

Brands (Cont)

	C	F	Cb
Healthy Choice: *Per 1/2 Cup*			
Vanilla	**100**	2	18
Rocky Road	**140**	2	28
Other flavors, average	**120**	2	22
Lowfat: All varieties, average	**110**	1.5	21
Hood: *Per 1/2 Cup*			
Chocolate	**140**	7	17
Chocolate Chip; Maple Walnut	**160**	9	18
Cookie Dough; Cookies 'n Cream	**160**	8	21
Grasshopper Pie	**160**	7	22
Heavenly Hash; Vanilla Fudge	**140**	6	21
Strawberry	**130**	7	16
Vanilla; Van. Choc. Strawberry	**140**	7	16
Light: Almond Praline	**110**	5	23
Carrib. Coffee	**110**	5	18
Vanilla; Van.Choc.Strawberry	**110**	4	18
Other Flavors, average	**140**	5	22
Lowfat: No Added Sugar, 1/2 cup	**115**	3	18
Fat Free: Average all flavors	**120**	0	27
Icecream Bars ~ See Page 32			
I Can't Believe It's Yogurt			
See Fast-Foods Section			
It's Soy Delicious			
Chocolate; Vanilla	**130**	4	23
Chocolate; Vanilla	**130**	4	23
Jerseymaid (Vons): *Per 1/2 Cup*			
After Dinner Mint; Cookies & Crm	**170**	9	19
Choc Chip; Mint Choc Chip	**160**	9	17
Heavenly Hash; Nut Chunky Choc.	**170**	8	22
Mocha Almd Fudge; Rocky Road	**160**	7	20
Neopolitan; Vanilla	**140**	7	16
Strawberry	**140**	6	18
Luigi's Real Italian Ice			
Squeeze-Up Tube: 8 fl.oz each	**150**	0	37
Rice Cream (Non Dairy): *Per 1/2 Cup*			
Vanilla	**150**	6	23
Supreme: Average all flavors	**150**	6	23
Sealtest: *Per 1/2 Cup*			
Butter Pecan	**160**	9	16
Choc. Chip Cookie Dough	**160**	8	20
Fudge Royal; Heavenly Hash	**150**	7	20
Vanilla/Choc. Strawberry	**140**	7	16

	C	F	Cb
Snackwell's: *Per 1/2 Cup*			
Brownie; Rocky Road	**130**	2	26
Praline Caramel	**140**	2	28
Vanilla	**100**	2	18
Starbucks: *Per 1/2 Cup*			
Espresso Swirl	**220**	10	29
Biscotti Bliss	**240**	12	30
Cafe Almond Fudge	**260**	13	30
Chocolate Chocolate Fudge	**290**	17	28
Italian Roast	**230**	12	26
JavaChip	**250**	13	29
Vanilla MochaChip	**270**	14	31
Lowfat: Mocha Mambo; Latte	**170**	3	30
Bars ~ see Icecream Bars & Pops Section			
Stonyfield Farm			
Chocolate; Raspberry; Vanilla	**120**	2	22
TCBY ~ See Fast-Foods Section			
Tofutti Non-Dairy Dessert: *Per 1/2 Cup*			
Premium: Vanilla	**190**	11	20
Better Pecan; Alm. Bark	**220**	13	22
Choc. Cookie Crunch	**210**	11	26
Chocolate Supreme	**180**	11	18
Van. Fudge; Wildberry	**190**	9	24
Low Fat Supreme: Average	**110**	2	25
Cutie Pies: Average, 67g bar	**250**	19	18
Too Toos: Vanilla S'wich	**215**	10	28
Van. Choc. Swirl/Chip S'wich	**230**	11	30
Teddy Fudge: 52g bar	**70**	1	19
Turkey Hill: *Per 1/2 Cup*			
Black Cherry	**140**	7	18
Butter Pecan	**170**	11	16
Choco. Mint Chip, Cookies 'n Crm	**160**	10	17
Neapolitan, Vanilla & Choc.	**150**	8	18
Rocky Road	**170**	8	23
Vanilla, Vanilla Bean	**140**	8	16
Lite: Choco Mint Chip	**140**	5	19
Cookies 'n Cream	**130**	5	21
Vanilla & Choc., Van. Bean	**110**	3	18
Weight Watchers: *Per 1/2 Cup*			
Cookie Dough Craze	**140**	3.5	24
Oh! So Very Vanilla	**120**	2.5	20
Positively Praline Crunch	**140**	3	25
Reckless Rocky Road	**140**	3	23
Triple Chocolate Tornado	**150**	3.5	26
Bars ~ See Page 31-32			

Per Bar/Serving	C	F	Cb
Baby Ruth (*Nestlé*)	180	12	15
Baskin Robbins: Tiny Toons	140	17	20
Cappuccino Blast, average	120	4	20
Sundae Bar: Pralines 'n Cream	280	17	28
Ben & Jerry's: Vanilla Pop	330	22	29
Cookie Dough Pop	410	24	45
Totally Nuts	370	29	24
Big Bear: See Klondike	290	10	45
Big Ed's Super Saucer: 10 fl.oz	420	28	32
1/2 Sandwich, 5 fl.oz	210	14	16
Borden: Sundae Cone	210	10	27
Twin Pops	60	0	14
Bon Bons (*Nestlé*): Milk Choc., (8)	330	23	27
Dark Chocolate, 8 pces	310	21	26
Bounty: all varieties	70	5	7
Butterfinger Icecream Bar, 2.5 oz	190	13	16
Breyers: Vanilla Bar	250	17	21
w. chocolate coating	230	15	20
Sandwich (Vanilla)	250	11	32
Carnation: Orange Sherbet, 3 oz	90	1	19
Icecream Cup: Choc., 3 fl.oz	140	8	16
Strawb., Vanilla, 3 fl.oz	100	6	12
Choc./Vanilla Malt, 12 oz	270	6	48
Sundae Cup, all types, 5 fl.oz	210	9	30
Chipwich Jr: Choc. Chip S'wich	240	10	35
Chiquita: Swirls, all flavors	80	3	12
Cool Creations: Mini Sandwich	110	5	16
Cookies & Cream Sandwich	240	11	34
Pops, all types, 2 oz	60	0	14
Mickey Mouse: 2.5 oz Bar	120	8	10
4 oz Bar	170	11	17
Creamsicle: Sugar-free pops	25	0	15
Orange, 2.8 fl.oz	110	3	20
Crunch (*Nestlé*): King, 4 oz	270	19	21
Reduced Fat, 2.5 oz	130	7	14
Regular Icecream Bar, 3 oz	200	14	16
Crystal Light: Cool 'n Creamy	50	2	7
Dole Bars: Coconut, 4 oz	210	7	33
Fruit Juice, reg., 1.75 oz	45	0	11
No Added Sugar, 1.75 oz	25	0	6
Fruit 'n Juice: Small, 2.5 oz	70	0	16
Pine-Coconut, 4 oz	150	4	27
Other flavors, 4 oz	120	0	28
Dreyers: Icecream Bars, average	250	17	22
Fruit Bars, 3 fl.oz	90	9	23
Smoothie Bars: Average	95	0	21
Sundae Cone, 4 fl.oz	240	11	31

Per Bar/Serving	C	F	Cb
Dove Bar: Almond	340	22	30
Bite Size, 5 pces, average	350	22	36
Caramel Pecan	350	35	35
Mocha Cashew	260	17	25
Peppermint	390	17	31
Vanilla Dark Choc; Cookie	340	21	35
Single Vanilla Dark	200	12	24
Vanilla Milk Chocolate	350	24	29
Drumstick (*Nestlé*): Chocolate	320	17	36
Choc. Dipped	320	16	40
Original Vanilla	340	19	35
Vanilla Caramel/Fudge	360	20	39
Eskimo Pie: Arctic Madness, 2.5 oz	230	15	23
Bars: Milk/Dark Choc, 50g	160	11	15
Fudge Bar, 55g	60	1	11
Reduced Fat varieties	120	8	13
Crispy Bar, 47g	130	8	13
Pecan, 51g	190	15	12
Big Bar, 99g	300	20	26
Icecream Sandwich, 65 g	160	4	27
Cones, 74g	210	12	24
No Sugar Added: Bar, 49g	120	8	13
Pudding Bar, 59g	90	1.5	16
Flintstones: Push Up Sherbet	100	2	20
Push Up Pebbles, 2.75 oz	120	6	15
Cool Cream, 2.75 oz	90	2	18
Froz-Fruit: Cherry	60	0	15
Strawberry	80	0	20
Frosty Dreams (*Nestlé*)	100	2	19
Frosty Pops (*Nestlé*)	40	0	11
Fruit A Freeze: Coconut	130	5	20
Lime	65	0	16
Banana; Strawberry	90	1.5	19
Dark Choc-Dipped Strawberry	90	3.5	14
Fudge Bar (*Nestlé*)	110	1	23
Fudgesicle: Fudge Bar	90	1	17
Sugar-Free	40	1	8
Fudgetastics: Sticks Sundae	220	15	37
Good Humor: Candy Crunch	280	21	21
Chocolate Eclair; Colonel Crunch	170	9	21
Chocolate Taco	320	17	38
Classic Almond	210	12	21
Dinosaur	110	2	25
Giant Sandwich, 5 fl.oz	240	10	35
Icecream Sandwich	190	8	28
King Cone	300	14	38

Per Bar/Serving	C	F	Cb
Good Humor (Cont):			
Strawberry Shortcake, 3.75 fl.oz	210	9	29
Cups: Sundae Twist	160	3	33
Combo (6 fl.oz)	200	10	25
Haagen-Daz Bars:			
Uncoated Choc; Coffee; Vanilla	200	13	16
Vanilla & Dark Chocolate	400	27	33
Multipack, each	320	22	17
Sorbet Bars, average	90	0	22
Sorbet 'n Yogurt Bars, average	100	0	20
Also See Page 196			
Hood: Chocolate Eclair, 1 bar	150	10	14
Cooler Cup, 2.1 oz	80	1	18
Crispy Bar	180	13	15
Fabukous Fudgies, 1 bar	100	3	19
Fabulous Fudge P'nut Butter	110	4	17
Fudge Bar	100	1	21
Hendrie's Cherry Choc. Dips	120	9	11
Hoodsie Cup Van./Choc.	100	5	12
Orange Cream Bar	90	2	18
Rockets, each	120	5	18
Vanilla Bar	160	12	11
Icecream Sandwich *(Nestle)*	170	6	26
Jell-O: Pop Bars	31	0	7
Jigglers, all varieties, 6 oz	215	1.5	50
Pudding Bars	80	2	13
Klondike: Almond Bar	310	21	26
Big Bear Van. Icecream S'wich	290	10	46
Choc Chip Cookie Sandwich	520	21	77
Gold Bar	340	23	30
Krunch	200	13	17
Lite Bar	110	6	14
Original Vanilla; Chocolate	290	20	25
Sandwich: Chocolate	270	10	41
Lite	100	2	18
Vanilla	250	9	37
The One	290	20	25
Kool-Aid Pops	40	0	10
Krispy Frostick:	150	10	13
Juice Flavored Sticks	50	0	13
M&Ms: Cookie Icecream S'wich	240	12	32
Mars Almond Bar	210	14	20
Matterhorn: Cone, 10 fl.oz	510	38	19
Milky Way: Choc, Reduced Fat	140	7	19
Caramel Swirl, 1 bar	180	10	21
Snack Bar, Vanilla/Chocolate	70	4	9
Minute Maid: Fruit Juice Pops	60	0	15

Per Bar/Serving	C	F	Cb
Nestlé Icescreamers:			
Push Up Pop	90	1.5	19
Shock Tarts, 1 pop	45	0	11
Tiger Tails, 1 pop	60	0	15
Oreo: Choc; Vanilla	160	9	19
Big Stuf, 1 sandwich	240	10	33
Cookies n' Cream, 1 bar, 59g	180	12	18
Pathmark: Vanilla w. choc. coat.	150	10	14
Polar Bar: Vanilla w. choc. coat.	240	18	15
Choc. Chip Cookie Dough	450	28	48
Pops (water/juice), average	60	0	14
Popsicles: Fudgesicle Fudge Pop	90	1.5	16
Sugar-free Ice Pop	15	0	4
Reece's: Peanut Butter Icecream	160	11	22
Rice Dream: Cones, all types	270	14	37
Vanilla Bar, 1 bar	220	14	25
Vanilla Nutty Bar, 1 bar	260	18	23
Mocha/Vanilla Pie	290	15	37
Smart Ones (*Weight Watchers*):			
Chocolate Mousse	40	1	9
Chocolate Treat	100	0.5	20
English Toffee Crunch	110	6	12
Mocha Java	80	1.5	15
Orange Vanilla Treat	40	0.5	10
Vanilla Sandwich	150	3	28
Snackwell: Icecream Sandwich	90	1.5	18
Yogurt Bars, 1 bar, 80g	120	2	22
Snickers: Pralines n' Creme	220	13	22
Icecream Bar	180	11	18
Snack, 4 bars	390	25	38
Starbuck's:			
Coffee & Almond Bars, 81g	280	18	26
Coffee Frappuccino Bars	110	2	20
Mocha Frappuccino Bar	120	2	21
Java Ice Cream Bar	270	16	29
Starburst: Juice Bars	20	0	5
Super Sundae Bar, 86g	310	20	26
3 Musketeers: 2 fl.oz bars	170	10	21
Snack Bars, regular	60	4	16
Tandem *(Nestlé)*: Sandwich	380	21	39
Twin Pop *(Nestlé)*	60	0	14
Vitari: soft serve, 4 fl.oz, average	80	0	20
Welch's:			
Fruit Juice Bars, 92g	80	0	19
Tropical Coolers, 92 bar	45	0	11
No Sugar Added, 1 bar	25	0	6
Fruit Smoothie, 1 ctn	240	0	59

Quick Guide

Cream

	C	F	Cb
Average All Brands			
Half & Half Cream: 1 Tbsp	20	2	0.5
2 Tbsp, 1 oz	40	4	1
Light, coffee/table (20% fat): 1 T.	30	3	0.5
2 Tbsp, 1 oz	60	6	1
Medium (25% fat), 1 Tbsp	40	4	0.5
Sour Cream:			
Regular, 1 Tbsp	30	3	0.5
2 Tbsp, 1 oz	60	6	1
1 cup	490	48	8
Lowfat/Light, 1 Tbsp	20	2	1.5
2 Tbsp, 1 oz	40	2.5	2
Half & Half, 1 Tbsp	20	2	1
Fat Free: (*HeluvaGood)*, 2 Tbsp	20	0	6
(Kroger), 2 Tbsp, 32g	25	0	5
(Naturally Yours; Oak Farms), 2 T.	20	0	3
(Knudsen), 2 Tbsp, 32g	35	0	6
Sour Cream Substitute:			
(Albertson's/ IMO), 2 T., 1 oz	50	5	2
(Tofutti) Sour Supreme, 1 oz	50	5	1
Whipping Cream:			
Heavy (37% fat):			
1 Tbsp fluid/2 T. whipped	50	5.5	1
1/4 cup whipped	100	11	2
1/2 cup fluid/1 c. whipped	400	44	8
Light (30% fat):			
1 Tbsp fluid/2 T. whipped	45	5	0.5
1/2 cup fluid/1 c. whipped	350	37	4

Whipped Toppings

	C	F	Cb
Cream (Pressurized): *Average All Brands*			
1 Tbsp	10	1	0.5
1/4 cup	40	4	2
Cream Toppings: ***Jewel,*** Lite, 2 T.	20	1	2
Cool Whip: Extra Creamy, 2 T.	25	1.5	2
Lite, 2 Tbsp, 9g	20	1	2
Free, 2 Tbsp, 9g	15	0	3
Non Dairy, 2 Tbsp	22	2	2
Kraft: Whipped, 2 Tbsp	20	2	1
Real Cream, 2 Tbsp	20	2	1
Reddi-Wip: Original Light, 2 T.	20	2	1
Deluxe, 2 Tbsp	30	3	0.5
1/4 cup/4 Tbsp	60	6	1
Fat Free, 2 Tbsp, 8g	10	0	2
Vetra: Light, sweetened, 2 T., 6g	15	1	1

Non-Dairy Coffee Creamers

Powder	C	F	Cb
Coffee-Mate:			
Regular, 1 tsp	10	0.5	1
1 heaping tsp	15	1	2
Fat Free, 1 tsp	10	0	2
Lite, 1 tsp	10	0.5	2
Flavors: 1 1/3 Tbsp	60	3	9
Fat Free: Average, 1 1/3 Tbsp	50	0	11
Cremora: Same as *Coffee Mate*			
N-Rich: Same as *Coffee Mate*			
Liquid/Refrigerated: *Per Tbsp*			
Coffee-Mate Non-Dairy Creamer:			
Plain: Regular/Plain, 1 Tbsp	20	1	2
Fat Free, 1 Tbsp	10	0	2
Lite, 1 Tbsp	10	0.5	1
Flavors: All flavors, 1 Tbsp	40	2	5
Fat Free, all flavors, 1 Tbsp	25	0	5
Hood (Non Dairy), 1 Tbsp	25	0	5
International Delight:			
Regular/Flavors, 1 Tbsp	35	1.5	6
Fat Free flavors, 1 Tbsp	30	0	7
Mocha Mix: Original, 1 Tbsp	20	1.5	1
Fat Free, 1 Tbsp	10	0	1
Lite, 1 Tbsp	10	0.5	1
Morning Blend (Ralph's):			
Non-Dairy Creamer: Reg., 1 Tbsp	15	1.5	0
Fat Free, 1 Tbsp	5	0	2
Rich's Coffee Rich: Regular, 1 T.	25	1	2
Light	15	0.5	0.5
Rich's Farm Rich: Regular, 1 Tbsp	20	1	2
Light/Fat Free	10	0	0.5

Coconut Cream/Milk

	C	F	Cb
Coconut Cream (Canned),			
Plain/unsweetened, 2 Tbsp, 1 oz	70	6	4
1/2 cup	280	24	16
Sweetened: *Coco Lopez,* 1 oz	120	5	20
1/2 cup, 4 oz	480	20	80
Coconut Milk, can, 1/2 cup	225	24	3
Coconut Water (center), 1 cup	45	0.5	9

Quick Guide

Butter & Margarine

Butter, Margarine, Blends	C	F	Cb
Average All Brands			
Regular: 1 tsp (5g)	35	4	0
1 Pat (5g)	35	4	0
1 Tbsp, approx. 1/2 oz	100	11	0
2 Tbsp, 1 oz	205	23	0
1 Stick, 1/2 cup, 4 oz	810	92	0
1 Pound, 2 cups, 16 oz	3240	368	0
Light (Regular) 40% Fat:			
1 tsp, 5g	17	2	0
1 Tbsp, 1/2 oz	50	6	0
2 Tbsp, 1 oz	100	11	0
Whipped (Regular):			
1 tsp (4 g)	27	3	0
1 Tbsp (10g)	70	7.5	0
1 Stick, 1/2 cup, 2 2/3 oz	570	60	0
Light (Whipped) 40% Fat:			
1 tsp, 5g	10	1	0
1 Tbsp. 9g	35	3.5	0
2 Tbsp, 18g	70	7	0
Unsalted: Same as Salted			

Clarified Butter

	C	F	Cb
100% Fat: 1 Tbsp, 1/2 oz	130	15	0
2 Tbsp, 1 oz	260	30	0

Flavored Butter/Spread

	C	F	Cb
Average All Brands			
Honey Butter (60% Fat):			
1 Tbsp, 1/2 oz	90	7	4
Downey's, 1 Tbsp, 1/2 oz	60	1	11
Garlic Butter (80% Fat):			
1 Tbsp, 1/2 oz	100	11	0
Sweet Cream Butter:			
Regular, 1 Tbsp	100	11	0
Stick (70% Fat), 1 Tbsp	90	10	0
Tub (60% Fat), 1 Tbsp	80	9	0

Other Spreads & Fats

	C	F	Cb
Copha, Dripping, Lard, Suet, Shortening:			
1 Tbsp, 1/2 oz	120	13	0
Chicken, Duck, Goose Fat:			
1 Tbsp, 1/2 oz	115	13	0

Light & Reduced Fat Spreads

Per 1 Tbsp (Unless Stated)	C	F	Cb
Benecol: Regular, single serve, 8g	45	5	0
Light, single serve, 8g	30	3	0
Blue Bonnet: Lowfat Margarine	45	4.5	0
45% Veg. Oil Spread	70	7	0
Breakstone's Whipped Butter	60	7	0
Brummel & Brown: Spread	50	5	0
Chiffon: Whipped, 1 Tbsp	70	7	0
Country Crock: Regular	60	7	0
Light	50	5	0
Country's Delight (70% Veg.)	90	10	0
Country Morning: Light	50	6	0
Downey's Honey Butter	60	1	0
Dutch Farms: 52% Veg. Spread	70	7	0
Fleischmann's: Soft Spread	80	9	0
Original	90	10	0
Fat Free Spread	5	0	0
'I Can't Believe It's Not Butter': Reg.	90	10	0
Light	50	5	0
Imperial: Diet, 1 Tbsp	50	6	0
Jewel: Soft Spread	60	7	0
Unbelievably Butter	90	9	0
Kraft: 'Touch of Butter' (bowl)	50	6	0
Land O'Lakes: Tub	80	8	0
Honey Butter	90	7	4
Light Whipped Butter	35	3.5	0
Light Butter	50	6	0
Mazola: Diet	50	6	0
Mother's; Mrs Filbert's, 1 Tbsp	70	8	0
Miracle: Soft	60	7	0
Stick	70	7	0
Nucoa: HeartBeat Margarine	25	3	0
Olivio: Vegetable Spread	80	8	0
Parkay: Squeeze, 1 Tbsp	80	9	0
Stick, 1/3 Less Fat	70	7	0
Tub, 1 Tbsp	60	7	0
Tub, Light/Soft Diet	50	6	0
Whipped	70	7	0
Promise: Regular	90	10	0
Extra Light	50	6	0
Buttery Light	45	5	0
Ultra, w. canola oil	35	4	0
Smart Balance: Regular	80	9	0
Light, 1 Tbsp	45	5	0
Smart Beat: Fat Free	10	0	3
Take Control: Veg Oil Spread	50	6	0
Weight Watcher's: Light, all types	45	4	2

Butter Substitutes

	C	F	Cb
Bake It Perfect (Fat Free Spread), 1 T.	5	0	0
Best O'Butter, $^1/_2$ tsp	4	0	0
Butter Buds: 1 serving, $^1/_2$ tsp	4	0	0
Butterlike Saute Butter, 1 Tbsp	35	2	0
Butter Sprinkles (Watkins): 1 tsp	5	0	0
Earth Balance, Non GMO,1 tsp	35	3.5	0
Molly McButter: $^1/_2$ tsp	5	0	0
Mrs Bateman's Baking Buttter, 1 T.	35	1	0

Spreads Comparison

	C	F	Cb
Mayonnaise: Regular, 1 Tbsp	100	11	0.5
Light, average, 1 Tbsp	50	5	1
Fat Free (e.g. *Wt. Watcher's*), 1 T.	12	0	3
Miracle Whip *(Kraft)*:			
Regular, 1 Tbsp	70	7	2
Light, 1 Tbsp	40	3	3
Free, 1 Tbsp	15	0	3
SmartBeat Dressing: 1 Tbsp	12	0	2

Extra Listings for Mayonnaise & Dressings
~ See Page 82 ~

	C	F	Cb
Peanut Butter, 1 Tbsp	100	8	3.5
Avocado, mashed, 1 Tbsp	25	2.5	2
Birdseye:			
No Fat Veggie Dip, 2 T., 1.1 oz	25	0	5

Animal Fats/Lards

Average All Types	C	F	Cb
Beef Tallow/Drippings, Lard (Pork), Chicken, Duck, Goose, Turkey.			
1 Tbsp (13g)	115	13	0
$2^1/_4$ Tbsp, 1 oz	255	28	0
1 cup, $7^1/_4$ oz	1850	205	0
$^1/_2$ pound, 8 oz	2040	227	0
Ghee/Butter Oil: 1 Tbsp, 13g	110	13	0
$2^1/_4$ Tbsp, 1 oz	250	28	0

Vegetable Shortening

Average All Types (example, *Crisco*)

	C	F	Cb
1 Tbsp	113	13	0
$2^1/_4$ Tbsp, 1 oz	250	28	0
1 cup, $7^1/_4$ oz	1810	205	0

Vegetable Oils

Includes almond, avocado, canola, corn, coconut, flaxseed, grapeseed, linseed, mustard, olive, palm, peanut, rice-bran, safflower, sesame, sunflower, soybean, wheatgerm. Note: Oil is 100% fat.

	C	F	Cb
1 tsp, 5g	45	5	0
1 Tbsp, $^1/_2$ oz	120	14	0
2 Tbsp, 1 oz	250	28	0
1 cup, $7^3/_4$ oz	1930	205	0

Fish Oils

Average All Types (Includes cod liver, herring, salmon, sardine):

	C	F	Cb
1 Tbsp, $^1/_2$ oz	125	14	0

Cooking Sprays

	C	F	Cb
Cooking Sprays (*Pam, Mazola, Weight Watchers, Wesson*):			
Per serving	2	0	0
2-3 second spray	6	1	0
Parkay Buttery Spray	0	0	0

Olestra (Olean)

	C	F	Cb
Olestra *(Olean)*	0	0	0

Olean is *Proctor & Gamble's* brand name for olestra - a no-calorie cooking oil that gives snacks (like potato chips, tortilla chips and crackers) taste and texture without adding fat or calories.

Quick Guide

Firm/Hard Cheeses

(American, Cheddar, Colby, Coon, Swiss)

	C	F	Cb
Regular Cheese:			
1 oz slice/piece	110	9	0.5
8 oz package	880	72	4
16 oz (1lb) package	1760	144	8
Cubes: 1" cube, 3/4 oz	55	5	0.5
1 1/4" cube, 1 oz slice	110	9	0.5
Diced: 1 cup, 4 1/2 oz	500	40	2
Grated: 1 Tbsp, 1/4 oz	27	2	0
Shredded:			
1/4 cup, 1 oz	110	9	0.5
1 cup, 4 oz	440	36	4
Sliced: 1 thin (3 1/2" sq.), 3/4 oz	85	7	0.5
Rectangular (7"x 4"x 1/8"), 1 1/2 oz	165	14	1
Round (3 1/4" diam. x 1/8"), 3/4 oz	85	7	0.5
Semi-circular, 1 1/4 oz (5 1/2" long, 3 1/2" radius, 1/8"thick)	140	11	0.5
Light: Average All Brands, oz	70	4.5	1
Fat Free: Average All Brands, 1 oz	50	0	2
Lowfat: Average All Brands, 1 oz	50	1.5	1

Cheese

Per 1 oz Unless Indicated

	C	F	Cb
American:			
Regular, 1 slice, 1 oz	110	9	1
Kraft Deluxe, 0.7 oz slice	70	6	0.5
Grated, 1 Tbsp, 1/4 oz	23	2	0
Light (*Borden*), 1 oz	70	4	0.5
Land O'Lakes, 1 oz	70	5	0.5
Smart Beat, 0.6 oz slice	35	2	0
Fat Free: Single, 0.75 oz	30	0	3
Alpine Lace, 1 oz	45	0	2
HealthyChoice, Singles, 0.7 oz	25	0	2
Weight Watchers, all types, 3/4 oz	30	0	3
***Babybel** (Laughing Cow)*, 1 oz	90	7	0
Crumbled, 1/2 cup, 2 1/2 oz	250	20	2
Dorman's Castello, 1 oz	135	12	1
***Bonbel** (Laughing Cow)*, 1 oz	100	8	0
Mini, 3/4 oz	75	6	0
Brick, 1 oz	100	8	0
Brie, 1 oz	95	8	1
Camembert, 1 oz	90	7	1
Caraway, 1 oz	105	8	1
Cheddar:			
Regular, 1 oz	110	9	0.5
(Also see 'Quick Guide')			
Reduced Fat/Light, 1 oz	80	5	0.5
Weight Watchers, 1 oz	80	5	1
Fat Free: *Alpine Lace*, 1 oz	45	0	2
Weight Watchers, 1 sl., 3/4 oz	30	0	3
Cheese Balls (*Kaukauna*), 1 oz	100	7	0.5
Cheese Nut, Average, 1 oz	100	7	2
Cheese Logs, Average, 1 oz	100	7	0.5
Cheshire, 1 oz	110	9	1.5
Colby, Regular, 1 oz	110	9	0.5
Reduced Fat (*Alpine Lace*), 1 oz	80	5	1
Colby-Jack, 1 oz	110	9	0.5
Cottage Cheese: ***Average All Brands***			
Creamed: 2 Tbsp, 1 oz	30	1	1
1/2 cup, 4 oz	120	5	4
w. fruit, 1/2 cup, 4 oz	130	4	15
Reduced Fat (2%), 2 T., 1 oz	25	<1	1
1/2 cup, 4 oz	100	2	4
Low Fat (1%), 2 Tbsp, 1 oz	20	<1	1
1/2 cup, 4 oz	80	1	3
NonFat, 2 Tbsp, 1 oz	20	0	1
1/2 cup, 4 oz	80	0	3
Borden Dry Curd (0.5%), 1/2 c., 4 oz	80	0	0
Friendship : Low Fat P'apple, 4 oz	120	1	17
NonFat Plus Peach, 1/2 c., 4 oz	110	0	15
Pot Style, 1/2 cup, 4 oz	90	3	3
w. Pineapple, 4 oz	140	4	16
Knudsen: 1.5% Fruit, 4 oz	110	2	12
Free, 1/2 cup, 4.3 oz	80	0	4
Cottage Dbles, 1 ctn, 5.5 oz	140	2.5	18
On the Go!, 1 cup, 4 oz	110	1.5	13
Light N' Lively: Garden Salad, 4 oz	90	2	5
Peach and Pineapple, 1/2 cup, 4.3 oz	120	1	14
Chevre: See Goat's Milk Cheese			
Cream Cheese: See Page 39			
Edam: Regular, 1 oz	100	8	0
Farmer (*Friendship*), 2 Tbsp, 1 oz	50	3	0
Feta: Regular, *Frigo*, 1 oz	100	8	1
Crumbled, 1/2 cup, 2 1/2 oz	190	15	2.5
Reduced Fat (*Alpine Lace*),	60	4	1
Fontina (*Sargento/Classica*), 1 oz	110	9	0.5
Gjetost (Goat's Milk, fresh), 1 oz	85	7	0.5
Sargento, 1 oz	130	8	12
Goat's Milk: Soft: *Chevre*, 1 oz	70	6	0.5
Chavril, 3 Tbsp, 1 oz	60	4.5	0.5

Goat's Milk Cheese (Cont)	C	F	Cb
Semi-Soft: 1 oz	100	8.5	1
Hard: Sargento, 1 oz	130	10	0.5
Gorgonzola: 1 oz	110	9	0.5
Galbani Dolcelatte: 1 oz	95	8	1
Gouda: 1 oz	100	8	0.5
Gruyere, 1 oz	115	9	0
Havarti, 1 oz	120	11	0
Italian (*Classica Italiano*), 1 oz	110	10	1
Jarlsberg, 1 oz	100	7	1
Jarlsberg Lite shredded, 1 oz	70	4	1
Kefir, 2 Tbsp, 1 oz	60	4	1
Limburger, 1 oz	90	8	0
Mascarpone, 1 oz	130	13	1
Mexican (*Sargento* Recipe Blend),			
Shredded, 1/4 cup, 1 oz	110	9	0.5
Monterey, 1 oz	105	8.5	0
Monterey Jack: regular, 1 oz	110	9	0
Light Naturals (Kraft), 1 oz	80	5	0
Alpine Lace, *Monti-Jack Lo*, 1 oz	80	5	0
Weight Watchers, 1 oz	90	6	1
Mozzarella:			
Regular: *Kraft/Dorman's*, 1 oz	90	7	0.5
Land O'Lakes/Polly-O, 1 oz	80	6	0.5
Shredded, 1/4 cup, 1 oz	80	6	0.5
Light: *Polly-O Lite*, 1 oz	60	2.5	0.5
Kraft Light Naturals, 1 oz	80	5	0.5
Sorrento Lite, 1 oz	60	3	0.5
Part Skim (*Alpine Lace*), 1 oz	70	5	0.5
Polly-O, 1 oz	90	6	0.5
Fat Free: *Healthy Choice*, 1/4 c.,1oz	45	0	1
Polly-O, 1 oz	35	0	1
Kraft, shredded, 1/4 cup, 1 oz	50	0	2
Muenster: regular, 1 oz	110	9	0
Reduced Fat: *Dorman's*, 1 oz	80	5	0
Neufchatel: *Dominick's*, 1 oz	70	6	2
Philadelphia, 1 oz	70	6	0.5
Flavored: Fruit/Herbs	80	7	1
Chocolate (*Hickory Farms*), 1 oz	110	8	1
Parmesan: Fresh/Block, 1 oz	110	7	0
Shredded/Grated, 1 Tbsp	22	1.5	0
Grated (Packaged): 1 Tbsp	26	2	0
1oz quantity	130	9	1
1/2 cup, 1 3/4 oz	230	16	2
w.Romano (*Frigo*), grated, 1 oz	130	9	1

Note: Packaged grated and shredded Parmesan have more calories (per unit weight) than block Parmesan due to a lower moisture content.

Pizza, shredded:	C	F	Cb
Frigo, 1/4 cup, 1 oz	90	7	1
1 cup, 4 oz	360	28	4
Lowfat *(Frigo)*, 1 oz	65	3	1
Port Du Salut, 1 oz	100	8	0.5
Port Wine (*Hickory Farms*), 1 oz	100	7	2.5
Pot (*Sargento*), 1 oz	25	0	1
Provolone: Regular, 1 oz	100	8	1
Reduced Fat, *Alpine Lace*, 1 oz	70	5	1
Pub (*Hickory Farms*), 1 oz	95	7	1
Quark: 40% fat, 1 oz	47	3	1
20% fat, 1 oz	32	1.5	1
Skim, 1 oz	22	0	1.5
Queso: Anego/Asadero/Blanco	105	9	1
Queso Chichuahua/De Papa	110	9	2
Queso De Taco, 1 oz	105	9	1
Ricotta Cheese:			
Whole Milk, 2 Tbsp, 1 oz	50	3.5	1
1/2 cup, 4 1/2 oz	225	16	4.5
Part Skim, 2 Tbsp, 1 oz	40	2.5	1
1/2 cup, 4 1/2 oz	180	12	4.5
Light/Low Fat, 2 Tbsp. 1 oz	30	1.5	2
1/2 cup, 4 1/2 oz	140	6	9
Fat Free *(Polly-O)*, 1/2 c., 4 1/2 oz	100	0	4
Baked Ricotta, 2 oz portion	130	9	3
Romano: Block/Loaf, 1 oz	110	8	1
Grated (Pkg), 1 oz	120	9	1
1 Tbsp	26	2	0.5
Roquefort, 1 oz	105	9	0.5
Slim Jack (*Dorman's*), 1 oz	90	7	1
Sheep's Milk (*Hollow Rd Farm*)	45	3	1
Smoked: *Sargents* Smokestick	100	7	1
Hickory Farm, Smoky Lyte, 1 oz	80	6	1
Stilton, 1 oz	118	10	1
String (*Frigo/Kraft/Sargento*), 1 oz	80	5	1
String Lite (*Frigo*), 1 oz	60	2	1
Mootown Light (*Sargento*), 1 stick	50	2.5	0.5
Swiss: Regular, 1 oz	110	9	1
Reduced Fat: *Alpine Lace*, 1 oz	90	6	1
Dorman's/Kraft Light Naturals, 1oz	90	5	1
Weight Watchers, 3/4 oz slice	30	0	2
Taco, shredded, 1/4 cup			
(*Frigo/Kraft/Sargents*)	110	9	1
Tilsit (*Sargents*), 1 oz	100	7	0.5
Tybo (*Dorman's/Sargents*), 1 oz	100	7	0.5
Vermont (*Churny*), 1 oz	100	9	1
Wensleydale, 1 oz	108	9	0
Whey Cheese, 1 oz	125	8	9

Cheese Products

	C	F	Cb
Cheese Food:			
Average all flavors, 3/4 oz slice	**70**	5	1.5
1 oz slice	**90**	6	2
Alouette: Fr. Onion/Garl.,2 T., 0.8oz	**70**	7	1
Light Garlic, 2 Tbsp, 0.8 oz	**50**	4	1
Cracker Barrel, Cheddar, 1.1 oz	**100**	8	4
Delico: Alouette Cajun, 2 T, 0.8 oz	**70**	7	1
Garden Vegetable, 2 T, 0.8 oz	**60**	6	1
Handi-Snacks:			
Cheez 'n Breadsticks, 1 pkg	**130**	7	11
Cheez'n Pretzels, 1 oz pkg	**110**	6	11
Cheez'n Crackers, 1.1 oz pkg	**130**	8	10
Mozzarella Stringchse Stick, each	**80**	6	0.5
Healthy Choice: Amer. Singles, 1 sl.	**30**	0	2
Heluva Good Cheese:			
American, 1 slice	**45**	5	2
Cheddar w. H/radish, 2 Tbsp, 1oz	**90**	7	3
Jalapeno: Aver., all brands, 1 oz	**90**	7	2
Kraft: American grated, 1T., 0.2 oz	**25**	2	1
Singles, 1 slice, 3/4 oz	**70**	6	1
Free Singles, 1 slice, 0.7 oz	**30**	3	3
Pimento Spread, 2 Tbsp, 1.1 oz	**80**	6	3
Velveeta (Process Cheese Spread)			
Regular, 3/8" slice, 1 oz	**100**	6	3
Light, 3/8" slice, 1 oz	**60**	3	3
Lifeway: Farmers Cheese, 2 oz	**75**	5	2.5
Precious: String Chse Stuffsters, 1 oz	**70**	4.5	1
Roka Blue, 2 Tbsp, 1.1 oz	**80**	7	2
Rondele: Soft Spread., 2 T, 1 oz	**100**	9	1
Light, 2 Tbsp, 0.9 oz	**60**	4	2
SmartBalance: Crmy Cheddar, 1 sl.	**40**	2	2
SmartBeat: All flav., 1 sl., 0.6 oz	**35**	2	2
Spreadery: Vermont, 2 Tbsp, 1 oz	**80**	5	3
Neufchatel, all flavors, 2 T, 1 oz	**80**	7	1
Velveeta: Cheese, 1 slice, 1 oz	**100**	6	3
Light, 1 oz	**60**	3	3
Shredded, 1/4 cup, 1.3 oz	**130**	9	3
WisPride: Hickory Smoked Cup;			
Port Wine Ball/Cup, 2 T., 1.1 oz	**100**	7	4
Light, 2 T., 1.1 oz	**80**	3	5

Cheese Whiz (Sauce)

	C	F	Cb
Regular, 2 Tbsp, 33g	**90**	7	20
Light, 2 Tbsp, 33g	**80**	3	6
Squeezable, 2 Tbsp, 33g	**100**	8	4

Cheese Substitutes

Per 1 oz Unless Indicated	C	F	Cb
Almond Rella (Nu Soya):			
Cheddar; Garlic & Herb, 1 oz	**60**	3	3
Borden: Taco-Mate, 1 oz	**100**	7	2
Delicia: American Colby	**80**	6	1
Dorman's Lo Chol: All types	**100**	7	1
Formagg:			
American Wh./Yellow, 1 sl. 0.7oz	**60**	4	0.5
Cheddar, 1 slice, 0.7 oz	**60**	4	0.5
Mozzarella (Old World), 1 oz	**60**	3	1
Parmesan Grated, 1 Tbsp, 1/4 oz	**22**	1.5	1.5
Provolone (Vintage), 1 oz	**60**	3	1
Swiss White, 1 slice, 0.7 oz	**60**	4	0.5
Frigo: Cheddar; Mozzarella, 1 oz	**90**	7	1
Georgio's: Imitation Cheddar;			
Mozzarella., shredded, 1/4 c., 1 oz	**90**	7	1
Golden Image:			
American 1 slice, 0.7 oz	**70**	5	1
Mild Cheddar, 1 slice, 0.7 oz	**70**	5	1
Harvest Moon : *Per 1/4 cup, 1.3 oz*			
Shredded: American; Cheddar	**120**	9	3
Mozzarella	**110**	9	3
Nu Tofu: Mozzarella, 1 oz	**70**	4	2
Fat Free: Mozz./Ched./Jack, 1 oz	**40**	0	2
Sargento *Classic Supreme:*			
Cheddar, shredded, 1 oz	**90**	6	2
Mozzarella, shrd, 1/4 cup	**80**	6	0.5
Smart Beat, all varieties, 0.6 oz sl.	**35**	2	2
Soya Kaas: Regular, 1 oz	**70**	5	1
Fat Free, all varieties, 1 oz	**40**	2	1
Soyco: Almond/Oat/Rice Slices,			
1 slice, 0.7 oz	**40**	2	1
Veggy Singles, 1 slice, 0.7 oz	**40**	2	1
Grated Parmesan, 2 tsp, 5g	**15**	0.5	0
Tofu Rella: *Per 1 oz*			
Tofu Rella, average all varieties	**180**	2	39
Zero-Fat Rella, all varieties	**45**	0	3
Almond/Hemp/Rice Rella,			
average all varieties	**70**	3.5	3
Tofutti *Better Than Cream Cheese*	**80**	8	1
Weight Watchers: Fat Free Slices,			
All varieties, 3/4 oz slice	**30**	0	3
Grated Italian Topping, 1 Tbsp	**20**	0	2
White Wave, *Soy A Melt:*			
Cheddar/Mozz./Mont. Jack, 1 oz	**80**	5	1
Fat Free, 1 oz	**40**	0	3
Singles: Amer./Mozzrlla, 3/4 oz sl.	**60**	4	1

Snack & Cheese Dips, Spreads

Cream Cheese

	C	F	Cb
Regular/Soft: 2 Tbsp, 1 oz	100	10	1
3 oz pkg	300	30	2
w. Chives/Herbs/Pimento, 1 oz	90	9	0.5
w. Fruit/Strawb./P'apple, 1 oz	90	8	5
Lox, 1 oz	90	9	0.5
Philadelphia Brand:			
Plain/Soft, 2 Tbsp, 1 oz	100	10	1
1/3 Less Fat, 1 oz	70	6	1
Light, 1 oz	70	5	2
Fat Free, 2 Tbsp, 1 oz	30	0	3
Flavor./Herbs/Fruit/Salmon, 1 oz	100	10	2
w. Smoked Salmon 1 oz	100	9	1
Light Blueberry, 2 Tbsp	70	4.5	5
Snack Bars: aver., all types, ea.	200	13	20
Whipped, 3 Tbsp, 1 oz	110	11	1
Alpine Lace: Fat Free, 2 T., 1 oz	30	0	1
Dominick's: Fat Free, 2 Tbsp, 1 oz	35	0	4
Light, 2 Tbsp, 1 oz	60	5	2
Weight Watchers, 2 Tbsp, 1 oz	40	2.5	1

Dips/Spreads

Per 2 Tbsp (1 oz) Unless Indicated

	C	F	Cb
Avocado/Guacomole	50	4	4
Baba Ghannouj (Eggplant/Sesame)	70	6	2
Birdseye: No Fat Veggie Dip, 1.1 oz	25	0	5
Breakstone: Sour Cream, all flav.	50	4	4
Chalco: Quéso Quesadilla; Cotija	120	10	0
Fresco, 2 Tbsp, 1 oz	70	8	0
Chef's Kitchen *(Jewel):* Dilly Dip	150	16	1
French Onion/Quarter; Spinach	70	6	2
Chi-Chi's: Con Quéso, 2 Tbsp	90	7	4
Hot/Medium/Mild/Acante, 2 T.	10	0	2
Dominick's: Port Wine & Cheddar	100	8	4
Eagle: Bean	35	2	2
French Onion Dip, aver. all brands	60	6	3
Frito Lay: Chili Cheese	45	3	3
French Onion	60	5	4
Bean/Jalapeno Bean	40	1	6
Jalapeno & Cheddar	50	3	3
Guacamole, 2 Tbsp, 1 oz	50	4	4
Guiltless Gourmet: Nacho Dip	25	0	5
Other varieties	30	0	5
Heluva Good Cheese:			
Cheese 'N Salsa	80	3	3
Clam/French Onion	50	5	2
Bacon/Homestyle/Ranch	60	5	2
Light Fr. Onion/Jalapeno Cheddar	40	2	3

Dips/Spreads (Cont)

Per 2 Tbsp (1 oz)

	C	F	Cb
Hummus, 2 Tbsp, 1 oz	50	1	5
1/2 cup, 4.5 oz	220	4.5	23
Hy-Top: Pimiento, 1 oz	90	8	3
Kaukauna: Nacho Cheese	90	7	4
Knudsen: Nacho Cheese	60	4	3
Sour Cream Bacon & Onion	60	5	2
Sour Cream French Onion	50	4	2
Kroger: The Big Dipper; all flavors	60	5	2
Kraft: Average all flavors	60	5	4
Premium: Bac. & On./Nacho Ch.	60	5	2
Other flavors	50	4	2
Philly flavors: Pineapple	100	9	1
Chive & Onion; Salmon	110	10	2
Cheesecake; Strawberry	110	9	5
Fat Free: Strawberry	45	0	6
Garden Veges	30	0	2
Lay's: Lowfat Sr. Cream, Onion	40	1	0
Louise's: (Fat Free) Honey Mustard	40	0	0
Sour Cream & Onion/Wh.Cheese	25	0	0
Marzetti: Blue Cheese	200	21	1
Light Ranch Veggie	60	7	5
Other flavors, average	140	14	2
Nalley's: All flavors, average	120	12	3
Naturally Fresh: All flavors, 1 oz	80	0	19
Old Dutch: Cheddar, Nacho	35	3	3
Old El Paso:			
Black Bean	25	0	5
Cheese'n Salsa: Mild; Medium	40	3	3
Lowfat, medium	30	1.5	3
Chunky Salsa varieties	15	0	3
Jalapeno Dip	30	1	4
Olys Bagel Spread: Berry	100	8	3
Honey Cinnamon; Raisin	100	8	6
Garden Veg; Garlic & Herb	90	9	1
Prices: Orig. Pimiento Cheese Spr.	80	7	2
Ruffles: French Onion; Ranch	70	6	4
Sealtest: French Onion	50	4	2
Snyder's Mustard Pretzel	90	4	13
Supremo Chihuahua: Quéso Bianco	100	8	0
Quéso Fresco; Rancherito	80	6	0
Tostitos Dip: Con Quéso	40	2	5
Medium/Mild/Hot	15	0	3
Tzatziki (Cucumber/Yoghurt Dip)	40	3	1
Wise: Jalapeno Bean	25	0	5
Taco	12	0	3

Salsa: See Page 78

Egg & Egg Dishes

Chicken Eggs

	C	F	Cb
Fresh Eggs			
Raw (weight with shell):			
Small, 40g	**65**	4	0
Medium, 44g	**70**	4	0
Large, 50g	**75**	4.5	0
Extra Large,56g	**80**	5	0
Jumbo, 63g	**90**	5.5	0
Egg Yolk, 1 extra large	**63**	5	0
Egg White, 1 extra large	**16**	0	0
Dried Egg Powder			
Whole Egg: 1/4 cup, 1 oz	**170**	12	0
1 Tbsp	**30**	2	0
Egg White, 1/4 cup, 1 oz	**105**	0	0
Egg Yolk, 1/4 cup, 1 oz	**195**	18	0
1 Tbsp	**27**	2.5	0

Egg Substitutes

1/4 Cup (Equivalent to 1 Egg) ~ Zero Cholesterol.

	C	F	Cb
Better 'n Eggs (Papetti), 1/4 cup, 2 oz	**30**	0	0
Egg Beaters (Fleischmann's):			
Regular, 1/4 cup	**30**	0	1
Cheese Omelete, 1/2 cup	**110**	5	2
Vegetable Omelete, 1/2 cup	**50**	0	5
Egg Watchers (Tofutti), 2 oz	**30**	0	1
Eggstra, 1/2 envelope	**50**	2	0
Healthy Choice, 1/4 cup, 2 oz	**25**	0	0
Egg Substitute (Jewel), 1/4 cup	**30**	0	1
Scramblers (Morn Star), 1/4 cup	**35**	0	0
Second Nature: Regular, 1/4 cup	**60**	2	3
Fat Free, 1/4 cup, 60ml	**30**	0	1
Simply Eggs, 1/4 cup	**35**	1	1

Other Eggs

	C	F	Cb
Duck, 1 large, 2 1/2 oz	**130**	9.5	0
Goose, 1 large, 5 oz	**280**	19	0
Quail, 3 eggs, 1 oz	**42**	3	0
Turkey, 1 large, 3 oz	**135**	9.5	0
Turtle, 1 egg, 1 3/4 oz	**75**	5	0

Omega-3 Fat Enriched

	C	F	Cb
Eggs Plus (Pilgrim's Pride): 1 large	**70**	4.5	0

Note: Cholesterol content same as regular eggs, but Omega-3 fats inhibit blood cholesterol increase. (Also see Cholesterol ~ Page 249)

Cooked Eggs

	C	F	Cb
Boiled Egg: Same as raw egg			
Fried Egg:			
With fat: 1 large egg	**100**	8	0.5
2 small eggs	**175**	13	1
No fat/nonstick pan, 1 large	**80**	5.5	0
Deviled Egg, 2 halves	**145**	13	0.5
Eggs Benedict (2) on toast or English muffin	**860**	56	25
Eggs Florentine (2) on toast or English muffin	**890**	59	25
Pickled Egg, 1 large	**80**	5.5	0
Poached Egg: 1 large	**80**	5.5	0
Scotch Egg, 1 egg	**300**	21	16
Scrambled Eggs: 1 large egg:			
w. 1 Tbsp milk + 1 tsp fat	**120**	9	1
w. 1 Tbsp skim milk/no fat	**85**	5.5	1
2 large eggs:			
w. 2 Tbsp milk + 2 tsp fat	**260**	20	2
w. 2 Tbsp skim milk/no fat	**180**	11	2

Omelets

	C	F	Cb
1 Egg: Plain (w. 1 tsp fat)	**125**	10	0.5
with 1/2 oz cheese	**175**	15	0.5
w. 1/2 oz cheese +1/2 oz ham	**200**	16	0.5
2 Eggs: Plain (w. 2 tsp fat)	**250**	20	1
with 1 oz cheese	**360**	29	2
w. 1 oz cheese+1 oz ham	**410**	32	2
3 Eggs: Plain (w. 1 Tbsp fat)	**360**	29	1.5
w. 2 oz cheese	**580**	47	2.5
w. 2 oz cheese+2 oz ham	**680**	53	2.5
Extras: Tomato/Onion/Veges	**20**	0	4.5
Egg Substitute (*Eggbeaters*):			
2 eggs (1/2 cup) + 1 tsp fat	**100**	4	2
3 eggs (3/4 cup) + 2 tsp fat	**160**	8	3
Extras: 1 oz cheese	**110**	9	1
1 oz ham	**50**	3	1
Tom./Onion/Veges	**20**	0	4.5

Egg Nog

Per 1/2 Cup (4 fl.oz)

	C	F	Cb
Regular: *Borden*	**160**	9	16
Crowley	**190**	9	23
Hood (Goldeen)	**180**	8	22
Light: *Borden/Hood*	**120**	2	23
Fat Free: *Hood*	**100**	0	21

Breakfast Sides

	C	F	Cb
Toast: Plain, 1 thick slice	85	1	13
with 2 tsp butter/marg.	155	9	13
with 3 tsp/1Tbsp fat	190	13	13
English Muffin: Plain, 2 oz	130	1	26
with 3 tsp fat	230	12	26
Bacon, 2 strips	70	5	0
Ham: Lean, 2 oz	100	3	0
Hash Browns: 1/2 cup	125	6.5	14
1 cup serving	250	13	28
Sausages, 2 links (1 oz ea.)	180	16	1.5

Frozen Egg Dishes

	C	F	Cb
Downyflake: Scrambled Eggs			
w. Ham & Hash Browns, 1 pkg	360	26	17
w. Ham & Pecan Twirl	470	28	40
w. Hash Browns & Sausage	420	34	17
Pillsbury Toaster Scrambles, 1	170	11	14
Swanson Great Starts: *Per Packet*			
Scrambled Eggs: w. Burrito	200	8	25
w. Bacon & Home Fries	290	19	17
w. Home Fries	200	12	15
w. Sausage & Hash Browns	360	26	21
Low Fat	240	13	18
Low Fat/Chol Eggs: w. Pancakes	220	7	30
w. Canadian Bacon	240	6	33
Egg, Bacon, Cheese Muffin	290	15	25
Egg, Sausage & Cheese	460	28	37
French Toast Sticks w. Syrup	320	10	50
Pancakes w. Sausage	490	25	52
Sandwich Egg, Cheese	350	20	30
Sausage, Egg & Chse on Biscuit	460	28	37
Quaker Scrambled Eggs			
w. Cheese/Fried Potatoes	250	13	22
w. Sausage & Hash Browns	290	20	14
w. Sausage & Pancakes	270	14	21
Weight Watchers: Omelet	220	5	30

Frozen Egg Rolls

Average All Brands (Chun King/La Choy)

	C	F	Cb
Chicken Egg Rolls: Mini, 5 rolls	165	6	24
Restaurant Style, 1 roll, 3 oz	170	5	25
Pork & Shrimp Egg Rolls:			
Mini, 5 rolls	175	5	23
Pork Restaurant Style, 1 roll	170	6	24
Shrimp Egg Rolls: Mini, 5 rolls	155	5	23
Restaurant Style, 1 roll	150	4	24

Fast Food/Restaurants

	C	F	Cb
Bojangles:			
Bacon/Egg/Chse S'wich	550	42	27
Burger King:			
Bisc. w. Bacon/Egg/Cheese	510	31	39
Croissan'wich Saus./Egg/Chse	550	42	22
Carl's Jr: Scrambled Eggs	160	11	1
Denny's: Eggs Benedict	695	45	34
Omelette: Ham 'n Cheddar	580	45	7
Veggie-Cheese	490	40	10
Farmer's	915	70	29
Sirloin Steak & Eggs	620	49	1
Hardees: Bacon & Egg	570	33	45
Ham, Egg & Cheese	540	30	48
Ultimate Omelet	570	33	45
McDonald's: Egg McMuffin®	290	12	27
Bacon, Egg & Cheese Biscuit	540	34	36
Scrambled Eggs (2)	160	11	1
Perkins: Country Club Omelet	930	79	6
Quincy's: Scrambled Eggs	95	7	1
Roy Rogers: Ham & Egg Bisc.	460	23	48

New Diet Aid – The Refrigerator Air-Bag!

Note: Cooking reduces weight of meat by 20-45% due to water and fat losses. Average weight loss is 30%. Actual loss depends on cooking method and cooking time. Examples:

4 oz raw wt. = approx. 3 oz cooked wt.
4 oz cooked wt. = approx. 5 1/2 oz raw wt.

What 3 oz Cooked Meat Looks Like

- Half the size of this book (4 1/4" x 3" x 3/8" thick)
- Rectangular piece (4" x 2 1/2" x 1/2" thick)
- Pack of cards (3 1/2" x 2 1/2" x 5/8" thick)

Quick Guide

Steak

Sirloin (Choice Grade)
External fat trimmed to 1/4"
Broiled, Edible Portion (no bone)

	C	F	Cb
Small Serving, 3 oz			
(3 oz cooked, from 4-4 1/2 oz raw)			
Lean + fat (1/4"), 3 oz	230	14	0
Lean + marbling, 3 oz	195	10	0
(External fat trimmed **before** cooking)			
Lean only, 3 oz	170	7	0
(No external fat or marbling)			
Medium/Regular Serving, 5 oz			
(from approx. 7 oz raw)			
Lean + fat (1/4"), 5 oz	470	29	0
Lean + marbling, 5 oz	400	20	0
Lean only, 5 oz	350	14	0
Large Serving, 8 oz			
(from 11-12 oz raw)			
Lean + fat, 8 oz	610	38	0
Lean + marbling, 8 oz	520	26	0
Lean only, 8 oz	454	18	0
Extra Large Serving, 12 oz			
(from approx. 16-17 oz raw)			
Lean + fat (1/4"), 12 oz	915	57	0
Lean + marbling, 12 oz	780	39	0
Lean only, 12 oz	680	27	0
Pan Fried			
Sirloin (choice), medium serving:			
Lean + fat (1/4"), 5 oz	450	32	0
Lean only, 5 oz	330	15	0

Other Steaks

	C	F	Cb
Filet Mignon (Tenderloin):			
1 medium steak, 6 oz raw wt.			
Broiled, with 1/4" fat trim			
Lean + fat (1/4"), 4 oz	340	24	0
Lean only, 3 1/2 oz	210	10	0
Broiled, (1/4" fat removed before cooking)			
Lean + marbling, 3 1/4 oz	220	12	0
Lean only, 3 oz	180	8	0
New York/Club Steak:			
Top Loin/Short Loin			
1 steak, regular (9 1/4 oz raw, 1/4" fat)			
Broiled: Lean + fat (1/4"), 6 1/4 oz	510	35	0
Lean + marbling, 5 1/2 oz	330	16	0
Lean only, 5 1/4 oz	310	14	0
Porterhouse Steak:			
1 medium, 6 oz raw wt. (no bone)			
Broiled:			
Lean + fat (1/4"), 4 1/4 oz	370	27	0
Lean only, 3 1/2 oz	220	11	0
T-Bone Steak:			
1 medium, 8 oz raw wt.			
Broiled: Lean + fat	380	27	0
Lean only	220	10	0

Beef - Average All Cuts

	C	F	Cb
Average All Retail Cuts			
Edible weight (no bone)			
Raw			
(1 lb raw yields approx. 11-12 oz cooked)			
Lean + fat (1/4" trim), 1 oz	70	5.5	0
1/2 Pound, 8 oz	560	44	0
Lean only, 1 oz	40	2	0
1/2 Pound, 8 oz	320	16	0
Fat only, 1 oz	190	20	0
Cooked (No Added Fat)			
Lean + fat (1/4"), 1 oz	86	6	0
Small serving, 3 oz	260	18	0
Lean + marbling, (no ext. fat), 1 oz	78	5	0
Small serving, 3 oz	235	15	0
Lean only, 1 oz	60	3	0
Small serving, 3 oz	180	9	0
Fat only, 1 oz	193	20	0

Beef - Individual Cuts

Average All Grades Edible Weight (no bone)	C	F	Cb
Brisket, whole, braised:			
Lean + fat (1/4"), 3 oz	**330**	27	0
Lean + marbling, 3 oz	**250**	17	0
Lean only, 3 oz	**205**	11	0
Chuck, blade, braised:			
Lean + fat (1/4"), 3 oz	**290**	22	0
Lean + marbling, 3 oz	**285**	20	0
Lean only, 3 oz	**210**	11	0
Flank: Raw, 4 oz	**200**	12	0
Braised, 3 oz	**225**	14	0
Broiled, 3 oz	**190**	11	0
Ribs, whole (ribs 6-12):			
Average all grades, roasted			
(1 lb raw yields 10 1/4 oz roasted)			
Lean + fat (1/4")			
(3.6 oz w. bone, 3 oz no bone)	**300**	25	0
Lean only, 3 oz (no bone)	**200**	11	0
Round, bottom, braised:			
Lean + fat (1/4"), 3 oz	**235**	14	0
Lean only, 3 oz	**180**	7	0
Round, eye/tip, roasted:			
Lean + fat (1/4"), 3 oz	**200**	11	0
Lean, 3 oz	**150**	5	0
Round, top: *Per 3 oz*			
Braised, Lean + fat	**210**	10	0
Lean only	**175**	5	0
Broiled, Lean + fat	**185**	8	0
Lean only	**155**	4	0
Pan-fried, Lean + fat	**235**	13	0
Lean only	**190**	7	0

Ground Beef

Raw: Reg. (73% lean), 4 oz	**350**	30	0
Lean (80% lean), 4 oz	**300**	24	0
Extra lean (85% lean), 4 oz	**250**	17	0
Healthy Choice (97% lean), 4 oz	**130**	4	0
Baked/Broiled: Reg., 3 oz	**250**	18	0
Lean, 3 oz	**230**	16	0
Extra lean, 3 oz	**200**	12	0
Pan-fried: Regular, 3 oz	**260**	19	0
Lean, 3 oz	**230**	16	0
Extra lean, 3 oz	**200**	12	0
Ground Beef Patties: Average			
Frozen, raw, 4 oz	**320**	26	0
Broiled, 3 oz	**240**	17	0

Quick Guide

Roast Beef

Round (Eye/Tip, average) Average All Cuts	C	F	Cb
Small Serving, 3 oz			
(2 thin slices/1 thick slice)			
Lean + fat (1/4"), 3 oz	**200**	11	0
Lean only, 3 oz	**150**	5	0
Medium Serving, 5 oz, (3-4 thin slices)			
Lean + fat, 5 oz	**330**	18	0
Lean only, 5 oz	**250**	8	0
Large Serving, 8 oz, (3 thick slices)			
Lean + fat, 8 oz	**530**	29	0
Lean only, 8 oz	**400**	13	0

Roast Dinner Extras

Gravy: Thin, 2 Tbsp	**20**	1	0.5
Thick, 2 Tbsp	**50**	2	0.5
1 Ladle/4 Tbsp	**100**	4	1
Veges: Beans, green, 1/2 cup	**20**	0	5
Cauliflower w. cheese sauce, 4 oz	**135**	9	15
Corn, kernels, 1/4 cup	**35**	0	9
Carrots, 1/4 cup	**20**	0	3
Peas, 1/4 cup	**35**	0	6
Pumpkin baked: w.fat, 4 oz	**90**	7	5
No added fat, 2 pces, 4 oz	**25**	0	5
Potato:			
Roasted w. fat, 1 small	**155**	8	30
Baked in Jacket, 1 large	**220**	0	50
with 1 Tbsp whipped butter	**295**	8	50
with Sour Cream, 2 Tbsp	**270**	6	51
Sweet Potato/Yam, 1 medium	**80**	0	20

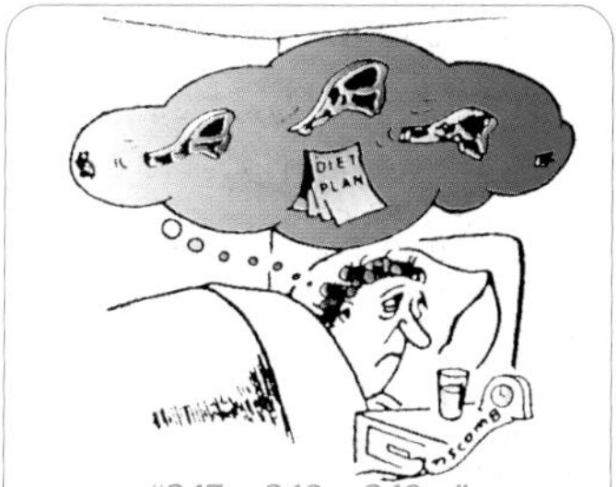

"347 ~ 348 ~ 349..."

Lamb

	C	F	Cb
Choice Grade			
Leg (Whole), roasted:			
Lean + fat, 3 oz	**220**	14	0
Lean only, 3 oz	**160**	7	0
Leg (Sirloin Half), roasted:			
Lean + fat, 3 oz	**250**	18	0
Lean only, 3 oz	**175**	8	0
Leg (Shank Half), roasted:			
Lean + fat, 3 oz	**190**	11	0
Lean only, 3 oz	**155**	6	0
Loin Chop, broiled:			
1 chop (raw wt., 4 1/4 oz):			
Lean + fat (2 1/4 oz edible)	**200**	15	0
Lean only (1.6 oz edible)	**100**	5	0
Rib Chop, broiled/roasted:			
1 chop (raw wt., 3 1/2 oz)			
Lean + fat (2 1/2 oz edible)	**255**	21	0
Lean only (1 3/4 oz edible)	**120**	7	0
Shoulder (Arm/Blade):			
Braised: Lean + fat, 3 oz	**290**	21	0
Lean only, 3 oz	**240**	14	0
Broiled: Lean + fat, 3 oz	**240**	16	0
Lean only, 3 oz	**180**	9	0
Roasted: Similar to Broiled			
Cubed Lamb (Leg/Shoulder):			
For stew or kabob			
Raw, lean only, 8 oz	**310**	12	0
Braised, lean only, 3 oz	**190**	8	0
Broiled, lean only, 3 oz	**160**	6	0
New Zealand Lamb (Imported):			
Similar calories and fat to domestic.			

Veal

	C	F	Cb
Edible Weights			
Leg (Top Round):			
Braised: Lean + fat, 3 oz	**180**	6	0
Lean only, 3 oz	**170**	5	0
Pan-fried, breaded:			
Lean + fat, 3 oz	**195**	8	9
Lean only, 3 oz	**175**	6	9
Pan-fried, not breaded:			
Lean + fat, 3 oz	**180**	7	0
Lean only, 3 oz	**155**	4	0
Roasted: Lean + fat, 3 oz	**135**	4	0
Lean only, 3 oz	**130**	3	0

Veal (Cont)

	C	F	Cb
Loin Chop: 1 chop, 7 oz raw wt.			
Braised: Lean + fat	**230**	14	0
Lean only	**155**	6	0
Roasted: Lean + fat	**175**	10	0
Lean only	**125**	5	0
Rib, roasted: Lean + fat, 3 oz	**195**	12	0
Lean only, 3 oz	**150**	7	0
Shoulder, Arm/Blade, roasted:			
Lean + fat, 3 oz	**155**	7	0
Lean only, 3 oz	**145**	6	0
Sirloin, roasted:			
Lean + fat, 3 oz	**170**	9	0
Lean only, 3 oz	**145**	6	0
Cubed for Stew, braised:			
Leg/Shoulder, lean only, 3 oz	**160**	4	0
(1 lb raw yields approx. 9 1/4 oz cooked)			

Pork

	C	F	Cb
Figures based on NLMB data (1990)			
Fresh Pork (Cooked Wt., no bone)			
(4 oz raw wt. = approx. 3 oz cooked wt.)			
Blade Steak, broiled:			
Lean + fat, 3 oz	**220**	15	0
Lean only, 3 oz	**190**	11	0
Country Style Ribs, broiled:			
Lean + fat, 3 oz	**270**	22	0
Lean only, 3 oz	**205**	13	0
Leg (Ham), roasted:			
Lean + fat, 3 oz	**250**	18	0
Lean only, 3 oz	**180**	9	0
(Ham, cured ~ See Cold Meats)			
Loin Chops, broiled: Average			
(From 1 chop: 5 oz raw wt. w.bone or 4 oz raw wt., no bone)			
Lean + fat, 3 oz	**200**	11	0
Lean only, 3 oz	**165**	7	0
Rib Chops, broiled:			
Lean + fat, 3 oz	**215**	13	0
Lean only, 3 oz	**180**	7	0
Rib Roast, roasted:			
Lean + fat, 3 oz	**210**	13	0
Lean only, 3 oz	**175**	9	0
Loin Roast, roasted:			
Lean + fat, 3 oz	**190**	10	0
Lean only, 3 oz	**160**	7	0

Pork (Cont)

	C	F	Cb
Sirloin Chop, broiled:			
Lean + fat, 3 oz	175	8	0
Lean only, 3 oz	155	6	0
Sirloin Roast, roasted:			
Lean + fat, 3 oz	215	14	0
Lean only, 3 oz	180	9	0
Tenderloin, roasted:			
Lean + fat, 3 oz	140	4	0
Lean only, 3 oz	135	4	0
Ground Pork			
Raw: Average, 1/4 lb, 4 oz	300	24	0
Broiled, 3 oz	245	18	0
Pan-fried, drained, 3 oz	250	19	0

Bacon

	C	F	Cb
Raw: 1 med. slice (20 lb), 3/4 oz	125	13	0
1 thick slice (12 lb), 1 1/3 oz	210	22	0
(1 lb raw yields approx. 5 oz cooked)			
Broiled/Pan-Fried: 1 med. sl., 6 g	36	3	0
3 medium slices, 18g	110	9	0
2 thin slices, 1/2 oz	80	7	0
1 thick slice, 12g	70	6	0
Canadian-style: Cooked, 1 slice	43	4	0
As purchased, 1 slice, 1 oz	45	4	1
Bacon Bits, 1 Tbsp, 1/4 oz	20	1	0
Breakfast Strips: Broil., 1 sl., 12 g	50	4	0

Ham

	C	F	Cb
Boneless Ham, cooked:			
Regular, (approx. 11% fat):			
Unheated (as purch.), 1 oz	52	3	0
Roasted, 3 oz	150	8	0
Extra Lean (5% fat):			
Unheated, 1 oz	37	2	0
Roasted, 3 oz	125	5	0
Whole Ham, cooked:			
Lean + fat (as purchased)			
Unheated, 1 oz	70	5	0
Roasted, 3 oz	345	26	0
Lean only, unheated, 1 oz	40	2	0
Roasted, 3 oz	135	5	0
Canned Ham: Similar to boneless ham			
Chopped, canned, 3 oz	260	21	0
Ham Patties, ckd, 1 pty, 2 1/4 oz	205	18	1
Ham Steak, extra lean, 2 oz	70	2	0

Luncheon Slices~ See Cold Meats: Page 48

Game Meats

	C	F	Cb
Bison Steak, lean, 6 oz (raw)	210	4	0
Boar (wild), roasted, 3 oz	140	4	0
Caribou, roasted, 3 oz	140	4	0
Deer/Venison, roasted 3 oz	135	3	0
Rabbit: Roasted, 3 oz	130	6	0
Stewed, 1 cup, diced, 5 oz	300	14	0

Variety & Organ Meats

	C	F	Cb
Brains: Braised, 3 oz	130	9	0
Pan-fried, 3 oz	200	14	0
Chitterlings, pork, simmered, 3oz	260	25	0
Ears, pork, simmered, 1 ear	180	12	0
Feet, pork: Simmered, 3 oz	165	11	0
Cured, pickled, 3 oz	170	14	0
Hormel, 2 oz	80	6	0
Head Cheese (Pork Snouts/Ears/Vinegar/Spices):			
1 oz slice	50	4	0
Heart: Average, braised, 3 oz	140	5	0
Jowl, pork, raw, 4 oz	750	80	0
Kidneys, simmered, 3 oz	130	4	0
Liver: Raw, 4 oz	160	5	3
Braised, 3 oz	140	4	3
Pan-fried, 3 oz	200	9	3
Pancreas, braised, 3 oz	200	13	0
Pork Cracklins, 0.5 oz	80	6	0
Pork Hocks, 1 piece, 6 oz	340	23	0
Scrapple, pork, 1 oz	60	4	4
Spleen, braised, 3 oz	130	4	0
Stomach, pork, raw, 4 oz	180	11	0
Sweetbreads: Beef, ckd., 3 oz	270	20	0
Lamb, cooked, 3 oz	150	5	0
Tail, pork, simmered, 3 oz	340	31	0
Tongue, braised, 3 oz: Veal	170	9	0
Beef/Lamb/Pork, average	240	17	0
Tripe, beef, raw, 4 oz	110	5	0
Lean + fat	310	25	0

'In eating, one third of the stomach should be filled with food, one third with drink, and the rest left empty.'

~ Gitten, the Talmud

Sausages, Franks

Fresh Sausages

	C	F	Cb
Pork/Beef: *Average All Types*			
Small: Raw, 4" link, 1 oz	**120**	12	1.5
Broiled/Pan-fried	**50**	4	1.5
Medium: Raw, 2 oz	**235**	23	2.5
Broiled/Pan-fried	**100**	8	2.5
Large: Raw, 3 oz	**360**	36	3.5
Broiled/Pan-fried	**150**	12	3.5
Italian: Raw, 3.2 oz	**315**	28	1.5
Cooked, 2.4 oz	**215**	17	1.5

Note: Fat is lost in broiling/pan frying.
(Cooked wt. = approx. 60-70% raw wt.)

Franks & Weiners

	C	F	Cb
Beef: *Average All Brands*			
Regular/Smoked: *Per Frank*			
4 oz link	**280**	22	5
2.6 oz link	**240**	19	2
2 oz link (8/16 oz pkg)	**180**	17	2
1.6 oz link (10/16 oz pkg)	**140**	13	1
1.5 oz link (8/12 oz pkg)	**135**	12	1
1.2 oz link (10/12 oz pkg)	**110**	10	1
1 oz link (16/16 oz pkg)	**90**	8	0.5
Small/Cocktail (50/lb), each	**30**	3	0.5
Light/Fat Reduced:			
Best's Kosher, (97% FF), 1.7 oz	**50**	1	5
Oscar Mayer, 2 oz link	**110**	8	2
Hebrew National (97% FF), each	**45**	1.5	2
Healthy Choice (Jumbo Frank)	**70**	1.5	0
Pork: *Country Style,* 2 oz panfried	**240**	22	1
Chorizo, 5 sausages, 2.5 oz	**280**	26	3
El Popular, 2 oz cooked	**210**	17	3
Jimmy Dean, cooked, 2 oz	**240**	21	0
Oscar Mayer (2), 1.7 oz, ckd	**170**	15	1
Light, 2 oz link	**110**	8	2
Turkey Franks: *Ball Park,* 1.75 oz	**40**	0	6
Empire Kosher, 2 oz	**90**	6	1
Foster Farms, 2 oz	**130**	11	0
Louis Rich: Reg. (10/16 oz), 2 oz	**110**	8	2
(8/12oz pkg), 1 1/2 oz	**80**	6	2
Mr Turkey, smoked, 2 oz	**90**	5	3
Shelton's: 1 frank, 1.2 oz	**80**	6	1
Chicken Franks *(Shelton's),* 1.2 oz	**95**	8	1
Empire Kosher, 2 oz	**100**	7	1
Foster Farms, 2 oz	**140**	12	0
Scott Petersen, 1.2 oz	**80**	6	1
Zacky Farms, 2 oz	**150**	13	0

Smoked Sausages

	C	F	Cb
Butterball (w. Turkey), 2 oz	**60**	0	6
Eckrich, 2 oz	**180**	16	4
Healthy Choice, 2 oz	**70**	1.5	6
Lemington Foods: 2 oz link	**180**	15	3
Skinless, 3 oz link	**250**	21	5
Bacon & Cheddar, 3 oz pce	**250**	20	7
Scott Petersen: Skinless, 3 oz link	**280**	24	5

Vegetarian Sausages

	C	F	Cb
Lightlife: Bkfst Links, 1 link, 35g	**70**	3	4
Lean Italian Links, 1 link, 40g	**80**	3	5

Breakfast Sausages/Biscuits

	C	F	Cb
Healthy Choice			
Breakfast Sausage, 2 patties, 1.6 oz	**50**	1.5	3
Jimmy Dean			
Sausage Biscuit 2	**390**	25	29
Mini Burgers, 2	**270**	14	23
Saus. Egg & Cheese, Biscuit, 1	**390**	27	28
Minyard: Pork Sausage Biscuit, 1	**200**	12	16
Owens Border Breakfast			
2 Sausages, Egg, Cheese, Tacos	**330**	11	42
2 Hot Sausages, Biscuits	**370**	23	26
Knob Sausages, 2 oz, ckd	**210**	18	0
Swift Premium			
Morning Makers: *Per 3.5 oz*			
Egg & Cheese, 1 pce	**240**	8	30
Ham, Egg & Cheese	**250**	10	31
Sausage, Egg & Cheese	**250**	8	32

WILL-POWER TONIC
~ RECIPE ~

- 1 Cup of Desire
- 1 Quart of Determination
- 1 Tbsp of Common Sense
- 1 Tbsp of Stick-to-itiveness
- 1 Tbsp of Foresight
- 1 Cup of Energy

Bagel, Corn & Hot Dogs

Hot Dogs, Ready-To-Go	C	F	Cb
(Includes Ketchup/Relish; No Mayo)			
Small (1 oz frank/ 1 oz roll)	200	8	24
Regular (1 1/2 oz frank/ 2 oz roll)	310	13	39
Large (2 oz frank/ 2 oz roll)	360	18	40
Super/Giant (3 oz frank/3 oz roll)	540	26	59
Corn Dogs			
Beef/Pork Frank: Average, 2.6 oz	250	17	21
Mini, each	65	4.5	5
Turkey: *Gobblers! (Shelton's)*	220	11	27
Bagel Dogs			
Best's Kosher: 1 dog, 1 oz	320	11	43
Mini, 1 piece, 0.8 oz	60	2	8
Vienna Beef: 1 piece, 1 oz	85	3.5	7
Weinerschnitzel (Franchise Outlets)			
Carbohydrate figures ~ author estimates only.			
Chili Dog, 1 serve	295	16	38
w. Lowfat Frank	230	5	38
Chili Cheese Dog	350	21	40
w. Lowfat Frank	280	9	40
Corn Dog	290	23	25
Deluxe Dog	275	14	38
w. Lowfat Frank	220	3.5	38
Kraut Dog	265	14	37
Mustard Dog	260	14	37
Relish Dog	280	14	37
Western Dog	380	23	40

Also See Fast-Foods Section

Toppings/Extras

	C	F	Cb
American Chse, 1 slice, 1 oz	110	9	1
Catsup, 1 Tbsp	16	0	4
Chili (w. Beans), 1/4 cup	70	3.5	9
Mustard, 1 Tbsp	20	0	1
Pickle Relish, 1 Tbsp	20	0	5
Sauerkraut, 1/2 cup	20	0	5

Deli & Luncheon Meats

Beef Jerky:	C	F	Cb
Bridgeford Beef Jerky, 1 oz	50	1	3
Beef Stick (5.5 oz stick), 1 oz	140	12	0
Beef Steak, 1 oz	50	1	0
Beef & Cheese (Giant Size), 1/2 pkg, 1.5 oz	170	14	1
Pepperoni Sticks, 2, 1 oz	140	12	0
Pepperoni (1" diam.), 1 oz	130	12	0
Teriyaki, 1.25 oz pkg	80	1	8
Original; Hot 'n Spicy	70	1	5
Berliner (pork/beef), 1 oz	65	4	0.5
Beerwurst (Beef):			
Small (2.75"diam), 1/16" slice	20	2	0
Large (4"diam), 1/8" slice	75	7	0.5
Beerwurst (Pork):			
Small (2.75"diam), 1/16" slice	15	1	0
Large (4"diam), 1/8" slice	55	4	0.5
Bologna, Beef & Pork:			
Regular: 1 thin slice, 1 oz	90	8	1
1 thick slice, 1.6 oz	145	13	1
Light *(Oscar Mayer)*, 1 sl., 1 oz	60	4	2
Red. Fat *(Hebrew Nat.)*,1 oz	65	6	0
Fat Free *(Osc. M.)*, 2 sl., 1.6 oz	40	0	1
Healthy Choice, 1 oz	35	1	3
Weight Watchers, 2 sl., 3/4 oz	35	2	0
Turkey, average, 1 oz	60	5	0.5
Chicken *(Tyson)*, 1 slice	45	4	0.5
Ring *(Boar's Head)*, 2 oz	160	13	0.5
Blood Sausage, 1 oz	100	9	0.5
Bratwurst:			
Average, 1 oz	90	8	0.5
Boar's Head, cook., 1 wurst, 4 oz	300	25	0
Bob Evan's, Beer, 2.6 oz link	270	21	1
Braunschweiger (Pork/Liver/Sausage), *Oscar Mayer*, 1 oz slice	100	9	1
Chicken, *Average All Brands*			
1 thick or 2 thin slices, 1 oz	30	1	1
Chicken Roll, 1 slice, 1 oz	90	4	1.5
Corned Beef:			
Average, full fat, 1 oz	70	5	1.5
Healthy Choice, Hillshire Farm,1oz	30	1	0.5
Hebrew National, 4 slices, 2 oz	90	4.5	0
Loaf, jellied, 1 oz	45	2	0
Hash, canned, average, 1 oz	50	3	2
Dutch Brand Loaf, average, 1 oz	70	5	1.5

Continued Next Page

Deli & Luncheon Meats (Cont)

Ham, Luncheon:	C	F	Cb
Baked/Boiled, sliced, 1 oz	30	1	0.5
Chopped: *Eckrich* (97% FF), 1 oz	25	1	1
Armour,canned, 1 oz	35	1.5	0.5
97% Fat Free, 1 oz	25	1	1.5
Healthy Choice Deli Traditions:			
Baked, 6 sl., 2 oz	60	1.5	1
Larger Slice, 1 slice, 1 oz	30	1	1
Hormel (Black Label), 1 oz	70	6	0
Oscar Mayer, 1 oz slice	60	3	1
Honey, average, 1 oz	30	1	0.5
Healthy Choice Deli Traditions:			
6 slices, 2 oz	60	1.5	3
Prosciutto, average, 1 oz	70	5	1
Ham & Cheese Loaf, aver., 1 oz	70	5	0.5
Head Cheese *(Osc. Mayer)*, 1 oz sl.	50	4	0
Honey Loaf *(Osc. Mayer)*, 1 oz sl.	35	1	2
Italian Sausage, 2.6 oz	270	21	1
Kielbasa (Polish Sausage), 1 oz	85	7	0.5
Scott Petersen, 3.4 oz link	320	27	4
Beef, 2.8 oz link	290	25	4
Boar's Head, 1 oz	60	5	0
Kippered Beefsteak:			
(Hickory Farms), 3 slices, 0.75 oz	50	1	1
Knackwurst, 1 oz	90	8	0.5
Liverwurst, 1 oz	95	8	0.5
Liver Pate, fresh, average, 1 oz	110	10	3.5
Luncheon Loaf *(Foods Co)*, 1 oz	80	7	2
Mortadella, 1 oz	90	7	0.5
Olive Loaf, average, 1 oz	70	5	3
Oscar Mayer, 1 oz slice	70	6	2
Pastrami (Beef), average, 1 oz	40	2	0.5
Healthy Deli, 1 oz	34	1	0.5
Hillshire (DeliSelect), 6 sl., 2 oz	60	1	1
Turkey Pastrami, 1 slice, 1 oz	30	1	1
Peppered Beef, 1 oz slice	40	2	1
Pepperoni: 5 slices, 1 oz	135	12	0
Pickle Loaf, average, 1 oz	80	6	1
Pickle & Pimiento Loaf			
(Oscar Mayer), 1 oz	80	6	3
Polish Sausage: See Kielbasa			
Proscuitti, average, 1 oz	70	5	0
Hormel, 1 oz	90	7	0
Roast Beef, lean, 1 oz	40	1	0.5

Salami:	C	F	Cb
Beef: average, 1 oz	80	7	1
Beer: average, 1 oz	70	6	0.5
Cotto: *Oscar Mayer,* 1 slice, 1 oz	70	5	1
Dry: Hard, aver. 3 slices, 1 oz	110	10	0.5
Oscar Mayer, 2 slices, 1.6 oz	120	10	1
Genoa: average, 1 oz	110	10	0
Stick *(Best's Kosher)*, 2, 1.75 oz	180	15	2
Italian: *(Bridgeford)*, 1 oz	120	11	0
Turkey: average, 1 oz	55	4	1
Spam: Original, 2 Tbsp, 1 oz	70	6	0
Summer Sausage: *Bridgeford,* 1 oz	100	9	0
Oscar Mayer, 1 slice, 0.8 oz	70	7	0
Treet *(Armour)*, canned, 1 oz	100	9	1.5
Turkey: average, 1 oz slice	30	1	0.5
3/4 oz slice	22	0.5	0.5
Turkey Breast:			
Butterball Fat Free, 6 sl, 2 oz	50	0	2
Deli Thin Smoked, 1 sl., 1 oz	25	0	2
Hillshire Deli Select, 6 sl., 2 oz	50	0.5	2
Louis Rich Carvery Board,			
3 slices, (52g), 1.8 oz	50	0.5	1
Free, 2 slices, 2 oz	50	0	2
Healthy Choice, 6 sl., 2 oz	60	1.5	3
Hearty Deli Rst'd, 3 sl., 2 oz	60	0.5	1
Honey Roasted, 6 sl., 2 oz	60	1.5	4
Turkey Ham, 1 slice, 1 oz	35	1.5	0.5
Turkey Pastrami, 1 oz	35	1.5	0.5
Turkey Roll, 1 oz	40	2	0.5
Turkey Loaf, 1 oz	30	1	0.5

Meat Spreads

Average All Brands
Per 1/4 cup (2 oz)

	C	F	Cb
Chicken	120	8	2
Ham, deviled	160	14	0
Liverwurst	170	14	3
Roast Beef	140	11	0
Sandwich Spread	140	10	8
Turkey	110	7	2

Paté

Paté	C	F	Cb
Canned: *Average All Brands*			
Chicken Liver, 1 Tbsp, 1/2 oz	30	2	1
2 Tbsp, 1 oz	60	4	2
Foie Gras, goose liver, 1 oz	130	12	2
Sells, liverpate, 2 1/8 oz	190	16	3
Fresh (Refrigerated):			
Average all types, 1 oz	110	10	4
Marcel Henri, 2 oz serving	220	20	2
Pate de Campagne, 1 oz	105	9	1
Chicken Liver w. Port Wine, 1 oz	100	9	1
Duck Truffle w. Port Wine, 1 oz	120	12	1
Coeur de France:			
Smoked Salmon Pate, 1 oz	45	3.5	1
Spinach Pate w. Roquefort, 1 oz	50	4	1
Garden Fresh Vegetable Pate:			
Mushroom, Artichoke & Spinach in Puff Pastry, 2 oz	110	7	8

Lunch Packs

Lunch Packs	C	F	Cb
Lunchables *(Oscar Mayer)*			
Per Package:			
Beef Tacos/Butterfinger/Drink	490	15	69
Bologna/Chse/Crackers/Cookies	470	31	31
Bologna/Chse/Crack./M&M's/Drink	530	27	60
Chsy Chip Nachos/Choc Fudge/Drink	540	26	70
Cinnamon & Fruit Roll/Drink	510	12	98
Cinnamon Rolls	370	11	65
Deluxe Turkey/Chicken	390	22	26
Grilled Burgers/Choc Balls/Cola	460	14	67
Ham & Swiss/Crackers/Drink	350	9	51
Hot Dogs/Choc Balls/Drink	450	19	64
Lean Ham/Chedd./Crackers/Cookie	420	21	39
Lean Ham/Chse/Crack./Snickers/Drk	440	18	54
Lean Ham/Swiss Chse/Crackers	340	18	21
Lean Turkey/Cheese/Cracker/ Reese's Peanut Butter/Drink	430	18	51
Lean Turkey Brst./Chedd. Crackers	340	19	22
Lean Turkey/Chse/Crack/Skittles/Drink	410	14	61
Waffles & Sausage/ Fruity Pebbles Bar/Drink	510	13	94
Nachos: Cheese & Salsa	380	21	39
Cheesy Crisp	380	23	35
w. Capri Sun/Nestle Crunch	570	29	70
Tacos: Beef Taco & Cheese	310	11	34
w. Capri Sun/Butterfinger	470	13	67
Mega Lunchables: *Per Package*			
2 Pepp. Pizza/Reese's P.B.Cup/Cola	760	28	105
2 Extra Cheesy Pizza/M&Ms/Drink	700	25	104
Soft Pizzastix + Twix	650	16	111
Ultimate + Shock Tarts/Cola	780	32	113
Sandwiches:			
Ham, Turkey, Cheddar	470	22	47
Oven Rst. Turkey & Chse Sub	410	17	45
Smoked Ham & Cheddar Sub	380	14	44
Smoked Turkey & Chedd. Bagel	380	4	63
Pizza:			
Deep Dish w. Reese Cup	760	28	105
Sauce & Mozzarella Cheese	300	13	38
Pepperoni Flavored Sausage, 3	310	14	30
Pizza/Nestlé Crunch/Drink	450	15	62
Munch-A-Bunch *(Jewel): Per 4 oz Package*			
Bologna/Chse/Crackers/Cookies	430	29	27
Other varieities, average	350	19	29
Smuckers: **Snackers,** 3.96 oz pkg	610	24	88

Chicken

Quick Guide

Chicken

From 3lb ready-to-cook chicken

	C	F	Cb
Breast/Wing Quarter			
Roasted: With skin	300	15	0
Without skin	190	5	0
Fried, batter dipped	480	26	18
Leg Quarter: Thigh & Drumstick			
Roasted: With skin	265	15	0
Without skin	180	8	0
Fried, batter dipped	430	26	16

KFC ~ See Fast-Foods Section.

Average - All Meats

Average of Light & Dark Meats

Per 4 oz Serving (no bone)

	C	F	Cb
Roasted: With skin	270	15	0
Without skin	215	8	0
Stewed: With skin	250	14	0
Without skin	200	8	0
Fried: Batter-dipped	330	20	11
Flour coated	305	17	3.5

Chicken Parts

Broilers or Fryers: Edible Weights (no bone)

	C	F	Cb
Breast: *Per* $^{1}/_{2}$ *Breast*			
Raw: With skin, 5 oz	245	13	0
Without skin, $4^{1}/4$ oz	130	2	0
Roasted: With skin, $3^{1}/2$ oz	195	8	0
Without skin, 3 oz	140	3	0
Stewed: With skin, 4 oz	210	8	0
Without skin, $3^{1}/4$ oz	140	3	0
Fried: Batter-dipped, 5 oz	370	19	12
Flour coated, w. skin, $3^{1}/2$ oz	220	9	7
Drumstick: *Per Drumstick*			
Roasted: With skin, 2 oz	125	6	0
Without skin, $1^{1}/2$ oz	75	2	0
Fried: Batter-dipped, $2^{1}/2$ oz	195	11	7
Flour coated, $1^{3}/4$ oz	120	7	1
Stewed: With skin, 2 oz	115	6	0
Without skin, $1^{1}/2$ oz	80	3	0
Thigh Portion: Edible Wt. (no bone)			
Raw: With skin, 3.3 oz ($4^{1}/4$ oz with bone)	200	14	0
Without skin, 2.4 oz	80	3	0
Roasted: With skin, $2^{1}/4$ oz	155	10	0
Without skin, 2 oz	110	6	0

Thigh Portion (Cont)	C	F	Cb
Stewed: With skin, $2^{1}/2$ oz	160	10	0
Without skin, 2 oz	105	5	0
Fried: Batter-dipped, 3 oz	240	14	8
Flour coated, $2^{1}/4$ oz	165	9	2
Wing: *Per Wing*			
Raw Weight 3.2 oz (with bone)			
Raw: With skin	110	8	0
Without skin	35	1	0
Roasted: With skin	105	7	0
Without skin	45	2	0
Fried: Batter-dipped	160	11	5
Flour coated	105	7	1
Stewed: With skin, 4 oz	100	7	0
Neck: Simmered, with skin	95	7	0
Without skin	30	2	0
Skin Only: *Skin from* $^{1}/_{2}$ *Chicken*			
Raw skin, $2^{3}/4$ oz	275	26	0
Roasted skin, 2 oz	255	22	0
Stewed skin, $2^{1}/2$ oz	260	24	0
Fried, Flour coated, 2 oz	280	24	5
Fried, Batter-dipped, $6^{3}/4$ oz	750	55	45

Roasters

	C	F	Cb
Average of Light & Dark Meat:			
Roasted: With skin, 4 oz	250	15	0
Without skin, 4 oz	190	8	0
Light Meat: Without skin, rst.	175	5	0
Dark Meat: Without skin, rst.	206	10	0

Stewing Chicken

	C	F	Cb
Stewed: *Per 4 oz Serving*			
Average of Light & Dark Meat:			
With skin	325	21	0
Without skin	270	14	0
Light Meat: Without skin	240	9	0
Dark Meat: Without skin	295	17	0

Capon Chicken

	C	F	Cb
Roasted: With skin, 4 oz	260	13	0
$^{1}/_{2}$ Chicken, with skin	1460	74	0

Chicken Offal & Stuffing

	C	F	Cb
Giblets, simmered, 1 cup	230	7	1.5
Fried, flour-coated, 1 cup	400	20	6
Gizzard, simmered, 1 cup	220	5	1.5
Heart, simmered, 1 cup	270	12	0.5
Liver: Raw, 4 oz	140	5	3.5
Simmered, 1 cup	220	8	1
Liver Pate Fresh, 1 Tbsp, $^{1}/_{2}$ oz	60	8	2
Stuffing: Average, $^{1}/_{2}$ cup	200	2	22

Chicken Products

Tyson	C	F	Cb
Chicken Chunks: Regular, (6)	280	20	19
Breast, (6)	220	19	11
Southern Fried, (6)	260	19	11
Breast Patties: Regular, each	190	12	11
Chick 'n Quick/Chedd., 74g ea.	220	14	12
Crispy Baked, each	80	0	9
Thick 'n Crispy, each	200	19	10
Southern Fried, each	180	12	8
Nuggets: Breaded White Meat, (6)	250	18	12
Wings: Flavored, average, (3)	170	10	1
BBQ Style, (3)	200	13	2
Stir Fry Kit: Chicken, 2 3/4 c. froz.	430	4.5	73
Wraps: Southwest Black. 1 1/2	560	12	82
Mandarin Sesame, 1 1/2 wraps	560	12	82
M/wave S/wiches: Breast, 119g	320	15	33
Stove Top: *Per Serving*			
Chicken Stuffing Mix: 1 oz	110	1	20
1/2 cup prep.	170	9	20

Duck, Goose, Quail

	C	F	Cb
Duck: roasted, with skin, 3 oz	285	24	0
Without skin, 3 oz	170	10	0
1/2 whole duck, with skin	1300	108	0
Goose: roast, with skin, 3 oz	260	19	0
Without skin, 3 oz	200	11	0
Pheasant: 1/2 bird, raw	720	37	0
Quail: 1 whole, raw	210	13	0

Turkey

Fryer-Roasters	C	F	Cb
Roasted: *Per 3 oz Serving*			
Light Meat: With skin	140	4	0
Without skin	120	1	0
Dark Meat: With skin	155	6	0
Without skin	140	4	0
1/4 of Whole Turkey: (Approx. 3 1/4 lbs raw wt. w/out neck and giblets; 2 lb 6 oz cooked wt.)			
Roasted: With skin	1400	46	0
Without skin	1030	18	0
Ground Turkey, Raw: (4oz raw wt. = 3oz ckd wt.)			
Regular (85% lean), 4 oz	180	10	0
Lean (90% lean), 4 oz	160	8	0
Breast, no skin, 4 oz	115	1	0

Turkey Parts

Roasted, Edible Weights (no bone)	C	F	Cb
Breast (1/4): (from 17 1/4 oz raw wt. w/bone)			
With skin, 12 oz (no bone)	525	11	0
Without skin, 10 3/4 oz	415	2	0
Back (1/2): With skin, 4 1/2 oz	265	13	0
Without skin, 3 1/2 oz	165	5	0
Leg (Thigh & Drumstick): (from 1 lb raw wt. w/bone)			
With skin, 8 1/2 oz (no bone)	420	13	0
Without skin, 7 3/4 oz	355	8	0
Wing: (from 7 1/4 oz raw wt. w/bone)			
With skin, 3 oz (no bone)	185	9	0
Without skin, 2 oz	100	2	0
Neck: Simmered, 1 neck (9 oz w. bone)	275	11	0
Giblets, simm., 1 cup, 5 oz	240	7	3

Young Hens (Roasted)

	C	F	Cb
Light Meat: With skin, 3 oz	175	8	0
Without skin, 3 oz	135	3	0
Dark Meat: With skin, 3 oz	200	11	0
Without skin, 3 oz	165	7	0
Young Toms — Similar to Young Hens			

Turkey Products

	C	F	Cb
Banquet ~ Frozen Meals, Page 55			
Circle L: Boneless Turk Bacon,3 oz	120	9	1
Louis Rich			
Fat Free Breast of Turkey			
Rotiss'd/Smoked/Rstd, 2 oz	60	0	1
Turkey Ham & Chunks, cooked:			
Breast & White Turkey, 2 oz	60	1	2
Turkey Ham/Pastrami, 2 oz	70	3	1
Turkey Salami, 2 oz	100	8	0
Luncheon Slices ~ See Cold Meats, Page 48			
Franks: Medium, 1 1/2 oz	80	6	2
Large, 2 oz	110	8	3
Smoked Sausage/Kielbasa, 1 oz	45	2	2
Turkey Nuggets, cooked, each	65	4	4
Turkey Patties, cooked, each	220	13	13
Turkey Sticks, cooked, each	75	5	4
Swanson ~ Frozen Meals, Page 59			
Turkey Store			
Gobble Stix: Honey, each	25	0	1
Lean Burger Patties, 1 patty	180	8	5
Lean Italian Sausage, 1 link	190	8	2

Quick Guide

Fresh Fish

	C	F	Cb
Low Oil (Less than 2.5% fat)			
White/pale colored flesh. Examples: Cod, Flounder, Haddock, Halibut, Monkfish Perch, Pike, Pollock, Snapper, Sole, Whiting.			
Per 4 oz Edible Portion			
Raw, 4 oz (no bones)	90	1	0
Steamed, Broiled, Baked	130	1	0
Fried: Lightly Floured	210	8	3.5
Breaded	260	12	8
In Batter	320	16	27
Medium Oil (2.5-5% fat)			
Pale colored flesh. Examples: Bluefin Tuna, Catfish, Kingfish, Salmon (Pink), Swordfish, Rainbow Trout, Yellowtail.			
Raw, 4 oz (no bones)	140	5	0
Baked, Broiled, 4 oz	175	6	0
Fried, 4 oz	230	11	8
High Oil (Over 5% fat)			
Darker colored flesh. Examples: Albacore Tuna, Bluefish, Herring, Mackerel, Orange Roughy, Salmon (Atl./Chinook/Sockeye), Sardines, Trout, Whitefish.			
Raw, 4 oz (no bones)	230	16	0

Cooking Yields (Fin Fish):
4 oz Raw wt. = 3 1/2 oz Cooked wt.
4 oz Cooked wt. = 5 oz Raw wt.

Calorie & Fat Variations
The amount of fat/oil in fish varies with the species, season and locality. Within the same fish, fat/oil content is generally higher towards the head.

Fish & Shellfish

Edible Weights: (no bones/shell)

	C	F	Cb
Abalone: Raw, 4 oz	120	1	7
Anchovy: Paste, 1 Tbsp, 1/4 oz	15	1	0.5
Cnd. in oil, drnd., 5 only, 3/4 oz	40	2	0
Pickled, 1 oz	50	3	0
Barracuda (Pacific), raw, 4 oz	130	3	0
Bass: Black, raw, 4 oz	105	1	0
Striped, raw, 1 fillet, 5 1/2 oz	150	4	0
Blue Fish, raw, 1 fillet, 5 1/4 oz	185	6	0
Butterfish, raw, 4 oz	165	9	0
Calamari, breaded/fried, 1 serve	360	21	0
Carp, raw, 4 oz	145	6	0
Catfish: Raw, 4 oz	130	5	0
Fried, bread., 1 fillet, 3 oz	200	12	7
Caviar: black/red, 1 Tbsp, 16g	40	3	0.5
Clams: Raw, 3 oz (4 lge/9 sm)	65	1	2
Fried, breaded, 3 oz	170	10	9
Canned, 3 oz	125	2	4
Minced, 1/4 cup, 2 oz	25	0	0.5
Cod, Atl./Pacific: Raw, 4 oz	95	1	0
Baked/Broil., 1 fill., 6 1/4 oz	135	2	0
Canned, 3 oz	90	1	0
Minced, 1/4 cup, 2 oz	25	0	0
Crab: Alaska King, raw, 4 oz	95	1	0
1 leg, cooked, 4 3/4 oz	130	2	0
Blue, raw, 1 crab (1/3 lb whole crab, 3/4 oz flesh)	18	<1	0
Canned, 1/2 cup, 2 1/2 oz	65	<1	0
Dungeness, 1 crab, 5 3/4 oz edible (from 1 1/2 lb whole crab)	140	2	2
Imitation Crab Legs/Stix, 3oz	80	1	8.5
Crayfish, raw, 4 oz (edible)	100	1	0
Croaker, raw, 4 oz	120	3	0
Cuttlefish, raw, 4 oz	90	1	1
Dolphinfish, raw, 4 oz	95	1	0
Eel: Raw, 4 oz	210	13	0
Smoked, 2 oz	190	16	0
Flounder/Sole, raw, 4 oz	120	<1	0
Gefilte Fish: See Kosher Foods ~ Page 157			
Grouper, raw, 4 oz	105	1	0
Haddock: Raw, 4 oz	100	<1	0
Broiled, 1 fillet, 5 1/4 oz	170	1	0
Smoked, 2 oz	22	<1	0
Halibut, raw, 4 oz	125	3	0
Herring: Atlantic, raw, 4 oz	180	10	0
Pickled, 2 pieces, 1 oz	60	4	2

Herring (Cont): Pickled	C	F	Cb
In Sour Cream, 1 oz	50	5	1
Party Snacks, 1/4 cup, dr., 2 oz	120	5	0
Rollmops, 1 1/2 oz	110	8	6
Canned: Plain w. liq., 4 oz	235	15	0
in Tomato Sauce, 4 oz	200	12	1
Smoked, kippered, 4 oz	245	14	0
Jellyfish: Raw, 4 oz	30	<1	0
Salted, 4 oz	40	<1	0
Kingfish, raw, 4 oz	120	3.5	0
Ling, raw, 4 oz	100	<1	0
Lobster, Northern: Raw, 4 oz	105	1	0.5
1 Lobster, 6 1/4 oz (from 1 1/2 lb whole lobster)	135	1.5	0.5
Cooked, 1 cup, 5 oz	140	1	2
Lobster Newberg, 3/4 cup	360	20	9
Lobster Thermidor, 1 serv.	370	22	15
Lobster Salads, 1/2 cup	220	13	5
Lox, Regular/Nova, 2 oz	65	2	0
Mackerel: Atlantic, raw, 4 oz	235	16	0
Jack, can., 1/2 cup, 3 1/3 oz	150	6	0
King, raw, 4 oz	120	2	0
Pacific/Jack, raw, 4 oz	180	9	0
Spanish, raw, 4 oz	160	7	0
Mahi-Mahi, raw, 4 oz	140	5	0
Monkfish, raw, 4 oz	75	1	0
Mullet, striped, raw	135	4	0
Mussels: Raw, 4 oz (edible)	100	2	4
1 cup, 5 1/4 oz (edible)	130	3	5
Cooked, moist heat, 3 oz	150	4	6
Ocean Perch, raw, 4 oz	90	1.5	0
Octopus, common, raw, 4 oz	95	1	2
Orange Roughy, raw, 4 oz	145	9	0
(Cals may be much lower. Over 90% of total fat is waxester which may not be metabolized)			
Oysters: Common, raw, 3 oz	70	1	3.5
Eastern raw:			
6 medium, 3 oz	60	2	3
1 cup, 8 3/4 oz	170	6	8.5
Fried/bread., 6 medium, 3 oz	170	11	10
Pacific, raw, 1 med., 1 3/4 oz	40	1	2
Oysters Rockfeller, 3 oysters	220	13	12
Perch, average, raw, 4 oz	105	2	0
Pollock, raw, 4 oz	100	1	0
Pompano, Florida, raw, 4 oz	190	10	0
Porgy/Scup, raw, 4 oz	130	4	0
Rockfish, Pacific, raw, 4 oz	110	2	0
Roe, raw, 1 oz	40	2	0.5

Salmon:	C	F	Cb
Raw: Chinook, 4 oz	205	7	0
Atlantic; Coho/Silver, 4 oz	160	7	0
Chum; Pink, 4 oz	135	4	0
Red/Sockeye, 4 oz	190	10	0
Smoked Salmon: Average, 2 oz	65	1	0
Pacific Supreme, 2 oz	100	4	0
Canned Salmon: *Average All Brands*			
Pink: 1 oz	40	2	0
1/4 cup, 63g (2.2 oz)	90	5	0
3 3/4 oz can, whole	155	8.5	0
7 1/2 oz can, whole	300	17	0
Skinless/boneless, 1/4 c., 2 oz	70	2	0
Red Sockeye: 1 oz	50	3	0
1/4 cup, 63g (2.2 oz)	110	7	0
3 3/4 oz can, whole	190	12	0
Atlantic, 1/2 cup, 3 1/2 oz	230	14	0
Chinook/King, 1/2 cup	210	14	0
Chum, 1/2 cup, 3 1/2 oz	140	5	0
Coho/Silver, 1/2 cup	155	5	0
Atlantic Steaks: Small, 8 oz	320	14	0
Medium, 12 oz	480	21	0
Large, 16 oz	640	28	0
Salmon Cake, take-out, 3 oz	240	15	6
Sardines: Canned: *Average All Brands*			
In Oil, undrained, 1 oz	85	7	0
Drained of oil, 1 oz	60	3	0
3 3/4 oz can, drained, (3 1/4 oz)	190	11	0
1 lrg/2 med. 3"/5 small, 0.8 oz	50	3	0
In Tom./ Mustard Sce, 1 oz	45	3	0
3 3/4 oz can (8 sardines)	170	11	0
Scallop: Raw, 6 lg./14 sm., 3 oz	75	<1	2.5
Breaded/fried, 6 lge, 3 oz	200	10	9
Shark: Raw, 4 oz	150	6	0
Batter-dipped, fried, 4 oz	260	16	7
Shrimps: Raw, in shell, 1/2 lb	140	2	1.5
Raw, shelled, 3 oz (12 lge)	90	1.5	0.5
Bread./fried, 3 oz (11 lge)	210	11	10
Canned, 2 oz	60	1	0.5
Smelt, Rainbow, raw, 4 oz	115	3	0
Snapper, raw, 4 oz	115	1	0
Sole, Lemon, raw, 4 oz	90	1	0
Squid, raw, 4 oz	105	1	3.5
Surimi, Imt. Crablegs/Shrimp, 4 oz	110	1	7.5
Swordfish, raw, 4 oz	140	5	0
Trout, Rainbow, raw, 4 oz	135	4	0
Smoked, 2 oz	110	6	0

Fish (Cont)

	C	F	Cb
Tuna:			
Raw, Bluefin, 4 oz	**165**	6	0
Skipjack, Yellowfin	**120**	1	0
Canned: ***Average All Brands***			
In Water, drained:			
Chunk/Solid, 2 oz can	**60**	0.5	0
3 oz can	**90**	1	0
6 oz can	**150**	1.5	0
In Oil, drained:			
Chunk Light, 2 oz	**110**	5.5	0
6 oz can, drained	**275**	14	0
Solid White, 2 oz	**90**	2.5	0
6 oz can, drained	**225**	6.5	0
Tuna Salad: Deli Style, 1/2 c., 4oz	**300**	24	15
Whitefish, raw, 4 oz	**155**	7	0
Whiting, raw, 4 oz	**100**	1.5	0

Frozen Fish Products

	C	F	Cb
Fisher Boy			
Quik Stix: 6 sticks, 3 oz	**200**	11	16
Quik Bake Crunchy Fish Portions:			
2 portions, 3.2 oz	**200**	10	19
Fish Rings, 7 rings, 3.2 oz	**230**	12	20
Salmon Fillet, 1 pce, 3.8 oz	**100**	2.5	1
Gorton's			
Fish Sticks: Breaded, 6, 3 oz	**210**	12	17
Crunchy Fish Fillets: Breaded *(Per Fillet)*			
Lemon Pepper	**135**	9	9
Garlic & Herb; Hot & Spicy	**125**	7	10
Grilled: It. Herb; Lemon Pepper	**130**	6	2
Cajun Blackened; Lemon Butter	**120**	6	1
Battered: Parmesan	**130**	7.5	10
Plain, 1 fillet	**120**	6.5	10
Garlic & Herb, 1 fillet	**125**	6.5	11
Lemon Pepper, 1 fillet	**135**	9	9
Homestyle Baked:			
Au Gratin, 1 fillet, 4.6 oz	**230**	12	14
Primavera, 1 fillet, 4.6 oz	**120**	5	4
Fish Portions: 1 portion, 2 1/2 oz	**170**	11	12
Popcorn Shrimp: 20 shrimp, 2 oz	**240**	13	22
Tenders: 3 1/2 piece, 4 oz	**250**	14	20
Kroger Fish Portions: *Per 2 Pieces, 4 oz*			
Batter Dipt, 2 pces, 4 oz	**260**	14	22
Crispy Crunchy, 2 pces, 4 oz	**270**	18	18
Louis Kemp: Crab Delights,			
Surimi, 1/2 cup, 2.5 oz	**80**	0	10

Frozen Fish Products (Cont)

	C	F	Cb
Mrs Paul's			
Battered: Fish Sticks, 6	**240**	11	13
Fish Portions, 2	**280**	17	22
Batter Dipped: Fish Sticks, 2	**330**	17	28
Crispy Crunchy: Fish Sticks, 5	**200**	14	20
Fish Fillets, 2	**250**	13	11
Breaded Fish Portions, 2	**240**	12	20
Crunchy Batter: Fish Fillets, 2	**280**	13	23
Flounder Fillets, 2	**260**	14	24
Haddock Fillets, 2	**250**	12	25
Healthy Treasures:			
Fish Sticks, breaded, 4 sticks	**140**	6	14
Fish Cakes, 2 cakes, 4 oz	**190**	7	24
Light Seafood Entrees: Fish Dijon	**200**	5	17
Fish Florentine	**220**	8	10
Fish Mornay	**230**	10	12
Sea-Pak			
Crunchy Clam Strips, 1 pkt, 5 oz	**410**	2.5	41
Oven Crunchy Butterfly Shrimp,			
4 shrimp, 3 oz	**200**	9	20
Popcorn Fish, 7 pces, 3 oz	**240**	11	23
Popcorn Shrimp, 15 pces, 3 oz	**210**	12	18
Van De Kamp's			
Fish Sticks: Breaded, 6 stix, 4 oz	**290**	17	23
Battered Fillets: 2.6 oz Fillet	**180**	11	12
Crisp & Healthy: Breaded,			
1 fillet, 1.8 oz	**85**	1.5	12
Grilled: Italian Herb, 1, 4 oz	**130**	6	2
Breaded Butterfly Shrimp, 7, 4 oz	**300**	14	32
Lemon Pepper, 1, 3.6 oz	**130**	6	0
Salmon, Creamy Dill, 1	**90**	2.5	1
Tuna, Barbecue, 1, 1.8 oz	**100**	0.5	5
Tuna, Sesame Teriyaki, 1	**110**	1.5	4

Banquet

	C	F	Cb
Meals: *Per Meal*			
Beef Enchilada	**380**	12	54
Boneless Pork Rib	**400**	19	39
Chicken Fingers & BBQ Sce, 9 oz	**340**	16	36
Chicken Fried Beef Steak	**400**	20	39
Chicken Nugget	**410**	21	42
Chicken Parmigiana	**290**	15	27
Fettuccine & Meatballs, Wine Sce	**280**	7	42
Fish Stick Meal, 6.6 oz	**300**	13	33
Fried Rice w. Chicken & Egg Rolls	**330**	9	51
Meat Loaf	**280**	16	23
Mexican Style Enchilada Combo	**360**	11	55
Our Original Fried Chicken	**470**	27	35
Pepperoni Pizza Meal	**480**	23	56
Pork Cutlet	**410**	24	39
Roasted Honey Turkey	**270**	12	29
Salisbury Steak Meal, 9.5 oz	**340**	19	28
Turkey Mostly White Meat	**290**	10	34
White Meat Fried Chicken	**470**	28	40
Yankee Pot Roast, 9.4 oz	**230**	10	20
The Hearty One: *Per Meal*			
Beef Enchilada, 15.65 oz	**520**	16	73
Boneless Pork Rib Dinner, 15.25 oz	**720**	38	62
Chicken Fried Beef Steak, 16 oz	**820**	50	63
Fried Chicken Dinner, 14.7 oz	**910**	55	70
Salisbury Steak Dinner, 16.5 oz	**780**	54	47
Turkey Dinner, 17 oz	**630**	10	57
Family Pack: *Per Serving*			
Big Wings: Firehouse, (2) 3 oz	**200**	14	1
Smokehse BBQ, 2 pces, 2.75 oz	**200**	14	4
Hot 'n' Spicy Wings (4) 2.75 oz	**220**	15	6
Pot Pies, each: Beef	**330**	15	38
Chicken	**350**	18	36
Turkey	**370**	20	38

Budget Gourmet

	C	F	Cb
Dinner: *Per Meal*			
Angel Hair Pasta w. Tom. Meat Sce, 8 oz	**230**	5	38
Beef Cheddar Melt w. Pot. Wedges, 9 oz	**350**	21	24
Italian Style Meatballs & Vege.	**280**	12	28
Low Fat Pasta in Wine & Mushr.	**270**	7	39
Mandarin Chicken	**240**	6	35
Potatoes Mozzarella in Sce	**300**	16	33
Light Entrees: Beef Stroganoff	**290**	7	30
Orange Glazed Chicken	**300**	2	51

Budget Gourmet (Cont)

	C	F	Cb
Regular Entrees			
Chicken & Egg Noodles	**370**	21	31
Chicken w. Fettuccine	**340**	14	40
Pepper Steak w. Rice	**290**	8	37
Roast Beef Supreme	**300**	13	35
Swedish Meatballs	**550**	34	42
Three Cheese Lasagna	**390**	16	36
Value Classics			
Chinese Style Veg. & White Chick.	**250**	6	40
Fettucini Alfredo w. Four Cheeses	**480**	22	40
Fettucini Primavera w. Chicken	**260**	7	36
Homestyle Macaroni & Cheese	**280**	9	38
Lasagna Mozzarella	**360**	11	40
Lasagne w. Meat Sauce	**300**	9	40
Macaroni & Chse w. Cheddar	**310**	7	45
Rigatoni in Cream Sce & Chicken	**230**	5	37
Spaghetti Marinara	**290**	6	43
Spicy Szechuan Vege & Chicken	**290**	9	41
Stir Fry Rice & Vegetables	**410**	18	44
Hearty (14 oz)			
Chicken a la King	**520**	21	56
Fettucini Alfredo w. 4 Chs/Chick.	**520**	25	50
Golden Fried Chicken Supreme	**390**	19	42
Oriental Rice w. Veg. & Chicken	**645**	33	67
Penne Pasta w. Chicken	**450**	11	63
Tex-Mex Rice & Beans	**470**	14	69

Chef Boyardee

	C	F	Cb
Overstuffed Beef Ravioli, 9 oz	**280**	5	46

Don Miguel

Same Figures as El Charito

Empire Kosher

	C	F	Cb
Express Meal			
Chicken Fajita, 1	**130**	2.5	15
Chicken w. Pasta, 1 cup	**140**	2	17
Chicken Stir-Fry, 1 cup	**160**	2.5	20
Pierogies: Potato Cheese, 5.3 oz	**250**	4	44
Potato Onion, 5.3 oz	**245**	4	47
Pies: Chicken Pie, 8 oz	**440**	21	41
Turkey Pie, 8 oz	**470**	23	45
Blintzes: Cheese, 2	**200**	6	29
Blueberry, 2	**190**	4	36
Potato Pancakes: mini, 12, 3 oz	**150**	7	19

El Charrito

Regular Dinners: Per 12 oz	C	F	Cb
Beef Enchilada Dinner	490	15	65
Cheese Enchilada	470	15	70
Chicken Enchilada	390	7	65
Mexican Style (13.25 oz)	610	30	67
Queso Beef; Saltillo Dinner	460	14	69
Queso Dinner	420	10	72
Lean Ole Dinners: Beef Enchilada	380	7	60
Cheese Enchilada	360	4.5	66
Combo Enchilada	380	7	66
Grande Dinners: Saltillo, 20.75 oz	750	26	105
Beef Enchilada, 21 oz	830	35	99
Mexican Style Dinner, 20 oz	840	42	89
Entrees: *Per 8 oz (227g)*			
Beef Enchilada	270	9	38
Cheese/Chicken Enchilada	250	8	38

Green Giant

Create A Meal: *Prepared*	C	F	Cb
Beef & Broccoli Stir Fry, 1 1/3 cup	290	13	15
Beefy Noodle, 1 1/4 cup	350	14	31
Cheesy Pasta & Veg, 1 1/4 cup	420	21	29
Chicken Alfredo, 1 1/4 cup	400	13	36
Garlic & Ginger Stir Fry, 1 1/2 cup	270	7	25
Garlic Herb Chicken, 1 1/4 cup	380	15	30
Homestyle Stew, 1 cup	340	16	24
Lo Mein Stir Fry, 1 1/4 cup	320	7	33
Mushroom Wine Chicken, 1 1/4 c.	390	13	31
Oven Roasted: Garlic Herb, 1 3/4 c.	350	9	35
BBQ Chicken, 1 1/3 cup	350	9	37
Chicken & Stuffing, 1 1/3 cup	370	11	36
Lemon Pepper Chick., 1 2/3 cup	310	8	30
Parmesan Herb Chicken, 1 3/4 cup	340	11	29
Skillet Lasagna, 1 1/4 cup	340	13	31
Sweet & Sour Stir Fry, 1 1/4 cup	340	7	43
Szechuan Stir Fry, 1 1/4 cup	310	14	20
Teriyaki Stir Fry, 1 1/4 cup	230	6	18

Healthy Choice

	C	F	Cb
Entrees: Beef Macaroni	220	4	34
Breaded Chicken Brst Strips, 8 oz	270	5	34
Cheesy Rice & Chicken	230	4	34
Chicken & Vegetable Marsala	230	1.5	32
Chicken Cantonese	280	6	34
Chicken Enchiladas	270	4	43
Chicken Olé	270	4	42

Healthy Choice (Cont)

Entrees (Cont):	C	F	Cb
Herb Breaded Pork Patty, 8 oz	280	6	38
Homestyle Chicken & Pasta, 9 oz	270	6	32
Honey Mustard Chicken	260	2	38
Lasagna Bake	280	6	43
Macaroni & Cheese	250	6	36
Manicotti w. 3 Cheeses	300	9	40
Sesame Chicken	240	3	40
Stuffed Pasta Shells	370	6	60
Tuna Casserole, 9 oz	240	7	30
Duos: Grilled Chick. Brst & Pasta	240	6	26
Breaded Chicken & Macaroni Chse	270	5	34
Salisbury Steak & Mashed Pot.	210	6	23
Turkey Breast w. Mash. Potatoes	200	5	19
Bowl Creations: *Per Bowl*			
Chicken Breast. & Veg. w. Pasta	230	5	29
Chicken Broccoli Alfredo	260	5	33
Chili & Cornbread	350	8	49
Colonial Chicken Pie	310	7	40
Country Chicken Bake	230	8	22
Fiesta Chicken	220	2	34
Garlic Lemon Chicken w. Rice	300	4	48
Roasted Potatoes w. Ham	210	4	26
Shrimp & Vegetables	250	4	39
Turkey Divan, 9.5 oz	250	6	31
Meals: Beef Pot Roast	330	9	41
Beef Stroganoff	310	6	44
Chicken Enchilada	310	7	46
Chicken Teriyaki w. Rice	270	4	41
Country Breaded Chicken	360	9	51
Country Herb Chicken	320	6	49
Country Inn Roast Turkey	250	4	28
Grilled Glazed Pork Patty	280	4	48
Herb Baked/Lemon Pepper Fish	340	7	54
Mesquite Beef w. BBQ Sauce	310	8	38
Roasted Chicken	220	5	25
Traditional Beef Tips	260	6	32
Traditional Breast of Turkey	290	4.5	40
Traditional Meatloaf	320	5	52
Medleys: Beef Teriyaki	330	7	48
Chicken Carbonara	310	7	39
Chicken Piccata	270	5	40
Country Glazed Chicken	250	5	31
Mandarin Chicken	280	3.5	43
Oriental Style Chicken	240	5	28
Rigatoni w. Broccoli & Chicken	280	7	34
Spiral Pasta & Beef Tips	300	7	40

Kid Cuisine

	C	F	Cb
Cheese Pizza	430	11	71
Circus Show Corn Dog, 8.8 oz	490	20	30
Cosmic Chicken Nuggets	440	16	50
Fantastic Fish Sticks, 7 oz	370	14	48
Game Time Taco Roll-Up, 7.35 oz	420	18	55
Hamburger Pizza	390	12	60
High Flying Fried Chicken	440	19	48
Magical Macaroni & Cheese	410	13	63
Parachuting Pork Ribettes, 7.55 oz	380	15	43

King Kold

	C	F	Cb
Potato Blintzees, 2.5 oz	110	3	18
Cheese Blintzees, 2.5 oz	110	1.5	14
Crepes, lowfat, w strwb. fill., 2.5 oz	110	1	19

La Choy

See Egg Rolls ~ Page 41

Lean Cuisine

	C	F	Cb
Everyday Favorites			
Angel Hair Pasta	220	3	41
Baked Chicken Florentine	220	4.5	32
Cheese Cannelloni	230	4	28
Cheese Ravioli	270	7	40
Chicken Enchilada Suiza w. Rice	280	5	48
Chicken Fettucini	280	6	36
Chicken Lasagna	270	8	30
Classic Cheese Lasagne	300	8	35
Country Veges. & Beef	210	4	33
Fettucini Alfredo	300	7	47
Fettucini Primavera	270	7	38
Hunan Beef & Broccoli	240	3.5	40
Lasagna w. Meat Sauce	290	6	37
Macaroni & Cheese	290	7	43
Macaroni Beef	270	5	42
Rst Chick. w. Lem. Pepper Fettuccine	260	7	34
Santa Fe Style Rice & Beans	300	5	54
Spaghetti w. Meat Sauce	300	4	50
Stuffed Cabbage w. Whipped Pot.	180	5	24
Swedish Meatballs w. Pasta	280	7	33
Teriyaki Stir-Fry	290	4	48
Entrees			
Chicken & Vegetables	250	6	31
Chicken Chow Mein w. Rice	220	5	33
Grilled Chicken w. Penne Pasta	250	5	29

Lean Cuisine (Cont)

	C	F	Cb
Entrees (Cont)			
Roast Potato w. Broc./Ched. Sce	260	6	39
Spaghetti w. Meat Balls	280	6	40
Vegetable Egg Roll, 9 oz	340	6	64
Vegetable Lasagna	260	7	35
Hearty Portions			
Cheese & Spinach Manicotti	340	6	52
Chicken & BBQ Sauce	380	8	54
Chicken Fettuccine w. Broccoli	390	9	48
Rigatoni w. Meatballs	440	9	62
Roast Chicken w. Mushroom	290	5	40
Roast Turkey Breast Dinner	380	6	57
Salisbury Steak Dinner	340	7	40
Cafe Classics			
Baked Chicken	230	4	31
Baked Fish	270	6	36
Beef Peppercorn, 8.75 oz	220	7	23
Beef Portabello, 9 oz	220	7	24
Beef Pot Roast	210	6	25
Cheese Lasagna w. Chicken	290	8	33
Chicken a l'Orange	250	2	40
Chicken Breast in Wine Sauce	210	6	23
Chicken Carbonara	280	8	33
Chicken in Peanut Sce	290	6	35
Chicken Mediterranean	270	4	40
Chicken Parmesan	220	5	27
Chicken Piccata	270	6	41
Chicken w. Basil Cream Sce	270	7	35
Fiesta Chicken	270	5	36
Glazed Chicken w. Veg. Rice	240	6	25
Glazed Turkey	240	5	37
Grilled Chick. w. Pasta, 9 3/8 oz	260	8	28
Herb Roasted Chicken	210	5	27
Honey Roasted Pork, 9.5 oz	250	6	32
MeatLoaf w. Whipped Potatoes	250	6	30
Oriental Beef, Vege & Rice	240	3.5	35
Salisbury Steak	280	8	29
Shrimp & Angel Hair Pasta, 10 oz	290	6	42
Skillet Sensations: *Per 1/2 Pkt*			
Beef Teriyaki & Rice	280	3	48
Chicken Oriental	280	3	46
Chicken Primavera	320	4.5	50
Garlic Chicken	340	4.5	56
Herb Chicken & Rst. Potatoes	270	5	39
3 Cheese Chicken	370	9	45

Marie Callender's

Meals & Dinners	C	F	Cb
Beef Pot Roast & Noodles, 1/2 pkt	**290**	9	33
Beef Tips & Mush. Sce, 13.6 oz	**430**	19	39
Cheese Ravioli in Marinara Sauce w. Spirals & Garlic bread, 1 c. + 1 oz brd	**370**	14	57
Cheesy Rice Chick. Broccoli, 12 oz	**390**	13	44
Chicken Cordon Bleu, 1 dinner	**590**	25	58
Chicken Parmigiana, 1 dinner	**620**	28	63
Chili/Cornbread, 1 c. + 1 1/2 oz br.	**350**	13	45
Chunky Chicken & Noodle, 1 meal	**520**	30	42
Country Fried Chick. & Gvy,1 din.	**610**	27	63
Country Fried Pork Chop, 1 dinner	**550**	27	50
Escalloped Noodles/Chicken, 1 c.	**270**	16	38
Fettucine Alfredo & Garlic Brd, 1 cup + 1 oz bread	**460**	27	71
Fettucine w. Broccoli & Chick.,1 c.	**410**	24	32
Grilled Chick. Brst w. Mash. Pot.	**340**	18	20
Ham Steak w. Macar. & Chse, 1 din.	**450**	9	63
Lasagna w. Meat Sauce, 1 cup	**370**	18	34
Meatloaf & Gvy w. Mashed Pot.	**540**	30	42
Roast Chicken & Vegies, 1/2 pkt	**260**	6	30
Salisbury Steak & Gravy, 1 dinner	**550**	25	51
Spagh. & Meat Sce,1 c. + 1 oz brd	**260**	10	51
Sweet & Sour Chicken, 1 dinner	**530**	9	56
Turkey with Gvy/dress., 1 dinner	**530**	17	52
Pot Pies: Chicken; Yankee, 10 oz	**680**	44	58
Turkey, 10 oz	**710**	46	56
Chicken & Broccoli, 10 oz	**780**	48	88
Chicken Au Gratin, 10 oz	**720**	48	53

Michelina's

Per Serving	C	F	Cb
Black Bean Chili w. Rice, 8 oz	**300**	4	58
Chicken a la King	**280**	8	39
Chili-Mac, 8 oz	**280**	9	36
Fettucine & Meatballs in Marsala	**250**	7	34
Fettucine Alfredo	**380**	15	45
Four Cheese Lasagna, 8 oz	**290**	7	42
Gr., Egg Noodles & Swedish M'ball	**360**	13	45
Lasagna Pollo	**280**	9	33
Lasagna Primavera	**270**	10	34
Lasagna w. Meat Sce, 9 oz	**290**	7	40
Linguini w. Clams & Sauce	**310**	4.5	55
Macaroni Cheese	**360**	14	40
Meatloaf, Gravy, Mash. Potato	**290**	16	22
Noodles Stroganoff w. Beef, 8 oz	**350**	15	39

Michelina's

Per Serving	C	F	Cb
Noodles w. Chicken, 8 oz	**300**	10	40
Penne Pasta w. Mushroom Sce	**280**	8	41
Penne Pollo	**290**	8	39
Pepper Steak & Rice	**260**	4.5	46
Rigatoni Pomodoro	**220**	2.5	40
Risotto Parmigiana	**460**	21	50
Salisbury Steak Mashed Potato	**300**	13	33
Shells & Cheese	**360**	12	45
Spagh. & Meatballs Pomodoro Sce	**300**	8	43
Spaghetti Marinara, 8 oz	**250**	2.5	47
Spaghetti w. Tomato Basil Sce	**250**	3	46
Stuffed Cheese Rigatoni	**260**	8	36
Yu Sing: Chicken Fried Rice	**360**	8	58
Chicken Lo Mein	**220**	3.5	34
Garlic Chicken	**250**	2.5	42
Sweet & Sour Chicken	**340**	4	67
Teriyaki Beef	**240**	2	51

Ortega

	C	F	Cb
Beef Taco Filling, 1/3 cup, 2 oz	**100**	6	4
Nacho Beef Bake, 1/4 pkt, 9 oz	**400**	20	36
Spanish Rice & Beans, 10 oz pkt	**400**	17	44
Beef Enchilada, 9.3 oz pkt	**360**	13	49
Cheese Enchilada, 9 3/4 oz pkt	**410**	15	55
Chicken Enchilada, 9 1/2 oz pkt	**400**	16	51
Skillet Fajitas: Steak, 1/2 c., 2 oz	**35**	1	3
Chicken, 3/4 cup, 2 1/2 oz	**45**	1	4
Nachos Ckn Supr., 1/2 pkt, 11 oz	**380**	11	49

Stouffer's

	C	F	Cb
Entrees: Beef, Rst Pot. & Peppers	**300**	6	44
Broccoli & Beef	**320**	5	51
Cheddar Cheese & Chicken Bake	**450**	21	41
Cheddar Pasta w. Beef & Tom.	**450**	19	45
Cheese Ravioli	**380**	13	51
Cheesy Spaghetti Bake	**460**	21	47
Chicken & Dumplings	**280**	8	33
Chicken a la King	**350**	13	41
Chicken Pie, 10 oz	**540**	33	38
Chili w. Beans	**270**	10	30
Classic/Cheese Manicotti	**360**	16	34
Creamed Chicken	**260**	19	8
Creamed Chipped Beef	**160**	11	6
Escalloped Chick. & Noodles, 10 oz	**430**	27	30
Fettucini Alfredo	**520**	28	50

Stouffer's (Cont)

	C	F	Cb
Entrees (Cont):			
Fish Fillets w. Mac. Cheese, 9 oz	**430**	21	37
Five Cheese Lasagna	**360**	13	40
Grilled Chicken & Vegetables	**400**	9	54
Lasagna Bake	**370**	12	47
Lasagna w. Meat Sauce, 10 1/2 oz	**370**	14	40
Macaroni & Beef	**420**	20	40
Macaroni & Chse, w. Broccoli	**350**	16	36
Macaroni Cheese, 1 cup	**380**	17	40
Meat Lasagna, 1 cup	**270**	10	28
Penne Pasta & Chicken Bake	**340**	14	37
Roasted Garlic Chicken	**320**	11	39
Salisbury Steak, 16 oz	**570**	24	47
Salisbury Steak & Macaroni Chse	**410**	19	34
Spaghetti w. Meat Sauce	**350**	12	46
Spaghetti w. Meatballs	**440**	15	56
Stuffed Pepper, 10 oz	**200**	5	27
Swedish Meatballs	**480**	24	43
Tuna Noodle Casserole	**320**	10	37
Turkey Tetrazzini	**360**	17	33
Veal Parmagiana	**630**	26	68
Veg. & Chicken Pasta Bake	**380**	11	46
Vegetarian Lasagne	**410**	18	42
Yankee Pot Roast	**320**	9	41
Side Dishes: Corn Souffle	**170**	7	21
Creamed Spinach	**160**	12	8
Escalloped Apples	**180**	3	38
Potatoes au Gratin	**130**	6	15
Scalloped Potatoes	**140**	5	18
Spinach Souffle	**150**	10	10
Welsh Rarebit	**120**	9	5
Hearty Portions: Beef Pot Rst, 16 oz	**370**	11	44
Chicken Fettuccini, 16 3/4 oz	**640**	24	67
Country Fried Beef Steak, 16 oz	**560**	25	61
Fried Chicken Breast, 15 1/8 oz	**520**	16	66
Meatloaf w. Potatoes, 17 oz	**480**	23	46
Pork w. Roast Potatoes, 15 3/8 oz	**570**	15	75
Roast Turkey Breast	**490**	20	52
Skillet Sensations: *Per 1/2 Pkg*			
Chicken & Dumplings	**280**	8	33
Chicken Alfredo	**490**	16	63
Homestyle Beef	**360**	11	34
Homestyle Chicken	**390**	13	47
Teriyaki Chicken	**340**	3	59
Family Style Favorites: *Per Serving*			
Chick. & Broc. Pasta Bake, 1/5 pkt	**340**	17	28
Grandma's Chick. & Veg. Rice Bake	**360**	15	36

Stouffer's (Cont)

	C	F	Cb
Homestyle: Beef Pot Roast	**250**	8	30
Baked Chicken in Gravy/Potato	**260**	11	18
Breaded Pork Cutlet	**420**	23	27
Chick. Breast w. Mushr. Gravy	**360**	15	32
Fried Chicken & Mashed Potato	**400**	17	38
Meatloaf & Whip. Potato	**360**	21	28
Salisbury Steak in Gravy/Onions	**350**	16	27
Veal Parmigiana	**410**	16	48

Swanson

	C	F	Cb
Pot Pies:			
Pot-Topped Beef, 12 oz	**450**	22	47
Potato-Topped Chicken, 12 oz	**440**	21	51
Deep Dish Chick., 1/2 pkt, 8.5 oz	**430**	20	48
Hungry Man Dinners:			
Boneless Pork Rib	**770**	38	78
Boneless Rst. Chick. Herb Gravy	**500**	12	65
Boneless White Meat Fried Chick.	**430**	16	49
Classic Fried Chicken, 16 1/2 oz	**790**	40	75
Country Fried Beef Steak	**660**	33	66
Fisherman's Platter, 13 oz	**640**	25	80
Fried Chicken Dinner, 11 oz	**430**	16	50
Mexican Style	**690**	27	87
Salisbury Steak	**610**	33	46
Sirloin Beef Tips	**440**	15	53
Stuffing Baked Turkey	**450**	15	59
Traditional Pot Roast	**360**	6	48
Turkey, mostly white meat	**510**	15	64
4 Compartment Meals			
Boneless Pork Rib, 10.5 oz	**470**	19	58
Boneless White Meat Fr. Chicken	**430**	16	49
Chicken Nuggets	**590**	25	71
Classic Fried Chicken, 11 1/2 oz	**600**	31	58
Country Fried Beef Steak w. Gravy	**460**	22	47
Fish 'N Chips	**490**	20	59
Herb Roasted Chicken	**310**	7	44
Mexican Style Comb., 13.25 oz	**470**	18	59
Salisbury Steak	**340**	15	35
Stuffed Baked Turkey	**450**	15	59
Turkey Brst. w. Stuffing & Gravy	**330**	6	50
Veal Parmigiana, 11 1/4 oz	**390**	18	40
Yankee Pot Roast	**250**	4.5	39

Thai Chef

Per Meal	C	F	Cb
Peanut Satay Chicken, 12 oz	400	14	50
Lemon Basil Chicken,12 oz	390	10	55
Thai Sweet & Sour Veges,12 oz	340	5	70
Vegetarian Mussaman, 12 oz	390	9	71

Taj

Per Meal	C	F	Cb
Asparagus Subzi/Dal Baahar	385	13	58
Bean Masala/Chunna Bahji	330	6	60
Chicken Masala/Korma	330	9	35
Eggplant Bhartha	300	7	55
Mushroom/Green Pea Masala	390	13	61
Palak Paneer	320	7	25
Raj Mah	340	5	62
Shahi Paneer	410	24	42
Vegetable Korma	340	12	54

Topps

	C	F	Cb
Chicken Nuggets, 4, 2.5 oz	200	12	12
Hamburger: 100% Pure Ground Beef			
Grilled or Panfried, 2.7 oz	230	17	1
Kabobs: Beef, 1 kabob, 1.5 oz	170	7	2
Chicken, 1 kabob	120	1.5	0

Tyson

See Page 51

Wolfgang Puck's

Per Meal	C	F	Cb
Breaded Chick. Parmagiana, 12 oz	540	21	58
Chick. & Spinach Pasta Wrap	460	11	68
Chicken Bolognese & Spaghetti	480	22	48
Chicken Pappardelle	460	18	47
Eggplant Parmesan	370	28	14
4 Cheese Lasagna; Meat Lasagna	490	22	51
4 Cheese Macaroni	610	33	51
Italian Sausage Pasta Wrap	700	29	67
Meat Lasagne, 12 oz	490	22	51
Meatloaf in Wine Sauce	560	32	36
Mushroom & Spinach Ravioli	260	18	54
Mushroom Lasagna/Tortellini	440	17	53
Penne Pasta w. Beef & Vege	410	18	38
Radiatore Pasta Primavera	310	10	41
Spicy Chicken Lasagna	470	21	45

Weight Watchers

Smart Ones: *Per Meal*	C	F	Cb
Angel Hair Pasta	180	2	32
Broccoli & Chse Baked Pot., 10 oz	250	6	39
Chick. Chow Mein; Fiesta Chicken	205	2	34
Chicken Enchiladas Suiza, 9 oz	270	9	33
Chicken Oriental	230	4.5	34
Cr. Rigatoni w. Broccoli & Chicken	240	3.5	39
Fettucini Alfredo w. Broc., 9.25 oz	270	6	39
Fiesta Chicken, 8.5 oz	210	2	35
Grilled Salisbury Steak	260	10	24
Honey Mustard Chicken, 8.5 oz	210	3.5	38
Lasagna Bolognese	240	2.5	43
Lasagna Florentine, 10.5 oz	290	8	36
Lemon Herb Chicken Piccata	210	2	31
Mac. & Chse; Ravioli Florentine	220	2	43
Pasta & Spinach Romano	260	8	35
Penne Pasta w. Sundr. Tom., 10 oz	300	8	43
Ravioli Florentine, 8.5 oz	220	2	43
Roast Turkey Medallions, 9 oz	200	2	33
Santa Fe Style Rice & Beans, 10 oz	300	8	49
Spaghetti & Meat Sce, 11.5 oz	280	5	43
Spaghetti Bolognese	280	5	43
Spaghetti Marinara, 9 oz	280	7	46
Spicy Penne & Ricotta	280	6	45
Spicy Penne Mediterranean	260	6	40
Spicy Szechuan Veg. & Chicken	220	2	39
Swedish Meatballs, 9 oz	290	7	34
Tuna Noodle Gratin	270	6	40
Ziti Mozzarella, 9 oz	290	7	47
Main Street Bistro Selections: *Per Meal*			
Basil Chicken, 9 oz	280	7	35
Bean & Beef Salsa Verde Bowl	290	8	37
Beef & Vege Rice Bowl	260	5	38
Chicken & Veges Carribean	230	3	37
Chicken Carbonara, 9.5 oz	300	6	36
Chicken Fettuccine	300	8	39
Fajita Chicken Supreme, 9.25 oz	280	7	33
Fire-Grilled Chick. & Vegies, 10 oz	280	5	40
Golden Baked Garlic Chick., 10 oz	280	6	40
Oven Rst Veg. Primavera, 10 oz	300	8	46
Oven Roasted Chicken	300	7	38
Slow Roast Turkey Breast, 10 oz	220	7	20
Southwestern Style Chicken Bowl	230	2.5	35
Yukon Gold Pot. & Corn Chowder	260	8	38
Pizza: 5.5 oz each	390	12	50

Pockets

Per Serving	C	F	Cb
Big Stuffs: Ham & Cheese	420	16	50
Cheese & Steak; Pepperoni	440	20	48
Croissant Pockets			
Supreme Pizza	390	20	40
Pepperoni Pizza	360	16	41
Philly Steak & Cheese	350	16	37
Ham & Cheddar	320	12	40
Egg, Sausage & Cheese	340	15	40
Chick. Broccoli & Chse; Turk./Ham	290	4	37
Delistuffs			
Ham & Cheese	340	13	41
Cheese Steak; Pepperoni Pizza	350	14	40
Hot Pockets			
Beef & Cheddar	350	16	36
Pepperoni Pizza	350	15	41
Sausage Pizza; Beef Fajita	340	6.5	38
Ham & Cheese	320	12	40
Meatballs w. Mozzarella	320	11	39
Other flavors	300	6	38
Pizza Minis: Pepperoni	250	11	31
Sausage/& Pepperoni	230	8	31
Double Cheese	240	10	32
Toaster Breaks: *Per Piece, 2.1 oz*			
Pizza: Pepperoni; Dble Cheese	190	9	22
Sausage & Pepperoni	180	8	22
Melts: Grilled Cheese	210	10	24
Ham & Cheese	180	8	22
Philly Steak & Cheese	190	10	20
Lean Pockets			
Chicken Parmesan	280	7	41
Philly Steak & Chse; Turkey/Broc.	260	7	35
Other flavors	270	7	40
Taj Samosa Pockets: *Per 9 oz*			
Aloo (potato)	170	8	26
Gobi (mixed vegetable)	150	5	22
Subzi (cabbage/potato)	150	5	22

Pizza & Egg Rolls

	C	F	Cb
Totino's: Pizza Rolls, 6 rolls, 3 oz			
Sausage	210	10	20
Pepperoni	230	12	20
Chun King: Munchers (Mini Egg Roll), 6 rolls, 3 oz	210	9	15

Burritos & Waffles

Per Serving	C	F	Cb
Belgar Chef			
Waffles	180	2	34
El Monterey: King Size, 8 oz			
Beef & Bean/Green Chili	580	27	30
Old El Paso			
Burrito: Bean & Cheese	300	9	44
Beef & Bean	320	10	47
Pizza, all types	250	9	30
Chimichanga, all types	350	18	38
Tina's Burrito			
Bean & Cheese, 8.5 oz	420	15	5
Microwaveable Pouch, 5 oz			
Chicken Burrito	240	4	15
Red Hot Beef	370	15	10
Beef & Bean	380	15	15
w. Green Chili	370	15	10

Frozen Pizza

Amy's: *Per Serving*	C	F	Cb
Cheese; Spinach; Pesto	**300**	12	38
Roasted Vegetable, 4 oz	**270**	8	43
Soy Cheese; Veggie Combo, aver.	**280**	10	37
Mushroom & Olive	**250**	9	33
Celeste			
Large Pizza: *Per 1/4 Pizza*			
Cheese	**320**	16	32
Deluxe; Pepperoni	**350**	20	34
Suprema, 1/5 pizza	**290**	16	27
Large Premium Pizza: *Per 1/4 Pizza*			
Cheese	**350**	18	33
Deluxe; Pepperoni	**390**	22	34
Sausage/Pepperoni	**380**	22	33
Pizza For One: *Per Pizza*			
Cheese; Vegetable	**420**	21	45
4-Cheese Orig.; Pepperoni	**475**	27	41
Deluxe; 4-Cheese Zesty	**470**	25	45
Sausage	**530**	27	52
Suprema	**500**	27	49
Rising Crust: *Per 1/6 Pizza*			
4-Cheese	**320**	11	39
Pepperoni	**380**	16	43
Suprema; Three Meat	**385**	17	40
Connie's Pizza (Chicago Deep Dish)			
Cheese, 1/4 pizza, 4.5 oz	**300**	12	34
Sausage, 1/4 pizza, 4.6 oz	**300**	11	39
Spinach Mushroom, 1/4 pizza, 5 oz	**310**	12	30
Di Giorno			
Rising Crust Pizza			
Large: *Per 1/6 Pizza*			
Four Cheese	**320**	11	39
Pepperoni; Three Meat	**390**	17	41
Supreme	**400**	17	41
Small (Individual) Size:			
Pepperoni, 12.75 oz	**300**	13	33
Supreme, 14.3 oz	**300**	14	34
Vegetable, 13.8 oz	**900**	39	90
Dominick's			
Per 1/6 Pizza			
Four-Cheese, 5 oz	**290**	9	38
Italian Sausage/Supreme, 5 oz	**320**	13	38
Healthy Choice: ***French Bread Pizza***			
Cheese; Pepperoni, 6 oz	**340**	5	50
Supreme, 6.35 oz	**330**	5	51
Vegetable, 6 oz	**280**	4	44

Freschetta	C	F	Cb
Per 1/2 Pizza: 4 Cheese	**390**	14	47
Pepperoni	**420**	17	48
Per 1/3 Pizza: Garlic Chicken	**260**	9	32
Supreme	**290**	12	33
Per 1/5 Pizza, Large: 4 Cheese	**380**	15	45
Vegetable Primavera	**350**	13	45
Sauce, Stuffed Crust: 4 Cheese	**310**	10	41
55g & Pepperoni	**340**	13	41
Supreme	**350**	13	40
Per 1/6 Pizza, Large: 4 Meat	**340**	14	39
55g & Pepperoni; Pepperoni	**350**	15	39
Special Deluxe; Supreme	**350**	15	40
Home Run Inn: *Per 1/4 Pizza*			
Cheese, 4.5 oz	**390**	30	34
Sausage, 5 oz	**400**	22	32
Sausage & Mushroom, 5.5 oz	**390**	23	29
Jack's Pizza			
Original 12": *Per 1/4 Pizza*			
Canadian Style Bacon	**280**	10	31
Cheese, 1/3 pizza	**360**	13	41
Hamburger; Saus.; Spicy Italian, 1/4	**300**	14	28
Pepperoni	**330**	15	31
Original 9": *Per 1/2 Pizza*			
Pepperoni; Sausage, average	**380**	18	37
Great Combinations (12"): *Per 1/4 Pizza*			
Bacon Cheeseburger; Dble Cheese	**380**	19	32
Pepperoni; Sausage, average	**400**	19	41
Sausage & Mushroom	**310**	15	29
Other types, average	**350**	18	30
Great Combinations (9"): *Per 1/2 Pizza*			
Double Cheese	**430**	21	38
Pepperoni & Sausage	**380**	18	36
Naturally Rising (12"): *Per 1/6 Pizza*			
Canadian Style Bacon; Cheese	**290**	10	35
Other types, average	**340**	16	34
Naturally Rising (9")			
Cheese, 1/3 pizza	**300**	10	38
Comb. w/Saus. & Pepperoni, 1/4	**300**	14	29
Pepperoni; Sausage, 1/3 pizza	**360**	16	38
The Works, 1/4 pizza	**280**	12	29
Pizza Bursts: All types, 6 pieces	**250**	13	26
Jeno's: ***Crisp 'n Tasty:*** *Per Pizza*			
Canadian Style Bacon; Cheese	**450**	19	17
Combination; Sausage; Supreme	**520**	28	17
Hamburger; Three Meat	**500**	25	16
Pepperoni	**510**	27	17

Lean Cuisine	C	F	Cb
French Brd Pizza: Deluxe, 6 1/8 oz	300	6	46
Pepperoni, 5 1/4 oz	310	7	46
Sundried Tomato, 6 oz	340	8	48
Marie Callender's: ***French Bread Pizza***			
Hearty Pepperoni	570	28	50
Smothered 4 Cheese	530	24	50
Super Supreme	510	23	50
Pepperidge Farm			
Croissant & Pastry Pizza:			
Cheese	390	20	39
Deluxe	450	27	40
Pepperoni	420	23	39
Pillsbury			
Microwave: Cheese, 1/2 pizza	240	10	28
Pepperoni, Combination, 1/2 pizza	310	15	29
Sausage, 1/2 pizza	280	13	29
French Bread Pizza: Cheese (1)	370	15	41
Sausage & Pepperoni, 1 pizza	430	19	46
Sausage, 1 pizza	410	16	48
Power Dogz Pizza For Kids			
Gonzo's Cheeseburger Max, each	460	20	48
KT's Poppin' Pepperoni, each	500	24	46
Shaggy's Cheezy Cheese, each	420	14	46
Red Baron: 4 Cheese, 1/4 pizza	430	21	45
Pepperoni, 1/4 pizza, 154g	450	23	41
Special Deluxe, 1/5 pizza	340	17	34
Supreme, 1/5 pizza	350	18	38
Deep Dish Singles: Pepperoni	540	31	47
Supreme, 1/5 pizza	490	27	46
Stouffer's: ***French Bread Pizzas,*** *1/2 Pkg*			
Bacon Cheddar/Deluxe Pizza	430	21	45
Cheese; Vegetable Deluxe	370	16	47
Cheeseburger; Pepperoni	430	20	45
Extra Cheese	400	16	50
Pepperoni & Mushr./Sausage	440	21	50
Sausage & Pepperoni/White Pizza	460	23	45
Three Meat	460	21	48
Tombstone: ***Original 12" Pizza***			
Canadian; Extra Cheese, 1/4	350	14	36
Pepperoni, 1/4 pizza	400	21	35
Other varieties, average, 1/5	320	15	29
12" Special Order: *Per 1/5 Pizza*			
Four Cheese	400	19	37
Other varieties, average	360	18	32

Tombstone (Cont)	C	F	Cb
Original 9" Pizza (Cont):			
Deluxe; Hamburger; Saus., 1/3	280	13	27
Extra Cheese, 1/2 pizza	380	16	40
Pepperoni varieties, aver., 1/3	310	16	27
Double Top:			
Two Cheese, 1/5 pizza	380	19	29
Other varieties, average, 1/6	330	18	25
Oven Rising: *Per 1/6 Pizza*			
All types, average	330	15	34
Thin Crust: 3 Cheese; Italian, 1/4	370	22	26
4 Meat Combo, 1/4 pizza	380	23	26
Pepperoni, 1/4	400	25	25
Supreme; Supreme Taco, 1/4	370	23	27
For One: average all types	550	32	42
For One (1/2 Less Fat): Cheese	360	10	43
Vegetable, 1 pizza	360	9	48
Totino's			
Party Pizza: *Per 1/2 Pizza*			
Cheese; Can Bacon; Vegetable	320	14	34
Combination; Zesty Italiano	390	21	35
Hamburger	380	20	34
Sausage & Mushr.; Three Meat	380	19	34
Sausage; Bacon; Pepperoni	380	21	34
Supreme	380	20	35
Pizza Family Size			
Cheese, 1/3 pizza	360	16	39
Combination, 1/4 pizza	310	17	29
Pepperoni, 1/3 pizza	410	22	38
Sausage, 1/4 pizza	300	16	29
Pizza Rolls: *Per 6 Rolls*			
Combination	230	12	23
Pepperoni	240	12	24
Sausage	230	11	24
Supreme; Cheese	210	10	25
Three Meat	220	10	24
M'wave Pizza For One: Cheese	240	11	26
Pepperoni; Sausage	290	16	26
Supreme	300	17	26
Wolfgang Puck's			
Per 1/2 Pizza: Mushroom& Spinach	270	8	36
Pepperoni & Mushroom	390	15	43
Spicy Chicken	360	16	36
Supreme	400	17	37
4 Cheese	360	15	40
Per 1/4 Pizza: BBQ Chicken	370	13	41
Pepperoni	360	15	34

B & M	C	F	Cb
Baked Beans: *Per 1/2 Cup (4 1/2 oz)*			
Bacon & Onion w. Brown Sugar	190	2	36
Baked Beans w. Pork	180	2	33
Barbeque; Vegetarian	170	1	33
w. Natural Honey; Red Kidney	170	2	30
Yellow Eye Baked Beans	180	3	30
Betty Crocker			
Chicken Helper: *Per 1 Cup Prepared*			
Chicken & Herb Rice	260	7	26
Southwestern Chicken	240	5	29
Average other flavors	300	9	28
Potato Buds: Plain, 1/3 cup mix	80	0	18
As prepared, 1/2 cup	160	8	19
Suddenly Salad: *Per 3/4 Cup, Prepared*			
Classic	250	8	38
Ranch & Bacon	330	20	30
Roasted Garlic & Parmesan	260	11	33
Campbell's: *Per 1/2 Cup, 4 1/2 oz*			
Barbecue; Old Fashioned Beans	170	2.5	29
Brown Sugar & Bacon Beans	170	3	29
Chili Beans	130	3	21
New England Beans	180	3	32
Pork & Beans in Tomato Sauce	130	2	24
Chef Boyardee			
Microwave Cup Meals: *Per Bowl*			
Beef Ravioli	190	3.5	28
Lasagna; Pasta w. Chick. & Veg.	220	6	34
Pasta w. Meatballs	230	8	30
Rice w. Beef & Veges.	250	7	38
Spaghetti & Meatballs	210	7	28
Pull Ring 7 oz Can: Beef Ravioli	170	4	27
Spaghetti w. Meatballs	210	8	27
Homestyle 15 oz Can: *Per Cup, 9 oz*			
Cannelloni; Rigatoni	250	10	31
Chicken Alfredo w. Pasta	250	12	24
Ravioli Primavera	230	6	40
Pull Ring 16 oz Can: *Per Cup*			
Beef/Cheese Ravioli	220	5	38
99% Fat Free Beef Ravioli	210	1	41
Spaghetti w. Meatballs	270	10	32
Lasagna Dinner Kit: *Per Serving*	290	7	44
Cheese Pizza Kit: *Per Serving*	300	5	51
Chef Jr: Micro Ravioli, 8 3/4 oz	210	5	33
Flying Saucers & Aliens, 9 oz	240	1.5	47
Other varieties, 1 cup, 9 oz	200	0.5	43

Dennison's Chili	C	F	Cb
15 oz Can: *Per 1 Cup Serving*			
Chili Con Carne With Beans:			
Original; Hot, 1 cup	350	15	36
Chunky; Hot & Chunky	320	12	32
Beef Chili w. Beans (99% Fat Free)	220	2	27
Mild Green w. Beans	370	17	32
Vegetarian w. Beans (99% FF)	180	1	35
No Bean Chili Con Carne	330	18	21
Dinty Moore *(Hormel Foods)*			
1 1/2 lb Can: Beef Stew, 1 cup	230	14	16
7 1/2 oz Can: Beef Stew	190	10	15
Noodles & Chicken	200	9	21
American Classics: *Per 10 oz Microwave Bowl*			
Beef Pot Roast	200	3	19
Chicken & Noodles	270	8	28
Chicken Breast & Gravy w. Pot.	240	4	25
Hearty Lasagna	340	16	28
Roast Beef & Gravy w. Potato	240	5	24
Salisbury Steak w. Potato	300	13	24
Turkey & Dressing w. Gravy	290	8	32
Dr. McDougall's: *Per Cup*			
Pasta w. Beans, Mediterranean	180	1	29
Pinto Beans & Rice, Sthwestern	190	2	38
Ramen Noodles; Chicken; Beef	140	1	39
Rice & Pasta Pilaf	210	1	36
Eden: *Per 1/2 Cup, 4 1/2 oz*			
Baked Beans w. Sorghum, Mustard	150	0	27
Black Soy Beans	90	1.5	9
Chili Beans w. Jalapeno & Peppers	130	0	21
Ginger Blacks w. Ginger, Lemon	120	0	21
Lentils w. Onion, Bay Leaf	90	0	13
Fantastic			
Cup Meals: *Per Packet*			
Bombay Curry Rice & Beans	250	1.5	53
Cajun Rice & Beans	230	3	46
Cha-cha Chili	220	1	37
Chili Ole, average	260	2.5	48
Ready, Set, Pasta!, average	230	3.5	41
Spanish Rice & Beans	210	1.5	49
Tex Mex Rice & Pinto Beans	240	2.5	48
Vegetarian Chili	160	1	27
Noodles: Average	140	1	27
Couscous: Black Bean Salsa	240	1.5	46
Creole Vegetable	220	1.5	41
Nacho Cheddar	120	2	21
Sweet Corn	180	1	36

Franco-American: *Per Cup*	C	F	Cb
Life w. Louise Pasta	190	2	36
Spaghetti in. Tom Sce w. Cheese	210	2	41
Spaghettios: in Tomato & Cheese	190	2	36
w. Sliced Franks/Meatballs	260	11	32
Beef Ravioli	230	3.5	42
Hamburger Helper: *Per Cup, Prepared*			
Bacon Cheeseburger; 3-Cheese	380	17	35
Beef Pasta; Beef Stew, average	260	10	25
Cheddar & Broccoli	350	15	33
Cheddar Cheese Melt	310	12	31
Cheeseburger Macaroni	360	15	33
Cheesy Hashbrowns; Chili; Pizza	290	10	31
Double Cheese Pizza	330	13	35
4-Cheese Lasagna; Stroganoff	330	14	31
Lasagna; Ravioli; Sthwestern Beef	290	10	32
Philly Cheesesteak	330	17	25
Hormel: *Per Cup*			
Kid's Kitchen: Beans 'N Wieners	310	13	37
Beefy Macaroni	190	6	23
Cheesy Macaroni 'N Beef	260	7	33
Cheezy Mac 'N Cheese	260	11	30
Mini Beef Ravioli	240	7	34
Noodle Rings & Chicken	150	5	16
Spaghetti Rings w. Meatballs	230	7	35
Microwave Cup: Beef Stew	190	10	15
Chicken & Noodles	200	9	16
Low Calorie	110	2.5	16
Chili w. Beans	220	6	27
Chili no Beans	190	8	15
Lasagna w. Meat Sauce	210	6	29
Scalloped Potatoes & Ham	240	14	20
Spaghetti w. Meat Sce	220	7	31
Chili, 15 oz Can: *Per Cup*			
With Beans: Reg./Hot/Chunky	270	7	34
Homestyle Chili	330	19	24
Turkey (99% Fat Free)	200	3	26
Vegetarian (99% Fat Free)	200	1	38
No Beans, 1 cup	210	9	17
Hungry Jack Potatoes			
Casseroles: 1/2 cup, average	150	5	24
Idaho Mashed: 1/2 cup, aver.	155	5	21
Inst. Potato Flakes: 1/3 cup	80	0	18
Pot. Pancake Mix, 2 T., Made Up	90	1.5	16
Green Giant: *Per Cup, 4.5 oz*			
Pork & Beans w. Tomato Sce	240	2	46
Spicy Chilli Beans	220	2	40

Hy Top: *Per Serving*	C	F	Cb
Deluxe Shells & Ched. Chse Dinner	410	16	51
Refried Beans, 1/2 Cup	150	2.5	24
Cans: *Per 1 Cup*			
Spagh. Rings & Tom. Meatballs	410	16	51
Spagh. Rings in Tomato Sce	190	0.5	40
Spaghetti w. Tom. Sce & Chse	180	0	39
1 1/2lb Can: Beef Stew, 247g	190	7	18
15oz Can: Corned Beef Hash	430	28	28
Chili w. Beans, 270g	510	32	34
Kraft Pasta Dinners: *Per Cup, Prepared*			
Deluxe: Four Cheese	320	10	44
Sharp Cheddar	270	4	38
Macaroni & Cheese:	320	10	44
Light	290	4.5	48
Light (Only 1 T. fat + skim milk)	290	6	47
Child's/Cartoon Pack	410	19	47
Easy Mac, 1 pouch	250	7	38
Velveeta: All varieties	360	13	46
Oven Classic Chicken Bake: *1/6 Pkt, Prepared*			
Au Gratin; Traditional Roast	340	11	33
Herb & Garlic	320	8	34
Homestyle BBQ	360	8	43
Honey Mustard	380	10	43
Lemon	370	7	48
Roasted Garlic	310	10	28
Lipton Packet Meals: *Per Cup, Prepared*			
Rice & Sauce: Spanish	270	7.5	47
Cheddar Broccoli; Chicken	280	9	46
If no fat used in prep'n, deduct 55 Cals and 6g Fat			
Noodles & Sauce: Butter/& Herb	310	14	42
Chicken Flavor; Chick. Broccoli	300	11	42
If no fat used in prep'n, deduct 55 Cals and 6g Fat			
Pasta & Sauce: Creamy Garlic	350	13	47
Crmy Mushr./Tom.; Zesty Ched.	320	11	43
Mild Ched. Chse; Rst Garlic Chick.	290	10	40
Roasted Garlic Olive Oil w. Tom.	270	8.5	42
Other varieties, average	290	9	40
If no fat used in prep'n, deduct 55 Cals and 6g Fat			
Recipe Secrets: Golden Onion	50	1	9
Onion	20	0	4
Onion & Mushroom; Savory Herb	30	0.5	6
Vegetable	30	0	9
Sizzle & Stir: *1/6 Pkt, Prepared*			
3 Cheese Alfredo Chkn & Penne	410	15	29
Savory Herbed Chicken & Pasta	340	9	28
Spanish Chkn; Teriyaki Stir Fry	360	9.5	34

Lunch Basket: *Per Serving*	C	F	Cb
Microwave: Dumplings 'n Chicken	140	5	21
Hearty Beef Stew	170	9	17
Lasagna w. Meat Sauce	160	3	29
Pasta 'n Chick. w. Veg	150	5	22
Manischewitz: Taco Dinner	290	12	38
Vegetarian Chili, 3/4 cup	145	1.5	31
Maruchan: *Per Pkt*			
Instant Noodles: all flavors, aver.	280	12	37
Instant Wonton, all flavors	200	12	19
Oriental Noodle, all flavors	290	12	38
Ramen flavors, 1/2 pkt, 1 1/2 oz	180	7	26
Wonton flavors, 1/3 pkt	90	5	9
Near East: *Prepared as Directed, Per Cup*			
Couscous: Original Plain	230	2	46
Chicken & Herbs	270	6	51
Toasted Pine Nut	230	6	40
Creamy Parmesan	280	7	48
Roasted Garlic; Broccoli	220	4	41
Roasted Pecan & Garlic	240	9	37
Rice Pilaf	190	0.5	42
Nile Spice: *Per Cup*			
Couscous: Lentil Curry	200	1.5	36
Minestrone	180	1.5	34
Parmesan	200	3	34
Nissan: Cup Noodles, all types, aver.	300	14	38
Old El Paso: *Per Serving*			
Refried Beans:			
Regular, Black, 1/2 cup	100	0.5	17
w. Green Chilies, 1/2 cup	100	0.5	19
w. Cheese, 1/2 cup	130	3.5	18
w. Sausage, 1/2 cup	200	13	14
Fat Free varieties, 1/2 cup	100	0	18
Mexe/Pinto Beans, 1/2 cup	110	0.5	19
Black/Garbanzo Beans, 1/2 cup	100	1	17
One Skillet Mexican (Prepared):			
Rice Burrito, (1)	190	4	35
Salsa; Taco, average, (2)	460	16	56
Dinner Kits (Prep'd): Soft Taco	390	19	33
Burrito (1)	270	12	27
Hard & Soft Taco (2)	360	17	32
Shells, Taco Sce, Seasoning (2)	310	18	19
Fajita (2)	330	10	35
Taco Dinner (2)	300	17	19

Old El Paso(Cont):	C	F	Cb
Side Dishes: *Per Serving*			
Canned: Chili with Beans, 1 cup	240	11	19
Spanish Rice, 1 cup	140	1	30
Tamales in Chili Gravy (1)	320	19	31
Boxed: Chsy Mexican Rice 1/3 pkt	250	2	55
Spanish Rice, 1/3 pkt	280	4.5	55
Pasta-Roni: *Per Cup, Prepared*			
Broccoli	340	15	41
Broccoli Au Gratin	280	10	41
Chicken; Shells & White Cheddar	310	13	41
Chicken & Broccoli; Parmesano	370	16	49
Chicken & Garlic (Lowfat)	210	3	39
Creamy Garlic	420	25	41
Fettucini Alfredo: Reduced Fat	310	8	50
Garlic & Olive Oil w. Vermicelli	360	16	48
Homestyle Chicken	230	6	39
White Cheddar & Broccoli	400	19	48
Pritikin: Vegetarian Chili, 1 cup	160	1	27
Progresso: Beef Rav., 1 c., 9 oz	260	5	45
Cheese Ravioli, 1 cup, 9 oz	220	2	43
Italian Style Zucchini, 1/2 c., 4.2 oz	50	2	7
Ramen Noodles: *Per Serving*			
Beef/Chicken Flavor, 3 oz	190	8	27
Baked Noodle: 1/2 Block, 1 1/2 oz	140	1	30
Noodles: Fat Fried Shrimp, 1 1/2 oz	170	6	26
Other Flavors, 1 1/2 oz	160	6	26
Fried Cup: Beef, 1 packet, 2.2 oz	290	11	41
Lowfat: Average, 2 oz	215	1.5	45
Rice-A-Roni: *Per Cup, Prepared*			
Beef; Herb & Butter	310	9	52
Broccoli Au Gratin	370	17	47
1/3 Less Salt	320	11	50
Chicken	310	9	52
1/3 Less Salt	280	5	53
Lowfat	210	3	41
Chicken & Broccoli	230	6	41
Chicken & Garlic	260	9	41
Chicken & Mushroom	360	14	52
Fried Rice	320	11	51
Long Grain & Wild Rice	240	6	43
Red Beans & Rice	290	7	51
Rice Pilaf; Risotto	310	9	51
Savory Chicken Vegetable	210	3	41
Spanish Rice	270	8	46
White Cheddar & Herbs	340	13	48

(Reduced Fat Recipe: If only 1 Tbsp fat is used instead of 2 Tbsp, deduct 35 calories and 4g fat.)

Stagg Chili	C	F	Cb
15 oz Can: Per 1 Cup			
Chili w. Beans: Classic/Dynamite	**330**	17	28
Country Brand/Laredo	**320**	16	29
Rancho House Chicken	**290**	9	32
No Beans: Steakhouse/Double	**330**	21	16
99% Fat Free: 4-Bean Chili	**200**	1	37
Turkey Ranchers/Silvarado Beef	**240**	3	31
Sweet Sue			
Chicken & Dumplings, 1 cup	**240**	7	31
Canned Whole Chicken:			
w/out giblets, 2 oz	**80**	5	0
Taco Bell: *Per 1/2 Cup*			
Home Originals: Refried Beans	**140**	2.5	22
Fat Free Beans w. Green Chilles	**120**	0	23
Trader Joe's			
Quiche: Broccoli & Cheddar, 6 oz	**490**	33	33
Mexicaine, 6 oz	**510**	36	29
Spinach & Mushroom, 6 oz	**470**	30	32
Tuna Helper (Betty Crocker)			
Prepared as Directed: Per Cup			
Cheesy Pasta	**310**	14	32
Creamy Pasta	**300**	13	31
Tuna Melt; Creamy Broccoli	**310**	12	34
Uncle Ben's			
Noodle Bowls: *Per Bowl, 12 oz (340g)*			
Honey Ginger Chicken	**430**	5	69
Spicy Thai Style Chicken	**400**	8	60
Rice Bowls: *Per Bowl, 12 oz (340g)*			
Barbeque Seasoned Beef	**430**	4.5	85
Chicken & Vegetable	**360**	5	56
Honey Dijon Chicken	**400**	3.5	73
Spicy Beef & Broccoli	**370**	4.5	62
Spicy Peanut Chicken	**420**	8.5	58
Sweet & Sour Chicken	**360**	3	65
Szechuan Chicken	**360**	4	58
Teriyaki Chicken	**380**	3.5	66
Teriyaki Stir Fry Vegetable	**360**	3	74
Wolf			
Chili w. Beans: 227g Can	**300**	16	27
15 oz Can, 1 cup, 254g	**330**	18	30
Chili No Beans: 227g Can	**390**	27	18
15 oz Can, 1 cup, 248g	**420**	30	20
Chunky Beef w. Beans:			
15 oz Can, 1 cup, 254g	**300**	15	28
No Beans, 1 cup, 246g	**330**	22	18

Soybean Products

	C	F	Cb
Cheeses (Soy): See Page 38			
Miso, 1/2 cup, 5 oz	**280**	8	39
Cold Mountain: Red, 1 T., 0.5 oz	**25**	1	3
Mellow White, 1 Tbsp, 0.5 oz	**35**	0.5	6
Natto, 1/2 cup, 3 oz	**190**	10	13
Tempeh, 1 piece, 3 oz	**170**	6	14
Fried, 3 oz	**250**	14	14
SoyBoy, White Wave ~ See Page 70			
Soybean Protein (TVP), 1 oz	**90**	0	7
Soy Drinks ~ See Page 24			

Tofu

Azumaya Tofu:			
Soft (Silken), 3 oz	**45**	2	4
Firm, 3 oz	**60**	2.5	3
Extra Firm, 3 oz	**75**	3.5	10
Age (Tofu Puff), 1/2 oz	**40**	1.5	2
Nama-Age (Fried Tofu), 3 oz	**130**	5	8
Calco: Tasty Tofu, 3 oz	**50**	3	2
Hinoichu Tofu:			
Soft, 3 oz, 1" slice	**45**	2.5	5
Reg. (Japanese), 3 oz, 1" slice	**60**	3	6
Firm (Chinese), 3 oz, 1" slice	**60**	3	6
Extra Firm, 3 oz	**90**	5	10
Mori-Nu Tofu (Silken):			
Soft, 4 oz	**60**	3	3
Firm, 4 oz	**70**	3	3
Extra Firm, 4 oz	**70**	2	3
Nasoya Tofu:			
Soft, 3 oz	**60**	3	2
Silken, 3 oz	**50**	2	2
Firm, 3 oz	**80**	4	2
Extra Firm, 3 oz	**90**	5	1
Chinese 5 Spice Tofu, 3 oz	**80**	4	2
Pulmuone Tofu:			
Soft, 3 oz	**45**	2	5.5
Silken, 3 oz	**45**	2	5.5
Firm, 3 oz	**55**	2.5	6
SoyBoy:			
Firm Organic, 3 oz	**100**	5	2
X-Firm Organic, 3 oz	**120**	6	2
X-Firm LowFu, 3 oz	**90**	2	6
TofuLin, 2 oz	**100**	5	4
Baked, Seasoned, Smoked, 2 oz	**100**	5	3
Carribean Tofu, 2 oz	**100**	5	3
Tofu Stir Fried, 4 oz	**120**	8	3

Amy's (*Frozen*): *Per Serving*	C	F	Cb
Pot Pies:			
Broccoli, 7 1/2 oz	430	22	46
Country Vege, 7 1/2 oz	370	16	47
Mexican Tamale, 8oz	220	3	41
Non-Dairy Vegetable, 7 1/2 oz	320	9	50
Shepherd's Pie, 8 oz	160	4	27
Vegetable, 7 1/2 oz	420	19	54
Entrees:			
Cheese Enchilada, 4.75 oz	210	12	13
Blk Bean Vege. Enchilada, 4.75 oz	130	4	20
Cheese Lasagna, 10.25 oz	310	11	37
Macaroni & Cheese, 9 oz	410	16	47
Macaroni & Soy Cheeze, 9 oz	360	14	42
Pasta Primavera, 9 1/2 oz	320	12	39
Ravioli w. Sauce, 8 oz	340	12	44
Vege./Tofu Lasagne w. Chse, 9 1/2 oz	300	10	41
Burritos:			
Bean & Rice, 6 oz	270	6	48
Bean & Cheese, 6 oz	280	8	43
Black Bean Vegetable, 6 oz	320	8	54
Breakfast, 6 oz	210	6	38
Asian Meals:			
Asian Noodle Stir Fry	240	4.5	41
Thai Stir Fry, 9.5 oz	270	11	36
Skillet Meals: *Per 1 Cup*			
Country Cheddar	250	11	27
Pasta & Vegetables Alfredo	220	8	27
Teriyaki Stir Fry	320	2.5	64
Whole Meals: Cannelloni, 9 oz	330	12	34
Black Bean Enchilada, 10 oz	250	8	41
Country Dinner, 11 oz	380	12	60
Cheese Enchilada, 9 oz	330	14	38
Chili & Cornbread, 10.5 oz	320	6	59
Veggie Loaf, 10 oz	260	5	47
Pocket Sandwich:			
Broccoli & Cheese	270	10	37
Cheese Pizza, 4 1/2 oz	290	9	38
Mediterranean Vegetable, 4 1/2 oz	220	7	33
Roasted Vegetable, 4 1/2 oz	220	8	35
Spinach Feta, 4 1/2 oz	200	7	27
Tamale,4 1/2 oz	250	7	39
Vegetable Pie, 5 oz	230	6	37
Veggie Pizza, 4 1/2 oz	240	6	35
Pizza: Cheese; Spinach	320	11	40
Peasto w. Tomato & Broccoli	300	11	39
Roasted Vegetable, 4 oz	270	8	43
Soy Cheese, 4.3 oz	280	11	37

Boca Burger	C	F	Cb
Breakfast Patties, 1	70	3	4
Chef Max's Favorite, 2.5 oz patty	110	2	10
Hint of Garlic, 2.5 oz patty	100	1	9
Vegan Original, 1 patty	80	0	8
Celentano (Frozen)			
Eggplant: Rollettes, 10 oz Tray	220	12	19
Parmagiana, 1/2 Tray, 7oz	320	21	22
Lasagna Primavera, 10 oz Tray	230	4	37
Spinach & Broccoli: Manicotti	230	4	36
Stuffed Shells, 10 oz Tray	210	4	31
Dr McDougall's/Eden			
See Page 64			
Gardenburger: *(Wholesome & Healthy Foods Inc.)*			
Gardenburger: *Per 2 1/2 oz Patty*			
Classic Greek	120	3	17
Fat Free	100	0	7
Five Roasted Vegetable	110	2.5	16
Original	130	3	18
Santa Fe	130	2.5	20
Savory Mushroom	120	3	18
Sautéed Onion	100	0	8
Tayburn Smoked Cheddar	140	3	23
Veggie Medley, 2 1/2 oz	100	0	17
Zesty Bean, 2 1/2 oz	120	2.5	19
GardenDog: 2 oz	120	2.5	4
GardenSausage: 2 1/2 oz patty	130	3	18
Lifeburger: 3 oz patty	100	0	9
Harvest Burger *(Green Giant)*			
Original, each	140	4	8
Southwestern, each	140	4	9
Health Valley			
Fat-Free Beans & Chili:			
Chili Burrito/Enchilada, 1/2 cup	80	0	15
Chili in a Cup, all types, 3/4 cup	120	1	21
Chili, Fajito flavored, 1/2 cup	80	0	15
Honey Baked Beans, 1/2 cup	110	0	25
Mild/Spicy Vegetarian Chili: all flavors, 1/2 cup	80	0	15
Ken & Robert's			
Veggie Burger, 2.5 oz	130	1	26
Veggie Pockets, average, 4.5 oz	250	8	39

Litelife (Frozen)	C	F	Cb
Smart Deli Slices, 3 slices, 1 1/2 oz	50	0	2
Smart Dogs, 1 link, 1 1/2 oz	45	0	1
Tofu Pups, 1 link, 1 1/2 oz	60	2.5	2
Wonderdogs, 1 1/2 oz	55	1	1
Loma Linda			
Frozen: Corn Dogs, 1 corn dog	150	4	22
Chik Nuggets, 5 pieces, 3 oz	240	16	13
Canned & Dry Prod.: Linketts, (1)	70	4.5	1
Big Franks, 1 link	110	7	2
Lowfat, 1 link	80	3	3
Chicken Supreme Mix, 1/3 cup mix	90	1	6
Dinner Cuts, 2 slices, 3 1/4 oz	90	1.5	3
Fried Chik'n/Gravy, 2 pcs, 3 oz	160	10	4
Gravy Quik: Aver.,1 Tbsp mix	20	0	4
Little Links, 2 links	90	6	2
Nuteena, 3/8" slice, 2 oz	160	13	6
Ocean Platter, 1/3 cup dry mix	90	1	8
Patty Mix, 1/3 cup dry mix, 1 oz	90	1	7
RediBurger, 5/8" slice, 3 oz	120	2.5	7
Sandwich Spread, 1/4 cup, 2 oz	80	4.5	7
Savory Dinner Loaf, 1/3 cup, drain.	90	1.5	7
Soyagen, all varieties. 1/4 c. drain.	130	6	12
Swiss Stake, 1 piece, 3 1/4 oz	120	6	8
Tender Bits, 6 pieces, 3 oz	110	4.5	7
Tender Rounds, 6 pieces, 2 3/4 oz	120	5	5
Vege Burger, 1/4 cup, 2 oz	70	1.5	2
Vita Burger Chunks, 1/4 cup	70	1	6
Vita Burger Granules, 3 Tbsp	70	1	6
Morningstar Farms			
America's Orig. Veggie Dog, each	80	0.5	6
Better'n Burger, 1 pattie	80	0	8
Better'n Eggs, 1/4 cup, 2 oz	20	0	0
Breakfast Links, 2 links	60	2	2
Breakfast Patties, 1 pattie	80	3	3
Breakfast Strips, 2 strips	60	4.5	2
Buffalo Wings, 5 nuggets, 3 oz	200	9	16
Burger-Style Recipe Crumbles, 2/3 c.	80	2.5	4
Chik Nuggets, 4 pieces	160	4	17
Chik Patties, 1 pattie	150	6	15
Corn Dog, 1 link	150	4	22
Mini, 4 pieces, 2.7 oz	170	4.5	21
Garden Grille, 1 pattie, 3 oz	120	2.5	16
Garden Vege patties, 1 pattie	100	2.5	9
Grillers, 1 pattie, 2 1/4 oz	140	6	5
Ground Meatless, 1/2 cup, 2 oz	60	0	4
Hard Rock Café Veggie Burger, 1	170	6	18

Morningstar Farms (Cont)	C	F	Cb
Harvest Burgers, all types, 1, 3.2 oz	140	4.5	8
Prime Patties, 1 pattie, 2 3/4 oz	140	2	6
Recipe Crumbles, 1/2 cup, 2 oz	70	0	5
Saus. Recipe Crumbles, 2/3 c., 2 oz	90	3	5
Scramblers, 1/4 cup, 2 oz	35	0	2
Spicy Bl. Bean Burger, 1 pattie	110	1	16
Breakfast Scramblers: *Per Sandwich*			
Bagel/Scramblers/Pattie/Cheese	320	4.5	40
Engl.Muf./Scramblers/Pattie/Chse	280	3	35
English Muffin/Scramblers/Pattie	240	2.5	32
Stuffed Sandwich, all types, aver.	290	8	42
Dry Products			
Garden Vegie Burger Kit, 1/4 pkg	80	0	6
Sth.West.Veggie Burger, 1/4 pkg	90	0	9
Midland Harvest			
Fat Free & Lowfat Dry Mix:			
Taco Filling & Dip, 2.7 oz	50	0	7
Chili Fixin's, 8 oz	160	1	24
Sloppy Joe Fixin's, 3.6 oz	70	0	11
Burger Loaf Dry Mix: Per 3.2 oz	120	4	8
Frozen Patties: Sausage, 2 oz	80	4	5
Other varieties, 3.2 oz	120	4	8
Natural Touch			
Frozen Products			
Dinner Entree, 1 pattie, 3 oz	220	15	2
Garden Vege pattie, 1 pattie	110	2.5	8
Lentil Rice Loaf, 1" slice, 3 oz	170	9	14
Nine Bean Loaf, 1" slice, 3 oz	160	8	13
Okara Pattie, 1 pattie, 2 1/4 oz	110	5	4
Spicy Bl.Bean Burger, 1 pattie	100	1	15
Vegan Burger, 1 pattie, 2 3/4 oz	70	0	6
Vegan Burger Crumbles, 1/2 cup	60	0	4
Vegan Saus.Crumbles, 1/2 cup	60	0	4
Vege Frank, 1 link	100	6	2
Canned & Dry Products			
Kaffree Roma, 1 rounded tsp, 2g	10	0	2
Roma Cappuccino, 3 Tbsp, 10g	50	3	5
Loaf Mix, 4 Tbsp dry mix, 1 oz	100	0.5	10
Original Veggie Burger, 1/4 pkg	80	0	6
Sthwestern Veggie Burger, 1/4 pkg	90	0	9
Roasted Soy Butter, 2 Tbsp	170	11	10
Stroganoff Mix, 4 Tbsp dry mix	90	3.5	10
Taco Mix, 3 Tbsp dry mix, 0.6 oz	60	1	5
Vegetarian Chili, 1 cup, 8 oz	170	1	21

New Menu (Vitasoy)	C	F	Cb
VegiBurgers, 3 oz	**110**	1	12
VegiDogs, 1 link, 1.5 oz	**45**	0	1
Tofumate (Season. Mixes): 1/4 pkt	**25**	0	4
SoyBoy			
Breakfast Links, 1 link, 1 oz	**65**	2.5	6
5-Grain Tempeh	**135**	6	9
Leaner Weiners, 1 weiner, 1.5 oz	**55**	0	2
Not Dogs, 1 link, 1.5 oz	**95**	3	10
Ravioli Rosa/Verde, 1 cup, 3.5 oz	**180**	3	29
Soysage, 2 oz	**120**	5	12
Soy Tempeh, 3 oz	**150**	6	9
Tofu Ravioli, 1 cup, 3.5 oz	**180**	3	31
White Wave			
Stir Fry: Chick'n & Herbs, 3 oz	**110**	4	7
Italian Style, 4 1/2 oz	**150**	6	14
Mexican Fajita, 3 oz	**180**	3.5	6
Thai Peanut, 4 oz	**230**	6	12
Seitan: Chicken w. Broth, 5 oz	**130**	0	12
Traditional, 4 oz	**140**	0	4
Tempeh: Five Grain, 1/3 pkg	**140**	4	15
Original, 1/3 pkg	**150**	6	10
Sea Veggie, 1/3 pkg	**120**	3	11
Wild/Soy Rice, 1/3 pkg	**140**	5	13
Tofu: Baked: All variet., 2 oz pce	**120**	6	3
Organic: Soft/Firm, 1/5 pkg, 3.2 oz	**90**	6	1
Fat-Reduced, 1/5 pkg, 3.2 oz	**90**	4	4
Extra Firm, 1/4 pkg, 3 oz	**80**	5	1
Worthington			
Frozen Products			
Beef Style Meatless, 3/8" slice	**110**	7	4
Bolono, 3 slices, 2 oz	**80**	3.5	2
Chic-Ketts, 2 slices (3/8"), 2 oz	**120**	7	2
Chick., Sliced or Roll, 2 sl., 2 oz	**80**	4.5	1
ChikStiks, 1 piece, 1 1/2 oz	**110**	7	3
Corned Beef Meatless, 4 sl., 2 oz	**140**	9	5
Crispy Chic Patties, 1 pattie	**170**	9	15
Dinner Roast, 3/4" slice, 3 oz	**180**	12	5
Fillets, 2 pieces, 3 oz	**180**	10	8
FriPats, 1 pattie	**130**	6	4
Golden Croquettes, 4 pieces	**210**	10	14
Leanies, 1 link	**100**	7	2
Prosage Links, 2 links	**60**	2.5	2
Prosage Patties, 1 pattie	**100**	3	3
Prosage Roll, 5/8" slice, 2 oz	**140**	10	2
Salami, Meatless, 3 slices, 2 oz	**130**	8	2
Smkd Beef, Meatless, 6 sl., 2 oz	**120**	6	6

Worthington (Cont)	C	F	Cb
Frozen Products (Cont)			
Smkd Turkey., Meatless, 3 sl, 2 oz	**140**	10	3
Stakelets, 1 piece, 2 1/2 oz	**140**	8	6
Stripples, 2 strips, 1/2 oz	**60**	4.5	2
Tuno, 1/2 cup (drained), 2 oz	**80**	6	2
Veelets, 1 pattie, 2 1/2 oz	**180**	9	10
Veggie Dog, 1 link	**80**	0.5	6
Vegetarian Egg Rolls, 1 roll	**180**	8	20
Wham, 2 slices, 1 1/2 oz	**80**	5	1
Canned & Dry Products			
Chili, 1 cup, 8 oz	**290**	15	21
Low Fat Chili, 1 cup, 8 oz	**170**	1	21
Choplets, 2 slices, 3 1/4 oz	**90**	2	3
Country Stew, 1 cup, 8 1/2 oz	**210**	9	20
Cutlets, 1 slice, 2 1/4 oz	**70**	1	2
Diced Chik, 1/4 cup, 2oz	**40**	0	1
FriChik, 2 pieces, 3 oz	**120**	8	1
Low Fat FriChik, 2 pcs, 3 oz	**80**	3	2
GranBurger, 3 Tbsp, 0.6 oz	**60**	0.5	3
Multigrain Cutlets, 2 sl., 3 1/4 oz	**100**	2	5
Numete, 3/8" slices, 2 oz	**130**	10	5
Prime Stakes, 1 piece, 3 1/4 oz	**120**	7	4
Protose, 3/8" Slice, 2 oz	**130**	7	5
Saucettes, 1 link	**90**	6	1
Savorex, 1 tsp	**10**	0	1
Savory Slices, 3 slices, 3 oz	**150**	9	6
Sliced Chik, 3 slices, 3 oz	**70**	0.5	2
Super Links, 1 link	**110**	8	2
Turkee Slices, 3 slices, 3 1/4 oz	**190**	14	3
Vegetable Skallops, 1/2 c., 3 oz	**90**	1.5	3
Vegetable Steaks, 2 pieces	**80**	1.5	3
Vegetarian Burger, 1/4 c., 2 oz	**60**	2	2
Veja Links, 1 link, 1 oz	**50**	3	1
Low Fat Veja Links, 1 link	**40**	1.5	1
Yves			
Canadian Veggie Bacon, 3 sl., 2 oz	**80**	0	2
Garden Vegetable Patties, 1, 3 oz	**70**	0	12
Jumbo Veggie Dogs, 2.6 oz each	**90**	0	5
Tofu Weiners, 1.3 oz each	**45**	0.5	2
Veggie Breakfast Links, 2, 1.8 oz	**65**	0	4
Veggie Ground Round:			
Burger Burgers, 1 patty, 3 oz	**70**	0	7
Deli Slices, 3.5 slices, 1.8 oz	**60**	0	2
Original & Italian, 1/3 cup	**60**	0	3
Pepperoni, 3.5 slices, 1.8 oz	**70**	0	4
Veggie Pizza Pep'roni, 16 sl., 1.7 oz	**70**	0	5
Veggie Weiners/Chili Dogs, 1.6 oz	**55**	0	3

Homemade & Restaurant

Restaurant & Take-Out *Per 8 fl.oz*	C	F	Cb
Bean Medley	200	3	34
Beef Consomme	30	0	2
Borscht (w. Cream)	130	8	14
Bouillabaisse	400	15	10
Chicken & Corn	290	14	20
Chicken & Wild Rice	80	4	9
Chicken Consomme	50	0	2
Chicken Curry	180	8	18
Chicken Jambalaya	160	7	8
Chicken Noodle	80	2	12
w. Chicken	160	4	12
Chicken Soup	80	2	6
Chili with Beans	250	12	25
Clam Chowder	240	15	17
Corn & Crab	120	3	18
Corn Chowder	150	8	16
Cream of Broccoli	200	12	20
Cream of Potato	220	12	25
Cream of Mushroom	290	21	20
Creamy Pumpkin	210	10	26
Fish Chowder	220	15	6
French Onion	420	15	25
Gazpacho	60	0	13
Lentil Soup	250	9	28
Lobster Bisque	320	15	10
Matzo Ball (w.1 large ball)	180	7	24
Minestrone	140	2	14
Mulligatawny	300	15	8
Pea & Ham	240	10	25
Potato & Bacon	170	7	19
Shark Fin Soup	220	6	4
Split Pea Soup	150	6	18
Vegetable (Fat Free)	75	0	18
Vegetable Beef	80	2	10
Vichyssoise	200	9	15
Watercress	90	4	13

• Ethnic & Restaurant Section: Pages 155-159
• Fast Foods/Restaurant Section: Pages 161-247
(*Arby's, Au Bon Pain, Boston Market, Dunkin' Donuts, Denny's, Schlotzsky's, Sizzler, Souplantation, Sweet Tomatoes*)

Homemade Soups:
Calculate calories, fat and carbohydrates from ingredients.

Bouillon Cubes & Powders

	C	F	Cb
Bouillon Cubes: Aver. all types			
Regular, 1 cube	8	0	1
Low Sodium (LiteLine)	12	0	1
Powders: Average, 1 tsp	8	0	1
Herb-Ox: Instant Broth & Seasoning,			
Beef, 1 envelope	10	0	2
Chicken, vegetarian	10	0	2
Herbs, Spices: 1 tsp	5	0	1
Soup Oyster Crackers 40 small/20 large, 1/2 oz	60	2	8

Amy's

Per 1 Cup (1/2 Can)	C	F	Cb
Black Bean Vegetable	110	1	22
Cream of Mushroom, 3/4 cup	120	9	10
Cream of Tomato, 1 cup	100	2	17
Lentil	130	4	19
Minestrone	90	1.5	17
No Chicken Noodle	90	3	12
Split Pea	100	0	19

Barnum & Bagel

Frozen Soup: *Per 1 Cup Serving*	C	F	Cb
Chicken Noodle	100	1.5	17
Chicken Matzo Ball	100	5	11
Minestrone	140	2	24
Mushroom Barley; Vegetable	130	1	26
Sweet & Sour Cabbage	160	1	36

Bean Cuisine

Made as Directed: Per 1 Cup Serving	C	F	Cb
Florentine/Country Bean; Barcelona	210	1.5	29
Basque Beans; Italian Market Bean	195	1.5	30
13 Bean Bouillabaisse	240	0	18

Betty Crocker

Bowl Appetit!: *Per 2.7 oz Serving*	C	F	Cb
Cheddar Broccoli Rice	300	8	52
Herb Chicken Veg. Rice	260	4	50
Macaroni & Cheese	370	12	54
Pasta Alfredo	360	11	51
Southwestern Rice	260	3	52
3-Cheese Rotini	370	12	52
Tomato Parmesan Penne	350	8	57

Campbell's

Red & White Label	C	F	Cb
Per 1 Cup Prepared (from 1/2 Cup Condensed)			
Bean & Bacon	**180**	5	25
Beef Broth	**15**	0	1
Beef w. Vegetable & Barley	**80**	2	11
Broccoli Cheese	**110**	7	9
Californian Veg.; Chicken Gumbo	**60**	1	10
Cheddar Cheese	**130**	8	11
Chicken Broth	**30**	2	1
Chicken Noodle/w. Stars	**70**	2	9
Chicken Vegetable	**80**	2	12
Clam Chowder Manhattan	**60**	0.5	12
Clam Chowder New England	**100**	2.5	15
Cream of Asparagus; Celery	**110**	7	9
Cream of Broccoli; Shrimp	**100**	6	9
Cream of Chicken & Broccoli	**120**	8	11
Cream of Chicken Dijon	**130**	8	12
Cream of Mushroom	**110**	7	9
Double Noodle in Chicken Broth	**100**	2.5	15
French Onion	**70**	2.5	10
Golden Mushroom	**80**	3	10
Minestrone	**100**	2	16
Split Pea w. Ham; Green Pea	**180**	3.5	28
Tomato	**80**	0	18
Tomato Bisque	**130**	3	24
Tomato Noodle	**120**	1	25
Tomato Rice (Old Fashioned)	**120**	2	23
Vegetable	**90**	1	16
Vegetable & Beef; Turkey Noodle	**80**	2	10
Won Ton	**45**	1	5
Healthy Request (Blue Label): *Per 10 3/4 oz Can*			
Average all varieties	**80**	2	10
16 oz Can: *Per 1/2 Can Serving*			
Hearty Chicken & Rice	**110**	2.5	16
Hearty Chicken Noodle	**100**	3	14
New England Clam Chowder	**120**	3	17
Split Pea & Ham	**170**	1.5	29
Simply Home: *Per 1 Cup Serving*			
Chicken & Pasta; Chicken Noodle	**90**	1	14
Chicken w. Rice	**100**	1	19
Country Vegetable	**110**	0.5	23
Minestrone	**140**	1	27
Soup To Go: *Per 10 3/4 oz Ctn*			
Chicken Rice	**140**	1.5	25
Garden Vegetable	**130**	1	25
Hearty Chicken Noodle	**100**	1.5	16
Vege. Beef w. Pasta	**130**	1.5	22

Campbell's (Cont)

Chunky (Red Can):	C	F	Cb
19 oz Can: *Per 1/2 Can Serving*			
Baked Potato w. Cheddar, Bacon	**180**	8	23
Baked Potato w. Steak, Cheese	**200**	9	21
Beef w. White & Wild Rice	**140**	1.5	23
Cheese Tortellini	**110**	2	18
Chicken Broccoli Cheese	**200**	12	14
Chicken Chowder Mushroom	**210**	12	18
Chicken Corn Chowder	**250**	15	18
Classic Chicken Noodle	**130**	3	16
Grilled Chicken Veg. & Pasta	**110**	2	17
Grilled Sirloin Steak & Vegies	**120**	2	20
Hearty Chicken & Vegetable	**90**	2	12
New England Clam Chowder	**300**	18	26
Potato Ham Chowder	**220**	14	16
Savory Chicken & Rice	**140**	3	18
Sirloin Burger	**180**	7	20
Tomato Chse Ravioli & Veges	**150**	3	26
Vegetable	**160**	4	15
Vegetable Beef	**150**	5	17
10 1/2 oz Can: Mega Noodle, 1 c.	**120**	3	20
Fun Shapes,1 cup	**120**	3	20
Select: *Per 1 Cup (approx. 1/2 Can)*			
Chicken & Pasta w. Garlic	**110**	2	17
Chicken Rice/Vegetables	**100**	1.5	18
Creamy Potato w. Garlic	**180**	9	21
Fiesta Vegetable	**120**	0.5	24
Grilled Chicken w. Tomato & Veg.	**100**	1.5	17
Minestrone	**120**	2.5	21
New England Clam Chowder	**190**	13	14
Fat Free	**110**	3	17
Tomato Garden	**100**	0.5	22
Vegetable	**110**	1	20
Soup & Recipe Mixes (Dry): *Per 1 Tbsp*			
Chicken Noodle/w. Broth	**30**	0.5	5
Onion	**20**	0	5

College Inn

Beef/No Fat Broth, 1 cup	**20**	0	0
Chicken Broth/Lower Sodium, 1 c.	**25**	1.5	1

Cup-A-Ramen

Beef; Cajun Chicken, 1 cup	**310**	16	36
Chicken ; Shrimp, 1 cup	**320**	17	36

Dominick's

	C	F	Cb
Canned:			
Tomato, condensed, 1/2 cup	80	0.5	18
Chicken Broth: Regular, 1 cup	15	0.5	0
Reduced Salt, 1 cup	15	0	0

Dr McDougall's

	C	F	Cb
Cup Mix:			
Minestrone & Pasta, 1 cup	180	1	31
Ramen Noodles, 1 container, 43g	150	0.5	29
Split Pea w. Barley, 1 cup	200	2	36
Tamale Pie w. Baked Chips, 1 cup	200	1.5	39
Tortilla Soup w. Baked Chips, 1 c.	190	1.5	37

Fantastic Cup Soups

	C	F	Cb
Per 1 Cup			
Country Lentil	230	1	41
Creamy Soups: Average	150	2.5	27
5 Bean	230	1	43
Jumpin' Black Bean	210	1	39
Minestrone	150	1	29
Split Pea	190	1	35
Vegetable Barley	150	0.5	29

Goodman's

	C	F	Cb
Soup Mixes (Prep.): *Per 1 Cup*			
Alphabet Vegetable	45	0	9
Noodle Soup: Regular	45	0.5	9
Salt Free	50	0.5	9
w. Vegetables	45	0	9
Onion Soup	30	1	5

Hain

	C	F	Cb
Canned: Per 1 Cup			
Homestyle Naturals:			
Chicken Broth	25	2	3
Chicken Noodle	150	3	24
Chunky Tomato	80	0.5	18
Minestrone	110	2	20
Healthy Naturals:			
Black Bean	90	0	18
Mushroom Barley	130	1.5	26
Vegetable Broth	30	0	8
Vegetarian Lentil	120	1	20
Vegetarian Split Pea	170	1	30
Wild Rice	80	1.5	15

Healthy Choice

	C	F	Cb
Baked Potato, 1 cup	140	2	25
Bean and Ham, 1 cup	160	1.5	29
Chicken Corn Chowder, 1 cup	160	2.5	26
Chicken with Rice, 1 cup	100	2	13
Chili Beef, 1 cup	170	1.5	29
Country Vegetable, 1 cup	100	0.5	22
Garden Vegetable, 1 cup	120	1	24
Lentil, 1 cup	150	1	29
New England Clam Chowder, 1 c.	120	1	22
Old Fashioned Chick. Noodle, 1 c.	150	2.5	23
Split Pea & Ham, 1 cup	160	0.5	25
Turkey w. White & Wild Rice, 1 c.	90	2	14
Zesty Gumbo, 1 cup	90	1.5	15

Health Valley

	C	F	Cb
Bean Vegetable, 1 cup	140	0	32
Beef Broth, 1 cup	20	0	0
Chicken Broth, 1 cup	45	1.5	0
Garden/Tomato Vegetable, 1 cup	80	0	17
Real Minestrone; Italian Plus, 1 c.	80	0	20
Split Pea & Carrots, 1 cup	110	0	17
Country Corn & Vegetable, 1 cup	70	0	17
Carotene varieties, average, 1 cup	70	0	17
Lentil & Carrots, 1 cup	90	0	25
Pasta Soups: Pasta Fagioli, 1 cup	120	0	25
Other varieties, 1 cup	110	0	23
Organic: Black Bean; Split Pea	110	0	25
Mushroom Barley; Potato Leek	60	0	15
Lentil; Tomato; Minestrone, 1 c.	90	0	20
Vegetable, 1 cup	80	0	18
Dry Soups: 1/3 cup, average	120	0	24

"He misses the way you used to bend over and pat him."

Hormel

	C	F	Cb
Microwave Cup Hearty Soup: *1 cup, 7 1/2 oz*			
Chicken w. Vegetable & Rice	110	2	17
Beef Vegetable	90	1	15
Beef & Ham	190	4	29
Chicken Noodle	110	2.5	13
Chicken w. Vegetable & Rice	110	2	17
Beef Vegetable	90	1	15
Beef & Ham	190	4	29
Chicken Noodle	110	2.5	13

Hy-Top Soups

Condensed (10 1/2 oz Can): *Per 1/2 Cup*			
Chicken w. Rice	70	1.5	11
Chicken Noodle	60	2	8
Cream of Chicken	100	5	10
Cream of Mushroom	110	7	10
Tomato	70	0	16
Vegetable	80	2	12

Knorr's Soup

Taste Breaks: *Per 1.6 oz Cup*			
Black Bean	190	1	36
Chicken Noodle/Vegetable	120	2	21
Corn Chowder	140	3	26
Hearty Lentil	200	1	38
Navy Bean	130	0.5	25
Potato Leek	130	2.5	22
Split Pea	150	0.5	29
Vegetarian Vegetable	160	1	32
Noodle Cups: *Per 2.1 oz Cup*			
Fettuccine Alfredo	230	4	41
Fettuccine w. Creamy Basil Sce	220	4	40
3-Cheese Macaroni	230	3.5	41

Lipton

Cup-a-Soup: *Per Envelope*			
Broccoli & Cheese	70	3	9
Cream of Chicken	70	2	12
Creamy Chicken Vegetable	80	4.5	10
Chicken Noodle	50	1	8
Recipe Secrets Mixes: *.Per Serving*			
Golden Onion	50	1	9
Onion Mushroom	30	0.5	5
Savory Herb w. Garlic; Vegetable	30	0	7
Noodle	60	2	9

Manischewitz

	C	F	Cb
Condensed:			
Per 1/3 Cup (Unprepared)			
Chicken	15	0.5	2
w. 3 Matzo Balls	80	4	9
Four Bean	70	1	13
Lentil	140	2	24
Minestrone	90	1.5	16
Per 8 fl.oz Serving (Prepared)			
Borscht w. Beets	90	0	21
Borscht Low Calorie	25	0	6
Instant Cup (Mrs Manischewitz): *Per Cup*			
Black Bean	200	1	37
Chicken Noodle	140	2	26
Chicken Rice	130	1	28
Hearty Lentil	140	1	26
Minestrone	210	1.5	39
Potato Leek	100	1	39

Near East

Per Serving			
Black Bean; Split Pea	195	1.5	34
Chicken; Sweet Corn	120	2.5	20
Chili & Corn	160	3	25
Country Mushroom	140	2.5	26
Italian Tomato	140	4	21
Lentil; Mediterranean Pasta	180	2	34
Minestrone; Parmesan Pasta	160	3	32
Potato Leek; Tomato & Rice	130	3	21
Primavera Pasta	190	2.5	36
Red Beans & Rice	190	2.5	36

Nile Spice

Per Cup			
Chicken Flavored Vegetable	110	1.5	21
Lentil	180	1.5	31
Minestrone	140	1	30
Potato Leek	110	3	19
Red Beans & Rice	170	1	36
Split Pea	200	1	35
Tomato & Rice	140	2.5	27

Pacific Foods

Ready To Eat: *Per Cup (8 fl.oz)*			
All Natural Chicken Broth	15	0	2
Organic Vegetable Broth	0	0	0

Progresso

Progresso	C	F	Cb
Per 1 Cup Serving			
Basil Rotini Tomato	120	1.5	22
Bean & Ham	160	2	25
Beef Barley	130	4	13
Beef Minestrone/Noodle	140	3	16
Cheese & Herb Tortellini Tomato	140	3	23
Chickarina	130	5	12
Chicken & Wild Rice	100	1.5	15
Chicken Barley	110	1.5	16
Chicken Broth	20	1.5	1
Chicken Minestrone	110	1.5	15
Chicken Noodle	90	2	9
Chicken Rice w. Vegetable	90	2	13
Chicken Vegetable	90	1.5	13
Creamy Cheddar Chicken	210	9	25
Creamy Tomato & Garlic	150	6	23
Escarole in Chicken Broth	25	1	3
French Onion	50	1.5	9
Green Split Pea	170	3	25
Hearty Black Bean	170	1.5	30
Hearty Chicken & Rotini	90	1.5	12
Hearty Penne in Chicken Broth	80	1	14
Herb & Rotini Vegetable	100	1	19
Home Style Chicken w. Veges	90	1.5	11
Italian Herb Shells Minestrone	120	1.5	22
Lentil	140	2	22
Macaroni & Bean	160	4	23
Manhattan Clam Chowder	110	2	11
Minestrone	120	2	21
Minestrone Parmesan	100	2.5	16
New England Clam Chowder	190	10	21
Oregano Penne Italian Style Vege.	90	2	15
Peppercorn Penne Vegetable	110	2	19
Potato Broccoli	165	6.5	21
Potato w. Ham & Cheese	170	7	21
Roasted Chicken Garden Herb	70	1.5	9
Roasted Chicken Italiano	80	1.5	10
Roasted Chicken Rotini	80	1.5	11
Roasted Garlic Pasta Lentil	120	1.5	20
Roasted Potato & Garlic	180	9	23
Southwestern Style Corn Chowder	200	7	29
Spicy Chicken & Penne	110	1.5	14
Split Pea w. Ham	150	4	20
Steak & Baked Potato	130	2.5	18
Steak & Mushrooms/Vegetables	100	2	12
Tomato; Tomato Basil	100	2	19
Tomato Vegetable Italiano	90	2	15

Progresso (Cont)

Progresso (Cont)	C	F	Cb
Tortellini in Chicken Broth	70	2	10
Turkey Noodle	90	1.5	11
Turkey Rice w. Vegetable	110	1	18
Vegetable	90	1	17
Vegetarian Vegetable	100	0.5	20
Zesty Herb Tomato	130	3.5	21
99% Fat Free: *Per 1 Cup Serving*			
Beef Barley	130	2	20
Beef Vegetable	160	2	24
Chicken Noodle	90	1.5	13
Chicken Rice w. Veges	110	2	16
Creamy Chicken Broccoli	90	2	13
Lentil; Minestrone	130	1.5	20
New England Clam Chowder	110	1.5	18
Roast Chicken, all types	90	1.5	12
Split Pea	170	1.5	29
Tomato Garden Vegetable	100	1.5	19
Vegetable	70	1	13
White Cheddar Potato	100	1.5	20

Pritikin

Per Cup			
Black Bean w. Rice	200	1	37
Chicken Flavored Vegetable	160	1	27
Minestrone	130	0.5	25
Potato Broccoli	110	0	22

Ralph's

Chicken Broth, 1 cup	30	1	3
Fat Free/Reduced Salt, 1 cup	20	0	2

Ramen Noodles

See Page 66

Rokeach

15 oz Can (Ready to Serve): *Per Serving*			
Barley & Mushroom	110	1	23
Chicken Consomme	50	4	0
Cream of Mushroom	120	7	13
Minestrone	170	1	32
Potato	100	1	20
Seven Bean	130	1	24
Split Pea & Egg Barley	190	1.5	35
Vegetable	110	1.5	22

Shari's

	C	F	Cb
Cream of Tomato, 1 cup	80	0	17
Great Plains Split Pea, 1 cup	150	0	26
Indian Black Bean & Rice, 1 cup	150	1	30
Italian White Bean, 1 cup	170	1	32
Spicy French Green Lentil, 1 cup	130	0	22
Spicy Mexican Bean, 1 cup	210	1	38
Tomato w. Red Bell Pepper, 1 cup	100	0	19
Vegetarian French Onion, 1 cup	60	0	9

Shelton's

Canned: Per Cup

Black Bean & Chicken	170	4	22
Turkey Meatball; Chicken Noodle	90	3	11
Chicken Tortilla	110	1.5	16
Chicken Broth	35	2.5	0

Streit's

Instant Soups: Per Serving

Chicken Flavor; Mushr. & Barley	70	0.5	11
Garden Vegetable	70	0.5	13
Mild Chili; Split Pea	60	0	14
Tomato Minestrone; Veg. Chicken	80	0.5	18

Swanson

Canned: Per Cup

Beef Broth	20	1	1
Chicken Broth	30	2	1
100% Fat Free	15	0	1
Vegetable Broth	20	1	3

Tabatchnick

Frozen: Per Serving (1 bag, 7½ oz)

Barley Mushroom	70	0	13
Cream of Broccoli/ Spinach	90	4	11
Old Fashioned Potato	70	0	16
Pea	180	2	31
Vegetable	110	1	20
Yankee Bean	160	2	27

Uncle Ben's

Hearty Soup Mix: Per Serving (⅓ pkg)

Black/Red Bean & Rice	150	2	28
Southwest Vegetable	90	1	19
White Bean & Pasta	100	1.5	18

Weight Watchers

	C	F	Cb
Chicken Noodle, 10½ oz	150	2	25
Chicken & Rice, 10½ oz	110	1.5	17
Minestrone, 10½ oz	130	2	23
Vegetable, 10½ oz	130	1	27
Instant Beef/Chicken Broth, 1 pkg	10	0	2

Westbrae

Canned: Per Cup Unless Indicated

Alabama Black Bean Gumbo	80	0	23
Calif. Unchicken Broth, ¾ cup	15	0.5	2
Chattanooga Corn Chowder	110	1	23
French Country Onion, ¾ cup	60	0	12
Great Plains Savory Bean	70	0	20
Irish Isle Potato Leek	110	1	22
Monte Carlo Cr. Mushroom, ¾ c.	70	3	10
Natural Wellington Unbeef	60	0	13
Rocky Mount. Crmy. Unchick., ¾ c.	70	3	10
Santa Fe Vegetable	120	0	23
Savanna Unchicken Rice	60	0.5	11
Spicy Southwest Vegetable	90	0	23
Tuscany Tomato	60	0	9
Versailles Garden Vegetable	70	0	15

Wolfgang Puck

Canned: Per 1 Cup

Chicken & Egg Noodles	150	5	16
Chicken & Vegetables	140	5	17
Chicken w. Pasta & Mushrooms	130	4.5	15
Chicken w. Sweetcorn	200	10	20
Creamy Chicken	210	12	15
Hearty Potato & Cheddar	260	18	16
Hearty Vegetable Beef	140	6	13
New England Clam Chowder	240	13	18
Old World Minestrone	180	7	24
Rst Chicken w. Wild Rice	150	5	18
Spicy 7 Bean w. Italian Sausage	230	11	22
Thick Country Vegetable	170	7	23

Enjoy nutritious soup as part of a meal or as a snack. Soup is an excellent filler for dieters - especially to beat the 4.30pm snack syndrome. Choose low fat varieties.

Herbs & Spices

	C	F	Cb
Per 1 Teaspoon: Average all types	5	0	1
Allspice, ground	5	0	1
Chili Powder	8	0	1
Cinnamon, ground	6	0	2
Curry Powder	6	0	1
Garlic Powder	9	0	2
Nutmeg, ground	12	0	1
Onion Powder	7	0	2
Parsley, dried	4	0	1
Pepper, black/red/white, aver.	6	0	1
Saffron	2	0	0
Tumeric, ground	8	0	1
Seeds: Fenugreek	12	1	2
Mustard, Poppyseed	15	1	1
Other types, average	7	0	1
Parsley Patch, Sesame, 1 tsp	16	1	1
Salt-free blends, average	10	0	2
All-purpose, 1 tsp	6	0	1

Seasonings & Flavorings

	C	F	Cb
Accent Flavor Enhancer, 1 tsp	10	0	0
Angostura Bitters, 1 tsp	12	0	3
Bacon Bits, average, 1 Tbsp	30	1	0
Bacon Chips (*Durkee*), 1 Tbsp	45	1	2
Best O'Butter, 1 tsp	10	<1	2
Braggs Liquid Aminos, 1 tsp	5	0	0
Butter Buds, 1 tsp	8	<1	2
Garlic Bread Sprinkle, 1 tsp	8	<1	1
Garlic Salt, 1 tsp	2	0	0
Italian Seasoning, 1 tsp	4	0	1
Lemon Pepper Season., 1 tsp	7	0	1
Meat Tenderizer, aver., 1 tsp	7	0	1
Molly McButter, 1 tsp	5	1	1
Mrs Dash Blends, 1 tsp	0	0	2
Perc Salt-free Seasoning, 1 tsp	8	0	2
Salad Sprinkles (*Lawry's*), 1 tsp	16	<1	2
Salad Supreme (*McCormick*), 1 tsp	10	<1	2
Salt: Regular, Sea Salt, Lite Salt	0	0	0
Seasoning Mixes, aver., 1/4 pkg	70	1	9
Taco Seasoning, aver., 1/4 pkg	30	<1	4
Old El Paso: Chili Season. Mix, 1 T.	15	0.5	3
Cheesy Taco Season. Mix, 1 Tbsp	15	0.5	3
Taco/Burrito Seasoning Mix, 2 tsp	15	0	4
Enchilada Seasoning Mix, 2 tsp	10	0	2
Fajita Seasoning Mix, 1 tsp	10	0	3
Vegit Seasoning Mix, 1 tsp	5	0	1

Condiments, Sauces

Average of Brands & Homemade

	C	F	Cb
Apple Sauce:			
Sweetened, 1/4 cup, 2 1/4 oz	45	0	11
Unsweetened, 1/4 cup, 2 oz	27	0	12
Eden; Tree of Life, 1/2 cup	50	0	15
Bac O's (*Betty Crocker*), 1 tsp, 1/2 oz	60	3	4
Barbecue: Average, 1 Tbsp	25	0	6
Bearnaise Sce, 1/4 cup, 2 1/2 oz	190	19	5
Braggs Liquid Aminos, 1 tsp	5	0	0
Catsup (Ketchup): Reg., 1 Tbsp	15	0	4
Cheese, h/made, 1/4 cup, 2 1/2 oz	150	10	12
Chili Sauce: *Heinz,* 1 Tbsp	15	0	4
Del Monte, 1 Tbsp	20	0	5
Wolf Hot Dog, 1 Tbsp	15	1	2
Cocktail Sce: 1/4 cup	110	0	15
Cranberry, jellied, 1/4 c., 2 1/2 oz	110	0	27
Escoffier Sauces, 1 Tbsp	20	0	4
Honey Mustard *(French's)*: 1 tsp	5	0	1
Horseradish: 1 tsp	2	0	0
Sauce: *Sauceworks,* 1 tsp	20	2	0
Ketchup: Regular, 1 Tbsp	16	0	4
Heinz Lite, 1 Tbsp	8	0	2
Mayonnaise: See Page 82			
Mushroom Sauce, 1/2 cup, 2 oz	50	2	5
Mustard, average, 1 tsp	0	0	0
Pizza Sauce, cnd., 1/4 cup, 2 oz	25	0	5
Seafood Cocktail Sce, 1/4 cup	60	0	14
Soy Sauce, all types, av., 1 Tbsp	10	0	0
Sour Cream Sce, 1/2 cup	250	15	22
Spaghetti Sce: 1/2 cup, 4 1/2 oz	135	6	19
Steak Sauce: *Heinz/A.1.,* 1 Tbsp	15	0	3
Lea & Perrins, 1 Tbsp	25	0	6
Str'berry Puree Sce: Unsweet., 2 T.	9	0	2
Sweet & Sour Sauce:			
Contadina, 2 Tbsp	40	1	8
Kikkoman Lite Soy, 1 Tbsp	10	0	1
La Choy, 2 Tbsp, 34g	60	0	14
Tabasco Sauce, 1 Tbsp	2	0	0
Taco Sauce, average, 2 Tbsp	10	0	1
Tartar Sauce: *Heinz,* 2 Tbsp, 30g	140	14	4
America's Choice, 2 Tbsp, 27g	160	17	1
Hellman's: Regular, 2 Tbsp, 30g	80	7	3
Lowfat, 2 Tbsp, 30g	40	1.5	7
Teriyaki Sauce: *Kikkoman,* 1 Tbsp	15	0	2
Vinegar: White or wine, 1 fl.oz	4	0	1
White Sauce, 1/2 cup, 5 oz	130	7	12
Worcestershire Sauce, 1 tsp	5	0	1

Pickles • Gravy • Sloppy Joe

Pickles & Relish

Item	C	F	Cb
Average All Brands			
Bread & Butter Pickles, 4 sl.,1 oz	20	0	5
Chutney, 2 Tbsp, 1 1/4 oz	40	0	12
Dill Pickle:			
Slices, 4 slices, 1 oz	3	0	0.5
1 large, (3 3/4" x 1 1/4" diam.), 2 1/4 oz	12	0	3
Extra lrg (4" x 1 3/4" diam.), 5 oz	30	0	6
Halves: Small, 1 oz	3	0	0.5
Large, 2 1/2 oz	8	0	2
Sweet, small, 1/2 oz	22	0	6
Gherkins, sweet, 1 med., 1 oz	15	0	7
Green Chilies, chopped, 2 Tbsp	5	0	1
Horseradish, 1 Tbsp	10	0	2
Jalapenos, pickled, 2 whole	5	0	1
Jalapeno Relish, 1 Tbsp, 1/2 oz	5	0	1
Mustard, aver. all brands, 1 tsp	5	0	0.5
Peppers: Hot/Mild, 1 oz	8	0	2
Pickled: Beets, 1/2 cup, 4 oz	75	0	19
Onions, 1 medium, 3/4 oz	10	0	2
Cocktail Onion, 1 onion	2	0	0
Red Cabbage, 1/2 cup, 3 oz	60	0	13
Pickles:			
Sweet, 2 Tbsp, 1 oz	35	0	0
Large (3" x 3/4 diam.), 1 1/4 oz	40	0	10
Pickle in a Pouch, 1 large	12	0	3
Relishes: Sandwich Spread, 1 tsp	20	1	5
Cranberry-Orange, 1 Tbsp	30	0	7
Hot Dog (*Heinz*), 1 Tbsp	17	0	28
Sweet Pickle, 1 Tbsp	20	0	5
Sauerkraut, 1/2 cup, 3 1/2 oz	25	0	5
Sweet Cauliflower	35	0	8

Salsa

Item	C	F	Cb
Average all types			
Regular, no oil, 2 Tbsp	15	0	3.5
w. Oil, homemade, 2 Tbsp	40	3	8
Chef's Kitchen, 2 Tbsp	10	0	2
Del Monte, all flavors, 2 Tbsp	10	0	2
Kaukauma, 2 Tbsp	15	0	3

Pasta Sauces: *See Page 79*

Gravy

Item	C	F	Cb
Homemade Gravy:			
Thin, little fat, 2 Tbsp, 1 oz	20	1	3
Thick, 2 Tbsp, 1 1/4 oz	50	2	9
1/4 cup, 2 1/2 oz	100	4	18
Franco-American (Canned)			
Au Jus Gravy, 1/4 cup, 2 oz	10	0	2
Beef/Mushrm; Turkey Gravy, 2 oz	25	1	3
Chicken Gravy, 2 oz	40	4	3
Golden Pork Gravy, 2 oz	45	4	3
Fat Free, Average, 2 oz	25	0	4
Pillsbury (Gravy Mixes)			
Brown; Homestyle, 1/4 cup	15	0	3
Chicken, as prep., 1/4 cup	20	0	4

Sloppy Joe Sauce

Item	C	F	Cb
Per Serving			
Del Monte: 1/4 cup, 67g	50	0	11
Heinz: 1/2 cup, 125g	70	0.5	14
Hunt's Manwich: 1/4 cup, 64g	30	0	6
Libby's: 1/3 cup, 78g	45	0	10

Tomato Products

Item	C	F	Cb
Whole/Chopped/Crushed/Diced			
1 cup, 8 1/2 oz	50	0	10
In Aspic, 1/2 cup	50	0	12
w. Green Chili, 1 cup, 8 1/2 oz	45	<1	11
Stewed, 1/2 cup	40	2.5	9
Wedges in Tom Juice, 1 cup	70	0.5	15
Salsa, average, 1 Tbsp	15	0	3.5
Tomato Ketchup, regular, 1 Tbsp	16	0	4
Tomato Paste, 2 Tbsp	25	0	5
Regular, 6 oz, 3/4 cup	150	0	34
Tomato Puree, 1/2 cup	50	0	10
Tomato Sauce:			
Regular, 1/2 cup	40	0	9
Spanish Style, 1/2 cup	40	0	9
w. Mushrooms, 1/2 cup	40	0	9
w. Onions, 1/2 cup	50	0	11
Tomato Seasoning, 3 tsp	20	0	4
Sundried Tomatoes:			
Natural, 5-6 pces, 0.4 oz	22	0	5
In Oil, drained, 6 pces, 1/2 oz	60	4	5

Sauce Mixes

	C	F	Cb
Knorr (Mix)			
Made As Directed: *Per 1/4 Cup, 2 oz*			
Au Jus	8	0.2	1
Bearnaise	170	17	5
Classic Brown Gravy	25	1	3
Demi-Glace	30	1	4
Hollandaise	170	18	5
Hunter; Lyonnaise	25	0.3	4
Mushroom Sauce	60	3	5
Napoli Sauce	100	3	17
Pepper Sauce	20	1	3
McCormick			
Grillmates:			
Marinade, aver. all flavors, 2 tsp	15	0	2
Sauce Blend Seasoning Mixes:			
Lemon Herb Chicken, 1 Tbsp	30	0	5
Chicken Fried Rice, 1 Tbsp	35	0	6
Stir Fry Chicken, 1 Tbsp	20	0	4
Chicken Teriyaki, 1 1/3 Tbsp	40	1	5

Marinades

	C	F	Cb
KC Masterpiece: *Per 1 Tbsp*			
Garlic & Herb	30	1.5	4
Honey & Teriyaki	35	0.5	7
Original BBQ	40	1.5	7
Lawry's 30 Minute: *Per 1 Tbsp*			
Hawaiian; Dijon & Honey	20	0	3.5
Carribean Jerk; Teriyaki	25	0	6
Mediterranean; Lemon Pepper	10	0	2
Mesquite	5	0	1
Thai Ginger; Herb & Garlic	10	0	2

Pizza & Enchilada Sauce

	C	F	Cb
Per 1/4 Cup			
Pizza Squeeze *(Contadina)*	35	1.5	6
Progresso Pizza Sauce	10	0	2
Ragu: Pizza Sauce	30	1	4
Pizza Quick; average all types	40	1.5	6
Enchilada Sauce *(Old El Paso)*	10	0	2

Brands

	C	F	Cb
Amy's: *Per 1/2 Cup*			
Family Marinara	50	1	8
Garlic Mushroom	120	7	10
Tomato Basil	80	3	11

Brands (Cont)

	C	F	Cb
Barilla: *Per 1/2 Cup*			
Arrabbiata; Siciliana	80	3.5	9
Marinara; Ortolana	80	4	10
Mushr. & Garlic; Pepperonata	70	2	12
Puttanesea	80	2.5	13
Classico: *Per 1/2 Cup*			
Florentine Spinach & Cheese	80	4.5	8
Italian Sausage & Fennel	90	5	7
Mushroom & Olive	50	1	8
Roasted Peppers & Onions/Garlic	60	2	9
Spicy Red Pepper	60	2.5	6
Sun Dried Tomato; 4 Cheese	80	4	8
Tomato & Basil	50	1	9
Contadina: *Per 1/2 Cup*			
Alfredo Sauce	360	32	10
Lite	160	10	10
Garden Vegetable Sauce	40	0	9
Marinara Sauce	80	4	9
Mushroom Alfredo	200	14	12
Mushroom Marinara Sauce	70	2.5	11
Pesto with Basil, Red. Fat	460	26	22
Pesto w. Sundried Tomato	380	30	20
Roasted Garlic Marinara	60	2	10
Del Monte: *Per 1/2 Cup*			
Chunky: Average all varieties	60	1.5	11
D'Italia Pasta: Four Cheese	60	2	8
Other varieties	50	1.5	9
Spaghetti Sauce: Traditional	60	0.5	15
Garlic & Onion	60	1.5	11
w. Mushroom/Meat	70	1.5	14
Dominick's: *Per 1/2 Cup*			
All Natural: Garlic & Onion	80	4	10
Marinara	80	4	10
Mushr. & Olive; Tomato & Basil	80	1	8
Italian Classics: Four Cheese	80	2.5	12
Portabella Mushroom	60	2	9
Puttanesea	70	3	8
Spicy Roasted Garlic	70	2	10
Sun Ripened Tomatoes	80	4	8
Tomato Basil	50	1	8
Estee: Spaghetti Sce, 1/4 cup, 4 oz	60	2	13
Frank Sinatra: *Per 1/4 Cup*			
Alfredo	160	14	4
Pesto	160	14	3

Brands (Cont)

	C	F	Cb
Five Brothers: *Per 1/2 Cup*			
Alfredo w. Mushrooms	**160**	12	6
Creamy Alfredo/Pesto	**200**	18	4
Fresh/Summer Tomato Basil	**60**	1.5	10
Grilled Summer Vegetable	**80**	5	12
Marinara w. Burgundy Wine	**80**	3	12
Mushroom & Garlic	**90**	3	13
Oven Roasted Garlic & Onion	**70**	1.5	10
Imported Romano & Garlic	**90**	4	10
Garden Valley: *Per 1/2 Cup*			
Chunky Vege. Primavera	**35**	0.5	12
Four Cheese	**35**	1	8
Millina's Finest; Roasted Garlic	**50**	0	12
Sundried Tomato; Tom. Mushroom	**50**	0	11
Sweet Tomato Basil	**60**	0	13
Hagerty Foods: *Per 4 oz*			
Asparagus Garlic	**95**	7	9
Caponata	**60**	3.5	8
Healthy Choice: *Per 1/2 Cup*			
Garlic & Herbs	**50**	0	10
Marinara w. Burgundy	**50**	5	11
Roasted Garlic & Romano	**60**	1	11
Sundried Tomato & Herb	**60**	0.5	12
Hy Top: *Per 1/2 Cup, 125g*			
Spaghetti Sauce: All flavors	**90**	4	11
Mama Coco's: *Per 1/2 Cup*			
Basil & Garlic	**70**	4	9
Marinara	**100**	7	8
Mushroom	**110**	8	8
Newman's Own: *Per 1/2 Cup*			
Bombolina	**100**	5	12
Other flavors	**60**	2	9
Prego: *Per 1/2 Cup*			
Extra Chunky: Garden Comb.	**90**	2	16
Garlic Supreme	**120**	3	23
Mushroom & Green Pepper	**120**	4.5	18
Mushroom Supreme	**120**	4.5	21
Zesty Mushroom	**120**	4	20
Tomato, Onion & Garlic	**110**	3.5	19
Regular:			
Diced Onion & Garlic	**110**	3	19
Flavored w. Meat	**140**	6	21
Fresh Mushroom; Traditional	**150**	5	23
Hamburger	**120**	4	17
Italian Sausage & Garlic	**120**	5	16
Mushroom & Garlic	**110**	2	20
Mushroom/Tomato Parmesan	**120**	3.5	19
Pepperoni	**120**	4.5	18
Roast Red Pepper/Herb & Garlic	**110**	3.5	17
Roast Garlic Parmesan	**120**	1.5	23
Three Cheese	**100**	2	18
Progresso: *Per 1/2 Cup, 4 1/4 oz*			
Pasta Sauces: Alfredo (Authentic)	**200**	15	7
Creamy Clam	**110**	6	8
Lobster	**100**	7	6
Marinara (Authentic)	**100**	4	12
Pizza	**40**	0	8
Red Clam	**60**	1	8
White Clam (Authentic)	**150**	10	5
White Clam, regular	**140**	10	5
Ragu: *Per 1/2 Cup*			
Cheese Creations:			
Creamy Tomato Romano	**120**	5	14
Classic Alfredo	**240**	24	6
Four Cheese	**240**	22	4
Light Parmesan Alfredo	**160**	12	4
Mushroom Green Pepper	**110**	3.5	18
Roasted Garlic Parmesan	**240**	22	6
Tom. Garlic Onion; Super Mushr.	**120**	3.5	19
Rinaldi: Meat/Mushroom, 1/2 c.	**90**	4	11
Seeds of Change: *Per 1/2 Cup*			
Average all varieties	**50**	0.5	9
Sutter Home: *Per 1/2 Cup*			
Italian Style Pasta Sauce	**80**	2	12
Sicilian Style; Spicy Mediterranean	**80**	2	12
Marinara Pasta Sauce	**70**	2	11

Brands (Cont)

	C	F	Cb
Taj: *Per 1/2 Cup*			
Bombay Curry Simmer Sauce	90	5	10
Calcutta Masala Simmer Sauce	100	5	13
Kashmir Tandoori Marinade Sce	50	3	5
Seasoning Mixes: *Per 2 tsp*			
Meat Loaf; Sloppy Joe's	30	0	4
Beef Stew	15	0	3
Chili	40	1	6
Chicken/Taco Seasoning	25	0	4
Spaghetti Sauce: Italian Style, 1 T.	25	0	5
Timpone's: *Per 1/2 Cup*			
Spaghetti Sauce: Classic	50	2.5	8
Mom's	70	3.5	8
Tomaso's: *Per 1/2 Cup*			
Basil & Fresh Garlic; Spicy Eggplant	60	3	7
Black Olive Fresh Basil	40	2	5
Extra Garlic	55	2	8
Fresh Mushroom & Artichoke	50	2	7
Sugo Rosa	105	7.5	8
Tree of Life: *Per 1/2 Cup*			
Pasta Sauce Plus: All varieties	45	0	9
Organic: Classic Tomato	40	0	8
Average other varieties	30	0	7

Other Sauces

	C	F	Cb
Bookbinders: *Per 1/2 Cup*			
White Clam Sauce	300	30	4
Bullseye: BBQ, 1 Tbsp	25	0	6
Estee: Barbecue Sauce, 1 Tbsp	18	<1	3
Steak Sauce, 1 Tbsp	14	<1	3
French's Grill & Glaze			
Honey Mustard, 2 Tbsp	90	1	18
Teriyaki, 2 Tbsp	60	0	13
Green Giant			
Sloppy Joe S'wich Sce, 1/4 c., 2.5 oz	50	0	11
Sloppy Joe Sauce & Meat	200	11	11
Heinz			
Per 1 Tbsp: Approx. 1/2 oz			
Barbecue Sauces: All flavors	35	0	9
Chili Sauce	15	0	4
Horseradish Sauce	70	7	13
Mustard: Pourable/Mild	8	<1	5
Spicy Brown	13	1	6

Other Sauces (Cont)

	C	F	Cb
Heinz (Cont)			
Per 1 Tbsp: Approx. 1/2 oz			
Seafood Cocktail Sauce	20	0	10
Steak Sauce 57	15	0	4
Tartar Sauce	70	7	2
Tomato Ketchup	16	0	26
Worcestershire Sauce	8	0	11
Hunt's BBQ: Original, 36g, 2 T.	50	0	13
Hickory & Brown Sugar, 38g, 2 Tbsp	70	0	18
Kraft			
Sauceworks: Cocktail, 2 Tbsp	30	0.3	6
Horseradish, 1 tsp	20	1.5	0
Sweet 'n Sour, 1 Tbsp	30	0	7
Tartar: 1 Tbsp	50	5	2
Lemon & Herb, 1 Tbsp	75	8	0
Barbecue Sauces: Average, 2 T.	50	0.5	9
Other Sauces: Mustard, 1 Tbsp	10	0	0
Horseradish: Reg./Cream Style, 1 T.	10	0	0
Sandwich Spread & Burger, 1 Tbsp	50	4	3
Sweet 'n Sour, 1 Tbsp	40	0.5	9
Nonfat Tartar, 1 Tbsp	12	0	5
Knudsen			
Potato Toppings: Aver., 2 T., 1 oz	50	4.5	2
Las Palmas			
Red Chile Sauce, 1/4 cup, 2 oz	15	0.5	2
Enchilada Sauces: Green Chile	25	1.5	3
Hot/Original, 1/4 cup, 2 oz	15	0.5	3
Salsa: Mexicana. Mild, 2 Tbsp, 1 oz	5	0	1
Mexicana Hot/Medium, 2 Tbsp	10	0	2
Old El Paso			
Salsa: Thick 'n Chunky, 2 T., 1 oz	10	0	2
Homestyle; Green Chili; Verde 2 Tbsp, 1 oz	10	0	2
Taco Sce: All varieties, 2 Tbsp, 1 oz	10	0	2
Enchilada Sces: All types, 1/4 c., 2 oz	20	1	3
Grilling Sauces: All types, 2 Tbsp	60	0	14
Tom. & Gr. Chiles/Jalapenos, 1/4 c., 2 oz	10	0	2
Open Pit: Honey, 2 Tbsp	40	0	10
Hickory; Original BBQ, 2 Tbsp	50	0.5	11
Thick & Tangy, 2 Tbsp	50	0	12
President's Choice: *Per 2 Tbsp*			
Honey Dijon	50	0.5	11
Hot & Spicy	55	0	13
Original BBQ	60	0	12

Quick Guide

Mayonnaise

	C	F	Cb
Regular			
Average All Brands, 1 Tbsp	100	11	0
(*Bestfoods, Kraft*), 1 Tbsp	100	11	0
1/2 cup, 4 oz	800	88	0
Light/Reduced Fat			
Kraft; Best Foods, 1 Tbsp	50	5	1
1/2 cup, 4 oz	400	40	8
Hain, 1 Tbsp	60	6	2
Hellman's; Estee, 1 Tbsp	50	5	1
Smart Balance, 1 Tbsp	50	5	2
Smart Beat, 1 Tbsp	40	4	1
Weight Watchers, 1 Tbsp	25	2	1
Fat Free			
Kraft; Weight Watchers, 1 Tbsp	10	0	3
1/2 cup, 4 oz	80	0	16

Mayonnaise Type Dressing

	C	F	Cb
BAMA Dressing, 1 Tbsp, 0.5 oz	50	4	3
Miracle Whip Salad Dressing:			
Regular, 1 Tbsp, 0.5 oz	70	7	2
Light, 1 Tbsp, 0.5 oz	40	3	3
Free, 1 Tbsp, 0.5 oz	15	0	3
Nayonaise (Nasoya)			
(Tofu Base/Dairy Free/Eggless)			
Regular, 1 Tbsp, 0.5 oz	35	3	1
Fat-Free, 1 Tbsp, 0.5 oz	10	0	2

Enjoy a healthy salad but don't drown it in high-fat salad dressings.

Quick Guide

Salad Dressings

Average All Brands
Per 2 Tbsp (Approx 1 oz)

	C	F	Cb
Blue Cheese: Regular	150	16	2
Light/Reduced Fat	80	8	1
Caesar: Regular	140	14	2
Light/Reduced Fat	50	5	0.5
French: Regular	130	11	5
Light/Reduced Fat	50	3	4
Fat/Oil-Free	40	0	4
Italian: Regular	130	11	3
Light/Reduced Fat	70	7	2
Fat/Oil-Free	10	0	2
Ranch: Regular	180	18	3
Light/Reduced Fat	90	8	3
Fat-Free	50	0	2
Russian: Regular	130	10	3
Light/Reduced Fat	50	5	2
Fat-Free	30	0	2
Thousand Island: Regular	130	12	5
Light/Reduced Fat	50	4	3
Fat-Free	35	0	3

Brands ~ Salad Dressings

Per 2 Tbsp (Approx 1 oz)

	C	F	Cb
Benecol: *Per 2 Tbsp*			
Creamy Italian	100	10	3
French Style	130	11	6
Ranch	130	13	3
Thousand Island	130	12	5
Bernstein's			
Balsamic	110	11	2
Cheese: Garlic Italian; Fantastico	110	11	2
Creamy Caesar	120	13	1
Fat Free Cheese & Garlic Italian	10	0	2
French Herb Garden	130	11	2
Restaurant Recipe Italian	130	13	1
Best Foods			
Caesar, 2 Tbsp	100	9	6
Chardonnay Vinaigrette	50	4	4
Chunky Blue Cheese	140	15	1
Creamy Caesar	170	18	2
Creamy French	160	16	4

Per 2 Tbsp (Approx 1 oz)	C	F	Cb
Best Foods (Cont)			
Creamy/Garlic/Spr. Onion Ranch	140	15	1
Creamy Thousand Island	130	13	4
Fat Free Caesar; Dijonnaise	30	0	7
Fat Free Ranch	45	0	4
Fat Free Italian	15	0	4
Rst. Tomato & Balsamic Vinegar	100	9	3
Citrus Splash:			
Oriental Orange; Ruby Red Ginger	90	7	7
Or. Vinaigrette; Tangy Tangerine	80	7	6
Tangerine Balsamic	80	7	7
Brianna's			
Blush Vintage	100	6	12
Cardini's			
Caesar, 2 Tbsp	160	17	1
Herb Poppy Seed	35	1	7
Zesty Garlic	120	13	2
Summer Honey Mustard	150	14	5
Carolina's Swamp Stuffs' *Per 2 Tbsp*			
Blue Tick Dressing	220	16	6
Cedar Spray	40	3	2
Milk Weed	100	10	2
Pure Tar	60	5	2
Red Tide	30	3	2
Seaweed Splash	30	2	2
Swamp Sauce	20	0	6
Tadpole Tea	30	2	2
Girards: *Per 2 Tbsp*			
Caesar	150	16	1
Lite	80	7	2
Lite Champagne	60	5	2
Oriental	120	11	6
Original French	120	13	0
Spinach Salad	80	2	14
Fat Free: Caesar	40	0	9
Raspberry Vinaigrette	40	0	9
Red Wine Vinaigrette	40	0	2
Good Seasons (Mix): *Prepared, 2 T. (Approx 1 oz)*			
Blue Cheese, Cheese Garlic	145	16	2
Cheese Italian, Garlic & Herbs	145	16	2
Classic Dill, 1 pkg	28	0	5
Italian; Mild Italian; Zesty Italian	145	16	2
Italian Lite; Lite Cheese Italian	55	6	2
Ranch	115	12	2

Per 2 Tbsp (Approx 1 oz)	C	F	Cb
Hain			
Regular Pourable: *Per 2 Tbsp*			
Canola: Garden Tomato	120	12	2
Italian; French Mustard	100	10	2
Creamy Caesar: French	120	12	2
Creamy Italian	160	16	0
Garlic & Sour Cream	140	14	0
Poppyseed Rancher's	120	14	0
Savory Herb (No Salt Added)	180	20	0
Thousand Island	100	10	5
Traditional Italian	160	16	0
(No Salt Added)	120	12	2
Mix: *Made Up Per 2 Tbsp*			
No Oil Range: Bleu Cheese	28	2	2
Buttermilk	22	0	2
Caesar	12	0	2
French	24	0	6
Italian	4	0	2
Healthy Sensation			
Blue Cheese, French, 2 Tbsp	40	2	8
Honey Dijon	50	2	10
Italian	15	0	2
Ranch	30	0	6
Thousand Island	40	0	8
Hidden Valley			
B.L.T. Ranch	150	15	3
B.L.T. Ranch Lite	90	7	5
Fat Free: Caesar	30	0	6
Honey & Bacon French	50	0	11
Honey Dijon	35	0	7
Italian Herb & Cheese; Ranch	30	0	6
Italian Parmesan	20	0	4
Red Wine & Herb Vinaigrette	45	0	11
Roasted Garlic Italian	40	0	5
Honey & Bacon French	150	12	10
Original Ranch/w. Bacon	140	14	1
Light Original Ranch	80	7	3
Ranch Caesar Creamy	110	11	1
Ranch Cole Slaw	150	15	5
Ranch Garden Veg./Garlic & Spice	130	13	3
Hollywood			
Caesar; Creamy French	140	14	4
Italian; Creamy Italian	180	18	3
Italian Cheese	160	16	4
Poppy Seed Rancher's	150	16	2
Thousand Island	120	12	6

Per 2 Tbsp (Approx 1 oz)	C	F	Cb
Knott's Berry Farm			
Honey Dijon, 2 Tbsp	130	13	4
Raspberry Vinaigrette	30	2	8
Roasted Garlic Caesar	140	14	3
Sun Dried Tomato Vinaigrette	100	10	3
Kraft			
Regular Dressings: *Per 2 Tbsp*			
Bacon & Tomato	140	14	2
Buttermilk Ranch	150	16	2
Caesar; Salsa Ranch	130	13	2
Caesar Ranch; Pesto Italian	140	15	1
Catalina French/ with Honey	140	12	8
Chunky Blue Cheese	90	7	5
Coleslaw	150	12	8
Creamy Caesar; Cucumber Ranch	140	15	2
Creamy Garlic; Creamy Italian	110	11	3
French	120	12	4
Honey Dijon	150	15	4
House Italian	120	12	3
Peppercorn Ranch; Ranch	170	18	1
Free	50	0	11
Roka Brand Blue Cheese	90	7	5
Russian	130	10	10
Salsa Zesty Garden	70	6	3
Sour Cream & Onion Ranch	170	18	1
Thousand Island	110	10	5
Thousand Island w. Bacon	120	12	5
Zesty Italian	110	11	2
Kraft Free (Fat Free):			
Blue Cheese, Catalina, French	50	0	12
Honey Dijon, Peppercorn/Ranch	50	0	11
Italian	10	0	2
Red Wine Vinegar	15	0	3
Thousand Island; Sr Cream & Onion	45	0	11
Light Done Right!: Classic Caesar	70	6	3
Italian; Red Wine Vinaigrette	50	4.5	3
Raspberry Vinaigrette	60	4	6
Thousand Island	70	4	17
Special Collection:			
Balsamic Vinaigrette	110	12	1
Creamy Cucumber Dill	120	12	4
Creamy Parmesan Romano	170	18	1
Creamy Roasted Garlic	160	17	2
Greek Vinaigrette	120	13	2
Savory Mayo:			
Roast Garlic/Onion	100	10	1
Tangy Tomato Bacon	130	11	8

Per 2 Tbsp (Approx 1 oz)	C	F	Cb
Kraft (Cont)			
Taste of Life: Garden Italian	50	4.5	3
Country Ranch; Tomato & Garlic	60	4.5	4
Honey Catalina	80	5	8
Vinaigrette: Caesar Parmesan	60	5	1
Roast Garlic	50	4.5	3
LadyLee (Lucky Stores)			
Fat Free French	120	11	7
Fat Free Italian	10	0	2
Fat Free Ranch/Thousand Island	35	0	8
Lawrey's			
Caesar; Italian, 2 Tbsp	130	13	2
Creamy Caesar	130	14	8
Red Wine Vinaigrette	90	7	7
Manischewitz			
Garlic Ranch, 2 Tbsp	15	0	4
Maple Grove			
Fat Free: Caesar, 2 Tbsp	30	0	6
Honey Dijon	45	0	10
Marzetti			
Regular Dressings:			
Blue Cheese	160	17	0
Buttermilk: Bacon Ranch; Ranch	180	19	1
Blue Cheese	160	18	1
Caesar; Chunky Blue Cheese	150	16	1
California French; Celery Seed	160	13	11
Classic Caesar Ranch	190	20	2
Country French	150	13	7
Creamy Italian	150	16	1
Dijon Honey Mustard	140	13	6
Garden Ranch; Ranch	180	19	1
Honey French/Blue Cheese	160	13	11
Italian w. Olive Oil	120	13	1
Potato Salad Dressing	120	13	7
Red Wine Vinegar & Oil	130	14	2
Slaw	170	16	6
Southern Slaw	100	11	14
Thousand Island	150	15	5
Fat Free Dressings: Italian	15	0	3
California French; Honey French	45	0	11
Honey Dijon	60	0	14
Ranch; Peppercorn Ranch	30	0	7
Slaw; Sweet & Sour	45	0	12
Thousand Island	35	0	9

Per 2 Tbsp (Approx 1 oz)	C	F	Cb
Marzetti (Cont)			
Light Dressings: Blue Cheese	60	6	4
Buttermilk Ranch	90	9	3
California French	80	6	8
Chunky Blue Cheese	80	7	4
French	40	2	6
Honey French	80	4	12
Italian	60	5	3
Ranch	90	8	7
Red Wine Vinegar & Oil	20	1	3
Slaw	60	7	10
Sweet & Sour	100	6	11
Thousand Island	70	5	6
Newman's Own			
Balsamic Vinaigrette, 2 Tbsp	90	9	3
Creamy Caesar	170	18	1
Family Recipe Italian	120	13	1
Italian Light	20	0	3
Olive Oil & Vinegar, 2 T.	150	16	1
Ranch	180	18	2
Nasoya			
Vegi-Dressing *(Tofu Base/Dairy Free):*			
Thousand Island	60	4	6
Other flavors	60	5	3
(Nayonaise - See Mayonnaise)			
Pfeiffer			
California French, 2 Tbsp	140	12	9
French	150	13	7
Honey Dijon	140	13	6
Lite Italian	50	5	3
Ranch	180	20	1
Savory Italian	110	12	3
Thousand Island	140	14	4
Pritikin			
Dijon Balsamic; Zesty Italian	30	0	6
Honey Dijon	45	0	11
Honey French Style	40	0	10
Raspberry	35	0	11
Ralph's Chef Express			
Blue Cheese, 2 Tbsp	170	18	1
Lite Ranch	90	8	3

Per 2 Tbsp (Approx 1 oz)	C	F	Cb
Red Wing			
Chunky Blue Cheese, 2 Tbsp	130	13	3
Creamy Ranch	150	15	2
French Tradit'nal; Spicy Sw. French	130	11	8
Italian Traditional	100	9	4
"K" Dressing	140	14	8
Thousand Island	110	9	8
San-J			
Fat Free: Honey Curry, 2 Tbsp	25	0	6
Tamari Mustard	25	0	5
Thai Peanut (lowfat)	50	2.5	7
S & W			
Light: Oriental Rice Wine, 2 Tbsp	30	0	7
Red Wine Vinegar Herb	40	0	10
Low Calorie Range: Blue Cheese	50	4	4
Creamy Cucumber; Thousand Island	50	4	4
Creamy Italian	20	2	2
French	35	0	6
Italian No-Oil	4	0	0
Russian	50	2	8
Seven Seas			
Regular Dressings			
Chunky Blue	90	7	5
Creamy Caesar	140	15	1
Creamy Italian	110	12	2
Green Goddess	120	13	1
Herbs & Spices	120	12	1
Ranch	150	16	2
Red Wine Vin. & Oil; Viva Italian	110	11	2
Two Cheese Italian	70	7	3
Viva Caesar	120	12	2
Viva Russian	150	16	3
Free (Fat-Free): Italian	10	0	2
Ranch	50	0	12
Red Wine Vinegar	15	0	3
Reduced Calorie:			
Crmy Italian; Red Wine Vin. & Oil	60	5	2
Italian w./Olive Oil	50	5	2
Ranch	100	9	5
Viva Italian	45	4	2
Spike Splashes!			
Original, 2 Tbsp	100	11	1
Salt Free	100	10	2
Fat Free	10	0	2

Per 2 Tbsp (Approx 1 oz)	C	F	Cb
Spectrum			
Fat Free: Creamy Dill	25	0	4
Creamy Garlic	20	0	4
Sweet Onion & Garlic; Tstd Sesame	15	0	3
Lowfat: Blue Cheese Style	35	2	3
Creamy Roasted Pepper	45	2	5
Honey Dijon	35	2	4
Mango Madness	50	2	7
Southwestern Caesar	40	2	3
Zesty Italian	30	2	1
The Spice Hunter			
Mix: *~ As Prepared, Per 2 Tbsp*			
Caesar Salad, 2 Tbsp	150	13	1
Chinese Salad	140	12	2
Garlic & Herb	140	13	2
Tree of Life			
House Dressing: Cafe Venice	120	12	2
Maison Caesar	70	6	1
Shanghai Palace	80	7	3
Lowfat Free: Blue Cheese	15	1	2
Fat Free: Honey French	35	0	8
Italian Garlic	20	0	4
Oriental Ginger	15	0	3
Walden Farms			
Fat Free, Calorie Free Range			
Average All Types, 2 Tbsp	0	0	0
Weight Watchers			
Salad Celebrations Dressings			
Fat Free: Caesar (Single), 0.75 oz	5	0	1
Caesar, 2 Tbsp	10	0	1
Creamy Italian (8 oz), 2 Tbsp	30	0	7
French Style, 2 Tbsp	40	0	9
Honey Dijon, 2 Tbsp	45	0	11
Italian (8 oz), 2 Tbsp	10	0	2
Ranch Style, 2 Tbsp	35	0	7
Ranch (Single), 0.75 oz	25	0	6
Wishbone			
Vinaigrette: Berry	50	4.5	2
Roast Garlic	60	5	3
Sun-dried Tomato	50	5	2
Robusto Italian	90	8	4
Russian: Regular	110	6	15
Thousand Island: Regular	130	12	7
Lite	80	5	8
Thousand Island	35	0	9

Per 2 Tbsp (Approx 1 oz)	C	F	Cb
Wishbone (Cont)			
Chunky Blue Cheese: Regular	170	17	2
Lite	80	8	3
Caesar	110	10	2
Italian	35	2	5
Classic House Italian	140	14	2
Classic Lite Olive Oil	40	4	2
Creamy Caesar	180	18	1
Creamy Italian	110	12	4
Fat Free: Caesar	25	0	5
Honey Dijon	45	0	10
Italian	15	0	2
Parmesan - Onion	45	0	9
Ranch	40	0	9
Red Wine Vinaigrette	40	0	7
French: Lite	60	3	8
Fat-Free	12	0	2
Sweet 'N Spicy; Red French	140	12	6
Lite	35	0	7
Italian: Regular	80	8	3
Lite	15	0.5	2
Italian Cream Lite	50	4	4
Olive Oil Vinaigrette	60	5	4
Parmesan - Onion	110	10	5
Ranch: Regular	160	17	1
Lite	100	8	5
Just Too Good!: Blue Cheese	45	2	6
Classic Caesar, 2 Tbsp	40	2	5
Creamy Caesar	40	2	7
Country Italian	30	2	3
Honey Dijon	50	2	8
Italian	35	2	5
Ranch	40	2	5
Thousand Island	60	2	9

Quick Guide

Cooked Cereals

	C	F	Cb
Buckwheat Groats, roasted:			
Dry, 1/2 cup, 3 oz	280	2	60
Cooked, 1 cup, 7 oz	180	1	39
Bulgar: Dry, 1/2 cup, 2 1/2 oz	240	1	53
Cooked, 1 cup, 6 1/2 oz	150	<1	34
Corn/Hominy Grits:			
Dry, 1/4 cup, 1.4 oz	145	<1	33
3 Tbsp, 1 oz	110	<1	25
Cooked, 3/4 cup, 6 1/2 oz	110	<1	25
Instant, 1 pkt, 0.8 oz	80	<1	18
w. Imitation Bacon Bits, 1 oz	100	<1	22
Cream of Rice, ckd, 3/4 c, 6 oz	90	0	20
Cream of Wheat:			
Regular, ckd, 3/4 cup, 6 oz	180	<1	37
Quick, ckd, 3/4 cup, 6 oz	95	<1	20
Instant, ckd, 3/4 cup, 6 oz	110	<1	23
Farina: Cooked, 3/4 cup, 6 oz	85	0	18
Millet, dry, 1/4 cup, 1 oz	100	0	20
Oat Bran:			
Raw, 1/3 cup, 1 oz	75	2	14
Cooked, 1/2 cup	45	<1	8
Oatmeal:			
Dry, 1/3 cup, 1 oz	110	0	19
Regular, ckd, 3/4 cup, 6 oz	110	2	19
1 cup, 8 oz	145	3	25
Instant: Regular, aver., 1 oz	100	2	18
Flavored, average	150	2	32
Quaker: ***See Brands***			
Wheat Hearts, 1 oz dry, 3/4 c. ckd	110	1	21

Quick Guide

Cold Cereals

	C	F	Cb
Average All Brands			
Bran (processed), 1/3 cup, 1 oz	70	<1	20
Bran Flakes, 3/4 cup, 1 oz	90	<1	23
Corn Flakes, 1 cup, 1 oz	110	<1	24
Granola, 1/4 cup, 1 oz	130	4	21
Oat Bran Cereal, 1/3 cup, 1 oz	110	1	22
Puffed Rice, 1 cup, 1/2 oz	55	0	12
Puffed Wheat, 1 cup, 1/2 oz	55	0	12
Raisin Bran, 1/2 cup, 1 oz	85	<1	22
Rice Crisps, 1 cup, 1 oz	110	1	25
Shredded Wheat, 1 bisc., 3/4 oz	80	<1	18
Sugar-frosted Flakes, 3/4 c, 1 oz	110	<1	26
Wheat Flakes, 1 cup, 1 oz	105	<1	23

Brans & Wheatgerm

	C	F	Cb
Bran: Wheat, unprocessed, 1 Tbsp, 3g	10	0	3
Rice Bran, raw, 1 Tbsp, 5g	16	1	2.5
1/3 cup, 1 oz	90	6	14
Oat Bran, 1 Tbsp, 5g	15	<1	3
1/3 cup, 1 oz	75	2	15
Wheat Germ, 1 Tbsp, 1/4 oz	25	1	3.5
1/4 cup, 1 oz	108	3	15

Cereal Add-ons

	C	F	Cb
Milk: *Per 1/2 Cup, 4 fl.oz*			
Whole, 1/2 cup	80	4.5	6
2%, 1/2 cup	60	2.3	6
1%, 1/2 cup	50	1	6
Nonfat, 1/2 cup	43	0	6
Yogurt: *Per 1/2 Cup, 4 fl.oz*			
Plain: Whole	90	4	7
Skim	60	0	8
Yogurt, fruit: Whole, 1/2 cup	125	2.6	23
Lowfat, 1/2 cup	120	2	23
Nonfat, 1/2 cup	60	0	13
Soy Drink: Regular, 1/2 cup	65	2	4
Lite, 1/2 cup, 4 fl.oz	50	1	3
Fruit: Dried, average, 1 oz	80	0	21
Banana, 1/2 medium	50	0	23
Prunes in Syrup, 5, 3 oz	90	0	24
Honey: 1 Tbsp, 3/4 oz	65	0	17
Lecithin Granules, 1 Tbsp, 10g	50	5	1
Nuts: Almonds, 6 (1/4 oz)	40	4	5
Pollen (Bee) Granules, 1 T., 8g	25	1	2
Psyllium Husks, 1 Tbsp, 5g	10	0	1
Seeds: Sunflower, 1 Tbsp	65	6	2
Soy Grits, 1 Tbsp, 8g	32	1.5	3
Sugar: 1 heaping tsp	25	0	7
1 Tbsp, 12g	46	0	12

Start the day right with a high fiber breakfast of cereals, milk/soy and fruit.

It will help prevent high-calorie snacking.

Ready-To-Eat	C	F	Cb
Arrowhead: Amaranth, 1 c., 1.2oz	**130**	1	23
Bran Flakes, 1 cup, 1 oz	**90**	1	18
Corn Flakes, 1 cup, 1.2 oz	**130**	0	30
Kamut Flakes, 1 cup, 1.1 oz	**110**	1	25
Maple Buckwheat Flake, 1 c., 1.5 oz	**160**	1	35
Multi Grain Flakes, 1 cup, 1.2 oz	**140**	1.5	29
Nature O's, 1 cup, 1.1 oz	**130**	2	24
Oat Bran Flakes, 1 cup, 1.2 oz	**140**	2.5	24
Puffed Corn/Rice, aver., 1 c., 0.8 oz	**60**	0.5	12
Puffed Kamut, 1 cup, 0.6 oz	**50**	0	11
Puffed Millet/Wheat, 1 cup, 0.5 oz	**60**	0.5	12
Raisin Bran, 1 cup, 2 oz	**190**	1.5	40
Rice Flakes, 1 cup, 1.7 oz	**80**	1	19
Shredded Wheat, 1 cup, 2 oz	**200**	1	44
Spelt Flakes, 1 cup, 1.1 oz	**100**	0.5	23
Sweetened Nature O's, 1 c., 1.5 oz	**160**	2.5	31
Wild Wheat Flakes, 1 cup, 1.5 oz	**160**	0.5	37
Barbara's Bakery			
Breakfast O's, 1 cup, 1 oz	**120**	2	22
Brown Rice Crisps, 1 cup, 1 oz	**120**	1	25
Cinnamon Puffins, 3/4 cup, 1 oz	**100**	1	26
Corn Flakes, all types,1 cup, 1 oz	**110**	0	26
Fruity Punch, 1 cup, 1 oz	**110**	0.5	26
Organic Ultra Minis, 3/4 cup, 2 oz	**190**	1	46
Shredded Oats, 1 1/4 cup, 2 oz	**220**	2.5	46
Shredded Puffins, 3/4 cup, 1 oz	**90**	1	23
Shredded Spoonfuls, 3/4 cup	**120**	1.5	23
Shredded Wheat, 2 bisc., 1.4 oz	**140**	1	31
Stars: Cocoa/Honey Crunch, 1 c., 1oz	**110**	0.5	26
Toasted O's, average, 3/4 cup	**120**	2	24
Betty Crocker: Scooby Doo! 25g	**80**	0	21
Breadshop: Granola, 1/2 c. 1.7 oz	**220**	7.5	32
Cinnamon Grins, 3/4 cup, 1 oz	**110**	0.5	25
Crispy Rice'n Corn Flakes, 3/4 c., 1 oz	**110**	0	26
Health Nuggets, 1/2 cup	**170**	1	38
Kamut 'n Honey, 1 cup, 1 oz	**120**	3	22
Puffs 'n Honey, 3/4 cup, 1 oz	**120**	3	21
Cap'n Crunch: All types, 3/4 cup	**110**	2	22
Chex: Corn, 1 1/4 cup, 1 oz	**110**	0	26
Wheat, 3/4 cup, 1.8 oz	**190**	1	41
Country Inn			
Green Gables Inn, 1/2 cup, 1.8 oz	**210**	7	36
Greyfield Inn, 3/4 cup, 1.8 oz	**210**	5	39
Inn at Ormsby Hill, 1 cup, 2.1 oz	**220**	2.5	48

Dr McDougall's	C	F	Cb
Oatmeal & Wheat, 1 cup, 2.4 oz	**220**	2	57
Oatmeal & 4 Grains,1 cup, 2.3 oz	**210**	1.5	52
Dominick's: Corn Flakes, 1 1/4 cup	**120**	0	27
Crispy Corn & Rice, 1 1/4 cup, 1 oz	**120**	0	26
Crispy Rice, 1 1/4 cup, 1 oz	**130**	0	28
Frosted Flakes, 3/4 cup, 1 oz	**120**	0	28
Fruit Rings, 3/4 cup, 1 oz	**100**	1	23
Tasteeos, 1 1/4 cup, 1 oz	**120**	2	24
Erewhon, *Per 1 oz:* Crisp Brn Rice	**110**	1	24
Aztec; Raisin Bran; Super O's	**100**	0	24
Fruit 'n Wheat	**100**	1	21
Wheat Flakes	**100**	0	22
Estee: Corn Flakes, 1 oz pkg	**90**	0	24
Raisin Bran, 1 oz pkg	**90**	1	21
Familia: Muesli, 1/2 cup, 2.1 oz	**210**	3	45
No Added Sugar, 1/2 cup	**200**	3	41
Glenny's: Maple Frosted Corn, 1 oz	**110**	0	20
Oat/Rice Mini Puffs, 1 oz	**110**	0	21
General Mills: Basic 4, 1/2 c, 1 oz	**100**	1.5	21
Body Buddies; Boo Berry 1 c, 1 oz	**120**	1	26
Cheerios: Regular, 1 cup, 1 oz	**110**	2	22
Apple Cinnamon, 3/4 c., 1 oz	**120**	2	25
Frosted; Team, 1 cup, 1 oz	**120**	1	25
Honey Nut, 1 cup, 1 oz	**120**	1.5	24
Multi-Grain, 1 cup, 1 oz	**110**	1	24
Chex: Corn, 1 cup, 1 oz	**110**	0	26
Honey Nut, 3/4 cup, 1 oz	**120**	0.5	26
Multi-Bran, 1 cup, 2 oz	**200**	1.5	49
Rice, 1 1/4 cup, 1 oz	**120**	0	27
Wheat, 1 cup, 2 oz	**180**	1	41
Cinnamon Grahams, 3/4 c., 1 oz	**120**	1	26
Cinnamon Tst Crunch, 3/4 c., 1 oz	**130**	3.5	24
Cocoa Puffs, 1 cup, 1 oz	**120**	1	27
Cookie Crisp; Count Choc, 1 c., 1 oz	**120**	1	26
Count Chocula, 1 cup, 1 oz	**120**	1	26
Country Corn Flakes, 1 c., 1 oz	**120**	0	26
Crispy Wheaties 'N Rais., 1 c., 2 oz	**190**	1	45
Fiber One, 1/2 cup, 1 oz	**60**	1	24
Frankenberry, 1 cup, 1 oz	**120**	1	27
French Toast Crunch, 3/4 c., 1 oz	**120**	1.5	26
Golden Grahams, 3/4 cup, 1 oz	**120**	1	26
Grand Slams, 1 cup, 1 oz	**120**	1	27
Honey Nut Clusters, 1 cup, 2 oz	**210**	2	47
Jurrasic Park Crunch, 1 cup, 1 oz	**120**	1	26
Kaboom, 1 1/4 cup, 1 oz	**120**	1.5	24

Ready-To-Eat (Cont)

General Mills (Cont)	C	F	Cb
Kix, 1 1/3 cup, 1 oz	**120**	0.5	26
Berry Berry, 3/4 cup, 1 oz	**120**	1.5	26
Lucky Charms, 1 cup, 1 oz	**120**	1	25
NesQuik: Choc Puff, 3/4 cup, 1 oz	**120**	2	25
Oatmeal Crisp Almond, 1 c., 2 oz	**220**	5	41
Apple Cinn.; Raisin, 1 cup, 2 oz	**210**	2	44
Raisin Nut Bran, 3/4 cup, 2 oz	**200**	4	41
Reese's P'nut Butter Puffs, 3/4 cup	**130**	3	24
Sunrise, 3/4 cup, 1 oz	**110**	0.5	26
Total Corn Flakes, 1 1/3 cup, 1 oz	**110**	0	26
Total Raisin Bran, 1 cup, 2 oz	**180**	1	43
Total Whole Grain, 3/4 cup, 1 oz	**110**	1	24
Trix, 1 cup, 1 oz	**120**	1.5	26
USA Olympic Crunch, 1 cup, 1 oz	**120**	1	26
Wheaties, 1 cup, 1 oz	**110**	1	24
Honey Frosted, 3/4 cup, 1 oz	**110**	0	27

Hansen's Natural: *Per 1/2 cup, 2 oz*			
Orange & Chocolate Cereal	**230**	9	35
Stawb. & Yogurt Cereal	**230**	9	30
Toasted Nut Crunch Cereal	**230**	6	39
Tropical Cluster Cereal	**210**	5	36

Health Valley			
Amaranth Flakes, 3/4 cup	**100**	0	24
Bran Cereal (w. Fruit), 3/4 cup	**160**	0	40
Corn Bran Flakes, 3/4 cup	**100**	0	24
Fiber 7 Flakes (100% Orig.), 3/4 c.	**100**	0	24
Golden Flax, 1/4 cup	**190**	3	38
Granola O's, all types, 3/4 cup	**120**	0	26
Healthy Crunches & Flakes, 3/4 c.	**130**	0	31
Healthy Fiber Flakes, 3/4 cup	**100**	0	23
Hot Cups: Maple; Banana, 1 pkt	**240**	2.5	46
Apple; 10 Grain, 1 pkt	**220**	2.5	42
98% Fat Free Granola 2/3 cup	**180**	1	43
Oat Bran Flakes, all types, 3/4 c.	**105**	0	26
Oat Bran/10 Bran O's, 3/4 cup	**100**	0	23
Puffed: Honey Sweetened, 1 cup	**110**	0	28
Raisin Bran Flakes, 1 1/4 cup	**190**	0	47
Real Oat Bran, 1/2 cup	**200**	3	34

Healthy Choice			
M/grain Rais. & Almd, 3/4 c., 1 oz	**100**	1	22
Flakes, 1 cup, 1.1 oz	**100**	0	26

Heartland			
Granola: Lowfat, 1/2 cup, 2 oz	**210**	3	40
Original; Raisin, 1/2 cup, 2 1/4 oz	**300**	11	41

Kashi	C	F	Cb
Breakfast Pilaf, 1/2 c., ckd, 5 oz	**170**	3	30
Honey Puffed Kashi, 1 cup, 1 oz	**120**	1	25
Kashi Go, 1/2 cup, 5 oz	**270**	3	59
Kashi Golean, 1/2 cup, 1 oz	**90**	0.5	21
Kashi Good Friends, 3/4 cup, 1 oz	**90**	1	24
Kashi Medley, 1/2 cup, 1 oz	**100**	1	20
Kashi Pillows, 3/4 cup, 2 oz	**200**	1	45
Puffed Kashi, 1 cup, 0.9 oz	**70**	0.5	13

Kellogg's: Apple Jacks, 1 c., 1 oz	**120**	0	30
All-Bran: 1/2 cup, 1 oz	**80**	1	23
with Extra Fiber, 1/2 cup, 1 oz	**50**	0.5	20
Apple Cinn. Rice Krispies, 3/4 c.	**110**	0	26
Apple Cinn. Squares, 3/4 c., 2 oz	**180**	1	44
Apple Raisin Crisp, 1/2 cup, 1 oz	**90**	0	23
Blueberry Squares, 3/4 cup, 2 oz	**180**	1	43
Bran Buds, 1/3 cup, 1 oz	**80**	0.5	24
Cinnamon Mini Buns, 3/4 cup	**120**	0.5	27
Complete Oatbran Flakes, 3/4 cup	**110**	0.5	23
Wheatbran Flakes, 3/4 cup	**90**	0.5	3
Cocoa Krispies, 3/4 cup	**120**	1	27
Common Sense O/Bran, 3/4 cup	**110**	1	23
Corn Flakes, 1 cup, 1 oz	**110**	0	24
Honey Crunch, 3/4 cup, 1 oz	**120**	1	26
Corn Pops, 1 cup, 1 oz	**120**	0	28
Cracklin' Oat Bran, 3/4 cup, 2 oz	**190**	7	35
Crispix, 1 cup, 1 oz	**110**	0	25
Double Dip Crunch, 3 3/4 cup	**110**	0	26
Froot Loops: 1 cup	**120**	1	28
other types, 1 cup, 1 oz	**120**	1	28
Frosted: Bran, 3/4 cup, 1 oz	**100**	0	26
Flakes, 3/4 cup, 1 oz	**120**	0	28
Krispies, 3/4 cup, 1 oz	**100**	0	24
Mini-Wheats: 3/4 cup, 1.8 oz	**180**	1	42
Bite Size, 1 cup, 1 oz	**200**	1	48
Fruity Marshmallow Krispies, 3/4 c.	**110**	0	25
Healthy Choice: Almd Crunch, 1 c.	**210**	2.5	45
Golden Multi-Grn Flakes, 3/4 c.	**110**	0	26
Tst Brown Sugar Sq., 1 cup	**190**	1	44
Just Right, all varieties, 1 cup, 2 oz	**210**	2	49
Low Fat Granola: 1/2 cup, 2 oz	**190**	3	39
w. Raisins, 2/3cup, 2 oz	**220**	3	47
Müeslix: Apple & Almond, 3/4 c.	**200**	5	39
Raisin & Almond, 2/3 cup	**200**	3	40
Nut & Honey Crunch, 1 1/4 c., 2 oz	**220**	2.5	46
Nutri-Grain: Almond, 1 1/4 c., 2 oz	**180**	3	38
Golden Wheat, 3/4 cup, 1 oz	**100**	1	24
Twists, 1 bar, 1.3 oz	**140**	3	26

Breakfast Cereals (Cont)

Kellogg's (Cont)	C	F	Cb
Pop Tarts: Lowfat, each, average	190	3	39
Toaster Pastries, average, 1 oz	210	6	37
Mini Pastries, aver., 1 pouch	170	7	31
Pastry Swirls, 2.2 oz	260	11	37
Snak Stix, 1 pastry, 1.8 oz	190	4	37
Product 19, 1 cup, 1 oz	100	0	25
Raisin Bran, 1 cup, 2 oz	190	1.5	47
Raisin Bran Crunch, 1cup, 1.85 oz	190	1	44
Raisin Squares, 3/4 cup, 2 oz	180	1.5	41
Rice Krispies, 1 1/4 cup	120	0	29
Treats, 3/4 cup	120	1.5	26
Bars: Original, 1 bar	90	2	18
Caramel/Peanut Butter, (1)	110	4	19
Double Choc Chunk, (1)	100	4.5	15
Scotcheroos, (1)	120	5	18
Razzle Dazzles, 3/4 cup, 1 oz	110	0	25
Smacks, 3/4 cup	100	0.5	24
Special K, 1 cup, 1 oz	110	0	22
Special K Plus, 1 cup	210	2	47
Strawberry Squares, 3/4 c., 2 oz	170	2	40
Temptations: Fr. Van. Alm., 3/4 c.	100	1.5	21
Honey Rst. Pecan, 2/3 c., 1 oz	120	0.5	24
Nabisco: 100% Bran, 1/3 cup, 1 oz	70	1	21
Cocoa Blasts, 1 cup	130	1	29
Cream of Wheat: All types, 1 pkg	150	1.5	32
Fruit Wheats, 1/2 cup, 1 oz	90	0	23
Shredded Wheat: 1 biscuit	80	0.5	19
Spoon size, 2/3 cup, 1 oz	90	1	23
Shredded Wheat'n Bran, 2/3 cup	90	0	23
Shredd. Wheat w. Oatbran, 1 oz	100	1	22
Toaster Pastry, 1.7 oz ea., average	190	5	34
Team Flakes, 3/4 cup, 1 oz	110	0	24
Nature's Path: Corn Flakes, 3/4 c.	115	0.5	26
Heritage: all varieties, 3/4 c., 1 oz	115	0	24
Heritage Muesli, 1/2 cup, 2 oz	215	3	41
Honey'd Raisin Bran, 3/4 cup, 1 oz	110	0	25
Millet Rice, 3/4 cup, 1 oz	120	1	25
Multigrain, 2/3 cup, 1 oz	110	0.5	24
New Morning			
Bran Flakes; Crispy Rice, 1 c., 1 oz	110	1	23
Cocoa Crispy Rice, 1 cup, 2.1 oz	210	1.5	45
Corn/Honey Frost. Flakes, 1 c., 1 oz	120	1	25
Ginky O's; Orig. Otios, 1 c., 1 oz	120	1	21
Granola Clusters, 3/4 c., 1.9 oz	200	2	42
Otiola: Blueberry, 1 cup, 1.9 oz	200	1.5	41

New Morning (Cont):	C	F	Cb
Otios: Cocoa, 1 cup, 1.76 oz	170	1.5	21
Apple Cinnamon, 1 cup, 1 oz	90	1.5	21
Honey Almond, 1 cup, 1 oz	100	1	22
Original, 1 cup, 1 oz	120	1	21
Raisin Bran, 1 cup, 30g	90	0.5	22
Ultimate Oat Bran Flakes, 1 c., 28g	110	1	21
Pillsbury: Toaster Strudel, 54g	180	8	26
Post: Alpha Bits, 1 cup	110	1	24
Cinna-Crunch Pebbles, 1 1/4 cup	130	1.5	27
Cocoa Pebbles, 7/8 cup	115	1	25
Great Grains, 2/3 cup, 1.8 oz	210	5	39
Fruit & Fiber, 1 cup	210	3	46
Grape Nut 'O's, 1 cup, 1.1 oz	120	0	28
Grape Nuts; Raisin, 1/4 cup	105	0	23
Honey Bunches of Oats, 3/4 cup	120	1.5	25
Honey Nut Shredd. Wheat, 1 c.,1.8oz	200	2	43
Natural Bran Flakes, 2/3 cup	90	0	23
Oat Flakes, 2/3 cup	105	1	22
Oreo O's, 3/4 cup	110	2.5	21
Raisin Bran, 2/3 cup, 1.4 oz	120	1	32
Cinna-Cluster, 1 cup, 2 oz	220	3	48
Waffle Crisp, 1 cup	130	3	24
Quaker			
Breakfast/Cereal Bars: each	130	3	26
Ready to Eat: Oat Bran, 1 1/4 cup	210	3	41
Cap'n Crunch, aver. all types, 3/4 c.	105	1.5	22
Life, all types, 3/4 cup	120	1.5	26
Oatmeal Squares, 1 cup	225	2.5	45
100% Natural Granola, 1/2 cup	220	9	31
Lowfat, 2/3 cup	210	3	44
w. Raisins, 1/2 cup	230	9	34
Popeye: Puffed Rice; Wheat, 1 cup	50	0	12
Quisp, 1 cup	110	1.5	23
Shredded Wheat, 3 bisc.	220	1.5	50
Toasted Oatmeal, 1 cup	190	2.5	39
Unprocessed Bran, 1/3 cup	30	0	11
Bagged: Cocoa Blasts, 1 cup	130	1	29
Apple Zaps; Fruitany O's, 1 cup	120	1	27
Frosted Flakers, 3/4 cup	120	0	28
Frosted/Honey Nut Oats, 1 cup	110	1	24
Frosted Oats/ Sweet Crunch, 1 cup	110	1.5	23
Fruitangy Oh's, 1 cup	120	1	27
Honey Crisp Corn Flakes, 3/4 cup	110	0	27
Honey Dipps, 1 1/4 cup	130	1.5	28
Marshmallow Safari, 3/4 cup	120	1.5	25
Rice Crisps, 1 cup	110	0	26

Quaker (Cont)	C	F	Cb
Grits: *Per Packet*			
Regular: All types, aver., 1/4 cup	130	0.5	31
Instant: All types, average	100	1	22
Instant Quaker Oatmeal: *Per Pkt*			
Oatmeal: Regular, 1 oz	100	2	19
Baked Apple, 1.4 oz	150	1.5	31
Cinn. Roll; Fr. Vanilla, 1 1/2 oz	160	2	33
Cookie Blast, average, 1 1/2 oz	160	2.5	32
Honey Nut, 1 1/2 oz	170	3.5	31
Maple/Br.Sug; Rais./Spice	160	2	33
Raisin/Date/Walnut, 1 1/4 oz	140	2	27
Dinosaur Eggs, 50g pkt	200	4	38
Kid's Choice: 1 pkt, aver., 1 1/2 oz	160	2.5	32
Sea Adventures, 1 pkt, 1 1/2 oz	190	4	37
Quick'n Hearty *(Microwave Oatmeal): Per Pkt*			
Regular, 1 oz	110	2	19
App.Spice; Cinnamon Dble Raisin	170	2	35
Br.Sugar Cinnamon; Honey Bran	150	2	30
Quaker/Hot: Multigrain, 1/2 cup	130	1.5	29
Oat Bran, 1/2 cup	150	3	25
Whole Wheat Hot Nat. 1/2 cup	130	1	30
Oats: Quick; Old Fash., Steel, 1/2 c.	150	3	27
Other Quaker Brands			
Honey Graham Oh's, 3/4 cup	110	2	23
King Vitaman, 1 1/2 cup	120	1	26
Kretschmer: Wheat Bran, 1/4 cup	30	1	10
Wheat Germ, all types, 2 Tbsp	50	1	6
Mother's: Hot Cereals, 1/2 cup	130	1.5	27
Oatbran; Oatmeal, 1/2 cup	150	3	3
Sun Country Granola: Almd, 1/2 c.	270	9	38
w. Raisins & Dates, 1/2 cup	260	8	43
Ralston: Bran Flakes, 3/4 c., 1 oz	110	1	24
Chex Multi Bran, 1 1/4 cup, 2 oz	220	2	46
Cocoa Crispy Rice, 1 c., 1 3/4 oz	200	1	45
Cookie Crisp, 1 cup, 1 oz	120	2	25
Frosted Flakes, 3/4 cup, 1 oz	120	0	28
Hot Ralston, 1/2 cup, 1.5 oz	150	1	31
Muesli: Blueberry, 1 cup, 2 oz	200	3	41
Cranberry, 3/4 cup, 2 oz	200	3	40
Strawberry, 1 cup, 2 oz	210	3	41
Raisin Bran, 3/4 cup, 2 oz	190	1	41
Sun Flakes, 3/4 cup	110	1	33
Tasteeos, 1 1/4 cup, 1 oz	130	3	22
Stone-Buhr: Bran, 1/4 c., 0.5 oz	65	0	14
7 Grain, 1/3 cup, 1 1/2 oz	140	2	31
Uncle Sam: Wheat/Flaxseed, 1 c.	190	5	38

Grains & Flours	C	F	Cb
Per 1/2 Cup (8 level Tbsp)			
Amaranth, 1/2 cup, 3 1/2 oz	350	6	60
Arrowroot, 1/2cup, 2 1/4 oz	230	0	57
Barley: Regular, 1/2 cup, 3 1/4 oz	325	2	56
Pearled, raw, 3 1/2 oz	350	1	78
Flakes, 1/2 cup, 1 1/2 oz	150	0.5	33
Buckwheat: Regular, 1/2 c., 3 oz	290	3	61
Groats, roasted, dry, 3 oz	285	2	60
Roasted, cooked, 3 1/2 oz	90	0.5	19
Flour, whole-groat	200	2	42
Bulgur: Dry, 1/2 cup, 2 1/2 oz	240	1	54
Cooked, 1/2 cup, 3 1/4 oz	75	0.5	17
Carob Flour, 1/2 cup, 1.8 oz	95	0.5	25
Corn kernels (blue/yellow), 3 oz	300	4	66
Corn Bran, 1/2 cup, 1.4 oz	85	0.5	32
Corn Flour/Masa, 2 oz	210	2	44
Corn Grits:			
Dry, 1/2 cup, 2 3/4 oz	290	1	62
Cooked, 1/2 cup, 4 1/4 oz	75	0.5	16
Corn Germ, toasted	245	13	21
Cornmeal: Average All Types			
3 Tbsp, 1 oz	100	0.5	22
1/2 c., 2.2 oz	220	2	46
Mixes: same as above	220	2	46
Cornstarch: 1 Tbsp, 8g	30	0	7
1/2 cup, 2 1/4 oz	230	0	57
Couscous: Dry, 3 1/4 oz	345	0	72
Cooked, 4.1 oz	60	0	12
Farina: Dry, 3 oz	325	0	70
Cooked, 4.1 oz	60	0	13
Flax Seeds, 2 oz	280	20	22
Garbanzo (Chick Pea), 1/2 c., 2 oz	200	3	35
Matzo Meal, 1/2 cup	260	1	55
Millet: raw, 1/2 cup, 3 1/2 oz	375	4	76
Cooked, 1/2 cup, 4 1/4 oz	145	1	29
Oat Bran: Raw, 1/2 cup, 1.7 oz	115	2	31
Cooked, 1/2 cup, 4 oz	115	1	33
Oats, rolled/oatmeal:			
Dry/Groats, 1/2 cup, 1.5 oz	155	3	28
Cooked, 1/2 cup, 4.2 oz	75	1	13
Polenta: See Cornmeal			
Made Up, 1/2 cup, 5 oz	220	2	24
Potato flour, 1/2 cup, 3.2 oz	315	0	72
Psyllium Husks, 1 Tbsp (5g)	10	0	2
Quinoa, 1/2 cup, 3 oz	320	5	53
Eden, 1/2 cup, 3 oz	340	5	62
Rice: See Next Page			

Grains & Flours (Cont)

	C	F	Cb
Rice Bran, 1/3 cup, 1 oz	90	6	14
Rice Flour, 1/2 cup, 2 3/4 oz	290	2	63
Rice Polish, 1/2 cup	220	7	39
Rye Grains:			
1/2 cup, 3 oz	280	2	59
Flakes, 1/2 cup, 1 1/2 oz	150	0.5	32
Flour, dark, 2 1/4 oz	210	2	44
Medium light, 1.8 oz	185	1	40
Semolina, 1/2 cup, 3 oz	305	1	61
Sorghum, 1/2 cup, 3.4 oz	325	3	72
Soybean Flakes, 1/2 cup, 1 1/2 oz	190	8	14
Soy Flour, 1/2 cup, 2 oz	250	11	18
Tapioca, pearl, Dry: 1/2 cup, 2. 7oz	260	0	67
3 Tbsp, 1 oz	100	0	26
Teff (Seed) Flour, 2 oz	200	0.5	41
Tortilla Flour Mix, 1/2 cup, 2 oz	225	12	37
Triticale, 1/2 cup, 3.4 oz	325	2	70
flour, whole-grain, 1/2 cup	220	1	47
Wheat: Average, 1/2 cup, 3 1/2 oz	320	2	28
Wheat Bran, unproc., 1/2 c., 1 oz	65	1	20
Wheat Flakes, 1/2 cup, 1 1/2 oz	160	0.5	32
Wheat Germ: Crude, 2 oz	200	8	29
toasted, 1/2 cup, 2 oz	215	12	28
Wheat Flour: Whole grain, 2.1 oz	205	1	44
White, all types, 1/2 c., 2.2 oz	220	0.5	46

Also See *Arrowhead Mills Cereals* ~ Page 88

"I got the idea while down at the bank."

Brown Rice

Average Short or Long Grain	C	F	Cb
Raw/Dry: 1/2 cup, 3 1/2 oz	350	2.5	72
1 cup, 7 oz	700	5	144
Cooked: Hot, 1/2 cup, 3 1/2 oz	110	0.5	23
1 cup, 7 oz	220	1.5	46
Cold, 1/2 cup, 2 1/2 oz	90	0.5	19

White Rice

	C	F	Cb
Raw: Short/Med. Grain, 1 c., 7 oz	720	1	156
Long Grain, 1 cup, 6 1/2 oz	670	1	144
Glutinous, 1 cup, 6 1/2 oz	680	1	150
Cooked (Boiled/Steamed):			
Short/Medium Grain:			
Hot, 1/2 cup, 3 1/4 oz	120	0	27
1 cup, 6 1/2 oz	240	0.5	54
Cold, 1/2 cup, 2 3/4 oz	90	0	20
Long Grain: Hot, 1/2 c., 2 3/4 oz	100	0	22
1 cup, 5 1/2 oz	200	0.5	44
Cold, 1/2 cup, 2 1/2 oz	80	0	17
Glutinous, 1 cup, 6 oz	170	0.5	36
Parboiled, ckd, hot, 1/2 c., 3 oz	90	0	20
Precook./Instant: Dry, 1/2 c., 3 1/2 oz	370	0	80
Cooked, Hot, 1/2 cup, 3 oz	90	0	20
Wild Rice: Raw, 1 cup, 5 1/2 oz	570	13	120
Cooked, hot, 1 cup, 5 3/4 oz	165	0.5	35

Rice Dishes

	C	F	Cb
Chinese Fried Rice: 1/2 c., 2 1/2 oz	160	5	21
1 cup, 5 oz	320	13	42
2 cups, 10 oz	640	26	84
Mexican Rice: 1 cup	500	12	90
Taco Bell, 1 serving	190	10	20
Taco John's, 1 serving	350	18	40
Taco Time, 1 serving	160	2	28
Rice-A-Roni ~ See Page 66			
Rice Pilaf: Restaurant, 1 cup	270	7.5	43
Boston Market, 2/3 cup	180	5	32
Denny's, 1 serving	110	2	21
Sizzler, side serving	260	5	47
Rice w. Raisins/Pinenuts, 1 cup	400	11	70
Risotto, 1 cup	420	18	65
Saffron Rice, 1 cup	370	12	66
Spanish Rice, 1 cup	390	9	72
El Pollo Loco, 1 serving	130	3	24
Sticky Thai Rice, 1 cup	750	28	121
Sushi Rice, 1 Tbsp	25	0	6

- Macaroni includes all shapes and sizes; (e.g. spaghetti, fettuccini, shells, tubes, ziti, twists, sheets, cannelloni, manicotti, elbows).
- All regular macaroni products have the same cals/fat/carb. on a weight basis.
- 1oz Dry = approx. 2 1/2 -3 oz cooked.

Dry Spaghetti/Macaroni

	C	F	Cb
1 oz quantity	105	0.5	21
1lb box/pkg., 16 oz	1680	7	336
Elbows, 1 cup, 3 3/4 oz	395	2	77
Shells, small, 1 cup, 3 1/4 oz	340	2	66
Spirals, 1 cup, 3 oz	315	2	61

Cooked Spaghetti/Macaroni

	C	F	Cb
Plain, All Types (no added fat):			
Firm/Al Dente (8-10 mins.), 1 oz	42	0.5	8.5
Medium (11-13mins.), 1 oz	37	0.5	7.5
Tender (14-20mins.), 1 oz	32	0.5	7
(Longer cooking increases water absorbed)			
Spaghetti, 1/2 cup, 2 1/2 oz	90	0.5	18
Medium serving, 1 cup, 5 oz	185	1	37
Large (restaurant), 2 c., 10 oz	370	2	74
Elbows/Spirals, 1 cup, 5 oz	185	1	38
Small Shells, 1 cup, 4 oz	150	0.5	31
Protein-fortified: Dry, 1 oz	107	0.5	21
Cooked, 1 cup, 5 oz	230	0.5	44
Spinach/Vegetable: Dry, 1 oz	105	0.5	21
Cooked, 1 cup, 5 oz	180	0.5	37
Whole-wheat: Dry, 1 oz	100	0.5	21
Cooked, 1 cup, 5 oz	175	0.5	37

Fresh Pasta (Refrigerated)

	C	F	Cb
Plain/Spinach/Tomato, average:			
As purchased, 4 oz	325	2.5	64
Cooked, 1 cup, 5 oz	190	1	38
Home-made, without egg:			
Cooked, 1 cup, 5 oz	175	1	35
Buitoni			
Angel Hair, 1 1/4 cup, 3 oz	230	2.5	43
Fettuccine/Linguini: 1 1/4 cup, 3 oz	240	2.5	45
Spinach, 1 1/4 cup, 3 oz	260	4	43
Ravioli: Beef, 1 1/4 cup, 3.6 oz	330	9	46

Buitoni (Cont):	C	F	Cb
Ravioli: Chk., Herb Parm., 1 1/4 c., 3.6oz	310	9	44
Dblestuff. Mozz. Herb, 1 1/2 c., 4 oz	360	12	44
Four Cheese, 1 cup, 3 oz	290	9	38
Light, 1 cup, 3 oz	230	4	37
Garden Vegetable, 1 cup, 3 oz	250	5	39
Mini 3 Cheese, 1 cup, 3.5 oz	260	5	41
Mini Beef, 1 cup, 3.5 oz	270	5	44
Rst Chick. & Garlic, 1 1/4 c., 4.5 oz	330	11	45
Tortellini: Chse & Rst Garlic 1 c., 3 oz	270	8	38
Chkn & Prosciutto, 1 c., 3.6 oz	360	13	45
Herb Chicken, 3/4 cup, 3 oz	260	7	40
Mozzarella & Herb, 1 cup, 3.6 oz	320	9	45
Mozzarella & Pepp., 1 c., 3.6 oz	350	10	49
Mushroom & Chse, 1 c., 3.6 oz	290	6	46
Spinach Cheese, 3/4 cup, 3 oz	260	6	40
Sundried Tomato, 1 cup, 3.6 oz	320	10	46
Sweet Italian Saus., 1 c., 3.6 oz	320	8	49
Three Cheese, 3/4 cup, 3 oz	250	6	39

Noodles

	C	F	Cb
Plain/Egg: Dry, 1 oz	108	1	20
1 cup, 1 1/3 oz	145	1.5	28
Cooked, 1 oz	38	0.5	7
1/2 cup, 2 3/4 oz	105	1	20
1 cup, 5 1/2 oz	210	2	40
Yolk Free: *Cooked, Per Cup*			
'No Yolks' (*Foulds*)	210	2	40
Passover Gold (*Manischewitz*)	200	0	42
Chinese: Cellophane/Rice, dry, 1 oz	100	0	25
Chow Mein/hard, dry, 1 oz	150	5	17
Japanese: Soba, dry, 1 oz	95	0.5	21
cooked, 1 cup, 4 oz	110	0.5	24
Somen, dry, 1 oz	100	0.5	22
cooked, 1 cup, 6 oz	225	0.5	49
Japanese Style Pan Fried:			
Maruchan's Yaki-Sobu, 1 c., 5.6 oz	260	3	50
Udon *(Chikara)*, aver., 7.5 oz pkt	250	1	52
Stir Fry/Yakisoba, 1 serve, 3.5 oz	220	2	44

Egg Roll Skins/Won Ton

	C	F	Cb
Egg Roll Skins:			
(Golden Dragon) 1 pce, 1 oz	80	0	18
(Wung Hung) 4 skins, 4 oz	300	0	64
Won Ton Wrappers:			
(Dynasty) 10 wrappers, 2.1 oz	170	1	36
Egg Roll/Spring Roll Wrapper:			
(Dynasty) 3 wrappers, 2.1 oz	170	1	36

Note: All breads have similar calories on a weight basis. However, volume may vary. For example, 1 oz of bread may equal 1 slice regular bread or 2 slices of a lighter bread. It is best to weigh bread used and calculate on 1 oz bread = 70 calories.

Quick Guide

Bread

	C	F	Cb
Average All Varieties:			
Thin slice (1/4") 1 oz	70	1	13
Extra thin slice 3/4 oz	55	<1	10
Light thin slice, 0.6 oz	40	<1	7.5
Toasting slice, 1.2 oz	85	1	16
Thick slice (3/8"), 1.5 oz	105	1.5	20
Large thick (1/2"), 2 oz	140	2	26
1-lb Loaf, 16 oz	1120	6	208
Toast has same calories as bread used.			
1 thin slice + 1 tsp of fat	105	5	13
1 thick slice (3/8") +2 tsp fat	175	10	20

Breads

	C	F	Cb
Batard (8 oz), 1/4, 2 oz slice	140	0.5	28
Boule, 1/2" thick, 2 oz slice	130	0	29
Bran style, 1 oz slice	70	1	14
Buttermilk, average, 1 oz slice	80	2	13
Caraway Rye, 1 oz slice	70	0	15
Challah, 1 oz slice	85	2	14
Corn Bread, aver., 1 pce., 3 oz	180	7	36
Cracked Wheat Sourdough, 1 1/2 oz	130	0.5	27
Croutons, 2 Tbsp	35	1	6
Dark Bread, 1 oz slice	70	1	14
Date & Nut, 1 oz slice	90	1	14
'Enriched' Breads, aver., 1 oz sl.	75	1	18
5-Grain Honey Whole Wheat,			
1 slice, 1 1/2 oz	110	1	23
Foccacia: Plain, 2 oz portion	150	4	23
Cheese & Garlic, 2 oz	170	8	21
Pesto, 2 oz	170	6	21
Tomato & Olive, 2 oz	120	2	20
French Stick, 1 oz slice	70	1	15
French Toast, 1 slice, 2 1/4 oz	160	7	18
Sticks (*Aunt Jemima*), 1 pce, 1 oz	75	3	12
Garlic Bread, 1 pce. w. fat, 1 oz	125	6	14
Garlic Toast, (*Pepp.Farm*), 1.4 oz sl.	160	10	15
Italian Bread, 1 oz slice	75	1	15
Light Bread, aver., 0.8 oz slice	40	<1	7.5
1 oz slice	70	1	13
Melba Toast, 2 pces	25	0	6

Breads

	C	F	Cb
MultiGrain: 1 slice, 1 oz	75	1	14
Fat Free, 1 oz	70	0	15
Nut/Health Nut, 1 oz slice	85	2	15
Oatmeal/Oatbran Bread, 1 oz sl.	70	1	13
Party Breads (*Pepp. Farm*): Rye, 1 sl.	15	<1	8
Dijon; Pumpernickel, 1 sl.	18	<1	3.5
Pita Bread, aver. all types, 2 oz	150	2	30
Mini/Pocket, 1 oz	75	1	15
Poppyseed (Vienna), 0.8 oz sl.	55	1	10
Pumpernickel, 1 oz slice	75	1	15
Cocktail size, 0.4 oz	30	<1	6
Raisin Bread, 1 oz slice	80	1	14
Raisin Walnut, 2 oz slice	160	3.5	29
Roman Meal, 1 oz slice	70	1	14
Country Potato & Oat, 1 1/2 oz	110	1.5	20
Rye, average., 1 thin slice, 1 oz	75	1	13
1 thick slice, 2 oz	150	2	25
Cocktail size, 0.4 oz	25	<1	4
Sandwich Bread, 1 oz slice	70	1	13
Sandwich Pockets: Reg., 2 oz	150	1	30
Sourdough, 1 oz slice	70	1	12
Wheat/Cracked Wheat, 1 oz sl.	75	1	14

Bread Rolls & Buns

	C	F	Cb
Brown 'n Serve, average, 1 oz	80	2	15
Dinner Rolls: 1 small, 1 oz	85	2	15
1 medium (3" diam),1 1/2 oz	130	3	23
English Muffins, aver., 2 oz	140	2	27
Frankfurter/Hot Dog: 1 1/4 oz	100	2	19
1 1/2 oz size	120	2	23
French: 1 medium, 1.3 oz	110	1	24
1 large, 3 oz	240	2	52
Hamburger: Regular, 1 1/2 oz	120	2	23
Large, 3 oz	240	4	46
Hoagie/Submarine, 4 3/4 oz	400	8	77
Kaiser Roll, 2 oz size	170	3	18
Onion Roll, 2 oz size	170	2	20
Parker House Roll, 0.7 oz size	65	1	12
Party Roll, 0.6 oz	55	1	10
Sandwich Roll, 1.6 oz size	120	2	23
Soft Pretzel Bun (*J & J*), 3 oz	235	3	50
Sourdough Roll, 1 1/4 oz	100	1	18
Sweet Rolls, 1 oz	100	2	20
w. Icing, average	160	6	20
Wheat Roll: Small, 1 oz	75	0.5	14
Medium, 1 1/2 oz	110	1	20

Quick Guide

Bagels

	C	F	Cb
Average All Brands			
Plain/Onion:			
1 mini/bagelette, 1 oz	80	<1	15
1 small bagel, 2 oz	160	1.5	30
1 medium bagel, 3 oz	240	2	45
1 large bagel, 4 oz	320	3	60
Bagel Chips (New York Style), 4 slices, 3/4 oz	90	2	17
Pizza Bagel, 6 oz each	380	7	60
Bagel Bites *(Ore-Ida)*, 4 pces	190	7	25
Bagel Crisps *(Burns Ricker)*, 1 oz	150	9	28

Bagel Brands

	C	F	Cb
Amy's Kitchen, aver., 3 1/2 oz	235	2	50
Awrey's, 2.7 oz each	190	0.5	42
Cosco Bakery: Plain, 4 oz	300	1	61
Everything, 4 oz	330	3.5	62
Lenders, all flavors, 3.6 oz	280	3	55
Oroweat: Oatmeal, 3.4 oz	270	4	49
Multi-Grain, 3.4 oz	260	1.5	51
Sara Lee: Mini, average, 1 oz	80	0	15
Toaster Size, all types, 2.2 oz	160	0.5	33
(95g) 3.4 oz Size: Egg	260	2	50
Other flavors, 3.4 oz	260	1	55
(113g) 4 oz Size:			
Apple Cinnamon	310	1.5	64
Banana Walnut	350	7	61
Chocolate Chip	320	3.5	61
Cranberry Orange	310	1.5	64
Honey & Oat	310	2	61
New York Style, 4 1/2 oz	330	1	69
Sun Dried Tomato Basil	300	1.5	61
The Works	330	3.5	62
Western: All flavors, aver., 3 oz	230	1	47

Bagels ~ see *Einstein Bros Bagels*, Pp 191
Bagel Sandwiches ~ See Pp 160

Bagel Spreads

	C	F	Cb
Cream Cheese: Plain, 1 oz	80	8	2
Reduced Fat, 1 oz	60	5	2
Flavors: Lox, 1 oz	75	6	1
Raisin Walnut, 1 oz	90	6	8
Strawberry, 1 oz	60	3	7
Sundried Tomato, 1 oz	80	7	2
Vegetable, 1 oz	60	6	1

Bread Products

	C	F	Cb
Bread Crumbs, dry:			
Plain or seasoned, 1 oz	110	1	20
1 rounded Tbsp, 10g	35	<1	6
1 cup, 3 1/2 oz	390	5	73
Corn Flake Crumbs, 1 oz	110	1	20
Graham Cracker Crumbs, 1 oz	115	1	21
Keebler, 1 cup, 4 1/4 oz	520	14	84
Bread Dough: Frozen, 1 slice	75	<1	14
Refrigerated, French, 1" sl.	60	1	13
Wheat/White, 1" sl.	80	2	14
Breadsticks: Boboli, 1.75 oz	130	2	22
Stella D'oro: Sesame, (1)	50	2	7
Plain/Onion/Wheat, 1 pce.	40	1	7
Keebler/Lance, 2 sticks	30	<1	6
Salt Sticks, plain, 1 oz	110	1	20
Croutons: Aver. all brands, 1 oz	100	3	17
2 Tbsp, 10g	35	1	6
Coating Mixes:			
Seasoned, average, 1 oz	110	3	20
Featherweight, 1.4 oz pkg	72	<1	17
Pretzels: See Snacks ~ Page 124			
Stuffing: Average, dry miz, 1 oz	110	1	10
Made-up, 1/2 cup, 4 oz	180	9	11

Croissants: *See Page 104*

Rice Cakes

	C	F	Cb
Average All Types/Brands:			
Regular size, 1 cake, 9g	35	0	7.5
Hain, Mini, average, 3g each	12	<1	2
Lundberg, all types, 15g each	60	<1	14
Quaker, large, all flavors, 13g each	50	0	11

Taco Shells

	C	F	Cb
Regular size, all types, each	55	3	6
Super Size, each	90	4	11
Mini Size, 1 taco	25	1.5	2
Salad Shell, flour (*Azteca*), 1.4 oz	180	11	19
Tortilla (Soft Taco), each	85	2	15
Corn Tortilla: 6", 1.2 oz each	45	0.5	9
Flour Tortilla: each, 1.75 oz	160	3	28
Lowfat	110	1.5	22
Burritos, 1 tortilla, 2.3 oz	190	5	32
Lowfat	110	1.5	22
Tostada Shells, each	55	3	6

Crispbreads

Per Crispbread/Cracker	C	F	Cb
Ak-Mak: Sesame, 5 crackers, 1 oz	35	0	7
Finn Crisp: Original, rye,1	35	0	7
Other types,1	19	0	3
Kavli Norwegian: Thin,1	17	0	3
Thick,1	20	0	3
Malsovit, Meal Wafers.1	75	4	7
New York Flatbread Crisps, 1	35	0	7
Ry-Krisp: Natural, 1 crispbread	20	0	3
Seasoned,1	30	0	5
Sesame,1	25	1	3
Ryvita: Dark/Light, 1 piece	26	0	4
WASA: Breakfast; Sesame	50	0	9
Extra Crisp; Light Rye	25	0	5
Hearty Rye	45	0	9
Organic Rye	25	0	7
Sourdough Flatbread, 3	50	0	11
Sourdough Rye	35	0	7

Matzos

Manischewitz			
American Matzos, 1 board, 1 oz	115	2	22
Passover Matzos, 1 board, 1.1 oz	130	0	27
Passover Egg Matzos, 1.1 oz	130	2	27
Egg 'n Onion Matzo, 1 oz	112	1	23
Thin Salted Tea Matzos, 0.9 oz	100	0	21
Unsalted; Whole Wheat, 1 oz	110	0	24
Dietetic Matzo Thins, 0.83 oz	90	0	19
Crackers: Miniatures, 1 cracker	9	0	20
Passover Egg Matzo, 1 cracker	11	0	20
Matzo Meal, 1 cup, 4 3/4 oz	515	2	110
Matzo Farfel, 1 cup, 2.7 oz	180	0.5	60
Grape Matzo, 1 oz each	110	0	25

Paul "Cookie" James

Quick Guide

Crackers

Average All Brands: Per Cracker	C	F	Cb
Cheese Crackers:			
Plain, 1" square	5	0	0.5
Small, octagonal	10	0	1
Round (2" diam.)	15	0	1.5
Sandwich (Peanut Butter)	35	1	4
Graham, 2 1/2" square,1 cracker	30	0.5	5
Melba Toast, plain, 1 piece	20	0	4
Oyster & Soup crackers, 1/4 oz (40 small oysters/20 lge hexagons)	60	2	10
Rice Crackers: 1 small	9	0	2
Rice Snax (*Amsnack*), 1/2 oz	60	1	12
Saltines, 2 crackers	25	1	4.5
Snack-type, 1 round cracker	15	0	3
Soda, 1 cracker, 1/2 oz	60	2	10
Water (*Carr's*), regular, 1 cracker	32	0	7
Bite-size, 1 cracker	13	0	4
Wheat, thin, 1 cracker	9	0	1
Zweiback Toast, 1 piece	30	0	5

Quick Guide

Cookies

Average All Brands: Per Cookie	C	F	Cb
Biscotti: Almond, 2.5 oz	55	2	8
Chocolate Chip Cookies:			
Small/Thin 0.5 oz	55	3	7
Regular, 1 oz	110	6	15
Large, 2.5 oz *(Mrs Field's)*	280	14	40
Jumbo, 4 oz	450	22	64
Oatmeal/Oatmeal Raisin:			
Small/Thin 0.5 oz	50	1.5	8
Regular, 1 oz	95	3.5	15
Large, 2.5 oz *(Mrs Field's)*	240	9	39
Jumbo, 4 oz	380	14	62
Peanut Butter:			
Small/Thin 0.5 oz	60	3	7
Regular, 1 oz	125	6.5	14
Large, 2.5 oz *(Mrs Field's)*	310	16	34
Jumbo, 4 oz	500	25	54
Lowfat Cookies			
Choc Chip (Lowfat), 1 oz (1)	100	1	21
Oatmeal Raisin (Fat-free), 1 oz (1)	90	0	20
Peanut Butter (Lowfat), 1 oz (1)	105	2	14

Brands	C	F	Cb
Per Cookie/Cracker (Unless Indicated)			
Archway			
Apple/Date-filled Oatmeal	**100**	3	16
Apricot/Strawb.-filled Oatmeal	**100**	3.5	16
Aunt Bea's Pound Cake Cookie	**100**	4	16
Coconut Macaroon	**100**	6	12
Chocolate Chip: Drop	**100**	3.5	15
Ice Box	**120**	6	15
N' Toffee	**130**	6	18
Fat-Free: Oatmeal Raisin (1)	**110**	0	25
Cinnamon Honey Heart (3)	**110**	0	25
Devil's Food Cookie (1)	**70**	0	16
Frosty Lemon/Orange	**110**	4.5	17
Fruit & Honey Bar	**100**	3.5	18
Ginger Snaps: Regular (5)	**150**	5	23
Reduced Fat (5)	**140**	3.5	25
Iced (5)	**150**	5	23
Lemon Snaps (5)	**150**	7	20
Molasses	**100**	3	18
Oatmeal: Regular; Raisin	**110**	3.5	17
Iced	**120**	5	19
Ol' Fashioned Peanut Butter	**120**	6	15
Old Fashioned Windmill	**90**	3.5	14
Peanut Butter Choc	**150**	7	17
Peanut Jumble	**110**	6	13
Pecan Icebox	**120**	6	15
Ruth's Golden Oatmeal	**120**	5	18
Sugar Cookies (1)	**100**	3	16
Austin: *Per Serving*			
Big Munch Wafer Bar, each	**200**	2.5	24
Cheese/Toast/Wheat Crackers, w. filling			
all types, average	**200**	2.5	29
Reduced Fat	**170**	1.5	25
Sandwich Cookies, all types	**240**	2	36
Smackers Crackers, all types	**130**	1	32
Zoo Animal Crackers, all types	**125**	1	20
Zoo Animal Pretzels	**200**	0	40
Bakery Wagon			
Iced Molasses, lowfat	**90**	1.5	18
Iced Oatmeal	**120**	4.5	18
Lemon Heaven	**120**	3.5	20
Peanut Butter	**130**	6	15
Sugarless Molasses	**120**	3	21
Fat-Free: Cobbler	**70**	0	16

Barbara's Bakery	C	F	Cb
Animal Cookies, each	**16**	0.6	2
Cheese Bites, all types, 26 crackers	**120**	1.5	24
Coconut Almond, 1 bar, 1 oz	**120**	4.5	20
Crisp Cookies, all types (1)	**80**	4	11
Espresso Bean; Lemon Yog., 1 bar	**120**	3.5	22
Fat Free: Mini, all types, each	**18**	0	4
Fig Bars, average	**60**	1	15
Rite Lite Rounds, 5 crackers	**55**	0.5	12
Roasted Peanut, 1 bar, 1 oz	**130**	4.5	20
Snackimals, 1 cookie	**15**	0.5	2
Wafer Crisps (3)	**60**	1	12
Wheatines, all types, 1 large square	**50**	1.5	10
Breadshop: Animal Cookies	**8**	0	1.5
Bremner			
Wafers: All varieties, 1 wafer	**10**	0.3	2
Breton: Low Sodium Wheat (3)	**70**	3	8
Vivant Vegetarian (3)	**60**	2.5	9
Cape Cod: Choc Chip Cranberry	**140**	6	20
Carr's: Cheddar (3)	**80**	4	8
Croissant (3)	**70**	3	10
Wholewheat Crackers (2)	**80**	3.5	11
Cheeze-It: Heads & Tails (31), 1 oz	**140**	6	18
Dare: Breton Wheat (3)	**60**	3	8
Delicious: Butter Finger (3)	**130**	6	18
Land O' Lakes (2)	**120**	6	15
Raisinets Oatmeal (3)	**140**	4.5	22
Skippy Peanut Butter (3)	**150**	10	13
Dominick's			
Grahams: Cinnamon (8)	**140**	5	22
Fudge (3)	**140**	7	19
Honey (8)	**150**	6	22
Lowfat (9)	**120**	1.5	25
Saltine Crackers (5)	**60**	2	10
Sugar Wafers (5)	**140**	7	25
Unsalted Tops (5)	**70**	2	10
Cookies: Choc Chip: Chewy (1)	**100**	5	14
Chunky (1)	**80**	4.5	10
Reduced Fat (3)	**150**	6	23
Old Fashioned: Assort.; Oatmeal	**80**	3.5	11
Pecan Shortbread	**100**	6	11
Sandwich Cremes: Chocolate	**70**	2.5	11
Vanilla	**80**	3	13
Striped Shortbread (3)	**160**	4	21
Vanilla Wafers (6)	**160**	6	23

Per Cookie/Cracker (Unless Indicated)

Entenmann's	C	F	Cb
Chocolate Brownie (2)	**150**	2	21
No Fat, 2 cookies	**100**	0	24
Original Choc Chip (3)	**150**	7	20
Soft Baked: Choc Chip	**100**	5	13
Gourmet English Toffee	**100**	5	13
Milk Choc Chip	**100**	5	13
Oatmeal Raisin, Fat Free (2)	**100**	0	23
White Choc Macadamia Nut (1)	**100**	6	12
Estee			
Chocolate Chip; Fudge Cookies	**38**	2	5
Coconut Cookies, Oatmeal Raisin	**35**	1.5	5
Fig Bars, each	**50**	0.5	11
Sandwich Cookies	**55**	2	6
Shortbread; Vanilla; Lemon	**35**	1.5	5
Famous Amos: Butter Shorties	**80**	4.5	10
Chocolate Chip (1)	**32**	1.5	5
4 cookies, 1 oz	**130**	7	19
with Pecans (1)	**35**	2	4.5
Choc Cake Sandwich (3)	**150**	7	23
Choc Chip & Pecans (4), 1 oz	**140**	8	18
Chocolate Chunk	**80**	4	10
Oatmeal Raisin (4), 1 oz	**135**	5	20
Pecan Shorties	**90**	5	10
Vanilla Sandwich (3)	**160**	6	23
Lowfat: Iced Lemon (7), 1.1 oz	**130**	1.5	25
Iced Gingersnaps (7), 1.1 oz	**120**	1.5	25
Frookie			
Cookies: Average all types	**45**	2	7
Animal Frackers	**10**	0.3	1.5
Apple Cinnamon Oatbran	**45**	2	7
Fruitins: Apple; Fig	**60**	1	12
Large Frooks: All types	**120**	4	18
Grandma's			
Choc Chip; Nutty Fudge	**190**	9	25
Fudge Choc Chip; Oatmeal Raisin	**170**	7	26
Old Time Molasses	**160**	4	29
Peanut Butter varieties, aver.	**190**	9	23
Cookie Bits: Average, (9)	**150**	7	22
Sandwich: Fudge (3)	**180**	5	31
Fudge Vanilla (3)	**120**	4	21
Vanilla (3)	**180**	5	32
Peanut Butter (5)	**210**	10	28
Rich & Chewy, 1 pkt	**270**	12	39
Sugar Wafers (3)	**160**	7	23
Tiny Bites (12)	**280**	12	39

Hain	C	F	Cb
Cheese Bites (22)	**120**	1.5	23
Cookie Jar Bits (Rice Cakes):			
Average all flavors, 17 bits	**60**	0.5	12
Mini Rice Cakes: Plain (8)	**60**	0	13
Oyster Crackers, Fat-Free (36)	**60**	0	13
Veg/Rice/Sesame Crackers (11)	**140**	6	19
98% Fat-Free, all types (11)	**110**	0	23
Health Valley			
Graham: Amaranth; Oat Bran	**15**	0	3
Original Amaranth/Oat Bran	**20**	0.5	4
Healthy Pizza, all flavors (6)	**50**	0	11
Lowfat, all flavors (6)	**60**	1.5	10
Original Rice Bran	**18**	0.5	3
Whole Wheat, all flavors	**10**	0	2
Cookies (each):			
Apple Spice; Hawaiian Fruit	**35**	0	8
Apricot Delight; Date Delight	**35**	0	8
Healthy Biscotti, all flavors	**60**	1.5	12
Healthy Choc./Chips, all flavors	**35**	0	8
Jumbo, all flavors	**80**	0	19
Raisin Oatmeal	**35**	0	8
Raspberry Fruit Center	**70**	0	18
Tarts: All types, 1 tart	**150**	0	35
Hy-Top			
Assorted Cookies (5), 1 oz	**120**	4	19
Assorted Sandwich Creme, aver.	**80**	3	12
Chewy-a-riffic	**90**	3.5	12
Chip-a-riffic (3)	**170**	9	23
Chocolate Chip (5), 1 oz	**110**	5	16
Cookie Time Assortment	**80**	3	12
Honey Cinnamon Grahams (2)	**120**	4	21
Oatmeal	**80**	3.5	11
Iced Oatmeal	**70**	3	11
Pecan-a-riffic	**100**	5	11
Sugar	**80**	3	12
Vanilla Wafers (8), 1 oz	**130**	5	21
Jewel			
Animal Crackers (9)	**140**	3.5	25
Chip-A-Riffic (3)	**180**	9	24
Choc/Vanilla Sandwich Creme (2)	**130**	5	20
Chocolate Chip: Regular (3)	**170**	9	23
Chewy (1)	**90**	3.5	12
Chunky (1)	**80**	4.5	10
Choc Chunk, 1 1/2 oz	**200**	9	26
Chocolate Sandwich Creme (2)	**120**	5	19
Cinnamon Grahams (8)	**140**	5	22

Per Cookie/Cracker (Unless Indicated)

Jewel (Cont)

	C	F	Cb
Cookie Jar Assortment (3)	150	9	23
Duplex Sandwich Creme (2)	120	5	19
Fudge Creme Wafer (3)	150	8	18
Fudge Marshmallow	110	4	18
Oatmeal; Oatmeal Old Fashioned	80	3.5	11
Peanut Butter (2)	140	5	21
Peanut Butter Chip, 1 1/2 oz	210	12	21
P'nut Butter Fudge Wafer (2)	140	8	14
Saltine Crackers; Unsalted Tops (5)	60	1.5	11
Striped Shortbread (3)	170	8	20
Sugar Wafers (5)	140	7	20
Unsalted Top Crackers (5)	70	2	10
White Choc Macadamia, 1 1/2 oz	200	10	26

Keebler

Crackers:

	C	F	Cb
Club: Orig.; 50% Red. Sodium (4)	70	3	9
33% Reduced Fat (5)	70	2	12
Grahams: Regular (8), 1 oz	130	3.5	23
Lowfat varieties (9), 1 oz	115	1.5	24
Snackin' (21), 1 oz	120	3.5	22
Munch'ems, average (40), 1 oz	140	5	20
Sandwich, 1 pkt, 1.3 oz	190	10	23
Snax Stix, average (20)	130	5	18
Toasted: Reduced Fat (5)	60	2	10
Regular varieties (5)	80	3.5	10
Town House: Regular (5)	80	4.5	9
Reduced Fat (6)	70	2	11
Wheatables: Reduced Fat (13)	130	4	21
Other varieties (12)	140	6	20
Cookies: Classic Collection (1)	80	3.5	12
Chips Deluxe: Soft & Chewy (1)	80	3.5	11
Peanut Butter Cup; Rainbow (1)	80	4.5	9
Chocolate Lovers; Coconut (1)	90	5	11
Crunchy Walnut; Chips Deluxe (1)	90	6	9
Cookie Stix (5)	140	6	22
Country Style Oatmeal (2)	120	6	15
Danish Wedding (4)	120	5	20
E.L. Fudge Sandwich (2)	120	6	17
Fudge Shoppe: S'mores (3)	160	8	22
Deluxe Grahams, Reg.(3)	140	7	19
Double Fudge 'n Caramel (2)	140	7	20
Fudge Sticks (3)	150	8	20
Fudge Stripes (3)	160	8	21
Reduced Fat (3)	140	5	21
Grasshopper (4)	150	7	20

Keebler (Cont)

Cookies (Cont):

	C	F	Cb
Ginger Snaps (5)	150	6	24
Golden Fruit (1)	80	2	14
Iced Animal, (6)	150	5	24
Krisp Kreem, (5)	140	7	19
Lemon Coolers (5)	140	5	23
Sandies: 25% Red. Fat	80	3	11
Regular varieties, average	80	5	9
Soft Batch, 0.5 oz all types, each	80	3.5	10
Choc Chunk types, 1 oz	130	7	17
Homestyle Oatmeal Raisin, 1 oz	130	4.5	20
Vienna Fingers: Regular (2)	140	6	21
Reduced Fat (2)	130	4.5	22
Wafers: Golden Vanilla Wafers (8)	150	7	20
Reduced Fat (8)	130	3.5	25
Rainbow (artif. flavored) (8)	130	5	20
Sugar: Vanilla (3)	130	6	19
Peanut Butter (4)	160	9	18

Lance

	C	F	Cb
Big Town, 1 pkg	250	11	38
Chocolate Chip, each	130	6	18
Dunking Sticks, each	180	10	22
Fig Bar, each	180	3.5	34
Fat Free: Apple/Cranberry, ea.	160	0	38
Oatmeal, each	130	6	18
Creme, each	240	10	35
Apple Bar, each	190	6	32
Peanut Butter, each	140	8	14
Peanut Butter Creme Wafer, 1 pkg	230	12	26

Lenell

	C	F	Cb
Almonettes (2)	80	4	10
Deluxe Assortment (2)	90	5	11
Icebox Pinwheels (2)	90	5	11
Jelly Stars (3)	100	5	13
Peanut Butter (3)	100	5	13

Lil' Dutch Maid

	C	F	Cb
Butter; Chip Delight (2)	80	3	11
Coconut Macaroons (2)	130	5	20
Creme: Chocolate/Duplex (2)	90	3	13
Strawberry/Vanilla, (2)	90	4	13
Oatmeal (2)	70	3	11
Iced Oatmeal (2)	80	3	11
Sugar (2)	80	4	10

Per Cookie/Cracker (Unless Indicated)

Little Debbie	C	F	Cb
Apple Flips	150	5	24
Chse Crackers w. P'nut Butter (4)	140	8	16
German Choc Cookie Rings	140	8	18
Ginger Cookies	90	3	15
Marshmallow Pies, each	160	6	27
Nutty Bar (2), 2 oz	310	18	32
Toasty Crackers w. P'nut Butter (4)	140	7	16
Yo-Yo's	130	6	21
Peanut Clusters, each	190	11	23
Figaroos, each, 1.5 oz	150	3.5	31
Peanut Butter & Jelly Sandwich	130	5	22
Lotte			
Chocolate (13), 1 oz	190	10	13
Koala Vanilla (13)	190	11	15
Koala Yummies (13), 1 oz	200	11	13
Peanut Butter (13)	190	10	11
Strawberry (13)	190	10	14
Lu Marie Lu			
Le Petit Beurre (4)	150	4	25
Le Petit Ecolier (2)	130	6	17
Le Truffe (4)	170	9	20
Pim's, Orange (2)	90	2.5	17
Mrs Fields' Cookies			
Per 1 Cookie, 2.5 oz			
Butter; Butter Toffee	290	12	40
Chewy Fudge	300	14	40
Coconut Macadamia	280	13	39
Debra's Special; Milk Choc	280	12	39
Milk Choc w. Walnuts	320	17	37
Milk Choc Macadamia	320	18	38
Oatmeal Raisin	240	9	39
Peanut Butter	310	16	34
Pumpkin Harvest	270	14	31
Semi-Sweet Chocolate	280	14	40
with Pecans	300	16	37
with Walnuts	310	16	38
Triple Chocolate	300	14	41
White Chunk Macadamia	310	17	37
Nibblers: *Per 2 Cookies, 1 oz*			
Debra's Special	100	4.5	13
Milk Choc w/Walnuts	120	6	14
Milk Chocolate; Peanut Butter	110	6	15
White Chunk Macadamia	120	7	13

Per Cookie/Cracker (Unless Indicated)

Mama's	C	F	Cb
Cremes: All varieties (3)	150	6	23
Manischewitz			
Matzo Boards ~ See Page 96			
Biscotti: Toffee Crunch Macaroons	50	2.5	7
Choc. Chip Cappucino	70	2.5	10
Chocolate Macaroons, each	45	2	8
Matzo Cracker, Miniatures	9	0	2
Whole Wheat Crackers	9	0	2
Marie Lu: Original Biscuit (3)	170	6	25
Matt's: Choc Chip	140	6	19
Oatmeal Raisin	120	4	20
Peanut Butter	140	6.5	18
Mother's Brand			
1.2.3. Cookies (1)	10	0.5	2
ABC Cinnamon Grahams (1)	12	0.5	1.5
ABC Sugar Cookies (1)	12	0.5	1.5
Almond Shortbread	60	4	6
Butter Cookies; Wafers, all types	25	1	4
Checkerboard Wafers	20	1	3
Chocolate Chip: Cookies	80	4	10
Cookies (bag) (1)	30	1	5
Cookie Parade Assortment, each	35	1.5	5
Chocolate Chip Parade	35	1.5	5
Angel Cookies	60	3	7
Circus Animal Cookies	25	1	3
Cocodas Coconut	30	2	4
Dinosaur Grrrahams	65	1.5	12
Double Fudge	90	4.5	12
English Tea/Taffy Sandwich	90	3.5	13
Flaky Flix Fudge/Vanilla	70	3.5	8
Gaucho Peanut Butter S'wich	95	5	11
Iced Raisin; Macaroon	80	4	9
Marias	55	2	9
Oatmeal Cookies: Regular	55	2.5	9
Iced; Chocolate Chip	65	2	11
Oatmeal Raisin Cookies	30	2	4
Oatmeal Walnut Choc. Chip	65	3	9
Striped Shortbread Cookies	55	2.5	7
Sugar Cookies	70	3	10
Taffy	90	4	13
Wallops, all types	80	1.5	15
Walnut Fudge	65	3.5	8
Zoo Pals	10	0.5	1

Per Cookie/Cracker (Unless Indicated)

Murray	C	F	Cb
Butter Cookies (8)	**130**	4	20
Sugar Free: All types (3)	**120**	6	20
Oatmeal (6)	**120**	4	23
Peanut Butter (6)	**130**	7	17
Wafers: Lemon/Strawb./Vanilla (8)	**150**	8	21
Ginger Snap Cookies (6)	**110**	4	21

Nabisco: *Per Cookie/Cracker, Unless Indicated*

	C	F	Cb
Crackers: Cheese Nips (29), 1 oz	**140**	6	20
Air Crisps: Ritz, 1 oz (23)	**140**	5	22
Potato varieties, 1 oz (22)	**120**	3.5	21
Pretzel Original, 1 oz (23)	**110**	1	22
Wheat Thins, 1 oz (23)	**130**	4.5	21
Bacon Flavored Thins (7), 1/2 oz	**80**	4	9
Better Cheddars: Reg; Low Salt	**7**	0.3	1
Chicken in a Biskit (7), 1/2 oz	**80**	5	9
Garden Crisps (7), 1/2 oz	**60**	2	10
Oysterettes (19), 1/2 oz	**60**	2.5	10
Ritz; Wheatsworth; Stoneground (1)	**16**	1	2
Ritz Bits S'wiches: Chse (14), 1.1 oz	**170**	10	17
Cheese, 1 3/4 pkg	**270**	16	28
Royal Lunch (1)	**50**	2	8
Snackwell's Red. Fat Fr. Onion (32)	**120**	2	24
Sociables (7)	**80**	4	9
Swiss (7), 1/2 oz	**70**	3.5	10
Tid Bit, cheese (16), 1/2 oz	**70**	4	8
Triscuit Thin Crisps (14)	**130**	5	20
Triscuit Wafers: All types	**20**	1	1
Uneeda, Unsalted Tops	**30**	1	5
Vegetable Thins (7), 1/2 oz	**80**	4.5	9
Waverly (5)	**70**	3.5	10
Wheat/Oat Thins: (8), 1/2 oz	**70**	2	10
Big Wheat Thins (11)	**140**	6	20
Zings! 1 pkg, 1.8 oz	**240**	11	34
Cookies:			
Barnum's Animal Crackers	**12**	0.5	23
Biscos: Sugar Wafers	**17**	1	24
Waffle Cremes	**35**	2	22
Brown Edge Wafers	**28**	1	4
Bugs Bunny Graham Cookies	**12**	0.5	5
Café Creme: Vanilla Fudge (2)	**200**	10	27
Vanilla; Cappuccino (2)	**160**	8	22
Cameo Creme Sandwich	**65**	2.5	10
Choc Cherry Bar, 1 bar	**130**	2	26
Chocolate Chip Bite Size	**10**	0.3	2

Nabisco (Cont): *Per Cookie/Wafer*

	C	F	Cb
Chocolate Chip Honey Grahams	**5**	0.2	1
Chocolate Snaps	**17**	0.5	3
Chocolate Wafers (Red. Fat)	**14**	0.2	3
Chips Ahoy: Chewy	**60**	3	8
Choc. Chip; Sprinkled; Red. Fat	**50**	2	7
Chunky	**80**	4	10
Mini	**12**	0.5	2
Soft Cookies (2-Pack), 1 cookie, 39g	**160**	7	26
Other types, average	**95**	5	11
Cookie Break; Van. Crm. S'wich	**53**	2	8
Famous Chocolate Wafers	**28**	1	5
Fig Newtons, each	**55**	1	11
Fat Free, each	**35**	0	11
Grahams	**15**	0.5	3
Honey Maid: Grahams, all types (2)	**30**	0.5	6
Low Fat Cinnamon Grahams (2)	**28**	0.4	6
Ideal Bars: Chocolate & Peanut	**90**	5	10
Lorna Doone: Shortbread	**35**	2	4
Marshmallow Puffs; Mystic Mint	**90**	4	14
Marshmallow Twirls	**140**	6	20
Newtons: Tropical; Strawb., aver (2)	**90**	1	21
Cobblers, all varieties	**50**	0	12
Nilla Wafers: Regular; Cinnamon	**15**	0.5	3
Reduced Fat (1)	**15**	0.3	3
Nutter Butter: Chocolate	**65**	4	9
Bites, each	**15**	0.6	2
Peanut Butter Sandwich	**65**	3	10
Soft Cookies (2-Pack), 1 cookie, 39g	**170**	8	22
Oatmeal Crunch	**15**	0.5	3
Old Fash. Ginger Snaps	**30**	0.6	5
Oreo: Regular, 3 cookies	**160**	7	23
Reduced Fat, 3 cookies	**130**	3.5	25
Double Stuf, 2 cookies	**140**	7	19
Fudge-Covered, 1 cookie	**110**	6	14
Mini Oreos, 9 pieces, 1 oz	**140**	6	21
Pecanz	**90**	5	9
Pinwheels: Choc./Marshmallow	**130**	5	21
Snackwell's Red. Fat Vanilla Creme	**65**	1.5	10
Teddy Grahams Snacks: All types	**5**	0.1	1

Pepperidge Farm	C	F	Cb
American Collection: Sante Fe	**120**	4.5	18
Average other flavors	**140**	7	16
Biscotti: Figaro	**110**	4	14
Caruso; La Scala; Tosca	**90**	3	13
Chocolate Chunk Minis (4)	**150**	8	20
Fruit Cookies: Cherry Cobbler	**70**	2.5	11
Average other flavors	**50**	2	7

Per Cookie/Cracker (Unless Indicated)

Pepperidge Farm (Cont)

	C	F	Cb
Distinctive: Bordeaux; Pirouette	35	2	5
Brussels	50	2.5	7
Brussels Mint; Milano	65	3	7
Chantilly Hazelnut Raspberry	80	3	12
Chessman; Toy Chest Butter	40	1.5	6
Double Choc. Milano	75	4	8
Endless Choc. Milano	180	10	21
Geneva	55	3	6
Hazelnut Milano	65	3.5	8
Lido	90	4.5	11
Linzer Strawberry Filled	100	4	15
Milk Choc. Bordeaux	60	3	7
Milk Choc. Milano	170	9	21
Mint/Orange Milano	70	4	8
Goldfish: Plain, 55 pces, 30g	140	6	19
Chocolate (19)	140	5	22
Choc. Chunk; Van.; Cinnamon (19)	150	7	21
International: Esprits Noir	90	5	10
Chocolat A L'Orange; Medaillon	75	3	12
Nantucket: Choc Chunk Minis (4)	150	8	20
Old Fashioned: Hazelnut	55	2.5	7
Brownie; Butterscotch Oatmeal	55	3	6
Chocolate Chip; Irish Oatmeal	45	2.5	6
Gingerman; Molasses Crisps	30	1	5
Lemon Nut Crunch	60	3	6
Oatmeal Raisin	55	2	8
Pecan Shortbread	70	4.5	7
Shortbread	70	3.5	8
Sugar	45	2	7
Sausalito: Choc Macadamia (4)	160	9	18
Soft Baked: Caramel; Choc Chunk	130	6	13
Choc. Macadamia/Walnut	130	6	16
Oatmeal Raisin	110	4	17
Vanilla Raspberry Tart	60	1.5	12

President's Choice

	C	F	Cb
Animal Crackers (14)	150	5	25
Butter Pecan (2)	190	13	17
Choc Chip Pecan (2)	160	9	18
Decadent: Choc Chip, all var., (2)	160	8	19
Family Arrowroot (5)	140	4	25
Grandma's Butter First (2)	180	10	20
Peanut Butter First (3)	160	9	16
Peanut Butter Persuasion (2)	160	8	18
Raisins First (2)	120	6	15
Temptations: Key Lime (2)	150	7	20
Other varieties (2)	140	5	21

Pirouline

	C	F	Cb
Pirouline, 8 rolls, 1 oz	130	3.5	23

Sinful

	C	F	Cb
Sinful: Chocolate Chip (2)	150	7	19
All Butter Raisin & Oatmeal (2)	130	6	20
Butter w. Soft Creme Raspberry (1)	70	3	12
Choc w. Vanilla Creme (2)	120	5	16

Salerno

	C	F	Cb
Almond Windmill (2)	120	4.5	17
Bonnie Shortbread (4)	160	7	22
Butter Cookies: Original (6)	160	7	22
Reduced Fat (6)	150	5	22
Coconut Bar (4)	150	8	18
Creme Wafer Sugar-free (5)	190	13	18
Dinosaur Graham	70	2.5	11
Farm Animal Crackers (13)	140	5	22
Grahams: Cinnamon (2)	130	3.5	22
Chocolate (2)	130	3	24
Iced Oatmeal (2)	120	5	18
Mini Butter: Flavored (25)	150	6	20
Angel/Chocolate Creme (9)	140	6	20
Mini Dinosaur (15)	140	5	21
Mint Creme Patties (2)	130	7	16
Oyster Crackers: Regular (42)	60	1.5	11
Fat-Free (42)	60	0	12
Royal Crispy Stix (3)	150	8	18
Royal Stripes (3)	180	8	24
Saltine Crackers: Regular (5)	60	1.5	11
Fat-Free (5)	50	0	11
Unsalted Tops (5)	60	1.5	11
Santa's Favorites, aniseed (6)	150	5	22
Scooter Pie Choc Marshmallow	140	5	23
Sugar Wafers, assorted (5)	180	11	20
Vanilla Wafers (7)	130	5	21

Snackwell's

	C	F	Cb
Snackwell's: Caramel Delights	70	2	13
Chocolate Chip (2)	20	0.5	3
Choc/Creme Sandwich; Oatmeal	55	1.5	10
Coconut Creme (2)	110	4	19
Streusel Squares	150	3	31

Stella D'Oro (Cont)

	C	F	Cb
Angel Bars	**80**	5	7
Almond Toast Cookie	**55**	1	10
Anginetti (4)	**140**	4	23
Anisette Sponge (2)	**90**	1	19
Anisette Toast (3)	**130**	1	27
Apple Pastry	**80**	3	14
Breakfast Treats	**100**	3	16
Biscotti (Hazelnut)	**100**	3.5	15
Castelets, regular/chocolate	**70**	3	9
Dutch Apple Bars	**110**	3	19
Egg Biscuits, Low Sodium	**40**	1	7
Egg Jumbo	**50**	1	9
Fruit Delight Apple Cinnamon	**70**	0	17
Golden Bars; Love Cookies	**110**	4	16
Kichel, low sodium	**7**	0.4	0.5
Lady Stella Assortment (3)	**130**	5	19
Margherite, chocolate/vanilla	**70**	2.5	11
Peach Apricot/Prune Pastry	**90**	4	14
Swiss Fudge	**70**	3	9

Sunshine

***Crackers:** Per Cracker, Unless Indicated*

	C	F	Cb
Cheez-It Crackers	**6**	0.3	0.5
Big Cheez-It	**12**	1	1
Heads & Tails, 1 pkt, 1.5 oz	**210**	9	28
Hi-Ho Crackers	**17**	0.5	2
Reduced Fat	**14**	0.5	2
Krispy: Regular	**12**	0.3	2
Oyster & Soup, 17 crackers	**60**	1.5	11
Reduced Fat	**10**	0	2
Party Mix, 1 pkt, 1.7 oz	**230**	9	32
Reduced Fat, 1/2 cup, 1 oz	**130**	3	21

Voortman

	C	F	Cb
Lemon Lucullan Delights (1)	**110**	5	16
Mini Chips, 1 oz (5)	**135**	6	19
Mini Wafers, 1 oz (5)	**150**	8	19

Waldbaum's

	C	F	Cb
Champagne Biscuits Saviordi (4)	**110**	0.5	25

Weight Watchers

	C	F	Cb
Apple Raisin Bars, each	**70**	2	14
Chocolate Chip (2)	**140**	5	22
Choc. S'wich Cookies (2)	**140**	3.5	23
Fruit Filled, 1 bar	**70**	0	16
Oatmeal Raisin (2)	**120**	2	22
Vanilla Sandwich Cookies	**140**	3	25

Thaw, Bake & Serve

	C	F	Cb
Big Country: Aver. all types (1)	**100**	4	15
Cookietree: *Per Cookie*			
Buttersugar; Cinn. Apple Oatmeal	**120**	5	17
Choc. varieties; Pecan/Macadam.	**130**	7	17
Cookie w. *M&M's*; Dble Fudge	**120**	6	17
Fat Free varieties, average	**125**	0	28
Peanut Butter/Chocolate	**130**	7	17
Raisin Oatmeal	**110**	3.5	18
Guiltless Indulgence (1.3 oz Cookie)			
Fat Free varieties, aver.	**120**	0	28
Lowfat Fudge/Choc., aver.	**130**	2	28
Grands!: *Per Biscuit*			
Blueberry; Golden Corn	**210**	9	28
Butter Tastin'; Buttermilk	**200**	10	24
Reduced Fat	**190**	7	27
Cinn. Raisin; Extra Fluffy; Wheat	**200**	8	28
Extra Rich	**220**	12	25
Flaky; Homestyle	**200**	10	25
Southern Style	**200**	10	24
Hungry Jack: Aver. all types (1)	**100**	4.5	14
Jewel			
Buttermilk Biscuits (2)	**100**	1.5	20
Old Fashioned Biscuits (2)	**100**	1.5	20
Pillsbury Cookies: *Per 1 oz*			
Buttermilk; Country, each	**50**	1	3
M & Ms	**130**	6	17
Choc. Chip/Dbl Choc Chip Chunk	**140**	7	17
Choc. Chip. Reduced Fat	**110**	4	18
Chocolate Chip w. Walnuts	**130**	7	16
Holiday, all types (2), 1 oz	**130**	7	16
Oatmeal Choc. Chip; Reeses	**125**	6	16
Peanut Butter	**120**	6	18
SnackWells, Choc. Chip, Red. Fat	**110**	3	19
SnackWells, Chocolate Fudge	**90**	1.5	18
Sugar (2), 1 oz	**130**	5	20
Tender Layer Buttermilk	**160**	4.5	9
One Step Pan Cookies	**130**	6	19
Toll House (*Nestlé*)			
Choc Chip	**140**	6	20
Reduced Fat Choc Chip	**130**	3.5	23
Choc. Chip White; Chunk	**150**	6	22
Peanut Butter Choc Chip	**150**	7	20
Sugar	**120**	5	18

Ready-to-Eat

Angel Food:	C	F	Cb
Plain, no oil, 2 oz	120	0	25
Plain with oil, 2 oz	160	1.5	25
w. Cream Frosting	230	7	37
Apple Fritters, 3 oz	360	22	38
Apple Pie: See Pies/Tarts Page 107			
Baklava, 1 1/2" square, 1 1/2 oz	110	6	13
Banana w. Butter Cream, 3 oz	300	13	40
Black Forest, 3 oz	230	10	34
Brownie, 3.5 oz	420	25	52
Bundt, 3 oz	300	17	35
Carrot Cake: Plain, 3 oz	230	8	41
w. Cream Cheese Frosting	380	21	42
Cheesecake: Small serving, 3 oz	260	18	24
Large serving, 5 oz	430	30	40
w. Lowfat Cheese/fruit, 3 oz	150	8	30
Cheesecake Factory: 1 sl., 7 oz	700	48	56
Lite, 1 slice, 7 oz	570	28	60
Denny's Cheesecake, 1 slice	470	27	48
Cherry Cobbler, 5 oz	350	10	62
Chocolate Cake: Plain, 2 oz	220	11	40
w. Chocolate Frosting, 3 oz	320	15	42
& Cream Filling, 3 1/2 oz	360	21	43
Cinnamon Crumb Cake, 4 oz	450	23	57
Cinnamon Roll, Large, 6 oz	630	27	87
Coffee Cake, 2 1/2 oz	230	7	38
Cream Cheese Crumb, 4 oz	410	20	52
Cream Puff (custard fill), 4 1/2 oz	300	18	26
Creme Horns, each	190	13	19
Croissants: See Next Column			
Cupcake: Plain, 1 1/2 oz	140	6	25
w. Frosting	170	7	30
Danish Pastry: Small, 2 oz	220	10	25
Large, 4 oz	440	20	51
Date Nut Roll, 1/2" slice	80	2	12
Devil's Food, w. Frosting, 3 oz	460	25	55
Donut Holes, 1 1/4" balls, 2 oz (5)	220	10	30
Donuts: See Page 106			
Eclair, Choc., Cust. fill, 3 1/2 oz	240	14	23
Fig Bars, average, each	150	3	30
Fig Cake, 1/2 piece	110	2	21
Fruit Cake, Dark/Light, 1 1/2 oz	165	7	26
Fudge Nut Brownie, each	340	13	56
Gingerbread: From mix, 3" sq.	200	6	37
Honey Bun, each	330	13	47
Key Lime Pie, 4.5 oz	440	22	54
Kolacky, Apricot/Rasp., 1/2 oz (1)	60	3.5	8

Ready-to-Eat (Cont)

	C	F	Cb
Lemon Cake, 2 1/2 oz piece	220	9	40
Lemon Poppy Seed Creme, 3 oz	310	15	40
Mississippi Mud Pie, 4 oz	380	24	37
Mud Cake, 1 piece, 3 1/2 oz	350	16	48
Muffins: See Next Page			
Orange Creme (Ring), 3 oz	300	15	40
Pineapple Upside Down, 2 1/2 oz	230	9	37
Peach Melba, 3 1/2 oz	300	8	52
Strawberry Creme, 3 oz	290	14	40
Strudel Bites, 3/4 oz	85	4	12
Pecan Twirls, 1 piece	110	5	16
Pecan Pie, 3 oz	330	13	51
Pies & Tarts: See Page 107			
Pound Cake, 3 oz	420	27	42
Sponge: Plain, 2 1/2 oz	190	3	36
w. Cream & Strawberry	325	8	38
w. Chocolate Icing	300	12	38
Raisin Bun, 1 bun, 2 1/4 oz	180	2	37
Strudel, fruit, average, 3 oz	280	8	45
Sweet Roll, average, 1 1/2 oz	155	7	24
Swiss Rolls, each	170	9	23
Tarts: See Page 107			
Tiramisu, 1 piece, 5 oz	400	29	30
Toaster Strudel, 2 oz	190	10	26
Turnovers, fruit, average, 3 oz	270	12	36

Croissants

Average All Brands	C	F	Cb
Plain/All Butter:			
Petite, 1 oz	120	7	14
1 Medium, 1 1/2 oz	180	10	21
1 Large, 2 1/2 oz	300	18	35
Sweet: *Per Croissant, 3 1/2 oz*			
Almond Croissant	420	25	39
Apple Croissant	250	10	30
Chocolate Croissant	400	24	36
Sandwich (Ham/Cheese), 5 oz ~ See Page 160			
Au Bon Pain: See Page 164			
Burger King: Croissan'wich-See Page 173			
Dunkin' Donuts: Plain	290	18	26
Almond	350	22	34
Chocolate	400	25	37
Sara Lee:			
All Butter, 1 1/2 oz	180	9	19
All Butter Petite, 1 oz	120	6	13

Quick Guide

Muffins: Ready-to-Eat

	C	F	Cb
Average All Types:			
Small, 1 oz	**80**	3	12
Medium, 2 oz	**160**	6	24
Large, 3 oz	**240**	9	36
Extra Large, 4 oz	**320**	12	48
Jumbo, 6 oz	**480**	18	60
English: Average, 1 muffin	**150**	2	29

Brands ~ Ready-To-Eat

	C	F	Cb
Awreys			
Blueberry, 2.25 oz	**210**	9	29
Raisin Bran, 2.5 oz muffin	**190**	7	30
Carl's: Blueberry Muffin	**340**	14	49
Bran Muffin	**370**	13	61
Dunkin' Donuts: See Page 188			
Hostess: Mini, average, each	**55**	3	7
Blueberry; Raspberry, each, 4 oz	**440**	19	62
Jewel: English Muffin, 2 oz	**130**	1	25
McDonald's: Apple Bran, 4 oz	**300**	3	61
Oroweat:			
Cinnamon Rais., 2.4 oz	**170**	1	35
Extra Crisp; Sourdough, 2 oz	**130**	0.5	26
Health Nut, 2.3 oz	**170**	3	30
Otis Spunkmeyer: *Per Whole Muffin (4 oz)*			
Banana Nut, 4 oz	**480**	24	60
Cheese Streudel	**440**	20	60
Wild Blueberry	**420**	22	48
Our Daily Muffin: Each, 3 oz	**120**	0	31
Pepperidge Farm: Average	**150**	3	28
Ralphs: Banana, 4.5 oz muffin	**470**	21	62
Blueberry, 4.5 oz	**410**	16	60
Bran & Raisin, 5 oz	**380**	8	78
Sara Lee: Blueberry	**220**	11	27
Corn	**260**	14	30
Snackwell's: Blueberry, 1/6 pkt	**120**	0	28
Weight Watchers: *Per Muffin*			
Chocolate Chocolate Chip	**190**	2	39
English Muffin Sandwich	**210**	5	28
Fat Free, average, all flavors	**165**	0	39
Low Fat, average, all flavors	**175**	3	37

Muffin Mixes

	C	F	Cb
Prepared: Per Muffin			
Betty Crocker: Banana Nut	**150**	5	24
Cinnamon Streusel	**170**	7	22
Lemon Poppyseed	**190**	7	30
Twice the Blueberry	**140**	4	25
Fat Free, all flavors	**120**	0	26
Duncan Hines: Blueberry, reg.	**120**	3	21
Bakery Style: Blueberry	**190**	6	32
Cinnamon Swirl	**200**	7	32
Cranberry Orange Nut	**200**	8	29
Pecan Crunch	**220**	11	27
Cinnamon Topp. Oatbran Honey	**140**	5	21
Oat Bran Blueberry	**110**	4	17
Oatmeal & Apples/Walnuts	**210**	9	30
Pillsbury: Blueberry Lowfat	**160**	2	34
Cinnamon	**160**	4	27
Other varieties	**180**	5	30
Robin Hood: Blueberry; Corn	**160**	6	24
Other flavors	**170**	8	23
Sweet Rewards: Fat Free	**120**	0	28

Sweet Rolls & Buns

	C	F	Cb
Cinnabon			
Classic Cinnabon, 1 serving	**730**	24	114
Caramel Pecanbon, 1 serving	**1100**	56	141
Minibon, 1 serving	**300**	11	45
Entenmann's: Cinn. Bun, 2.15 oz	**230**	10	32
Reduced Fat, 2.15 oz	**160**	3	32
Pecan Danish Ring, 1/6, 2 oz	**250**	15	25
Twist: Raspberry, 1/8, 2 oz	**220**	11	27
Nonfat, 1/8, 2 oz	**140**	0	32
Cinnamon Danish, 1/8, 2 oz	**240**	13	29
Lemon Danish, 1/8, 2 oz	**210**	11	26
Walnut Danish Ring, 1/8, 2 oz	**240**	15	25
Hostess: Honey Bun: Glazed	**320**	19	34
Iced/Frosted, 3.4 oz	**410**	24	42
Jewel Bake Shop			
Cinnamon Swirl Bread, 1 oz sl.	**160**	2.5	30
Gourmet Cinn. Rolls, 6 oz roll	**640**	29	88
Little Debbie: Pecan Spinwheels, 1 oz	**110**	4	16
Mickey: Cinnamon Pastry, 4 oz	**200**	5.5	35
Cinnamon Nut, 2 1/2 oz	**230**	8	37
Raisin Cinnamon, 2 1/2oz	**200**	4.5	35
Pillsbury: Cinnamon Roll, 1.5 oz	**150**	5	23
Reduced Fat, 1.5 oz	**140**	3.5	24

Donuts

Quick Guide

	C	F	Cb
Donuts			
Average All Brands			
Plain, 1 3/4 oz	210	12	25
Sugared, 1 3/4 oz	220	11	27
Glazed, 2 oz	250	12	34
Chocolate Iced, 2 oz	260	14	29

Brands

	C	F	Cb
Buttercrumb			
Cinnamon, 1 cake, 1.6 oz	170	6	28
Dolly Madison Donuts			
Regular, 1 3/4 oz	270	12	40
Gem varieties, 1/2 oz each	65	3	8
Powdered Mini, 1/2 oz each	60	3	8
Dunkin' Donuts: *See Fast-Foods Section ~ Page188*			
Dutch Mill: Plain, 1 3/4 oz	210	12	25
Sugared, 1 3/4 oz	220	11	27
Glazed, 2 oz	250	12	34
Double-Dipped Chocolate, 2 oz	280	17	31
Entenmann's Donuts			
Cinnamon Powdered, 1 3/4 oz	240	15	24
Frosted Devil's Food, 2.4 oz	310	19	34
Glazed Buttermilk, 2 1/4 oz	270	13	35
Light, 2 oz	190	7	31
Light Fantastic Fudge, 2 oz	210	9	40
Light Fantastic Fudge, 2 oz	210	9	40
Milk Chocolatey, 2.4 oz	310	19	35
Rich, Frosted, 3 pces, 2 oz	280	18	26
Hostess Donuts			
Cinnamon Sweet Roll, 2 oz	220	7	36
Regular: Plain, 1 oz	140	7	15
Chocolate Frosted, 1 1/2 oz	180	11	19
Pwd Sugar/Cinnamon, 1 1/2 oz	210	10	25
Old Fashioned; Glazed, 1 1/2oz	180	9	23
Blueberry, 1 1/2 oz	210	13	21
Hostess O's, Raspberry, 2 oz	230	10	34
Donettes: Frosted, 1/2 oz	77	4.5	8
Crumb; 1/2 oz	57	2.5	8
Powdered, 1/2 oz	84	4	12
Jewel			
Cinnamon Spiced, 2 oz	230	15	24
Little Debbie Donuts			
Donut Sticks, 1.6 oz pkg	210	13	21
3 oz pkg	390	23	39

Brands (Cont)

	C	F	Cb
Mickey			
Egg Fluff, 2, 1.65 oz	210	11	25
French Twirl, 2, 1.65 oz	240	16	21
Jumbo, aver. all types, 1, 1.5 oz	190	11	21
Mini, 2, 1 oz	130	8	15
Sara Lee Donuts			
Choc. Frosted Mini, 3/4 oz each	100	5.5	13
Powdered Mini, 1/2 oz each	85	4.5	9
Glazed, 1/2 oz each	110	5	14
Reduced Fat, 1/2 oz each	55	2.5	8
Tastykake Donuts			
Plain, 1 1/2 oz	190	10	22
Cinnamon, 1 1/2 oz	180	8	26
Frosted Rich, 2 oz	260	16	28
Honey Wheat, 2 oz	210	8	32
Powdered Sugar, 1 1/2 oz	180	9	24
Van De Kamp's Donuts			
Old Fashioned: Plain	270	11	40
Chocolate, 2.4 oz	340	22	34
Powdered, 2 oz	240	11	35
Assorted, 2 1/4 oz	280	17	32
Mini Donuts: Chocolate, 4, 2 oz	290	17	32
Crumb, 4	220	8	35
Powdered, 4	250	12	33
Lowfat: Maple Buttermilk, 1	200	2	43
Chocolate Buttermilk, 1	200	2	43
Double Chocolate, 1	190	2.5	41
Powdered, 1	150	1.5	32
Zingers			
Devil's/Vanilla Food, 2 cakes	280	8	50

Quick Guide

Pies

Average All Brands *1/8 of 9" Pie, 4 oz Serving*	C	F	Cb
Apple; Blueberry; Cherry	290	13	46
Boston Cream Pie	330	14	55
Chocolate Pie	300	18	35
Custard; Coconut Custard	250	13	27
Lemon Chiffon Pie	360	14	50
Lemon Meringue	270	11	42
Mince Pie	300	13	46
Pecan Pie	470	24	52
Pumpkin Pie	240	13	28
Strawberry Pie	230	9	86

Brands

Per Serving	C	F	Cb
Denny's: Apple Pie	470	22	64
Cherry Pie	630	25	100
Chocolate Peanut Butter	655	39	64
Chocolate Silk Pie	650	43	60
Dutch Apple Pie	440	19	65
Hershey's Choc Chunks N' Chips	600	36	58
Oreo® Cookies & Creme	690	30	73
Pumpkin Pie	235	7	38
Entenmann's			
Homestyle Apple, 1/6 pie, 4.3 oz	340	12	56
Hostess			
Fruit; Cherry, 4.5 oz pie	470	22	65
Lemon, 4.5 oz pie	500	24	66
Long John Silver: *Per Serving*			
Chocolate Cream Pie	280	17	29
Double Lemon Pie	350	18	41
Key Lime Cream Cheesecake	310	19	33
McDonald's: Apple Pie, 2 3/4 oz	260	13	34
Mickey			
Apple/Cherry Fruit Pie, aver.	500	30	55
Sweet Rolls: Cinn. Pastry, 4 oz	200	5.5	35
Cinnamon Nut, 2 1/2 oz	230	8	37
Raisin Cinnamon, 2 1/2 oz	200	4.5	35
Mrs Bairds: Apple Pie, 4.2 oz	400	19	56
Cherry Fruit Pie, 4.2 oz	400	19	56
Tastykake: Fruit, average	310	11	50
French Apple	360	12	61
Coconut Creme	390	20	47

Pastry & Pie Crusts

Pie Crust:	C	F	Cb
Baked, 9" diameter shell			
1 Pie Shell, 6 1/2 oz	900	60	79
2-crust Pie, 9", 11 1/4 oz	1500	93	137
Betty Crocker, 9", 1/8 shell	110	8	9
Boboli, thin Pizza Crust, 1/5, 2 oz	160	4	24
Jewel, 1/8 of 9" crust	130	8	13
Keebler Graham Cracker, 1/8 of 9"	110	5	14
Mrs Smith's Deep Dish, 9" (1/8)	110	7	11
Nabisco Oreo, 1/6 of 9" crust	140	7	18
Pet-Ritz, all types, 1/8, 3/4 oz	90	5	11
Pillsbury (All Ready), 1/8 pie, 1 oz	120	7	13
Piecrust Sticks, 8 oz	960	64	90
Choux Pastry, raw, 1 oz	60	4	3
Filo Pastry: 4 sheets, 2 1/2 oz	210	2.5	40
Athens: 1/8 pkg, 2 oz	180	1	35
Mini Dough Shells, 2, 8g	45	2	1
Pepp. Farm, 2 sheets, 1 1/2oz	120	1	25
Flaky Pastry, 1 sheet, 6 oz	780	72	18
Puff *(Pepp.Farm),* 1/2 sheet, 4.5 oz	510	33	42
1/6 sheet, 1 1/2 oz	170	11	14
Bake & Fill Shell, 1.7 oz	190	13	16
Pizza Crust, 1/8 whole	90	1	16
***Bisquick* Baking Mix:**			
Original, 1/3 cup, 1 1/2 oz	170	6	25
Reduced Fat, 1/3 cup, 1 1/2 oz	150	2.5	28

Pie Filling

Canned: Average All Brands	C	F	Cb
Apple, 4 oz	120	0	28
1 Can, 21 oz	600	0	145
Apricot, 4 oz	150	0	36
Blackberry, Blueberry, 4 oz	120	0	28
Bosenberry, Cherry, 4 oz	120	0	28
Chocolate, Coconut, 4 oz	140	3	33
Lemon, 4 oz	200	2	47
Mincemeat, 4 oz	190	1	45
Peach, 4 oz	120	0	28
Pumpkin, 4 oz	170	0	40
Libby, 1/2 cup	100	0	23
Raisin, 4 oz	130	0	30
Raspberrry, Black/Red, 4 oz	190	0	45
Strawberry, 4 oz	120	0	28

Cakes & Pastries	C	F	Cb
Amy's: Apple Pie, 8 oz	280	12	42
Banquet: Crm Pies, aver., 1/3 pie	350	21	42
Eli's Frozen Cheesecakes: *Per 1/8 Pkg, 3 oz*			
Cookies N Creme; Choc. Caramel	320	23	11
Keylime; Original, average	320	22	26
Entenmann's			
All Butter Loaf, 1/6 loaf, 2 oz	210	9	30
Banana Cake, 1/8 cake, 2.5 oz	290	15	39
Brownie: Ultimate Fudge, 1	220	13	27
Light: Fudge, 1/10 strip, 1.4 oz	110	0	27
Lemon; Coffee, 1/8 strip, 1.9 oz	130	0	29
Cheese Coffee, 1/8 cake, 1.7 oz	160	7	21
Cheese-Filled Crumb Coffee 1/8 cake, 2 oz	200	9	25
Chocolate Fudge, 1/6 cake, 3 oz	310	14	46
Creme-Filled: Choc Cupcakes, 1	160	0	39
Golden Cakes, 1 cake, 2.3 oz	280	15	34
Crumb Coffee, 1/10 cake, 2 oz	250	12	33
Golden Loaf, (Light) 1/8, 1.7 oz	130	0	28
Louisiana Crunch, 1/9, 3 oz	330	14	48
Marshmallow Ice Devil's Food, 1/8	300	14	42
Mocha Cake, 1/6 cake, 3 oz	340	17	45
New York Crumb Coffee, 1/10, 2 oz	250	12	33
Ultimate Choc Crumb, 1/9, 2 oz	250	13	34
Ultimate Crumb, 1/10, 2 oz	250	13	33
Grands!: Blueberry Biscuits, 2 oz	210	9	29
Cinnamon Rolls, 3.5 oz roll	300	7	54
Hostess: Angel Food Cake, 1/8	160	1.5	33
Brownie Bites, each	57	3	7
Carrot Cake, 2 pces, 3.5 oz	300	7	55
Suzy Q's, 2 cakes, 2 oz	230	9	35
Twinkies, 2 pces, 1.5 oz	150	5	25
Per Cake: Chocodiles	240	11	33
Chocolicious	190	7	30
Chocolate/Orange Cupcake, aver.	170	6	28
Crumb Coffee	130	5	19
Dessert Cups, each	100	2	17
Ding Dongs; King Dongs	180	9	22
Ho Ho's, each	125	6	17
Honey Bun: Glazed	320	19	34
Iced/Frosted	410	24	42
Light: Brownie	140	2.5	28
Cupcakes; Twinkies	135	1.5	28
Crumb Cakes	90	0.5	19
Snoballs	180	5	31

Jewel Bake Shop	C	F	Cb
Choc Mini Cupcakes, 1 cake	100	12	30
Cinnamon Swirl Bread, 1 oz slice	160	2.5	30
Creme Horns, 1 horn	190	13	19
Elephant Ears, 2.5 oz	340	22	34
Fancy Jelly Roll, 1/6 roll, 2.7 oz	190	2.5	38
French Torpedo Roll, 2.7 oz	170	1	35
Gourmet Cinn. Rolls, 6 oz roll	640	29	88
Key Lime Meringue Pie, 1/6 whole, 5 oz	340	12	55
Kroger			
Angel Food Cake, 1/5, 2 oz	150	0	35
Dessert Shells, 2 shells, 1.65 oz	150	1.5	31
Gourmet Rugala, (18g), 0.6 oz	80	5	8
Little Debbie (Fresh)			
Cakes:			
Coffee, 2, 2 oz	230	7	39
Choc Chip Snack, 2, 2.4 oz	290	14	42
Chocolate Cup, 1.5 oz	180	9	26
Creme-filled Strawb. Cupcake ,1	200	9	29
Devil Cremes, 1.65 oz cake	190	8	29
Devil Squares, 2 cakes, 2.2 oz	270	13	37
Frosted Fudge , 1.5 oz cake	200	10	25
Swiss Cake Rolls, 2 cakes	260	12	39
Zebra Cakes, 2 cakes, 2.6 oz	330	16	45
Fudge Brownies, 2 oz, 1	270	13	39
Honey Buns, 1.75 oz bun	220	13	24
Muffin Loaves, 2 oz loaf	230	11	30
Oatmeal Creme Pies, 1	170	7	26
Pecan Spinwheels, 1 oz roll	110	4	16
Manischewitz			
Cheesecake, 3 oz	250	19	16
Marie Callendar (Frozen)			
Cobbler, all types, 1/4 pie, 4.25 oz	390	19	45
Pepperidge Farm			
Cakes Supreme: *Per 3 oz Slice*			
Lemon Mousse	290	12	35
Chocolate Mousse	250	10	35
Boston Creme	260	9	32
Cream Cakes Supreme:			
Cream Cheese Carrot, 1/9, 3 oz	320	20	38
Pineap./Strawb. Cr., 2.7 oz slice	240	10	38
Old Fashioned Cakes: *Per 3 oz Slice*			
Butter Pound	290	13	39
Deluxe Carrot	310	16	39
Turnovers: All types, aver., 3 oz	290	15	48

Pepperidge Farm (Cont)	C	F	Cb
Layer Cakes: *Per 3 oz Slice*			
Chocolate Fudge	**300**	16	37
Devil's Food; Coconut; Golden	**290**	14	40
German Choc. 1/8 cake, 2.5 oz	**250**	13	31
Strawberry Stripe, 1/8	**250**	11	35
Vanilla	**290**	13	41
Fruit Squares: *Single, 2.5 oz*			
Apple; Blueberry; Cherry	**210**	10	27
Rich's			
Chocolate Eclairs (Frozen), 57g ea.	**190**	9	24
Sara Lee (Frozen)			
Cakes: *Per Serving*			
All Butter Pound, 1/6, 2.7 oz	**320**	16	38
Reduced Fat, 1/4, 2.7 oz	**280**	11	42
All Butter; Chocolate, 1/4, 2.7 oz	**320**	16	40
Banana Sundae, 1/10, 3 oz	**270**	14	32
Butter Streusel Coffee, 1/6, 2 oz	**220**	12	25
Carrot Cake Bites, 1 pce, 1/2 oz	**80**	5	7
Choc Layer, 1/8, 3 oz slice	**340**	17	46
Dble Choc Layer, 1/8, 2.8 oz	**260**	13	33
Free & Light, 1/4, 2.7 oz	**200**	4	39
Golden Butter, 1/4, 2.7 oz	**300**	13	41
Pecan Coffee, 1/6, 2 oz	**230**	12	24
Red, White, Blueb. 1/10, 3 oz	**210**	8	31
Strawberry, 1/4, 2.7 oz	**290**	11	44
Dessert Cakes: *Per 1/6 Whole*			
Carrot, 3.2oz	**320**	17	39
Banana, 2.3 oz	**230**	8	37
Layer Cakes: *Per 1/8 Whole*			
Strawberry Shortcake, 2.5 oz	**180**	7	27
Other flavors, average, 3 oz	**260**	13	32
Cheesecake: *Per Serving*			
Cherry/Strawberry, aver., 4.75 oz	**340**	12	53
Chocolate Chip, 4.3 oz	**410**	21	47
Peanut Butter Cup, 3.5 oz	**380**	22	34
New York Style: Classic, 1/6	**500**	30	50
Mixed Berry Swirl, 1/6	**490**	28	52
Choc Chip Cookie Crumble, 1/6	**520**	27	61
Original: 1/5 whole, 4.3 oz	**350**	18	39
Classics: Choc. Mousse, 1/5	**400**	25	37
French, 1/5, 4.7 oz	**410**	25	41
Strawberry, 1/6 whole	**320**	14	43
Bars: 1 bar, 2.75 oz	**190**	14	14
Bites:			
Choc-Dipped Orig., 5 pces	**480**	33	40
Tstd Almond, 5 pces	**450**	29	42

Sara Lee (Cont)	C	F	Cb
Cheesecake Singles: *Per Slice*			
Caramel Choc Pecan, 110g	**400**	25	37
Strawberry Drizzle, 113g	**380**	20	46
Cream Pies (9"): *Per Serving*			
Choc. Silk; Coconut Crm, 1/5, 5 oz	**500**	32	49
Lemon Meringue, 1/6, 5 oz	**350**	11	59
Homestyle Pies (9"): *Per 4 1/2 oz (1/8 of Pie)*			
Apple; Cherry	**340**	16	46
Blueberry; Dutch Apple	**355**	15	53
Mince/Raspberry, averge	**390**	18	52
Peach	**330**	13	50
Pecan	**520**	24	70
Pumpkin	**260**	11	37
Individual Slices: *Per Slice*			
Apple/Cherry Pie, 4 oz	**300**	11	47
Carrot; Cookies N Cream, 3.5 oz	**335**	20	40
Lemon Icebox Pie, 3.5 oz	**260**	10	41
Southern Pecan Pie, 4 oz	**470**	23	62
Strawberry Swirl Ch'cake, 3.5 oz	**300**	17	31
Round Danish: *Per 1/6 Whole*			
Butter Streusel/Pecan	**225**	12	24
Cheese	**180**	6	28
Raspberry	**200**	8	27
Deluxe Cinnamon Roll	**320**	15	41
Weight Watchers: *Per Serving*			
Brownie à la Mode	**190**	4	34
Chocolate Mousse	**190**	5	31
Chocolate Eclair	**150**	4	25
Choc. Chip Cookie Dough Sundae	**180**	4	33
Choc. Rapsberry Royale	**190**	3	39
Double Fudge Brownie Parfait	**190**	2.5	39
Double Fudge Cake	**190**	4.5	36
French Style Cheesecake	**180**	5	28
Mississippi Mud Pie	**160**	5	24
New York Style Cheesecake	**150**	5	21
Strawberry Parfait Royale	**180**	2	35
Triple Chocolate Eclair	**160**	5	25

Made As Directed	C	F	Cb
Betty Crocker			
Cakes (Super Moist): *Per 1/12 Cake (Prep'd)*			
Chocolate Chip	270	13	34
Peanut Butter Choc; White	240	10	35
Other flavors, average	250	11	34
Per 1/10 Cake (Prepared):			
Carrot	320	13	42
Cherry; Sour Cream	280	12	43
Strawberry Swirl	290	12	43
Light: White	210	3.5	43
Devil's Food; Yellow	230	4.5	43
If using *No Cholesterol Recipe*, deduct 40 calories; and 4 grams fat.			
Angel Food Cakes: 1/12 mix	140	0	32
Brownie Mixes: *Per 1/20 Pkg (Prep'd)*			
Chocolate Chunk	180	9	24
Dark Chocolate	170	7	25
Fudge	170	7	23
Original Supreme	160	6	27
Peanut Butter; Walnut	180	9	23
Turtle (Caramel & Pecan)	170	8	23
Classic Dessert:			
Boston Cream Pie (1/10)	200	4.5	38
Choc. Pudding Cake (1/8)	170	3.5	33
Date Bar, 1/12 mix, dry	160	7	23
Gingerbread Cake (1/8)	230	7	38
Golden Pound (1/8)	290	13	41
Lemon Chiffon (1/16)	140	3	26
Lemon Pudding (1/8)	180	4	33
Pineapple Upside Down (1/6)	400	15	63
Creamy Chilled:			
Banana Cream (1/9)	250	11	35
Chocolate French Silk (1/8)	270	11	39
Coconut Cream (1/8)	290	13	38
Cookies & Cream (1/6)	380	16	53
Sunkist Lemon Supreme (1/9)	320	13	52
Stir 'n Bake Mixes: *Per 1/6 Pkg*			
Carrot Cake w. Crm Chse Frosting	250	7	46
Chocolate Brownies	220	8	35
Coffee	200	6	36
Devil's Food Cake w. Choc. Frost.	240	8	42
Supreme Dessert Bars: *Per Bar*			
Caramel Oatmeal; Choc. Chunk	180	9	24
Strawberry Swirl Cheesecake	180	19	20
Sunkist Lemon	140	4	23
Other varieties, average	170	8	24

Made As Directed	C	F	Cb
Aunt Jemima			
Coffee Cake, 1/8 cake	170	5	30
Duncan Hines			
Angel Food, 1/12 Whole	140	0	30
Other flavors, average, 1/12	190	5	34
Cookies: All flavors, 1 cookie	65	3	8
Estee			
Brownie, 1 pce, 2"x 2"	50	2	12
All cakes, 1/5 cake	200	4	38
Choc. Chip Cookie, 1 cookie	45	2.5	6
Jell-O-No Bake: *Prepared As Directed*			
Cheesecakes:			
Cherry/Strawberry, 1/8 pkg	340	13	52
Peanut Butter Cup, 1/8 pkg	380	23	44
Real/Homestyle, 1/6 pkg	360	17	48
Cookies & Creme: 1/6 pkg	390	8	29
Double Layer Lemon, 1/8 pkg	260	13	35
Manischewitz			
Apple Cake w. real apple, (1/6)	260	10	43
Nancy's			
Petite Desserts, 1 tartlets, 0.6 oz	80	4.5	9.5
Pillsbury			
Moist Supreme: *Per 1/12 Cake (Prepared)*			
Angel Food	140	0	31
Devil's Food	270	14	33
French Vanilla; German Choc.	250	11	34
Funfetti	240	9	38
Other flavors, average 1/12	260	12	35
Streusel Coffee: 1/16 Cake	260	11	37
Bundt: Hot Fudge, 1/12	350	20	39
Chocolate Caramel Nut, 1/16	290	18	28
Strawberry Cream Cheese, 1/16	300	17	34
Deluxe Brownies: *Per 2" Square*			
Fudge, 1/16	150	6	22
Fudge, 1/20	190	9	24
Thick 'n Fudgy: Cheesecake Swirl	170	9	21
Double Choc.	150	6	23
Chocolate Chunk	160	7	22
Deluxe Bar Mixes: *Per Serving*			
Apple Streusel	150	6	23
Chips Ahoy	150	5	25
Fudge Swirl Cookie	180	8	25
Lemon Cheesecake	190	10	22
Other flavors, average	175	7	26

Cakes & Dessert Mixes (Cont)

	C	F	Cb
Robin Hood			
Devil's Food, 1/5 cake	310	17	36
Yellow 1/5 cake	280	13	37
Sweet Rewards			
Fat Free, all flavors (1/8)	170	0	40
Reduced Fat, all flavors (1/12)	200	5	37
Brownie Mix: Supreme, 1 pce	150	4	27
Lowfat Fudge, 1/18 pkg	130	2.5	27
Snackwell's			
Brownie: Devil's Food (1/12)	150	2.5	28
Fudge (1/12)	150	2.5	29
Cakes: Devil's Food, 1/6 cake	200	4	38
White; Yellow, 1/6 cake	210	4.5	39
Cookies: Choc. Chip, 1 oz (1/18)	110	3	19
Chocolate Fudge, 1 oz (1/18)	90	1.5	18
Streusel Squares, 1.5 oz piece	150	3	31

Cake Frostings

	C	F	Cb
Betty Crocker			
Ready-to-Spread:			
Creamy Deluxe, all flav., 2 Tbsp	140	5	24
Whipped Deluxe, 2 Tbsp	100	5	15
Sweet Rewards: Red. Fat, 2 Tbsp	125	2	25
Frost. Mixes: C'nut Pecan, 2 T. prep	160	8	21
Duncan Hines: *Per 2 Tbsp, 1.2 oz*			
Coconut Pecan	150	9	18
Pillsbury: *Per 2 Tbsp (approx. 1/12 Tub)*			
Caramel Pecan	150	8	19
Cream Cheese; Lemon	150	6	24
Chocolate; Choc. Fudge/Mocha	140	6	21
Coconut Pecan	160	10	17
Dark Choc	130	6	20
All other flavors	150	6	25
Decorators, Choc., 1 Tbsp	70	2	11
Sweet Rewards			
Average all flavors, 1 Tbsp	120	2.5	24

Baking Ingredients

	C	F	Cb
Almond Paste:			
(Marzipan), 1 oz	125	7	12
Baking Powder: Regular, 1 tsp	3	0	0.5
Cream of Tartar, 1 tsp	2	0	0.5
***Bisquick* Baking Mix:**			
Original, 1/3 cup, 1 1/2 oz	170	6	25
Reduced Fat, 1/3 cup, 1 1/2 oz	150	2.5	28
Butter/Margarine: 1/2 cup, 4 oz	820	91	0
Carob Flour, 1/2 cup	90	<1	26
Chocolate Baking Bars: ***Average All Brands***			
Unsweetened, 1 oz	150	15	8
Grated, 1 cup, 4 1/2 oz	680	68	36
Semi-sweet, 1 oz	160	8	18
Bitter-sweet/White Baking 1 oz	160	9	17
Chocolate Baking Chips: ***Average All Brands***			
Milk Choc./Semi Sweet 1 oz	140	8	16
1/4 cup, 1 1/2 oz	210	12	24
1 cup, 6 oz	840	48	96
Cocoa Powder, Baking: *Nestle,* 1 T.	15	1	3
1/3 cup, 1 oz	80	4	12
Hershey's, 1 Tbsp	20	0.5	3
1/3 cup, 1 oz	115	3.5	21
Coconut, dried: Unsweet., 1 oz	190	18	7
Sweetened/flaked, 1 oz	135	9	14
1/2 cup, 1.3 oz	175	12	18
Toasted (*Baker's*), 1 oz	170	13	17
Creamed, 1 oz	195	19	19
Coconut Cream *(Coco Lopez)*, 2 T.	120	5	5
Cornstarch, 1 Tbsp	30	0	7
Flour: All Purpose, 1 cup, 5 oz	400	0	84
Flavor Extracts, ***Average All Brands***			
Imitation, 1 tsp	15	0	3.5
Pure Extract, 1 tsp	20	0	4
Almond, Vanilla, 1 tsp	10	0	3
Fruit Pectin: Swtnd, 1 Tbsp, 1/2 oz	35	0	10
Unsweetened, 1 Tbsp	2	0	0.5
Gelatin, dry, 1/4 oz pkg	30	0	0
Lemon/Orange Peel, 1/4 cup	30	0	4
Nuts & Seeds ~ Pages 127-128			
Pie Crusts & Fillings ~ Page 107			
Rennin, 1 pkg (11g)	12	0	3
Vinegar, aver. all types, 1 oz	4	0	2
Whey, sweet, dry, 1 oz	90	<1	20
Yeast: Active, dry, 1/4 oz pkg	15	0	2
Fleischmann's, 0.6 oz pkg	15	0	2
Bakers, compressed, 1 oz	25	0	3
Brewers; Torula, 1 oz	80	<1	11

Puddings, Desserts, Gelatin

Ready-To-Serve

	C	F	Cb
Instant Pudding & Pie Filling			
Per 1/2 Cup			
Regular: average all flavors	**170**	4	30
Reduced Calorie: *D-Zerta*	**70**	<1	12
Estee	**70**	0	12
Jell-O, sugar-free	**80**	2	11
Royal, sugar-free	**100**	2	17
Del Monte Pudding Snacks: *Each*			
Chocolate; Chocolate Fudge	**130**	4	24
Butterscotch; Tapioca; Vanilla	**120**	3	22
Fat Free Vanilla	**90**	0	20
Dr McDougall's: Rice Pudd., 3 oz	**310**	1.5	69
Jell-O Pudding Snacks *(6 Pack)*			
Choc./Caramel, 4 oz (113g) each	**160**	5	28
Fat Free, 4 oz snack	**100**	0	23
Chocolate/Vanilla; Van. Swirls	**160**	5	27
Cheesecake Snacks, aver., 4 oz	**150**	4.5	25
Jewel: Chef's Kitchen			
Rice Pudding, 1/2 cup, 4.5 oz	**230**	8	35
Tapioca Pudding, 1/2 cup, 4.5 oz	**170**	8	35
Kozy Shack: Banana; Van., 4 oz	**130**	3	22
Lite, 4 oz	**110**	1	22
Rice Pudding, 4 oz cup	**140**	3	24
Creme Caramel Flan, 1 cup, 4 oz	**150**	4	25
Choc./Tapioca Pudding, 4 oz	**140**	3	25
Manischewitz: Choc., 1/2 cup	**110**	0.5	26
Passover Gold Noodle, 1/2 cup	**140**	2	28
President's Choice			
Key Lime Pie (36oz) 1/8 pie, 4.5 oz	**440**	22	54
Mississippi Mud Pie (36oz) 1/9, 4 oz	**380**	24	37
Swiss Miss Pudding Snacks			
Swirls, 4 oz	**160**	6	26
Choc. Pudding Snacks, 3 1/2 oz	**150**	5	23
Tapioca: 1 pudding cup, 3 1/2 oz	**120**	3.5	21
Fat Free varieties, 3 1/2 oz	**90**	0	20
Weight Watchers (Frozen)			
Chocolate Mousse, 2 3/4 oz	**190**	5	31

Other Desserts ~ See Page 109

Pudding Bars (Frozen)

	C	F	Cb
Jell-O Pudding Pops: Regular	**80**	2	12
Deluxe Chocolate covered	**200**	10	27

Homemade Puddings

	C	F	Cb
Apple Tapioca, 1/2 cup	**150**	0	32
Bread Pudding, 1/2 cup	**250**	8	40
Blancmange, 1/2 cup	**140**	5	19
Chocolate, 1/2 cup	**190**	6	30
Corn Pudding, 1/2 cup	**135**	4	21
Crème Brûlée, 1/2 cup	**400**	35	16
Plum Pudding, 2 oz	**170**	3	32
Rennin Dessert, 1/2 cup	**115**	4	16
Rice with Raisins, 1/2 cup	**200**	4	38
Sponge Pudding, 3 1/2 oz	**340**	16	45
Tapioca Cream, 1/2 cup	**110**	4	15
Trifle, 1/2 cup	**180**	7	26

Custards

	C	F	Cb
Custard Mix			
Jell-O (Americana) Golden Egg:			
Dry, 1/6 pkg	**80**	0	19
Prep. w. 2% milk, 1/2 cup	**140**	2.5	19
Jello Flan, w. 2% milk, 1/2 cup	**140**	2.5	20
Royal-Flan: Prep. w 2% milk, 1/2 c.	**130**	2.5	18
Homemade Custard			
Baked, plain, 1/2 cup, 4 1/2 oz	**150**	7	16
w. skim milk, artif. sweetened	**70**	3	4
Boiled, 1/2 cup	**165**	7	18

Meringues

	C	F	Cb
Meringue Swirl, 1/2 oz	**50**	0	8
Meringue Shell, 1 oz Shell	**100**	0	16

(Add extra calories/fat/carbohydrate for fillings)

Gelatin/Jell-O

	C	F	Cb
Gelatin Mix:			
Average, (Jell-O, Royal)			
Regular, all flavors, 1/2 cup	**80**	0	18
Sugar Free/Low Cal., 1/2 cup	**8**	0	0
Creme Gelatin/Parfait: *Per 1/2 Cup*			
Winky: Strawberry (109g)	**110**	1.5	22
Rainbow (130g)	**100**	0	24
Reser's: Dessert Parfait (110g)	**100**	2	19
Mrs Crockett's Kitchen: Str. Parfait	**160**	4	26
Snack Cups (*Del Monte/Jell-O):*	**70**	0	17

Non-Dairy Desserts

	C	F	Cb
Imagine (4 Pack):			
Aver. all flavors, 1 cup, 3.75 oz	**160**	3	34

Quick Guide

Pancakes

	C	F	Cb
Plain: *Average All Types*			
Small (3" diam.), 3/4 oz	50	2.5	6
Medium (4" diam.), 1 1/4 oz	80	3	11
Large (5" diam.), 2 1/2 oz	160	6	21
Add Extra for Syrups/Butter			
Pancake Syrup: Regular, 1 Tbsp	50	0	13
1/4 cup	200	0	52
Lite, 1 Tbsp	25	0	6
1/4 cup	100	0	24
Butter/Margarine: Regular, 1 T.	100	11	0
Whipped, 1 Tbsp	70	7.5	0

Restaurant Style Pancakes

	C	F	Cb
Denny's			
Hot Cakes, Plain, 3	490	7	95
w. Syrup & Butter	725	17	130
Original Grand Slam Breakfast	795	50	65
w. Syrup & Margarine	1030	60	101
Maple Flav. Syrup, 1 serving	145	0	36
Whipped Margarine, 1/2 oz	90	10	0
Hardees			
3 Pancakes (no fat)	280	2	56
w. Sausage Pattie	430	16	56
w. 2 Bacon Strips	350	9	56
IHOP (International House of Pancakes)			
Pancakes (Syrup/Butter extra):			
Buttermilk, 1 (2 oz)	110	3	17
Short Stack, 3	330	9	51
Full Stack, 5	550	15	85
Buckwheat, 1 (2 oz)	110	4	15
Country Griddle, 1 (2 oz)	120	3.5	19
Harvest Grain 'N Nut, (2 1/4 oz)	180	9	20
Crepes (Egg Pancakes), 1 (2 oz)	100	5	12
Waffles (Plain): Regular, 1 (3 oz)	310	15	37
Belgian: Regular, 1 (4 oz)	390	19	48
Crepe: Egg, 1 (2 oz)	120	6	14
McDonalds			
Hotcakes, Plain (3)	340	8	56
w. Marg. (2 pats) & Syrup (1)	600	17	104
Perkins			
Buttermilk, 3, plain	440	12	70
Harvest Grain: Plain, 3	270	2	56
w. lowcal Syrup	295	2	63
5-Stack w. lowcal Syrup	475	3.5	93

Brands

	C	F	Cb
Aunt Jemima			
Frozen: Lowfat, 3	130	2	33
Original; Blueberry, 3	200	3	40
Pancake & Waffle Mix:			
Original, 1/3 cup, prepared	240	6.5	38
Complete, 1/3 cup	160	2.5	32
Mini Pancakes (13)	240	4	46
Thaw & Pour B'milk Pancake Batter:			
1/2 cup, 4 x 4" pancakes	260	3.5	51
Betty Crocker Pancake Mixes			
Complete Original, 3	200	3	40
Complete Buttermilk, 3	200	2.5	40
Bisquick (Shake 'N Pour)			
Pancake & Waffle Mixes:			
Average, all types, 3	200	3	38
Hungry Jack Pancakes			
Mixes: *Per 1/3 Cup (prep.)*			
Buttermilk: Complete, 1/3 cup	160	1.5	32
Original, w. 2% Milk, Oil, Egg	290	13	32
w. Skim Milk, Oil, Egg Whites	220	6	32
Extra Lights: Complete	150	2	30
Microwave: Buttermilk, 3	270	4.5	51
Original, 3 pancakes	270	4.5	51
Northern Pines: Complete Gourmet			
3 x 4" pancakes, 3.5 oz	380	7	71

Waffles

	C	F	Cb
Homemade: 7" waffle, 2 1/2 oz	245	13	26
From Mix: 7" waffle, 2 1/2 oz	205	8	28

Frozen Waffles

	C	F	Cb
Aunt Jemima			
Blueberry, 1 waffle	95	3	15
Buttermilk, 1	100	3	17
Dominick's: 1 waffle	58	1	10
Eggo *(Kelloggs)*: Banana Bread, 1	95	3	6
Chocolate Chip, 1 waffle	100	3.5	16
Cinnamon Toast, 1 set	96	3	15
Homestyle, average, 1	95	3.5	15
Nut & Honey, 1	110	4.5	15
Nutri-Grain, 1	85	2.5	14
Special K (fat free), 1	60	0	13
Waf-fulls, all types, 1, 2 oz	160	5	26
Hungry Jack: Blueberry, 1 waffle	105	4	17
Buttermilk; Homestyle, 1	95	3	15
Mini Funfetti, 1	65	2	11

Sugar, Sweeteners, Jams

Sugar

White Sugar, granulated:	C	F	Cb
1 level teaspoon, 4g	15	0	4
1 heaping teaspoon, 6g	25	0	6.5
1 cube, 1/2"	24	0	6.5
Single portion, 1 packet	25	0	6.5
1 Tablespoon, 12g	46	0	12
1 ounce, 1 oz	110	0	20
1 cup, 7 oz	770	0	203
1 pound	1760	0	464
Brown Sugar:			
1 Tbsp, 13g	50	0	13
1 ounce, 1 oz	109	0	28
1 cup, not packed, 5 oz	540	0	140
1 cup, packed, 7 3/4 oz	845	0	218
Powdered/Confectioners:			
Sifted, 1 cup, 3 1/2 oz	385	0	98
Unsifted, 1 cup, 4 1/4 oz	460	0	117
Other Sugars			
Glucose, 1 oz	110	0	27
Tablets (*Dex 4*), 1	15	0	4
Barley/Wheat/Rye Malt,			
1 Tbsp, 3/4 oz	60	0	14
Cinnamon Sugar, 1 tsp	15	0	4
Dextrose, 1 oz	110	0	27
Fructose: 1 tsp	15	0	4
3 Tbsp, 1 oz	110	0	27
Estee, 1 pkg	10	0	2
FruitSource: 1 oz (powder)	110	0	27
Sorbitol, 1 oz	110	0	27
Turbinado Sugar, 2 Tbsp, 1 oz	110	0	27
Unrefined Cane Sugar, 1 oz	110	0	27

Sugar Substitutes

	C	F	Cb
Diabetic Sweet: 1 pkt	0	0	1
Equal: Tablet/Liquid	0	0	0
Granulated, 1 pkg	4	0	1
NutraSweet Spoonful, 1 tsp	2	0	0.5
Nutra Taste, 1 pkt	0	0	0
Sprinkle Sweet, 1 tsp	2	0	0.5
Stevia, 1 pkt	0	0	0
Sugar Delight, 1 pkt	8	0	2
Sugar Like (Bateman's), 1 tsp	4	0	1
Sugar Twin: 1 pkt	3	0	0
Sugar Substitute, 1 tsp	2	0	0
Sweet 'N Low, 1 pkt	0	0	1
Sweet One, 1 pkt	0	0	0
Weight Watchers Sweetener, 1 tsp	4	0	1

Honey, Jam, Preserves

Honey	C	F	Cb
1 tsp, 1/4 oz	22	0	5.5
1 Tbsp, 3/4 oz	65	0	17
1 ounce, 1 oz	86	0	23
1 cup, 12 oz	1030	0	269
Single Portion, 1/2 oz pkg	43	0	11
Jams/Jellies/Preserves			
Regular, 1 tsp, 1/4 oz	18	0	5
1 Tbsp, 3/4 oz	55	0	16
1 ounce	75	0	22
Single Portion, 1/2 oz pkg	38	0	11
Smucker's, aver. all types, 1 Tbsp	50	0	13
Apple/Fruit Butters, 1 T., 0.6 oz	20	0	6
Fruit Spreads:			
Regular, 1 tsp	16	0	4
Low Sugar, 1 tsp	8	0	2
Low Cal. *(Featherweight),* 1 tsp	4	0	1
Jelly: Regular, average, 1 tsp	18	0	4.5
Imitation, Low Calorie, 1 tsp	4	0	1
Marmalade, citrus, 1 tsp	18	0	5

"They say he's good!"

Quick Guide

Syrups

	C	F	Cb
Average All Types			
(Corn/Rice/Maple/Pancake/Waffle)			
Regular/Dark/Light Color:			
1 Tbsp	55	0	14
2 Tbsp	110	0	27
1/4 cup	220	0	55
1 cup	880	0	22
Single Portion: 1 oz pkg	115	0	29
1 1/2 oz: pkg	170	0	42
Lite (e.g *Weight Watchers*),			
1 Tbsp	25	0	6
2 Tbsp	50	0	12
1/4 cup	100	0	25

Brands ~ Syrups

Per 2 Tbsp (1 fl.oz Serving)
(For 1/4 cup serving, double the figures.)

	C	F	Cb
Arrowhead Mills: Sorghum Pure	60	0	16
Aunt Jemima:			
Original; Butter Rich	105	0	26
Lite; Butterlite	50	0	13
Bernard Jensen's: Rice Bran	53	0	15
Cary's: Sugar Free	18	0	5
Pure Maple	105	0	26
Cozy Cottage: Sugar Free	10	0	3
Eden: Barley Malt/Wheat	120	0	28
Estee: Maple/Blueberry	40	0	10
Hungry Jack: Regular	100	0	25
Lite	50	0	12
Karo, all types	120	0	30
Knott's Berry Farm: All types	105	0	26
Log Cabin: Regular	100	0	27
Lite	50	0	13
Lundberg: Brown Rice Syrup	85	0	21
Mrs. Butterworth's: Lite	60	0	15
Original; Country Best Recipe	115	0	29
Northern Pines: Maple Leaf	80	0	20
Smucker's:			
Fruit Syrup; Regular	105	0	26
Light	65	0	16
Spring Tree: Maple Syrup	105	0	26
Sucanat: 100% Pure Cane Syrup	60	0.5	14
Tree of Life: Maple	100	0	26
Rice Syrup	120	0	30
Weight Watchers Syrup	50	0	12

Molasses

Average All Brands	C	F	Cb
Dark/Light: 1 Tbsp	55	0	14
1 cup, 11 1/2 oz	880	0	224
Blackstrap: 1 Tbsp, 3/4 oz	47	0	13
1 cup, 11 1/2 oz	750	0	208

Icecream Toppings

Per 2 Tbsp

	C	F	Cb
Hershey: Choc. Fudge	100	4	14
Kraft: Butterscotch	130	2	28
Caramel	120	0	28
Chocolate; Pineapple; Strawb.	110	0	28
Hot Fudge	140	4	24
Marzetti: Caramel Apple	60	7	23
Caramel Apple Reduced Fat	30	3	26
RW Knudsen: All flavors	75	0	19
Smuckers: Butterscotch Caramel	140	1	30
Chocolate Fudge	130	1	28
Dove: Dark Choc.	140	5	22
Milk Choc.	130	4	21
Fat Free, all flavors	130	0	31
Guilt Free, all flavors	100	0	24
Hot Caramel	120	3	28
Hot Fudge	140	4	22
Light Hot Fudge	90	0	23
Marshmallow	120	0	30
Magic Shell Toppings	200	16	25
Microwave: Choc./Fudge	130	2	28
Fat Free	110	0	27
Peanut Butter Caramel	150	4.5	24
Pecans/Walnuts in Syrup	170	10	20
Pineapple; Strawberry	120	0	28
Sundae Syrups, all flavors	110	0	27

Quick Guide

Chocolate

Average All Brands

	C	F	Cb
Milk Chocolate, regular:			
Plain/Nuts/Fruit, average, 1 oz	150	10	15
1 1/2 oz Bar	225	15	23
2 oz Bar	300	20	30
4 oz Block	600	40	60
8 oz Block	1200	80	120
1 Pound, 16 oz	2400	160	240
Dark/White Chocolate, 1 oz	150	10	16
Chocolate-coated:			
Almonds, 5-6, 1 oz	160	11	11
Clusters, nut, 2, 1 oz	160	11	15
Coffee Beans, 1.4 oz	180	10	24
Creme/Cordial Centres, 1 oz	120	4	27
Fudge, 1 oz	125	5	18
Macadamias, 2-3 pces., 1 oz	180	13	11
Mints, 1 med., 11g	45	1	9
Nougat & Caramel, 1 oz	120	4	21
Peanuts, 12 med., 1 oz	160	11	15
Raisins, 30 med., 1 oz	120	4	21
Cooking Chocolate:			
Sweet/Semi-sweet, 1 oz	160	8	18
Chips, 1/4 cup, 2 1/2 oz	210	12	24
Unsweetened, 1 oz	150	15	8
Carob: plain, 1 oz	160	11	9

Also See Baking Ingredients: Page 111
Carob Candy: See Page 122

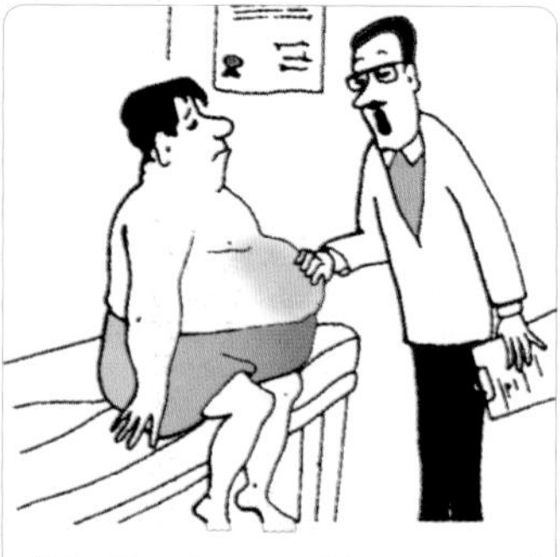

"It's time to curb this inflation"

Brands & Generic

Per Piece/Serving	C	F	Cb
Abba Zabba, 2 oz bar	250	5	48
Absolutely Almond, 2.5 oz bar	380	23	40
Aero Bar *(Nestlé),* 1.45 oz bar	210	13	26
After Dinner Mints, 1 small	45	1	9
After Eight Mint, each	35	1.2	6
Allen Wertz: Simply Sugar Free			
Coffee Time (decaf), 4	45	15	12
Coffee Toffee, 6	120	3	33
Other types, 4	120	2.5	37
Almond Joy, 1.76 oz bar	240	13	29
King Size, 2 pces, 1 1/2 oz	220	12	26
Snack, 2, 1.3 oz	190	10	23
Almond Roca, 1 pce	70	5	6
Almonds, sugar-coated, 7, 1 oz	130	5	20
Altoids *(C & B),* each	3	0	1
Amazin' Fruit, 1 bag	180	0	41
Andes: Creme de Menthe; Cherry Jubilee			
Choc covered Patty, (3), 1 1/2 oz	180	3	35
Thins, aver. all flav., (8), 1.4 oz	210	13	22
Anthon Berg: Cognac, each	180	8	25
After Dinner Sweet:			
Marzipan w. Madeira, 1.4 oz	175	7.5	26
Marcipan Brod, each	120	7	13
Asteroid *(Nestlé),* 54g	260	10	40
Baby Ruth, King Size, 3.7 oz bar	495	21	67
2.1 oz bar	280	12	36
Fun size, each	100	4.5	17
Snack, 1 bar, 3/4 oz	100	5	12
Baci *(Perugino),* each	85	5	8
Bar None, 1.5 oz bar	240	14	23
Barley Sugar, 1 pce., 0.2 oz	23	0	6
Big Hunt, 2 oz	230	3	47
Bit-O-Honey, 1.7 oz	200	3.5	41
Chews, 6 pces, 1.4 oz	170	3	34
Blow Pops, each	50	0	14
Bonus Bar, 2.1 oz bar	290	16	34
Boston Baked Beans, 30 pces, 1 oz	135	5	20
Brach's: Almond Supremes,11	220	15	18
But'rscotch Disks, 3, 0.6 oz	70	0	16
Choc Bridge Mix, 16, 1.4 oz	190	9	25
Circus Peanuts, each	25	0.6	3
Clusters, 3	220	14	19
Double Dip Choc Peanuts, 15	220	14	19
Golden Butter/Internation. Toffee	25	0.6	5
Lemon Drops, 4, 0.6 oz	50	0	13
Malted Milk Balls, 15	190	9	27

Per Piece/Serving	C	F	Cb
Brach's (Cont):			
Milk Maid Caramel, 18	170	5	30
Orange Slices Hi-C, each	50	0	13
Breath Savers, all types, each	10	0	2
Brite Crackers, 1 bag, 1.5 oz	140	0	32
Brock: Candy Corn, (10) 0.7 oz	75	0	18
Gummy Bears; Sour Balls, each	26	0	6
Lemon Drops, each	20	0	5
Orange Slices, each	35	0	9
Spice Drops, each	12	0	3
Starlight Mints, each	20	0	5
Toffee, each	25	0.8	5
Bubble Gum ~ *See 'Gum'*			
Buncha Crunch, 1/2 cup, 1.4 oz	200	10	26
Burnt Peanuts, 40 pces, 40g	190	8	32
Butterfinger: King Size, 3.7 oz bar	480	18	75
2.1 oz bar	270	11	41
Fun size, each	100	3.5	15
Mini, each	20	1	7
Snack, 2, 1.3 oz	170	7	27
Butterfinger B.B's, 1.7 oz bag	230	10	33
Buttermints, 18 pces, 1 1/2 oz	160	0	40
Butterscotch, 5 pces	115	5	30
Buttons *(Walgreens)*, 3, 18g	70	0	16
Chips, 1 oz	150	7	36
Discs *(Sathers)*, 3, 0.6 oz	110	0	16
Candy Cane, Medium, 5", 1/2 oz	50	0	12
Candy Corn, 1 oz	110	0	27
4 oz pkt: 24 pces, 1 1/2 oz	150	0	37
Candy Necklaces, 20g each	80	0.5	20
Caramels: each	30	1	6
Chocolate, each	25	0.3	6
Creams, 3 pces, 1 1/4 oz	130	3	23
2.75 oz pkt, 5 pces, 1 1/2 oz	160	3.5	30
Hershey's Classic Caramels:			
Traditional, 6 pces	160	5	27
Choc Creme Filled, 6 pces	160	6	26
Caramel Nips, each	30	1	6
Caramel Popcorn, 1 cup, 1 oz	120	1.5	26
Caramel Truffles *(Godiva)*, 1 pce	110	6.5	11
Caramello *(Hershey's)* 1.6 oz bar	220	10	29
Cellas Choc Cherries,.1 pce	55	2	9
Certs: Breath Mints, 1 pce	6	0	2
Sugar-free, 1 piece	7	0	2
Candy Jar Mix *(Jewel)*, 3, 17g	70	0	17
Charleston Chew, 1 bar, 53g	230	7	40
Cherry Sours *(Sathers)*, 11, 1 1/2 oz	150	0	38
Chews, all types, 1 oz	110	1	25

Per Piece/Serving	C	F	Cb
Chocolate Mints, each	55	4	4
Chocolate Parfait Nips, each	30	1	5
Chuckles, each	35	0	10
Chunky Bar *(Nestlé)*, 1.4 oz	210	11	24
Cinnamon Bears *(Walgreens)*, 5	150	0	38
Cinn. Buttons *(Walgreens)*, 3 pce	70	0	17
Cinnamon Drops *(Sathers)*, 19 pce	150	0	36
Coconut Stacks, 4, 41g	190	6	33
Coffee Go Coffee/Cappuccino, ea.	18	0.4	4
Coffee Rio-Gold, each	15	0.5	3
Collard & Bowser: Eng. Toffee, 2	80	4	12
Corn Nuts, 1/3 cup, 1 oz	130	4	20
Cote d'Or: Bouchee, each	130	8	12
Chokotoff, each	210	9	30
Nougatti	150	8	19
Bar & Nuts,1.3 oz	220	18	12
Cracker Jack, 1.25 oz box	150	2.5	29
Crisped Rice: Almond, 1 bar	130	6	18
Choc Chip, 1 bar	115	4	18
Crows, 7 oz pkg	150	0	37
Crunch: 5 oz bar	725	38	90
King Size, 2.75 oz bar	400	21	51
1.55 oz bar	230	12	29
Fun size, each	50	2.5	7
Snack, 3, 1 1/2 oz	220	11	28
Crunch Berries Treats, 1.6 oz bar	190	4.5	36
Decadence *(NuBar)* Bar, 1.3 oz	140	2.5	30
Dots, 12 dots	150	0	37
Double Dip Stick, 1 stick	16	0.5	3
Dove: Dark/Milk, 1.3 oz bar	200	12	22
Bar, 6 oz	920	56	104
Miniatures, each	30	2	3
Dum Dum Pops *(Spangler)*, 1 pop	25	0	6
English Toffee, 1 pce	48	3	5
Eda's Sugar Free, all flav., 5, 1/2 oz	40	0	15
Estee Dietetic Candies:			
Caramels, all flavors, 1 pce.	30	1	5
Chocolate, Dark/ Mint, 1/2 bar	200	14	23
Gummy Bears; Gum Drops, 1 pce.	7	0	1.5
Hard Candies: Butterscotch, 2	25	0	6
Assorted Fruit Lollipops, 5	60	0	15
Peppermint, 3	30	0	7
Mint/Toffee, 5	60	0	15
Lollipop	30	0	8
Milk Chocolate, 1/2 bar, 4 oz	230	17	17
Peanut Butter Cups, 1 cup	40	3	3
Fructose Sweetened, 1 cup	40	2	3
Peanut Brittle, 1/3 box, 1.5 oz	240	9	28

Per Piece/Serving	C	F	Cb
5th Avenue, 2.1 oz bar	290	13	40
King Size bar	460	20	64
Fanny May: Single wrapped pces			
Mint Meltaway Patty, 1.5 oz	250	17	22
Pixie, 1.5 oz	215	12	24
Trinidad, 1.5 oz	205	11	24
Ferrero Rocher, each	75	5	6
3 pces, 1.3 oz	220	15	17
Fifty 50 Snack Bars: P'Nut But, 2	200	14	16
Almond Choc., 7 pce, 1 1/2 oz	210	15	20
Crunch Choc., 7 pce, 1.1 oz	160	11	19
Fruit & Nut Choc., 7 pce, 1 1/2 oz	200	14	21
Milk Choc., 3 pce, 1/2 bar, 43g	210	14	25
Mini bars, 8 bars, 1 oz	140	9	16
Fondant: Choc-coated, 1.2 oz	130	3	28
Mint, 1 oz	105	0	27
Franklin Crunch 'N Munch:			
All varieties, aver. 1.25 oz	170	7	30
Fran's: Gold Bar, 1.75 oz	260	14	34
Gold Bites (Almonds), 1	130	7	17
Fruit Crystals *(Walgreens)*, 3 pces	70	0	17
Fruit Drops, each	6	0	1
Fruit Gems *(Sunkist)*, 3, 1.1 oz	105	0	26
Fruit Leathers, average, 0.5 oz	45	0	12
Fruit Pastilles, 1 roll, 1.4 oz	100	0	26
Fruit Rolls, 1 roll	80	0	20
Fruit Roll-Ups, 1/2 oz	50	0	12
Fruit Runts *(Walgreens)*, 1T., 1/4 pkt	60	0	14
Fruit Waves, 0.5 oz	50	0	12
Fudge: Chocolate/Vanilla, 1 oz	115	3	20
with Nuts, 1 oz	120	4	21
Choco. Marshmallow, 1 oz	120	5	18
w. Nuts, 1 oz	125	5.5	18
Peanut Butter, 1 oz	105	2	21
Ghirardelli: Milk/Dark Chocolate,			
1.25 oz bar	185	12	20
w. almonds, 1.5 oz bar	220	14	25
Choc Nuts & Chews, 1 pce	55	3.5	5
Godiva: Hearts, each	45	2	4
Almond Butter Dome, 1 pce	80	6	6
Bouchee au Chocolate, 1 pce	220	13	23
Cordial Assortment, each	60	2.5	9
Gold Ballotin, 1 pce	70	3.5	9
Milk/Dark/IvoryAssortment, each	75	4	8
Nut & Caramel, each	75	4	6
Truffle Amaretto, 1 pce	110	6.5	12
Golden Almond Bar, 1 bar	520	34	40

Per Piece/Serving	C	F	Cb
Golden 111 Bar, 1 bar	500	30	52
Go Lightly: Box Candies, 4	60	0	15
Bags: Assorted Taffy, 6	140	3	36
Vanilla Caramels, 5	150	6	31
Super Free Choc Crunch, 7,1 1/2 oz	180	13	23
Goobers Peanuts, 1 pkg, 1.4 oz	210	13	20
Good & Fruity, 1 box, 1.8 oz	140	1	35
Good & Plenty: 1/5 bar, 1.4 oz	130	0	38
Candy Bar, 1/5 bar, 1.4 oz	130	0	31
GooGoo Cluster, 1 bar, 1.75 oz	240	11	32
GUM: *Per Piece*			
Bazooka, each	30	0	7
Beechies	6	0	2
Big League Chew	10	0	2
Bubble Gum Balls *(Walgreens)*	5	0	2
Bubble Yum	25	0	6
Sugarless	10	0	3
Candilicious	30	0	2
Carefree (Sugarless/Regular	5	0	2
Chiclets	5	0	1
Clorets, stick	10	0	2
Dentyne	6	0	2
Estee, bubble/regular	5	0	2
Extra *(Wrigley's)*,			
Sugar-Free Bubble Gum, 1	5	0	2
Freshen-Up	13	0	2
Hubba Bubba: Regular	23	0	6
Sugar-free, average	14	0	0.5
Ice Breakers, 1 stick	5	0	2
Sonic Boom Bubble Gum	15	0	3
Sticklets	7	0	2
Trident: Slab	5	0	1
Soft Bubble Gum	9	0	1
Wrigley's, all flavors	10	0	2
Gum Drops, 1 small	15	0	3
1 large, 0.4 oz	40	0	7
6 oz pkt: 4 pces, 1.4 oz	130	0	31
Gummi Bears: 1 bear	17	0	4
8 bears, 1 1/2 oz	140	0	32
Gummi Novelties *(Walgreens)*, 6	150	0	22
Gummi Savers, each	12	0	3
Gummi Sweet Tarts, 1 bug, 1.5 oz	150	0	34
Gummi Watch, 1, 2 oz	105	0	24
Gummi Worms, each	25	0	5
Guylian: No Sugar Added			
Milk Chocolate, 8 squares, 1 oz	126	9	15
Dark Chocolate, 8 squares, 1 oz	117	9	14

Per Piece/Serving	C	F	Cb
Halvah *(Joyvah)*:			
Plain/Marble, 1/2 bar, 2 oz	390	25	18
Choc.coated Sesame, 1/2 bar, 2 oz	380	23	20
Hard Candy, all flavors, 1 oz	110	0	28
1 regular piece	18	0	5
Heath: Original, 1.4 oz bar	210	13	25
Sensations Singles, 1.4 oz	210	14	25
Hershey's:			
Bar, 1.55 oz bar	240	14	25
King Size bar	410	25	38
w. Almonds, 1.45 oz bar	230	14	20
Bites: Almond Joy (20), 40g	220	14	22
Cookies 'n' Creme (20), 40g	210	10	23
Cookies 'N Mint, 1.55 oz bar	230	12	27
Crunchy Cookie Cups, 1.4 oz	210	12	23
Hugs: w. Almonds (9), 1.4 oz	230	13	22
Kisses: Milk Choc./Almond (8)	210	13	23
Milk Chocolate, 1.55 oz bar	200	12	25
2.6 oz bar	400	23	42
7 oz bar, 1/5 bar	200	12	21
Miniatures, 5 pces, 1.5 oz	230	13	25
Nuggets: Milk Choc./Alm. (4)	210	13	23
Cookies 'N Mint, (4)	200	10	24
Cookies & Creme, (4) 1.4 oz	200	11	25
P'nut B. Crispy Rice, 2 bars, 1.1 oz	230	13	25
Special Dark Choc., 1.45 oz bar	230	13	25
Sweet Escapes: 1.4 oz bar, aver.	180	7	27
Choc Toffee Crisp, 1 bar, 18g	80	3.5	12
Triple Choc Wafer, 1 bar, 20g	80	2.5	14
C'mel & P'nut But., 1 bar, 18g	70	2.5	12
Whoppers (18), 40g	190	7	30
Honeycomb: Plain, 1 oz	115	0	27
Choc-coated, 1 oz	125	1	28
Hot Tamales, 1 box, 60g, 2.1 oz	220	0	55
Sathers, 19 pces, 1.4 oz	150	0	36
Ice Blue Mints *(Walgreens),* 3, 17g	70	0	17
Jawbreakers *(Sathers),* 3, 17g	70	0	17
Jellies, 3 medium, 1 oz	120	0	30
Jells Raspberry *(Joyva),* each	70	1	8
Jelly Beans: Small, 22 beans, 1 oz	100	0	24
Regular, 12 beans, 1 oz	100	0	24
1 bean	8	0	2
Jumbo, 1 bean	20	0	5
Jewel, 13 beans, 1.4 oz	140	0	36
Sathers/Walgreens, 17, 40g	150	0	37
Jelly Bellys, each	4	0	1
35 pces, 1.4oz	140	0	37
Jelly Rings, *(Jewel),* 3, 1.5 oz	160	0	39
Jolly Rancher: Candy (3), 0.6 oz	70	0	17
Jolly Jellies, 7 oz	120	0	30
Sugar Free, 4 pces, 0.5 oz	35	0	14
Junior Mints, 1.6 oz box	180	3	38
16 pces, 1.4 oz	160	2.5	34
Juicefuls: Red Raspb., (3), 0.6 oz	60	0	15
Assorted Fruits, 1 pce	20	0	5
Jujubes, each	3	0	0.5
Juju Mix *(Sathers),* 11 pce, 1 1/2 oz	150	0	36
Juju Toys: 6 pce, 1.5 oz	150	0	37
Jujufruits, each	10	0	2
Kit Kat: 2.6 oz bar	365	21	50
King Size, 2.8 oz bar	410	22	48
1.5 oz bar	215	12	27
Multipack, each	80	4	10
Snack, 3 (2 pce bars), 1.65 oz	240	12	30
Krackel, 2.6 oz bar	390	21	45
Snack size, 0.35 oz	55	3	5
Kudos: 1 oz bar, aver. all types	120	5	20
M&M's Milk Choc Minis, 0.8 oz	90	2.5	17
Snickers, 0.8 oz	100	3.5	16
Lance: Popscotch, 1.2 oz pkg	160	6	24
Chocolaty Peanut Bar, 2 oz bar	320	18	30
Peanut Bar, 1.8 oz pkg	260	14	24
Lemon Drops, 3, 1/2 oz	50	0	12
Sugar Free *(Walgreens),* 5, 1/2 oz	35	0	14
Lemonhead, 10, 1/2 oz	60	0	14
Licorice: Average all types, 1oz	100	0	25
Bites *(Switzer),* each	12	0	1
Chews *(Panda),* each	10	0	2
Tid Bits, each	5	0	1
Twists: Black/Red, aver. 1 pce	30	0	7
American Licorice Co.: Laces, 1	35	0	8
Stick, (1) 0.5 oz	45	0	11
Choco Sticks, (4) 1.4 oz	145	0	35
Red Bites, 1.4 oz	140	0	34
Super Red Ropes, 1 rope, 2 oz	200	0	46
Vines, 1 pce	70	0	17

"You can begin to control what you eat when you write it down everyday."

Per Piece/Serving	C	F	Cb
Lifesavers: Large size, 1 candy	**15**	0	4
Regular, all flavors, 1 candy	**9**	0	2
1 Roll (14 candies), 1.14 oz	**130**	0	32
Sugar-free Delites: *Per Candy*			
Orchard Fruits; Summer Blend	**5**	0	2
Butter Toffee; European Collect.	**9**	0.5	3
Gummi Savers, 1.5 oz roll	**140**	0	32
Lollipops Fruit, 1 pce, 0.4 oz	**45**	0	11
Lik-m-aid *(Nestlé)*, 1.7 oz	**60**	0	15
Lindt: Lindor, Balls, average	**73**	4	8
Dark Choc Truffles, each	**70**	6	4
Lollipops, each, 0.2 oz	**20**	0	7
Lollipops C Pops *(Glenny's)*, each	**35**	0	8
Mamba, 9 pces, 1 1/2 oz	**160**	2	36
M&M's: Plain, 1.7 oz pkg	**240**	10	34
Milk Chocolate, 1 pce	**4**	0.2	0.5
20 pces, 0.6 oz	**80**	4	10
34 pces, 1 oz	**135**	6.5	17
68 pces, 2 oz	**270**	13	34
Almond Choc., 1.3 oz pkg	**200**	11	21
1.5 oz pkg	**230**	13	25
Crispy, 1.5 oz	**200**	9	30
King Size, 1/2 pkg, 1.6 oz	**240**	12	28
1.5 oz pkg	**220**	11	26
Mini Milk Choc. Candies, 1 tube	**180**	8	24
1.5 oz pkg	**70**	3	7
Peanut: 1.7 oz pkg	**250**	13	30
Fun Size, 0.7 oz pkg	**110**	5	13
Peanut Butter: 1.6 oz pkg	**240**	13	27
Fun Size, 0.7 oz pkg	**110**	6	12
Mars Bar: All varieties, 1.8 oz	**240**	13	31
Fun size, 1 bar	**95**	5	12
Marshmallows: Firm/Soft, 1 oz	**90**	0	23
Regular size, 6 pce, 33g	**110**	0	26
Mini-Marshmallow, 1/2 c., 30g	**100**	0	24
Choc-coat. Twists *(Joyva)*, ea.	**95**	2	10
Kraft: Mini, 1/2 cup	**80**	0	21
Creme, 2 Tbsp	**40**	0	10
Jet-Puffed, 5 pces	**90**	0	23
Funmallows, each	**25**	0	6
Miniature, 1/2 cup	**100**	0	25
Teddy Bear, 1/2 cup	**50**	0	12
Marshmallow Egg, 1 egg	**110**	0	26
Marzipan: 1 oz	**140**	7	16
Mauna Loa: Choc., 2.5 oz bar	**420**	29	36
Choc. coated Macadamias, 9	**230**	17	19
Mega Fruit Gummi, each	**10**	0	2

Per Piece/Serving	C	F	Cb
Mike & Ike, 1 pkg, 2.1 oz	**220**	0	55
Milk Choc. *(Hershey's):* 1.55 oz bar	**240**	14	25
with Almonds, 1.45 oz bar	**230**	14	20
Milk Choc. Crisp, 1.45 oz bar	**205**	11	22
Milk Duds, 13 pces, 1.3 oz	**160**	6	30
Milk Shake Bar, 1.8 oz bar	**220**	7	37
Milky Way: 2 oz bar	**270**	10	41
Fun size, 1.4 oz each	**90**	3.5	14
Miniatures, 5, 43g	**190**	7	30
Snack, 2, 40g	**180**	7	28
Milky Way Lite, 1.6 oz	**170**	5	34
Miniatures, 1.4 oz pkg, 5	**150**	4.5	29
Midnight Bar, 1.75 oz	**220**	8	36
Mints: uncoated, 1 oz	**100**	0	23
1 small mint (3/4 " diam)	**7**	0	2
1 large mint 1 1/2" diam.)	**30**	0	7
Mon Cheri *(Ferrero)*, 4 pces, 45g	**260**	18	20
Mounds, 1.9 oz bar	**250**	13	31
Mr Goodbar: King Size, 2.6 oz bar	**410**	25	37
1.75 oz bar	**270**	17	25
Necco Candy Wafers, 3, 57g	**15**	0	4
Neuhaus, average all types	**80**	5	7
Nips *(Pearson)*, all flavors, 2, 14g	**60**	2	10
Nite Bite, *(Glucose Bar))*	**100**	3.5	15
Nothing But Nuts Butter Toffee			
3 Tbsp, 1 oz	**200**	15	9
Nougat, 2 pces, 1 oz	**115**	1	25
Chocolate Covered, 1 oz	**120**	4	20
Nougat Nut Cream, 3.5 oz	**340**	31	50
Now & Later *(Nabisco)*, 1 pkg	**270**	2.5	63
Nutrageous Bar *(Reeses)*, 3.4 oz	**520**	30	52
King Size, 3.4 oz bar	**480**	24	54
Oh Henry! 1.8 oz bar	**240**	10	32
100 Grand, 1.5 oz bar	**200**	8	30
Orange *(Lindt)*, 6 block, 40g	**190**	10	24
Orange Slices: *(Jewel)*, 3, 41g	**140**	0	36
(Walgreens), 3, 43g	**150**	0	36
Pastel Mints *(Walgreens)*, 33 pce	**150**	0	38
Patteez *(Sweet n' Low)*, 1/2 ctn, 5	**120**	2.5	32
PayDay Bar: 1.85 oz bar	**260**	13	29
King Size, 3.4 oz	**480**	24	54
Peanut Bar, 1.6 oz bar	**210**	14	20
Peanut Butter Bars, 3 pces, 18g	**80**	1.5	15
Peanut Brittle, 1 oz	**130**	5	20
Peanut Chews *(Goldenberg's)*, ea.	**60**	3	21
Peanuts, choc-covered, each	**25**	1.5	2
Pearson's Mint Patties, 5, 38g	**150**	2.5	31

Per Piece/Serving	C	F	Cb
Pecan Roll, 1/3 bar, 40g	200	10	26
Peppermints, 7 small, 0.5 oz	50	0	12
Peppermint Twists, 2, 13g	60	0	12
Pez, 1 roll	30	0	6
Planters: Choc. Peanuts, 25, 7 oz	220	13	20
Orig. Peanut Bar, 1.6 oz	230	14	22
Popcorn ~ See Snacks Page 123			
Positively Pecan, 2.5 oz bar	390	24	38
Pralines, small, 0.3 oz	35	2	5
1 large piece, 1.4 oz	180	10	24
Pretzels: choc-covered:			
3 minisize, 1.15 oz	150	5.5	23
1 regular, 1 oz	130	4.5	20
Pretzel Flipz *(Nestlé)*, 8, 1 oz	130	5	19
Raisinets, 1 pkg, 1.7 oz	210	8	33
Raspberry Cream, each	80	2.5	5
Reese's: Chocolate Bar, 2.8 oz	420	24	43
Candy (Multipack), each	95	5.5	9
Miniatures, each	40	2.5	4
Peanut Butter Bites (18), 39g	210	12	22
Mini, 1 pce	42	2.5	5
Peanut Butter Cups, 1.8 oz cup	280	17	28
Mini, 1 pce	42	2.5	5
Reese's Pieces, 50, 1.4 oz	190	8	24
Snack, 2, 34g	190	11	19
Rice Crunchy Bars: 1 bar, 19g			
Average all flavors	60	0	14
Rice Krispies Treats: 1.3 oz bar	150	3.5	29
Chocolate Chip, 1.3 oz bar	160	5	28
Riesen Choc. Chew, 5, 1.4 oz	180	7	29
Ritter Sport: Plain Choc, 50g	260	16	26
w. Hazelnuts, 1/2 pkg, 50g	290	19	24
Rolo, each	32	1.5	5
Root Beer Barrels, 3, 0.5 oz	60	0	16
Russell Stover Candy: Creams, ea.	60	2	10
Almond Delight, 2 oz	290	17	32
Caramel Bar, 46g	230	11	20
Jelly Cups (P/Nut Butter), 2, 34g	140	9	14
Mint Dream	160	8	19
Pecan Delight (Sugar Free), 2 oz	260	18	27
Pecan Delight, 2 oz bar	310	20	27
Pecan Roll, 50g	260	18	23
Salt Water Taffy *(Sathers)*, 5, 43g	150	2.5	34
Seashells *(Guylian)* 1 shell	65	4	6
Sesame Crunch, 3 pces	80	4	7
Simply Lite: Li'l Bits Chocolatey/P'nut Butter, 1/2 ctn, 36 pieces	130	5	18

Per Piece/Serving	C	F	Cb
Simply Sugar Free: See *Allen Wertz*			
Sixlets *(Hershey)*, 1 pkg	240	9	37
Skittles, all flavors, 1.5 oz pkg	170	2	39
1.6 oz pkg, each	60	0.5	14
King Size, 2.17 oz, 1 pack	240	2.5	54
Skor Toffee Bar, 1.4 oz	220	14	23
Smarties Candy Rolls, 1 roll	25	0	5
Snackwell's Raisin Dips, 5 oz	160	5	34
Snickers:			
Bar: 2.1 oz bar	280	14	35
King Size, 1/2 bar, 1.2 oz	170	8	21
Munch Bar, 1.4 oz bar	230	15	17
Fun size, each	95	5	12
Miniatures, each	42	2.5	5
Creme Egg, each	170	10	19
Snack, 2, 40g	190	10	24
Sno Caps, 2.3 oz pkg	300	13	48
Soft 'N Chewy Butter Toffee, ea.	32	0.5	7
Sonic Boom Pops *(Walgreens)*, ea.	60	0	14
Sour Brite Crawlers, 13 pces	140	0	31
Sour Punch, all types, 1 pkg	190	9	45
1 straw	20	0	5
Spearmint Leaves: *(Jewel)*, 5, 40g	140	0	35
(Walgreens), 5, 1 1/2 oz	150	0	38
Spice Drops, 14 pces, 1 1/2 oz	140	0	36
Spree *(Nestlé)*: Snack, 1, 1/2 oz	50	0	13
Starburst: Candy Canes, 0.5 oz	70	0	18
Fruit Chews, each	20	0.4	4
2 oz pkg	240	4.5	48
Fruit Twist, each	35	0	8
Fruit Twist, 2 oz pkg	190	1	45
Jellybeans, 1.5 oz	150	0	38
Jellybean Egg, 2 oz	200	0	51
Trop. Fruit Chews, 2.7 oz pack	240	5	48
Starlight Mints: 3 pces, 1/2 oz	60	0	16
Suckers *(Walgreens)*, 1 sucker, 11g	45	0	11
Sweet 'N Low: Chews, each	11	0.2	3
Sugar-Free Hard Candy, each	8	0	2
Sweet Escapes: *See Hershey's*			
Sweet Success Bars, 1 bar	120	4	23
Sweet Tarts *(Nestlé)*, 7, 1/2 oz	50	0	13
Symphony: All types, 1/5 bar, 7 oz	220	14	24
Taffy, 1 pce, 1/2 oz	55	0.5	12
3 Musketeers, 2.1 oz bar	260	8	46
Fun size, each	70	2	13
Miniatures, each	25	0.5	5
Snack, 2, 33g	140	4.5	26

Per Piece/Serving	C	F	Cb
Tang-a-Roos: 1 roll	**24**	0	6
Tarts: *(Walgreens),* 4 pce, 15g	**60**	0	15
Tails: *(Walgreens),* 8 pce, 15g	**60**	0	15
Tastetations *(Hershey's)*: Pep'mint	**20**	0	8
Butterscotch; Caramel; Choc	**20**	0.5	4
Terry's Orange Milk Choc, 1 pce	**50**	3	5
Tic Tac, all varieties, each	**1.5**	0	0
Toblerone: 50g (1.76 oz) bar	**270**	15	32
1 bar, 100g, (3.5 oz)	**540**	30	63
1/3 bar, 33g	**180**	10	21
Toffees: Regular, 1 oz	**150**	9	15
Tongue Torchers *(Walgreens),* 3	**70**	0	17
Tootsie Roll Midgies *(Walgreens)*, 6	**160**	3	33
Tootsie Roll Pops, 1/2 oz pop	**50**	0	12
Treasures *(Nestlé):* Nestlé Crunch, 3	**160**	8.5	20
Butterfinger Pieces, 3	**180**	9	23
Creamy Caramel, 3	**180**	9	22
Peanut Butter Miniatures, 3	**180**	12	17
Truffles: Regular, 1 pce, 0.4 oz	**60**	4	5
Large (*Godiva*), 0.75 oz	**110**	6.5	12
Extra Large (*J.Schmidt*), 1 1/2 oz	**220**	13	24
Turtles *(Nestlé),* each	**85**	4.5	10
Twix: Caramel (1), 1 oz	**140**	7	18
King Size: 1 cookie, 3.35 oz	**120**	6	16
4 cookies	**480**	24	64
Fun Size, 0.5 oz	**80**	4	10
2 oz pkg, 2 bars	**280**	14	37
Peanut Butter, 0.9 oz	**140**	8.5	14
Snack, 1 cookie, 0.5 oz	**80**	5	8
Twizzlers Strawberry, 1 oz pce	**110**	0	30
Velamints: Sugar Free, 1 pce	**10**	0	2
Werther's Original, 3 pce, 15g	**60**	1	13
Whatchamacallit Bar, 1.7 oz	**220**	10	29
Whitman's: Sampler, 3 pces, 1.4 oz	**200**	11	25
Assorted, 1 pce	**60**	3	9
Dark Chocolate, 1 pce	**65**	3	8
Pecan Roll, 2 oz roll	**300**	20	26
Snoopy Treats, 2 pces	**190**	10	24
Yogurt Candy: Plain, 1 oz	**120**	6	15
Coated Raisins, 1 oz	**120**	4	21
York Mints: 1.5 oz patty	**145**	5	34
Snack size, 0.5 oz	**55**	1	11
Peppermint Patties, 3	**150**	2.5	30
Zachary Old Fash. Creme Drops, 3	**170**	3	36
Zero Bar, 1 pce, 0.7 oz	**85**	3	14

Carob Candy

Per Piece/Serving	C	F	Cb
Carob: Plain/Natural, 1 oz	**160**	11	9
Carob coated: Raisins, 1 oz	**130**	8	15
Almonds/Peanuts, 1 oz	**150**	10	14
Malt Balls, 1 oz	**135**	8	15
Caramels, 1 oz	**110**	4	18
Dates, 1 oz	**125**	5	20
Soybeans	**145**	9	16
Trail; Party Mix, 1 oz	**140**	9	15
Carob Chips, unsweetened, 1 oz	**140**	7	19
Carob Bars, average all brands:			
Plain/Nut, 1 oz	**160**	11	13
Fruit & Nut, 1 oz	**155**	10	13
Mint/Orange, 1 oz	**160**	11	14
Caroby Natural Touch, 3 oz	**450**	27	36
Carafection: Cashew Coconut Crunch,			
1/2 Bar, (42g) 1.5 oz	**250**	14	5

Cough Drops & Lozenges

Per Piece/Serving	C	F	Cb
Beech Nut, 1 tablet	**10**	0	2
Hall's, 1 tablet	**15**	0	4
Hall's Plus, 1	**18**	0	5
Helps Cough, all flavors, 1	**14**	0	3
Listerine Loz. (Amer.Chicle)	**9**	0	2
Ludens Throat Drops, all flavors, 14	**10**	0	2
Pine Bros, 1 cough drop	**10**	0	2
Rite Aid, Menthol Cough, 1 drop	**12**	0	3
Rolaids/Sodium Free, 1	**4**	0	1
Sathers Peppermint Lozenges, 1	**13**	0	3
Squibb Cough/Throat Loz.'s, 1	**16**	0	4
Sucrets (Beecham) Lozenges, 1	**10**	0	2
Wintergreen Loz. (Walgreens), 1	**13**	0	3

Cough Medications - Page 128

Real women don't have hot flashes. . . . They have power surges!

Home-Popped Popcorn

Popping Corn Kernels:	C	F	Cb
2 Tbsp, 1 oz	100	1	22
(makes approx. 3½ cups)			
Air-popped (no oil), plain, 1 oz	100	0	22
1 cup (6g)	20	0	4
Oil-popped, plain, 1 oz	140	8	10
1 cup (11g)	55	3	4
Popcorn Oil, 1 Tbsp	120	14	0

Microwave Popcorn

Average All Brands (Popped)			
Butter: Regular, 1 cup	35	2	4
Light, 1 cup	25	1	4
Act II Popcorn:			
Butter, 1 cup, 0.3 oz	35	2	4.5
4 cups, popped, 1 oz	140	8	18
Light Butter, 1 cup, 0.2 oz	24	1	4.5
5 cups, popped, 1 oz	120	4	22
Butter Lovers,1 cup, 0.3 oz	45	3	4.5
3.5 cups, 1 oz	160	10	15
Butter Lovers (Reduced Fat), 1 c.	30	1.5	4.5
4.5 cups, 1 oz	130	6	20
American Fare (K-Mart):			
Butter, 1 cup, 0.3 oz	37	2.5	4
3.5 cups, 1 oz	130	9	14
Light Butter, 1 cup, 0.3 oz	28	1	5
3.5 cups, 1 oz	100	4	17
Healthy Choice: Butter, 6 cups	100	2.5	22
Natural, 6 cups, 1 oz	100	2	22
Newman's Own: Butter, 1 oz	170	11	16
Light Butter Flavor, 3½ cups	110	3	20
Orville Redenbacher:			
Movie Theater Butter, 1 cup	30	2	3
4 cups, popped, 1 oz	120	8	12
Light Movie Theater Butter, 1 cup	20	1	2
4 cups, 1 oz	80	4	8
Double Feature Jumbo, 1 cup	30	2	3
Smart Pop!: Lowfat, 1 cup	15	0	3
Butter Light, 1 cup	20	0.5	3

Bagged Popcorn

Average All Brands (Ready-to-Eat)			
Regular: Plain, ½ oz pkg	80	5	7
1 oz pkg	160	10	14
Box (store/airport), 2 oz	320	20	28
Bag (9" high x 5" wide), 3 oz	480	30	42

Bagged Popcorn (Brands)

Act II Popcorn:	C	F	Cb
Butter Toffee: ¾ cup, 1 oz	110	1	27
w. Peanuts, ¾ cup, 1 oz	120	2.5	24
Caramel w. P'nuts, ¾ cup, 1 oz	120	2.5	24
Supreme w. Pecans, Almonds, ¾ c.	130	5	22
Boston's: Fat Free, ⅔ cup, 1 oz	100	0	23
Lite, 2 cup, 1 oz	140	6	19
Gourmet Super Prem., 2 c., 1 oz	160	11	13
40% Less Fat, 2¾ cup, 1 oz	140	6	17
Cracker Jack: Original, ½ c., 1 oz	120	2	23
Fat Free varieties, ¾ cup, 1 oz	110	0	26
Crunch 'N Munch: ½ cup, 1 oz	140	5	22
Caramel w. P'nuts, ⅔ c., 1.2 oz	140	3.5	25
Fiddle Faddle: ¾ cup, 1 oz	140	6	21
Orville Redenbacher Clusters,			
Butter Toffee, ⅔ cup, 1.1 oz	140	4.5	24
Slimmons (Fat Free): ¾ c., 1 oz	110	0	25
Weight Watchers: Butter, ⅔ oz	90	2.5	14

Movie Theater Popcorn

	C	F	Cb
Small (7 cups): Plain	400	27	30
with Butter	580	47	30
Medium (16 cups): Plain	900	60	70
with Butter	1170	90	70
Large (20 cups): Plain	1150	76	90
with Butter	1500	116	90

Potato Chips/Crisps

Average All Brands			
Regular: Plain or flav'd, 1 chip	9	1	1
17 chips, 1 oz bag	150	10	15
4 oz quantity	600	40	60
Pringles, 12 crisps, 1 oz	150	10	15
6.75 oz can	1000	65	100
Ruffles, Buffalo Style, 1 oz	160	10	16
Reduced Fat:			
Pringles (Right Crisps), 1 oz	140	7	20
Crunch Tators, 1 oz	140	7	19
Kettle Fry (Eagle), 1 oz	150	8	16
Lowfat/Baked varieties, 1 oz	110	1.5	23
Fat Free (*Childer's/Louise's*), 1oz	100	0	22
Pringles (Fat Free), 1 oz	70	0	15
Lay's Wow!, 20 chips, 1 oz	75	0	18
Ruffles Wow!, 17 chips, 1 oz	75	0	17
Cheddar Sour Crm,15, 1 oz	75	0	16

Pretzels

Pretzels	C	F	Cb
Average All Brands			
Hard Baked Pretzels:			
1 oz	110	2	22
Sticks, thin, 2 1/4" (9/oz), 1	12	0	3
Twists, thin, 1/4" thick, (5/oz), 1	25	0.2	5
Dutch (2 3/4" x 2 5/8") 1/2 oz, 1	55	1	11
Fat Free: Snyders (1), 1 oz	100	0	22
Utz Wheels/Nuggets, 1 oz	100	0	22
Rold Gold: Sticks, 48, 1 oz	100	0	23
Sourdough Nuggets, 12, 1 oz	100	0	23
Thins, 12, 1 oz	110	0	24
Twists, 16, 1 oz	110	1	22
Tiny Twists, 18, 1 oz	100	0	23
Low Fat Pretzels:			
American Fare Mini Twists, 1oz	120	1	23
Rold Gold: Crispy Thins, 9, 1 oz	110	0.5	22
Choc-coated: (*Nestlé*), 1 oz	130	6	20
White Fudge covered (*Nestlé*), 1 oz, 7 pieces	140	6	19
Soft Pretzels (Twists) average:			
Plain: Regular, 2.5 oz	190	0	41
King Size, 5 oz	390	0	83
Big Cheese, 5 oz	380	7	61
Peanut Butter filled (*Tr. Joe's*) 1oz	160	7	18
Toffee (*Crunch 'n Munch*), 12	120	1	25
Auntie Annie's: See Fast-Foods Pg. 167			
Snyder's of Hanover: Logs (7) 1oz	120	1	21
Homestyle (15), 1 oz	120	1	24
Super Pretzel: Jalapeno, 5 oz	360	0	78
Bavarian Twist, 3 oz	210	3	41
Cinnamon Raisin w. Icing, 5 oz	420	4	76
Sweet Dough Twist, 3.7 oz	300	3	60

Tortilla Chips

Tortilla Chips	C	F	Cb
Tortilla Chips: Average, 1 oz	150	8	22
(1 oz = approx. 11 chips or 12 strips)			
Utz: Lowfat Baked, 8 chips, 1 oz	120	1.5	23
Boston: Baked, 13 chips, 1 oz	110	1.5	23
Doritos: 18 chips, 1 oz	140	6	20
Light, 13 chips, 1 oz	130	5	20
Wow! Nacho Cheesier, 1 oz	90	0.5	16
Keebler Suncheros Light, 1 oz	150	8	18
Kettle: Average, 1 oz	140	6	18
Padrino Reduced Fat, 1 oz	130	4	22

Snacks

Snacks	C	F	Cb
Bacon Cheese Crackers, 1 oz	140	6	14
Banana Chips, 1/3 cup, 1 oz	140	7	18
Beef Jerky: Average, 1 oz	70	1	0
Beef Sticks *(Frito-Lay's)* 0.3 oz	50	4	1
Bugles: Original, 1 1/3 cup, 1 oz	160	9	18
Baked Bugles, 1 1/2 cup, 1.1 oz	130	3.5	23
Cajun Jerky, 1 1/2 oz	150	6	6
Carrot Chips *(Hain)*	160	9	26
Cheddar Lites *(Health Valley)* 1 oz	120	3	21
Cheese Crackers, 1 oz	130	6	18
Cheese Filled *(Frito-Lay's)*	210	11	24
Cheese Curls, 1 1/4 cup, 1 oz	160	9	19
Reduced Fat *(Utz),* 1 oz	140	6	21
American Fare, 1 1/4 cup, 1 oz	140	5	22
Cheese Puffs, average, 1 oz	150	10	15
Lowfat, 1 oz	140	5	20
Health Valley, 1 1/2 cup	110	3	21
No Fries, 1 oz	110	0	23
Cheese Straws, 4 pieces	110	7	8
Cheese Twists: 23 twists, 1 oz	150	8	19
Cheetos: Regular all flavors	160	10	15
Light, cheese flavored	140	6	19
Cheez Balls: 45 balls, 1 oz	150	10	15
Reduced Fat, 45 balls, 0.73 oz	100	4.5	13
Cheez Bopps (*Boston's*), (28) 1 oz	130	6	17
Cheez Curls/Doodles, 1 oz	160	10	16
Cheez Mania *(Planters)*, 35, 1 oz	160	3	15
Chex Mix: *General Mills,* 1.1 oz	150	10	15
Bold 'N Zesty (40% less fat), 1/2 c.	140	6	20
Chedder (50% less fat), 1/2 c.	130	5	20
Traditional (60% less fat), 2/3 c.	130	4	21
Chex *(Ralston)* 2/3 cup, 1 oz	130	5	20
Churros *(Mex. Pastry)* 10",1.2 oz	140	9	12
Cinna Chips *(T.J. Cinn.)* 3, 1 oz	110	4	19
Combos (Oven Baked): *Per Bag, 1.8 oz*			
Cheddar Cheese Crackers	240	11	31
Cheddar/Nacho Cheese Pretzels	240	8	35
Pepperoni Pizza	240	11	30
Corn Chips: Aver. all types, 1 oz	160	10	15
8 oz bag	1280	80	120
Doritos, (12), 1 oz	150	7	20
Corn Crunchies/Spirals, 1 oz	160	10	15
Corn Crisps *(Pringle),* 1 oz	140	7	18
Corn Nuts, 1/3 cup, 1 oz	130	4	20
Corn Puffs *(Health Valley)* 2 c. 1 oz	120	1.5	25
Dunkaroos, 1 tray, 1 oz	130	5	20

Snacks (Cont)

	C	F	Cb
French's Potato Sticks 3/4 c., 1 oz	180	12	16
Fruit a Freeze: Bars, each, 3 oz	170	9	23
Funyun's Onion flavor., 1 oz	140	7	18
Goldfish (*Pepperidge Farm*) 1 oz	140	7	18
Gold-N-Chees (*Lance*), 1 3/8 oz	180	7	25
Lance Sandwich: Bonnie, 1 pkg	160	7	23
Capt. Wafers; Choc-O-Mint, pkg	190	10	23
Sour Dough w. Cheddar, 1 pkg	240	15	23
Other varieties, average, 1 pkg	200	10	22
Munchos, 16 pieces, 1 oz	160	10	16
Nabisco: Oreo, 1.3 oz	160	7	24
Chips Ahoy, 1.3 oz	150	5	25
Sweet Crispers (18), 1 oz	135	3	25
Nibblers (*Snyder's*): Regular (13)	130	3	23
Sourdough Fat Free (16)	120	0	25
Onion Rings (*Lance*), 1 pkg	120	6	16
Oriental Mix (rice snacks), 1 oz	155	7.5	15
Original Party Mix (*Flavor House*):			
1/3 cup, 1 oz	160	10	13
Party Mix (*Flavor Tree*) 1/4 cup	160	11	14
Pork Skins/Rind:			
Baken-ets, 1 oz	160	10	0
Grande, 2/3 cup	80	5	0
Lance, 1 pkg	65	4	1
Potato Puffs (*Health Valley*), 1 oz	110	3	21
Potato Sticks (*French's*), 3/4 c., 1.1oz	180	12	16
Ranch Puffs (*No Fries*), 1 oz	110	0	23
Rice Chips: Bar-B-Q/Onion, 1/2 oz	70	3	9
Santitas (*Frito Lay*), 1 oz	140	6	20
Sesame Sticks, 1 oz	155	8	18
Snack Crackers (*No Fries*), 1 oz	110	0	24
Soy Nuts, dry roasted, 1 oz	130	6	9
Spicers Wheat Snacks, 1 1/2 oz	150	7.5	18
Sunchips (*Frito Lay*), 1 oz	140	7	18
Toast/Cheese Crackers, 1 pkg	205	10	23
Tostitos, average, 1 oz	140	8	18
Trail Mix (Nuts/Seeds/Dried Fruit):			
Regular, 3 Tbsp, 1 oz	130	8	13
Tropical, 3 Tbsp, 1 oz	120	5	19
w. Chocolate Chips, 1 oz	140	9	13
Turkey Jerky Teriyaki (*Oberto*)	80	0.5	0
Vegetable Snacks/Chips, 1 oz	130	4	24
***Weight Watchers*:** Chse Curls, 1/2 oz	70	2.5	10
Apple Chips: 3/4 oz pkg.	70	0	18
Yogurt Raisins, 1 oz	120	4	21

Granola & Sports Bars

Per Bar	C	F	Cb
Advantage Bar, 60g	240	10	2
Amway: Positrim Food Bar,			
Cocoa Almond, 1 wrap (2 bars)	190	7	28
Peanut Butter, 1 wrap (2 bars)	210	9	28
Arbonne: Nutrition Bar, 50g	190	4.5	24
Ashfi /Herbal Energy, 51g	190	4	29
Balance + Bar, 50g (1.76 oz)	200	6	22
Snack, Honey, Peanut, 25g	100	3	11
Barbara's Bakery: Real Fruit	50	0	13
Cereal Bars, fruit filled	110	0	27
Granola Bars	80	2	15
Bariatrix: Nutra Bars, 47g	170	5	23
Proti Bars (15g Protein), 41g	130	5	15
Right Choice Bars, 40g	140	3	24
BioX Bio Protein: 81g	300	7	37
Boost: Choc./Strawb. Crunch	190	6	30
Boulder Bar Endurance, 2.5 oz	220	4	13
Burn-IT: 50g bar	180	3	13
Cap'N Crunch, all types, 0.8 oz	90	2	17
Carnation Breakfast Bars, 35g (1.2 oz):			
Granola (Honey/Choc), average	130	2.5	26
Choc Chip/P.nut Butter, chewy	150	5	24
Clif Bar: 2.4 oz, 68g bar	250	6	40
Crunchy, all types, 1 bar	240	5	39
Luna: 48g bar	180	5	24
Apr.; Cranb. Apple Cherry, 1 bar	220	2	44
Choc Almond Fudge, 1 bar	230	4.5	39
Carrot Cake; Choc Chip, 1 bar	240	4	43
Cookies 'n Cream, 1 bar	230	3.5	39
Ginger Snap, 1 bar	230	3.5	42
Choc Brownie, 1 bar	240	4	41
Edgebar, 2 oz, 57g bar	220	2	42
Energia Bar, 2.25 oz	230	2	41
Ensure Choc Fudge Bar	130	3	20
Entenmann's: Multi-Grain, 1.3 oz	140	3	25
Extreme Ripped Force, 45g	160	3	33
Fi-Bar Nectar Granola Bars, 1 oz	100	0	22
Chewy & Nutty Bar, 1.2 oz	140	4.5	23
Fi-Pro-Tein (*R-Kane*), 1.2 oz bar	107	1	16
Figurines Diet Bar, aver., 1 bar	110	6	12
Fruitein Energy Bar, 1.3 oz	130	3	18
Gatorbar, 2.25 oz	210	1	26
GeniSoy: Peanut Butter Fudge	230	5	31
Other varieties, average	220	3.5	32
Glucerna: Nutr'l Bar, 38g	140	4	24
Hain: Mini Munchies Rice	90	1.5	2

Per Bar	C	F	Cb
Hansen's: Chocolate, 50g	180	2	38
Yogurt varieties, 50g	190	4	38
Hardbody, 2.5 oz, 71g	280	7	41
Health Valley: Fruit/Granola Bars	140	0	34
Cereal: Strawberry Cobbler	130	2	27
Healthy Recipes *(Novartis)*	150	4	21
HeartBar, Orig., Cranberry, 50g	190	3	27
HMR Benefit Bar, 1.1 oz	160	5	22
IDN *(Nu Skin)*: AppSignal, 2 wafers	25	0	5
Glycobar, 42g (1.48 oz)	170	5	28
ProGRAM-16 Bar, 65g (2.28 oz)	250	5	34
Jewel Granola Bars: Cereal	140	3	27
Choc Chip/P'nut Butter	130	4.5	20
Lowfat varieties	110	2	22
Jolt Bar *(Nutra Tech)* 40g	140	3	24
Kashi Golean, 2.75 oz	280	5	52
Kudos: *M&M's*	90	2.5	17
Snickers, 23g	100	3.5	16
Choc Chip/Fudge; P. Butter, 28g	125	5	20
Lean Body, 76g	300	6	15
Met-Rx Food Bars, average, 100g	320	3	50
Source One: Per pkg, all types	190	3	30
MightyBite Choc. bar, 25g	100	4	11
Mountain Lift Energy Bar	220	4.5	34
Myoplex Plus Deluxe, 90g	340	7	43
Nature Valley Granola: Oats	180	6	27
Lowfat varieties	110	2	21
NiteBite (Time-release Glucose Bar)			
Choc. Fudge; P'nut Butter, 25g	100	3.5	15
NuBar Decadence, 1.3 oz	140	2.5	30
Nutiva (Hemp, Sunflower), 40g	205	14	15
Nutra Blast, average, 47g	160	4	27
Nutri-Grain: Cereal/Twist bars	140	3	27
Low Fat Granola Bars, 21g	80	1.5	16
Fruit-full Squares, 49g bar	190	6	33
Odwalla, 2.2 oz	245	5	45
100% Bar, 50g	190	6	31
Optizone, 50g	190	6	20
Perfect Rx Nutrition Bar, 100g	340	3	50
Planters: Peanut Bar, 1.6 oz	230	11	22
Pounds Off Bar: All flavors	220	4	35
Power Bar: Harvest, 2.3 oz	240	4	45
Athletic: All varieties, 65g	230	2.5	45
Essentials, 53g	180	4	28
Perform. Energy: Oatmeal Raisin	230	2.5	43
Protein Plus, 2.75 oz	290	5	38
PR Bar Ironman, 49.6g	200	6	22
Prozone Nutrition Bar, 50g	195	6	18

Per Bar	C	F	Cb
Promax: Dble Fudge Brownie, 75g	270	5	34
Other flavors	280	5	36
Pure Protein Sports Bar, 78g (2.75 oz):			
Chewy Choc Chip, 1 bar	285	5	16
Peanut Butter, 1 bar	280	7	9
Other varieties, average	270	4	15
Quaker: Chewy Granola Bars			
Butterfinger; Nestlé Crunch	120	3.5	21
Peanut Butter; Grand Slam	110	3	20
Restart: Peanut Butter, 1.25 oz	140	4	10
Strawb. Banana; Chocolate	130	2.5	21
Rice Krispies Bar *(Kellogg's)*, 28g	120	4	20
Coco Pops Bar, 22g	100	3.5	16
Treats Squares, 22g	90	2	18
Slim-Fast Bars, 1.2 oz	140	5	20
Meal on the Go, 56g	220	5	36
Snackwell's: Cereal Bars	120	0	29
Hearty Fruit & Grain	130	3	26
Chewy Granola, Fudge-Dip., 1 oz	130	3	26
Source One (Met-Rx), 1 pkg, 62g	190	3	30
Spirutein Energy Bar, 1.4 oz	150	4	19
Energy: Cocoa, 65g (2.3 oz)	210	3	41
Steel Bar, 3 oz, 85g	330	6	52
Steel Pro, 85g	330	6	15
Sweet Rewards: Choc. Chip	110	2	23
Brownie; Fat Free	120	2	30
Sweet Success (*Nestlé*): Choc Bars	100	3.5	23
Snack Bars, 33g (1.2 oz)	120	4	23
Thermo Speed Bar, 85g	280	5	24
Think! Interactive Bar, 2 oz, 56g	220	3	43
Thunder Bar, all flavors	220	2	44
Tiger's Milk: 35g Bar	130	2.5	24
Peanut Butter varieties	150	6	19
Protein Rich	145	5	18
Tiger Sport, 65g	230	2	43
Twinlab: Ultra Fuel, $2\frac{1}{2}$ oz	230	0	42
Ironman Triathlon, 56.8g	230	7	25
Ultimate Protein Bar:			
Choc./Dream; P'nut Butter, 78g	280	6	20
Berries 'N Yogurt, 40g (1.4 oz)	140	3	14
Chocolate Choc Dream, 40g	140	2.5	10
Ultra Slim-Fast: Rich Caramel, 1 oz	110	3.5	22
Peanut Butter Crunch, 1 oz	120	4	20
Universal Muscle, 56.7g	280	5	35
Verve (Wholefoods Mkt), 2.4 oz	240	5	41
White Lightning, 85g	320	5	27
You Are What You Eat, 56g	220	5	39
Zone Force/Perfect, aver., 50g	195	6	21

Per 1 oz Unless Indicated	C	F	Cb
Acorns, raw 1 oz	**105**	7	12
Almonds, Dried/Dry roasted:			
Whole, 24-28 med., 1 oz	**170**	15	7
1/2 cup, 2 1/2 oz	**420**	37	17
Chopped, 1/2 cup, 2 1/4 oz	**380**	34	16
Sliced, 1/2 cup, 1 2/3 oz	**280**	25	12
Choc. coated (5-6), 1 oz	**160**	11	14
Oil rstd. (Blue Diamond), 1 oz	**175**	17	3.5
Almond Meal (partially defattened)			
1 cup (not packed), 2 1/4 oz	**260**	11	11
Honey roasted, 1 oz	**170**	13	8
Brazil Nuts, 8 medium, 1 oz	**185**	19	3.5
Cashews, Dry or Oil roasted:			
14 large/18 med./26 small, 1 oz	**165**	14	10
1/2 cup, 2.4 oz	**400**	33	23
Honey roasted, 1 oz	**170**	12	10
Chestnuts, aver. all: Dried, 1 oz	**105**	1	22
Raw/Fresh, 5-6 nuts, 1 oz	**60**	0	13
Canned, water chestnuts			
sliced/whole/drained, 1 oz	**23**	0	5
Coconut:			
Flesh (no shell), 1 oz	**100**	10	4
Raw: 1 pce. (2"x2"x1/2"), 1.6 oz	**160**	15	7
1/2 medium (4 1/2" diam.)	**650**	62	30
Dried (Desiccated):			
Unsweetened, 1 oz	**187**	18	17
Sweetened, shredded, 1 oz	**140**	9	13
Grated, 1/2 cup, 1.3 oz	**185**	12	18
Cream (can.), 1/2 c., 5.2 oz	**285**	26	12
Milk (canned), 1/2 c., 4 oz	**225**	24	3
Water (center liq.), 1/2 cup, 4 1/4 oz	**23**	0	4.5
Filberts or Hazelnuts:			
Shelled, 18-20 nuts	**180**	18	4.5
Chopped, 1/4 cup	**180**	18	4.5
Ground, 1/4 cup	**120**	12	3
Ginko Nuts, can., 14 med., 1 oz	**32**	0	6
Hickory, 30 small nuts	**190**	18	5
Macadamia Nuts, shelled:			
Raw, 7 med./14 small, 1 oz	**200**	21	4
1/2 cup, 2.3 oz	**460**	48	10
Oil roasted, 1 oz	**205**	22	3.5
1/2 cup, 2.4 oz	**490**	52	8
Choc. coated, 2-3 pces, 1 oz	**180**	13	15
Mixed Nuts: 18-22 nuts, 1 oz	**175**	13	7
Planters: Dry roasted	**170**	15	7
Honey roasted (dry rst'd)	**170**	13	7
Oil roasted, all types	**180**	16	7
Kettle: Choc Lover's Mix, 1 oz	**130**	17	16

Per 1 oz Unless Indicated	C	F	Cb
Nut Toppings:			
Chopped, 1 Tbsp, 1/4 oz	**40**	4	1.5
Peanuts:			
Raw/Dried: In shell, 1 oz	**117**	10	3
Shelled, 1 oz	**160**	14	4.5
Boiled: 1/2 cup, 1.1 oz	**102**	7	7
Roasted, 30 lge./60 sml., 1 oz	**165**	14	6
1 cup, 5.1 oz	**840**	71	31
Chopped, 3 Tbsp, 1 oz	**165**	14	6
Planters: Oil Roasted, 1 oz	**170**	15	5
Beer Nuts, 1 oz pkg	**180**	14	7
Choc-coated, 1/2 cup, 2 1/2 oz	**380**	25	36
Cocktail, oil roasted, 1 oz	**170**	14	5
Dry Roasted, 1 oz	**160**	14	6
Honey roasted, 1 oz	**170**	13	8
Honey/Dry roasted, 1 oz	**160**	13	7
Spanish Oil Roasted, 1 oz	**170**	14	5
Sweet 'n Crunchy, 1 oz	**140**	8	16
Pecans:			
Kernel halves, 1 oz	**190**	19	5
(20 Jumbo or 31 large halves)			
1 cup halves, 3.8 oz	**720**	73	20
Chopped, 1/2 cup, 2 oz	**380**	30	10
Oil roasted, 1 oz	**195**	20	4.5
Honey roasted, 1 oz	**200**	18	5
Pilinuts, dried, 1/4 cup, 1 oz	**205**	23	1
Pinenuts, dried, 1 Tbsp, 10g	**50**	5	1.5
Pistachios:			
Unshelled, 1/2 cup, 2 oz	**165**	14	7
Shelled, 1/4 c., 45 nuts, 1 oz	**165**	14	7
Lance, 1 1/8 oz package	**180**	14	8
Planters: **Dry Roasted,** 1oz	**170**	15	6
Fruit 'n Nut Mix, 1 oz	**150**	9	13
Nut Topping, 1 oz	**180**	16	6
Tavern Nuts, 1 oz	**170**	15	6
Sesame Nut Mix:			
(Planters), 1 oz	**160**	12	8
Soybean Nuts:			
Dry roasted, 1 oz	**130**	6	9
1/2 cup, 3 oz	**390**	18	28
Oil roasted, 1 oz	**140**	7	9
Walnuts:			
Black, 15-20 halves, 1 oz	**175**	16	3.5
Chopped, 1/4 cup	**190**	18	4
Ground, 1/4 cup	**120**	12	2.5
English/Persian:			
14 halves, 1 oz	**185**	18	5
Chopped, 1/4 cup	**195**	19	5

Seeds

Seeds	C	F	Cb
Alfalfa Seeds, sprout., 1/2 c., 1/2 oz	**5**	0	1
Caraway, Fennell, 1 tsp	**10**	0.5	1
Cottonseed Kernels, rst., 1 Tbsp	**50**	4	2
Flax Seeds, 3 Tbsp, 1 oz	**140**	10	11
Lotus Seeds, dried, 1/2 c., 1/2 oz	**50**	0.5	10
Poppy Seeds, 1 tsp	**15**	1	1
Pumpkin & Squash Seeds, whole:			
Roasted/Tamari, 1 oz	**125**	5.5	3
1/2 cup (32g)	**140**	6	3.5
Dried, 1 oz	**155**	13	5
Safflower Kernels, dried, 1 oz	**150**	11	10
Sesame Seeds: Dried, 1 Tbsp, 9g	**50**	4.5	2
Roasted/Toasted, 1 oz	**160**	14	7
Sunflower Kernels/Seed:			
Dry roasted, 1 Tbsp, 8g	**45**	4	1.5
1/4 cup, 1 oz	**160**	14	6
Oil roasted, 1/4 cup, 1 oz	**180**	17	6
Watermelon, dried, 1/4 cup, 1 oz	**160**	14	4.5

Quick Guide

Peanut Butter

Average All Brands:	C	F	Cb
1 tsp, 6g	**35**	3	1.5
1 Tbsp, 0.6 oz, (17g)	**105**	8.5	3.5
2 Tbsp, 1.2 oz, (34g)	**210**	17	7
1 oz Quantity (28g)	**170**	14	6
1/2 cup, 5 oz	**850**	70	30
Jif "Sensations" Berry Blend, 1 T.	**100**	8.5	5
Chocolate Silk, 1 Tbsp, 0.6 oz	**95**	7.5	7
Peanut Wonder, 1 Tbsp	**50**	2	5.5
Smucker's Honey Swtnd., 1 Tbsp	**100**	8	4
Goober Grape/Strawb., 1 Tbsp	**90**	5	4
Skippy, honeynut, 1 Tbsp, 16g	**95**	8	4

Other Nut & Seed Butter

	C	F	Cb
Almond Butter, 1 Tbsp, 1/2 oz	**105**	9	2.5
Almond Butter Honey Roasted	**90**	7	5.5
Beanut Butter, 1 Tbsp, 1/2 oz	**88**	5.5	7
Cashew Butter, 1 Tbsp	**92**	7	4.5
Cashew Peanut Date Butter	**95**	7	4
Hazelnut Butter, 1 Tbsp	**100**	10	2.5
Pecan Butter, 1 Tbsp	**110**	11	3.5
Pistachio Butter, 1 Tbsp	**100**	8.5	5
Sesame Butter/Tahini, 1 tsp	**30**	3	1
1 Tbsp, 1/2 oz	**90**	8.5	2
Sunflower Seed Butter, 1 Tbsp	**95**	8	4

Supplements

Supplements	C	F	Cb
Aloe Vera Juice, undil., 2 fl.oz	**5**	0	1
Cod Liver Oil, 1 Tbsp	**120**	13	0
Evening Primrose Oil, capsules, 1	**5**	0.5	0
Fiber Supplements: Tabs, 1	**1**	0	0
Bios Life 2, 1 packet	**10**	0	2
Metamucil, 1 packet	**5**	0	1
Regular, 1 rounded Tbsp	**34**	0	8
Sugar-Free, 1 Tbsp	**6**	0	1
Fish Oil Capsules, aver., each	**10**	1	0
Flax Oil Capsules, 2	**10**	1	0
Garlic Tablets/Capsules, each	**3**	0	0
Lecithin Granules, 1 Tbsp, 10g	**50**	5	1
Protein; Powders, aver., 1 oz	**100**	0.5	0
Tablets, 20 tabs., 1/2 oz	**70**	0	0
Seaweed: Dried, 1 oz	**85**	0.5	22
Soaked, drained, 1 oz	**15**	0.5	3
Spirulina, 1 tablet	**2**	0	0.5
Vitamins/Minerals: Tabs/Caps, 1	**2**	0	0
Vitamin E Capsules, each	**5**	0.5	0
Yeast: Tablets, 2 tabs.	**4**	0	0.5
Flakes, 1 heaping Tbsp, 1/3 oz	**30**	0.5	4
Powder, 1 heaping Tbsp, 1/2 oz	**50**	0.5	6

Cough & Pharmaceutical

	C	F	Cb
Cough/Cold Syrups: 1 tsp	**36**	0	9
Regular, average, 1 Tbsp	**120**	0	30
Sugar-free, 1 Tbsp	**0**	0	0
Cough Drops/Lozenges ~ See Page 122			
Antacids: Average, 1 tablet	**4**	0	1
Liquid, 1 Tbsp	**6**	0	1
***Sudafed* Syrup,** 1 tsp	**14**	0	3
***Tylenol* Liquid:** Child, 1 tsp	**17**	0	4
Extra Strength, 1 tsp	**11**	0	3

Nut eaters are healthier and live longer say medical researchers.

Nuts are a nutritious source of protein, vitamins, minerals and fiber.

Their fat and fiber content can help to lower blood cholesterol, but watch the quantity if overweight.

Weights As Purchased	C	F	Cb
Acerola, 1 cup, 20 pcs, 3 1/2 oz	30	0	7.5
Apples: whole, average all varieties:			
1 small (4 per lb), 4 oz	70	0	17
1 medium (3 per lb), 5 1/2 oz	90	0	23
1 large (2 per lb), 8 oz	135	0	34
I extra large, 11 oz	185	0	46
without skin, 1/2 medium	35	0	9
Caramel Apple, 1 medium	170	0	42
Nut Coated, 1 medium	230	5	46
Apricots: 1 small (12 per lb)	17	0	4
1 medium (8 per lb), 2 oz	25	0	6
1 large (5-6 per lb), 3 oz	35	0	8
Atemoya, 1/3 cup	95	0	22
Avocado (w/out seed/skin):			
Average, 1/2 medium, 3 1/2 oz	160	15	6
1 salad slice, 1/2 oz	25	2	1
Mashed/Puree, 2 Tbsp, 1 oz	50	4.5	2
1/4 cup, 2 oz	90	9	5
Californian, 1/2 medium, 3 oz	150	15	6
Mashed/Puree, 1/2 c., 4 oz	200	20	8
Florida, 1/2 medium, 5 1/2 oz	170	13	14
Mashed/Puree, 1/2 c., 4 oz	125	10	10
1/2 cup cubed, 3 oz	95	8	8

Note: Avocados are nutritious and contain no cholesterol. Fat is mainly monounsaturated and benefits blood cholesterol. Excellent substitute for butter or margarine on bread.

Banana: 1 small (4 lb), 4 oz	55	0	12
1 medium (3 per lb), 5 oz	80	0	18
1 large (2 1/2 per lb), 7 oz	105	0	24
W/out skin, 1 medium., 3 1/4 oz	80	0	18
1/2 cup, mashed, 4 oz	105	0	24
Berries: Average all types, (Black/Boysenberries/Blueberries)			
1/2 cup, 2.5 oz	40	0	10
1 pint, 14 oz	220	1	56
Breadfruit, 1/2 cup, 4 oz	115	0	28
Cantaloupe, 1/2 med. (5" diam.)	100	0	25
1 slice, 2.5 oz (w/out skin)	20	0	6
1 cup pieces/balls, 5.5 oz	55	0	13
Carambola (Star Fruit), 1 med	50	0	4
Cassava, 1/3 cup	120	0	27
Cherimoya (Custard Apple), 5 oz	130	0	33
Cherries: Sweet, 8 fruit, 2 oz	40	0	10
1/2 lb (30 cherries)	145	0	38
Sour, 8 fruit, 2 oz	25	0	6
1/2 lb (30 cherries)	100	0	23

Weights As Purchased	C	F	Cb
Coconut: Fresh, 1 piece, 1 oz	100	10	4
Shredded, fresh, 1/2 cup	140	14	6
Sweetened, dried, 1/2 cup	235	16	22
Crabapples, 1/2 cup slices, 2 oz	40	0	9
Cranberries, 1/2 cup, 2 oz	20	0	5
Currants: *Per 1/2 cup*			
European Black, raw, 2 oz	35	0	8
Red & White, raw, 2 oz	30	0	7
Custard Apple, raw, 4 oz	115	1	27
Dates ~ See Dried Fruits			
Durian, flesh, 4 oz	140	2	26
Elderberries, 1/2 cup, 2 1/2 oz	55	0	13
Feijoas, 1 medium, 2 1/2 oz	35	0	7
Figs, green/black: 1 med., 2 oz	40	0	10
1 large, 3 oz	60	0	15
Fruit Salad, fresh, average,			
1/2 cup, 3 1/2 oz	60	0	15
1 cup, 7 oz	120	0	30
Gooseberries, raw, 1/2 c., 2 1/2 oz	30	0	7
Grapefruit: average all types,			
1/2 fruit, 8 1/2 oz (4 1/2 oz flesh)	40	0	10
1 cup sections w. juice, 8 oz	75	0	17
Grapes: Average, 1 cup, 5 1/2 oz	100	0	24
1 small bunch, 4 oz	70	0	15
1 medium bunch, 7oz	125	0	31
1 large bunch, 16 oz	285	0	71
Granadilla, flesh, 3 1/2 oz	95	0	23
Groundcherries, 1/2 cup, 2 1/2 oz	35	0	8
Guava: 1 fruit, 4 oz	80	0	15
1/2 cup, 3 oz	40	0	9

Continued Next Page

Weights As Purchased	C	F	Cb
Honeydew, 1 wedge (7"x2" wide),			
8 oz (with skin)	45	0	10
1 cup cubes/balls, 6 oz	60	0	14
Honey Murcots, 1 only, 5 oz	45	0	11
Jaboticaba, flesh, 4 oz	75	2	15
Jackfruit, flesh, 1/8 average, 4 oz	105	0	25
Jambos (Brazil Cherry), flesh, 4 oz	35	0	8
Java-Plum, 4 plums, 1/2 oz	25	0	6
Jujube, 3 oz	65	0	16
Kiwifruit, 1 medium, 3 oz	45	0	11
1 large, 4 oz	60	0	15
Kumquats, 5 medium, 3 1/2 oz	60	0	15
Kiwano, 1/2 medium, 5 oz	35	0	8
Langsat, Duku, 1 medium, 2 oz	25	0	5
Lemon, 1 medium, 4 oz	20	0	5
1 wedge, 1 oz	5	0	1.5
Peel, 1 Tbsp	4	0	0.5
Limes, 1 only, 2 oz	20	0	7
Loganberries, froz., 1/2 c., 2 1/2 oz	40	0	9
Logans, 5 fruit, 1/2 oz	10	0	2.5
Loquats, 4 fruit, 2 1/4 oz	20	0	6
Lychees, 4 fruit, 2 1/4 oz	25	0	6
Mamey Apple, 1 whole, 3 lb	430	4	100
1/4 fruit (1 cup flesh), 7 oz	100	1	24
Mandarin: 1 small, 3 oz	25	0	6
1 medium, 4 oz	35	0	8
1 large, 6 oz	55	0	13
Mango, flesh, 1/2 cup sl., 3 oz	25	0	6
1 whole, medium, 11 oz	140	0	34
Melons: Average all types			
1 cup, cubes/balls, 6 oz	60	0	14
Monstera Deliciosa (Taxonia),			
Edible part, 4 oz	50	0	11
Mulberries, 20 fruit, 1 oz	15	0	3
Nashi Fruit (Asian Pear),			
1 medium, 4 1/2 oz	50	0	11
Nectarines, 1 medium, 4 oz	50	0	12
1 large, 5 1/2 oz	70	0	17
Oheloberries, 1/2 cup, 2 1/2 oz	20	0	5
Olives (Pickled): Green, 10 lrg, 1 1/2 oz	45	5	0.5
Ripe, Grk. Style, 10 med., 1 oz	70	7	2
Ripe (Black), Californian:			
1 small/medium	4	0.5	0.3
1 large/extra large	6	0.5	0.5
1 jumbo	7	0.5	0.5
1 colossal	9	1	0.5
1 super colossal	13	1	1

Weights As Purchased	C	F	Cb
Oranges, average all varieties:			
1 small, 5 oz (with skin)	50	0	12
1 medium (3" diam.), 7 oz	70	0	17
1 large, 10 oz	100	0	24
Flesh only, 1 cup, 6 oz	80	0	19
Californian Valencia,			
1 medium (2 3/4" diam.), 6 oz	60	0	15
Californ. Navels (3" diam.), 7 oz	60	0	15
Sunkist Navel, 14 oz	130	0	32
Florida Orange, 1 medium, 7 oz	70	0	17
Peel, 1 Tbsp	0	0	0
Papaya, 1/2 cup, cubed, 2 1/2 oz	30	0	7
1 medium, 16 oz	120	0	28
Passionfruit, 1 medium, 1 1/4 oz	20	0	4.5
PawPaw (see Papaya)			
Peaches: 1 med. (4 per lb), 4 oz	35	0	8
1 large, 6 oz	55	0	13
Pears: Bartlett, 1 small, 4 oz	60	0	15
1 medium, 6 oz	90	0	22
1 large, 8 oz	120	0	30
Bosc, 6 oz	90	0	22
D'Anjou, 1 medium, 8 oz	120	0	30
Red Pear, 5 oz	80	0	20
Seckel (Wash'ton), 2 1/4 oz	35	0	9
Asian (Nashi), 1 large, 7 oz	80	0	20
Pepino, 1/2 medium, 4 oz	20	0	4
Persimmons: Native, 1 oz	30	0	7
Japan. (2 1/2"d. x 2 1/2"h), 7 oz	120	0	30
Seedless (Maui), 1 md., 5 oz	100	0	25
Pineapple (flesh only), 1 slice			
(3/4" thick, 3 1/2" diam.), 3 oz	40	0	10
1 cup, diced, 5 1/2 oz	80	0	20
1 medium, 1 1/2 lb	525	0	130
Pitanga, 3 fruit, 1 oz	6	0	1
Plaintains, 1/2 cup slices, 2 1/2 oz	90	0	22
Plums, average all types:			
Mini/Damson, (1" diam.), 1/2 oz	8	0	2
Small (1 3/4" diam.), 2 oz	30	0	7
Medium (2 1/4" diam.), 3 oz	45	0	10
Large (2 1/2" diam.), 4 oz	65	0	15
Pomegranates, 1/2 fruit, 5 oz	55	0	13
Pummelo, flesh, 1/2 cup, 4 oz	35	0	8
Prickly Pears, 1 fruit, 5 oz	50	0	11
Quinces, 1 medium, 3 1/2 oz	55	0	14
Rambutan (Rambotang),			
Red/Yellow, 1 med., 2 oz	15	0	4
Raspberries, 1/2 cup, 2 oz	30	0	7

Weights As Purchased	C	F	Cb
Rhubarb, raw, 1/2 cup, 2 oz	15	0	3
Sapodilla (Chico), 1 md., 7 1/2 oz	140	2	34
Sapotes, 1/2 medium, 5.5 oz	150	0.5	38
Soursop, 1 cup pulp, 8 oz	150	0	38
Strawberries:			
1 cup, 5 1/2 oz	45	0	10
6 medium/3 large, 2 oz	15	0	3
1 pint, 12 oz	95	0	22
Chocolate Dipped, 2 medium	45	2.5	6
Sugar Apples, 1/2 cup pulp, 4 oz	120	0	30
Tamarillo, 1 medium, 3 oz	20	0	4
Tamarind: 1 fruit, 1/4 oz	5	0	0
Tangelo: 1 small, 4 oz	30	0	1.5
1 medium, 5 oz	40	0	2
1 large, 7 oz	55	0	2.5
Tangerine, 1 medium, 4 oz	50	0	12
Tangor, 1 medium, 4 oz	35	0	7
Tomato:			
Cherry, 1 med., 3/4 oz	5	0	1
1 small, 3 oz	25	0	6
1 medium, 5 oz	35	0	7
1 large, 7 oz	45	0	9
1 medium slice	5	0	1
Canned Tomatoes/Products ~ Page 78-81			
Tree Tomato (Tamarillo), 3 oz	20	0	5
Ugli Fruit, Tangelo type, 5 oz	40	0	2
Watermelon (flesh only): 1 sl, 8 oz	70	0	15
1 cup cubed, 5 1/2 oz	50	0	12
Wax Jambu (Rose Apple), 2 oz	10	0	2

"You have a Vitamin E deficiency."

Dried Fruit

Dried Fruit	C	F	Cb
Apples, 5 rings, 1 oz	75	0	18
Apricots, 8 halves, 1 oz	65	0	15
Banana Chips, 1/2 cup, 1 1/2 oz	160	5	18
Banana Flakes, 4 Tbsp, 1 oz	80	0	20
Currants, 1/4 cup, 1 1/4 oz	100	0	24
Dates: 5 medium dates, 1 1/2 oz	120	0	28
Large Calif., 3 dates, 2 oz	160	0	37
1/2 cup, chopped, 3 oz	240	0	57
Figs, 3 medium figs, 2 oz	145	0	34
Longans; Lychees, 1 oz	80	0	19
Mango Slices, 4 strips, 1 oz	70	0	15
Mixed Fruit, 1 oz	70	0	16
Papaya Spears, 1 oz	75	0	17
Peaches, 2 halves, 1 oz	60	0	14
Pears, 3 halves, 2 oz	75	0	17
Pineapple, 1 oz	80	0	18
Prunes: with pits, 1 oz	60	0	14
1 Medium (60/lb)	16	0	4
1 Large (50/lb)	22	0	5
1 Extra Large (40/lb)	27	0	6
Without pits, 4 med., 1 oz	70	0	17
Cooked: w. sugar, 1/2 c, 5 oz	200	0	45
w/out sugar, 1/2 c, 4 1/2 oz	125	0	28
Raisins, 2 Tbsp, 1 oz package	85	0	19
1/2 cup, 2 1/2 oz	215	0	50

Candied Glacé Fruit

Apricot, 1 medium, 1 oz	100	0	25
Cherry, 3 large, 1/2 oz	50	0	12
Citron/Fruit Peel, 1 oz	90	0	21
Fig, 1 piece, 1 oz	90	0	21
Ginger, 1 oz	95	0	23
Pineapple, 1 slice, 1 1/4 oz	120	0	30

Fruit Leather/Rolls

Average All Brands: 1 oz	100	0	24
Fruit By The Foot, 1 leather	80	0	18
Fruit Roll-Ups, 1 roll, 1/2 oz	50	0	12
Stretch Island Leathers, 2 pces, 1 oz	90	0	21
Sunkist Fruit Roll, 1 roll	75	0	18

Other Fruit Confectionery/Snacks/Bars
~ See Snacks/Granola Bars Page 124-126

Canned Fruit & Snacks

Canned Fruit

Solids & Liquids: *Per 1/2 Cup (Approx. 4 1/2 oz)*	C	F	Cb
Apples: sweetened	70	0	17
Apricots: In water/diet	35	0	9
In juice/light	60	0	15
In syrup	105	0	27
Blackberries/Blueberries			
In heavy syrup	115	0	30
Cherries, pitted, in water	55	0	14
In light syrup	85	0	21
In heavy syrup	110	0	28
In extra heavy syrup	130	0	33
Fruit Cocktail: In water/diet	40	0	11
In juice/light	55	0	15
In light syrup	80	0	21
In heavy syrup	95	0	25
Fruit Salad: In water/diet	35	0	9
In juice/Light	60	0	16
In heavy syrup	95	0	25
Gooseberries: Light syrup	90	0	23
Grapefruit: Juice pack	45	0	15
In light syrup	75	0	20
Mixed Fruit: In water/diet	40	0	10
In fruit juices	60	0	15
In light syrup	60	0	15
In heavy syrup	100	0	25
Mandarin Oranges: In water	40	0	11
In light syrup	80	0	21
Peaches (halves or slices):			
In water/diet	30	0	8
In juice/light	50	0	14
In light syrup	70	0	20
drained, 1/2 peach	40	0	11
In heavy syrup	100	0	26
Pears: In water/diet	35	0	10
In juice/light	60	0	16
In heavy syrup	100	0	26
Pineapple:			
(Chunks/Crushed/Spears/Wedges/Slices)			
In own juice	70	0	18
In heavy syrup	90	0	23
Slices, drained, 2 slices			
In own juice	30	0	8
In heavy syrup	45	0	11

Canned Fruit (Cont)

Per 1/2 Cup	C	F	Cb
Plums: In water	50	0	14
In juice	75	0	20
In light syrup, 3 plums	85	0	21
In heavy syrup, 1/2 cup,	160	0	41
3 plums	120	0	31
Prunes: In heavy syrup	120	0	32
4 prunes	70	0	18
Raspberries, in heavy syrup	120	0	30
Strawberries: In water	25	0	7
In heavy syrup	120	0	31
Tropical Fruit Salad:			
In light syrup	80	0	18
In heavy syrup	95	0	21

Fruit Snack Cups

Del Monte Fruit Cups: Per 4 oz	C	F	Cb
Diced Peaches/Pears/Mixed,			
In heavy syrup	80	0	20
In extra light syrup	50	0	13
In fruit juices	50	0	13

A Well-Balanced Diet!

Vegetables - Fresh or Frozen

Edible Portion *(Raw Weight Unless Indicated)*	C	F	Cb
Alfalfa Sprouts, 1/2 cup, 1/2 oz	5	0	1
Artichokes, Globe/French:			
1 medium, 4 1/2 oz	65	0	15
Artichoke Heart, 1/2 cup, 3 oz	40	0	10
Asparagus, raw/froz.: 4 med. spears	15	0	3
Cuts & tips, 1/2 cup, 3 oz	25	0	5
Bamboo Shoots, ckd, 1/2 c, 4 oz	15	0	3
Beans: Green/Snap, 1/2 c, 2 oz	20	0	4
Broadbeans, ckd, 1/2 cup, 3 oz	90	0	16
Butterbeans, 1/2 cup, 3 oz	90	0	20
Lima, baby, 1/2 cup, 3 oz	90	0	17
Dry Beans, average all types: (Kidney, Brown, Haricot, Lima, Mung, Navy, Pinto, Red, White)			
Raw, 2 Tbsp, 1 oz	95	0.5	18
1 cup, 7 oz	665	3	126
Cooked, 1 oz	35	0	7
1/2 cup, 3 oz	105	0	21
Soybeans: Mature, dry, 1 oz	110	5	7
Dry, 1/2 cup, 3 1/2 oz	385	18	22
Cooked, 1/2 cup, 3 oz	105	5	6
Bean Sprouts, aver., 1/2 c., 3 oz	25	0	3
Beets, cooked, 1/2 c, slices, 3 oz	25	0	6
1 beet, 2" diam., 2 oz	17	0	4
Beet Greens, ckd, 1/2 c., 2 1/2 oz	20	0	4
Bell Pepper: See Peppers			
Black Eyed Peas, ckd, 1/2 c., 2 oz	160	0	32
Bok Choy (Chinese Chard), 3 oz	12	0	2
Broccoli: Raw, 1/2 cup, 1 1/2 oz	12	0	3
1 spear (5 oz edible)	40	0	8
Cooked, 1/2 cup, 3 oz	25	0	5
Brussel Sprouts, ckd, 1/2 c, 3 oz	35	0	7
Cabbage, average all varieties:			
Raw, shred., 1/2 cup, 1 1/4 oz	8	0	1
Cooked, 1/2 cup, 2 1/2 oz	15	0	2
Carrot: Ckd, 1/2 cup sl., 2 1/4 oz	35	0	8
Raw, 1 medium (7 1/2"), 3 oz	33	0	8
Raw, 1 lb, (5-6 med)	175	0	40
4 sticks (4"), 1 1/2 oz	15	0	3
Shredded, 1/2 cup, 2 oz	25	0	6
Cauliflower, cooked:			
3 floret, 1/2 c. 1" pcs, 3 oz	15	0	3
1/2 medium (15 oz raw)	100	0	20
Celeriac, 1/2 cup, raw, 2 3/4 oz	30	0	7
Celery, 1 stalk, 7 1/2", 1 1/2 oz	5	0	1
Diced, 1/2 cup, 2 1/4 oz	10	0	3

Edible Portion *(Raw Weight Unless Indicated)*	C	F	Cb
Chard (Swiss), 1/2 cup, ckd, 3 oz	20	0	4
Chick Peas (Garbanzo Beans):			
Dry, 1 cup, 6 oz	550	10	92
Cooked, 1 cup, 6 oz	270	4	45
Chicory/Witloof ~ See Endive			
Chicory, Greens, 1/2 cup, 3 oz	20	0	4
Chives, chopped, 1 Tbsp	1	0	0
Collards, 1/2 cup, 3 oz	15	0	4
Corn, yellow/white:			
Raw, kernels, 1/2 c., 2 3/4 oz	65	1	14
Ear (5"x 1 3/4"), 5 1/2 oz	80	1	17
Trimmed to 3 1/2" long	60	1	14
Cooked, kernels, 1/4 c., 1 1/2 oz	35	<1	7
(Also see Frozen & Canned Corn Page 135)			
Cress, Garden, 1/2 cup, 1 oz	10	0	2
Cucumber, 1 whole, 11 oz	40	0	12
1/2 cup slices, 2 oz	5	0	1
Dandelion Greens, 1/2 cup, 1 oz	15	0	3
Eggplant: 1 whole, 4 1/2 oz	40	0	10
1/2 cup, 1" pieces, 1 1/2 oz	10	0	2
1 slice, fried, 1 oz	40	4	10
Endive, Belgian/French:			
1 med. head (6"), 2 1/2 oz	12	0	3
Fennel, 2 oz	10	0	2
Garlic, 1 clove	4	0	1
Ginger: 1/4 cup slices, 1 oz	20	0	4
Crystallized (sugared), 1 oz	95	0	20
Horseradish, 1 pod, 3/4 oz	4	0	1
Jerusalem Artichoke, 1/2 cup	60	0	14
Jicama, raw, 1/2 cup	25	0	5
Kale, 1/2 cup, 2 oz	20	0	4
Kohlrabi, 1/2 cup, cooked, 3 oz	25	0	6
Leek, cooked, 1 whole, 4 oz	40	0	9
Lentils, green/brown: Dry, 1 oz	95	0	17
Dry, 1 cup, 6 1/2 oz	620	0	108
Cooked, 1/2 cup, 3 1/2 oz	115	0	20
Lettuce: 1 c., chop./shred., 2 1/2 oz	10	0	2
Butterhead, 2 leaves, 1/2 oz	2	0	0.5
Cos/Romaine, 1/2., shred., 2 1/2 oz	4	0	1
Iceberg: 1 leaf, 3/4 oz	3	0	1
1 medium head, 15-16 oz	60	0	15
Lotus Root, 10 slices, ckd, 3 oz	60	0	15
Mung Bean Sprouts, 1/2 cup	15	0	3
Mushroom: Raw, 1/2 cup, 1 oz	10	0	2
Cooked, 1/2 cup, 2 1/2 oz	20	0	3
Mustard Greens, 1/2 cup, 1 oz	7	0	1

Edible Portion (Raw Weight Unless Indicated)	C	F	Cb
Okra, ckd., 1/2 cup, slices, 2 3/4 oz	25	0	6
Onions: Raw, 1 medium, 4 oz	40	0	9
1/2 cup, chopped, 3 oz	30	0	7
Dehydrated flakes, 1/4 c, 1/2 oz	45	0	11
Rings, breaded/fried, 2 rings	80	5	9
Ore-Ida, 4 pces	220	11	27
Scallions, 1/2 cup, 2 oz	15	0	4
Spring, 1/4 cup, chopped, 1 oz	6	0	1
Parsley, chopped, 1/2 cup, 1 oz	10	0	2
Parsnips, 1 medium, 4 oz	80	0	20
Cooked, 1/2 cup slices, 2 3/4 oz	65	0	16
Peas: Green, 1/4 cup, 1 1/2 oz	35	0	6
raw, with pods, 1/2 lb	70	0	13
Snow Peas (8-9 pods), 1 oz	10	0	2
Split, dry, hulled, 1 oz	50	0	10
cooked, 1 cup, 7 oz	230	1	41
Peppers: Bell, 1 medium, 5 oz	25	0	6
1/2 cup, chopped, raw, 1 3/4 oz	12	0	3
1 ring (3" diam. x 1/4" thick)	2	0	0
Sweet, 1 medium, 5 oz	35	0	10
Chili: Green/Red, 1 1/2 oz	18	0	4
Habanero, 1 only, 8g	11	0	2
Pigeon Peas, cooked, 1/2 cup	85	1	16
Pimientos, 3 medium, 3 1/2 oz	25	0	5
Poi, 1/2 cup, 4 1/4 oz	135	0	33
Potatoes: Raw (with skin)			
1 Baby, Gourmet, 2 oz	45	0	11
1 small, 3 oz	65	0	15
1 medium, 5 oz	110	0	26
1 peeled, 4 oz	90	0	21
1 large, 8 oz	180	0	41
1 Extra large. (Russet), 12 oz	270	0	62
Mashed w. milk and fat, 1/2 c.	110	4	14
Baked (no fat); large, 10oz raw:			
Plain, with skin, 7 oz	220	0	51
without skin, 5 1/2 oz	145	0	34
With Toppings:			
+ 2 tsp fat	290	8	51
+ Sour Cr./Chives, 2 Tbsp	270	6	53
+ Plain Yoghurt, 2 Tbsp	240	1	55
+ Grated Cheese, 1 oz	330	9	56
+ Cottage Cheese, 2 oz	280	2	56
Roasted (w. fat), 1 small	155	8	36
Garlic Potatoes, 4 oz	120	2	22
Hash Browns: w. Butt. Sce, 2 1/2 oz	125	6	10
Homemade, 1/2 cup, 2 1/2 oz	165	10	10

Edible Portion (Raw Weight Unless Indicated)	C	F	Cb
Potatoes (Cont):			
French Fries: small serve, 2 1/2 oz	220	12	14
medium serve, 4 oz	350	20	22
Froz., uncooked, 18 fries, 4 oz	185	7	22
Oven-heated, 18 fries, 4 oz	185	7	22
Take-Out: 1 cup, 5 oz	440	25	28
McDonald's: Small, 2 1/2 oz	210	10	26
Large, 5.2 oz	450	22	57
Supersize, 6.2 oz	540	26	68
Fried: 18 fries, 3 oz	275	15	16
Au Gratin, 1/2 cup, 4.3 oz	160	9	22
Pancakes, 1 only, 5 oz	90	5	9
Kugel, 5 oz	300	20	26
Puffs, fried, 4 puffs, 1 oz	65	3	37
Scalloped, 1/2 cup, 4 1/4 oz	105	4	13
Stuffed Baked Potatoes:			
See *1-Potato-2* ~ Fast-Food Section			
***Ore-Ida* Frozen Potatoes (As Purchased):**			
Steak Fries, 8 fries, 3 oz	110	3.5	17
Frozen Crispers, 3 oz	220	13	24
Country Fries, 15 fries, 3 oz	120	3.5	19
Crispy Crunchies, 13 fries, 3 oz	160	8	20
Fast Fries, 22 fries, 3 oz	150	6	20
Pixie Crinkles, 22 pces, 3 oz	130	1.5	21
Golden Curls, 17 pces, 3 oz	160	7	22
Golden Fries, 16 pces, 3 oz	120	4	20
Golden Patties, 1, 2.5 oz	140	7	16
Hash Browns: Average, 3 oz	80	0	17
Oven Chips, 7, 3 oz	180	8	25
Potatoes O'Brien, 3/4 c., 2 oz	60	0	14
Season'd Crinkle Cuts, 15, 3 oz	120	3	23
Shoestrings, 3 oz	150	5	22
Sweet Potatoes: 1 patty, 60g	70	0	17
Center Cut: Prime, 2 pce	70	0	16
Petite, 5 pce, 117g	80	0	18
Mashed/Casserole, 1/2 cup	80	0	20
Tater Tots, 9 pces, 3 oz	150	8	20
Taters, 4 pces, 3 oz	150	7	20
Twice Baked, all types, 1, 5 oz	190	7	26
Waffle Fries, 9, 3 oz	150	7	21
Zesties, 12 pces, 3 oz	160	9	21
Potato Salad, 1/2 cup, 4 1/2 oz	180	10	14
Pumpkin, mashed, 1/2 c., 4 oz	25	0	6
Purslane, cooked, 1/2 c., 2 oz	10	0	2
Radish: aver., 10 only, 1 1/2 oz	10	0	2
Oriental, 1/2 c. slices, 1 1/2 oz	10	0	2

Edible Portion *(Raw Weight Unless Indicated)*	C	F	Cb
Rutabagas, ckd., 1/2 c. cubes, 3 oz	**30**	0	7
Salsify, ckd, 1/2 c. slices, 2 1/2 oz	**45**	0	11
Sauerkraut, 1/2 cup, 4 oz	**25**	0	5
Seaweed, aver. all: Dried, 1 oz	**50**	0	13
Soaked, drained, 1 oz	**15**	0	4
Nori/Laver, dried, 6 sheets, 1/2 oz	**35**	0	5
Shallots, chopped, 1 Tbsp	**7**	0	1
Soybeans ~ See Beans Page 68-70, 133			
(Soy Products/Tofu/Tempeh ~See Pages 67)			
Sorrel, raw, 1/2 cup, 4 oz	**23**	0.7	4
Spinach, cooked, 1/2 cup, 3 oz	**20**	0	4
Creamed, 1/2 cup, 4 1/2 oz	**140**	12	10
Squash: Summer, average			
raw, 1/2 cup slices, 2 1/4 oz	**13**	0	3
cooked, 1/2 cup slices, 3 oz	**18**	0	4
Winter, cooked:			
Acorn, 1/2 cup cubes, 3 1/2 oz	**55**	0	15
1/2 medium (10oz raw wt.)	**85**	0	22
Butternut, 1/2 c. cubes, 3 1/2 oz	**40**	0	11
1/4 medium (9oz raw wt.)	**95**	0	26
Hubbard, 1/2 c. cubes, 3 1/2 oz	**50**	0	11
Spaghetti, 1/2 cup, 2 3/4 oz	**23**	0	5
Succotash, ckd, 1/2 cup, 3 1/3 oz	**110**	1	23
Sweetcorn ~ See Corn.			
Sweet Potatoes: Cooked with Skin			
No fat, 1 only, 4 oz	**120**	0	28
No skin, mash, 1/2 c., 5 1/2 oz	**170**	0	40
Swedes, 1/2 cup, 3 oz	**45**	0	10
Taro, cooked, 1/2 cup, 2 oz	**95**	0	23
Tomatoes: See Fruit ~ Page 131			
1 small, 3 oz	**20**	0	5
1 medium, 5 oz	**35**	0	8
1 large, 7 oz	**45**	0	10
Cooked, 1/2 cup, 4 1/4 oz	**30**	0	7
Fried, 1 small, 3 oz	**60**	4	5
Tomatillo, 1 oz	**7**	0	1
Turnips: White, ckd, 1/2 cup, 3 oz	**15**	0	4
Greens, ckd, 1/2 cup, 2 1/2 oz	**15**	0	3
Water Chestnuts, 4 nuts	**40**	0	10
1/2 cup slices, 2 1/4 oz	**65**	0	15
Watercress, 10 sprigs, 1 oz	**4**	0	1
Yam, cooked, 1/2 cup, 2 1/2 oz	**80**	0	20
Baked Yam, medium, 8 oz	**260**	0	62
Yardlong Bean, 1 pod, 1/2 oz	**7**	0	1
Zucchini, 1 medium, 10 oz	**45**	0	10
1/2 cup slices, cooked, 3 oz	**13**	0	3

Frozen Vegetables (Mixed)

Birdseye	C	F	Cb
Brocc./Carrots/W. Chestnuts, 1 cup	**35**	0	6
Broccoli/Corn/Red Peppers, 3/4 cup	**50**	0.5	11
Broccoli/Cauli./Carrots, 1 cup	**30**	0	4
Brussels Sprouts/Cauli./Carrots	**35**	0	5
Carrots/Corn/Green Beans, 2/3 cup	**60**	0.5	11
Cauliflower/Carrots/Pea Pods, 1 cup	**30**	0	5
Chopped Spinach, 1/3 cup	**20**	0	2
Baby: Corn Blend, 2/3 cup	**60**	0.5	11
Bean & Carrot Blend, 1 cup	**30**	0	5
Broccoli Blend, 1 cup	**70**	1.5	8
Broccoli Florets, 1 cup	**25**	0	4
Gold & White Corn, 2/3 cup	**80**	1	15
Pea Blend, 3/4 cup	**40**	0	7
Sweet Pea, 2/3 cup	**70**	0.5	12
Pasta Secrets: Primavera, 1 cup	**230**	10	26
Zesty Garlic, 1 cup, cooked	**240**	10	31
Stir Fry: *Prepared (Includes Pasta)*			
Asparagus, 2 cup	**90**	0.5	16
Green Bean, 1 3/4 cup	**100**	0.5	19
Voila: Garlic Chicken, ckd, 1 cup	**260**	11	27
Pesto Chicken, ckd, 1 cup	**250**	9	25
Green Giant			
Vegetables: Asparagus Cuts, 2/3 c.	**25**	0	4
Corn: Nibblers, 1 ear	**70**	0.5	14
Extra Sweet Niblets, 2/3 cup	**70**	1	13
Sthwestern & Rst Peppers, 3/4 c.	**90**	1	18
Green Bean Casserole, 2/3 cup	**100**	5	11
Honey Glazed Carrots, 1 cup	**90**	3.5	13
Le Sueur Baby Sw. Peas, 2/3 cup	**60**	0.5	11
Spinach, 1/2 cup	**25**	0	3
Veges In Cheese & Cream Sauce: *Prepared*			
Alfredo Vegetables, 3/4 cup	**80**	3	9
Broccoli & Cheese, 2/3 cup	**70**	2.5	9
Brocc., Cauliflower, Carrots, 2/3 c.	**70**	2.5	10
Cauliflower in Cheese Sce, 1/2 cup	**60**	2.5	8
Creamed Spinach, 1/2 cup	**80**	3	9
Cream Style Corn, 1/2 cup	**110**	1	23
Green Bean Casserole, 2/3 cup	**90**	5	9
Rice & Vegetables: *Prepared*			
Cheesy Rice & Brocc., 1 pkt, 10 oz	**300**	5	56
Oriental Rice, 1 pkt, 10 oz	**340**	12	52
Rice Medley, 1 pkt, 10 oz	**280**	4	52
Rice Pilaf, 1 pkt, 10 oz	**230**	3.5	44
White & Wild Rice, 1 pkt, 10 oz	**280**	6	51

Continued Over Page

Frozen Vegetables (Cont)

Green Giant (Cont)	C	F	Cb
Pasta Accents: *Per 1 Cup, Cooked*			
Alfredo Broccoli	105	4	14
Cr. Cheddar w. Broc./Carrots	125	4	18
Garden Herb	115	3.5	16
Garlic Seas. w. Broc./Corn/Carrots	130	5	18
Primavera	140	4.5	19
Three Cheese	150	4.5	21
White Cheddar	135	4	18
La Choy			
Mixed Fancy Vegetables, 1/2 cup	12	0	3
Veg-All			
Succotash, 1/2 cup	80	1	17
Westpac			
Just Add: *As Prepared, Per 10 oz*			
Beef: Oriental Garlic & Ging. 1 1/4 c.	280	7	25
Chicken, 1 1/4 cup	290	2	34
Hamburger: Vegetable Stroganoff	320	12	32

Canned/Bottled

Solids & Liquid	C	F	Cb
Artichoke Hearts: Plain, 1 oz (1)	30	0	8
Marinated, 1 oz	60	5	2
Asparagus (Tips/Cuts/Spears), 1/2 cup, 4 1/2 oz	20	0	3
Bamboo Shoots, 1 cup, 4 1/2 oz	25	0	4
Bean Salad, 1/2 cup, 3 oz	90	0	23
Bean Sprouts, 2/3 cup	10	0	2
Beans:			
Green, 1/2 cup, 4 1/4 oz	20	0	4
Baked Beans, 1/2 cup, 4 1/2 oz	120	<1	18
Butter Beans, 1/2 cup, 4 1/2 oz	90	0	20
Italian, cut, 1/2 cup, 4 1/2 oz	30	0	7
Kidney Beans, 1/2 cup, 4 1/2 oz	105	<1	20
Lima Beans, 1/2 cup, 4 1/2 oz	80	0	15
Pinto Beans, 1/2 cup, 4 1/2 oz	100	<1	20
Wax Beans, cut, 1/2 cup, 4 1/2 oz	20	0	4

(Also see Canned Products ~ Pages 68-70)

Beets:			
Sliced/Whole, 1/2 c., 4 1/2 oz	35	0	7
Crinkle/Pickled (*Del Monte*) 1/2 c.	80	0	20
Carrots:			
Sliced, 1/2 cup	35	0	8
Honey Glazed (*Green Giant*) 1/2 c.	45	3.5	13

Canned/Bottled (Cont)

	C	F	Cb
Corn: Whole kernel, sweet: 1/2 cup, 4 1/2 oz	80	0.5	20
Drained Solids, 1/2 cup, 3oz	65	0.5	15
Creamed style, 1/2 cup, 4 1/2 oz	100	0.5	24
Eggplant, 2 Tbsp, 1 oz	25	2	5
Garbanzo/Chick Peas, 3 oz	100	2	20
Green Chilies: diced, 2 Tbsp, 1 oz	5	0	1
Hearts of Palm, (1), 1.2 oz	9	0	2
Mushrooms: 1/2 cup, 2 1/2 oz	20	0	4
in Butter Sauce, 2 oz	30	1	3
Olive Salad (*Progresso*), drain, 2 T.	25	2.5	1
Onions: Pickled, 1 med., 3/4 oz	10	0	2
Cocktail, 1 onion	2	0	0.5
Peas, 1/2 cup, 3 oz	60	0	11
Peppers: Hot Chilli, 1 only, 1 oz	8	0	2
Sweet, undrained, 2 1/2 oz	15	0	3
Jalapeno, w. liq., 1/2 c. chopped	17	0	3
Cherry (*Progresso*), dr., 2 T., 1 oz	25	2	2
Fried, drain, 2 Tbsp, 1 oz	60	5	3
Pepper Salad (*Progresso*), dr., 2 T.	15	1	1
Potatoes, 1/2 cup, 3 oz	55	0	12
Salsa: Average all types, 2 Tbsp	15	0	3.5
Sauerkraut, undrained, 1/2 c., 4 oz	25	0	6
Spinach, 1/2 cup, 3 1/2 oz	25	0	3.5
Straw Mushrooms, 1/2 cup, 4.3 oz	20	0	3
Succotash: *Per 1/2 cup, 4 1/2 oz*			
w. Cream Style Corn	100	1	23
w. whole kernels, undrained	80	1	17
Sweetcorn: See Corn.			
Sweet Potato, 1/2 cup, 3 1/2 oz	105	0	24
Candied (*Green Giant*) 3/4 cup	240	7	41
Tomatoes, Sundr.: Natural, 5-6 pce	22	0	5
In Oil, drained, 6 pces, 1/2 oz	60	4	6
Tomato Products ~ See Page 78-81			
Vegetables, mixed, 1/2 cup, 4 oz	45	0	8
Yams in Light Syrup, 1/2 cup, 4 oz	105	0	25
Zucchini in Tom. Sce., 1/2 c., 4 oz	30	0	8

Take-Out Vegetable Dishes

Appetizers: Caponata, 1/4 cup	30	1	5
Curried Vegetables, 8 oz serving	400	33	22
Pakoras, 1, 2 oz	110	5	12
Ratatouille, 1 cup, 9 oz serving	200	16	10
Samosa, 2, 4 oz	500	45	25
Succotash, 1/2 cup	110	1	23
Spring Roll, 2, 3 oz	200	9	28

Average All Outlets *Per Serving*	C	F	Cb
Antipasto Salad, 1 cup	140	10	2
Bean Salad, 1/2 cup	110	4	17
Bulgur Salad, 1/2 cup	70	2	12
Caesar Salad, Classic, 1 cup	200	14	15
Side Salad, no dressing	25	0	6
Carrot Raisin: No dress., 1/2 cup	20	0	5
with dressing, 1/2 cup	65	5	5
Chef Salad: Regular, no dressing	620	37	8
w. 2oz 1000 Island	860	61	8
Chicken Salad Platter, 6 oz	200	8	12
Coleslaw: Traditional, 1/2 cup	150	8	18
w. low cal dressing	60	1	12
Corn, Mexican, 1/2 cup	240	12	33
Cucumber, non-oil dress, 1/2 cup	60	0	14
w. Oil dressing, 1/2 cup	140	12	8
Eggplant Salad, 1/2 cup	75	5	7
Fettucini w. veges, 1/2 cup	110	5	15
Garden Salad, no dressing	35	0	8
Greek Salad, 1 cup	120	10	7
Greek Vegetables, 1/2 cup	140	12	7
Lettuce, hearts, 1/4 head	20	0	4
Lobster Salad Platter, 6 oz	200	8	12
Macaroni Salad, 1/2 cup	140	8	16
Nicoise, 1 cup	450	32	18
Pasta Salad, 1/2 cup	160	8	16
Pineapple Coconut Slaw, 1/2 cup	150	10	14
Potato Salad: Dijon	140	7	17
w. Mayonnaise, 1/2 cup	170	10	17
Lowfat, 1/2 cup	110	1.5	21
Rice Salad, 1/2 cup	150	10	13
Saffron Rice, 1/2 cup	130	3	24
Spinach Salad	180	13	13
Tomato & Mozzarella, 1/2 cup	180	14	10
Tabouli, 1/2 cup	150	6	22
Three Bean Salad, 1/2 cup	80	5	9
Tortelini w. Basil Pesto, 1/2 cup	170	10	19
Waldorf w. mayo, 1/2 cup	160	12	12

Signature Salads: Per 6 oz Serving
(Supplied to Deli's and Institutions)

	C	F	Cb
Antipasto Salad, 6 oz	510	50	4
Artichoke Salad, marinated	400	41	8
California Medley	120	7	15
Cheese Agnolotti	250	8	23
Chicken Salad	420	33	11
Crabmeat Flavored	450	38	20
Egg Salad	300	23	14

Signature Salads (Cont):	C	F	Cb
Fresh Button Mushroom	190	16	6
Garden Olive, 6 oz	630	67	3
Ham Salad	400	32	14
Prima Pasta Salad	360	30	18
Seafood Pasta Del Mar	170	10	21
Seafood with Crab & Shrimp	420	34	20
Shrimp Salad	360	32	8
Tuna Salad	450	36	14

Fast-Food Restaurant Chains ~ *See Page 161*

Fresh Salad Packs

Pre-Packaged (Supermarkets)

	C	F	Cb
Dole: Complete: Caesar, 3 1/2 oz	170	13	8
Oriental, 3 1/2 oz	120	6	13
Romano, 3 1/2 oz	150	12	9
Spinach Bacon, 3 1/2 oz	170	10	18
Sunflower Ranch, 3 1/2 oz	160	16	5
Lunch For One: Ranch, 1 kit	350	29	20
Special Blends (no added dressing):			
Aver. all varieties, 2 cups, 3 oz	15	0	3
Regular Salad Packs (no added dressing):			
Classic Coleslaw, 3 oz	25	0	5
Classic Iceberg, 3 oz	15	0	4
Zesty Italian, 7 oz	110	0	4
Fresh Express: *Per 1 1/2 cups*			
Salad Kits: Caesar Salad	170	14	9
Fat Free Caesar Salad	70	0	1
Taco Fiesta	110	8	7
Garden Salad; Italian Salad Mix	20	0	3
European/Riviera Salad Mix	15	0	3
Hearts of Romaine Salad Mix	20	0.5	3
Garnden w. Romaine Salad	20	0	3
Ready Pac: Aver. all types	15	0	2
Weight Watchers			
Caesar/Garden/European, 3.5 oz	60	0	12
Caesar Salad w. cookies, 4 oz	160	3	30
Garden Salad w. cookies, 4 oz	120	1.5	24
European Salad w. cookies, 4 oz	160	3	11

Salad Toppings

	C	F	Cb
Bacon Bits, aver., 1 Tbsp	30	1.5	2
Chow Mein Noodles, dry, 1/2 c.	120	5	13
Croutons, 2 Tbsp, 10g	35	1	6
Olives, 5 medium	25	2	0
Potato Chips, 1 oz	150	10	15
Sunflower Seeds, 1 Tbsp, 8 g	45	4	1.5
Tortilla Chips, 1 oz	150	8	16

Quick Guide

Orange Juice

Per 8 fl.oz Unless Indicated

	C	F	Cb
Average ~ Fresh or Sweetened:			
1/2 Cup, 4 fl.oz	55	0	13
Small Glass, 6 fl.oz	82	0	20
Regular Glass, 8 fl.oz	110	0	26
8 3/4 fl.oz Box	120	0	28
10 fl.oz Bottle	140	0	32
11 1/2 fl.oz Can	160	0	36
16 fl oz Bottle	220	0	52
64 fl.oz Bottle	880	0	208

Other Juices

Average All Brands
Per 8 fl.oz Unless Indicated

	C	F	Cb
Aloe Vera Juice, unsweet., 2 oz	5	0	1
Apple Juice: 8 fl.oz	115	0	30
10 fl.oz Bottle	145	0	36
64 fl.oz	920	0	232
Blueberry Juice, 8 fl.oz	90	0	25
Carrot Juice: Fresh, 6 fl.oz	60	0	14
Sweetened, 6 fl.oz	75	0	17
Cranberry Juice, Cocktail/Blend 8 fl.oz	120	0	34
Grape Juice, 8 fl.oz	160	0	40
Grapefruit Juice, 8 fl.oz	100	0	23
Lemon Juice: 1 Tbsp	4	0	1.5
1 cup, 8 fl.oz	60	0	21
Concentrate, 1 tsp	0	0	0
Lime Juice, 1 Tbsp	4	0	1.5
Orange Juice, 8 fl.oz	110	0	26
Passion Fruit Juice (Fresh):			
Purple, 1 cup, 8 fl.oz	125	0	34
Yellow, 1 cup, 8 fl.oz	150	0	36
Papaya/Peach Nectar, 8 fl.oz	140	0	35
Pear Nectar, 8 fl.oz	150	0	40
Pineapple Juice, 8 fl.oz	110	0	27
Prune Juice, 8 fl.oz	180	0	43
Strawb./Raspberry Juice, 8 fl.oz	100	0	23
Tangerine Juice, 8 fl.oz	100	0	25
Tomato Juice, 8 fl.oz	50	0	12
Vegetable Juice, 8 fl.oz	50	0	12
Fruit Blends, average, 8 fl.oz	120	0	31
Fruit Nectars, average, 8 fl.oz	140	0	35

Juice Brands

Per 8 fl.oz Unless Indicated

	C	F	Cb
Apple & Eve			
Naturally Cranberry	120	0	30
Cranberry/Raspberry Apple	120	0	30
Arizona			
Crazy Carrot; Lemonade/Pink	110	0	27
Grape/Kiwi/Strawberry	120	0	29
Mucho Mango	100	0	25
Bright & Early			
Orange Juice (Chilled/Frozen)	120	0	30
Grape Juice (Frozen)	140	0	33
Campbell's			
Tomato Juice, 8 fl.oz	50	0	10
10.5 fl.oz	60	0	12
V-8 Healthy Request, 8 fl.oz	50	0	12
V-8 Splash Tropical Blend, 8 fl.oz	120	0	30
Capri Sun			
Average all flavors, 6.75 oz	100	0	28
Chiquita			
Frozen Concentrates, prepared:			
Average all varieties, 8 fl.oz	130	0	32
Del Monte			
Pineapple Juice: Fresh, 8 fl.oz	110	0	27
From Concentrate, 8 fl.oz	130	0	32
Prune Juice, 8 fl.oz	170	0	42
Tomato Juice:			
Fresh, 8 fl.oz	40	0	10
From Concentrate, 8 fl.oz	50	0	12
Snap-E-Tom Cocktail, 6 fl.oz	40	0	10
Fruit Smoothie Blenders: *Per 6.5 fl.oz*			
Mango-Pineapple-Banana; Strawberry-Peach-Banana	180	0	45
Peach-R'berry/P'apple-Or.-Ban.	210	0	53
Dole			
100% Fruit Juice Blends:			
Average all varieties, 8 fl.oz	120	0	29
Fruit Drink Blends:			
Average, 8 fl.oz	130	0	31
Spicy Vegetable Blend, 12 fl.oz	80	0	16
Dominick's			
Orange Juice (100% Pure), 8 fl.oz	110	0	27
Tropical Fruit Blend	130	0	32

Per 8 fl.oz Unless Indicated	C	F	Cb
Eden: Organic Apple, 8 fl.oz	80	0	23
Five Alive: Citrus beverage, 8 fl.oz	120	0	30
Fresh Samantha			
Banana Strawberry	150	1	12
Carrot/Orange; The Big Bang	100	0	8
Grapefruit	90	0	7
Mango Mama/Tangerine	120	0	10
Raspberry Dream	120	1	10
Protein Blast	160	1	10
Desperately Seeking C	110	0	5
Fruitopia			
Average all flavors, 8 fl.oz	110	0	28
Iced Teas ~ See Page 148			
Goya Nectar			
Apricot Nectar, 1 can	130	0	31
Pear Nectar, 1 can	240	0	59
Hawaiian Punch			
Fruit Juicy, Red, 6 fl.oz	90	0	22
Box, 8.45 fl.oz	120	0	30
Hi-C: Orange Juice			
Chilled/Premium Choice, 8 fl.oz	110	0	30
10 fl.oz bottle	140	0	36
Calcium Rich, 8 fl.oz	120	0	33
Other Juices Drinks: Aver., 8 fl.oz	130	0	32
8.45 fl.oz box, average	135	0	33
11.5 fl.oz can	180	0	45
Hood: Grapefruit Juice (Select)	100	0	23
Natural Blenders, average	130	0	32
Orange Juice: Select	120	0	30
Calcium Rich	120	0	30
Jui2ce			
All flavors, 8 fl.oz bottle	95	0	23
Juicy Juice			
Apple Grape, 8.45 fl.oz box	120	0	10
Berry, 8.45 fl.oz box	130	0	30
Punch, 8.45 fl.oz box	140	0	32
Tropical, 8.45 fl.oz box	150	0	26
Kern's Nectars			
Pineapple Coconut Nectar, 6 fl.oz	140	0	26
11.5 fl.oz box	210	0	48
Other nectars, average, 6 fl.oz	110	0	27

Per 8 fl.oz Unless Indicated	C	F	Cb
Kool Aid			
Koolers, average, 8.45 fl.oz	140	0	37
Fruit Drinks, average, 8 fl.oz	100	0	25
Sugar Free, 8 fl.oz	5	0	0
Knott's: Sparkling Ciders, 325 ml	110	0	25
Knudsen			
Fruit Juices: Apple	110	0	28
Apple Blends, all varieties	120	0	30
Black Cherry; Prune	180	0	43
Grape; Pomegranate	150	0	37
Grapefruit	100	0	23
Just Cranberry; Tomato	60	0	14
Orange	100	0	23
Pear	120	0	30
Nectars: Coconut	140	5	26
Other Nectars, average	130	0	36
Blends: Average all flavors	120	0	30
Citrus Juices:			
Rio Red Grapefruit	140	0	35
Lemonade (Natural)	120	0	30
Simply Nutritious: *Per 8 fl.oz*			
Ginseng Boost	110	0	27
Lemon Ginger Echinacea	120	0	30
Mega C	130	0	31
Mega Green; Gingko Alert	120	0	30
Morning Blend; VitaJuice	120	0	30
Floats: Orange	140	0	33
Spritzers:			
Average all flavors, 12 oz	170	0	43
Lights, all flavors, 12 oz	110	0	28
TeaZers: All flavors, 12 oz	110	0	28
Very Veggie: 8 fl.oz	50	0	10
Krasdale			
Cranberry Apple	170	0	42
Cranberry Juice Cocktail	130	0	32
Cranberry Raspberry	150	0	37
Libby's			
Orange Juice, 8 fl.oz	105	0	25
Juicy Juice, average, 8 fl.oz	140	0	34
Nectars, 1 can, 11.5 fl.oz	220	0	52
Mauna La'i Hawaiian			
All flavors, 8 fl.oz	130	0	32
Mistic (Mega 24 fl.oz)			
Average All flavors, 8 fl.oz	120	0	30
24 fl.oz	360	0	90

Per 8 fl.oz Unless Indicated	C	F	Cb
Minute Maid			
100% Juices: *Per 8 fl.oz*			
Apple/ Orange Juice	115	0	27
Fruit Drinks/Punch: *Per 8 fl.oz*			
Average all flavors	115	0	30
Chilled Singles: *Per 16 fl.oz Bottle*			
Berry/Tropical Punch	240	0	60
Lemonade/ Orange Juice	220	0	55
Juices to Go: *Per 10 fl.oz Bottle*			
Average all flavors	160	0	40
Boxed Juices: *Per 8.45 fl.oz*			
Cherry Grape; Tropical Punch	130	0	32
Orange Juice; Apple Juice	120	0	31
Berry; Fruit	120	0	31
Calcium Juices: *Per 8 fl.oz*	120	0	29
Mott's			
Apple Raspb., Fruit Punch, 10 fl.oz	145	0	36
Apple Cranberry, Grape Apple 10 fl.oz	180	0	42
Clamato Tomato Cocktail, 8 fl.oz	60	0	11
Fruitsations: all flavors, 4 oz	85	0	22
Grapefruit (from conc.), prep.	120	0	28
Juice Paks: All flavors, 8.45 fl.oz	120	0	30
Mini Motts, 4.23 oz	60	0	14
Orange Juice (from conc.)	130	0.5	30
Naked Juice			
Apple Juice, 8 fl.oz	120	0	29
Banana Blueberry; Boysenberry	140	2	34
Banana Date	240	4	46
Berry Blast; Wise Guy	130	0	30
Carrot Beet/Celery/Spinach	100	0	21
Chocolate Dream	190	2	38
Grapefruit Juice	110	0	23
Green Machine	140	0.5	35
Mighty Mango; Orange Jce Nirvana	110	0	24
Papaya Strawberry	100	0	24
Protein Drink (6g protein)	170	1.5	33
Protein Zone (17g protein)	220	4	32
Strawberry Banana/Lemonade	140	0	33
Turbo C	110	0	27
Vanilla Creme	150	1	28
Watermelon	80	1	18
Zippitea	80	0	32
Newman's Own			
Lemonade, 10 fl.oz	140	0	34

Per 8 fl.oz Unless Indicated	C	F	Cb
Ocean Spray			
Apple Juice (from conc.)	110	0	28
Bl. Cherry; Crazy Kiwi; Mega Melon	130	0	33
Cranberrry:			
Cranberry Grape	170	0	41
Cranberry Juice Cocktail	140	0	34
Light Style (Low Calorie)	40	0	10
Other Cranberry flavors, aver.	150	0	35
Caribbean Colada; Cran-Mango	130	0	32
Cranicot; Cranapple; Cranblueberry	160	0	41
Crantastic Fruit Punch	150	0	37
Fruit/Holiday Punch; Tangerine	130	0	32
Grapefruit: 100% Juice	100	0	24
Other flavors, average	125	0	31
Lemonade flavors, average	130	0	32
Orange Juice (from concentrate)	120	0	31
Kiwi Strawb.; Summer Cooler	120	0	31
Ruby Red & Strawberry	140	0	34
Ruby Red & Mango/Tangerine	130	0	33
Odwalla: *Per 8 fl.oz Unless Indicated*			
Boyzenberry Mango	140	0	34
C Monster, 16 fl. oz	300	0	72
Fruitshake Blackberry	160	0	40
Grapefruit Juice	90	0	34
Guanaba Dabba Doo!	130	0	30
Lotta Colada	160	0	33
Mango Tango	150	0	37
Mo Beta, 16 fl. oz	280	0	70
Orange Juice	120	0	34
Raspberry Smoothie	140	0	35
Strawberry Banana	100	0	25
Strawberry Go Man Go	100	0	25
Super Protein, 16 fl.oz	400	0	40
Vegetable Cocktail	70	0	18
Orange Julius: *Per 16 fl.oz*			
Orange	265	0	65
Pina Colada	300	0	75
Strawberry	340	0	85
Raspberry Cream Supreme	510	20	82
Tropical Cream Supreme	510	25	71
Realemon - Realime (*Borden*)			
Lemon/Lime Juice (from concentrate)			
1 teaspoon	0	0	0
2 Tbsp, 1 fl.oz	6	0	2
1/2 cup, 4 fl.oz	24	0	8

Per 8 fl.oz Unless Indicated	C	F	Cb
Santa Cruz			
Natural 100%: Aver. all varieties	120	0	30
Sparkling varieties, 8 fl.oz	150	0	33
S&W: Apple Juice, 8 fl.oz	120	0	30
Orange Juice, 6 fl.oz can	90	0	22
Grapefruit Juice, unswt'd, 8 fl.oz	105	0	25
Tomato Juice, 8 fl.oz	30	0	7
Snapple			
Cranberry Royal, 10 fl.oz	150	0	38
Fruit Drink Blends, 8 fl.oz	120	0	30
Grapeade; Orangeade 8 fl.oz	120	0	30
Orange Juice, 10 fl.oz	130	0	30
Whipped Snapple (Fruit Smoother):			
Aver. all flavors, 297ml bottle	160	0	40
Squeezit			
Average all flavors, 6.75 fl.oz	90	0	23
Sunny D			
Enriched Citrus Beverage (5% Jce)	130	0	31
Sunny Delight			
Florida Citrus, 6 fl.oz	90	0	22
Calcium Rich, 6 fl.oz	150	0	37
Florida Citrus Punch, 6 fl.oz	90	0	22
Sunny Delight Lite, 6 fl.oz	20	0	5
Tropical Fruit Punch, 6 fl.oz	90	0	22
Sunsweet			
Prune Juice/w. Pulp, 8 fl.oz	180	0	43
Tang			
Fruit Box (8.45 fl.oz): Aver. all flav.	140	0	34
Pouches, average all flavors (1)	100	0	26
Mix: *Made up, 6 fl.oz*			
Regular (2 Tbsp dry)	90	0	22
Sugar Free	7	0	0
Tree of Life: Black Cherry	180	0	43
Concord Grape	160	0	40
Cranberry Nectar	150	0	38
Other varieties, average	130	0	33
Tree Top: *Per 6 fl.oz*			
Apple Juice; Apple Citrus/Pear	120	0	30
Apple Cranberry/Grape	130	0	32
Fruit Juice Punch, 10 fl.oz	150	0	37
Grape/Grape Fruit Juice; Sparkling	120	0	30
Orange Juice	120	0	28

Per 8 fl.oz Unless Indicated	C	F	Cb
Tropicana			
Blends: Berry; P'apple, 8 fl.oz	130	0	32
Pure Premium:			
Orange Juice + Fiber	120	0	30
Ruby Red	120	0	28
Season's Best: Orange Juice	110	0	27
7 fl.oz bottle	90	0	23
10 fl.oz bottle	130	0	33
11.5 fl.oz can	140	0	36
Grapefruit Juice, 8 fl.oz	160	0	40
Tropics:			
Average all flavors, 8 fl.oz	110	0	26
Twister: Average, 8 fl.oz	120	0	32
10 fl.oz bottle	150	0	40
11.5 fl.oz can	160	0	40
Light, average, 8 fl.oz	35	0	10
10 fl.oz bottle	50	0	11
V-8 Splash			
Regular, 1 cup, 8 fl.oz	110	0	28
Diet V-8 Splash, 1 cup	10	0	3
Veryfine			
Apple Cranberry	130	0	33
Fruit Punch	140	0	36
Grape Juice (100%)	150	0	37
Grape Drink	110	0	28
Grapefruit Juice (100%)	90	0	20
Pink	120	0	30
Guava Straw.; Lemon Lime	120	0	30
Orange Juice (100%)	120	0	24
Orange Drink	140	0	35
Papaya Punch	120	0	30
Pineapple Orange	130	0	32
Welch's			
Regular Juices:			
Average all blends, 8 fl.oz	160	0	40
Tomato, 8 fl.oz	50	0	10
8.45 fl.oz Box, average	150	0	37
Mini Drinks, 5.5 fl.oz	100	0	25
Frozen Juice Concentrates: *Per 8 fl.oz* (Reconstituted)			
Grape	160	0	41
White Grape Juice Blends	150	0	36
Cranberry/Raspberry	150	0	37
Lite Cranberry/Grape/Raspberry	50	0	13
Other flavors, average	130	0	33

Nutritional Shakes/Drinks

	C	F	Cb
Amway Positrim Drink Mix			
Regular Mix, 1 pkt, 43g	160	4	27
Fat Free Mix, 1 pkt, 65g	230	0	50
Arbonne Int'l Meal Shake	190	4.5	24
Balanced: Diet, 11 fl.oz can	180	1	34
Choc Royale; Fr. Vanilla 11 fl.oz	180	2	35
Strawb.; Vanilla 11 fl.oz can	230	3	36
Kids Chocolate, 8 fl.oz can	160	3	30
Bariatrix Shakes, 1 serving	100	2	6
Proti-Max Meal, 67g	250	3	20
Boost: Ready-To-Drink, 8 oz	240	4	41
Boost High Protein, 8 fl.oz	240	6	33
Boost Plus, 8 fl.oz can	360	14	45
Bulk Force, 1 pint bottle	750	0	163
Carnation Instant Breakfast			
Powder: 1 reg. envelope, 37g	130	1	28
No Sugar Added, 1 envel., 21g	70	1	12
Ready-To-Drink, aver., 10 oz	220	3	37
Choice dm *(Mead Johnson)*, 8 fl.oz	250	12	25
Ensure: Regular, 8 oz can	225	6	31
Ensure Bal'd Bkfst, choc pouch	140	0.5	30
Ensure Fiber, 8 fl.oz can	250	6	42
Ensure Light, 8 fl.oz can	200	3	33
Ensure Plus, 8 fl.oz can	360	13	47
Glucerna, 8 fl.oz can	220	11	22
Powder, made up, 1/2 cup	250	9	34
Genisoy: Shake, 1 scoop, 35g	120	0	17
Protein Powder, 1 scoop, 29g	100	0	0
Health Source Soy,			
2 scoops, 1 oz	100	1	4
Herbalife, (Thermogetics F.1), 1 oz	100	1	14
HMR 500 Shakes, 1 pkt	100	0	16
HMR 120, 1 serving	120	1.5	16
IDN *(Nu Skin):*			
Aloe Fountain, 2 fl.oz	20	0	5
Amino Build, 3 scoops, 1 1/2 oz	160	1	12
Appeal: French Delight, 2 oz pkt	210	2	33
Swiss Truffle, 2 oz pkt	220	2.5	33
Appeal Lite HT	120	1.5	26
Sports Drinks: See Next Page			
Mass Recovery, 1 pint bottle	380	0	60
Met-Rx: Nutrition Drink Mix, 72g	260	2	22
Metaform:			
Lean Mass, 2 scoops	140	0	11
Protein Powder, 76g pkt	270	2	21
Proton, 45g pkt (1.6 oz)	170	1	15
Nutrament (Mead Johnson): 12 fl.oz	360	10	52

	C	F	Cb
Optifast 800:			
Powder, 1 serving	160	3	20
Ready-To-Drink, Chocolate	160	3	20
ProBalance, 8.45 fl.oz	300	10	39
Pro-Cal 100 *(R-Kane),* 1 pkt	105	2	7
Pure Pro, 1 pint bottle	160	0	<1
Resource *(Novartis):*			
Plus, 8 fl.oz	360	11	52
Standard 8 fl.oz pak	250	6	40
Diabetic, 8 fl.oz pak	250	11	23
Fruit Beverage, 8 fl.oz pak	180	0	36
Yogurt Flav'd Beverage, 8 fl.oz	250	4	45
Rite Aid Nutritional Suppl. 8 oz	250	6	40
Sav-on Nut'l: 8 fl.oz can	360	13	47
Light, 8 fl.oz can	200	3	33
Slim-Fast: All flavors, 1 scoop	100	1	20
Prep. w. Fat Free milk, 8 fl.oz	190	1	32
Sustacal: Liquid, 8 fl.oz can	240	6	33
Basic, 8 fl.oz can	250	9	34
Sustacal Plus, 8 fl.oz	360	14	45
Powder, 2 oz + water	200	1	36
Sweet Success *(Nestlé):*			
Healthy Shake, 10 fl.oz can	200	3	37
Fruit Flavors, 10 fl.oz	200	0.5	39
Powder, 2 scoops, 32g (1.1 oz)	100	1	25
Total Balance, 9.5 oz can	230	7	25
Twin Lab RxFuel, 1 pkt	250	0	62
Ultra Slim-Fast: Powder, 1 scoop	120	0.5	24
Ready-To-Drink, 11 oz can	220	3	38
Walgreens Nutritional Supplements:			
Advanced Formula, 8 oz can	250	6	40
Plus, 8 oz can	355	13	47
Light, 8 oz can	200	3	33
Weider (Powders):			
Creatine ATP, 2 scoops, 2 oz	230	0	37
Complete Rx, 70g pkt (2.5 oz)	240	2.5	27
Lean Pro, 2 scoops, 50g (1.76oz)	180	1.5	22
Ultra Whey Pro, 1 scp, 30g (1oz)	110	1	2
Women's Natural Replace., 33g	120	1	13
Dynamic:			
Body Shaper, 35g	140	0.5	22
Muscle Builder, 2 scoops, 45g	190	0	27
Weight Gainer, 4 scoops, 85g	330	0.5	62
Victory Pure Protein: 2 scoops,			
Egg/Beef/Vege. average	140	0	14
Victory Mass 1000, 7 oz	740	2.5	148
Mega Mass 4000, 3 scoops	1640	4	319
Super Mega Mass 2000, 2 sc.	520	1.5	102

Sports Energy Drinks

(Fluid Replacement, Carbohydrate Rich)
Per 8 fl.oz Unless Indicated

	C	F	Cb
AllSport, all flavors, 8 fl.oz	70	0	18
Amino Force, 22 oz	390	0	75
Blue Thunder, 22 oz	400	0	68
Body Fuel (w. NutraSweet), 8 fl.oz	4	0	1
Body Works *(Shasta),* 12 fl.oz	90	0	22
Carboplex *(Nutra Life),* 31g	120	0	30
Cytomax, 8 fl.oz	65	0	13
Exceed (Weider): Powder, 2 Tbsp	70	0	17
Liquid, 12 fl.oz box	105	0	26
Gatorade: ThirstQuencher, 8 fl.oz	50	0	14
ReLode, 1 pkt	80	0	20
GatorLode, 11.6 fl.oz can	280	0	70
GatorPro, 11 fl.oz can	360	6	59
Hansen's: Anti-Ox, 243ml can	110	0	31
Energy (w. Taurine/Gingko), 246ml	120	0	32
Hydra Fuel *(Tury Labs)*	65	0	16
IDN *(Nu Skin):*			
Creatine Blast, 1 scoop, 1 1/2 oz	130	0	32
Splash C with Aloe, 1 scoop	80	0	20
Sportalyte, 1/2 pkt (makes 8 fl.oz)	70	0	17
Knudsen: Isotonic Sports, 8 fl.oz	60	0	15
Simply Nutritious, 1/2 bot., 16 fl.oz	60	0	14
Max, made-up, 8 fl.oz	96	0	24
Met-Rx ORS,			
Endura (Meta genics)	60	0	15
Pedialyte *(Abbott)*	25	0	6
Powerade, all flavors, 8 fl.oz	70	0	19
Pro-formance, all flavors	100	0	25
Recharge *(Knudsen),* all flavors	70	0	18
Red Bull Energy Drink, 8.3 fl.oz	113	0	28
Relode Gel, 0.75 oz pkt	80	0	20
Ripped Force, 16 oz	90	0	22
Snapple Sport, all flavors	80	0	20
Sobe (20 fl.oz): Energy; Proline	120	0	32
Elixir 3C: Orange	90	0	24
Cranberry Grapefruit	110	0	28
The Juice, 11 fl.oz	260	0	65
10-K *(Suntory)*	60	0	15
Thermo Force, 16 oz	260	0	65
Tiger's Milk (mix):			
Energy Booster, 3 heap Tbsp.	120	0	30
Twin Lab Ultra Fuel, 16 oz	400	0	100
Upper Deck: All flavors	80	0	19

Quick Guide

Fruit Smoothies

Average All Brands

	C	F	Cb
Fruit Only: 8 fl.oz cup	305	0	25
12 fl.oz	160	0	38
16 fl.oz	210	0	50
24 fl.oz	320	0.5	76
Fruit + Nonfat Milk/Soy:			
12 fl.oz	190	0.5	40
16 fl.oz	250	0.5	53
24 fl.oz	380	1	80
Fruit + Nonfat Frozen Yogurt/Sherbert:			
12 fl.oz	210	0.5	47
16 fl.oz	280	0.5	62
24 fl.oz	420	1	94

Brands - Fruit Smoothies

	C	F	Cb
Hansens: *Per 11 fl.oz*			
Fruit flavors, regular	170	0	43
Lite: Cranberry; Raspberry	50	0	13
Energy: Island Blast	170	0	42
Super Energy: Tropical Blast	170	0	40
Super Power: Berry Splash	170	0	41
Super Protein: Banana Citrus	290	1	59
Super Vita: Orange Carrot	170	0	40
Jamba Juice *(California):* See Page 202			
Jera's Juice *(Boston): Per 24 fl.oz*			
Mango Passion	300	0.5	71
Raspberry Madness	425	1	100
Spring Fever	400	1.5	91
Soy Smoothie	360	4.5	79
Whippy Snapple: *Per 10 fl.oz*			
Citrus	150	0	39
Pineapple Orange	100	0	41
Fruit Whips: *Per 8 oz bottle*			
Berry/lemon/Orange/Tropical			
All flavors, 236ml (8 oz)	125	0	29

Dehydration limits sporting performance. Drink adequate water before, during and after strenuous exercise. Lightly sweetened drinks may benefit endurance athletes.

Quick Guide

Cola & Soda Drinks

Average All Brands	C	F	Cb
Coca-Cola and Pepsi			
8 fl.oz Cup	100	0	25
12 fl.oz Can	150	0	37
16 fl.oz Bottle	200	0	50
20 fl.oz Bottle	250	0	63
24 fl.oz (*Pepsi*)	300	0	75
1 Liter Bottle	400	0	100
2 Liter Bottle	800	0	200

Other Soda Drinks

Club Soda, 12 fl.oz	0	0	0
Club Soda Cream, 12 fl.oz	170	0	42
Diet Soft Drinks: Aver., 12 fl.oz	0	0	0
Ginger Ale, 12 fl.oz	120	0	30
Lemon Lime, 12 fl.oz	220	0	55
Orange, 12 fl.oz	180	0	45
Root Beer, 12 fl.oz	165	0	41
Tonic Water, 12 fl.oz	135	0	34
Mineral Water: Plain, 12 fl.oz	0	0	0
Sweetened/flavored, 12 fl.oz	150	0	37
w. Fruit Juice, 12 fl.oz	120	0	30
Seltzers: Plain/Diet, 12 fl.oz	0	0	0
Sweetened/flavored, 12 fl.oz	150	0	37
w. Fruit Juice, 12 fl.oz	120	0	30

Movie Theater & Take-Out

Average All Flavors (Figures allow for 25% Ice)			
Small, 12 fl.oz	110	0	27
Regular, 16 fl.oz	150	0	37
Medium, 22 fl.oz	210	0	5
Large, 32 fl.oz	300	0	75
Cinnabon: Icescapes, 16 fl.oz			
Orange Cream	360	16	50
Root Beer	470	22	63
Mochalatta	390	12	62

Soda Brands

Per 12 fl.oz Unless Indicated			
A&W: Cream Soda	165	0	41
Diet Cream Soda/Root Beer	1	0	0
Root Beer	180	0	45
Albertson's: Cola	160	0	43
Lemon Lime	140	0	38
Other flavors, average	170	0	47

Soda Brands (Cont)

Per 12 fl.oz Unless Indicated	C	F	Cb
Arizona: Lite Choc. Fudge, 8 fl.oz	60	0	14
Strawb. Banana Colada, 8 fl.oz	140	0.5	33
Pina Colada, 8 fl.oz	140	1	34
Lemonade, 15 fl.oz Can	220	0	54
Barq's Root Beer	165	0	41
Big Red: 8 fl.oz	100	0	25
Barrelhead: Rootbeer	165	0	41
Bodyworks (Shasta), all flav.	90	0	23
Canada Dry: Birch Beer; Cactus	165	0	41
Club Soda	0	0	0
Collins Mixer	120	0	30
Ginger Ale, all flavors	135	0	37
Diet, all flavors	0	0	0
Half & Half; Hi-Spot; Wild Cherry	165	0	41
Lemon Sour	150	0	37
Seltzer, all flavors	0	0	0
Sour Mixer	135	0	34
Tahitian Treat	225	0	56
Tonic Water/Twist Lime	150	0	37
Diet	0	0	0
Clearly Canadian, 11 fl.oz, aver.	120	0	30
Coca-Cola: Classic	140	0	35
Coke II	160	0	40
Diet Coke; Diet Cherry Coke	1	0	0
Cherry Coke	150	0	42
Cragmont: Cola	165	0	41
Cherry	180	0	45
Diet, all flavors	0	0	0
Crush, all flavors	210	0	52
Crystal Light, all flavors	8	0	2
Diet Rite, all flavors	1	0	0
Doc Shasta	160	0	40
Dr Diablo, Cola	140	0	35
Dr Nehi	150	0	41
Dr Pepper: Regular	150	0	40
Diet (Reg.; Caffeine Free)	3	0	0.5
Fanta: Orange; Grape	180	0	45
Ginger Ale	130	0	33
Root Beer	165	0	41
Fresca	4	0	1
Hansen's: Average all flavors	130	0	37
Orange Creme Soda, 8 fl.oz	110	0	31
Health Valley: Ginger Ale	150	0	41
Sarsaparilla RootBeer	150	0	41
Rootbeer Old Fashioned	120	0	30
Wild Berry	140	0	35

Per 12 fl.oz Unless Indicated	C	F	Cb
Hires: Cream; Root Beer	180	0	45
Jolt Cola	150	0	41
Knudsen: Spritzers, average	170	0	43
Lights, all flavors	110	0	28
Kick (Royal Crown)	180	0	45
Lucozade, 7 fl.oz	136	0	34
Manischewitz, Seltzer	0	0	0
Mello Yello: Regular	180	0	45
Diet	5	0	0
Minute Maid: Diet Orange	3	0	0.5
Berry; Black Cherry; Orange	165	0	41
Fruit Punch; Grape	180	0	45
Lemonade	160	0	40
Peach; P'apple; R'berry; Grapefr.	165	0	41
Strawberry	185	0	46
Mountain Dew, 24 fl.oz Bottle	170	0	46
Mr Pibb: Regular	150	0	37
Diet	2	0	1
Mug: Root Beer	160	0	43
Diet	0	0	0
Natural Brew: Apple, Cream	170	0	43
Cafe Mocha, Cherry Amaretto	160	0	40
Ginseng Cola, Ginger Ale	170	0	43
Nehi (Royal Crown): Cream	180	0	45
Ginger Ale, Quinine Water	135	0	45
Other flavors, average	195	0	45
Orangina, 10 fl.oz Bottle	120	0	45
Orbitz, 300ml Bottle, average	130	0	30
Pepsi: Regular; Caffeine Free	150	0	41
Diet Pepsi	0	0	0
One	1	0	0
Wild Cherry	160	0	43
Perrier: Regular or flavors	0	0	0
Ramblin' Root Beer	180	0	45
RC Cola: Regular	160	0	40
Diet Cola	1	0	0
Cherry	165	0	41
Royal Mistic: Punch, 16 fl.oz	230	0	57
'N Juice, average	155	0	38
Sparkling, average, 11.1 fl.oz	115	0	28
Schweppes: Bitter Lemon	165	0	41
Ginger Ale, regular; Raspberry	120	0	30
Ginger Beer; Lemon Lime	150	0	37
Grapefruit; Lemon Sour	165	0	41
Seltzer	0	0	0
Tonic: Regular	120	0	30
Diet	0	0	0
Sensa (Guarana flavored)	135	0	34

Per 12 fl.oz Unless Indicated	C	F	Cb
Santa Cruz: Sparkling, all types	150	0	37
Orange	195	0	48
7UP: Regular	140	0	38
Cherry, Gold	155	0	38
Shasta: Black Cherry	170	0	46
Cherry Cola; Doc Shasta	160	0	40
Club Soda; Diet, all flavors	0	0	0
Cola, regular	170	0	46
Caffeine Free	160	0	40
Fruit Punch, Pineapple	200	0	50
Ginger Ale	130	0	33
Shasta Plus: all flavors	170	0	46
Slice: Lemon Lime	150	0	38
Diet Lemon Lime	0	0	0
Dr. Slice	140	0	40
Fruit; Grape; Pineapple; Red	190	0	51
CherryLime; Slice Cola	160	0	43
Snapple: Average all flavors	180	0	45
Spree (Shasta): all flavors	170	0	43
Sprite: Regular	150	0	37
Diet	4	0	1
Squirt: Regular Soda Citrus	150	0	40
Ruby Red Soda	170	0	46
Sunkist: Average all flavors	210	0	52
Diet Citrus	0	0	0
Diet Orange	7	0	1.5
Surge Citrus	170	0	46
TAB	1	0	0
Upper 10 (RC): Regular	150	0	37
Diet	4	0	1
Vernor's: Ginger Ale	150	0	37
Wink	195	0	48
Welch's: Sparkling, average	180	0	45

Fruitopia

(Contain 10% Fruit Juice): *Per 2 fl.oz*

Apple Raspb.; Trop. Consideration	115	0	45
Lemonade Love; Cranberry Lemon	170	0	43
Pink Lemonade; Tangerine Wave.	175	0	44
Other flavors, average	190	0	47

Kool-Aid, Tang

Bright & Early, 6 fl.oz	90	0	23
Kool-Aid, unsweetened, 6 fl.oz	2	0	0.5
Sugar, sweetened, 6 fl.oz	80	0	20
Sugar Free (NutraSweet), 6 fl.oz	4	0	1
Tang, all flavors, 6 fl.oz	90	0	23
Sugar-Free, 6 fl.oz	6	0	1.5

Instant Coffee

	C	F	Cb
Powder/Granules: Regular or Decaffeinated,			
1 level tsp	**2**	0	0.5
1 rounded tsp	**4**	0	1
Ground, 1 Tbsp	**5**	0	1
Brewed/Percolated, 1 cup, 8 fl.oz	**5**	0	1
Coffee With Milk/Cream/Creamers:			
1 Cup Coffee:			
w. Whole Milk: Dash, 1 Tbsp	**10**	0.5	1
2 Tbsp, 1 fl.oz	**20**	1	1.5
w. 2% Milk, 2 Tbsp	**15**	0.5	1.5
w. 1% Milk, 2 Tbsp	**12**	0.3	1.5
w. Fat Free Milk, 2 Tbsp	**10**	0	1.5
w. Half & Half: 2 Tbsp	**45**	4	1
w. Cream (light coffee): 2 Tbsp	**65**	6	1
w. *Coffee Mate:* Liquid, reg., 1T.	**40**	2	5
Liquid Fat Free, 1 Tbsp	**15**	0	2
Powder, 1 heaping tsp	**20**	1	2
Sugar ~ Add Extra: 1 heaping tsp	**25**	0	6
Single portion, 1 pkt	**25**	0	6

Flavored Coffee Mixes

	C	F	Cb
Caffé D'Vita: 1 tsp	**20**	1	4
Coffee Essence, 1 tsp	**16**	0	4
General Foods, Cafe Intl: Regular	**60**	3	10
Sugar-free, average	**30**	2	3
Maxwell House: Mocha, 1 envelope	**100**	2.5	17
Mocha, sugar-free, 1 envelope	**60**	3	7
Van., Irish Cream, 1 envelope	**90**	1	20
Nescafé: Frothé, all flavors, average	**90**	1.5	19
Chicory: Instant Coffee, 1 tsp	**6**	0	1
Coffee Essence, 1 tsp	**16**	0	4

Coffee Substitute Mixes

	C	F	Cb
Roasted Cereal Beverages:			
Cafix Instant Beverage, 1 tsp	**6**	0	1
Kaffree Roma (Natural Touch), 1 tsp	**6**	0	1
Postum, Instant Hot Beverage, 1 tsp	**12**	0	3
Teeccino Caffe, 1 tsp	**10**	0	2

Bottled Ready-To-Drink

	C	F	Cb
Coffee: Per Bottle			
Main St: Fr. Vanilla, 12 fl.oz	**190**	3	31
Nescafe: Caffe Latte, 9.5 fl.oz	**140**	3.5	23
Mocha, 9.5 fl.oz	**140**	3	26
Starbucks: All types,. 9.5 fl.oz	**190**	3	40

Coffee Shops/Restaurants

Per 8 fl.oz Cup (Unless Indicated)

	C	F	Cb
Coffee (Regular/Percolated/Filtered)	**5**	0	1
Americano Drip Coffee,1 cup	**5**	0	1
Cafe Au Lait: 1 cup, 8 fl.oz	**65**	2.5	6
Nonfat Milk,1 cup	**45**	0	7
Caffe Latté:			
8 fl.oz cup: w. Whole Milk	**100**	5	8
w. 2% Milk	**80**	2.5	8
w. Nonfat Milk	**60**	0	8
12fl. oz: w. Whole Milk	**180**	10	14
w. Nonfat Milk	**110**	0.5	15
Cafe Mocha (Mochaccino): 1 c.	**120**	3	15
12 fl.oz	**180**	4.5	15
16 fl.oz	**240**	6	15
Cappuccino:			
8 fl.oz cup: w. Whole Milk	**70**	3.5	6
w. 2% Milk	**60**	2	6
w. Nonfat Milk	**40**	0	6
12 fl.oz: w. Whole Milk	**110**	6	9
w. 2% Milk	**80**	3	9
w. Nonfat Milk	**60**	0	9
Mocha, with Cream			
8 fl.oz: w. Whole Milk	**180**	12	16
w. Nonfat Milk	**150**	8	16
Tall, 12 fl.oz: Whole Milk	**290**	18	25
w. Nonfat Milk	**230**	11	26
Iced Mocha (no cream)			
Tall, 12 fl.oz: w. Whole Milk	**190**	9	24
w. Nonfat Milk	**140**	2	24
Espresso: Regular	**4**	0	1
Doppio (Double)	**8**	0	2
Espresso Con Panna			
(w. dollop whipped cream)	**30**	3	1
Espresso Macchiato	**15**	0.5	2
Frappuccino: Tall, 12 fl.oz	**200**	3	39
Grande, 16 fl.oz	**270**	4	52
Frappuccino Mocha:			
Large/Tall, 12 fl.oz	**230**	3	44
Grande, 16 fl.oz	**310**	4.5	59
Iced Latte: Similar to Caffe Latte			
Intellicino: 12 fl.oz	**150**	7	15
Lowfat (2% milk)	**120**	3.5	5

Irish & Liqueur Coffees

	C	F	Cb
Irish Coffee (no sugar)	**175**	10	0
Liqueur Coffee, aver. all types	**200**	10	16

Cocoa & Hot Chocolate

	C	F	Cb
Cocoa:			
(w. Whipping Cream - *Starbucks*):			
8 fl.oz cup: w. Whole Milk	210	14	19
w. Nonfat Milk	80	8	17
Tall (12 fl.oz): w. Whole Milk	300	20	26
w. Nonfat Milk	120	11	26
Hot Chocolate:			
8 fl.oz cup: w. Whole Milk	200	10	25
w. Nonfat Milk	140	2	25
Tall (12 fl.oz): w. Whole Milk	300	15	38
w. Nonfat Milk	210	3	38
Cinnabon: Mocholatta Chill, 16 oz	410	18	54

Coffee Extras

Chocolate (Cocoa) Topping, 1/2 tsp	10	0	2
Flavored Syrups, 2 Tbsp	80	0	20
Sugar-free, 2 Tbsp	0	0	0
Hershey's Chocolate Syrup, 2 Tbsp	100	0	24
Half & Half Cream, 2 Tbsp	40	3	3
Light Whipped Cream, 2 Tbsp	30	2	2

Starbucks

Americano:			
Short, 8 fl.oz	5	0	1
Tall, 12 fl.oz	10	0	2
Grande, 16 fl.oz	15	0	3
Venti, 20 fl.oz	15	0	3
Drip Coffee:			
Short, 8 fl.oz	5	0	1
Tall, 12 fl.oz	10	0	1
Grande, 16 fl.oz	10	0	2
Espresso: Solo	5	0	1
Doppio	10	0	2
Espresso Con Panna (w. Whipped Cream):			
Solo	30	3	1
Doppio	35	3	2
Espresso Macchiato:			
Solo: w. Whole Milk	15	0.5	2
w. Lowfat Milk (2%)	10	0	2
w. Nonfat Milk	10	0	2
w. Soy Milk	10	0	1
Doppio: w. Whole Milk	20	0.5	3
w. Lowfat Milk (2%)	15	0	3
w. Nonfat Milk	15	0	3
w. Soy Milk	15	0	2

Starbucks (Cont)

	C	F	Cb
Coffee Frappuccino:			
Tall, 12 fl.oz	180	2	38
Grande, 16 fl.oz	240	2.5	50
Venti, 20 fl.oz	300	3	63
Mocha Frappuccino:			
Tall, 12 fl.oz	210	2	43
Grande, 16 fl.oz	280	3	58
Venti, 20 fl.oz	350	3.5	72
Rhomba Frappuccino:			
Tall, 12 fl.oz	240	5	43
Grande, 16 fl.oz	320	7	58
Venti, 20 fl.oz	400	8	72
Chai Tea Latté:			
Short: 8 fl.oz w. Whole Milk	160	7	18
w. Lowfat Milk (2%)	130	3.5	18
w. Nonfat Milk	110	0	19
w. Soy Milk	100	4	13
Tall: 12 fl.oz w. Whole Milk	220	9	26
w. Lowfat Milk (2%)	190	5	26
w. Nonfat Milk	150	0	27
w. Soy Milk	140	5	18
Grande: 16 fl.oz w. Whole Milk	320	13	26
w. Lowfat Milk (2%)	260	7	37
w. Nonfat Milk	210	0.5	37
w. Soy Milk	200	8	25
Venti: 20 fl.oz w. Whole Milk	400	17	46
w. Lowfat Milk (2%)	330	9	46
w. Nonfat Milk	270	1	47
w. Soy Milk	260	10	32
Tiazzi Blended Fruit Juice:			
Mango Citrus/Wild Berry, average			
Tall, 12 fl.oz	180	0	43
Grande, 16 fl.oz	250	0	60
Venti, 20 fl.oz	340	0	81

Rev. Dr Robert Schuller

*"Inch by inch
Life's a cinch"*

*"You'll never win
If you don't begin!"*

Teas

	C	F	Cb
Regular: Bag, Loose or Instant			
Brewed, 1 cup, 8 fl.oz	1	0	0
(Add extra for sugar/milk)			
Herbal: Average all varieties, 1 cup	1	0	1
Bigelow: Apple Orchard, 1 cup	5	0	1
Other Varieties	2	0	0.5
Celestial Seasonings:			
Bengal Spice; Spearmint	5	0	0.5
Lemon Zinger	4	0	1
Roastaroma	10	0	2
Other varieties	2	0	0.5
Chai Tea Latté (*Starbucks*): See Previous Page			

Quick Guide

Iced Tea

Average All Brands	C	F	Cb
Pre-Sweetened: 8 fl.oz	100	0	25
12 fl.oz	150	0	38
16 fl.oz	200	0	50
Unsweetened: 8 fl.oz	2	0	0

Iced Tea Mixes

Per Serving	C	F	Cb
4C Instant	90	0	22
Bigelow, Nice Over Ice	1	0	0.5
Celestial Seasonings, Iced Delight	4	0	1
Crystal Light, Sugar Free	3	0	0
Kool-Aid Fruit T's	70	0	17
Lipton: Instant	0	0	0
Instant Lemon/Raspberry	3	0	1
Lemon	55	0	14
Peach/Raspb, Sugar Free	5	0	1
Nestea: 100% Instant	2	0	0
Decaffeinated	6	0	1
Ice Teasers, all flavors	6	0	1
Peach, Raspberry	90	0	22

"A woman is like a teabag. You never know her strength until she's in hot water."

~ Nancy Reagan

Bottled & Canned Teas

Per 8 fl.oz Unless Indicated	C	F	Cb
Arizona: Green Tea w. Ginseng & Honey			
20 fl.oz Bottle: 1 cup, 8 fl.oz	70	0	18
Diet Green w. Ginseng	0	0	0
15.5 fl.oz Can: Average all flavors			
1/2 can, 7.75 fl.oz	95	0	28
w. Ginseng Extract	60	0	15
Herb Tea w. Honey, 8 fl.oz	70	0	17
Honey Lemon, 8 fl.oz	90	0	22
Brisk: 1 liter Bottle: Aver., 1 cup	90	0	24
12 fl.oz Can: Lemon, 1 Can	120	0	33
Raspberry, 1 Can	130	0	35
24 fl.oz Bottle: Lemon, 1 cup	80	0	22
Fruitopia: Average all flavors	110	0	28
Knudsen: Coolers, all flavors	90	0	23
Lipton (16 fl.oz Bottle): *Per 8 fl.oz*			
No Lemon	70	0	18
Lemon	90	0	21
Peach; Raspberry	110	0	26
Mistic: Tropical Cooler, 8 fl.oz	45	0	12
Nestea Iced Tea: Diet Lemon	3	0	0.5
Cool from Nestea, 1 cup, 8 fl.oz	80	0	20
12 fl.oz	120	0	33
Diet Cool from Nestea	2	0	0.5
Lemon/Peach/Raspberry	80	0	20
Sweetened Ice Tea	65	0	17
Oregon Chai: Herbal Bliss, 1/2 cup	70	0	18
Nirvana/Kashmir Green, 1/2 cup	80	0	20
Royal Mistic: Regular, 12 fl.oz	145	0	36
Diet, 12 fl.oz	8	0	2
Schweppes, 8 fl.oz	90	0	22
Shasta, 8 fl.oz	80	0	20
Snapple: Regular, sweetened	70	0	17
Diet/Unsweetened	0	0	0
Lemon; Peach, Raspberry	100	0	25
Sobe: Green Tea, 1 cup	90	0	23
Ssips (Johanna Farms), 8.45 fl.oz	100	0	25
Tropicana: Lemonfruit	100	0	25
Diet Lemon Fruit	15	0	4
Peach/Rasp./Tangerine, 8 fl.oz	120	0	28
10 fl.oz Bottle	140	0	35
11.5 fl.oz can	160	0	40
Twister: Apple Berry, 8 fl.oz	100	0	28
Lemon Citrus	110	0	28
Turkey Hill: Regular	90	0	22
Raspberry Cooler	110	0	28
Diet Decaffeinated	0	0	0

Health Hazards: Excess alcohol contributes to obesity, high blood pressure, stroke, heart and liver disease, some cancers, and even impotence.
Concentration and short-term memory are reduced as well as sporting performance.
Other alcohol hazards include stomach upsets, menstrual problems, anxiety, headaches, insomnia, work absenteeism and family arguments.

Alcohol contributes to obesity through its high calories and by lessening the body's ability to burn fat. Fat storage is promoted, particularly in the belly - a danger zone. Alcohol can also stimulate appetite.

Alcohol is potentially more harmful while dieting. Blood sugar levels may drop with resultant tiredness and further impairment of concentration, reflexes and driving skills - and maybe the dieter's resolve!

SAFE ALCOHOL LIMITS

Women: No more than **1 drink** per day.
Men: No more than **2 drinks** per day.
(At least 2 days a week should be alcohol-free.)

1 Drink = 12 fl.oz regular beer, or 5 fl.oz wine, or $1\frac{1}{2}$ fl.oz spirits (80 proof).
Each drink contains approximately 14g alcohol.

For some people, **safe drinking** will mean no alcohol drinks at all. (Even one drink may impair driving skills, particularly if tired; and 3-4 drinks daily has been linked to brain shrinkage in some social drinkers).

It is advisable not to drink at all if you are:

- pregnant or trying to conceive
- taking drug medication (unless approved by your doctor or pharmacist)
- have a condition such as liver or heart disease
- planning to drive or use machinery
- studying or needing to concentrate
- a child or adolescent

Women and adolescents are more prone to alcohol's ill-effects due to their lower body weight, smaller livers and lesser capacity to metabolise alcohol.

Note: You cannot save daily drinks for one occasion.
Binge drinking is particularly harmful ~
4 drinks 'in a row' for males or 3 drinks for females.

Excess alcohol contributes to obesity and high blood pressure

HOW TO CALCULATE ALCOHOL CONTENT

Percent alcohol on label refers to alcohol volume (ml alcohol/100ml).

100ml = $3\frac{1}{2}$ fl. oz

To convert to grams (weight) of alcohol, multiply the percent volume by 0.8 - since 1 ml of alcohol weighs only 0.8 grams (actually 0.789g).

EXAMPLE
12 fl.oz Can Beer (5% alcohol)

5% alc.volume = 5% of 12 fl.oz
= 0.6 fl.oz
= 18ml alcohol
(1 fl.oz=30ml)

Weight (18ml x 0.8)
=14.4g alcohol

Quick Guide

Beer: Alc ~ Alcohol (Grams)

Beer Contains Zero Fat

	C	Alc	Cb
Malt Liquor/Ale (5.6% Alc. Vol.)			
12 fl.oz Can/Bottle/Glass	180	16	17
22 fl.oz Can/Bottle/Glass	330	29	32
Regular Beer (5% Alc. Vol.)			
7 fl.oz Glass	80	8.5	4
12 fl.oz Bottle/Can/Glass	140	14	10
16 fl.oz. Bottle/Can	185	19	11
22 fl.oz Bottle	260	26	20
32 fl.oz Bottle	370	37	28
40 fl.oz. Bottle	470	47	35
Light Beer (4.2% Alc. Vol.)			
7 fl.oz Glass	65	7	4
12 fl.oz Bottle/Can/Glass	110	12	6
16 fl.oz Bottle/Can	145	16	8
22 fl.oz Bottle	200	22	11
Low Alcohol Beer (2.3% Alc. Vol)			
(Example: *Blatz LA*),12 fl.oz	75	7	6
Non-Alcoholic/Near Beer			
(Less than 0.5% alcohol by volume)			
Average All Brands, 12 fl.oz	70	1	16

Beer Brands

Per 12 fl.oz Serving
Percentage alcohol listed below is by volume - not by weight.

	C	Alc	Cb
Amber Ice (5.3% alcohol)	130	15	6
Anchor Steam (4.6%)	155	13	16
Anheuser Light (3.2% alcohol)	75	9	7
Artic Ice (5.3%)	150	15	8
Artic Ice Light 3.2 (3.9%)	100	11	6
Augsburger Bock (4.9%)	170	14	17
Augsburger Golden/Dark (4.9%)	170	14	17
Augsburger Red (4.9%)	160	14	14
Ballard Bitter (4.7%)	180	14	19
Beck's (5%)	150	14	12
Big Sky (4.8%)	150	14	12
Big Sky Light (4.5%)	105	13	5
Black & Tan (4.5%)	185	13	22
Black Label (5.6%)	155	16	11
Black Label Light (3.7%)	100	11	6
Blackhook Porter (4.9%)	160	14	14
Blatz (4.3%)	135	12	10
Blatz LA (2.3%)	75	7	6

Brands (Cont)

Beer Contains Zero Fat

	C	Alc	Cb
Blatz Light (3.7%), 12 fl.oz	100	11	3
Blue Moon Ale: Belgian (4.8%)	160	14	13
Honey Blond Ale (5.5%)	200	16	20
Nut Brown Ale (5.1%)	180	15	16
Raspberry Cream Ale (4.9%)	190	14	20
Bud Dry (4.9%)	130	14	8
Bud Light (4.2%)	110	12	7
Bud Ice (5.5%)	150	16	9
Bud Ice Light (4.1%)	95	12	4
Budweiser (4.9%)	150	14	11
Busch (4.9%)	145	14	11
Busch Light (4.2%)	110	12	7
Carling (4.4%)	140	13	10
Carlsberg (5%)	135	13	10
Castlemaine XXXX (4.7%)	140	13	9
Colt 45 MM (5.6%)	155	16	1
Coors (4.9%)	150	14	12
Coors Dry (4.9%)	120	14	6
Coors Light 3.2 (4%)	100	11	4
Corona Extra (4.6%)	130	13	9
Dos Equis Lager (5%)	130	14	9
Elk Mountain Amber Ale (5.5%)	190	16	18
Elk Mountain Red (4.9%)	160	14	13
Extra Gold (4.9%)	150	14	12
Extra Gold 3.2 (4%)	120	11	10
Faust (5%)	170	14	17
First Reserve (4.9%)	170	14	16
Fosters Lager (4.9%)	135	14	9
George Killian's: Irish Brown(5.2%)	185	15	15
Irish Red (5%)	160	14	13
Wilde Honey Ale (5.3%)	170	15	14
Goebel (4.1%)	130	12	12
Goebel Light (3.9%)	110	11	8
Grolsch Premium (5%)	140	14	10
Guinness Draught (4.3%)	155	12	17
Heileman's: Old Style (4.9%)	147	14	12
Old Style Light (4.1%)	110	12	6
Heineken (5.4%)	170	15	15
Heineken Dark (5.2%)	175	15	16
Herman Joseph's			
Special Premium (4.9%)	150	14	12
Highland Ale: Black (5.6%)	180	16	16
Amber (5.2%)	160	15	14
Hurricane (5.5%)	150	16	10
Icehouse, Miller (5.0%)	135	14	9
Icehouse, Miller (5.5%)	150	16	10

Brands (Cont)

Beer Contains Zero Fat *Per 12 fl.oz Serving*	C	Alc	Cb
Keystone Regular/Dry (4.9% alc.)	**125**	14	6
Ice (5.3%)	**145**	15	8
Light, 3.2 (4%)	**100**	10	4
Amber Light (3.8%)	**110**	11	8
King Cobra (5.9%)	**180**	17	15
Kirin Lager (Japan) (4.8%)	**135**	13	9
Labatt's Blue (5%)	**145**	14	9
Lowenbrau Dark/Special (4.9%)	**160**	14	15
Magnum Malt Liquor (5.9%)	**155**	17	23
Meister Brau (4.5%)	**130**	13	11
Meister Brau Light (4.5%)	**105**	13	5
Memphis Brown (4.6%)	**120**	13	6
Michelob: Regular (5%)	**160**	14	12
Light (4.3%)	**135**	12	12
Dry (4.9%)	**130**	14	8
Amber Bock (5%)	**160**	14	15
Centennial (5.5%)	**175**	16	15
Classic Dark (5%)	**160**	14	15
Golden Draft (4.8%)	**150**	14	13
Golden Draft Light (4.2%)	**110**	12	7
Hefeweizen (5%)	**165**	14	14
Malt (5.8%)	**160**	17	9
Miller, Regular (5%)	**150**	14	12
Miller Genuine Draft (5%)	**145**	14	11
Light (4.5%)	**100**	13	4
Miller High Life (5%)	**145**	14	9
Miller High Life Ice (5.5%)	**142**	16	7
Miller High Life Light (4.5%)	**100**	13	4
Miller Lite (4.5%)	**95**	13	4
Miller Lite Ice (5.5%)	**125**	16	4
Miller Lite Ice (5%)	**115**	14	3
Milwaukee's Best (4.5%)	**130**	13	11
Milwaukee's Best Ice (5.5%)	**135**	16	5
Milwaukee's Best Light (4.5%)	**100**	13	8
Minnesota's Best (4.9%)	**140**	14	10
Moosehead (5%)	**125**	14	14
Natural Ice, Budweiser (5.9%)	**160**	16	10
Natural Light, Budweiser (4.2%)	**110**	12	7
Natural Pilsner, Budweiser (4.9%)	**150**	14	12
Newcastle Brown Ale (4.5%)	**140**	12	13
Northstone Amber Ale (4.9%)	**150**	14	8
Old Milwaukee (4.5%)	**145**	13	15
Light (4.3%)	**122**	12	10
Ice (5.5%)	**155**	16	10
Red (4.5%)	**135**	13	11

Alc ~ Alcohol (Grams)

	C	Alc	Cb
Pabst (5%),12 fl. oz	**155**	14	14
Pete's Wicked Ale (5%)	**180**	14	20
Piels (4.7%)	**135**	13	10
Piels Light (4.5%)	**127**	13	9
Primo (4.3%), 12 fl.oz	**140**	12	13
Ranier (4.6%)	**142**	13	12
Red Bull Malt (7%)	**192**	20	12
Red Dog (5%)	**150**	14	12
Red Hook ESB (5.4%)	**175**	16	16
Red Hook Rye (5%)	**155**	14	14
Red Light (4.1%)	**105**	12	5
Red River Valley (4.9%)	**165**	14	15
Red Wolf (5.5%)	**155**	16	12
Samuel Adams (4.6%)	**170**	13	17
Samuel Adams Lager (4.7%)	**180**	13	19
Sapporo Draft (Japan) (4.5%)	**140**	12	12
Schaefer (4.3%)	**140**	12	12
Schaefer Light (3.9%)	**110**	11	8
Schlitz Ice (4.6%)	**145**	13	13
Schlitz Ice Light (4.3%)	**120**	12	8
Schlitz Malt (5.9%)	**180**	17	14
Schmidt (4.6%)	**142**	13	12
Sheaf Stout, 5.7%	**180**	16	17
Sierra Nevada: Pale Ale (5.6%)	**175**	16	16
Big Foot Ale (10.1%)	**210**	29	2
Pale Bock (6.6%)	**190**	19	20
Porter (6%)	**185**	17	18
Silver Thunder (5.9%)	**165**	17	11
Stella Artois, 5%, 330ml	**135**	14	9
Southpaw Light (5%)	**125**	14	6
Stroh's (4.4%)	**145**	13	13
Stroh's Light (4.3%)	**115**	13	7
Stroh's Signature (4.9%)	**160**	14	15
Wheat Hook (4.8%)	**150**	14	12
Winterfest (5.7%)	**185**	16	18
Zeigenbock (5%)	**155**	14	13
Zima Clear Malt (4.6%)	**150**	14	13

Homebrewed Beer: Similar to regular beers, according to alcohol content.

Non-Alcoholic Brews

Less Than 0.5% Alcohol *Average All Brands* *(Busch, Kaliber, O'Douls, Old Milwaukee NA, Stroh's NA, Sharp's, Haakebeck, Texas Select)*	C	Alc	Cb
12 fl.oz Can/Bottle	**70**	1	15

Alcoholic Lemon Brews

	C	Alc	Cb
Average All Brands (4.8% Alcohol) *(Includes Hooper's Hooch, Lusty, Saxer)*			
12 fl.oz Bottle/Can	150	13	12

Cider

Alc ~ Alcohol (Grams)

	C	Alc	Cb
Alcoholic Cider: Average,			
5.5% alcohol, Dry, 12 fl.oz	130	16	12
Sweet, 12 fl.oz	160	16	12
Hardcore Crisp Hard Cider (6% alc)			
12 fl.oz	190	17	19
Hornsby's Draft Cider (6% alc)			
12 fl.oz bottle	170	17	15
Woodchuck Draft Cider (5% alc)			
Amber, 8 fl.oz	135	14	14
Dark & Dry, 8 fl.oz	120	14	11
Granny Smith, 8 fl.oz	110	14	7

Quick Guide

Table Wine

Average All Varieties (11.5% Alcohol)	C	Alc	Cb
4 fl.oz (1/2 large wine glass)	85	11	2
6 fl.oz (3/4 large wine glass)	125	16	3
1/2 Carafe/Bottle, 375ml	265	34	6
1 Bottle, 750ml	530	68	13

Table Wines

	C	Alc	Cb
Red: Claret/Burgundy/Chianti, 4 fl.oz	80	11	0
Sparkling Reds, 4 fl.oz	90	11	3
Rose: Medium, 4 fl.oz	80	11	0
White: Dry (Chablis/Hock/Riesling)	75	11	0
Zinfandel Sweet			
(Moselle/Sauterne), 4 fl.oz	85	11	2
Sparkling, 4 fl.oz	95	11	4
Champagne: *Per 4 fl.oz Serving*			
Average 1 glass, 4 fl.oz	85	11	2
w. Orange Jce (3:1 orange)	75	8	4
w. Orange Jce (1:1 orange)	65	5	7
Cold Duck, 4 fl. oz	108	11	8
Sake: Rice Wine (16% alc.), 4 oz	125	15	5
Mulled Wine: (Gluhwein), 4 oz	180	14	20
Non-Alcoholic Wine, aver., 4 oz	50	0	12
Reduced Alcohol Wine (6%):			
Average all types, 4 fl.oz	50	0	12

Dessert Wines

	C	Alc	Cb
Madeira (18% alc), 2 oz	85	9	5
Marsala (18%), 2 oz	110	9	11
Port, Muscatel, (18%), 2 oz	85	9	5
Sherry (18%), 2 oz			
Dry, 1 Sherry glass	65	9	0.5
Sweet/Cream, average	85	9	5
Vermouth: Dry (18%), 2 oz	65	9	0.5
Sweet (15%), 2 oz	85	7	8

Cooking Wine

Average All Brands	C	Alc	Cb
Red/White, 2 Tbsp, 1 oz	20	3	1
Marsala. 2 Tbsp, 1 oz	35	4	2
Sherry, 2 Tbsp, 1 oz	40	4	2

Cooking with Wine

For alcohol to evaporate, sufficient heat and cooking time (at least 30 minutes) is required.

Red and white table wines would then contain negligible residual calories.

Sweetened wines (marsala/sherry) would contain 10 calories per 1 fl.oz used.

Flambé Desserts: Only surface alcohol is burnt off.

Spirits/Liquors

All Contain Zero Fat

Includes Bourbon, Brandy, Gin, Rum, Scotch, Tequila, Vodka, Whiskey.

Note: All spirits with same proof (alcohol) have similar calories and zero fat.

Average All Brands	C	Alc	Cb
80 Proof (40% Alcohol by Volume):			
1 fl.oz	65	9.5	0
1 1/2 fl.oz Jigger	100	14.5	0
1/2 Bottle, 375 ml	810	120	0
1 Bottle, 750 ml	1620	240	0
86 Proof (43% Alcohol):			
1 fl.oz	70	10	0
1 1/2 fl.oz Jigger	105	15	0
1/2 Bottle, 375 ml	870	125	0
1 Bottle, 750 ml	1750	250	0
100 Proof (50% Alcohol):			
1 fl.oz	.82	12	0
1 1/2 fl.oz Jigger	125	18	0
1/2 Bottle, 375 ml	1025	150	0
1 Bottle	2050	300	0

Coolers & Premix Cocktails

Zero Fat Unless Indicated
Calorie & Carbohydate estimates given where no data available.

	C	Alc	Cb
Bacardi Fruit Mixers (Frozen Conc.)			
Made up (2 oz mix + 1 oz Rum + Ice)			
Margarita	160	10	22
Pina Colada	230	10	40
Other varieties, average	200	10	32
(If 2 oz Rum used, add extra 70 cals/10g alcohol)			
Bartles & Jaymes:			
Wine Cooler/Cocktails (5%): *Per 12 fl.oz*			
Berry; Kiwi Strawberry	230	14	35
Fuzzy Navel	250	14	42
Margarita	270	14	47
Oriental Dragon Fruit	250	14	32
Original	200	14	30
Strawberry Daiquiri; Tropical	230	14	39
Malt Based Coolers (3.9% alc.): *Per 12 fl.oz*			
Berry; Black Cherry; Peach	210	11	33
Margarita; Pina Colada	270	11	48
Fuzzy Navel; Tropical	230	11	38
Strawberry Daiquiri	220	11	36
Boone's Farm Wine Coolers:			
Snow Crk Berry; Sun Peach (5%)	150	10	20
Sangria; Strawberry Hill (7.5%)	190	14	23
Breezer By Bacardi *(3.2% alc): Per 12 fl.oz*			
Passionfr.; Calypso Berry	220	9	39
Pina Colada (contains 6g fat)	250	9	33
Strawberry Daiquiri	250	9	47
Tahitian Tangerine	200	9	34
Heublein Premium Classics:			
Long Is. Ice Tea (15% alc), 2 oz	130	7	20
Manhattan (22.5%), 2 oz + ice	160	11	20
Mai Tai (22%), 2 oz + ice	160	11	20
Pina Colada, 4 oz (10g fat) + ice	280	4	40
Jack Daniels Country Cocktails *(5.9%)*			
Average all flavors, 200ml	170	9.5	25
Jose Cuervo Cocktails *(5.9%):*			
Margarita/ Lime, 200ml	180	9.5	27
Strawberry, 200ml bottle	170	9.5	25
TGI Friday's *Frozen Cocktails (12.5%):*			
Per Serving (3 fl.oz Premix & Ice)			
Margarita; Strawberry Daiquiri	145	9	20
Note: All drinks below contain 6g fat/serving.			
B52; Strawberry Shortcake	230	9	29
Mint Choc. Chip; P.Colada	250	9	32
Mudslide; Orange Dream	240	9	31

Premix Cocktails (Cont)

	C	Alc	Cb
The Club (Premix Cocktails): *Per 4oz*			
Long Island Ice Tea; Manhattan	220	16	30
Margar.;Scr'driver;Vod. Martini	210	7	40
Mudslide (9g fat)	270	12	41
P. Colada; Or. Craze; Whisk. Sour	260	10	40

Shooters

Alc ~ Alcohol (Grams)

	C	Alc	Cb
Kamakazi	150	20	2
Mud Slide	160	13	17
Fuzzy Navel	120	13	7
Pineapple Bomber	130	11	13
Turbo	110	14	3
Shots: Average all types, 1 1/2 fl.oz	110	14	3

Flavorings/Syrups

Non-Alcoholic, Fat Free

	C	Alc	Cb
Angostura Bitters, 1/4 tsp	3	0	0
Grenadine/Cassis, 2 Tbsp, 1 oz	70	0	17
Lime Juice, 2 Tbsp, 1 oz	10	0	2
Sugar Syrup, 2 Tbsp, 1 oz	70	0	17
Sour Mix, 2 Tbsp, 1 oz	10	0	2
Tonic Water, 8 fl.oz	90	0	22

Cocktail Mix 'N Drinks

No Alcohol Added

	C	Alc	Cb
Bloody Mary Mix *(Mr & Mrs T)*, 8 fl.oz	40	0	9
Pina Colada Mix: *Daily's*, 3 fl.oz	160	0	37
Mr & Mrs T, 4.5 fl.oz	180	0	43
Margarita Mix *(J.Cuervo)*, 4 fl.oz	100	0	24

Cocktails • Liqueurs

Cocktails

Alc ~ Alcohol (Grams)

Zero Fat Unless Indicated

(Made to Standard Recipes)	C	Alc	Cb
Bloody Mary	**120**	14	5
Bourbon & Soda	**110**	15	1
Brandy Alexander (16g fat)	**300**	16	11
Cerebral Hemorrhage (5g fat)	**290**	17	32
Collins (w. 2oz gin)	**180**	20	11
Daiquiri	**110**	14	3
Gin & Tonic	**170**	16	14
Harvey Wallbanger (2 oz Vodka)	**250**	30	11
Highball (1 1/2 oz Whiskey)	**110**	14	3
Irish Coffee (contains 9g fat)	**210**	14	8
Leprechaun's Libation	**285**	31	17
Mai Tai (2 oz Rum)	**260**	27	17
Manhattan	**130**	17	3
Martini	**160**	22	1
Mind Eraser	**160**	17	10
Mint Julep	**165**	20	8
Pina Colada (contains 12g fat)	**260**	14	12
Screwdriver	**180**	14	20
Spritzer (3 oz Wine)	**70**	8	3
Tequila Sunrise	**190**	20	14
Tom Collins	**120**	16	2
Whiskey Sour	**125**	15	5

Liqueurs/Cordials

Per 1 fl.oz	C	Alc	Cb
Baileys Irish Cream (34 Proof; 5g fat)	**95**	4	5
Lite (30 Proof; 2g fat)	**75**	4	7
Cherry Brandy (48 Proof)	**80**	6	9
Coffee Liqueur (53 Proof)	**90**	6.5	11
Amaretto (56 Proof)	**110**	6	17
Benedictine (80 Proof)	**90**	10	5
Cointreau (80 Proof)	**100**	10	7
Creme de Cacao (54 Proof)	**100**	6	15
Creme de Menthe (60 Proof)	**120**	7	14
Drambuie (80 Proof)	**105**	10	9
Grand Marnier (80 Proof)	**100**	10	7
Kahlua (53 Proof)	**90**	6.5	11
Kirsch (68 Proof)	**80**	8	6
Midori, aver. all types, (42 Proof)	**80**	5	11
Ouzo (80 Proof)	**90**	10	5
Sambuca (84 Proof)	**100**	10	7
Schnapps (80 Proof)	**100**	10	7
Southern Comfort (78 Proof)	**75**	9	3
Tia Maria (64 Proof)	**90**	8	9
Triple Sec (60 Proof)	**80**	7	4

Ten Hints to Avoid Harmful Drinking

1. **Add up the alcohol** you typically drink each day and on social occasions. How does this compare with 'low risk' amounts?
2. **Compare the alcohol content** of different drinks and select those with lower content. Request half ounces of alcohol in cocktails and mixed drinks. Dilute them and keep topping off with non-alcoholic drinks.
3. **Try low alcohol** or non-alcohol alternatives such as fruit juices and mineral water. Take your own to parties.
4. **Before drinking alcohol,** quench your thirst with water and non-alcoholic drinks - particularly after vigorous exercise or sport.
5. **Slow the rate of drinking.** Chugging or drinking fast is the major cause of illness and death from alcohol poisoning.
6. **Avoid drinking in 'rounds'.**
7. **Have a non-alcoholic 'spacer'** between drinks (e.g. mineral water, orange juice).
8. **Don't drink on an empty stomach.** Food slows the rate of alcohol absorption.
9. **Keep track of the number of drinks** and know when to stop. Stick to a set limit.
10. **Do not drive, swim, or operate machinery** while under the influence.

Note: Alcohol can be very dangerous when taken with prescription or street drugs or when you are very tired.

Coffee Liqueurs

Average All Types (Includes Benedictine, Cointreau, Kahlua):	C	Alc	Cb
1 serving	**200**	10	10

Ginseng Vials

Most contain up to 33% alcohol.
A 10ml (1/3 ounce) vial can contain up to 2.5 grams alcohol.

Note: Figures for these dishes are only a guide. Large variations occur with serving size, recipe ingredients and cooking methods.

Chinese & Asian Dishes

Appetizers	C	F	Cb
Curried Meat Triangles, 1 pce	150	5	12
Dim Sum (Dumplings), 1 ball	65	2	5
Egg Rolls, mini, 3 rolls	100	3	11
Spring Roll, Small, 1 1/2 oz	100	7	10
Medium, 3 oz	200	12	20
Large, 5 oz	350	15	33
Wonton, 1 only	55	3	4
Soup: Clear, 1 bowl	30	1	4
with Noodles	100	3	12
Chicken & Corn	150	8	8
Fortune Cookie: each	25	<1	5

Entrees & Main Dishes

Per Whole Dish (2-3 Serves)

Beef with Broccoli, 16 oz	650	30	31
Beef in Black Bean Sce, 17 oz	530	33	17
Chicken & Almonds, 18 oz	685	50	18
Chop Suey: Chicken, 20 oz	560	37	7
Pork, 20 oz	680	50	12
Chow Mein: Beef/Chick., 24 oz	940	60	50
Crispy Fried Chicken, 8 oz	485	33	12
Lemon Chicken, 10 oz	580	32	25
Omelet: Chick/Shrimp, 16 oz	990	82	10
Sweet & Sour: Fish, 20 oz	1160	58	106
Pork, 18 oz	950	50	92
Duck, 18 oz	1120	71	85
Vegetable Combination, 6 oz	250	17	13
Extra Listings: See Frozen Entrees/Meals.			
Rice: Plain, 1 cup, 5 oz	170	0	36
Fried: 1 cup, 5 oz	320	13	42
Large dish, 16 oz	1010	40	134
Noodles: Chinese Egg, boiled, 1 cup	200	3	42

Confucious say:

"Man who eat with one chopstick never have problem with obesity!"

Cajun & Creole

Per Serving	C	F	Cb
Alligator, 1 oz ckd	40	0.5	0
Baked Herb Chicken	850	53	2
Bouillabaisse	400	15	10
Cajun Fried Turkey	630	25	0
Cocktail Sauce, 1 Tbsp	15	0	3
Couche-couche, 1/2 cup	80	0	17
Crawfish Bisque	500	10	10
Crawfish, cooked, 2 oz	45	0.5	0
Creole Jambalaya	550	30	15
Dove, cooked, 1 oz	60	3.5	0
Frog's Legs, steamed (2)	45	0	0
Guinea Fowl, flesh, 1 oz, ckd	40	1	0
Hogshead Cheese, 1/4 cup	80	5.5	0
Jambalaya, Shrimp & Crabmeat	520	14	12
Red Beans & Rice	400	17	52
Roasted Quail, w. Bacon on Toast	550	25	15
Remoulade Sauce, 1 Tbsp	55	5.5	1
Shrimp Creole	450	20	10
Stuffed Smothered Steak, w. 1 cup rice	890	50	50
Squab, flesh, 1 oz cooked	60	3.5	0
Turtle, cooked, 1 1/2 oz	60	1.5	0

French Foods

Blanquette d'Agneau (Lamb Stew w. Veg)	800	30	17
Brioche, 1 cake	280	14	34
Bouillabaise (Fish Stew)	400	15	10
Coq au Vin (Chicken in Wine)	800	30	16
Coquilles St. Jacques, fried, 6 lge	300	14	2
Creme Caramel (Caram. Custard)	260	10	38
Crepe Suzette, 1x6"crepe/sauce	220	10	13
Duck a l'Orange	780	35	47
Escargots (Snails), in garlic but., (6)	200	10	4
Frogs Legs, fried, 4 med. pairs	400	20	10
Lamb Noisettes, fried, 2 chops	500	40	1
Mousse au Chocolat	380	15	33
Potage Creme Crecy (Carrot Soup)	360	18	14
Salade Nicoise (Tuna/Oliv./Veg.)	450	13	14
Veal Cordon Bleu (Veal/Ham/Ch)	650	25	18
Vichyssoise (Pot./Leek Soup), 1 c.	200	9	15

German

	C	F	Cb
Bavarian Bread Dumpling, 3 small	330	10	28
Beef: Goulash with Veges	520	20	46
Black Forest Cake, 1 slice	380	16	30
Bratwurst: Grilled, 1 medium, 6 oz	540	12	58
Chicken: Fried, Viennese-style	530	20	28
Livers w. Apple/On., 6 oz	460	28	10
Herring, Pickled: Rollmops, 4 oz	260	16	3
with Sour Cream, 4 oz	310	20	3
Hot Sausage Curry	300	7	6
Kugelhupf (Yeast Cake), 1 lge sl.	400	58	3
Sauerbraten Pork (Pot Roast)	650	35	15
Torte: Linzer (Alm./Raspb. Jam)	430	18	58
Sacher (Choc./Apricot Jam)	260	12	23
Weiner Schnitzel, 1 med.	750	35	38

Greek

	C	F	Cb
Baklava Pastry, 1 only, 3¾ oz	400	21	45
Calamari, deep fried, 1 cup	300	13	17
Galactobureko, 1 only (Filo, Custard, Pastry in Syrup)	360	15	48
Kataifi, (Filo, Nut, Pastry in Syrup)	350	11	56
Moussaka, 1 serve, 8 oz	350	22	22
Souvlakia (Lamb), each, 2 oz	120	6	1
Stuffed Tomatoes, 2 only	250	12	17
Taramosalata, 1 Tbsp, ½ oz	40	3	2
Tyropita (Filo/Egg/Cheese Pastry)	350	26	31
Tzatziki (Cucumber/Yog. Dip), 1 T.	20	1	1
Vine Leaves, stuffed, 3 rolls, 6 oz	200	5	13

Indian & Pakistan

Per Serving
(Meat dishes allow 4 oz meat/serving)

	C	F	Cb
Aloo Samosa, each (Savory Pastries w. Potato fill.)	150	12	12
Alu Gosht Kari (Meat/Pot. Curry)	600	40	23
Ande ki Kari (Egg, Tom Sce), each	250	23	7
Bhona Gosht (Mint Broil Lamb)	560	28	5
Chicken Pilaf (Murgh Biriyani)	700	53	50
Chapati/Roti, 7" diam. piece (Baked Whole Wheat Bread)	60	<1	11
Dal (Lentil Puree), 1 cup, no oil	230	1	37
1 Tbsp Tadka (oil topping)	120	13	0
Dhakla, 1 oz	105	5	13
Dhansak, ½ cup	105	3.5	11
Fish Jhol (Fish in Gravy)	230	10	5

Indian & Pakistan (Cont)

	C	F	Cb
Gosht Kari (Meat Curry/Tom./Pot.)	460	25	17
Imli Chatni (Chutney), 1 Tbsp	30	0	7
Lamb Pilaf	520	35	40
Machchi Molee (Fish, C'nut Milk)	690	45	15
Masala Gosht (Beef/Tom./Gravy)	400	25	18
Mulligatawney Soup, average	300	15	8
Murgh Tikka, 1 cup	300	4	7
Naan, 1 oz	75	2	11
Pappadom, 1 large/2 small	50	3	5
Pesrattu, 9" crepe	130	5	15
Pork Vendaloo Curry	620	47	3
Rajmah (Kidney Bean Curry)	400	17	56
Rogan Josh (Lamb/Yoghurt Sce.)	500	30	3
Saag Gosht (Beef/Spinach Sce.)	430	26	10
Shahi Korma (Braised Lamb)	430	28	3
Tandoori Chicken: Breast	260	13	5
Leg/Thigh portion	300	17	6

Italian Dishes

	C	F	Cb
Cannelloni, 1 tube, 6 oz	280	15	18
Chicken Cacciatore	370	22	4
Gnocchi, Spinach	300	18	17
Lasagne with meat, 10 oz	400	17	36
Manicotti, cheese/tomato	230	14	18
Minestrone Soup, 1 cup	260	6	28
Osso Buco (Veal/Tom./Mushr.)	550	28	5
Ravioli, 8 oz	300	12	30
Risotto (Chicken)	420	12	70
Spaghetti: Plain, 1 cup, 5 oz	185	1	44
Restaurant: 2 cups, plain	370	2	88
+ Bolognese (Meat Sce)	650	16	90
+ Marinara (Seafoods)	700	20	90
+ Napoletana (Tom. Sce)	540	13	105
Saltimbocca (Veal/Ham/Cheese)	430	28	5
Tortellini, 20 pieces	530	20	74
Veal Marsala	400	20	11
Veal Parmigiana	350	20	5
Pizza: *Per ½ Pizza (12")*			
Vegetarian/Cheese: Thin Crust	650	26	63
Thick Crust	850	35	108
Sausage/Pepperoni: Thin Crust	700	32	68
Thick Crust	900	62	135

(**Also see** *Pizza Hut, Domino's, Shakey's, Godfather's Pizza* ~ **Fast Foods Section.**)

Japanese

Sushi	C	F	Cb
Lunch Menu (Assorted Sushi)			
Regular, 1 serving	330	3	56
Deluxe, 1 serving	430	4	72
Sushi Rice, ckd, 1 Tbsp	25	<1	5
1 cup, 5 1/4 oz	380	3	82
Nigiri-Zushi: (Fish wrapped Sushi)			
Per 1 oz piece:			
Ebi-zushi (Jumbo Shrimp)	20	<1	3
Kani-zushi (Surimi Crab)	30	<1	5
Maguro-zushi (Tuna)	25	<1	4
Sake-zushi (Salmon)	35	1	4
Suzume-zushi (Baby Snapper)	30	<1	4
Tai-zushi (Red Snapper)	30	<1	4
Nori-Maki-Zushi: *Per Piece*			
(Seaweed-wrapped Sushi Rolls)			
Anago-maki (Conger Eel)	20	1	2
California-maki (Crab/Caviar/Avocado)			
1/2 roll	70	1	10
Futo-maki (Egg Omelet, Shellfish, Veg.),			
1 piece.	70	1	10
Kobana-maki (Egg Om., Cucum.)	35	<1	6
Kappa-maki (Cucumber)	15	0	3
Tekka-maki (Tuna)	20	<1	4
Uni-maki (Sea Urchin)	20	<1	4
Inari-Zushi (Bean Curd Pouches w. Sushi)			
1 pouch, 3 oz	130	2	23
Tamago-Yaki (Omelet-wrapped Sushi)			
1 piece	45	1	5
Sashimi (Slice Raw Seafood/Beef)			
Ika (Squid), 4 oz	105	2	0
Hamachi (Yellowtail), 4 oz	165	6	0
Naguro (Yellowfin Tuna), 4 oz	120	1	0
Niku (Beef), 5 oz	200	10	0
Saba (Mackerel), 4 oz	160	7	0
Suzuki (Sea Bass), 4 oz	110	<1	0
Tako (Octopus), 4 oz	95	1	0
Dipping Sauces: Aver., 2 Tbsp	30	0	7
Ginger Vinegar Dress., 2 Tbsp	20	0	5
Miso Soup w. tofu pces, 1 cup	85	3	11
Sukiyaki (Beef/Tofu/Veg.), 8 oz	400	24	32
Tempura (Batter-fried Shrimp & Veges.)			
3 large shrimp & veges	320	18	25
1 shrimp only	60	4	3
Teppan Yaki (Steak, Seafood & Veges.)			
10 oz serving	470	30	15
Teriyaki Beef, 4 oz serving	350	25	4
Sake Wine (16% alc.), 3 fl.oz	115	0	7

Kosher/Deli Foods

Bagel/Bialy,	C	F	Cb
1/2 small, 1 oz	80	1	16
Beiglach (Cheese Knish)	350	17	35
Blintzes, average, 1 only	120	1	25
w. Sour Crm. & Preserves	370	10	30
Borscht, (no cream), 1 cup	85	3	14
Diet/Reduced Cal., 1 cup	30	1	7
Cabbage Roll (meat/rice), 5 oz	170	6	21
Chicken Broth, 1 cup	80	8	0
with vegetables	100	8	5
with noodles	150	9	16
Lowfat, plain, 1 cup	25	1	0
Cholent, 1 med serve, 1 cup	350	16	48
Chopped Liver: 1 serve, 3 oz	110	6	5
with Egg Salad, 1/4 cup	100	7	3
Farfel, dry, 1/2 cup	90	<1	21
Hallah (Yeast Bread), 1 sl., 1 oz	85	2	14
Gefilte Fish Balls:			
Regular, medium, 2 oz	55	2	4
with jelled broth	80	2	6
Cocktail size, 1 oz	30	1	2
Sweet, medium, 2 oz	65	2	4
with jelled broth	95	2	9
Herring: Smoked, 2 oz	120	8	0
in Sour Cream, 2 oz	150	10	0
Kasha, cooked, 1/2 cup	100	<1	20
Kipfel (Vanilla/Almd. Cookie), 1 pce.	60	2	7
Knaidlach, 1 ball	40	2	5
Knish: Kasha/Potato, 1 only	130	4	22
Cheese, 1 only	350	17	35
Kreplach, beef, 1 piece	40	1	6
Kugel, potato/noodle, 1 serve	150	7	20
Latkes (Potato Pancake), 2 oz	200	11	22
3 Latkes w. Sour Cr./Apple Sce	750	25	95
Lochshen: Plain, 1 cup	130	2	26
Pudding, 1 cup	380	13	48
Lox (Smoked Salmon), 2 oz	65	2	0
Mandelbrot (Almond Bread), 1 slice,			
1/4" thick	45	2	5
Matzo: 1 board, 1 oz	110	<1	21
(Also see Matzoh ~ Page 96)			
Matzo Balls, 2 small, 1 large	90	3	12
Soup, with 1 large ball	180	7	24
New York Cheesecake, 4 oz	350	24	26
Pierogi, potato/cheese, 1 pce	90	4	11
Reuben Sandwich	920	60	28
Schmaltz (Rend'd chick. fat), 1 T.	90	10	0

Lebanese/Middle East

	C	F	Cb
Baba Ghannouj, 2 Tbsp, 1 oz (Eggplant/Seasame Dip)	70	6	2
Baklava, 1 pastry, 1 3/4 oz (Pastry, Nuts, Syrup)	245	18	18
Cabbage Rolls, 1 roll, 3 oz (Cabbage Leaf, Meat, Rice)	100	3	12
Cous Cous, 1 serve (Semolina, Milk, Fruit, Nuts)	400	21	43
Felafel (Chick Pea Fritter): Fried, 1 medium, 1 oz	60	4	4
Hummus, 1/4 cup, 2.2 oz	105	3	5
Fried Kibbi, 1 piece, 3 oz (Wheat, Meat, Pinenuts)	180	8	15
Kafta, 1 skewer, 1 1/2 oz (Ground Lamb Saus. on Skewer)	85	5	2
Kibbeh Naye, 1 cup, 9 oz (Raw Lamb, Bulgur & Spices)	450	18	28
Lebanese Omelet, 1 serving, 4 oz (Egg, Spinach, Pinenuts, Onion)	200	12	13
Pilaf, 1 cup (Rice, Onion, Rais., Apr. Spice)	400	11	60
Shawourma, 1 serve, 4 oz (Spit Roast Beef)	280	15	2
Shish Kabob, 1 stick, 2 1/2 oz	130	7	2
Spinach Pie, 1 piece, 3 1/2 oz	290	21	20
Sweet Almond Sanbusak, 1 pce (Pastry, Almonds, Spices)	200	15	11
Tabouli, 1 serve, 4 oz	170	14	7
Tahini Sauce, aver., 1 Tbsp	90	8	2

Mexican

	C	F	Cb
Black Bean Soup, 1 bowl	200	3	34
Bueso Fresco, 1/4 cup	80	4.5	8
Burritos (*Taco Bell*): Bean	380	12	54
Big Beef Supreme	520	23	51
Chili, plain, 1/4 cup	90	6	8
Chili con Carne, w. Beans, 1 cup	310	17	15
w/out Beans, 1 cup	370	28	10
Corn Chips, 1/2 cup, 1 oz	160	10	17
Empanadas, average, 1 small	230	10	28
Enchilada, average	330	10	49
Fajitas: Chicken (Soft)	200	7	20
Guacamole, 2 Tbsp, 1 oz	120	12	2
Horchata 1 cup, 8 fl. oz	120	0.5	27
Margarita (w. 1 1/2 oz Tequila)	160	0	6
Menudo, 1/2 cup	55	1.5	10

Mexican (Cont)

	C	F	Cb
Nachos: *Taco Bell*, Big Beef	430	24	43
Bellgrande (*Taco Bell*)	740	39	83
Del Taco: Regular	390	23	39
Macho Nachos	1090	61	110
Quesadilla: Cheese (*Taco Bell*)	370	20	32
Refried Beans, 3/4 cup, 6 oz	160	3	26
Sopaipillas (flky. pstry.puffs), 1 pc	100	7	10
w. honey & cream	200	14	18
Taco (*Taco Bell*): Regular	170	10	11
Chicken	180	5	23
Taco Supreme	230	13	13
Big Border Taco	280	16	17
Taco Salad w. Salsa	840	52	85
Taco Sauce, average, 1/4 cup	15	0	3
Taco Shell, regular	50	2	8
Tamales, Van Camp's (can), 1/2 c	150	8	14
Tostada *(Taco Bell)*	300	14	31
Tortilla, corn, 6" diam.	70	1	14
Tortilla Chips, 1 oz	150	8	18

Extra Listings of Mexican Dishes:

- Frozen Entrees/Meals ~ See Page 55
- Fast Foods Section *(Taco Bell, Del Taco).*
- Canned Bean/Chili Products ~ See Page 64

Polish

	C	F	Cb
Cabbage Rolls w. Sour Cr., 2 sm.	220	10	30
Chicken Casserole w. Mush., 1 c.	520	27	5
Kielbasa (Sausages, Onions, fried, 2 large.)	350	28	2
Meatballs in Sour Cream, 3 x 1 1/2" balls	300	16	11
Pierogi, Fruit/Veg, 3" ball	80	2	15
Pork Goulash (Pork/Veg. Stew)	550	21	38
Pot Roast with Vegetables	630	21	28

Brooklyn

Soul Foods

	C	F	Cb
Breakfast Sausage, fried, 2 patties	**250**	17	0
Cornbread, homemade, 3 oz	**200**	7.5	28
Fatback, raw, 1/4 oz	**60**	6.5	0
Ham Hock, 1 oz	**90**	6.5	2
Hog Maw, 1 oz	**45**	2.5	0
Hominy, 3/4 cup	**85**	1	17
Hush Puppies, 5 pces, 3 oz	**260**	12	35
Kale, ckd, 1/2 cup	**20**	0.5	4
Neck Bones, Pork, 1 oz	**65**	4	0
Opossum, 1 oz	**65**	3	0
Oxtail, 1 oz	**70**	3.5	0
Pig Ear, 1/4 ear	**50**	3	0
Pig Foot, 1/2 foot	**70**	4.5	0
Pig Tail, 1/3 tail	**115**	10	0
Poke Salad, ckd, 1/2 cup	**15**	0.5	3
Pork Brains, 1 oz	**40**	2.5	0
Pork Cracklings, 1/2 oz	**80**	6	0
Pork Chitterlings, simmered, 3 oz	**260**	25	0
Pork Skin, 1 cup	**70**	4.5	0
Sousemeat, 1 oz	**60**	4.5	0
Succotash, 1/2 cup	**80**	1	17
Sweet Potato Ple, 1/8 of 9" pie	**250**	12	34
Tongue Pork, 1/3 tongue	**75**	5.5	0
Tripe, 2 oz	**55**	2	0
Vienna Sausage, 2 small, 1 oz	**90**	8	1

Thai Foods

	C	F	Cb
Appetizers: Satay Pork, 1 oz	**100**	4	2
Spring Roll, 1 1/4 oz	**110**	6	13
Soups: Tom Yam (Hot & Sour):			
with Seafood, 1 cup	**100**	3	4
Vegetarian, 1 cup	**50**	0	11
Mud Crab w. Coconut, 1 cup	**400**	30	16
Curries: Chick. w. Ginger, 1 cup	**390**	34	4
Thick Red Curry w. Beef, 1 cup	**600**	50	7
Thai Chicken Curry, 1 cup	**340**	23	4
Massaman Curry, 1 cup	**680**	57	8
Green Curry w. Pork, 1 cup	**480**	44	5
Stir Fry: *Per 1 Cup*			
(Combinations include Meat & Seafood)			
Comb. w. Fried Rice Noodles	**470**	33	30
Comb. w. Steamed Rice Noodles	**360**	10	42
Comb. Stir Fry & Veges (no rice)	**410**	15	65
Stir Fry Vegetables	**100**	2	18
Salads: Thai Chicken, 1 serving	**330**	9	17
Thai Beef Salad, 1 serving	**260**	9	15

Spanish

	C	F	Cb
Arroz Abanda (Fish with Rice)	**340**	8	31
Arroz Con Pollo (Rice/Chick. Sal)	**500**	23	50
Clams Marinera, 8 clams	**330**	16	22
Cochifrito (Lamb w. Lemon/Garlic)	**650**	25	5
Cochinillo Asado, 2 sl. (Rst Suckling Pig)	**300**	15	3
Cocido Madrileno (Madrid-Style Boiled Dinner)	**450**	27	18
Flan de Leche (Caramel Custard)	**325**	9	52
Fritadera de Ternera (Sauteed Veal)	**450**	27	2
Gazpacho, 1 bowl	**60**	0	15
Paella a la Valenciana (Chicken & Shellfish Rice)	**900**	42	70
Pollo a la Espanola (Chicken)	**475**	30	4
Ternera al Jerez (Veal w. Sherry)	**660**	29	6
Zarzuela (Fish & Shellfish Medley)	**530**	27	40

Vietnamese

	C	F	Cb
Bo Xao Dau Phong: *Per Whole Dish* (Ginger Beef w.Onion, Fish Sce.)	**750**	30	10
Bo Nuong (Beef Satay), 2 sticks	**265**	9	4
Ca Chien Gung (Whole Snapper w. Ginger)	**600**	16	6
Canh Chay (Veg./Tofu Soup)	**80**	3	13
Cuu Xao Lan (Curried Lamb, Veges in Coconut)	**900**	40	80
Ga Chien (Crsp. Chick + Plum Sce)	**900**	40	105
Ga Nuong (Chicken Satay + Sce.)	**240**	10	4
Ga Xao Rau(Marinated Chicken Braised w.Veg.)	**800**	26	100
Rau Cai Xao Chay (Stir Fried Vege., Soy Sauce.)	**400**	15	65
Thit Heo Goi Baup Cai, each (Spicy Cabbage Rolls w.Pork)	**200**	7	11

Gourmet & Miscellaneous

	C	F	Cb
Ants Eggs/Larvae, 1 Tbsp	**20**	0	0
Ants, Choc. coated, 3 Tbsp	**140**	7	2
Bee Maggots, canned, 3 Tbsp	**65**	2	0
Caviar, black/red, 1 Tbsp	**40**	3	0
Caterpillars, canned, 2oz	**60**	2	0
Frogs Legs, fried, 1 pair (large)	**125**	7	0
Haggis, boiled, 4oz	**350**	24	22
Locusts, raw, 1oz	**35**	1	0
Silkworms, raw, 1oz	**60**	2	0
Snails (Escargots) ~ See French Foods			
Snake, roasted, 4oz	**160**	6	0

Sandwiches

	C	F	Cb
No Spreads Unless Indicated			
(Includes 2 Slices Bread ~ 3 oz)			
BLT (5 strips Bacon, 2 Tbsp Mayo)	600	40	46
Breaded Chicken & Salad	540	28	46
Chicken (5 oz) Salad w. Mayo.	580	30	49
Chopped Liver, Egg, Mayo.	630	25	44
Corned Beef (5 oz) w. Mustard	560	28	44
Cream Cheese w. Olives (5 large)	340	14	46
Egg Salad w. Mayonnaise	570	29	49
Egg Salad Club w. Bacon, Mayo.	780	53	49
Grilled Cheese (3 oz)	540	30	44
Ham (4 oz); Cheese (4 oz), Mayo.	910	56	44
Lobster Salad (4 oz) w. Mayo.	530	25	45
Overstuffed Tuna Salad (7 oz)	870	39	75
Reuben (6 oz Beef/Pastrami, 2 oz Cheese, 2 Tbsp Dressing)	920	60	28
Roast Beef (4 oz) w. Mustard	460	12	45
Roast Pork (4 oz) w. Apple Sauce	500	16	55
Shrimp Salad Club w. Bacon, Mayo.	800	57	48
Sloppy Joe w. Sauce (7 oz)	600	30	45
Steak Sandwich (5 oz cooked)	680	32	41
Triple Cheese (4 oz) Melt	720	45	46
Tuna (5 oz) Salad w. Mayo.	610	30	49
Turkey Breast (5 oz) w. Mayo.	460	18	44
Turkey Breast (5 oz) w. Mustard	360	7	44
Turkey Club w. Bacon, Mayo.	830	38	31
Vegetarian w. Avocado, Cheese	820	49	72

Subs: See *Subway* Page 238

Wraps & Roll-Ups

	C	F	Cb
Average All Types (Meat/Chicken/Fish/Veges)			
Regular size, approx. 9 oz	500	25	48
Large, approx. 15 oz	830	40	80
Jumbo, approx. 22 oz	1400	70	134

Au Bon Pain: See Page 164
Long John Silver: Page 208
Taco Bell Fajita Wraps: Page 240
Wendy's Pitas: Page 244

Bagels

	C	F	Cb
Plain, unfilled, 3 oz	240	2	45
w. 2 Tbsp Cream Cheese	340	12	46
w. 2 oz Lox (Smoked Salmon)	320	4	45

Au Bon Pain: Page 164
Einstein Bros Bagels: Page 191

Croissants

	C	F	Cb
Unfilled, medium 1 1/2 oz	180	10	20
w. Ham (2 oz), Salad	280	14	24
w. Ham (2 oz), Cheese (2 oz)	470	30	20
w. Chick (2 oz) Cheese (2 oz)	470	30	20
w. Turkey/Ham/Chse (2 oz ea.)	580	36	20
Au Bon Pain: Ham & Cheese	380	20	36
Spinach & Cheese	270	16	27

Vending Machines

	C	F	Cb
Brownie, frosted	180	9	24
Cheese Balls, 1 oz	150	8	16
Choc Chip Cookies, 4	130	7	19
Choc Milk, 8 fl.oz	225	9	26
Coca Cola Classic, 12 fl.oz	140	0	35
Diet Coke, 12 fl.oz	1	0	0
Corn Chips, 1 oz	160	10	15
Danish Pastry, 2 oz	220	10	25
Donut, plain, 1 3/4 oz	210	12	25
Fruit Pie, 4 oz	290	13	46
Granola/Cereal Bars	130	3	26
Hershey's, 1.55 oz	240	14	25
Hot Fries, 1 oz	140	10	11
Kellogg's Rice Krispies Treat	120	1.5	26
Lance: Captain's Wafers, 1 pkg	230	12	26
Big Town, 1 pkg	250	11	38
M & M's: Plain, 1.7 oz	240	10	34
Peanuts, 1.7 oz	250	13	30
Milk, whole, 8 fl.oz	150	8	12
Reduced Fat, 2%, 8 fl.oz	120	5	12
Milky Way, 2 oz	270	10	41
Onion Rings, 1 oz	120	6	16
Orange Juice, 8.75 fl.oz	120	0	28
Peanuts, roasted, 1 oz	165	14	6
Popcorn, plain, 1 oz	160	10	14
Pork Skins, 1 oz	160	10	0
Potato Chips, 1 oz	150	10	15
Reduced Fat, 1 oz	140	7	20
Pretzels, 1 oz	110	2	22
Raisins, 1/2oz pkg	40	0	9
Reece's Peanut Butter Cups, 1.8 oz	280	17	28
Snickers, 2.1 oz bar	280	14	35
Tortilla Chips, 1 loz	150	8	22

Fast-Food Chains & Restaurants

- **Cal** — **Calories**
- **Fat** — **Fat (grams)**
- **%FC** — **Percent Fat Calories**
- **S.Fat** — **Saturated Fat (grams)**
- **Chol** — **Cholesterol (milligrams)**
- **Sod** — **Sodium (milligrams)**
- **Pro** — **Protein (grams)**
- **Carb** — **Carbohydrates (grams)**

Arby's®

Breakfast Items	Cal	Fat	%FC	S.Fat	Chol	Sod	Pro	Carb
Bacon, 2 strips	90	7	70%	3	15	220	5	0
Biscuit (Plain)	280	15	48%	3	0	730	6	34
Blueberry Muffin	230	9	35%	2	25	290	2	35
Cinnamon Nut Danish	360	11	27%	1	0	105	6	60
Croissant (Plain)	220	12	49%	7	25	230	4	25
Egg	95	8	76%	2	180	55	0.5	0.5
French-Toastix, 6 pieces	430	21	44%	5	0	550	10	52
Ham	45	1	20%	1	20	405	7	0
Sausage	165	15	82%	6	25	320	7	0
Swiss Cheese, 1 slice	45	3	60%	2	12	175	4	0.5
Table Syrup	100	0	0%	0	0	30	0	25
Roast Beef Sandwiches								
Arby's Melt w. Cheddar	370	18	44%	6	31	940	18	36
Arby-Q	430	18	38%	6	37	1320	22	48
Beef 'N Cheddar	490	28	52%	9	50	1215	25	40
Bacon Cheddar Deluxe	540	34	56%	10	44	1140	22	38
Giant Roast Beef	555	28	45%	11	71	1560	35	43
Junior Roast Beef	325	14	39%	5	30	780	17	35
Regular Roast Beef	390	19	44%	7	43	1010	23	33
Super Roast Beef	525	27	46%	9	43	1190	25	50
Chicken Sandwiches								
Breaded Chicken Fillet	535	28	47%	5	45	1015	28	46
Chicken Cordon Bleu	625	33	48%	8	77	1595	38	46
Chicken Fingers (2 Pieces)	290	16	50%	2	32	675	16	20
Grilled Chicken: BBQ	390	13	30%	3	43	1000	23	47
Deluxe	430	20	42%	4	61	850	23	41
Roast Chicken: Club	545	31	51%	9	58	1105	31	37
Deluxe; Santa Fe	435	22	45%	6	54	820	29	35
Sub Shop Sandwiches								
French Dip	475	22	42%	8	55	1410	30	40
Hot Ham 'N Cheese	500	23	41%	7	68	1665	30	43
Italian	675	36	48%	13	83	2090	30	46
Philly Beef 'N Swiss	755	47	56%	15	91	2025	39	48
Roast Beef	700	42	54%	14	84	2035	38	44
Triple Cheese Melt	720	45	44%	16	91	1800	37	46
Turkey	550	27	44%	7	65	2085	31	47
Fish/Ham Sandwiches: Fish Fillet	530	27	46%	7	43	865	23	50
Ham 'N Cheese: Plain	360	14	35%	5	53	1285	24	34
Melt	330	13	35%	4	43	1015	20	34
Light Menu: Garden Salad	60	0.5	7%	0	0	40	3	12
Roast Beef Deluxe	295	10	31%	3	42	825	18	33
Roast Chicken Deluxe	275	6	23%	2	33	775	20	33
Roast Turkey Deluxe	260	7	21%	2	33	1260	20	33
Roast Chicken Salad	150	2	12%	<1	29	420	20	12
Side Salad	25	0.3	12%	0	0	15	1	4
Crouton 1 pkt	60	2	30%	<1	1	155	2	9

	Cal	Fat	%FC	S.Fat	Chol	Sod	Pro	Carb
Potatoes: Curly Fries	300	15	45%	3	0	855	4	38
Cheddar Curly Fries w. Sce	335	18	48%	4	3	1015	5	40
French Fries	245	13	48%	3	0	115	2	30
Potato Cakes	205	12	53%	2	0	400	2	20
Baked Potato (Plain)	355	0.3	0%	0	0	25	7	82
w. Marg/Sour Cream	580	24	37%	9	25	210	9	85
w. Broccoli 'n Cheddar	570	20	32%	5	12	565	14	89
Deluxe Baked Potato	735	36	44%	16	59	500	19	86
Soups: Boston Clam Chowder	190	9	43%	3	25	965	9	18
Cream of Broccoli	160	8	45%	4	25	1005	7	15
Lumberjack Mixed Vegetable	90	4	40%	2	5	1150	2	10
Old-Fashion Chicken Noodle	80	2	22%	0	20	850	6	11
Potato with Bacon	170	7	37%	3	20	905	6	23
Timberline Chili	220	10	41%	4	30	1130	18	17
Wisconsin Cheese	280	18	58%	7	35	1065	10	20
Desserts/Shakes								
Apple Turnover	330	14	38%	7	0	180	4	48
Cherry Turnover	320	13	37%	5	0	190	4	46
Cheesecake (Plain)	320	23	65%	14	95	240	5	23
Chocolate Chip Cookie	125	6	43%	2	10	85	2	16
Chocolate Shake	450	12	24%	3	35	340	15	76
Jamocha Shake	385	10	23%	3	36	260	15	62
Vanilla Shake	360	12	30%	4	36	280	15	50
Polar Swirl: Butterfinger	460	18	35%	8	28	320	15	62
Heath	545	22	36%	5	39	345	15	76
Oreo	480	22	41%	10	35	520	15	66
Peanut Butter Cup	515	24	42%	8	34	385	20	61
Snickers	510	19	33%	7	33	350	15	73
Dressings/Sauces								
Arby's Sauce	15	0.2	12%	0	0	115	0	4
Beef Stock Au Jus	10	0	0%	0	0	440	0	1
Barbeque Sauce	30	0	0%	0	0	185	0	7
Blue Cheese	290	31	96%	6	50	580	2	2
Cheddar Cheese Sauce	35	3	77%	1	4	140	1	1
Honey French	280	23	74%	3	0	400	0	18
Horsey Sauce	60	5	74%	1	5	150	0	2
Mayonnaise	110	12	98%	7	5	80	0	0
Light Cholesterol Free	12	1	75%	0	0	65	0	0.5
Italian Sub Sauce	70	7	90%	1	0	240	0	1
Parmesan Cheese Sauce	70	7	90%	1	5	130	1	2
Red Ranch Dressing	75	6	72%	1	0	115	0	5
Tartar Sauce	140	15	96%	2	30	220	0	0
Thousand Island Dressing	260	26	90%	4	30	420	0	7
Reduced Calorie:								
Honey Mayonnaise	70	7	90%	1	20	135	0	1
Italian	20	1	45%	0	0	1000	0	3
Buttermilk Ranch	50	0	0%	0	0	710	0	12

	Cal	Fat	%Fc	S.Fat	Chol	Sod	Pro	Carb
Bagels: Each								
Plain, 5 oz	350	1.5	3%	0	0	660	14	72
Asiago Cheese, 4.2 oz	380	6	14%	3.5	15	690	17	66
Cheddar & Scallion, 4.2 oz	310	7	20%	4.5	20	650	14	47
Chocolate Chip, 5 oz	380	7	16%	3.5	5	480	12	69
Cinnamon Raisin, 5 oz	360	1.5	3%	0	0	540	12	77
Cranberrry Walnut, 5oz	460	4	7%	0.5	0	590	15	93
Dutch Apple w. Walnut Streussel, 5 oz	350	5	13%	0	0	480	11	77
Everything, 4.2 oz	360	2.5	6%	0	0	710	14	72
Honey & Grain, 4.2 oz	360	2	5%	0	0	580	14	72
Jalapeno Double Cheddar, 4.2 oz	290	3.5	10%	2	10	600	12	53
Mocha Chip Swirl, 5 oz	370	3.5	8%	2	0	480	12	72
Onion, 5 oz	370	1.5	3%	0	0	660	14	78
Sesame, 4.2 oz	380	4	9%	0.5	0	540	15	71
Wild Blueberry, 4.5 oz	380	1.5	3%	0	0	570	14	80
Spreads: Per 2 oz								
Plain Cream Cheese	180	18	90%	11	50	150	4	2
Lite Bagel: Van. Hazelnut; Strawberry	150	11	66%	7	35	210	5	6
Lite Cream Cheese:	100	8	72%	5	20	280	6	4
Honey Walnut	150	11	66%	7	30	190	4	9
Raspberry	130	10	69%	7	30	200	6	7
Sundried Tomato	120	8	60%	5	20	320	6	6
Veggie	130	11	76%	7	35	230	5	4
Wraps Sandwiches: Per Sandwich								
Southwestern Tuna (no dressing)	760	46	54%	14	100	1030	40	48
Chicken Caesar (no dressing)	440	12	25%	5	70	900	37	43
Summer Turkey (no dressing)	430	4.5	9%	0	20	1380	35	62
Sandwiches: Buffalo Chicken	640	19	27%	3.5	85	1650	41	76
Chicken Foca-cha-cha	870	29	30%	5	130	2280	74	80
Fields & Feta	560	17	27%	4	10	850	20	89
For the Love of Olive	570	13	20%	1.5	40	2060	38	80
Fresh Mozzarella, Tomato & Pesto	650	30	42%	12	55	1090	30	69
Honey Dijon Chicken	730	18	22%	6	135	1990	57	85
Hot Roasted Turkey Club	950	50	47%	16	135	2240	50	80
Radically Roasted	620	10	15%	4.5	30	1540	33	69
Steak & Cheese Melt	750	32	38%	8	90	1600	40	79
Thai Chicken	420	6	13%	1	20	1320	20	72
Breads: Per 1.75 oz Slice								
French Bread	120	5	38%	0	0	320	4	25
French Parisienne Baguette	110	2	16%	0	0	260	4	22
Multigrain Batard	110	1	8%	0	0	310	5	22
Olive Batard	120	2	15%	0	0	310	5	22
Rye	110	1.5	12%	0	0	310	5	21
Sundried Tomato Batard	110	0	0%	0	0	270	4	22
Tomato Herb; Multigrain Loaf	130	1	6%	0	0	310	5	27
Rolls: Hearth, each	220	1.5	6%	0	0	410	9	43
Petit Pain, each	200	1	5%	0	0	570	7	41

	Cal	Fat	%Fc	S.Fat	Chol	Sod	Pro	Carb
Soups: Per 8 oz Serving								
Beef Barley	75	2	24%	0.5	15	660	6	11
Carribean Black Bean	120	1	7%	0	5	770	7	22
Chicken Noodle; Chicken Wild Rice	80	1.5	17%	0	15	670	8	10
Clam Chowder	270	19	63%	9	65	730	11	16
Cream of Broccoli	220	18	74%	9	40	770	5	14
Enchilada w. Tomatilla	170	8	42%	3	20	910	6	14
Garden Vegetable	30	0	0%	0	0	820	2	8
Potato & Cheese w. Ham	150	1	6%	5	25	820	5	14
Summer Asparagus	160	11	62%	6	30	880	5	15
Tomato Florentine	60	1	15%	0.5	5	1030	4	13
Vegetarian Chili	140	2.5	16%	0	0	1070	6	27
Salads: Per Serving								
Chicken Caesar	360	11	28%	6	65	910	36	28
Chicken Tarragon w. Almonds	470	23	44%	4	80	500	32	38
Field Green, Gorgonzola & Walnut	400	34	77%	13	50	800	2	9
Garden Salad: Small	100	1	9%	0	0	150	6	20
Large	160	1.5	8%	0	0	290	7	34
Mozzarella & Rst Red Pepper	340	18	48%	10	60	135	22	26
Oriental Chicken	270	4	13%	0.5	70	700	40	17
Pesto Chicken	230	11	43%	2	45	250	6	11
Tuna	490	27	50%	4.5	45	750	26	40
Desserts: Per Piece								
Apple Coffee Cake	480	24	45%	12	100	285	6	60
Apple Strudel	440	26	53%	8	0	780	5	48
Cherry Strudel	450	29	58%	12	0	730	5	45
Caramel Apple Bar	370	18	44%	3	25	200	4	54
Key Lime Blueberry Bar	340	15	40%	5	110	290	5	45
Mochaccino Bar	405	24	53%	10	37	295	5	44
Pear Ginger Tea Cake	380	20	47%	3	0	200	3	47
Southern Pecan Bar	560	35	56%	11	50	300	1	60
Walnut Fudge Brownie	380	18	43%	11	100	150	5	56
Specialties: Per Piece								
Pecan Roll, 6.8 oz roll	900	48	48%	15	50	480	1	111
Croissants: Per Croissant								
Hot: Ham & Cheese	380	20	47%	12	70	690	16	36
Spinach & Cheese	270	16	53%	9	40	330	9	27
Dessert: Plain	270	15	50%	9	40	240	6	30
Almond	560	37	59%	15	105	250	12	50
Apple	280	10	32%	6	25	180	4	46
Chocolate	440	23	47%	15	30	230	7	53
Cinnamon Raisin	380	13	31%	8	35	290	7	51
Raspberry Cheese	380	19	45%	11	60	300	6	47
Muffins: Per Muffin								
Lowfat: Chocolate Cake	290	3	9%	0.5	20	630	4	68
Triple Berry	270	4	10%	0.5	25	560	5	60

Gourmet Muffins~ Next Page

Au Bon Pain® (Cont)

	Cal	Fat	%FC	S.Fat	Chol	Sod	Pro	Carb
Muffins: Per Muffin								
Gourmet: Blueberry	410	15	33%	2.5	85	380	8	64
Carrot Pecan	480	23	43%	5	55	650	8	61
Chocolate Chip	490	20	37%	7	35	560	8	70
Corn	470	18	34%	2.5	65	570	8	70
Pumpkin w. Streussel Topping	470	18	34%	3	60	550	8	74
Raisin Bran	390	11	25%	4	45	1030	9	65
Cookies: Per Cookie								
Almond Biscotti	200	10	45%	3.5	35	45	4	24
Chocolate Almond Biscotti	240	13	49%	6	35	50	5	28
Chocolate Chip	280	13	42%	8	40	85	3	40
Cranberry Almond Macaroon	160	8	45%	5	0	115	2	22
English Toffee	220	12	49%	7	45	110	2	28
Ginger Pecan	260	15	52%	6	40	115	5	30
Oatmeal Raisin	250	10	36%	3.5	30	240	3	40
Shortbread	390	25	58%	15	65	190	3	39
Drinks: Per 16 oz								
Blast: Malt Shoppe	370	4.5	11%	2.5	15	220	11	71
Strawberry Banana Split	380	2	5%	1.5	10	125	7	82
Hot Hazelnut; Str'berry/ Van. Choc.	310	6	17%	3.5	25	180	11	57
Hot Caramel/Raspberry Mocha	330	6	17%	3.5	25	180	11	57
Frozen Blast: Original; Mocha	320	3	8%	2	10	150	9	64
Wilch Blast: Malt Shoppe	450	9	18%	6	35	350	19	74
Original Frozen Mocha	350	7	18%	4.5	30	240	16	56
Strawberry Banana Split	280	5	16%	3.5	25	190	13	45
Iced Cappuccino: Small, 9 fl.oz	110	4	33%	2.5	15	110	7	10
Medium, 12 fl.oz	150	6	36%	3.5	25	150	10	15
Large, 20 fl.oz	270	10	33%	6	40	270	18	26
Iced Tea: Peach, Small, 8 fl.oz	90	0	0%	0	0	15	0	22
Medium, 12 fl.oz	130	0	0%	0	0	20	0	33

Applebee's®

	Cal	Fat	%FC	S.Fat	Chol	Sod	Pro	Carb
Low Fat & Fabulous								
Asian Chicken Salad: Large	645	9.5	13%	na	na	na	32	108
Regular	370	5.5	13%	na	na	na	16	64
Blackened Chicken Salad: Large	410	5	11%	na	na	na	54	38
Regular	290	3	9%	na	na	na	38	28
Chicken Fajita Quesadilla	520	11	19%	na	na	na	42	63
Garlic Chicken Pasita	590	8	12%	na	na	na	39	89
Lemon Chicken Pasita	530	11	19%	na	na	na	29	78
Veggie Quesadilla	345	8	21%	na	na	na	22	46
Desserts, Sundaes								
Marble Cheesecake	260	2	8%	na	na	na	10	50
Strawberry Shortcake	250	2	7%	na	na	na	10	48
Brownie Sundae	415	2	4%	na	na	na	17	82

	Cal	Fat	%FC	S.Fat	Chol	Sod	Pro	Carb
Pretzels								
Almond Pretzel	350	1.5	4%	0.5	0	390	9	72
with Butter	400	8	18%	5	20	400	9	72
Cinnamon Sugar Pretzel	350	2	5%	0	0	410	9	74
with Butter	450	9	4%	5	25	430	8	83
Garlic Pretzel	320	1	3%	0	0	830	9	66
with Butter	350	4.5	11%	2.5	10	850	9	68
Glazin' Raisin Pretzel	470	0.5	1%	0	0	460	11	104
with Butter	510	4	7%	2	10	480	11	107
Jalapeno Pretzel	270	1	3.5%	0	0	780	8	58
with Butter	310	4.5	13%	2.5	10	940	8	59
Original Pretzel	340	1	2.5%	0	0	900	10	72
with Butter	370	4	10%	2	10	930	10	72
Parmesan Herb Pretzel	390	5	12%	2.5	10	780	11	74
with Butter	440	13	26%	7	30	660	10	72
Sesame Pretzel	350	6	15%	1	0	840	11	63
with Butter	410	12	26%	4	15	860	12	64
Sour Cream & Onion Pretzel	310	1	3%	0	0	920	9	66
with Butter	340	5	13%	3	10	930	9	66
Whole Wheat Pretzel	350	1.5	4%	0	0	1100	11	72
with Butter	370	4.5	11%	1.5	10	1120	11	72
Beverages								
Auntie Annie's Lemonade: 22 fl.oz	180	0	0%	0	0	0	0	43
Kiwi-Banana Dutch Ice: 14 fl.oz	190	0	0%	0	0	30	0	44
20 fl.oz	270	0	0%	0	0	40	0	63
Lemonade Dutch Ice: 14 fl.oz	315	0	0%	0	0	0	0	77
20 fl.oz	450	0	0%	0	0	0	0	110
Mocha Dutch Ice: 14 fl.oz	400	10	23%	9	0	100	0	74
20 fl.oz	570	15	23%	12	0	150	0	105
Orange Crème Dutch Ice: 14 fl.oz	280	0	0%	0	0	35	0	64
20 fl.oz	400	0	0%	0	0	50	0	92
Pina Colada Dutch Ice: 14 fl.oz	220	0	0%	0	0	15	0	53
20 fl.oz	535	0	0%	0	0	50	0	125
Raspberry Dutch Ice: 14 fl.oz	175	0	0%	0	0	30	0	40
20 fl.oz	250	0	0%	0	0	40	0	57
Strawberry Dutch Ice: 14 fl.oz	220	0	0%	0	0	40	0	50
20 fl.oz	315	0	0%	0	0	60	0	72
Wild Cherry Dutch Ice: 14 fl.oz	210	0	0%	0	0	25	0	48
20 fl.oz	300	0	0%	0	0	35	0	69
Dipping Sauces: Caramel Dip	135	3	20%	1.5	5	110	1	27
Cheese Sauce	100	8	72%	4	10	510	3	4
Chocolate Flavored Dip	130	4	27%	1.5	2	65	1	24
Hot Salsa Cheese	100	8	72%	4	10	550	2	4
Light Cream Cheese	70	6	77%	4	25	140	3	1
Marinara Sauce	10	0	0%	0	0	180	0	4
Strawberry Cream Cheese	110	10	82%	6	35	105	2	4
Sweet Mustard	60	1.5	22%	1	40	120	0.5	8

Baskin-Robbins®

	Cal	Fat	%Fc	S.Fat	Chol	Sod	Pro	Carb
***Regular Deluxe:** Per Regular Scoop*								
Banana Strawberry	285	15	47%	10	55	90	4	37
Baseball Nut	350	20	51%	11	66	120	5	40
Black Walnut	350	24	62%	11	66	100	6	28
Blueberry Cheesecake	330	18	49%	5	77	155	4	40
Cherries Jubilee	310	15	43%	10	66	90	4	35
Chocolate	330	20	54%	13	66	130	5	40
Chocolate Almond	395	24	55%	11	66	120	6	37
Chocolate Chip	330	22	60%	13	77	100	4	33
Chocolate Chip Cookie Dough	375	20	48%	13	77	155	4	44
Chocolate Fudge	350	20	51%	13	66	175	4	46
Chocolate Mousse Royale	375	22	53%	11	55	130	5	44
Chocolate Raspberry Truffle	395	20	45%	13	66	130	6	50
Chunky Heath Bar	375	22	53%	13	66	155	4	42
Cookies 'N Cream	375	24	57%	15	66	100	4	35
Egg Nog	330	17	46%	11	88	100	4	35
English Toffee	350	20	51%	13	66	155	4	42
Everybody's Favorite Candy Bar	375	20	48%	11	66	200	4.5	44
French Vanilla	350	22	56%	13	154	100	4	31
Fudge Brownie	375	24	57%	13	55	165	6	42
German Choc Cake	395	22	50%	13	55	165	6	44
Gold Medal Ribbon	330	17	46%	11	66	210	4	44
Jamoca	310	20	58%	11	77	100	4	31
Jamoca Almond Fudge	350	20	51%	10	55	90	6	37
Lemon Custard	330	17	46%	11	100	120	4	35
Mint Choc Chip	330	22	60%	13	77	100	6	33
Mississippi Mud	350	17	44%	10	55	185	4.5	48
Old Fashion Butter Pecan	350	24	62%	13	77	110	4	28
Oregan Blackberry	310	17	49%	11	66	110	4	44
Peanut Butter 'N Choc	395	26	59%	13	66	210	6	35
Pistachio-Almond	375	26	62%	11	66	100	6	28
Pralines 'n Cream	350	20	51%	11	66	185	4	42
Pumpkin Pie	285	15	47%	10	66	110	4	44
Quarterback Crunch	350	22	56%	15	66	165	4	40
Reeses Peanutbutter	395	24	55%	13	66	155	6	37
Rocky Road	375	22	53%	11	66	130	6	42
Rum Raisin	310	15	43%	10	66	90	4	40
Strawberry Shortcake	350	20	51%	13	66	155	4	40
Triple Chocolate Passion	395	24	55%	15	77	155	6	46
Vanilla	310	18	52%	11	88	90	6	31
Very Berry Strawberry	285	15	47%	9	55	90	2	35
Winter White Chocolate	330	20	54%	13	55	110	4	40
Winter Wondermint	270	14	47%	9	55	80	3	33
World Class Chocolate	350	20	51%	11	66	120	4	40
***Light Icecream:** Regular Serving*								
Espresso 'N Cream	220	6	25%	2	11	135	6	39

	Cal	Fat	%Fc	S.Fat	Chol	Sod	Pro	Carb
Non Fat Icecream: Regular Serving								
Average all flavors	235	0	0%	0	0	210	7	50
No Sugar Added: Regular Serving								
Average all flavors	220	5	20%	3	11	120	6	40
Ices, Sherbets, Sorbets: Regular Serving								
Ices: The Mask	265	0	0%	0	0	20	0	64
Other flavors	240	0	0%	0	0	20	0	60
Sherbets: Average all flavors	265	4	14%	2	11	60	2	57
Sorbets: Pink Raspberry; Black Tie	265	0	0%	0	0	25	0	66
Mixed Berry	240	0	0%	0	0	20	0	61
Yogurt Gone Crazy								
Maui Brownie Madness	310	6	17%	2	11	175	9	57
Perils of Praline	310	6	17%	4	11	230	9	55
Raspberry Cheese Louse	285	6	19%	4	22	200	9	53
FroZone Kids Flavors: Regular Serving								
Dirt 'N Worms	350	17	44%	10	55	175	4	48
Eerrie I Scream; Pink Bubblegum	330	17	46%	11	55	100	5	40
Neon Sour Apple/Watermelon Ice	240	0	0%	0	0	20	0	59
Polar Paws	350	22	56%	13	66	100	4	37
Skullicious	375	22	53%	15	66	120	4	40
Blasts: Per 8fl.oz								
Cappuccino: Non Fat	90	0	0%	0	0	60	3	22
w. Whipped Cream	160	7	39%	4	30	60	3	22
Chocolate: Non Fat	170	0	0%	0	0	105	4	40
w. Whipped Cream	250	7	25%	4	25	120	4	46
Mocha Cappuccino: Non Fat	120	0	0%	0	0	75	3	26
w. Whipped Cream	180	6	30%	4	25	70	3	28
Smoothies: Per 8 fl.oz								
Soft Serve: Aloha Berry Banana	180	0	0%	0	5	80	4	40
Bora Berry Bora	170	0	0%	0	5	75	4	38
Average other flavors	160	0	0%	0	5	75	3	35
Hard Serve: Aloha Berry Banana	210	0	0%	0	0	85	4	46
Bora Berry Bora; Tropical Tango	190	0	0%	0	0	70	4	43
Copa Banana; Sunset Orange	170	0	0%	0	0	75	4	38
Toppings								
Baby Gummy Bears, 75 pieces	130	0	0%	0	0	15	3	30
Butterscotch, 2 oz	200	2	9%	na	6	160	1	47
Hot Fudge, 1 oz	100	3	27%	na	0	45	1	17
No Sug.Add/Fat Free	90	0	0%	0	2	95	2	20
Praline Caramel, 1 oz	90	0	0%	0	0	105	0	19
Strawberry, 1 oz	60	0	0%	0	0	5	0	14
Whipped Cream, 2 tsp	30	3	90%	2	5	0	0	1
White & Colored Sprinkles	20	0.5	22%	0	0	0	0	3
Cones: Sugar Cone	60	3	45%	0	0	50	1	7
Cake Cone	25	0.5	18%	0	0	55	1	4
Waffle Cone: Large	120	1.5	11%	0	0	55	0	14
Fresh Baked	145	2	12%	0.5	13	5	2	30

Big Boy

	Cal	Fat	%FC	S.Fat	Chol	Sod	Pro	Carb
Sandwiches								
Turkey	225	5	20%	2	75	835	22	24
Chicken w. Mozzarella	405	13	29%	6	76	420	42	26
Dinners (w. Bread; No Dressing)								
Chicken Breast: w.Salad	350	13	34%	3	65	340	38	20
w.Mozzarella & Salad	370	12	29%	4	76	355	42	24
Cajun & Salad	350	13	34%	4	65	610	38	20
Chckn. & Veg. stir-fry (no bread)	560	14	22%	4	68	750	43	68
Fish: Cod Baked; Dijon, Salad	430	18	38%	4	68	570	44	21
Cod, Cajun, Salad	365	12	30%	4	68	460	43	20
Spaghetti Marinara & Salad	450	6	12%	3	8	760	15	87
Soup: Cabbage, 1 bowl	45	1	21%	2	1	730	2	9
1 cup	40	0	0%	0	1	625	2	8
Vegetables								
Vegetable Stir-fry	410	10	22%	2	0	705	9	74
Beans, green	30	0	0%	0	0	0	2	6
Carrots	35	0	0%	0	0	40	1	8
Corn	90	1	10%	0	0	0	3	21
Mixed Vegetables	30	0	0%	0	0	40	2	5
Peas	80	0	0%	0	0	130	6	13
Potato, Baked	165	0	0%	0	0	10	5	37
Rice	115	0	0%	0	0	640	3	25
Roll	140	0	0%	0	2	185	3	30
Salad: Chicken Breast, Dijon	390	11	25%	2	65	415	42	31
Dinner, without Dressing	20	0	0%	0	0	10	1	4
Dressing: Buttermilk	35	2	50%	1	10	150	0	4
Desserts: 'No-No' frozen dessert	75	0	0%	0	0	35	2	17
Yogurt, frozen, regular	70	0	0%	0	0	30	2	16
Shake	185	0	0%	0	2	130	8	36

Blimpie®

	Cal	Fat	%FC	S.Fat	Chol	Sod	Pro	Carb
Subs								
Per 6" Sub								
Blimpie Best	410	13	29%	5	50	1480	26	47
Cheese Trio	510	23	41%	13	60	1060	26	51
Club	450	13	26%	6	40	1350	30	53
Grilled Chicken	400	9	20%	2	30	950	28	52
5 Meatball	500	22	40%	8	25	970	23	52
Ham & Swiss	400	13	29%	7	35	970	25	47
Ham, Salami, Provolone	590	28	43%	11	70	1880	32	52
Roast Beef	340	4.5	13%	1	20	870	27	47
Steak & Cheese	550	26	42%	4	70	1080	27	51
Tuna	570	32	50%	5	50	790	21	50
Turkey	320	4.5	14%	1	10	890	19	51
Salad: Grilled Chicken, no dressing	350	12	31%	0	140	1190	47	13

	Cal	Fat	%FC	S.Fat	Chol	Sod	Pro	Carb
Cajun Spiced Chicken								
Breast	280	17	55%	3	75	565	18	12
Leg	265	16	55%	3	96	530	19	11
Thigh	310	23	67%	5	67	465	15	11
Wing	355	25	63%	5	94	630	21	11
Cajun Roast Chicken								
Breast, skin free	145	5	31%	1	84	560	24	<1
Leg, skin free	160	8	45%	2	125	565	23	<1
Thigh, skin free	215	15	63%	3	95	430	20	<1
Wing, skin free	230	15	59%	3	117	620	22	3
Southern Style Chicken								
Breast	260	16	55%	3	76	700	16	12
Leg	260	15	52%	4	94	445	19	11
Thigh	310	21	61%	5	78	630	16	14
Wing	340	21	56%	5	86	685	17	19
Sandwiches/Snacks								
Buffalo Bites	180	5	25%	2	105	720	27	5
Cajun Fillet: no Mayo	340	11	29%	5	45	400	22	41
w. Mayo	440	22	45%	7	55	505	22	41
Cajun Steak Sandwich	435	26	54%	8	55	985	18	39
Chicken Supremes	340	16	42%	6	58	630	21	26
Grilled Fillet, no mayo	235	5	19%	3	51	540	23	25
w. Mayo	335	16	43%	5	61	645	23	25
Biscuit Sandwiches								
Bacon	290	17	53%	5	10	810	8	26
Bacon, Egg & Cheese	550	42	69%	14	160	1250	17	27
Biscuit (plain)	245	12	44%	3	2	665	4	29
Cajun Fillet	455	21	61%	6	41	950	20	46
Country Ham	270	15	49%	4	20	1010	9	26
Egg	400	30	66%	6	120	630	8	26
Sausage	350	23	64%	7	20	810	9	26
Smoked Sausage	380	26	62%	9	20	940	10	27
Steak	650	49	68%	13	34	1125	14	37
Fixins'								
Bo Rounds	235	11	42%	4	13	330	3	31
Cajun Pintos	110	0	1%	0	0	480	6	18
Corn on the Cob	140	2	13%	0	0	20	5	34
Dirty Rice	165	6	33%	2	10	760	5	24
Green Beans	25	0	0%	0	0	710	0	5
Macaroni & Cheese	200	14	63%	5	26	420	7	12
Marinated Cole Slaw	135	3	20%	0	0	455	1	26
Multi-Grain Roll	150	3	18%	0	0	210	6	26
Potatoes, no Gravy	80	1	11%	0	0	380	2	16
Seasoned Fries	345	19	49%	5	13	480	5	40
Sweet Biscuits: Apple Cinnamon	330	13	35%	4	<1	560	4	37
Bo Berry™	220	10	41%	3	<1	410	3	29
Cinnamon	320	18	51%	4	<1	560	4	37

Boston Market®

	Cal	Fat	%FC	S.Fat	Chol	Sod	Pro	Carb
Entrees								
Chicken: 1/4 white meat w. skin, wing	280	12	38%	3.5	135	510	40	2
No skin or wing	170	4	21%	1	85	480	33	2
1/4 dark meat w. skin	320	21	59%	6	155	500	30	2
No skin	190	10	47%	3	115	440	22	1
1/2 chicken w. skin	590	33	50%	10	290	1010	70	4
Original Chicken Pot Pie, 1 pie	780	46	53%	13	135	1480	32	61
Teriyaki, 1/4 dark meat w. skin	380	21	50%	6	155	870	30	17
Hearth Honey Ham	210	9	38%	3.5	75	1490	25	9
Meat Loaf & Chunky Tom Sauce	400	25	56%	8	80	1700	23	19
Meat Loaf & Gravy	390	22	51%	8	120	1040	30	19
Meat Loaf w. Mash. Pots & Gravy	740	42	51%	17	90	2650	28	55
Turkey: Breast, no skin	170	1	5%	0.5	100	850	36	1
Oven Rstd Medallions: w. Gravy	210	4.5	19%	1	70	1050	28	8
w. Stuffing & Gravy	600	18	27%	3.5	75	2150	35	67
Soup: Chicken Noodle, 1 cup	130	4.5	31%	1	40	1310	11	12
Chicken Tortilla, 1 cup	220	11	45%	4	35	1410	10	19
Salads: Caesar Side Salad, 4 oz	200	17	76%	5	15	450	7	7
Caesar Entree, 10 oz	510	42	74%	11	35	1130	17	17
no dressing, 8 oz	230	12	47%	6	20	500	16	14
Chicken Caesar, 13 oz	650	45	62%	12	105	1580	43	17
Tossed: w. Caesar Dressing	380	31	73%	5	15	810	5	18
w. Fat Free Ranch	160	2.5	14%	0	0	940	5	29
Sandwiches								
Chicken Salad	680	30	39%	5	120	1360	39	63
Chicken w. Cheese & Sauce	750	33	38%	12	135	1860	41	72
No Cheese or Sauce	430	5	10%	1	65	910	34	62
Ham w. Cheese & Sauce	750	34	41%	12	100	1730	38	72
No Cheese or Sauce	440	8	16%	3	45	1450	25	66
Meat Loaf w. Cheese	860	33	35%	16	165	2270	46	95
No Cheese	690	21	27%	7	120	1610	40	86
Turkey: Club	650	26	36%	8	105	1590	39	64
Open-Faced	500	12	22%	2	80	2170	37	61
Turkey w. Cheese & Sauce	710	28	35%	10	110	1390	45	68
No Cheese or Sauce	400	4	8%	1	60	1070	45	61
Side Dishes:								
Corn, 3/4 cup	180	4	20%	1	0	130	5	30
Hot Cinnamon Apples, 3/4 cup	250	4.5	16%	0.5	0	45	0	56
Macaroni Cheese, 3/4 cup	280	11	35%	6	30	830	13	32
Mash Potatoes & Gravy, 3/4 cup	210	10	43%	5	25	740	4	26
Rice Pilaf, 2/3 cup	180	5	25%	1	0	600	5	32
Savory Stuffing, 3/4 cup	310	12	35%	2	0	1140	6	44
Zucchini Marinara, 3/4 cup	60	3	45%	0	0	330	1	7
Baked Goods: Brownie	450	27	54%	7	80	190	6	47
Choc Chip Cookie	340	17	45%	6	25	240	4	43
Corn Bread, 1 loaf	200	6	27%	1.5	25	390	3	33
Oatmeal Raisin Cookie	320	13	37%	3	25	260	4	48

	Cal	Fat	%Fc	S.Fat	Chol	Sod	Pro	Carb
Breakfast: Biscuit, 3 oz	300	15	45%	3.5	0	830	6	35
Biscuit with Egg	390	22	50%	5	150	1020	11	37
Biscuit with Sausage	510	35	61%	10	30	1190	13	35
Biscuit w. Sausage, Egg, Cheese	650	46	63%	14	190	1600	20	38
Croissan'wich®: w. Sausage/Cheese	410	29	63%	11	40	830	14	24
w. Sausage/Egg/Cheese	500	36	65%	13	190	1120	19	26
French Toast Sticks (5), 4 oz	390	20	46%	4.5	0	440	6	46
Hash Brown Rounds: Small, 2.6 oz	240	15	56%	4	0	450	2	23
Large, 4.5 oz	390	25	57%	7	0	760	3	38
Cini-Minis: 4 Rolls w/out Icing	440	23	47%	6	25	710	6	51
Vanilla Icing only, 1 oz	110	3	25%	1	0	40	0	20
Grape/Strawberry Jam	30	0	0%	0	0	0	0	7
Burgers: Triple Play Burger	770	49	57%	25	165	1290	50	32
Whopper® Sandwich	680	39	51%	12	80	940	29	53
without Mayonnaise	530	22	37%	9	70	840	29	53
Whopper® w. Cheese Sandwich	780	47	54%	17	105	1390	34	55
without Mayonnaise	620	30	43%	14	90	1280	33	54
Double Whopper® Sandwich	920	57	56%	20	150	1020	48	53
without Mayonnaise	760	40	47%	17	135	920	48	54
Double Whopper® w. Cheese	1020	65	57%	25	170	1460	53	55
without Mayonnaise	860	48	50%	23	160	1350	53	54
Whopper JR® Sandwich	420	24	51%	8	55	520	20	32
without Mayonnaise	350	16	41%	7	50	470	20	32
Whopper JR® w. Cheese Sandwich	470	28	53%	11	65	740	22	33
without Mayonnaise	390	19	44%	9	60	690	22	32
Bull's-Eye® BBQ Deluxe Sandwich	440	25	51%	8	55	470	20	34
without Mayonnaise	360	16	40%	7	50	410	20	33
Hamburger	340	16	42%	7	50	540	19	30
Double Hamburger	500	28	50%	12	95	590	33	30
Cheeseburger	380	19	45%	9	60	760	22	31
Double Cheeseburger	600	36	54%	18	120	1030	38	32
Bacon Cheeseburger	430	23	48%	10	70	900	25	31
Bacon Double Cheeseburger	640	39	55%	19	130	1180	41	32
Chicken & Fish Sandwiches								
BK Big Fish® Sandwich	710	38	48%	14	50	1200	24	67
BK Broiler® Chicken Sandwich	550	25	41%	5	105	1110	30	52
without Mayonnaise	390	8	18%	2	90	1010	29	51
Chicken Sandwich	660	39	53%	8	70	1330	25	53
without Mayonnaise	460	17	33%	5	55	1190	25	52
Chicken Club Sandwich	620	32	46%	8	75	1460	30	54
without Mayonnaise	530	21	35%	2	60	1390	30	54
Chicken Tenders® Sandwich	450	27	54%	5	30	680	14	37
without Mayonnaise	290	10	31%	3	20	570	14	36
Chicken Tenders®: 4 pieces	170	9	47%	3	25	420	11	10
5 pieces	220	12	49%	3	30	530	14	13
6 pieces	250	14	50%	4	35	650	16	15
8 pieces	340	19	50%	5	50	840	22	20

	Cal	Fat	%Fc	S.Fat	Chol	Sod	Pro	Carb
Sides: Jalapeno Poppers®,4 pces	230	15	50%	5	20	790	7	22
French Fries (Salted): Small, 2.6 oz	230	11	43%	3	0	510	2	31
Medium, 4 oz	370	17	41%	5	0	760	4	49
King Size, 6 oz	540	25	41%	7	0	1080	6	72
Onion Rings: Child's, 1.8 oz	190	9	42%	2.5	0	260	3	23
Medium, 3.3 oz	330	16	43%	4	0	470	5	41
King Size, 5.3 oz	530	26	44%	7	4	760	7	66
Mozzarella Sticks: 4 pieces	290	16	49%	6	20	670	12	25
Dipping Sauces (1 oz): Barbecue	35	0	0%	0	0	400	0	9
Honey Flavored	90	0	0%	0	0	10	0	23
Honey Mustard	90	6	60%	1	10	150	0	10
Ranch	120	13	97%	2	5	85	0	2
Sweet & Sour	40	0	0%	0	0	65	0	10
Desserts: Dutch Apple Pie, 4 oz	340	14	37%	3	0	470	2	52
Hershey's® Sundae Pie, 2.6 oz	310	18	52%	13	10	135	3	33
Beverages: Sprite, medium, 22 fl.oz	260	0	0%	0	0	na	0	66
Coca-Cola® (1/4 ice), med., 22 fl.oz	280	0	0%	0	0	na	0	70
Tropicana® Orange Juice, 10 fl.oz	140	0	0%	0	0	0	2	33
Reduced Fat Milk - 2% Fat, 8 fl.oz	130	5	35%	3	20	120	8	12
Chocolate Shake: Small, 10.7 oz	330	7	19%	4	25	250	9	58
Small, syrup added	390	7	16%	4	20	350	14	105
Medium, 14 oz	440	10	20%	6	30	330	12	75
Medium, syrup added	570	10	16%	6	30	520	14	105
Strawberry Shake: Med., syrup added	550	9	13%	5	30	350	13	104
Small, syrup added	390	7	16%	4	20	260	10	72
Vanilla Shake: Medium, 14 oz	430	9	18%	5	30	330	13	73
Small, 10.7 oz	330	7	19%	4	20	250	10	56
Condiments/Toppings: Ketchup, 1/2 oz	15	0	0%	0	0	180	0	4
American Cheese, 2 slices, 25g	100	8	72%	5	20	440	5	1
Bacon, 3 pieces, 8g	40	3	60%	1	10	150	3	0
Bull's Eye® BBQ Sauce, 1/2 oz	20	0	0%	0	0	130	0	5
Land O'Lakes Whipped Blend, 5g	25	3.5	97%	1	0	30	0	0

Carvel® Ice Cream

Soft Serving Ice Cream	Cal	Fat	%Fc	S.Fat	Chol	Sod	Pro	Carb
Chocolate: Regular	420	22	47%	13	55	220	9	48
Vanilla: Regular	440	22	45%	13	90	240	11	46
No Sugar Added: Regular	285	6.5	20%	4.5	33	190	11	55
Large	365	8.5	21%	5.5	42	240	14	70
No Fat (average all flavors): Regular	265	0	0%	0	0	100	6	58
Large	335	0	0%	0	0	135	8	73
Sherbet, all flavors: Regular	310	2	5%	1	11	100	4.5	68
Blue Ribbon Cakes: Average, 4 oz	220	11	45%	6	25	125	4	27
Flying Saucers: Chocolate; Vanilla	240	10	37%	5	30	180	5	33
Lil' Love/Piece of Cake: 4 oz	260	13	45%	8	30	140	5	31
Sheet Cake; Small Round: 4 oz	210	11	47%	7	25	120	4	25

Captain D's® Seafood

	Cal	Fat	%Fc	S.Fat	Chol	Sod	Pro	Carb
Platters								
Broiled Shrimp	720	8	10%	1	155	1760	32	131
Broiled Chicken	802	10	11%	2	82	1650	46	131
Broiled Fish	734	7	8%	1	49	1645	36	131
Broiled Fish & Chicken	777	10	12%	1	66	1650	41	131
Lunches								
Broiled Shrimp	421	7	15%	1	155	1725	25	64
Broiled Chicken	503	9	16%	2	82	1615	39	65
Broiled Fish	435	7	14%	1	49	1610	28	65
Broiled Fish & Chicken	478	8	15%	1	66	1610	34	68
Stuffed Crab	90	7	46%	na	na	250	8	16
Sandwiches								
Broiled Chicken	450	19	38%	na	105	860	40	29
Side Items								
Baked Potato	280	0	0%	0	0	20	6	64
Breadstick	110	4	33%	0	0	210	3	16
Cole Slaw	160	12	68%	na	16	245	3	12
Corn on the Cob	250	2	7%	na	0	15	9	60
Cheese, 1 oz	54	5	83%	na	14	205	3	<1
Crackers (4)	50	1	18%	na	3	150	1	8
Cracklins, 1 oz	220	17	70%	na	0	740	1	16
Dinner Salad	20	0	0%	0	0	15	1	4
French Fries	300	10	30%	na	0	150	3	50
Fried Okra	300	16	48%	na	0	445	7	34
Green Beans	45	2	39%	na	4	750	2	5
Hushpuppy	125	4	29%	na	0	465	2	20
Rice	124	0	0%	0	0	9	3	28
Vegetable Medley	35	1	25%	0	0	115	1	4
White Beans	125	0.5	3%	na	2	100	8	22
Salad Dressings: Per Serving								
Blue Cheese	110	12	98%	na	14	100	<1	<1
French	110	11	89%	na	7	190	<1	4
Light Italian	15	0.5	30%	0	0	na	0	3
Ranch	90	10	98%	na	15	230	<1	<1
Sour Cream, Imitation	30	3	90%	3	0	na	0	1
Sauces: Cocktail, 1 oz	35	0.4	8%	na	0	250	<1	8
Sweet & Sour	50	0	0%	0	0	5	0	13
Tartar	75	7	84%	na	10	160	<1	3
Desserts								
Carrot Cake	435	23	48%	na	32	415	8	49
Cheesecake	420	31	66%	na	141	480	7	30
Chocolate Cake	305	10	30%	na	20	260	4	49
Pecan Pie	460	20	39%	na	4	375	5	64

	Cal	Fat	%Fc	S.Fat	Chol	Sod	Pro	Carb
Breakfast								
French Toast Dips, no Syrup	370	20	48%	2.5	0	430	6	42
Sunrise Sandwich, no Bacon/Saus.	360	21	30%	5	225	700	14	28
Breakfast Burrito	480	30	56%	13	465	750	27	26
Scrambled Eggs	160	11	62%	3.5	425	125	13	1
English Muffin w. Marg.	210	9	38%	1	0	300	5	27
Breakfast Quesadilla	310	16	46%	6	230	670	14	27
Bacon, 2 Strips	50	4	72%	1.5	10	140	3	0
Sausage, 1 Patty	200	19	85%	17	30	480	8	2
Sandwiches								
Famous Star® Hamburger	580	32	50%	9	70	910	25	49
Super Star® Hamburger	650	30	41%	12	80	1430	32	63
Jr. Hamburger	330	13	35%	5	45	480	18	34
Western Bacon Cheeseburger®	650	30	41%	12	80	1430	32	63
Dble Western Bacon Cheeseburger®	900	49	53%	21	155	1770	51	64
Charbroiled BBQ Chicken Sandwich™	280	3	10%	1	60	830	25	37
Charbroiled Chicken Club Sandwich™	460	22	43%	7	90	1110	32	33
Charbroiled Santa Fe Chicken S'wich™	510	31	55%	7	95	1240	28	32
Ranch Crispy Chicken Sandwich	620	29	42%	6	50	1220	25	65
Bacon Swiss Crispy Chicken S'wich	720	36	45%	10	75	1610	32	66
Charbroiled Sirloin Steak Sandwich	580	26	40%	5	85	1110	33	50
Carl's Catch Fish Sandwich™	510	27	47%	7	80	1030	18	50
American Cheese	60	5	75%	3	15	280	3	0
Swiss-style Cheese	50	3.5	63%	2.5	10	250	4	0
Great Stuff Potatoes								
Plain, no margarine	290	0	0%	0	0	20	6	68
Bacon & Cheese	630	29	41%	7	35	1700	20	76
Broccoli & Cheese	530	21	35%	4.5	15	950	11	74
Sour Cream & Chive	430	14	29%	3	10	135	7	70
Bakery/Desserts: Per Serving								
Blueberry Muffin	340	14	37%	2	40	340	5	49
Bran Raisin Muffin	370	13	32%	2	45	410	7	61
Cheese Danish	400	22	49%	5	15	390	5	49
Chocolate Cake	300	10	30%	2.5	23	260	3	49
Chocolate Chip Cookie	370	19	46%	8	25	350	3	49
Strawberry Swirl Cheesecake	290	17	53%	9	55	230	6	30
Side Orders: Per Serving								
Breadstick, 1	35	0.5	12%	0	0	60	1	7
Chicken Stars, 6 pieces	280	19	61%	4.5	40	330	12	15
CrissCut Fries®, 5 oz	410	24	53%	5	0	950	5	43
French Fries, 3 oz	290	14	43%	3	0	170	5	37
Hash Brown Nuggets, 4 oz	330	21	57%	4.5	0	470	3	32
Onion Rings, 5 oz	430	21	44%	5	0	700	7	53
Zucchini, 5 oz	340	19	50%	4.5	0	860	5	37
Salads: Per Serving (no dressing)								
Charbroiled Chicken Salad-to-Go™	200	7	31%	3.5	75	440	25	12
Garden Salad-to-Go™	50	2.5	50%	1.5	10	60	3	4

Carl's Jr® (Cont)

	Cal	Fat	%Fc	S.Fat	Chol	Sod	Pro	Carb
Dressings								
Blue Cheese	320	35	99%	6	25	370	2	1
Fat Free French	60	0	0%	0	0	770	0	16
Fat Free Italian	15	0	0%	0	0	660	0	4
House	220	22	90%	4	20	440	1	3
1000 Island	230	23	86%	3.5	20	420	1	5
Sauces: BBQ	50	0	0%	0	0	270	1	11
Honey	90	0	0%	0	0	0	0	22
Mustard	50	0	0%	0	0	210	0	11
Salsa	10	0	0%	0	0	160	0	2
Sweet 'n Sour	50	0	0%	0	0	80	0	12
Shakes: Chocolate, small	390	7	16%	5	30	280	9	74
Strawberry, small	400	7	16%	5	30	240	9	77
Vanilla, small	330	8	22%	5	35	250	11	54

Chick-Fil-A®

	Cal	Fat	%Fc	S.Fat	Chol	Sod	Pro	Carb
Chick-Fil-A Sandwiches								
Chicken	290	9	27%	2	50	870	24	29
Chicken Deluxe	300	9	27%	2	50	870	25	31
Chicken (no bun/pickles)	160	8	44%	2	45	690	21	1
Chargrilled Chicken:	280	3	11%	1	40	640	27	36
Deluxe	290	3	10%	1	40	640	28	38
No bun, no pickles	130	3	23%	1	30	630	27	0
Club (no dressing)	390	12	28%	5	70	980	33	38
Chick. Salad (on whole wheat)	320	5	12%	2	10	810	25	42
Soup: Hearty Breast of Chicken	110	1	8%	0	45	760	16	10
Strips, Nuggets								
Chick-n-Strips (4-count)	230	8	30%	2	20	380	29	10
Nuggets (8-pack)	290	14	52%	3	60	770	28	12
Salads								
Chick-n-Strips Salad	290	9	28%	2	20	430	32	21
Chargrilled Chicken Garden	170	3	18%	1	25	650	26	10
Chicken Salad Plate	290	5	14%	0	35	570	21	40

Chilis®

	Cal	Fat	%Fc	S.Fat	Chol	Sod	Pro	Carb
Guiltless Grill								
Chicken Pita	600	9	14%	3	45	3010	39	90
Chicken Platter	565	9	14%	3	60	3285	38	83
Chicken Salad w. Dressing	275	5	16%	1	45	1475	29	27
Chicken Sandwich	530	8	14%	2	45	2925	44	70
Veggie Pasta	680	13	17%	4	125	760	34	102
w. Chicken	785	15	17%	5	165	1195	53	106

Church's® Fried Chicken

	Cal	Fat	%FC	S.Fat	Chol	Sod	Pro	Carb
Fried Chicken: Breast	200	12	54%	3	65	510	19	4
Leg	140	9	58%	2	45	160	13	2
Thigh	230	16	63%	4	80	520	16	5
Wing	250	16	58%	4	60	540	19	8
Tender Strip	80	4	45%	1	15	140	6	5
Side Items: Apple Pie	280	12	39%	3	5	340	2	41
Biscuit	250	16	58%	3	5	640	2	26
Cajun Rice	130	7	48%	2	5	260	1	16
Cole Slaw	92	6	59%	1	0	230	4	8
Corn on the Cob	140	3	19%	1	0	15	4.5	24
French Fries	210	11	47%	3	0	60	3	29
Okra	210	16	69%	3	0	520	3	19
Potatoes & Gravy	90	3	30%	1	0	520	1	14

Cousins Subs®

	Cal	Fat	%FC	S.Fat	Chol	Sod	Pro	Carb
Hot Dog	275	16	52%	5	24	770	10	22
Italian/Wheat Bread, aver., half loaf	250	3	11%	1	4	450	8	46
Cold Italian 7 1/2" Subs								
Cappocolla & Cheese/Genoa	570	35	55%	9	55	1600	32	30
Cousins Special	670	44	60%	13	71	1640	38	33
Genoa & Cheese	660	44	60%	15	29	1580	37	30
Regular	610	40	59%	12	65	1500	35	30
Cold 7 1/2" Subs								
BLT (no mayo or cheese)	340	14	4%	5	40	1420	20	34
Club Sub (no mayo or cheese)	340	10	26%	7	110	2050	36	29
Cold Veggie (no mayo or cheese)	290	11	34%	5	12	250	21	27
Ham (no mayo or cheese)	310	9	23%	3	55	1440	30	30
Ham & Cheese	620	14	33%	6.5	77	1750	35	30
Provolone (Cheese) Sub	650	45	42%	21	80	1550	31	30
Roast Beef (no mayo or cheese)	360	8	20%	3	25	1570	41	30
Seafood with Crab	550	34	55%	11	30	1620	25	38
Tuna	750	54	48%	16	90	1400	30	32
Turkey Breast (no mayo or cheese)	320	9	25%	3	70	1980	32	30
Hot 7 1/2" Subs								
Cheese Steak	470	17	32%	6	40	1540	33	46
Double	630	23	36%	8	54	2060	44	62
Chicken Breast (no mayo or cheese)	320	6	17%	2	10	1370	37	30
Gyro, regular	550	23	38%	8	30	1200	28	57
Hot Veggie (no mayo or cheese)	360	14	5%	6	15	320	26	33
Italian Sausage	800	56	64%	20	45	2200	44	51
Meatball & Cheese	660	41	57%	16	90	1610	42	30
Pepperoni Melt	700	46	39%	18	130	1900	41	30
Philly Cheese Steak	510	23	41%	15	45	1430	32	43
Steak (no mayo or cheese)	425	8	17%	4	40	1360	28	51

For mayonnaise add: 235 Cals; 26g Fat; 9g Sat.Fat; 30mg Cholesterol

Cousins Subs® (Cont)

	Cal	Fat	%FC	S.Fat	Chol	Sod	Pro	Carb
Mini 4" Subs: Italian Special	400	26	58%	8	40	970	22	20
Provolone (Cheese)	480	33	62%	15	59	1140	23	22
Ham (no mayo or cheese)	210	5	21%	2	35	960	20	20
Ham & Cheese (no mayo)	430	28	58%	10	63	1220	24	21
Meatball & Cheese	380	23	55%	9	50	930	24	17
Seafood w. Crab	320	20	56%	6	17	940	14	22
Tuna	520	37	64%	11	62	965	21	22
Turkey Breast (no mayo or cheese)	170	4	21%	2	30	745	17	16
For mayonnaise add: 125 Cals; 14g Fat; 4.5g Sat.Fat; 16mg Cholesterol								
French Fries: Small	275	13	43%	5.5	11	240	3.5	38
Medium	400	17	38%	8	16	355	8.5	55
Large	525	25	43%	11	21	465	9	72
Soups: Cheese, regular	210	14	60%	5	20	1120	7	15
Chicken Noodle, regular	105	3	20%	1	20	920	6	13
Chicken w. Wild Rice	185	10	48%	2	18	1070	7	15
Chilli	220	9	37%	3	39	945	16	20
Clam Chowder; Chse Broccoli, reg.	160	9	50%	2	13	640	8	19
Cream of Potato	190	9	43%	3	5	860	5	24
Red Beans & Rice	140	0	0%	0	0	720	6	28
Tomato Base	110	1	8%	0	10	720	4	22
Vegetable Beef	70	1	13%	0	10	890	4	12
Salads: Chef	190	8	38%	4	59	480	25	6
Garden	140	6	38%	0	0	180	15	6
Italian	290	18	56%	7	56	540	26	6
Seafood	175	6	31%	3	65	440	21	12
Side	80	2	22%	0	0	140	8	8
Tuna	260	15	53%	4	45	480	26	6
Cookies: Choc Chip; Cr'berry Walnut	210	11	47%	4	20	190	2	25

Dairy Queen®/Brazier®

	Cal	Fat	%FC	S.Fat	Chol	Sod	Pro	Carb
Burgers								
DQ® Homestyle: Hamburger	290	12	37%	5	45	630	17	29
Cheeseburger	340	17	45%	8	55	850	20	29
Double Cheeseburger	540	31	52%	16	115	1130	35	30
Bacon Double Cheeseburger	610	36	53%	18	130	1380	41	31
Ultimate Burger	670	43	58%	19	135	1210	40	29
Hot Dogs: Regular	240	14	52%	5	25	730	9	19
Chili 'n' Cheese Dog	330	21	57%	9	45	1090	14	22
Sandwiches: Chicken Breast Fillet	430	20	42%	4	55	760	24	37
Grilled	310	10	29%	2.5	50	1040	24	30
with Cheese	480	25	47%	7	70	980	27	38
Chicken Strip Basket: w. Gravy	1000	50	45%	13	55	2260	35	102
The Great Steakmelt™ Basket	750	37	44%	13	75	2000	31	70
French Fries: Small	350	18	46%	3.5	0	630	4	42
Medium	440	23	47%	4.5	0	790	5	53
Onion Rings	320	16	45%	4	0	180	5	39

	Cal	Fat	%FC	S.Fat	Chol	Sod	Pro	Carb
Ice Cream & Desserts								
Cones/Soft Serve:								
DQ® Vanilla Soft Serve, 1/2 cup	140	4.5	29%	3	15	70	3	22
DQ® Choc. Soft Serve, 1/2 cup	150	5	30%	3.5	15	75	4	22
Vanilla Cone: Small	230	7	27%	4.5	20	115	6	38
Medium	330	9	25%	6	30	160	8	53
Large	410	12	26%	8	40	200	10	65
Chocolate Cone: Small	240	8	30%	5	20	115	6	37
Medium	340	11	27%	7	30	160	8	53
Dipped Cone: Small	340	17	45%	9	20	130	6	42
Medium	490	24	44%	13	30	190	8	59
Novelties/Treats: Banana Split	510	12	21%	8	30	180	8	96
Buster Bar®	450	28	56%	12	15	280	10	41
Choc. Chip Cookie Dough Blizzard®:								
Small	660	24	33%	13	55	440	12	99
Medium	950	36	34%	19	75	660	17	143
Choc. Sandwich Cookie Blizzard®:								
Small	520	18	31%	9	40	380	10	79
Medium	640	23	32%	11	45	500	12	97
Chocolate Sundae: Small	280	7	22%	4.5	20	140	5	49
Medium	400	10	22%	6	30	210	8	71
Dilly® Bar: Chocolate	210	13	56%	7	10	75	3	21
DQ® 8" Round Cake, 1/8 Cake	370	13	32%	8	25	280	7	56
DQ® Fudge Bar	50	0	0%	0	0	70	4	13
DQ® Sandwich	150	5	30%	2	5	115	3	24
DQ® Treatzza Pizza™, 1/8 pizza:								
Heath®	180	7	35%	3.5	5	160	3	28
M & M's®	190	7	33%	4	5	160	3	29
DQ® Vanilla Orange Bar	60	0	0%	0	0	40	2	17
Lemon DQ Freez'r®, 1/2 cup	80	0	0%	0	0	10	0	20
Peanut Buster® Parfait	730	31	38%	17	35	400	16	99
Starkiss®	80	0	0%	0	0	10	0	21
Strawberry Shortcake	430	14	29%	9	60	360	7	70
Frozen Yogurt								
Cup of Yogurt: Medium	230	0.5	2%	0	5	150	8	48
DQ® Nonfat Frozen Yogurt, 1/2 cup	100	0	0%	0	0	70	3	21
Heath® Breeze®: Small	470	10	19%	6	10	380	11	85
Medium	710	18	23%	11	20	580	15	123
Strawberry Breeze®: Small	320	0.5	31%	0.5	5	190	10	68
Medium	460	1	31%	1	10	270	13	99
Yogurt Cone: Medium	260	1	5%	0.5	5	160	9	56
Yogurt Strawb. Sundae: Medium	280	0.5	2%	0	5	160	8	61
Malts, Shakes, Slushes, Smoothys								
Chocolate Malt: Medium	880	22	22%	14	70	500	19	153
Chocolate Shake: Medium	770	20	23%	13	70	420	17	130
Misty® Slush: Medium	290	0	0%	0	0	30	0	74
Straw. Banana DQ Glazier Smoothy™	670	14	19%	9	45	250	11	128

	Cal	Fat	%Fc	S.Fat	Chol	Sod	Pro	Carb
Breakfast: Breakfast Burrito	250	11	40%	6	160	520	10	24
Bacon & Egg Quesadilla	450	23	46%	12	260	920	21	40
Egg & Cheese Burrito	450	24	48%	13	530	740	23	39
Macho Bacon & Egg Burrito™	1030	60	52%	20	790	1760	40	82
Steak & Egg Burrito	580	34	53%	16	560	1270	33	41
Tacos: Big Fat Chicken Taco™	340	13	34%	4	45	840	18	38
Big Fat Crispy Chicken Taco™	620	38	55%	9	60	1070	21	52
Big Fat Steak Taco™	390	19	44%	6	45	960	18	38
Big Fat Taco™	320	11	30%	5	35	680	16	39
Chicken Soft Taco	210	12	51%	4	30	520	11	16
Taco; Soft Taco	160	10	56%	4	20	150	7	11
Ultimate Taco	260	17	59%	8	50	470	14	13
Burritos: Combo Burrito™	530	22	37%	13	55	1680	28	61
Bean & Cheese Red/Green Burrito	270	8	26%	5	15	1020	11	36
Chicken Works Burrito	520	23	40%	12	65	1620	26	57
Del Beef Burrito™	550	30	49%	17	90	1090	31	42
Del Classic Chicken Burrito™	560	36	58%	13	70	1100	24	41
Deluxe Combo Burrito™	570	25	39%	15	60	1700	29	64
Deluxe Del Beef Burrito™	590	33	50%	19	95	1110	32	45
Half Pound Red/Gree Burrito	430	12	25%	9	20	1670	20	65
Macho Beef Burrito™	1170	62	47%	29	190	2190	60	89
Macho Combo Burrito™	1050	44	38%	21	115	2760	49	113
Spicy Chicken/Veggie Works Burrito	490	18	33%	11	25	1660	18	69
Steak Works Burrito	590	31	47%	16	70	1820	27	58
Quesadillas: Chicken	530	31	52%	21	104	1240	33	41
Regular	500	27	49%	20	75	860	23	39
Spicy Jack Chicken	570	30	47%	16	105	1300	32	40
Spicy Jack Regular	490	26	48%	17	75	920	23	38
Salads: Deluxe Chicken Salad™	730	34	42%	15	70	2360	33	75
Deluxe Taco Salad™	780	40	46%	18	80	2250	33	76
Tostada	210	9	38%	5	15	640	9	24
Burgers: Cheeseburger	330	13	35%	6	35	870	16	37
Double Del Cheeseburger™	560	35	56%	12	85	960	26	35
Del Cheeseburger™	430	25	52%	7	45	710	16	35
Nachos: Regular	360	24	60%	8	5	630	5	40
Macho Nachos®	1100	63	51%	24	55	2640	31	113
Sides: Beans 'n Cheese Cup	260	3	10%	2	5	1810	16	44
Rice Cup	140	2	13%	1	2	910	3	27
Fries: Chili Cheese, 10.5 oz	670	46	62%	15	45	880	17	51
Deluxe Chili Cheese™, 12 oz	710	49	62%	16	50	880	17	53
Large, 7 oz	490	32	59%	5	0	380	5	47
Regular, 5 oz	350	23	59%	4	0	270	3	34
Small, 3 oz	210	14	60%	2	0	160	2	20
Shakes: Chocolate, small (11.5 fl.oz)	520	12	20%	9	35	270	12	89
Vanilla; Strawb.,small, 11.5 fl.oz	420	7	15%	5	35	250	12	75
Chocolate, large, 15 fl.oz	680	16	21%	12	45	350	16	117
Vanilla; Strawb., large, 15 fl.oz	550	10	16%	6	50	320	16	97

Denny's®

	Cal	Fat	%FC	S.Fat	Chol	Sod	Pro	Carb
Breakfast								
All American Slam	710	62	78%	20	685	1280	38	9
Cinnamon Swirl Slam	1125	78	62%	26	635	1375	38	68
Dagwood Breakfast Slam	1250	90	65%	38	802	3595	75	35
Denver Sam	1140	67	53%	19	795	3150	54	81
Farmer's Slam	1200	80	60%	24	704	2450	50	81
French Slam	1030	71	62%	20	777	1430	44	58
Grand Slam Slugger	790	46	52%	14	487	1440	32	58
Griddle Combo	830	60	65%	19	630	1020	35	40
Original Grand Slam	795	50	57%	14	460	2240	34	65
w. Syrup & Margarine	1030	60	52%	16	460	2385	34	101
Lumberjack Slam	1315	70	48%	18	481	1030	54	118
Scram Slam	740	62	75%	20	685	1295	40	14
Shamrock Slam	865	72	48%	23	515	1230	37	16
Slim Slam (no topping)	495	12	22%	3	34	1020	35	40
Breakfast Sides: Applesauce	60	0	0%	0	0	15	0	15
Bacon, 4 strips	160	18	98%	5	36	640	12	1
Bagel, 1 only	235	1	4%	0	0	495	9	46
Biscuit: Buttered	270	11	36%	4	0	790	5	40
w. Sausage Gravy	400	21	47%	6	12	1265	8	45
Cereal: Kellogg's Dry, average, 1 oz	100	0	0%	0	0	275	2	23
Country Fried Potatoes, 6 oz	515	35	90%	8	8	805	3	23
Cream Cheese, 1 oz	100	10	90%	6	31	90	2	1
Egg: 1 only	120	10	75%	3	210	120	6	1
Two Egg Breakfast	825	67	73%	17	538	1765	31	24
Egg Beaters (Egg Substitute)	70	5	64%	1	1	140	5	1
Flour Tortillas and Salsa	290	8	0%	1.5	0	1030	6	50
Grits, 4 oz	80	0	0%	0	0	520	2	18
Ham, griller slice, 3 oz	95	3	28%	1	23	760	15	2
Hashed Browns, 4 oz	220	14	57%	2	0	425	2	2
Covered, 6 oz	320	23	65%	7	30	605	9	2
Covered & Smothered, 8 oz	360	26	65%	7	30	790	9	26
Dble Covered & Smothered, 13 oz	460	26	50%	7	30	1215	12	48
Muffins: English, each	125	1	7%	0	0	200	5	24
Oatmeal (Quaker), 4 oz	100	2	18%	0	0	175	5	18
Oatmeal N' Fixins	460	6	11%	3	11	85	13	95
Sausage, 4 links	355	32	81%	2	64	945	16	0
Sausage Gravy, 4 oz	125	10	72%	2	12	475	3	6
Syrup: Blueberry/Strawberry, aver.	100	0	0%	0	0	35	12	13
Maple-flavored, 3 Tbsp	145	0	0%	0	0	25	0	36
Sugar-free	25	0	0%	0	0	70	0	9
Toast, 1 slice dry	90	1	10%	0	0	165	3	17
Toppings: Average, 3 oz	105	0	0%	0	0	15	0	26
Whipped Cream, dollop, 2 oz	25	2	72%	0	7	5	0	2
Whipped Margarine, 1/2 oz	90	10	100%	2	0	120	0	0
French Toast: Plain	505	24	43%	6	220	595	16	54
Cinnamon Swirl	1030	49	43%	21	280	675	23	124

	Cal	Fat	%Fc	S.Fat	Chol	Sod	Pro	Carb
Omelette (no extras):								
Eggs Benedict	695	45	58%	11	515	1720	35	34
Farmer's Omelette	915	70	72%	20	635	955	29	29
Ham'n Cheddar	580	45	70%	8	670	1180	37	7
Ultimate	585	47	76%	12	640	940	31	9
Vegge-Cheese	490	40	72%	13	645	535	26	10
Waffles: Plain	305	21	63%	3	146	200	7	23
w. Syrup & Butter	540	31	52%	5	146	345	7	59
Buttermilk Hot Cakes: Plain (3)	490	7	13%	1	0	1820	12	95
w. Syrup & Butter	725	17	21%	3	0	1965	12	130
Skillets: Big Texas Chicken Fajita	1220	70	51%	19	520	1820	49	25
Chicken Fried Steak	1745	104	53%	28	607	2185	60	120
Meat Lover's	1150	93	73%	26	460	2505	41	24
Steak & Eggs (no extras)								
Chicken Fried Steak	430	36	75%	12	440	860	22	10
Moons Over My Hammy	920	60	58%	24	580	2810	54	42
Pork Chop	675	47	62%	13	570	1580	55	7
Sirloin Steak	620	49	71%	18	570	630	44	1
Smoked Moons	840	53	56%	18	544	2260	47	42
T-Bone Steak	990	77	70%	31	655	1005	73	1
Turkey Monte Cristo	860	44	46%	19	265	1745	42	75
Soup: Cheese	295	23	10%	13	20	895	6	13
Chicken Noodle	60	2	30%	0	10	640	2	8
Chili w. Cheese topping	400	19	30%	8	57	1040	25	21
Clam Chowder	215	11	46%	9	5	905	5	22
Cream of Broccoli	195	12	55%	9	0	820	4	15
Cream of Potato	220	12	49%	9	0	760	4	23
Split Pea	145	6	37%	2	5	820	8	18
Vegetable Beef	80	1	11%	1	5	820	6	11
Sandwiches (no fries/sides): BLT	635	46	65%	8	55	1115	18	37
Bacon Cheddar Burger	875	52	53%	19	165	1670	53	58
Big Texas BBQ Burger	930	58	56%	24	163	2270	53	53
Buffalo Chicken Burger	805	45	50%	9	77	2145	37	67
Chicken Burger	630	32	46%	7	82	1970	35	53
Chicken Cordon Bleu	1025	42	37%	14	124	2825	60	97
Classic Burger	675	40	53%	15	105	1140	37	42
w. Cheese	835	55	59%	20	137	1595	47	43
Club Sandwich	720	38	47%	7	75	1665	32	62
Double Decker Burger	1245	80	58%	13	125	2200	50	80
Garden Burger	665	33	44%	8	32	1050	18	75
Garlic Mushroom Swiss Burger	870	51	53%	14	116	1530	43	58
Grilled Chicken	520	14	24%	3	70	1615	35	64
Grilled Chicken (Fit Fare®)	435	9	24%	3	82	2705	35	56
Ham & Swiss on Rye	535	31	52%	4	36	1640	23	40
Rueben	580	35	54%	6	69	2725	27	37
The Super Bird	620	32	46%	5	60	1180	35	48
Turkey Breast w. Multigrain	475	26	49%	5	57	1105	23	39

	Cal	Fat	%Fc	S.Fat	Chol	Sod	Pro	Carb
Salads (no dressing/bread unless indicated)								
Garden Deluxe Salad: w. Chicken Brst	265	11	37%	5	90	715	32	10
w. Buffalo Chicken Strips	515	35	61%	8	79	1200	33	26
w. Fried Chicken Strips	440	26	53%	6	73	1030	33	26
w. Salmon Fillet	340	9	24%	5	124	850	67	10
w. Turkey and Ham	320	11	31%	6	100	1705	43	12
Grilled Chick. Caesar w. Dressing	600	41	61%	10	100	1790	37	20
Side Caesar w. Dressing	360	26	65%	7	23	915	11	22
Side Garden Salad	115	4	31%	1	0	150	3	16
Dressings								
BBQ Sauce, 1.5 oz	50	1	18%	0	0	595	0	11
Blue Cheese, 1 oz	165	18	98%	3	20	205	1	1
Caesar, 1 oz	135	14	93%	2	2	380	1	1
French: Regular, 1 oz	105	10	86%	2	7	275	0	3
Guacamole, 1.5 oz	75	6	72%	2	0	265	1	4
Honey Mustard Fat-Free, 1 oz	40	0	0%	0	0	120	0	9
Horseradish Sauce, 1 oz	170	20	99%	3	45	230	1	3
Italian Dressing: Reduced Calorie	70	7	90%	1	0	150	0	1
Marinara, 1.5 oz	50	2	36%	1	0	205	1	7
Ranch, 1 oz	100	11	99%	2	8	215	1	1
Salsa, 2 oz	10	0	0%	0	0	220	0	15
Sour Cream, 1.5 oz	90	9	90%	6	20	25	1	2
Tartar, 1.5 oz	230	24	94%	3	17	185	0	5
Thousand Island, 1 oz	120	11	82%	2	15	170	0	5
Appetizers								
Buffalo Chicken Strips (5)	735	42	51%	4	96	1675	48	43
Buffalo Wings (12)	855	54	57%	17	500	5550	92	1
Chicken Strips (5)	720	33	41%	4	95	1665	47	56
Mozzarella Sticks (8)	710	41	52%	24	48	5220	36	49
Onion Rings	380	23	54%	6	6	2005	5	38
Sampler	1405	80	51%	24	75	5305	47	124
Entrees								
Charleston Chicken	330	18	49%	4	65	995	25	16
Chicken Fried Steak	265	17	58%	8	27	670	15	14
Chicken Pot Pie Dinner	1065	55	46%	17	124	2915	41	103
Chicken Strip w. Dressing	635	25	35%	1	95	1510	47	55
Fried Shrimp Dinner	330	10	41%	2	135	775	17	18
Grilled Alaskan Salmon Dinner	210	4	17%	1	102	105	43	1
Grilled Chicken Breast Dinner	130	4	28%	1	65	560	24	0
Grilled Chicken Stir-Fry (no bread)	864	10	10%	1	67	3655	43	149
Mandarin Glazed Salmon (no bread)	615	20	29%	4	81	2035	53	58
Pot Roast Dinner w. Gravy	290	11	34%	5	87	930	42	5
Roast Turkey & Stuffing w. Gravy	390	3	69%	1	115	2470	46	38
Sirloin Steak Dinner	340	28	74%	8	345	687	18	1
Steak & Shrimp Dinner	645	42	59%	14	150	1145	36	31
T-Bone Steak Dinner	860	65	29%	18	196	870	65	0
Vegetable Stir-Fry (no bread)	430	9	18%	1	1	1755	12	74

	Cal	Fat	%FC	S.Fat	Chol	Sod	Pro	Carb
Sides								
Broccoli in Butter Sauce	50	2	36%	2	5	280	3	7
Carrots in Honey Glaze	80	3	34%	1	0	220	1	12
Corn in Butter Sauce	120	4	30%	2	5	260	3	19
Bread Stuffing, plain	100	1	9%	0	0	405	3	20
Fries: Unsalted	325	14	39%	3	0	130	5	44
Chili Cheese, 12 oz	815	44	42%	17	74	915	20	77
Seasoned	260	12	42%	3	0	555	5	35
Smothered Cheese, 9 oz	765	48	56%	17	78	875	27	69
Gravy, all types, average	15	0.5	30%	0	0	120	0	2
Green Beans w. Bacon	60	4	60%	2	5	390	1	6
Green Peas in Butter Sauce	100	2	18%	2	5	360	5	14
Grilled Mushrooms	15	0	0%	0	0	0	2	2
Potato: Baked, plain w. skin	220	0	0%	0	0	15	5	51
Mashed	105	1	8%	0	0	380	3	21
Vegetable Rice Pilaf	85	1	10%	0	0	325	2	17
Desserts								
Banana Royale	550	25	41%	15	64	185	6	80
Chocolate Layer Cake	275	12	39%	3	26	375	4	42
Hot Fudge Cake	620	35	50%	17	60	170	7	73
Lowfat Choc Chip Yogurt	110	2	16%	0.5	5	60	4	20
Rainbow Sherbet	120	1.5	11%	1	5	30	1	25
Pies, 1/6 slice: Apple	470	24	46%	6	0	470	3	64
Cheesecake, no topping	470	27	52%	13	90	280	8	48
Cherry	630	25	36%	6	0	550	3	100
Chocolate Peanut Butter	655	39	53%	19	27	320	15	64
Chocolate Silk	650	43	59%	26	165	220	6	60
Dutch Apple	440	19	39%	5	0	290	3	65
Hershey's Choc Chunks N' Chips	600	36	54%	25	10	270	6	58
Oreo® Cookies & Creme	690	30	39%	17	20	390	10	73
Pecan	600	28	42%	4	50	430	5	81
Pumpkin	235	7	21%	2	36	215	3	38
Dessert Toppings								
Blueberry, 2 oz	70	0	0%	0	0	10	0	17
Chocolate, 2 oz	320	25	70%	0	0	85	2	27
Fudge, 2 oz	200	10	45%	7	3	95	1	30
Strawberry, 2 oz	80	1	11%	0	0	10	1	17
Sundaes								
Single Scoop, no topping	190	14	66%	6	37	45	3	14
Double Scoop, no topping	375	27	65%	12	75	85	6	29
Banana Split	895	43	43%	19	80	175	15	112
Butterfinger® Hot Fudge	780	38	43%	25	71	335	10	106
Drinks								
Butterfinger® Blender Blaster	770	38	44%	23	108	345	13	97
Flavored Coffee, average	70	1	13%	1	2	5	0	16
Floats, Rootbeer/Cola	280	10	43%	6	39	110	3	47
Malted Milkshake, van/choc.	585	26	40%	16	108	280	12	82

	Cal	Fat	%Fc	S.Fat	Chol	Sod	Pro	Carb
***14" Hand Tossed:** Per 2 Slices*								
Cheese Pizza (Base)	515	15	26%	7	32	1080	21	75
With Topping: Beef	625	25	36%	11	53	1390	27	75
Cheddar Cheese	590	21	32%	11	50	1190	26	75
Italian Sausage & Mushroom	635	24	34%	10	54	1420	27	80
Pepperoni	615	24	35%	10	52	1445	26	75
X-tra Cheese & Pepperoni	680	29	38%	13	68	1675	30	76
Ham	550	17	28%	7	44	1375	26	75
Vegi	605	22	33%	10	47	1370	26	78
***14" Thin Crust:** Per 1/4 Pizza*								
Cheese Pizza (Base)	385	17	40%	7	32	1170	17	43
With Topping: Beef	495	26	47%	11	53	1480	22	44
Cheddar Cheese	455	22	43%	11	50	1280	21	44
Pepperoni	480	25	47%	10	52	1535	21	44
X-tra Cheese & Pepperoni	550	30	49%	13	54	1765	25	45
Ham	415	18	39%	7	44	1465	21	44
Italian Sausage & Mushroom	500	25	45%	10	54	1515	22	48
Vegi	470	23	44%	10	47	1460	22	47
***14" Deep Dish:** Per 2 Slices*								
Cheese Pizza (Base)	675	30	40%	11	41	1575	26	80
With Topping: Beef	785	40	46%	15	62	1885	31	80
Cheddar Cheese	745	36	43%	15	80	1685	30	80
Pepperoni	775	39	45%	14	61	1940	30	80
X-tra Cheese & Pepperoni	845	44	47%	17	77	2170	27	82
Ham	705	31	40%	11	54	1670	30	80
Italian Sausage & Mushroom	795	39	44%	15	64	1920	32	85
Vegi	765	36	42%	14	57	1865	31	83
***14" Combination Toppings:** Per Serving (Add to Cheese Pizza Base)*								
America's Favorite	175	14	72%	6.5	37	580	10	4
Deluxe	110	9	73%	3.5	21	350	5	3
ExtravaganZZa	190	15	71%	6	37	700	10	4
Hawaiian	105	6.5	55%	3.5	26	465	8	5
Meatzza	240	19	71%	8.5	53	870	14	3
Pepperoni Extra	205	17	74%	8	44	730	11	2
***6" Deep Dish:** Per Pizza*								
Cheese Pizza (Base)	600	27	40%	10	36	1340	23	68
With Topping: Beef	645	31	43%	12	44	1465	25	68
Cheddar Cheese	685	34	45%	15	58	1475	28	68
Pepperoni	650	31	43%	12	46	1525	25	68
Ham	610	28	41%	10	43	1495	25	68
Italian Sausage & Mushroom	650	30	42%	11	45	1475	25	70
Sides: Breadstick, 1 stk	115	4	31%	1	0	150	3	18
Cheesy Bread, 1 piece	140	6	38%	2	6	180	4	18
Barbeque Wings, each	50	2.5	45%	0.5	26	175	6	2
Garden Salad: Small, no dressing	20	0.3	13%	0	0	15	1	4
Large, no dressing	40	0.5	11%	0	0	25	2	8
Hot Wings, each	45	2	40%	0.5	26	355	5	0.5

12" Hand Tossed: Per 2 Slices	Cal	Fat	%Fc	S.Fat	Chol	Sod	Pro	Carb
Cheese Pizza (Base)	375	11	26%	5	23	775	15	55
With Topping: Beef	455	18	35%	8	38	990	19	55
Cheddar Cheese	435	16	33%	8	38	865	18	55
Pepperoni	450	18	36%	8	38	1050	18	55
X-tra Cheese & Pepperoni	500	22	40%	10	49	1215	21	56
Ham	400	12	27%	5	32	990	18	55
Italian Sausage & Mushroom	460	17	33%	7	39	1015	18	58
Vegi	440	16	33%	7	34	985	19	57
12" Thin Crust: Per Slice (1/4)								
Cheese Pizza (Base)	275	12	39%	5	23	835	12	31
With Topping: Beef	355	19	48%	8	38	1050	16	31
Cheddar Cheese	335	17	45%	8	38	925	15	31
Pepperoni	350	19	49%	8	38	1110	15	31
X-tra Cheese & Pepperoni	400	23	50%	10	49	1275	18	32
Ham	300	13	39%	5	32	1050	15	31
Italian Sausage & Mushroom	355	18	46%	7	39	1075	15	33
Vegi	340	17	45%	7	34	1045	16	34
12" Deep Dish: Per 2 Slices								
Cheese Pizza (Base)	480	22	41%	8	30	1125	19	56
With Topping: Beef	560	29	46%	11	45	1340	22	56
Cheddar Cheese	540	27	45%	11	45	1215	23	56
Pepperoni	560	29	46%	10	45	1400	22	56
Ham	505	23	41%	8	39	1340	22	56
Italian Sausage & Mushroom	560	28	45%	10	46	1365	22	59
Vegi	550	27	44%	10	41	1335	22	58
12" Combination Toppings: Per Serving (Add to Cheese Pizza Base)								
America's Favorite	135	11	73%	5	29	450	7	3
Deluxe	90	7	70%	3	17	290	4	2
ExtravaganZZa	155	12	70%	5	30	570	8	3
Hawaiian	75	4.5	54%	2.5	18	325	6	4
Meatzza	185	15	72%	6	42	690	11	2
Pepperoni Extra	150	12	72%	6	32	530	8	1
Toppings: Anchovies	25	1	36%	0	9	395	2	0.5
Bacon	80	6.5	73%	2	10	180	4	0
Cheddar Cheese	55	4.5	74%	3	14	80	3	0.5
Extra Cheese	45	4	71%	2	9	115	3	0
Green Peppers, Onions, Mushrooms	5	0	0%	0	0	1	0	1
Olives: Green	12	1	75%	0	0	245	0	0.5
Ripe	13	1	69%	0	0	65	0	0.5
Dressings: Blue Cheese, 1 1/2 oz	220	24	98%	4	40	440	2	2
Creamy Caesar, 1 1/2 oz	200	22	99%	3	10	470	1	2
Honey French, 1 1/2 oz	210	18	77%	3	0	300	0	14
House Italian, 1 1/2 oz	220	24	98%	3	0	440	0	1
Lite Italian, 1 1/2 oz	20	1	45%	0	0	0	0	2
Ranch, 1 1/2 oz	260	29	100%	4	5	380	0	0.5
Fat Free Ranch, 1 1/2 oz	40	0	0%	0	0	560	0	10
1000 Island, 1 1/2 oz	200	20	90%	3	25	320	0	5

	Cal	Fat	%Fc	S.Fat	Chol	Sod	Pro	Carb
Cake Donuts: Each								
Blueberry	290	16	50%	3.5	10	400	3	35
Butternut	300	16	48%	4.5	0	360	3	36
Chocolate Frosted	300	16	48%	3	0	370	3	38
Chocolate Coconut	300	19	57%	6	0	370	4	31
Cinnamon	270	15	57%	3	0	360	3	31
Coconut	290	17	53%	5	0	360	3	33
Double Chocolate	310	17	50%	3.5	0	370	3	37
Dunkin' Donut	240	15	56%	3	0	340	3	25
Glazed	270	15	57%	3	0	360	3	33
Glazed Chocolate	290	16	50%	3.5	0	370	3	33
Jelly Stick	290	12	37%	2.5	0	390	3	44
Old Fashioned	250	15	54%	3	0	360	3	26
Powdered	270	15	50%	3	0	350	3	32
Sugared	250	15	54%	3	0	350	3	27
Toasted Coconut	300	17	51%	5	0	370	3	35
Whole Wheat Glazed	310	19	55%	4	0	380	4	32
Yeast Donuts: Each								
Apple N' Spice	200	8	36%	1.5	0	270	3	29
Bavarian Kreme	210	9	38%	2	0	270	3	30
Black Raspberry	210	8	34%	1.5	0	280	3	32
Boston Kreme	240	9	33%	2	0	280	3	36
Chocolate Frosted	200	9	40%	2	0	260	3	29
Chocolate/Vanilla Kreme Filled	270	13	43%	3	0	260	3	35
Glazed	180	8	40%	1.5	0	250	3	25
Jelly Filled	210	8	34%	1.5	0	280	3	32
Lemon	200	9	40%	2	0	270	3	28
Maple/Marble Frosted	210	9	38%	2	0	260	3	30
Strawberry	210	8	34%	1.5	0	260	3	32
Strawberry/Vanilla Frosted	210	9	33%	2	0	260	3	30
Sugar Raised	170	8	42%	1.5	0	250	3	22
Muffins: Each								
Apple Cinnamon Pecan	520	21	36%	6	70	610	8	73
Blueberry: Regular	490	18	33%	6	75	630	8	75
Reduced Fat	450	13	26%	9	65	600	8	75
Chocolate Chip: Regular	610	25	37%	10	75	590	10	88
Chocolate Hazelnut Chunk	580	26	40%	9	85	610	11	77
Corn: Regular	500	17	31%	5	80	920	9	80
Reduced Fat	460	12	23%	7	75	900	9	80
Cranberry Orange: Regular	520	16	28%	3.5	30	910	8	86
Honey Raisin Bran	520	16	28%	3.5	30	910	8	86
Crullers/Sticks: French (Cruller)	150	8	48%	2	20	115	2	17
Glazed	290	15	46%	3	0	350	3	37
Glazed Chocolate	280	15	48%	3	0	360	3	35
Plain	240	15	56%	3	0	340	3	25
Powdered	270	15	50%	3	0	340	3	30
Sugar	270	15	50%	3	0	340	3	30

	Cal	Fat	%Fc	S.Fat	Chol	Sod	Pro	Carb
English Muffins: Each								
Bacon & Cheese Omelet	400	21	47%	8	300	1440	21	32
Egg & Cheese	290	12	37%	5	275	910	16	28
Egg, Bacon & Cheese	360	18	45%	8	285	1210	20	29
Egg, Ham & Cheese	360	11	28%	5	235	1330	22	23
Egg, Sausage & Cheese	480	34	64%	12	310	1450	25	28
Plain	130	1	7%	0.5	0	520	4	26
Spanish Omelet	370	17	41%	5	285	1150	17	36
Three Cheese Omelet	400	22	50%	9	305	1450	19	32
Croissants: Each								
Egg & Cheese	430	27	57%	9	280	640	16	30
Bacon & Cheese Omelet	550	37	60%	13	305	1180	21	31
Egg, Bacon & Cheese	500	34	61%	12	290	930	20	30
Egg, Ham & Cheese	530	29	49%	9	295	1080	23	30
Egg, Sausage & Cheese	630	49	70%	15	320	1180	24	30
Plain	290	18	55%	6	5	270	5	26
Spanish Omelet	520	34	59%	11	290	900	18	36
Three Cheese Omelet	550	39	64%	15	310	1190	20	31
Bagels: Bacon & Cheese	600	21	32%	7	300	1620	26	78
Berry Berry	410	1.5	3%	0	0	670	12	87
Blueberry	340	1	3%	0	0	670	10	75
Cinnamon Raisin	340	1	3%	0	0	480	10	74
Egg & Cheese	360	11	28%	5	275	810	17	45
Egg, Bacon & Cheese	360	13	33%	6	260	640	17	44
Egg, Ham & Cheese	460	13	25%	6	275	1060	24	44
Egg, Sausage & Cheese	550	34	56%	12	295	1160	25	44
Everything; Poppyseed	360	2	5%	0	0	710	11	75
Garlic	360	1	2.5%	0	0	720	11	76
Onion	330	1	3%	0	0	660	10	70
Plain	340	1	3%	0	0	710	10	73
Salt	340	1	3%	0	0	3030	10	73
Sesame	380	4.5	10%	0.5	0	720	12	74
Spanish Omelet	570	17	27%	4.5	285	1330	23	82
Three Cheese Omelet	610	22	32%	9	305	1630	25	78
Wheat	330	1.5	4%	0	0	670	12	73
Cream Cheese, (per packet): Lite	130	11	76%	7	30	250	5	3
Average other flavors	180	17	85%	11	50	310	3	3
Cake Munchkins: Butternut (3)	200	11	49%	3	0	240	2	25
Chocolate Glazed (3)	200	10	45%	2	0	250	2	26
Cinnamon (4)	250	14	50%	3	0	330	3	30
Coconut (3)	200	12	49%	3.5	0	240	2	23
Glazed (3)	200	10	45%	2	0	250	2	27
Plain (4)	220	14	57%	3	0	310	2	22
Powdered Sugar (4)	250	14	50%	3	0	310	2	29
Yeast Glazed	200	9	41%	2	0	220	3	27
Yeast Jelly Filled	210	9	38%	2	0	240	3	30
Yeast Lemon Filled	170	8	42%	1.5	0	190	2	23

	Cal	Fat	%Fc	S.Fat	Chol	Sod	Pro	Carb
Fancies								
Apple Danish	380	16	38%	4	2	270	5	53
Apple Fritter	300	14	42%	3	0	360	4	41
Bismark Chocolate Iced	340	15	39%	3.5	0	290	3	50
Bow Tie	300	17	50%	3.5	0	340	4	34
Cherry Danish	350	15	39%	4	2	260	5	48
Cinnamon Bun	510	15	26%	4	10	420	8	85
Cinnamon Danish	480	24	45%	6	3	390	7	58
Coffee Roll	270	14	46%	3	0	340	4	33
Choc./Maple/Vanilla Frosted	290	15	46%	3	0	340	4	36
Eclair	270	11	36%	2.5	0	290	3	39
Glazed Fritter	260	14	48%	3	0	330	4	31
Cookies								
Chocolate varieties	220	12	49%	6	35	110	3	27
Oatmeal Raisin Pecan	220	10	40%	5	30	110	3	29
Peanut Butter varieties	240	14	51%	6	30	150	5	24
Soup								
Beef Barley	90	0.5	5%	0	10	970	7	15
Beef Noodle	90	1	10%	0	20	980	8	12
Chicken Noodle	80	1.5	17%	0	15	890	5	12
Chile	170	6	32%	2.5	20	860	8	20
Chile Con Carne w. Beans	300	15	45%	0	45	690	17	25
Cream of Broccoli	200	11	50%	6	25	1050	8	17
Cream of Potato	190	10	47%	5	25	770	6	19
Harvest Vegetable	80	2	23%	0	0	1120	4	12
Manhattan Clam Chowder	70	0.5	6%	0	5	890	5	11
Minestrone	100	1	9%	0	0	900	5	16
New England Clam Chowder	200	10	45%	3	30	1050	10	16
Split Pea w. Ham	190	9	43%	3	15	830	8	20
Cocoa: Dunkin' Hot	230	8	31%	2	0	310	2	38
Coffee (No Cream or Sugar)								
Decaf (10 oz)	0	0	0%	0	0	0	0	0
Dunkacinno	250	11	40%	3.5	10	240	2	34
Hazelnut (10 oz)	5	0	0%	0	0	10	0	1
Other varieties (10 oz)	5	0	0%	0	0	5	0	1
Cream, 1 oz	60	5.5	83%	3.5	20	10	1	1
Coolatta								
Coffee: w. Cream, 10 oz	410	22	48%	14	75	65	3	51
w. Milk, 10 oz	260	4	7.5%	2.5	15	75	4	52
w. 2% Milk, 10 oz	240	2	7.5%	1.5	10	80	4	52
w. Skim Milk, 10 oz	230	0	0%	0	0	80	4	52
Hazelnut: w. Cream, 16 oz	370	22	54%	13	75	70	3	42
w. Milk, 16 oz	230	4	16%	2.5	15	80	4	43
Mocha w. Milk, 16 oz	230	4	16%	2.5	15	80	4	43
Vanilla Bean, 16 oz	400	7	7%	4	0	170	1	94

	Cal	Fat	%FC	S.Fat	Chol	Sod	Pro	Carb
Bagels								
Average all types, 4 oz	330	1	3%	0	0	500	11	70
Chocolate Chip Bagel, 4 oz	370	3	8%	2	0	500	11	76
Egg Bagel, $3^1/2$ oz	340	3	8%	1	35	510	11	69
Sesame Dip/Sunflower	370	5	12%	1	0	700	12	70
Cream Cheese, Whipped								
Plain, 2 Tbsp	70	7	70%	5	20	65	1	1
Plain Lite, 2 Tbsp	60	5	70%	3	15	85	1	2
Smoked Salmon, 2 Tbsp	60	6	90%	4	20	120	1	1
Flavors, average, 2 Tbsp	70	7	70%	5	15	60	1	4
Spreads: Fruit, 2 Tbsp	75	0	0%	0	0	20	0	19
Honey Butter, 1 Tbsp	90	8	80%	4	15	35	0	4
Hummus, 2 Tbsp	60	4	35%	0.5	0	60	1	6
Peanut Butter, 2 Tbsp	190	15	71%	2	0	140	8	7
Sandwiches								
Baguette, Our Big Hero	920	30	29%	13	90	2640	45	98
BBQ Chicken	550	11	18%	2	50	1680	30	83
Chicago Bagel Dog Asiago	740	34	41%	15	80	1360	29	78
Classic NY Lox & Bagel	660	27	37%	19	85	1150	26	79
Egg Santa Fe	650	24	33%	8	300	1210	30	78
Ham Deli	450	6	12%	2	45	1300	20	74
Holey Cow	900	50	50%	13	105	1450	36	77
Mediterranean Hummus	540	13	22%	4	15	880	18	89
Roast Beef Deli	460	4	7%	2	45	880	31	76
Roast Chicken & Smoked Gouda	520	11	19%	4.5	80	1380	37	68
Smoked Turkey Deli	420	1.5	13%	0	30	1270	25	75
Tuna Salad Deli	500	7	13%	1.5	30	1060	32	77
Turkey Pastrami Deli	440	2	4%	0	40	1610	31	76
Turkey Pastrami Reuben Deli	660	19	26%	6	65	2590	39	83
Veg-Out	490	13	24%	7	30	850	17	77
Soups: Per Regular Cup								
Aztec Chicken Chili	190	6	28%	2	25	680	10	24
Chicken & Wild Rice	190	10	47%	2	25	990	8	18
Chicken Noodle	140	4.5	29%	0	35	880	5	19
Cream of Potato	180	8	40%	2.5	5	830	5	23
Red Beans & Rice	130	0	0%	0	0	660	6	26
Smoked Salmon Corn Chowder	190	8	40%	1.5	10	740	7	24
Tortilla	280	14	45%	4	0	2970	4	29
Turkey w. Chili Beans	240	12	45%	3	35	1160	12	20
Vegetarian Black Bean	160	3.5	20%	1	0	690	9	23
Very Veggie White Bean Chili	190	7	33%	3	10	960	5	27
Bagel Shtick								
Asiago	450	9	18%	5	15	770	20	72
Cinnamon Sugar	570	24	38%	4	0	800	11	79
Everything	380	4.5	10%	0	0	1130	12	73
Potato	350	4.5	12%	1	0	590	10	69
Sesame	420	8	17%	1	0	510	13	75

	Cal	Fat	%Fc	S.Fat	Chol	Sod	Pro	Carb
Bagel Chips								
Plain, 4 oz serving	90	3	30%	0	0	330	2	13
Flavors, average, 1 oz	90	3	30%	0	0	330	2	15
Roll-Ups: Albuquerque Turkey	690	33	43%	14	80	1800	28	71
Baja Shaved Beef	720	36	45%	14	85	1490	30	67
Pacific Smoked Salmon	590	31	47%	18	100	1260	22	55
Thai Noodle & Vegetable	630	21	30%	2	0	1310	24	97
w. Chicken	670	18	24%	1	40	1850	27	99
Cookies & Muffins								
Big Brownie	500	21	38%	4	30	280	4	70
Ice Cinnamon Bun, 4 oz	380	10	24%	2	0	310	8	64
Cookies: Black & White, 4 oz	390	12	28%	3	15	260	3	68
Chocolate Chunk, 4 oz	600	28	42%	10	45	480	8	78
Ginger White Chocolate, 4 oz	510	17	30%	8	25	350	7	81
Oatmeal Raisin, 4 oz	550	21	34%	5	40	320	8	82
Peanut Butter, 4 oz	620	35	50%	10	55	620	10	65
Sugar, 4 oz	610	32	47%	8	55	490	7	73
Muffins: Banana Nut, 5 oz	520	29	50%	5	95	430	9	59
Blueberry, 5 oz	460	24	47%	3	90	410	6	57
Chocolate Chip, 2 oz	240	13	45%	3	40	180	3	28
Lowfat Lemon Poppyseed, 5 oz	370	7	17%	1	0	560	8	69
97% Fat Free Apple Cinnamon, 5 oz	350	1.5	3%	0	0	85	8	77
Mocha Chocolate Chip, 5 oz	550	29	47%	8	95	430	7	66
Scones: All types, 5 oz	490	17	31%	8	45	500	9	75
Garden Salads								
Asian Chicken	480	4.5	8%	1	55	1520	24	84
Bagel Croutons, 1/4 bag	25	1	20%	0	0	75	1	4
Broccoli & Poppyseed Coleslaw	160	9	50%	2	25	250	3	16
Bros. Bistro	1050	52	45%	14	30	1640	28	117
Caesar Side; small	220	17	70%	3	10	520	4	12
Fresh Fruit Cup	110	0.5	4%	0	0	10	1	25
Greek Pasta Salad	450	30	60%	9	45	950	12	35
Grilled Chicken Caesar	480	37	69%	3	75	1100	26	11
Harvest Chick. w. Rosemary, Flatbrd	730	20	25%	5	55	1880	36	103
Idaho Potato Salad	150	7	42%	1.5	5	200	2	19
Mind Bageling Side	220	18	74%	3	0	380	2	13
Roasted Chicken Caesar	890	42	42%	9	85	2050	40	86
Traditional Potato, 1/2 cup	290	24	74%	3	15	600	3	21
Tuna	160	6	38%	1	30	540	21	3
Coffee & Tea: Per 12 fl.oz								
Almond Delight: Iced, 16 oz	180	4	20%	3	15	120	7	28
Non Fat, 12 oz	150	0	0%	0	5	130	8	29
Cafe Latte: Regular	140	5	32%	4	20	140	9	13
Non Fat, regular	100	0	0%	0	5	140	9	14
Cappuccino	90	3.5	25%	2	15	95	6	9
Mocha, 16 oz	210	6	26%	4	15	120	7	33

Other Coffees and Teas ~ See Pages 146-148

	Cal	Fat	%FC	S.Fat	Chol	Sod	Pro	Carb
Chicken: Breast	160	6	34%	2	110	390	26	0
Leg	90	5	50%	2	75	150	11	0
Thigh	180	12	60%	4	130	230	16	0
Wing	110	6	49%	2	80	220	12	0
Tortillas: Corn, each, 6"	70	1	13%	0	0	35	1	14
Flour, each, $6^1/2$"	90	3	30%	0	0	225	3	13
Burritos: Bean, Rice & Cheese	505	16	28%	6	17	1265	17	73
Chicken Lover's	475	19	36%	6	0.5	1375	29	47
Classic	580	22	34%	7	0	1595	31	66
Ultimate	635	23	32%	8	90	1235	39	66
Mexican Chicken Caesar	735	35	43%	8	80	1215	36	65
Southwest	625	27	39%	4	60	1795	30	69
Tacos: Chicken Soft Taco	235	12	46%	4	74	630	17	15
Taco Al Carbon	165	6	33%	2	68	20	13	14
Bowls: Flame Broiled Chicken Salad	355	13	33%	2	42	1080	25	6
Mexican Chicken Caesar Salad	735	35	43%	8	80	1215	36	65
Pollo Bowl: Regular	470	11	21%	2	42	1870	30	66
Smokey Black Bean	605	23	34%	7	54	1955	29	75
Southwest Chicken Salad	530	31	53%	5	52	1330	25	40
Specialties: Chicken Taquito	370	17	42%	4	25	690	15	43
Kids Dinosaur Chicken Bites	185	10	48%	2	64	345	12	11
Tortilla Chips (unsalted), 3 oz	425	24	51%	5	0	12	5	48
Tostada Salad (no Shell/Sour Cream)	305	11	32%	3	57	1175	29	28
Tostada Shell	440	27	55%	4	0	610	7	42
Side Dishes: Cole Slaw	205	16	70%	3	11	360	2	12
Corn Cobbette, $5^1/2$"	80	1	11%	0	0	10	3	18
French Fries, 5.5 oz	445	19	38%	5	0	605	6	61
Garden Salad	105	7	60%	3	15	100	5	7
Macaroni & Salad	245	12	44%	4	22	950	10	24
Pinto Beans	185	4	19%	0	0	745	11	29
Potato Salad	255	14	50%	2	15	525	3	30
Smokey Black Beans	105	16	47%	6	13	730	7	35
Spanish Rice	130	3	20%	1	0	400	2	24
Dressings: Light Italian, 2 oz	25	1	36%	1	0	990	0	3
Ranch, 2 oz	350	39	100%	6	5	500	1	2
1,000 Island; Creamy Cilantro, 2 oz	270	27	90%	4	30	460	1	9
Southwest; Bleu Cheese, 2 oz	300	32	96%	6	50	590	2	2
Condiments: Avocado Salsa, 1 oz	12	1	75%	0	0	205	0	2
Guacamole, 1 oz	30	2	60%	0	0	160	0	3
House/Spicy Chipotle Salsa, 1 oz	6	0	0%	0	0	95	0	2
Jalapeno Hot Sauce, 1 pkt (.5 oz)	5	0	0%	0	0	110	0	1
Light Sour Cream, 1 oz	45	3	60%	0	12	25	2	2
Pizo de Gallo Salsa, 1 oz	11	0.5	41%	0	0	130	0	15
Desserts: Banana Split	715	28	35%	11	56	310	12	107
Churros	180	11	55%	3	5	220	3	18
Foster's Freeze, no cone	180	5	25%	3	20	100	4	30
Smoothies, all types	360	7	17%	3	23	135	3	68

Fazoli's® Italian Food

	Cal	Fat	%FC	S.Fat	Chol	Sod	Pro	Carb
Soup; Bread								
Minestrone Soup	123	1	7%	na	1.5	910	1	23
Breadstick, dry	100	1	9%	na	0	180	4	18
Breadstick	172	8	42%	na	0	180	4	18
Salads: No Dressing								
Garden Salad	30	0	0%	0	0	20	2	6
Italian Chef Salad	262	21	72%	na	46	1445	15	13
Pasta Salad	600	26	39%	na	24	2020	19	68
Dressings: Per 1 oz								
Honey French	146	12	74%	na	0	205	0	9
House Italian	106	9.5	80%	na	0	510	0	5
Reduced Calorie Italian	65	4.5	62%	na	0	395	0	3
Ranch	155	13	75%	na	3	215	0	1
Thousand Island	130	13	90%	na	17	225	0	4
Pizza: Per Double Slice								
Cheese	464	15	27%	na	39	970	24	58
Combination	570	25	39%	na	60	1370	29	63
Pepperoni	526	22	37%	na	53	1225	26	61
Pasta: Per Serving								
Baked Spaghetti Parmesan	697	25	32%	na	60	770	38	76
Baked Ziti: Small	485	17	31%	na	35	575	23	56
Regular	747	26	31%	na	53	865	36	87
Cheese Ravioli: w. Tomato Sauce	476	15	28%	na	66	535	20	65
w. Meat Sauce	510	17	30%	na	72	795	20	65
Chicken Parmesan	465	9	17%	na	86	680	42	47
Fettucine Alfredo: Small	535	15	25%	na	14	170	17	80
Regular	800	22	25%	na	20	230	25	120
Fettucine Broccoli: Small	560	15	24%	na	14	190	20	85
Regular	825	23	25%	na	20	265	27	124
Small Spaghetti: w. Tomato Sauce	356	8	20%	na	0	230	12	62
w. Meat Sauce	370	8	19%	2	20	160	17	60
w. Meatballs	718	31	39%	na	61	725	27	80
Regular Spaghetti: w. Tomato Sauce	510	10	17%	na	0	245	16	93
w. Meat Sauce	553	12	19%	na	30	225	26	90
w. Meatballs	1022	42	37%	na	81	965	38	118
Lasagna: Regular	436	19	39%	na	144	967	21	41
Broccoli	423	18	38%	na	137	760	20	44
Sampler Platter	707	21	27%	na	82	730	26	97
Shrimp & Scallop Fettucine	650	20	27%	na	102	355	31	80
Desserts: Per Serving								
Cheesecake: Plain	338	26	70%	na	110	260	7	20
Turtle	373	27	65%	na	104	250	8	27
Lemon Ice, 12 oz	142	0	0%	0	0	10	0	36
Milk Chocolate Chunk Cookie	360	15	37%	0	30	345	6	54
Strawberry Topping, 1 oz	33	0	0%	0	0	37	0	8

Godfather's™ Pizza

	Cal	Fat	%FC	S.Fat	Chol	Sod	Pro	Carb
Original Crust: Per Slice								
Cheese Pizza: Mini, 1/4 pizza	130	3	26%	na	8	180	7	19
Medium, 1/8 pizza	230	5	26%	na	14	340	13	34
Large, 1/10 pizza	260	6	21%	na	18	395	12	36
Jumbo, 1/10 pizza	380	9	26%	na	27	580	22	53
Combo Pizza: Mini, 1/4 pizza	175	7	27%	na	16	380	10	21
Medium, 1/8 pizza	310	11	34%	na	27	660	17	36
Large, 1/10 pizza	340	12	33%	na	30	740	20	38
Jumbo, 1/10 pizza	505	18	26%	na	47	1095	30	56
Golden Crust: Per Slice								
Cheese Pizza: Medium, 1/8 pizza	210	10	31%	na	12	310	10	26
Large, 1/10 pizza	240	9	34%	na	14	365	12	28
Combo Pizza: Medium, 1/8 pizza	270	12	42%	na	22	560	13	28
Large, 1/10 pizza	305	14	42%	na	25	675	16	31

Golden Corral®

	Cal	Fat	%FC	S.Fat	Chol	Sod	Pro	Carb
Chicken								
Grilled	170	5	26%	na	100	520	32	0
Fried	370	19	46%	na	85	570	37	14
Shrimp, fried	250	12	43%	na	90	470	12	24
Steak: Ribeye, 6 oz	450	35	70%	na	120	220	34	0
Sirloin, 5 oz	230	14	55%	na	90	270	27	0
Chopped, 4 oz	320	23	65%	na	100	160	28	0
Tips w. Onions	290	13	40%	na	120	260	30	8
Baked Potato	225	2	8%	na	0	60	5	46
Texas Toast	170	6	32%	na	0	230	5	26

Haagen-Dazs®

	Cal	Fat	%FC	S.Fat	Chol	Sod	Pro	Carb
Ice Cream: Per 1/2 Cup								
Baileys Irish Cream	270	17	56%	10	38	85	5	23
Belgian Chocolate Chocolate	330	21	57%	12	85	60	5	29
Brownies a la Mode	280	18	58%	11	100	115	4	26
Butter Pecan	310	23	67%	11	110	160	5	20
Capppucino Commotion	310	21	61%	12	100	105	5	25
Caramel Cone Explosion	310	20	58%	12	95	130	5	27
Cherry Vanilla	240	15	60%	10	100	75	4	23
Chocolate	270	18	60%	11	115	75	5	22
Chocolate Chocolate Chip/Mint	300	20	60%	12	100	70	5	26
Coffee	270	18	60%	11	120	85	5	21
Coffee Chip	290	19	59%	12	100	75	5	25
Cookie Dough Dynamo	300	19	57%	12	95	140	4	29

Continued Next Page

	Cal	Fat	%Fc	S.Fat	Chol	Sod	Pro	Carb
Ice Cream: Per 1/2 Cup (Cont)								
Cookies & Cream	270	17	57%	11	110	115	5	23
Deep Chocolate Peanut Butter	350	24	62%	11	80	100	8	28
Dulce De Lache Caramel	290	17	53%	10	100	110	5	28
French Vanilla Coffee	270	18	60%	11	120	85	5	21
Macadamia Brittle	300	20	60%	11	110	120	4	25
Macadamia Nut	320	24	68%	12	110	115	5	20
Midnight Cookies & Cream	300	18	54%	11	90	140	5	29
Mint Chip	290	19	58%	12	105	105	4	26
Pralines & Cream	290	18	56%	9	95	180	4	27
Rum Raisin	270	17	57%	10	110	75	4	22
Strawberry	250	16	58%	10	95	80	4	23
Strawberry Cheesecake Craze	270	16	53%	9	100	140	4	27
Swiss Chocolate Almond	300	20	60%	11	100	65	6	23
Vanilla	270	16	53%	11	120	85	5	21
Vanilla Chocolate Chip	310	20	58%	12	105	90	5	28
Vanilla Swiss Almond	310	21	61%	11	105	80	6	23
***Lowfat Ice Cream:** Per 1/2 Cup*								
Chocolate Fudge Brownie	190	2.5	12%	1.5	30	110	7	34
Coffee Fudge	170	2.5	13%	1.5	25	95	5	32
Strawberry	150	2	60%	1	15	40	5	28
Vanilla Caramel	180	2.5	68%	1.5	20	120	6	32
Ice Cream Sandwich								
Vanilla	260	15	52%	9	65	125	4	32
Vanilla & Chocolate	270	14	46%	8	65	120	4	32
Ice Cream Bars: Single Pack								
Chocolate & Dark Chocolate	350	24	62%	15	85	60	5	28
Coffee Almond Crunch	360	26	65%	15	100	85	5	27
Strawberry White Chocolate	320	23	64%	14	70	75	4	24
Vanilla & Almonds	370	27	66%	14	90	80	6	26
Vanilla & Milk Chocolate	330	24	65%	14	90	75	5	24
Sorbet: Per 1/2 Cup								
Tropical Passionfruit	120	0	0%	0	0	0	0	28
Chocolate	120	0	0%	0	0	70	2	28
Mango; Raspberry; Zesty Lemon	120	0	0%	0	0	0	0	31
Margarita; Strawberry	130	0	0%	0	0	0	0	32
Soft Serve: Mango; Raspberry	100	0	0%	0	0	0	0	25
***Frozen Yogurt:** Per 1/2 Cup*								
Vanilla; Cherry Vanilla	140	0	0%	0	<5	45	6	30
Vanilla Fudge	160	0	0%	0	<5	100	6	34
Vanilla Raspberry Swirl	130	0	0%	0	<5	30	4	28
Soft Serve								
Coffee	140	4	26%	2.5	35	75	5	20
Nonfat Chocolate/Vanilla	110	0	0%	0	0	65	4	23
Nonfat Chocolate Mousse	80	0	0%	0	0	65	5	24

	Cal	Fat	%FC	S.Fat	Chol	Sod	Pro	Carb
Breakfast Items								
Biscuits: Rise 'N' Shine	390	21	48%	6	0	1000	6	44
Apple Cinnamon 'N' Raisin	200	8	36%	2	0	350	2	30
Sausage	510	31	55%	10	25	1360	14	44
Sausage & Egg	630	40	57%	22	285	1480	23	45
Bacon & Egg	570	33	52%	11	275	1400	22	45
Bacon, Egg & Cheese	610	37	55%	13	280	1630	24	45
Ham	400	20	45%	6	15	1340	9	47
Ham, Egg & Cheese	540	30	50%	11	285	1660	20	48
Country Ham	430	22	46%	6	25	1930	15	45
Ultimate Omelet	570	33	52%	12	290	1370	22	45
Big Country:								
Sausage	1000	66	59%	38	570	2310	41	62
Bacon	820	49	54%	15	535	1870	33	62
Frisco Breakfast Sandwich (Ham)	500	25	45%	9	290	1370	24	46
Hash Rounds	230	14	55%	3	0	560	3	24
Biscuit 'N' Gravy	510	28	49%	9	15	1500	10	55
Pancakes: Three Pancakes	280	2	6%	1	15	890	8	56
w. 1 Sausage Pattie	430	16	33%	6	40	1290	16	56
w. 2 Bacon Strips	350	9	23%	3	25	1130	13	56
Hamburgers & Sandwiches								
Hamburger	270	11	37%	3	35	670	14	29
Cheeseburger	310	14	41%	6	40	890	16	30
Mushroom 'N' Swiss	490	25	46%	12	80	1100	28	39
Cravin' Bacon Cheeseburger	690	46	60%	15	95	1150	30	38
1/4 Pound Double Cheeseburger	470	27	52%	11	80	1290	27	31
Frisco Burger	720	46	57%	16	95	1340	33	43
Roast Beef: Regular	320	16	45%	6	43	820	17	26
Big	460	24	47%	9	70	1280	26	35
The Boss	570	33	52%	12	85	910	27	42
The Works	530	30	51%	12	80	1030	25	41
Mesquite Bacon Cheeseburger	370	18	44%	7	45	970	19	32
Chicken Fillet Sandwich	480	18	44%)	3	55	1280	26	54
Grilled Chicken Sandwich	350	11	28%	2	65	950	25	38
Hot Ham 'N' Cheese	310	12	35%	6	50	1410	16	34
Fisherman's Fillet	560	27	43%	7	65	1330	26	54
Fried Chicken								
Breast, each	370	15	36%	4	75	1190	29	29
Wing, each	200	8	36%	2	30	740	10	23
Thigh, each	330	15	41%	4	60	1000	19	30
Leg, each	170	7	37%	2	45	570	13	15
French Fries: Small	240	10	37%	3	0	100	4	33
Medium	350	15	39%	4	0	150	5	49
Large	430	18	38%	5	0	190	6	59
Mashed Potatoes, 4 oz	70	0.5	6%	0.5	0	330	2	14
Gravy, 1.5 oz	20	0.5	22%	0	0	260	1	3
Baked Beans, 5 oz	170	1	5%	0	0	600	8	32

Hardee's® (Cont)

	Cal	Fat	%Fc	S.Fat	Chol	Sod	Pro	Carb
Salads & Dressings: ColeSlaw	240	20	75%	3	10	340	2	13
Side Salad; no dressing	25	0.5	18%	0	0	45	1	4
Garden Salad; no dressing	220	13	53%	9	40	350	12	11
Grilled Chicken Salad; no dressing	150	3	18%	1	60	610	20	11
Fat Free French Dressing	70	0	0%	0	0	580	0	17
Ranch Dressing	290	29	90%	4	25	510	1	6
Thousand Island Dressing	250	23	83%	3	35	540	1	9
Shakes & Desserts								
Vanilla	350	5	13%	3	20	300	12	65
Chocolate	370	5	12%	3	30	270	13	67
Strawberry	420	4	9%	3	20	270	11	83
Peach	390	4	9%	3	25	290	10	77
Cool Twist: Vanilla Cone	170	22	11%	1	10	130	4	34
Chocolate Cone	180	2	1%	1	5	110	5	34
Sundaes: Hot Fudge	290	6	19%	3	20	310	7	51
Strawberry	210	2	9%	1	10	140	5	43
Big Cookie	280	12	39%	4	15	150	4	41
Peach Cobbler: Small	310	7	20%	1	0	360	2	60

Harveys®

	Cal	Fat	%Fc	S.Fat	Chol	Sod	Pro	Carb
Breakfast Items								
Pancakes	90	1	10%	na	8	na	2	17
Sausage	170	14	75%	na	12	na	9	3
Toast, plain	250	3	11%	na	1	na	8	48
Burgers								
Hamburger: Regular	360	14	35%	na	17	na	12	40
Double	530	26	44%	na	34	na	31	44
Super	480	19	36%	na	112	na	37	38
Cheeseburger	420	18	39%	na	30	na	22	41
Chicken Fingers, 1 serving	240	12	45%	na	57	na	15	18
Sandwiches: Chicken	420	16	34%	na	110	na	19	46
Western	350	10	26%	na	265	na	15	58
Sides: French Fries	480	24	45%	na	5	na	10	56
Hash Browns	150	9	55%	na	2	na	2	15
Hot Dog	330	15	41%	na	50	na	12	32
Onion Rings	290	14	44%	na	5	na	4	36
Muffins								
Blueberry	260	6	21%	na	1	na	4	45
Bran	300	13	39%	na	1	na	5	42
Apple Turnover, each	180	7	35%	na	7	na	1	28
Drinks: Apple Juice	80	2	23%	na	0	na	2	20
Orange Juice	80	1	12%	na	0	na	1	18
Shakes: Chocolate	320	11	31%	na	36	na	12	74
Strawberry; Vanilla	300	10	30%	na	36	na	11	69

I Can't Believe It's Yogurt®

	Cal	Fat	%Fc	S.Fat	Chol	Sod	Pro	Carb
Original Frozen Yogurt								
Per Regular Serving (9 fl.oz)								
Awesome Amaretto	280	6	19%	4	20	230	6	51
Cookies 'N Cream	260	3	10%	1	5	200	7	54
French Vanilla	260	6	20%	4	45	200	7	47
Peanut Butter Bliss	310	12	46%	4	15	200	7	46
White Chocolate Mousse	280	7	22%	4	15	200	7	49
Nonfat Frozen Yogurt								
Average all flavors: Regular	220	0.5	2%	0	5	150	6	48
Small, 6.2 fl.oz	160	0	0%	0	0	100	4	32
Nonfat (w. NutraSweet)								
Average all flavors: Regular	190	0.5	2%	0	5	160	6	40
Small, 6.2 fl.oz	140	0.5	3%	0	5	110	4	29

In-N-Out Burger®

	Cal	Fat	%Fc	S.Fat	Chol	Sod	Pro	Carb
Burgers								
Hamburger	390	19	44%	5	40	640	16	39
Cheeseburger	480	27	50%	10	60	1000	22	39
Double Double® (2 patties/2 sl. chse)	670	41	55%	18	120	1430	37	40
French Fries, 125g	400	18	27%	5	0	245	7	54
Shakes (15 oz)								
Chocolate	690	36	55%	24	95	350	9	83
Vanilla	680	37	57%	25	90	390	9	78
Strawberry	690	33	51%	22	85	280	8	91

Int'l House of Pancakes ~ IHOP®

	Cal	Fat	%Fc	S.Fat	Chol	Sod	Pro	Carb
Pancakes: (Syrup/Butter extra)								
Buttermilk, 1 (2 oz)	110	3	25%	1	30	450	3	17
Short Stack, 3	330	9	25%	3	90	1350	9	51
Full Stack, 5	550	15	25%	5	150	2250	15	85
Buckwheat, 1 (2 oz)	110	4	33%	1	50	280	3	15
Country Griddle, 1 (2 oz)	120	3.5	26%	1	38	440	3	19
Harvest Grain 'N Nut, 1(2 1/4 oz)	180	9	45%	1.5	38	410	5	20
Crepes (Egg Pancakes), 1 (2 oz)	120	6	45%	1.5	66	230	3	14
Syrup: 1 Tbsp	50	0	0%	0	0	0	0	12
Whipped Butter, 1 Tbsp	70	7	90%	4.5	20	70	0	0
Waffles (Plain): Regular, 1 (3 oz)	310	15	43%	3.5	70	380	6	37
Belgian: Regular, 1 (4 oz)	390	19	44%	12	145	850	8	48

Jack in the Box®

	Cal	Fat	%Fc	S.Fat	Chol	Sod	Pro	Carb
Breakfast								
Biscuit	190	9	42%	2.5	0	500	3	24
Breakfast Jack	280	12	38%	5	190	750	17	28
French Toast Sticks	420	20	42%	4	5	420	7	53
Hash Browns	170	12	63%	2	0	250	1	14
Sausage Biscuit	380	27	73%	8	35	730	11	25
Sausage Croissant	660	48	65%	15	240	860	20	37
Sausage, Egg & Cheese Biscuit	510	36	63%	12	220	1050	19	27
Sourdough Breakfast Sandwich	450	24	48%	8	205	1040	21	36
Supreme Croissant	530	34	57%	10	225	1060	21	37
Ultimate Breakfast Sandwich	600	34	51%	10	410	1480	34	39
Country Crock Spread	25	3	100%	0.5	0	45	0	0
Grape Jelly, 1 packet	40	0	0%	0	0	5	0	10
Syrup	130	0	0%	0	0	5	0	30
Burgers								
Cheeseburger	330	15	41%	6	60	760	15	32
Bacon Bacon	760	50	59%	17	135	1570	39	39
Bacon Ultimate	1020	71	62%	26	210	1740	58	37
Double	440	24	49%	11	80	1110	24	31
Ultimate	950	66	62%	26	195	1370	52	37
Hamburger	250	9	32%	3.5	30	610	12	30
Hamburger w. Cheese	300	13	39%	6	40	840	14	31
Jumbo Jack: Regular	550	30	49%	10	75	880	27	43
w. Cheese	640	38	53%	15	105	1340	31	44
Sourdough Jack	690	45	58%	15	105	1180	34	37
Sandwiches								
Chicken Fajita Pita	320	10	28%	4.5	55	850	24	34
Chicken Sandwich	400	21	47%	3	40	770	15	38
Chicken Supreme	830	49	53%	7	65	2140	33	66
Grilled Chicken Fillet	480	24	45%	6	65	1110	27	39
Jack's Spicy Chicken	570	29	45%	2.5	50	1020	24	52
Finger Foods								
Bacon/Cheddar Potato Wedges	750	50	60%	16	45	1510	20	55
Chicken Breast Pieces: 5 piece	360	17	43%	3	80	970	27	24
Egg Rolls: 1 piece	150	8	48%	2	10	340	5	13
3 piece	440	24	49%	6	30	1020	15	40
Fish & Chips	780	39	45%	9	45	1740	19	86
Stuffed Jalapenos: 3 piece	230	13	50%	5	25	740	7	20
7 piece	530	31	52%	12	60	1730	16	46
Mexican Food								
Monster Taco	270	17	56%	6	30	630	12	19
Salsa	10	0	0%	0	0	200	0	2
Taco	170	10	52%	3.5	15	390	7	12
Teriyaki Bowls								
Chicken	670	4	5%	1	15	1730	26	132
Soy Sauce	5	0	0%	0	0	480	<1	<1

	Cal	Fat	%Fc	S.Fat	Chol	Sod	Pro	Carb
Salads: *No Dressing*								
Garden Chicken	200	9	40%	4	65	420	23	8
Side	50	3	51%	2	10	75	2	3
Salad Dressings								
Blue Cheese	210	15	64%	2.5	25	750	1	11
Buttermilk House	290	30	93%	11	20	560	1	6
Low Calorie Italian	25	1.5	54%	0	0	670	0	2
Thousand Island	250	24	86%	4	35	570	1	10
Croutons	50	2	36%	1.5	0	100	1	8
Curly Fries								
Chili Cheese	650	41	57%	12	25	1760	14	60
Seasoned	410	23	50%	5	0	1010	6	45
French Fries: Regular	350	16	41%	4	0	710	4	46
Jumbo Fries	430	20	43%	5	0	890	4	58
Super Scoop	610	28	41%	6	0	1250	6	82
Onion Rings	450	25	50%	5	0	780	7	50
Condiments								
Cheese: American, 1 slice	45	4	70%	2	10	230	2	1
Swiss-style, 1 slice	40	3	67%	2	10	210	2	1
Dipping Sauce: Barbecue	45	0	0%	0	0	310	1	11
Buttermilk House	130	13	90%	5	10	240	<1	3
Frank's Red Hot Buffalo	10	0	0%	0	0	840	0	2
Sweet & Sour	45	0	0%	0	0	160	<1	11
Tartar	210	22	94%	3	30	340	1	2
Packet Sauce: Chinese Hot Mustard	10	0	0%	0	0	50	0	1
Hot Sauce	5	0	0%	0	0	110	<1	1
Ketchup	10	0	0%	0	0	105	0	2
Mayonnaise	150	17	100%	2.5	15	120	0	0
Mustard	5	0	0%	0	0	55	0	0
Sour Cream	60	6	90%	4	20	30	1	1
Desserts: Cheesecake	320	18	50%	10	65	220	7	32
Double Fudge Cake	300	10	30%	2	50	320	3	50
Hot Apple Turnover	340	18	49%	4	0	510	4	41
Ice Cream Shakes								
Cappuccino, regular	630	29	41%	17	90	320	11	80
Chocolate, regular	630	27	39%	16	85	330	11	85
Oreo Cookie Classic, regular	740	36	43%	19	95	490	13	91
Strawberry, regular	640	28	39%	15	85	300	10	85
Vanilla, regular	610	31	46%	18	95	320	12	73
Drinks								
Barq's Root Beer, regular	180	0	0%	0	0	40	0	50
Coca Cola, regular	170	0	0%	0	0	12	0	46
Dr Pepper, regular	190	0	0%	0	0	25	0	49
Lowfat Milk (2%) 8 fl.oz	130	5	34%	3	25	85	9	14
Orange Juice, 10 fl.oz	150	0	0%	0	0	20	2	34
Sprite, regular	160	0	0%	0	0	40	0	41

Jamba Juice®

	Cal	Fat	%Fc	S.Fat	Chol	Sod	Pro	Carb
Smoothies: Per 24 fl.oz								
Aloha Pineapple™	430	2	4%	0	0	40	5	103
Banana Berry™	440	2	4%	0	0	30	7	96
Caribbean Passion®	415	2	5%	0	0	40	2	98
Chocolate Moo'd™	650	8	11%	4	10	30	15	131
Citrus Squeeze®: Orange-A-Peel™	420	2	4%	0	0	30	4	96
Coffee Moo'd™	595	6	9%	1	0	100	13	121
Coldbuster™	430	2	4%	0	0	100	5	97
Cranberry Craze®	395	2	4%	0	0	50	5	89
Jamba Powerboost™	455	2	4%	0	0	30	9	100
Kiwi-Berry®	420	0	0%	0	0	50	3	100
Lime Sublime™	410	2	4%	0	0	20	3	95
Mango-A-Go-Go™	460	2	4%	0	0	20	2	109
Mocha Moo'd™	625	7	10%	2	10	20	14	126
Orange Berry Blitz™	375	2	5%	0	0	30	5	84
Orchard Oasis™	435	2	4%	0	0	30	2	102
Peach Pleasure®	440	2	4%	0	0	30	3	104
Peanut Butter Moo'd™	755	19	22%	4	0	20	23	124
Peenya Kowlada®	565	5	8%	1	0	30	8	123
Protein Berry Pizazz™	475	1	2%	0	0	20	25	91
Raspberry Refresher™	440	3	6%	0	0	40	3	101
Razzmatazz™	440	2	4%	0	0	30	3	102
Strawberries Wild™	415	1	2%	0	0	40	6	96

Note: Figures for saturated fat, cholesterol and sodium are author estimates.

Original Recipe®	Cal	Fat	%FC	S.Fat	Chol	Sod	Pro	Carb
Breast	400	24	54%	6	135	1115	29	16
Drumstick	140	9	58%	2	75	420	13	4
Thigh	250	18	65%	4.5	95	750	16	6
Whole Wing	140	10	64%	2.5	55	415	9	5
Extra Crispy™ : Breast	470	28	54%	8	160	874	39	17
Drumstick	195	12	52%	3	77	375	15	7
Thigh	380	27	61%	7	118	625	21	14
Whole Wing	220	15	58%	4	55	415	10	10
Hot & Spicy Chicken: Breast	505	29	52%	8	162	1170	38	23
Drumstick	175	10	51%	3	77	360	13	9
Thigh	355	26	66%	7	126	630	19	13
Whole Wing	210	15	64%	4	55	350	10	9
Other Entrees: Chunky Pot Pie	770	42	49%	13	70	2160	29	69
Crispy Strips: Colonels, 3 pieces	300	16	48%	4	56	1105	26	18
Spicy, 3 pieces	335	15	40%	4	70	1140	25	23
Popcorn Chicken: Small, 3.5 oz	362	23	57%	6	43	610	17	21
Large, 6 oz	620	40	58%	10	73	1046	30	38
Wings: Hot Wings, 6 pieces	470	33	63%	8	150	1230	27	18
Honey BBQ Wings, 6 pces	607	38	56%	10	193	1145	33	33
Sandwiches								
Original Recipe Chicken: w. Sauce	450	22	44%	5	70	940	29	39
without Sauce	360	13	33%	3.5	60	890	36	36
Honey BBQ Flavored Chicken, w. Sce	310	6	17%	2	125	560	28	37
Triple Crunch Chicken: w. Sauce	490	29	53%	6	70	710	26	39
without Sauce	390	15	34%	4.5	50	650	25	29
Triple Crunch Zinger: w. Sauce	550	32	52%	7	65	630	26	39
without Sauce	390	15	34%	4.5	50	650	36	36
Tender Roast Chicken: w. Sauce	350	15	38%	3	75	880	32	26
without Sauce	270	5	16%	1.5	65	690	31	23
Side Dishes: Per Serving								
BBQ Baked Beans, 5.5 oz	190	3	14%	1	5	760	6	33
Biscuit, 2 oz	180	10	50%	2.5	0	560	4	20
Coleslaw, 5 oz	232	13	52%	2	8	284	2	26
Corn on the Cob, 5.7 oz	150	1.5	14%	0.5	0	20	5	35
Macaroni & Cheese, 5.4 oz	180	8	40%	3	10	860	7	21
Mashed Potatoes w. Gravy, 4.8 oz	120	6	45%	1	<1	440	1	17
Potato Salad, 5.6 oz	230	14	55%	2	15	540	4	23
Potato Wedges, 4.8 oz	280	13	42%	4	5	750	5	28
Desserts: Dble Choc Chip Cake, 2.7 oz	320	16	45%	4	65	230	4	41
Little Bucket Parfaits: Chocolate Crm	290	18	56%	11	15	330	3	37
Fudge Brownie	280	10	32%	3.5	145	190	3	44
Lemon Creme	410	14	30%	8	20	290	7	62
Strawberry Shortcake	200	7	31%	8	10	220	1	33
Colonels Pies: Apple Pie Slice, 4 oz	310	14	40%	3	0	280	23	44
Pecan Pie Slice, 4 oz	490	23	42%	5	85	510	5	68
Strawberry Creme Pie Slice, 2.7 oz	280	15	48%	8	15	130	4	32

	Cal	Fat	%Fc	S.Fat	Chol	Sod	Pro	Carb
Original Skinless Flame Broiled Chicken								
Leg & Thigh	175	8	41%	2	54	365	21	3
Breast & Wing (skin on wing)	220	8	33%	2	27	495	34	3
Original Breast Meat	160	4	32%	1	23	400	28	2
Half Original Chicken (skin on wing)	390	16	37%	4	81	860	55	6
Rotisserie Chicken: Leg & Thigh	300	18	54%	5	114	515	31	1
Breast & Wing	355	16	40%	4	140	675	50	1
Half Rotisserie Chicken	655	34	46%	9	254	1190	80	2
Fresh Roasted Carved Turkey								
Turkey Breast Sandwich	540	7	11%	0	118	800	49	68
1/2 Turkey Breast Sandwich	270	4	13%	0	60	400	25	34
1/4 lb Sliced White Meat	155	1	6%	0	95	60	34	0
1/4 lb Sliced Dark Meat	210	8	34%	3	96	90	32	0
Open-Faced Turkey S'wich: w. extras	670	21	28%	10	161	1395	51	69
Hand-Carved Turkey Dinner: w. extras	705	21	27%	10	160	1420	53	76
Turkey Pot Pie, 5.5 oz	905	45	45%	12	165	1380	42	83
Salads: Per Regular (no dressing)								
BBQ Chicken Salad, 15 1/2 oz	465	21	40%	8	121	740	40	30
Caesar Salad, 9 1/2 oz	170	8	42%	4	11	485	10	16
Chicken Caesar Salad, 12 oz	310	11	32%	4	83	545	36	16
Chinese Chicken Salad, 17 oz	295	8	24%	2	71	170	31	23
Koo Koo Roo House Salad, 16 oz	165	6	32%	2	7	360	9	21
Koo Koo Roo Slaw (side)	55	2	32%	0	0	230	1	10
Pesto Pasta Salad	170	5	26%	1	16	250	10	21
12 Vegetable Chopped Salad, 13 oz	80	1	11%	0	0	65	5	16
Soup: Ten Vegetable, 8 oz	120	3	22%	0	0	620	3	21
Sandwiches: BBQ Chicken	570	14	22%	7	115	1540	43	69
Original Chicken Breast	750	47	56%	9	128	1075	35	50
Chicken Caesar	730	37	45%	12	144	2140	51	49
Turkey Breast	540	7	11%	0	118	800	49	68
Dressings: Balsamic Viniagrette, 2 T.	90	9	90%	1	0	240	0	3
BBQ, 2 Tbsp	40	0	0%	0	0	280	0	10
Caesar, 2 Tbsp	160	17	95%	4	14	180	0	1
Chinese Chicken Salad, 2 Tbsp	110	8	65%	2	0	110	0	8
Chopped Salad, 2 Tbsp	100	7	63%	5	0	350	0	8
Cranberry Sauce, 1 oz	45	0	0%	0	0	15	0	11
Gravy, 2 oz	25	1	36%	0	0	310	1	3
Lahvash (flatbread), each	95	0	0%	0	0	145	4	20
Hot Sides								
Baked Yam	360	0	0%	0	0	25	5	86
Black Beans	140	2	13%	0	0	570	8	23
Confetti Rice	130	0	0%	0	0	165	3	30
Creamed Spinach	140	12	77%	6	38	395	3	9
Hand-Mashed Potatoes	185	5	24%	3	15	360	3	32
Italian Vegetables	35	2	50%	1	5	125	1	4
Macaroni & Cheese	270	11	36%	6	31	245	11	28
Roasted Garlic Potatoes	115	2	15%	1	3	165	2	22

Krystal®

	Cal	Fat	%Fc	S.Fat	Chol	Sod	Pro	Carb
Breakfast								
Biscuit: Plain	260	15	52%	4	0	570	4	27
Bacon, Egg & Cheese	390	25	57%	8	225	870	12	28
Chik	340	17	45%	6	25	990	11	34
Sausage	440	32	65%	11	55	850	12	27
Country Breakfast	660	42	57%	14	590	1450	24	46
Hash Browns	190	13	61%	5	10	340	1	17
Sunriser	240	14	52%	5	255	460	12	14
Sandwiches								
Krystal: Regular	160	7	39%	3	20	260	7	17
Double	260	13	45%	6	40	550	13	24
Bacon Cheese	190	10	47%	4.5	25	430	10	16
Chik	240	11	41%	3.5	25	640	11	24
Cheese	180	9	45%	4	25	430	9	16
Double Cheese	310	16	46%	7	65	800	16	26
Chili Cheese Pup	210	12	51%	5	40	510	9	17
Corn Pup	260	19	66%	8	50	480	5	19
Plain Pup	170	9	47%	3.5	25	500	6	15
Fries: Regular	370	18	44%	7	15	85	4	49
Chili Cheese	540	28	46%	13	45	800	13	59
Desserts/Drinks								
Chocolate Shake	380	11	26%	7	50	410	12	58
Krystal Chill	200	7	31%	3.5	25	1130	13	22
Apple Turnover	220	10	41%	3.5	0	300	3	31
Lemon Pie	360	10	25%	3.5	55	190	7	60

La Salsa Fresh Mexican Grill®

	Cal	Fat	%Fc	S.Fat	Chol	Sod	Pro	Carb
Estimates Only								
Taco: Mexico City Taco, Chicken	250	7	20%	2	50	130	17	27
Fish Taco (Sonora)	225	9	36%	4	45	440	15	21
La Salsa, Chicken w. Cheese	300	10	30%	4	55	220	17	35
Vegetarian w. Cheese	290	8	25%	3	5	285	12	39
Burrito								
Bean & Cheese	535	14	24%	6	10	920	16	27
Californian 'Veggie'	600	19	29%	8	20	800	20	87
El Champion Burrito (12", 2lbs)	1100	52	43%	18	200	1200	60	100
Burrito Grande	550	26	43%	9	95	530	30	50
Sides: Cheese, 0.5 oz	60	5	75%	3	20	150	3	30
Black Beans (no cheese), 5 oz	290	1	3%	1	0	110	15	38
Rice, 3.5 oz	170	3	16%	0	0	230	3	30
1/2 Rice & 1/2 Beans (no cheese)	310	3	10%	0	9	250	9	44
Salsa, 2 Tbsp	15	0	0%	0	0	300	0	3

Little Caesars® Pizza

Pizza: Per Slice	Cal	Fat	%Fc	S.Fat	Chol	Sod	Pro	Carb
12" Round: Cheese	160	6	33%	3	15	320	8	22
Pepperoni	180	8	40%	3	20	420	9	21
12" Square: Cheese	140	5	32%	2	10	280	7	19
Pepperoni	160	6	33%	2.5	15	350	8	19
12" Thin: Cheese	120	6	45%	2.5	15	280	6	12
Pepperoni	150	8	48%	3.5	20	380	7	12
14" Round: Cheese	170	6	31%	3	15	360	8	23
Pepperoni	200	8	36%	4	20	460	9	23
Meatsa	220	10	40%	4	25	570	11	24
Supreme	230	10	39%	4	25	550	11	25
Veggie	190	7	33%	3	15	500	9	25
14" Square: Cheese	140	5	32%	2	10	280	7	19
Pepperoni	160	7	39%	2.5	15	350	8	19
14" Thin: Cheese	140	5	32%	2	10	280	7	19
Pepperoni	160	7	39%	2.5	15	350	8	19
16" Round: Cheese	230	8	31%	3.5	20	440	11	30
Pepperoni	260	11	38%	4.5	25	570	12	31
18" Round: Cheese	240	8	30%	3.5	20	470	12	32
Pepperoni	270	11	36%	4.5	30	600	13	32
Baby Pan! Pan!	310	15	43%	5.5	30	640	14	32
Pizza By The Slice: Cheese	290	10	31%	4.5	25	570	14	39
Pepperoni	340	14	37%	6	35	770	16	39
Sandwiches (Cold): Ham & Cheese	600	22	33%	9.5	55	1410	33	68
Italia	690	31	40%	13	75	1660	34	68
Tuna	820	39	42%	4.5	80	1330	45	71
Turkey	600	21	31%	9.5	55	1570	38	66
Veggie	580	24	37%	9.5	30	940	26	70
Sandwiches (Hot): Meatsa	960	53	49%	23	115	2240	48	72
Pepperoni	980	56	51%	26	125	2290	48	71
Supreme; Cheeser	900	49	49%	21	105	2040	42	74
Vegetarian	760	36	42%	17	65	1360	38	74
Salads: Antipasto	80	6	67%	2.5	15	340	5	4
Caesar	80	3	33%	1.5	5	190	5	7
Greek	60	3	45%	0	10	330	3	5
Tossed	50	0.5	9%	0	0	60	2	9
Dresssings (1 oz): Blue Cheese	230	24	93%	5	30	450	2	2
Buttermilk Ranch	270	29	96%	5	4	380	0	1
Creamy Caesar; Golden Italian	220	23	94%	4	10	540	1	2
Fat Free Italian	25	0	0%	0	0	390	0	5
Honey French	220	18	73%	3	0	310	0	14
Low Calorie Caesar	230	25	97%	4	55	360	1	1
Thousand Island	220	21	85%	3	30	360	0	7
Italian Cheese Bread: 1 piece	120	6	45%	2	10	240	5	12
Crazy Bread: 1 stick, 1.2 oz	90	2.5	25%	0.5	0	120	3	14
Crazy Sauce: 4 oz	45	0	0%	0	0	250	1	9
Chicken Wings: 1 piece	50	4	72%	1	15	640	4	0
Cinnamon Stick	340	9	23%	1	0	440	8	57

	Cal	Fat	%FC	S.Fat	Chol	Sod	Pro	Carb
Flavorbaked: Fish, 1 piece	90	2.5	26%	1	35	320	14	1
Chicken	110	3	24%	1	55	600	19	0
Crispy Fry: Fish & Chips	710	42	53%	10	30	na	16	66
Lemon Crumb Baked: Fish, 1 piece	195	2	9%	na	145	635	35	10
Sandwiches: Ultimate Fish	430	21	44%	7	35	1340	18	44
Batter-Dipped Fish (no sauce)	320	13	37%	4	30	800	17	40
Flavorbaked Fish	320	14	39%	7	55	930	23	28
Flavorbaked Chicken	290	10	31%	2	60	970	24	27
Grab n Go: Battered Chicken, 1 serve	320	12	34%	3	20	850	14	41
w. Cheese	370	17	41%	8	35	1090	17	41
Battered Fish, 1 serve	300	11	33%	3	20	770	11	39
w. Cheese	350	16	41%	8	35	1010	14	39
Popcorn Munchers: Chicken, 4 oz	380	23	55%	4	35	1030	23	20
Fish/Shrimp, 4 oz	310	15	44%	3	75	1310	15	31
Batter-Dipped: Shrimp, 1 serve	35	2.5	64%	0.5	10	95	1	2
Chicken	120	6	45%	2	15	400	8	11
Fish	170	11	58%	2.5	30	470	11	12
Breaded: Chicken Strips/Fish	105	5	43%	1	15	350	6	11
Clams	300	17	51%	4	40	670	11	31
Wraps								
Chicken: Salsa, Regular, 11 oz	690	32	40%	7	20	1690	18	81
Large, 22 oz	1370	64	40%	13	35	3370	36	162
Cajun/Ranch/Tartar: Average								
Regular, 11 oz	730	36	45%	7	25	1830	18	82
Large, 22 oz	1450	72	45%	14	50	3650	36	165
Fish: Salsa, Regular, 11.5 oz	690	32	40%	7	25	1640	18	84
Large, 23 oz	1380	64	40%	14	45	3280	35	167
Cajun/Ranch/Tartar: Average								
Regular, 11.5 oz	730	36	45%	8	25	1780	18	85
Large, 23 oz	1450	72	45%	15	58	3550	35	170
Popcorn Shrimp: Salsa, Reg., 11 oz	690	32	40%	9	40	1660	16	84
Large, 22 oz	1380	64	40%	17	85	3310	32	170
Cajun/Ranch/Tartar: Average								
Regular, 11 oz	730	36	45%	9	45	1810	16	86
Large, 22 oz	1450	72	45%	18	95	3600	32	172
Side Items: Fries, regular	250	15	54%	3	0	500	3	28
Fries, large, 5 oz	420	24	51%	4	0	830	5	46
Cheese Sticks	160	9	50%	4	10	360	6	12
Corn Cobbette	140	8	51%	2	0	0	3	19
Hushpuppy, 1 piece	60	2.5	37%	0	0	25	1	9
Rice	140	3	19%	1	0	210	3	26
Slaw	140	6	39%	na	0	260	1	20
Soup: Broccoli Cheese, 8 oz	180	12	60%	4.5	15	1240	5	13
Salads: Garden Salad	45	0	0%	0	0	25	3	9
Grilled Chicken Salad	140	2.5	16%	0.5	45	260	20	10
Ocean Chef Salad	130	2	14%	0	60	540	14	13
Side Salad, no dressing	25	0	0%	0	0	15	1	4

	Cal	Fat	%Fc	S.Fat	Chol	Sod	Pro	Carb
Sandwiches/Burgers								
Big Mac®	590	34	52%	11	95	1310	28	38
Big X'tra!®	710	46	58%	15	95	1400	24	51
with Cheese	810	55	61%	19	120	1870	29	52
Cheeseburger	330	14	38%	6	45	830	15	36
Chicken McGrill®	450	18	36%	3	60	970	26	46
Plain (no mayo)	340	7	18%	1.5	50	890	26	45
Crispy Chicken Deluxe™	550	27	44%	4.5	50	1180	23	54
Filet-O-Fish®	470	26	49%	5	50	890	15	45
Hamburger	280	9	29%	4	30	590	12	35
Quarter Pounder®	430	21	43%	8	70	840	23	37
with Cheese	530	30	51%	13	95	1310	28	38
French Fries								
Small	210	10	43%	1.5	0	135	3	26
Medium	450	22	44%	4	0	290	6	57
Large	540	26	43%	4.5	0	350	8	68
Super Size	610	29	42%	5	0	390	9	77
McSalad Shaker™ Salads/Dressings								
Chef Salad	150	8	48%	3.5	95	740	17	5
Garden Salad	100	6	54%	3	75	120	7	4
Grilled Chicken Caesar Salad	100	2.5	22%	1.5	40	240	17	3
Croutons (1 pkg)	50	1	18%	0	0	105	1	9
Caesar Dressing (1 pkg)	150	13	78%	2.5	15	390	2	5
Fat-Free Herb Vinaigrette (1 pkg)	30	0	0%	0	0	220	0	7
Honey Mustard Dressing (1 pkg)	150	11	66%	1.5	15	290	1	13
Ranch Dressing (1 pkg)	170	18	95%	3	10	480	0	2
Red French Reduced Calorie (1 pkg)	130	6	41%	1	0	370	0	18
Thousand Island Dressing (1 pkg)	130	9	62%	1.5	15	360	0	11
Breakfast Menu								
Bacon, Egg & Cheese Biscuit	540	34	56%	10	250	1550	21	36
Biscuit, 2.7 oz	290	15	46%	3	0	780	5	34
Breakfast Burrito	320	20	56%	7	195	660	13	21
Egg McMuffin®	290	12	37%	4.5	235	790	17	27
English Muffin, 2 oz	140	2	13%	0	0	210	4	25
Ham, Egg & Cheese Bagel	550	23	37%	8	255	1490	26	58
Hash Browns, 2 oz	130	8	55%	1.5	0	330	1	14
Hotcakes: Plain, (3)	340	8	21%	2	15	630	9	56
w. Margarine, 2 pats	420	17	36%	4	15	750	9	56
w. Margarine, 2 pats & Syrup (1)	600	17	25%	4	20	770	9	104
Sausage Biscuit	470	31	59%	9	35	1080	11	35
with Egg	550	37	60%	10	245	1160	18	35
Sausage McMuffin®	360	23	58%	8	45	740	13	26
with Egg	440	28	57%	10	255	890	19	27
Sausage Patty	170	16	85%	5	35	290	6	0
Scrambled Eggs (2), 3 1/2 oz	160	11	62%	3.5	425	170	13	1
Spanish Omelette Bagel	690	38	49%	14	275	1560	27	59
Steak, Egg & Cheese Bagel	660	31	42%	11	285	1300	36	57

	Cal	Fat	%Fc	S.Fat	Chol	Sod	Pro	Carb
Chicken McNuggets/Sauces								
Chick McNuggets®4 Pces	190	11	52%	2.5	35	360	10	13
6 Pieces	290	17	53%	5.5	55	540	15	20
9 Pieces	430	26	54%	5	80	810	23	29
Barbeque Sauce (1 pkg), 1 oz	45	0	0%	0	0	250	0	10
Honey (1 pkg), 1/2 oz	45	0	0%	0	0	0	0	11
Honey Mustard (1 pkg), 1/2 oz	50	4.5	81%	0.5	10	85	0	3
Hot Mustard Sauce (1 pkg), 1 oz	60	3.5	0%	0	5	240	1	7
Light Mayonnaise (1 pkg)	40	4	90%	0.5	5	80	0	1
Sweet 'N' Sour Sauce (1 pkg), 1 oz	50	0	0%	0	0	140	0	11
Muffins/Danish: Apple Danish, 3.7 oz	340	15	39%	3	20	340	5	47
Cheese Danish, 3.7 oz	400	21	47%	5	40	400	7	45
Cinnamon Roll, 3.4 oz	390	18	41%	5	65	310	6	50
Lowfat Apple Bran Muffin, 4 oz	300	3	9%	0.5	0	380	6	61
Desserts/Sundaes/Cookies/Shakes								
Baked Apple Pie, 2 3/4 oz	260	13	45%	3.5	0	200	3	34
Chocolate Chip Cookie, 2 3/4 oz	170	10	53%	6	20	120	2	22
Fruit 'n Yogurt Parfait: w. granola	380	5	12%	2	15	240	10	76
no granola	280	4	13%	2	15	115	8	53
McDonaldland® Cookies, 1 pkg	180	5	25%	1	0	190	3	32
McFlurry™: Butterfinger®	620	22	31%	14	70	260	16	90
M&M®	630	23	32%	15	75	210	16	90
Nestlé Crunch®	630	24	34%	16	75	230	16	89
Oreo® Cookie	570	20	31%	12	70	280	15	82
Nuts (Sundae/Topping), 1/4 oz	40	3.5	79%	0	0	55	2	2
Vanilla Reduced Fat Icecream Cone	150	4.5	27%	3	20	75	4	23
Shakes: average all, small, 14 fl.oz	360	9	23%	6	40	200	11	59
Sundae: Hot Caramel Sundae	360	10	25%	6	35	180	7	61
Hot Fudge Sundae, 6.3 oz	340	12	16%	9	30	170	8	52
Strawberry Sundae	290	7	21%	5	30	95	7	50
Drinks: **Orange Juice,** 6 fl.oz	80	0	0%	0	0	20	0	20
1% Lowfat Milk, 8 fl.oz ctn	100	2.5	23%	1.5	10	115	8	13
Coca-Cola Classic (25% ice):								
Small,16 fl.oz	150	0	0%	0	0	15	0	40
Medium, 21 fl.oz	210	0	0%	0	0	20	0	58
Large, 32 fl.oz	310	0	0%	0	0	30	0	86
Super Size, 42 fl.oz	410	0	0%	0	0	40	0	113
Diet Coke: Small,16 fl.oz	0	0	0%	0	0	30	0	0
Medium, 21 fl.oz	0	0	0%	0	0	40	0	0
Large, 32 fl. oz	0	0	0%	0	0	60	0	0
Super Size, 42 fl.oz	0	0	0%	0	0	70	0	0
Sprite: Small, 16 fl.oz	150	0	0%	0	0	55	0	39
Medium, 21 fl.oz	210	0	0%	0	0	80	0	56
Large, 32 fl. oz	310	0	0%	0	0	115	0	83
Super Size, 42 fl.oz	410	0	0%	0	0	160	0	109
Hi-C Orange Drink: Small, 16 fl.oz	160	0	0%	0	0	30	0	44
Medium, 21 fl.oz	240	0	0%	0	0	40	0	64

Mrs Fields' Cookies®

	Cal	Fat	%Fc	S.Fat	Chol	Sod	Pro	Carb
Per 1 Cookie, 1.7 oz								
Butter; Butter Toffee	220	10	41%	6	40	140	2	30
Chewy Fudge	220	11	45%	7	25	60	2	30
Coconut Macadamia	210	9	38%	3.5	15	170	2	29
Debra's Special	210	9	38%	4.5	30	140	3	29
Milk Choc	230	11	43%	7	30	140	3	29
Milk Choc w. Walnuts	240	13	48%	7	30	135	3	28
Milk Choc Macadamia	240	13	49%	7	30	130	3	27
Oatmeal Raisin	180	7	35%	4	26	165	2	29
Peanut Butter	230	12	47%	6	35	190	4	26
Pumpkin Harvest	200	10	45%	6	30	200	3	24
Semi-Sweet Chocolate	230	10	39%	7	30	130	2	31
with Pecans	220	12	49%	6	20	115	2	28
with Walnuts	230	12	46%	6	25	125	2	29
Triple Chocolate	220	10	41%	7	30	140	3	31
White Chunk Macadamia	240	13	49%	7	30	125	3	28
Nibblers: Per 2 Cookies, 1 oz								
Debra's Special	100	4.5	40%	2	10	80	1	13
Milk Choc w. Walnuts	120	6	45%	3	10	65	1	14
Peanut Butter; Triple Choc	110	6	49%	2.5	15	95	2	13
Semi-Sweet Chocolate	110	5	40%	3	10	60	1	15
White Chunk Macadamia	120	7	53%	3.5	10	60	1	13

Mazzio's Pizza®

	Cal	Fat	%Fc	S.Fat	Chol	Sod	Pro	Carb
Appetizers: Per Serving								
Garlic Bread w. Cheese, 2 slices	700	35	45%	7	15	1280	21	74
Meat Nachos	500	37	67%	17	15	1200	21	21
Sandwiches: Ham & Cheese	790	39	44%	13	85	1900	40	71
BBQ Beef & Cheddar	580	24	37%	11	95	1260	39	51
Chicken & Cheddar	570	24	38%	8	70	1350	33	56
Deluxe Submarine	810	43	48%	13	75	2240	39	68
Pizza: Per Slice								
Original Crust: Cheese	270	9	30%	3	17	660	12	37
The Works	345	14	37%	5	31	920	16	38
Pepperoni	305	12	35%	5	24	800	13	37
Sausage	35	14	38%	5	28	900	15	37
Deep Pan: Cheese	350	13	33%	5	15	620	17	42
Combo	410	18	40%	6	20	930	19	42
Pepperoni	380	17	40%	5	25	740	18	38
Sausage	430	21	44%	8	25	1040	21	41
Thin Crust: Cheese	220	12	49%	4	17	440	9	22
Pasta: Chicken Parmesan	600	19	29%	3	50	1600	39	68
Fettuccine Alfredo, small	440	28	57%	16	55	680	14	34
Meat Lasagna, small	460	25	49%	10	85	1370	24	36
Spaghetti, small	290	10	31%	3	5	800	11	39

Nathan's® Famous

	Cal	Fat	%Fc	S.Fat	Chol	Sod	Pro	Carb
Hamburgers								
Regular	435	23	48%	10	77	280	25	32
Double Burger	670	41	55%	18	154	460	44	32
Super Burger	535	32	54%	9	86	525	27	34
Sandwiches								
Breaded Chicken Sandwich	510	25	44%	4	56	930	23	48
Charbroiled Chicken S'wich	290	6	19%	1	53	860	24	35
Cheese Steak Sandwich	485	26	48%	10	73	580	26	37
Chicken Salad	155	4	23%	1	49	345	20	9
Fillet of Fish S'wich	405	15	33%	2	32	715	20	46
Pastrami Sandwich	325	12	33%	4	48	1015	21	34
Turkey Sandwich	270	2	7%	0	27	1460	28	34
Platters								
Chicken, 2 piece	1095	66	54%	14	212	1420	54	72
4 pieces	1790	109	55%	23	425	2370	102	99
Fillet of Fish	1455	74	46%	10	147	1840	60	137
Fried Clam	1025	51	45%	7	49	1825	23	119
Fried Shrimp	795	34	38%	5	83	1435	23	100
French Fries	515	26	45%	4	0	60	9	62
Frank Nuggets (7)	360	24	60%	6	46	740	9	25
Frankfurter	310	19	55%	8	45	820	13	22

Olive Garden®

	Cal	Fat	%Fc	S.Fat	Chol	Sod	Pro	Carb
Lunch Entrees								
Capellini Pomodora, 13 oz	340	11	28%	1.5	5	700	9	52
Chicken Giardino, 13 oz	300	7	21%	3	35	910	20	40
Linguine alla Marinara, 10.5 oz	280	6	20%	1	0	510	8	48
Shrimp Primavera, 19 oz	450	9	19%	1.5	140	820	26	65
Dinner Entrees								
Capellini Pomodora, 20.5 oz	550	17	28%	2.5	5	1090	16	84
Chicken Giardino, 21 oz	460	8	16%	3	60	1000	36	59
Linguine alla Marinara, 26 oz	450	9	19%	1.5	0	770	14	79
Shrimp Primavera, 19 oz	603	13	19%	2	275	1220	44	84
Soup & Breadstick								
Minestrone Soup, 6 fl.oz	100	1	10%	0	0	610	5	18
Breadstick, plain, 1 stick	140	1.5	10%	0	0	270	5	26

Feedback welcome

Comments and suggestions are most welcome. Please write, fax or email the author

(Contact Details ~ Page 287)

1-Potato-2®

Per Baked Potato (No Skin)	Cal	Fat	%FC	S.Fat	Chol	Sod	Pro	Carb
Ultra-Lites: Chicken Stir-Fry	330	3	8%	1	21	1290	16	62
Chicken Fajita; Carribean Chicken	270	1.5	5%	0.5	21	555	16	50
Chick, Mushroom, Rst Red Pepper	245	2	7%	0.5	21	715	13	45
Crab & Broccoli DeLite	335	2.5	6%	1	35	740	19	55
Vegie & Herb Cheese	240	1.5	5%	1	5	425	13	44
Lite: Chicken Caesar & Broccoli	375	12	29%	3	31	845	19	50
Herb Roasted Vegetable	260	6	20%	1	1	210	6	47
Fresh Mex Chicken; Spinach Souffle	320	9	26%	4	60	570	15	44
Gourmet: Bacon & Cheese	660	47	64%	18	61	920	20	39
Bacon Double Cheeseburger	765	54	63%	21	88	1290	30	40
BBQ Chick, Cheddar, Bacon	685	43	57%	17	90	1765	32	44
Broccoli & Cheese	545	36	59%	14	42	575	16	42
Chicken Broccoli & Chedd.; 3 Cheese	590	37	56%	15	63	820	23	43
Chicken Caesar & Broccoli	710	51	65%	10	36	1375	16	50
Crab, Broccoli & Cheese	595	35	53%	14	55	1230	25	46
Mexican	670	46	62%	17	70	1070	18	48
Philly Steak & Cheese	675	40	53%	15	69	1410	34	46
Potato Skins (with Sour Cream)								
Bacon 'n Cheddar, 9 oz	975	53	50%	25	98	1340	27	100
Southwestern, 11 oz	910	46	45%	22	84	1425	23	105
Fresh Cut Fries: Small, 13 oz	615	39	57%	7	0	320	5	63
Medium, 16 oz	765	49	58%	8	0	400	7	79
Large, 25 oz	1225	78	57%	13	0	640	11	126
Topped Fries: Nacho Cheese	840	54	58%	11	13	625	10	81
Fresh Fries 'n Chicken Tenders	920	50	49%	9	48	895	26	93
Soups: Baked Potato Soup, 13 oz	640	26	36%	11	52	1630	20	81
Broccoli & Chse Potato Soup, 13 oz	665	29	40%	13	58	1435	21	80
Country Skillets: Idaho "Nachos"	1010	61	54%	20	82	840	30	89
BBQ Chick, Cheddar & Bacon	890	57	58%	16	63	760	24	74
Bacon, Ranch & Cheddar	1090	74	61%	20	71	940	22	87

Papa John's Pizza

Per Slice: 1/8 Large Pizza (14")	Cal	Fat	%FC	S.Fat	Chol	Sod	Pro	Carb
Original: All the Meats	410	18	40%	7	35	1040	21	42
Cheese; Garden	300	11	28%	3	20	550	14	37
Pepperoni	310	13	38%	5	25	760	15	35
Sausage	340	13	35%	6	25	810	15	40
The Works	370	17	41%	6	29	840	18	37
Thin Crust: All the Meats	330	20	54%	9	39	920	15	23
Cheese; Garden Special	240	12	46%	6	19	540	9	23
Pepperoni	270	15	50%	7	24	580	11	22
Sausage	270	15	50%	7	29	730	12	22
The Works	320	19	52%	8	35	760	14	24
Cheese Sticks, (2)	160	6	34%	1.5	10	290	7	21

	Cal	Fat	%Fc	S.Fat	Chol	Sod	Pro	Carb
Entrees								
Chicken Dinner	620	13	18%	na	136	1360	60	60
Fish Dinner	470	7	13%	na	133	1390	33	60
Fruit Cup	50	0.5	6%	na	0	10	1	12
'Lite & Healthy'	105	2	18%	na	0	495	3.5	15
Omelette								
Country Club	930	79	76%	na	1154	1135	47	6
Deli Ham & Cheese	960	79	74%	na	864	1830	53	8
'Denver' w. Fruit Cup	235	6.5	25%	na	154	795	23	22
'Everything'	695	54	69%	na	814	870	45	9
Granny's Country	940	82	78%	na	810	785	43	7
w. 9 oz Hash Browns	1245	90	64%	na	810	870	48	57
Ham & Cheese	645	51	72%	na	743	830	41	2.5
Mushroom & Cheese	685	60	78%	na	744	925	32	5
Seafood w. Fruit Cup	270	5.5	19%	na	197	595	29	28
Hash Browns, 3 oz	100	2.5	23%	na	na	30	1.5	17
Pita Stir-fry:	310	9	27%	na	26	750	44	41
w. Coleslaw	440	18	36%	na	36	880	45	54
& Pasta Salad	625	33	47%	na	37	1395	49	63
w. Pasta Salad	490	24	44%	na	27	1270	48	50
Salads: Chef's, Mini	215	11	46%	na	55	645	23	7
Muffins: Apple	545	24	40%	na	95	730	9	76
Banana Nut	585	29	45%	na	92	700	9	75
Blueberry	505	23	41%	na	88	670	7	71
Bran	475	17	32%	na	0	570	9	83
Carrot	560	23	37%	na	81	780	7	88
Choc Choc Chip	545	26	43%	na	83	630	10	73
Corn	680	17	22%	na	33	1550	12	121
Cranberry Nut	560	28	45%	na	88	670	9	71
Oat Bran: Regular	515	16	28%	na	0	590	10	87
Plain	585	26	40%	na	104	795	9	81
98% fat-free	495	1	2%	na	5	800	12	111
Pancakes								
Buttermilk, (3)	440	12	24%	na	24	990	13	70
Harvest Grain:								
w. Low-Cal Syrup (5)	475	3.5	6%	na	0	1640	11	93
Short Stack (3)	270	2	7%	na	0	1020	7	56
Syrup, low cal: 1.5 oz	25	0	0%	na	na	0	0	7
Pies (Per Slice): Apple Pie	520	26	45%	na	0	460	3	72
made w. *Equal*	420	24	51%	na	0	370	3	55
Cherry Pie	570	26	41%	na	0	700	4	84
made w. *Equal*	425	24	51%	na	0	510	4	55
Coconut Cream Pie	440	33	68%	na	5	490	6	56
French Silk Pie	550	37	60%	na	53	480	4	59
Lemon Meringue Pie	395	16	36%	na	0	530	2	63
Peanut Butter Brownie	455	35	69%	na	29	435	9	44
Pecan Pie	670	26	35%	na	17	670	7	106

	Cal	Fat	%FC	S.Fat	Chol	Sod	Pro	Carb
Pizza								
Per Slice								
Bacon: 1/8 large	330	12	33%	na	27	440	17	39
1/8 medium	250	9	32%	na	20	330	13	29
1/4 Express Lunch	180	7	35%	na	16	240	10	21
Beef: 1/8 large	295	8	24%	na	20	480	16	39
1/8 medium	220	6	25%	na	15	360	12	29
1/4 Express Lunch	165	5	27%	na	13	260	9	21
Black Olive: 1/8 large	280	7	22%	na	18	480	14	40
1/8 medium	210	5	21%	na	13	360	11	30
1/4 Express Lunch	160	4	22%	na	12	260	8	21
Cheese: 1/8 large	270	6	20%	na	18	270	14	39
1/8 medium	200	5	22%	na	13	200	11	29
1/4 Express Lunch	150	4	24%	na	12	150	8	21
Extra Cheddar: 1/8 large	300	9	27%	na	27	330	16	39
1/8 medium	225	7	28%	na	19	235	12	29
1/4 Express Lunch	180	6	30%	na	19	195	10	21
Extra Mozzarella: 1/8 large	320	10	28%	na	31	350	18	39
1/8 medium	235	7	27%	na	22	250	13	29
1/4 Express Lunch	175	6	31%	na	18	185	10	21
Green Pepper: 1/8 large	270	6	20%	na	18	270	14	39
1/8 medium	205	5	22%	na	13	200	11	30
1/4 Express Lunch	155	4	23%	na	12	150	8	21
Ham: 1/8 large	275	6	20%	na	21	330	15	39
1/8 medium	210	5	21%	na	15	245	11	29
1/4 Express Lunch	155	4	23%	na	14	190	9	21
Jalapeno: 1/8 large	270	6	20%	na	18	335	14	39
1/8 medium	205	5	22%	na	13	245	10	30
1/4 Express Lunch	150	4	24%	na	12	200	8	21
Mushroom: 1/8 large	205	5	22%	na	13	200	11	30
1/8 medium	180	4	20%	na	12	180	9	29
1/4 Express Lunch	155	4	23%	na	12	150	8	21
Onion: 1/8 large	270	6	20%	na	18	270	14	39
1/8 medium	205	5	22%	na	13	200	10	30
1/4 Express Lunch	155	4	23%	na	12	150	8	21
Pepperoni: 1/8 large	310	9	26%	na	24	555	15	39
1/8 medium	230	7	26%	na	18	430	12	29
1/4 Express Lunch	170	6	32%	na	15	290	9	21
Pineapple; Tomato: 1/8 large	275	6	20%	na	18	270	14	40
1/8 medium	205	5	22%	na	13	200	10	30
1/4 Express Lunch	155	4	23%	na	12	150	8	22
Salami: 1/8 large	290	8	25%	na	23	340	15	39
1/8 medium	215	6	25%	na	17	255	11	29
1/4 Express Lunch	165	5	27%	na	15	200	9	21
Sausage: 1/8 large	300	8	24%	na	21	520	16	39
1/8 medium	225	6	24%	na	15	375	12	29
1/4 Express Lunch	180	6	30%	na	14	360	10	21

	Cal	Fat	%FC	S.Fat	Chol	Sod	Pro	Carb
Medium Size Pizza: Per Slice								
Stuffed Crust: **Beef**	**465**	22	42%	10	30	1140	23	46
Cheese	**445**	19	38%	10	24	1080	22	46
Chicken Supreme	**530**	17	29%	8	32	1110	24	47
Ham	**405**	22	49%	12	40	1190	24	27
Italian Sausage	**480**	23	43%	10	35	1165	22	46
Meat Lover's®	**545**	29	48%	12	48	1430	26	46
Pepperoni	**440**	19	39%	9	27	1115	20	45
Pepperoni Lover's	**525**	26	45%	12	62	1415	26	46
Pork Topping	**460**	21	41%	10	30	1175	22	46
Super Supreme	**505**	25	44%	11	44	1370	25	46
Supreme	**490**	23	42%	10	33	1230	24	47
Veggie Lover's®	**420**	17	36%	8	19	1030	20	48
The Big New Yorker								
Cheese	**395**	17	39%	8	18	1100	20	42
Pepperoni	**380**	16	38%	7	22	1115	18	42
Supreme	**460**	22	43%	9	33	1310	10	44
The Edge								
Chicken Veggie	**120**	3	31%	1	10	310	6	16
Taco	**140**	5	32%	2	10	450	6	17
Thin 'n Crispy								
Beef	**305**	15	44%	7	24	815	15	45
Cheese	**245**	10	38%	5	11	655	13	44
Ham	**210**	7	30%	3	15	660	12	44
Italian Sausage	**325**	18	50%	7	32	865	15	45
Meat Lover's®	**340**	19	50%	8	35	970	16	45
Pepperoni	**235**	10	38%	4	14	670	12	44
Pepperoni Lover's	**290**	14	43%	6	22	860	15	28
Pork Topping	**300**	15	45%	6	23	875	15	45
Veggie Lover's®	**220**	8	33%	3	7	620	9	30
Hand Tossed								
Beef	**350**	12	31%	5	21	945	16	44
Beef Taco	**270**	8	26%	4	15	870	13	35
Cheese	**310**	9	26%	5	11	850	14	43
Chicken Supreme	**290**	6	18%	3	17	840	15	44
Chicken Taco	**290**	11	34%	5	15	940	12	35
Ham	**280**	6	20%	3	15	855	13	43
Italian Sausage	**365**	14	34%	6	26	975	16	44
Meat Lover's®	**375**	15	36%	6	30	1075	17	44
Meatless Taco	**250**	8	29%	4	10	790	14	35
Pepperoni	**300**	8	24%	4	15	865	13	43
Pepperoni Lover's	**370**	14	34%	6	26	1125	17	43
Pork Topping	**340**	12	32%	5	20	990	16	44
Super Supreme	**360**	12	30%	5	23	1025	16	45
Supreme	**330**	11	30%	5	18	930	15	44
Taco	**280**	11	35%	5	15	870	12	34
Veggie Lover's®	**280**	6	20%	3	7	770	12	45

Pizza Hut® (Cont)

	Cal	Fat	%FC	S.Fat	Chol	Sod	Pro	Carb
Medium Size Pizza: Per Slice								
Pan Pizza: Beef	400	18	40%	6	20	775	15	45
Beef Taco	300	12	36%	5	15	770	12	36
Cheese	360	15	37%	8	11	680	13	44
Chicken Supreme	345	12	31%	4	30	670	15	45
Chicken Taco	320	15	42%	5	15	830	12	36
Ham	330	12	33%	4	15	690	12	44
Italian Sausage	415	20	43%	7	26	805	15	45
Meat Lover's®	430	21	44%	7	29	610	16	45
Meatless Taco	290	12	37%	5	15	770	10	36
Pepperoni	355	14	35%	5	14	700	12	44
Pepperoni Lover's	370	16	39%	5	18	765	13	44
Pork Topping	395	18	41%	6	20	820	15	45
Super Supreme	400	18	40%	6	22	855	15	46
Supreme	385	17	40%	6	18	760	14	45
Taco	310	13	38%	5	15	800	12	36
Veggie Lover's®	330	12	33%	4	7	600	11	46
Pasta/Sandwiches								
Cavatini Pasta	480	14	26%	6	8	1170	21	66
Cavatini Supreme Pasta	560	19	31%	8	10	1400	24	73
Spaghetti w. Marina Sauce	490	6	11%	1	0	730	18	91
Spaghetti w. Meatballs	850	24	25%	10	17	1120	37	120
Spaghetti w. Meat Sauce	600	13	19%	5	25	910	23	98
Ham & Cheese Sandwich	550	21	34%	7	22	2150	33	57
Supreme Sandwich	640	28	39%	10	28	2150	34	62
Sides: Breadsticks, 1 serving	130	4	27%	1	0	170	3	20
Breadstick Dipping Sce, 1 oz	30	0.5	15%	0	0	170	0	5
Garlic Bread, 1 slice	150	8	48%	2	0	240	16	3
Hot Wings (4)	210	12	51%	3	130	900	22	4
Mild Wings (5)	200	12	54%	4	150	510	23	0

Pizzeria Uno®

	Cal	Fat	%FC	S.Fat	Chol	Sod	Pro	Carb
Thin Crust Pizza: 9" Individual								
Vegetarian: w. Cheese	850	22	23%	12	55	1660	46	127
No Cheese	620	5	7%	1	0	1100	20	124
Soup: Tomato Garden Veg.	125	1	7%	0	0	900	2.5	25
Light Lunch w. Soup	745	6	7%	1	0	2000	23	150
Entrees								
Veggie Burger Meal	610	15	22%	1	0	1800	15	104
Tomato Basil Chicken	570	8	13%	1.5	55	1280	42	83
Zesty Pasta Marinara	380	3.5	8%	0.5	0	800	13	75
Salads: Special House	90	1	10%	0	0	860	4	17
Light Lunch w. Salad	710	6	7%	1	0	1960	24	141
Pasta Green Salad	410	9	13%	1	0	700	14	69
Veggie Dip Platter	460	11	22%	2	0	770	14	77

Popeye's®

	Cal	Fat	%FC	S.Fat	Chol	Sod	Pro	Carb
Chicken								
Chicken Breast: Mild/Spicy	530	31	52%	11	195	1380	46	18
Chicken Leg: Mild/Spicy	200	12	54%	4	108	500	17	7
Chicken Thigh: Mild/Spicy	390	29	67%	10	150	887	25	12
Chicken Wing: Mild/Spicy	220	15	61%	5	90	510	14	10
Sides								
Biscuit, 2 oz	225	12	48%	4	1	429	3	25
Cajun Rice	180	7	35%	3	60	436	8	23
Cinnamon Apple Pie, 3 oz	90	10	100%	3	3	292	3	37
Coleslaw	235	17	65%	3	14	260	1	20
Corn on the Cob	255	4	14%	1	0	24	7	48
French Fries, 4.5 oz	380	18	42%	7	11	924	5	50
Mashed Potatoes: no Gravy	95	2	19%	1	2	384	1	17
w. Gravy	120	4	30%	1	7	570	3	18
Onion Rings, 4 oz	380	20	47%	8	15	270	7	43
Red Beans & Rice	340	19	50%	6	18	696	7	33

Quincy's® Family Steak House

	Cal	Fat	%FC	S.Fat	Chol	Sod	Pro	Carb
Breakfast: Bacon	35	3	77%	1	5	100	2	0
Corned Beef Hash	210	15	64%	8	45	795	10	11
Scrambled Eggs	95	7	66%	2	215	270	7	1
Country Ham	90	6	60%	2	35	1100	9	1
Oatmeal	175	2	10%	0	0	285	4	18
Pancakes	95	3	28%	1	30	250	3	12
Syrup	75	0	0%	0	0	15	0	20
Sausage Gravy	70	6	77%	2	10	150	2	3
Sausage Links	225	22	88%	8	20	390	7	0
Sausage Patties	230	23	90%	9	45	350	7	0
Steak Fingers	360	25	62%	11	50	690	16	18
Steak								
Chopped, 8 oz	500	42	76%	20	89	350	31	0
Country Style Steak w. Gravy	530	25	42%	7	54	1160	32	44
Cowboy Steak, 14 oz	580	33	51%	15	176	1310	61	9
Filet w. Bacon	340	17	45%	7	125	310	48	2
N.Y.Strip Steak, 10 oz	450	26	52%	13	148	155	53	1
Porterhouse Steak	680	46	61%	23	154	345	67	0
Ribeye, 10 oz	450	29	58%	13	116	155	48	0
Sirloin: Large	370	20	49%	9	119	390	46	2
Regular	285	16	50%	7	71	320	34	0
Sirloin Junior	195	10	46%	5	69	200	25	0
Sirloin Tips	205	8	35%	3	63	790	27	4
Smothered Strip Steak	620	41	59%	16	148	240	55	12
T-Bone, 13 oz	520	35	60%	18	118	265	51	0

Continued Next Page

	Cal	Fat	%FC	S.Fat	Chol	Sod	Pro	Carb
Soups: Chili with Beans	235	11	42%	2	15	920	13	21
Clam Chowder	180	9	45%	1	0	835	3	21
Cream of Broccoli	170	10	53%	1	0	770	2	18
Vegetable Beef	90	2	20%	1	0	325	5	14
Entrees								
Grilled Chicken, regular	125	2	14%	0.5	55	540	25	1
Homestyle Chicken Filet	220	9	37%	2	25	680	13	21
Grilled Salmon	230	4	16%	1	109	110	46	1
Sth Breaded Shrimp	545	31	51%	6	135	820	19	47
Steak & Shrimp	680	39	52%	12	170	820	48	33
Roasted Herb Chicken	875	65	67%	17	340	1240	70	4
Roasted BBQ Chicken	940	65	62%	17	340	1550	70	21
Grilled Trout	300	12	36%	3	115	520	41	2
Sandwiches: No Mayo/Extras								
Bacon Cheeseburger	665	41	55%	17	87	1000	37	33
Grilled Chicken Sandwich	325	4	11%	1	55	1185	33	39
Philly Cheese Steak	590	30	46%	11	87	1685	37	38
Smothered Steak	430	15	31%	6	69	850	34	36
Spicy BBQ Chicken	370	5	12%	1	55	1610	34	45
Breads: Banana Nut	165	7	38%	1	5	195	2	22
Biscuit	270	15	50%	4	11	610	5	29
Cornbread	140	5	32%	1	0	340	3	19
Yeast Roll	160	4	23%	<1	0	285	1	29
Sides: Baked Potatoes	370	0	0%	0	0	25	8	86
Corn on the Cob	140	1	6%	0	0	540	5	33
Rice Pilaf	105	2	17%	0	0	270	2	20
Salad Dressings: Bleu Cheese	155	16	93%	3	10	165	2	2
French: Regular	125	12	86%	1	0	500	0	4
Light	85	4	42%	0	0	285	2	13
Honey Mustard	100	6	54%	1	0	220	2	10
Italian: Regular	135	14	93%	2	0	230	0	3
Light	20	2	90%	0	0	485	2	2
Light Creamy Italian	65	4	55%	0	0	485	2	8
Light Thousand Island	65	4	55%	0	20	340	2	8
Parmesan Peppercorn	150	14	84%	0	0	280	1	4
Ranch	110	11	90%	2	10	195	1	1
Desserts: Banana Pudding	240	12	45%	9	10	240	3	30
Brownie Pudding Cake	310	5	15%	<1	0	395	4	66
Chocolate Chip Cookie	60	3	45%	1	5	35	1	8
Apple Cobbler	255	8	28%	2	5	285	1	49
Cherry Cobbler	410	8	18%	2	5	185	1	55
Peach Cobbler	305	8	24%	2	5	190	1	50
Frozen Yogurt	135	2	13%	1	5	85	5	25
Sugar Cookie	60	3	45%	1	5	30	<1	8
Toppings: Caramel	105	1	8%	<1	0	120	0	24
Fudge	105	4	34%	1	0	75	1	15
Pineapple	70	0	0%	0	0	20	0	20

Rally's Hamburgers®

	Cal	Fat	%Fc	S.Fat	Chol	Sod	Pro	Carb
Burgers/Sandwiches								
Rallyburger	435	22	46%	7	63	1175	20	35
with Cheese	490	27	50%	13	78	1375	23	35
Big Buford	745	48	56%	20	151	1860	41	35
Chicken Fillet Sandwich	400	15	34%	4	42	790	21	43
Chili w. Cheese & Onion, 7 oz	360	22	55%	9	74	1145	23	20
13 oz size	670	41	55%	17	137	2125	43	37
Super Barbecue Bacon	595	31	47%	12	88	1710	29	49
Super Double Cheeseburger	760	48	57%	26	154	1735	41	37
French Fries								
Regular	210	11	47%	4	7	295	3	26
Large	320	16	45%	5	10	440	5	39
X-Large	425	21	44%	7	13	585	7	52
Shakes								
Vanilla, small	320	11	31%	6	38	200	9	49
Other flavors, small	410	12	26%	7	38	260	10	73

Rax®

	Cal	Fat	%Fc	S.Fat	Chol	Sod	Pro	Carb
Sandwiches								
Regular Rax	340	22	59%	7	54	710	16	31
Deluxe	520	35	60%	12	69	785	18	34
BBC (Beef Bacon & Cheddar)	715	51	64%	20	102	1455	28	36
Grilled Chicken	525	33	56%	8	69	995	24	32
Jr. Deluxe	370	25	61%	10	42	510	11	25
Barbeque Beef	400	20	45%	7	40	1030	13	43
Mushroom Melt	600	37	56%	13	104	1690	30	35
Turkey Bacon Club	680	46	61%	15	76	1900	29	37
Turkey	485	32	60%	8	50	1285	17	32
Cheddar Melt	345	23	60%	12	41	540	10	26
Philly Melt	540	32	54%	16	78	1295	28	35
Potatoes								
Plain	210	0	0%	0	0	10	0	50
Cheese/Broccoli	280	6	19%	3	4	620	7	50
Cheese	270	6	20%	3	4	620	7	47
Cheese/Bacon	400	19	51%	14	82	875	7	50
Butter	305	11	32%	9	0	30	0	50
Sour Cream Topping	260	4	14%	3	0	30	4	50
Soups								
Cream of Broccoli	170	10	53%	1	0	770	2	18
Chili w. Beans	235	11	42%	2	15	920	13	21
Salads								
Grilled Chicken Caesar	160	5	28%	3	50	1150	23	6
Caesar Side Salad	40	2	45%	1	5	330	2	3
Side Salad	40	4	90%	1	0	90	0	2
Gourmet Garden	220	9	37%	3	5	840	23	12

Red Lobster®

Fish: Per Lunch Portion (5 oz raw wt.)	Cal	Fat	%Fc	S.Fat	Chol	Sod	Pro	Carb
(For **Dinner Portion** of 10 oz, double the figures.)								
Prepared with No Added Fat								
Add extra for butter sauce. [1 tsp = 30 cals; 3g fat (90%); 30mg sodium]								
Catfish	170	10	53%	3	85	50	20	0
Cod (Atlantic)	100	1	9%	0	70	200	23	0
Flounder	100	1	9%	0	70	95	21	1
Grouper	110	1	8%	0	65	70	26	0
Haddock	110	1	8%	0	85	180	24	2
Halibut	110	1	8%	0	60	105	25	1
Lemon Sole	120	1	7%	0	65	90	27	1
Mackerel	190	12	57%	4	100	250	20	1
Monkfish	110	1	8%	0	80	95	24	0
Norwegian Salmon	230	12	47%	3	80	60	27	2
Ocean Perch (Atlantic)	130	4	28%	1	75	190	24	1
Pollock	120	1	7%	0	90	90	28	1
Rainbow Trout	170	9	48%	3	90	90	23	0
Red Rockfish	90	1	10%	0	85	95	21	0
Red Snapper	110	1	8%	0	70	140	25	0
Sockeye Salmon	160	4	22%	1	50	60	28	2
Swordfish	100	4	36%	1	100	140	17	0
Tilefish	100	2	18%	1	80	60	20	0
Yellowfin Tuna	180	6	30%	2	70	70	32	0
Shellfish								
King Crab Legs 16 oz	170	2	11%	0	100	900	32	6
Snow Crab Legs, 16 oz	150	2	12%	1	130	1630	33	1
Calamari, breaded, fried, 5 oz	360	21	52%	6	140	1150	13	30
Langostino, 5 oz	120	1	8%	0	210	410	26	2
Maine Lobster, 18 oz	240	8	30%	2	310	550	36	5
Rock Lobster, 1 tail, 13 oz	230	3	12%	1	200	1090	49	2
Calico Scallops, 5 oz	180	2	10%	0	115	260	32	8
Deep Sea Scallops, 5 oz	130	2	14%	0	50	260	26	2
Shrimp, 8-12 pces., 7 oz	120	2	15%	0	230	110	25	0
Steaks/Chicken								
Sirloin, 8 oz	350	15	39%	na	150	110	51	0
Strip Steak, 7 oz	690	64	83%	na	140	70	29	0
Hamburger, 1/3 lb	320	23	65%	na	105	70	27	0
Filet Mignon, 8 oz	350	16	41%	na	140	105	47	0
Rib Eye Steak, 12 oz	980	82	75%	na	220	150	56	0
Skinless Chicken Breast, 4 oz	140	3	19%	na	70	60	26	0

		Cal	Fat	%Fc	S.Fat	Chol	Sod	Pro	Carb
Large Pizza: Per Slice **(Thin = 1/8 whole; Pan = 1/6 whole)**									
Bacon Super Deli:	Thin	400	26	58%	10	50	720	18	32
	Pan	520	28	48%	10	50	760	24	52
Cheese:	Thin	320	12	34%	8	40	480	14	32
	Pan	410	13	30%	10	40	500	20	52
Chicken & Garlic Gourmet:									
	Thin	340	14	37%	8	50	568	18	34
	Pan	460	16	31%	8	50	310	22	54
Classic Pesto:	Thin	340	16	42%	8	30	420	14	36
	Pan	460	18	35%	8	30	480	18	54
Garden Pesto:	Thin	340	16	42%	8	30	400	14	36
	Pan	460	17	33%	8	30	460	18	56
Gourmet Veggie:	Thin	320	13	37%	6	30	400	14	36
	Pan	440	15	31%	8	40	460	18	56
Guinevere's Garden Delight:									
	Thin	300	11	33%	6	30	500	14	36
	Pan	400	12	27%	8	30	500	18	54
Italian Garlic Supreme:									
	Thin	400	20	47%	8	50	440	16	34
	Pan	500	22	40%	8	50	480	20	54
King Arthur's Supreme:									
	Thin	400	20	45%	8	50	680	18	36
	Pan	480	20	37%	8	50	640	20	54
Maui Zaui:	Thin	340	13	34%	8	40	700	18	36
	Pan	620	20	29%	12	60	980	30	74
Pepperoni:	Thin	340	16	42%	6	40	480	16	34
	Pan	440	16	33%	8	40	480	18	52
Roastin Toastin Garlic:									
	Thin	380	18	42%	8	50	620	18	36
	Pan	510	22	39%	10	52	710	24	56
Salute Chicken & Garlic:									
	Thin	300	11	33%	6	40	500	16	36
	Pan	400	12	27%	6	40	540	18	56
Salute Veggie:	Thin	280	10	32%	4	20	340	12	38
	Pan	380	10	24%	6	20	380	16	56
Large 1/8 (16") Pizza									
Aloha Vinnie		430	14	29%	8	40	1140	19	55
Big Vinnie Pepperoni		460	19	37%	10	50	740	20	49
Sandwiches									
Chicken Club		800	38	43%	14	115	1510	39	72
Ham & Honey Mustard		760	33	39%	13	95	1630	36	76
Garden Vegetable		670	29	39%	10	55	990	25	75
Garlic Parmesan Twists (3)		430	15	31%	6	25	690	17	55
Turkey Pesto		830	40	43%	14	85	1200	42	71
Turkey Santa Fe		840	44	47%	16	95	1360	39	72

Roy Rogers®

	Cal	Fat	%Fc	S.Fat	Chol	Sod	Pro	Carb
Breakfast Items: Biscuit	390	21	48%	6	0	1000	6	44
Cinnamon 'N' Raisin Biscuit	370	18	44%	5	0	450	3	48
Sausage Biscuit	510	31	55%	10	25	1360	14	44
Sausage & Egg Biscuit	560	35	56%	11	170	1400	18	44
Bacon Biscuit	420	23	49%	7	5	1140	9	44
Bacon/Ham & Egg Biscuit	470	26	50%	8	150	1190	14	44
Ham & Cheese Biscuit	450	24	48%	8	25	1570	11	48
Ham, Egg & Cheese Biscuit	500	27	49%	10	170	1620	16	48
Sourdough Ham, Egg & Cheese	480	24	45%	9	185	1440	20	45
Big Country Breakfast: with Bacon	740	43	52%	13	305	1800	25	61
with Sausage	920	60	59%	19	340	2230	33	61
with Ham	710	39	49%	11	330	2210	24	67
3 Pancakes	280	2	6%	1	15	890	8	56
with 1 Sausage	430	16	33%	6	40	1290	16	56
with 2 Bacon	350	9	23%	3	25	1130	13	56
Bagel, all types, average	300	2	6%	0.5	0	520	10	60
Hashrounds	230	14	55%	3	0	560	3	24
Burgers								
Hamburger	260	9	31%	4	20	460	11	33
Cheeseburger	300	13	39%	7	25	690	13	34
1/4 lb Hamburger	430	18	38%	8	25	450	25	41
1/4 lb Cheeseburger	470	22	42%	10	30	680	27	42
Sourdough Bacon Cheeseburger	730	46	57%	18	65	1470	35	43
Sourdough Grilled Chicken	500	21	38%	6	45	1530	30	46
Bacon Cheeseburger	490	28	51%	13	35	800	30	29
Sandwiches: Roast Beef	260	4	14%	1	60	700	24	30
Chicken Fillet	500	24	43%	5	20	1050	19	49
Grilled Chicken	340	11	29%	2	30	910	25	32
Fisherman's Fillet (seasonal)	490	21	39%	5	15	1040	21	56
Chicken: Fried: Breast	370	15	36%	4	75	1190	29	29
Wing	200	8	36%	2	30	740	10	23
Thigh	330	15	41%	4	60	1000	19	30
Leg	170	7	37%	2	45	570	13	15
1/4 Roy's Roaster: White Meat	500	29	52%	9	240	1450	56	3
No Skin	190	6	28%	2	100	700	32	2
Dark Meat	490	34	62%	10	225	1120	43	2
No Skin	190	10	47%	3	110	400	24	1
Nuggets: 6 piece	290	18	56%	4	15	610	12	20
Salads: Grilled Chicken	120	4	30%	1	60	520	18	2
Garden	190	14	66%	9	40	280	12	3
Fries: Regular	350	15	39%	4	0	150	5	49
Large	430	18	38%	5	0	190	6	59
Baked Potato: w. Margarine	240	13	49%	2	0	220	3	27
Cornbread	310	17	49%	3	30	260	4	35
Coleslaw, 5 oz	295	25	78%	4	15	430	2	16
Desserts: Hot Fudge Sundae	320	10	28%	5	25	260	8	50
Strawberry Sundae	260	6	21%	3	15	95	6	44

	Cal	Fat	%Fc	S.Fat	Chol	Sod	Pro	Carb
HealthMex®								
All HealthMex® items have less that 22% of calories from fat.								
Bean & Rice Burrito	340	7	20%	1	5	990	11	58
Burrito w. Chicken/Mahi Mahi	380	9	20%	2	30	960	30	48
Combo	690	13	15%	3	72	1735	51	93
Taco w. Chicken	180	3	15%	1	20	340	14	24
Taco w. Mahi Mahi	190	2	10%	0	35	260	18	25
Taco Combo: w. Chicken	480	8	15%	1	47	1195	33	68
w. Chicken & Mahi Mahi	490	7	15%	1	62	1115	37	69
w. Mahi Mahi	500	7	15%	1	77	1035	41	70
Tacos: Carne Asada	210	7	30%	1	20	520	12	25
Carnitas	290	14	45%	2	45	125	15	24
Fish Taco	280	14	45%	3	30	280	11	28
Fish Taco Especial	370	21	50%	5	45	380	15	29
Grilled Chicken	200	5	20%	1	20	260	14	24
Grilled Mahi Mahi Fish	300	14	40%	3	55	270	21	23
Shrimp	260	13	45%	2	90	430	12	23
Burritos: Bean & Cheese	490	20	35%	4	45	1000	20	57
Carne Asada	470	21	40%	4	45	1460	25	48
Carnitas	640	36	50%	10	100	540	33	47
Chicken	540	25	40%	8	70	1000	35	47
Especial: w. Carne Asada	690	39	50%	6	75	1680	29	56
w. Chicken	670	36	50%	6	75	1220	34	55
w. Carnitas	820	51	55%	8	120	990	36	55
Fish	590	30	45%	4	45	830	21	60
Mahi Mahi	640	31	45%	9	100	870	39	52
Shrimp	480	22	40%	8	130	1200	19	52
Combos: Baja Grill Combo	1100	45	35%	12	65	2440	50	129
Cabo Combo	1190	55	40%	25	160	2200	41	137
Pesky's Combo	1170	61	45%	15	90	1480	41	115
Baja Bowls: Grilled Chicken	260	6	20%	2	30	1440	19	35
Grilled Steak	270	8	27%	3	30	1710	16	36
Los Otros: Nachos Grande	1400	91	60%	18	145	1900	44	109
w. Steak	1520	97	55%	21	180	2650	58	110
w. Chicken	1500	94	55%	19	175	2200	63	110
Kid Pesky® Meals								
Beans	80	1	20%	0	5	200	5	13
Bean/Cheese Burrito	480	20	35%	8	45	810	20	55
Cheese Quesadilla	520	29	50%	9	80	820	22	41
Chips	350	18	45%	6	3	500	6	44
Fish Taco	280	14	45%	9	30	140	11	26
Rice	50	2	35%	0	7	335	1	7
Taquitos	320	17	50%	6	840	420	20	22
Churro, mini	65	4	55%	1	5	60	1	7

Note: Rubio's uses only skinless chicken breast & lean trimmed steak.
Canola oil is used – no lard or MSG. Saturated fat counts are author estimates only.

	Cal	Fat	%Fc	S.Fat	Chol	Sod	Pro	Carb
Microwave Sandwiches								
Oscar Mayer:								
Big Bite w. Bun	300	19	57%	8	30	800	10	22
1/4 Pound Big Bite	480	36	66%	15	60	1370	16	23
Mesquite Jalapeno Bite	380	26	60%	10	0	1100	15	23
Spicy Bite	380	25	60%	10	55	1140	16	22
Croissants								
Egg, Cheese & Bacon	410	28	60%	10	155	880	16	26
Egg, Ham & Cheese	350	22	57%	7	155	950	17	25
English Muffin								
w. Egg/Cheese/Canadian Bacon	270	25	85%	7	240	940	18	21
Biscuit: Sausage/Egg/Cheese	560	41	66%	14	170	1330	16	36
Burritos								
Ramona: Beef & Bean	290	9	27%	4	76	290	16	37
Potato & Beef	340	14	37%	6	33	280	13	41
Bean & Cheese	340	13	34%	6	34	300	15	41
Reynoldos Jumbo Burritos:								
Beef & Bean	630	20	28%	5	10	1470	25	88
Beef & Potato	550	16	26%	5	15	1650	19	82
Bean & Cheese	680	25	33%	10	22	1335	25	88
Red Hot	600	20	30%	5	15	1810	22	82
Green	640	22	31%	7	22	1680	23	85
Chimichanga								
Don Miguel: Chicken	270	8	27%	1.5	20	580	11	37
Shredded Beef	260	9	31%	2	20	610	11	35
Hot & Spicy Beef	280	9	29%	2	15	580	10	39
Fountain Drinks								
(Figures Assume 1/4 Ice)								
Coca-Cola/Pepsi/Dr.Pepper/7Up:								
Gulp, 16 oz	150	0	0%	0	0	15	0	38
Big Gulp, 32 oz	300	0	0%	0	0	30	0	75
Super Gulp, 44 oz	410	0	0%	0	0	40	0	102
Double Gulp, 64 oz	600	0	0%	0	0	60	0	150
Diet Coke/Diet Pepsi:								
(Negligible Calories/Fat)								
Slurpees								
Average All Flavors:								
16 oz size	200	0	0%	0	0	15	0	50
22 oz size	275	0	0%	0	0	20	0	69
32 oz size	400	0	0%	0	0	30	0	100
44 oz size	550	0	0%	0	0	40	0	138

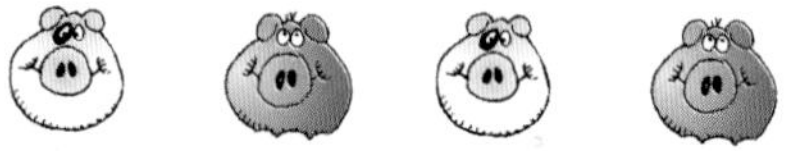

	Cal	Fat	%Fc	S.Fat	Chol	Sod	Pro	Carb
Light & Flavorful Sandwiches								
Albacore Tuna: Small	370	12	29%	7	30	1210	24	47
Regular	565	17	27%	9	50	1795	37	70
Chicken Breast: Small	360	7	17%	1.5	20	1615	24	50
Regular	540	10	16%	3	30	2490	35	75
Dijon Chicken: Small	305	2.5	7%	1	20	1205	25	47
Regular	475	4.5	8%	2	30	1815	39	70
Pesto Chicken: Small	345	6	16%	3	20	1270	24	49
Regular	515	8.5	15%	5	30	1900	36	73
Santa Fe Chicken, small	445	14	28%	4	30	1755	29	52
Smoked Turkey Breast: Small	340	4.5	12%	1	20	1405	22	50
Regular	500	6.5	12%	1	30	2105	33	76
The Vegetarian: Small	320	9.5	27%	1	0	805	12	48
Regular	510	16	28%	2	0	1230	20	71
Original Sandwiches								
Per Regular Sandwich								
Cheese Original	830	43	45%	13	60	2005	38	75
Deluxe	1030	53	45%	16	80	3970	57	79
Ham & Cheese	770	32	40%	12	60	3350	44	78
The Original	800	38	45%	15	60	2315	36	75
Turkey	900	42	45%	12	50	3075	50	78
Specialty Deli								
Per Regular Sandwich								
Albacore Tuna Melt	860	42	44%	14	60	2430	53	72
BLT	860	48	50%	20	60	1785	28	72
Chicken Club	865	37	38%	10	50	2480	52	78
Corned Beef	570	16	25%	8	80	2855	37	73
Corned Beef Reuben	840	36	40%	18	90	3560	47	76
Pastrami & Swiss	920	40	39%	18	80	4055	54	79
Pastrami Reuben	965	45	42%	10	50	3860	52	80
Roast Beef	650	20	30%	8	70	1795	42	72
Roast Beef & Cheese	870	37	40%	10	60	2510	56	75
Texas Schlotzsky's	850	41	45%	14	70	3290	44	78
The Philly	820	29	35%	8	40	2525	57	80
Turkey & Bacon Club	1000	53	45%	15	60	3080	56	73
Turkey Guacamole	760	30	35%	8	30	2870	35	85
Turkey Reuben	900	40	40%	10	50	3800	52	80
Vegetable Club	620	27	40%	7	0	1475	18	74
Western Vegetarian	630	30	40%	8	0	75	18	42
Leaf Salads: (No dressing, croutons, chow mein noodles, crackers)								
Caesar Salad	65	4.5	60%	1	0	175	5	2
Chicken Caesar Salad	145	5.5	34%	1	10	440	21	4
Chinese Chicken Salad	180	3.5	18%	1	10	265	18	14
Garden Salad	110	3	25%	0	0	120	4	14
Greek Salad	190	12	55%	3	10	595	9	14
Ham & Turkey Chef's Salad	250	13	45%	3	10	1490	23	14
Smoked Turkey Chef's Salad	230	10	40%	3	10	1340	23	14

	Cal	Fat	%Fc	S.Fat	Chol	Sod	Pro	Carb
Deli Salads								
Cole Slaw, 1/2 cup	**180**	13	65%	3	10	310	1	13
Macaroni Salad, 3/4 cup	**360**	25	63%	6	20	660	4	25
Potato Salad: Choice, 2/3 cup	**270**	19	63%	1	0	560	2	19
w. Mustard & Egg, 2/3 cup	**240**	16	63%	3	210	570	2	18
Diced w. Egg, 2/3 cup	**230**	14	55%	3	210	640	3	19
Deli-Style Potato Chips, 1.5 oz	**210**	10	43%	0	0	220	3	25
Bread (Regular Size)								
Dark Rye/Sourdough Bun	**330**	1.5	5%	0	0	790	11	68
Jalapeno Cheese Bun	**345**	3	7%	2	10	870	11	69
Wheat Bun	**330**	2	5%	0	0	840	13	64
Soups: *Per 8 oz Cup Serving*								
7-Bean Medley	**200**	3	15%	0	0	2000	10	34
Boston Clam Chowder	**440**	10	25%	3	30	1820	10	26
Chicken Noodle (Old Fashioned)	**180**	4	15%	1	10	1680	10	24
Cream of Broccoli	**380**	7	50%	2	10	1860	6	24
Minestrone	**140**	2	15%	0	0	1740	6	26
Vegetable Vegetarian	**100**	0	0%	0	0	1420	6	20
Sourdough Crust Pizzas (8")								
Bacon, Tomato & Mushroom	**640**	28	39%	8	40	725	28	69
Barbeque Chicken	**680**	18	24%	4	40	1275	39	76
Chicken & Pesto	**580**	16	25%	4	30	830	40	69
Double Cheese	**535**	19	32%	5	60	590	24	67
Double Cheese & Pepperoni	**680**	32	42%	8	80	1060	31	67
Fresh Tomato & Pesto	**530**	19	32%	8	80	455	23	67
Mediterranean	**510**	19	35%	4	30	815	20	67
New Orleans	**580**	17	25%	9	40	2840	37	70
Smoked Turkey & Jalapeno	**580**	17	25%	5	30	1465	36	71
Southwestern	**600**	19	29%	8	80	3410	36	72
Thai Chicken	**640**	18	25%	4	20	1290	39	83
The Original Combination	**600**	25	40%	12	60	845	24	70
Vegetarian Special	**500**	15	25%	4	20	570	25	68
Desserts: *Per Serving*								
Cookies: Chocolate Chip/Chunk	**160**	7	40%	3	20	140	2	24
Oatmeal Raisin	**150**	5	35%	2	10	140	1	24
Peanut Butter	**170**	8	40%	3	20	190	2	21
Other Cookies, average	**170**	8	40%	3	20	160	2	22
Fudge Brownie Cake	**410**	25	35%	6	40	135	5	46
New York/Strawberry Cheesecake	**310**	18	55%	8	50	230	7	31
Kid Schlotzsky's *(no Cookie/Drink)*								
Cheese Sandwich, small	**410**	17	40%	7	20	970	18	46
Ham & Cheese, small	**440**	18	35%	7	30	1340	22	47
Kid's Cheese Pizza	**450**	13	25%	4	20	395	18	66
Kid's Pepperoni Pizza	**490**	17	31%	10	40	520	19	66
Peanut Butter & Jelly, small	**500**	15	25%	4	0	750	14	78

Note: Figures for saturated fat and cholesterol are author estimates only.

	Cal	Fat	%Fc	S.Fat	Chol	Sod	Pro	Carb
Pizzas (12"): Per Slice (1/10 Pizza)								
Cheese only:								
Thin Crust	135	5	33%	3	15	320	8	13
Thick Crust	170	5	26%	3	15	420	7	22
Homestyle Pan	305	14	41%	7	20	590	14	31
Onion/Olives/Mushrooms:								
Thin Crust	125	5	36%	3	10	315	7	14
Thick Crust	160	4	22%	2	15	420	9	22
Homestyle Pan	320	15	42%	7	20	650	15	32
Sausage Pepperoni:								
Thin Crust	165	8	44%	5	15	395	9	13
Thick Crust	205	8	35%	5	20	425	11	22
Homestyle Pan	375	20	48%	11	25	680	17	31
Sausage Mushroom:								
Thin Crust	140	6	39%	3	15	335	8	13
Thick Crust	180	6	30%	3	15	420	10	22
Homestyle Pan	340	17	45%	8	25	680	16	31
Pepperoni:								
Thin Crust	150	7	42%	4	15	400	8	13
Thick Crust	185	6	29%	4	15	420	10	22
Homestyle Pan	345	15	39%	9	25	740	16	31
Shakey's Special:								
Thin Crust	170	9	48%	5	15	475	13	13
Thick Crust	210	8	34%	4	20	420	13	22
Homestyle Pan	385	21	49%	11	30	880	18	32
Other Items								
Spagh. w.Meat Sce/Garlic Bread	940	33	32%	10	na	1900	26	134
Potato Wedges, 15 pieces	950	36	34%	10	na	3700	17	120
Shakey's Super Hot Hero	810	44	49%	15	na	2690	36	67
Hot Ham & Cheese Sandwich	550	21	34%	10	na	2135	36	56
5-Piece Fried Chicken & Potato	1700	90	48%	30	na	5330	97	130
3-Piece Chicken & Potato	945	56	53%	18	na	2290	57	51

Note: Saturated fat figures are author estimates only.

	Cal	Fat	%FC	S.Fat	Chol	Sod	Pro	Carb
Main Menu								
All-American Burger	**690**	32	42%	na	150	930	54	44
Bacon Cheeseburger	**890**	49	50%	na	195	1490	66	44
Baked White Fish	**510**	8.5	15%	na	94	2230	48	58
Baked Potato, Plain	**345**	6.5	17%	na	0	615	6	67
Cajun Whitefish	**480**	11	20%	na	73	885	40	56
Charbroiled Blackened Chicken	**830**	26	28%	na	97	2015	47	100
Charbroiled Chicken Breast	**795**	23	26%	na	97	1830	47	99
Chicken Alfredo	**1705**	78	41%	na	430	3145	85	170
Chicken Parmesan Sandwich	**750**	30	36%	na	99	2520	42	80
Chicken Stir Fry	**1200**	35	26%	na	103	4315	48	172
Corned Beef Reuben Sandwich	**790**	53	60%	na	180	4145	40	37
Fish Sandwich	**830**	17	18%	na	67	2600	44	126
French Fries, 4 oz	**210**	11	47%	5	0	440	3	25
Fried Chicken Sandwich	**560**	15	24%	na	66	3170	31	77
Fried Fish Platter	**1050**	39	33%	na	97	2050	49	123
Grilled Shrimp	**720**	20	25%	na	195	1400	39	96
Half O'Pound Burger	**1350**	53	35%	na	225	1885	89	130
Ham Steak Dinner (no veges)	**670**	26	35%	na	100	3210	48	60
Hot Roast Beef Sandwich w. Veg.	**770**	24	28%	na	98	2900	44	95
Italian Feast	**1435**	45	28%	na	262	4630	64	204
Mushroom Swiss Burger	**970**	58	54%	na	175	1125	64	49
Original Slim Jim Sandwich	**1005**	34	31%	na	98	4395	54	123
Patty Melt	**945**	60	57%	na	190	1275	50	40
Roast Beef Platter (no veges)	**880**	30	31%	na	135	3255	59	96
Shrimper's Feast	**1035**	39	34%	na	182	2130	39	128
Shrimp Stir Fry	**875**	19	20%	na	200	3975	41	131
Spaghetti	**495**	16	29%	4	55	390	24	63
Steak (6 oz), 6 Grilled Shrimp	**1330**	57	39%	na	250	2220	76	128
Steak (6 oz), 5 Fried Shrimp	**1385**	58	38%	na	248	2250	76	139
Turkey Club/Whole Wheat	**950**	53	50%	na	178	2690	71	47
Ultimate Grilled Cheese S'wich	**895**	46	46%	na	102	3000	42	77
Children's Menu								
All-American Jnr Burger	**235**	11	42%	4	30	545	14	20
Kid's: Chicken Dinner	**245**	13	48%	4	40	150	21	11
Fish 'N Chips w. Fries	**335**	17	46%	5	41	460	13	33
Fried Shrimp	**195**	12	55%	4	70	635	10	12
Spaghetti	**250**	8	29%	2	27	195	13	32
Desserts, Icecream, Sundaes								
Apple Pie: a la Mode	**1205**	53	40%	na	49	1115	12	174
w. NutraSweet	**455**	18	36%	na	0	415	4	64
Cheesecake, 1 slice, 4 oz	**365**	26	64%	na	62	190	5	23
Carrot Cake	**500**	26	47%	6	37	475	9	56
Hot Fudge Sundae	**600**	30	45%	na	80	230	10	75
Original Strawberry Pie	**330**	17	46%	4	0	250	2	45
Strawberry Sundae	**610**	27	40%	na	88	190	9	85
Walnut Brownie	**575**	34	53%	15	35	435	10	61

	Cal	Fat	%Fc	S.Fat	Chol	Sod	Pro	Carb
Chowder: Smoked Salmon	165	7	38%	2	20	75	13	14
Clam: 1 cup	100	3.5	32%	1	12	525	3	14
Entrees: *Per Serving*								
Chicken: Tenderloin Strip								
w. Fries, 5 pces	795	38	43%	13	77	800	44	69
'Lite Catch', 3 pces	305	15	44%	5	58	675	26	17
Chicken: Strips, Create A Catch	80	4	45%	2	15	150	8	4
Strips, Fish, Fries	805	40	45%	13	100	860	80	72
Strips, Shrimp, Fries	800	39	44%	13	97	1035	36	77
Clam: Strips w. Fries	1005	70	63%	20	14	570	22	90
Strips, Fish, Fries	870	54	56%	18	61	670	25	81
Cod: 3 pces. w. Fries	665	32	43%	10	38	1055	27	68
4 pces. w. Fries	760	36	43%	12	50	1390	34	74
5 pces. w. Fries	855	41	43%	14	62	1725	42	80
Fish Meal: 1 fillet w. Fries	560	28	45%	9	55	410	17	51
2 fillets w. Fries	735	38	47%	13	108	765	28	71
2 pces w. Salad, Lite Catch	410	23	51%	7	120	940	25	27
3 fillets, w. Fries	910	48	48%	16	160	1120	39	82
3 fillets + Salad, small	410	23	51%	7	119	940	25	27
'Create a Catch'	175	10	51%	3	53	360	11	11
Fish, Oysters, Fries	885	44	45%	16	80	810	25	95
Oyster w. Fries, 'Basket'	1040	51	44%	17	52	855	28	118
Salmon, baked	270	11	37%	2	70	505	39	1
Shrimp, Fish, Fries:	730	37	46%	12	105	945	24	77
Jumbo, w. Fries, Basket	710	35	45%	11	73	910	20	79
Original, Fries, Basket	725	36	45%	12	102	1120	20	82
Skipper's Platter Basket	1040	63	55%	20	111	1200	32	97
Sandwiches								
Chicken, 'Create a Catch'	605	32	48%	11	82	975	31	44
Fish: 'Create a Catch', regular	525	33	57%	9	86	1190	19	43
Double	700	73	94%	19	139	1550	30	54
French Fries	385	18	42%	4	2	50	6	50
Potato, baked	145	0	0%	0	0	5	4	32
Salads: Coleslaw	290	27	84%	4	50	330	2	10
Green, small, Lite Catch	60	3	46%	1	13	225	3	6
Shrimp & Seafood	170	3	16%	1	80	660	23	15
Side	25	0	0%	0	0	10	0	4
Salad Dressings & Sauces								
Blue Cheese	220	23	93%	10	8	240	1	4
Italian Gourmet	140	15	96%	3	0	200	0	2
Low Cal	15	1	53%	0	6	80	0	2
Ranch House	190	20	96%	4	0	300	1	2
Thousand Island	160	14	79%	3	6	415	0	8
Barbeque Sauce, 1Tbsp	25	1	36%	0	0	225	0	5
Cocktail Sauce, 1 Tbsp	20	0	0%	0	0	215	0	5
Tartar Sauce, 1Tbsp	65	7	97%	2	4	100	0	0
Root Beer Float	300	10	30%	3	10	65	3	33

	Cal	Fat	%Fc	S.Fat	Chol	Sod	Pro	Carb
Hot Entrees								
Hamburger	**625**	33	47%	12	142	335	45	36
Dakota Ranch Steak: 6 oz	**315**	20	57%	8	100	255	30	0
8 oz	**420**	27	58%	11	135	340	37	0
9 1/2 oz	**500**	32	58%	13	160	400	47	0
Hibachi Chicken Breast w. Pineapple	**195**	3	14%	1	65	685	28	13
Lemon-Herb Chicken Breast	**140**	3	19%	1	65	380	27	0
Malibu Chicken Patty, each	**310**	19	55%	3	75	590	23	11
Salmon	**250**	12	44%	2	41	230	32	0
Santa Fe Chicken Breast	**150**	3	18%	1	65	350	30	0
Shrimp, Broiled	**150**	6	36%	0	218	375	23	0
Fried, 4 only	**225**	2	8%	0	118	705	18	35
Mini	**150**	1	6%	0	80	480	13	24
Shrimp Scampi	**145**	3	19%	1	150	385	27	0
Swordfish	**315**	14	40%	3	89	330	45	0
Accompaniments								
Cheese Toast, 1 pce	**275**	21	69%	5	5	495	6	16
French Fries	**360**	12	30%	6	0	245	5	45
Potato, Baked, Flesh Only	**105**	0	0%	0	0	5	2	24
Rice Pilaf	**260**	5	18%	1	0	865	4	47
***Condiments:** Per 1 1/2 oz*								
Sauces:								
Buttery Dipping	**330**	37	100%	7	0	0	0	0
Cocktail	**40**	0	0%	0	0	395	0	8
Hibachi	**60**	0	0%	0	0	710	0	11
Malibu	**285**	31	99%	6	28	355	0	0
Marinara, 1 oz	**15**	0	0%	0	0	90	0	3
Nacho Cheese, 2 oz	**120**	10	75%	5	30	600	5	3
Sour Dressing	**90**	9	91%	8	0	45	0	0
Tartar	**170**	17	90%	3	14	455	0	6
Margarine, Whipped, 1 1/2 T.	**105**	12	100%	2	0	145	0	0
Hot Bar								
Broccoli Cheese Soup, 4 oz	**140**	9	58%	2	8	355	3	10
Chicken Noodle Soup, 4 oz	**30**	1	29%	0	7	495	2	4
Chicken Wings, 1 oz	**75**	4	49%	1	20	135	4	4
Clam Chowder, 4 oz	**120**	6	46%	0	6	510	3	11
Focaccia Bread, 2 pces	**110**	7	58%	1	0	135	2	9
Meatballs, 4 balls	**155**	11	63%	5	30	460	9	5
Minestrone Soup, 4 oz	**35**	0	0%	0	0	445	1	7
Pasta, Fettucine, 2 oz	**80**	1	11%	0	5	5	3	15
Pasta, Spaghetti, 2 oz	**80**	0	0%	0	0	0	3	16
Potato Skins, 2 oz	**160**	8	45%	1	0	465	2	22
Refried Beans, 1/4 cup	**60**	1	15%	2	5	270	4	11
Saltine Crackers, 2 crackers	**25**	1	36%	0	2	75	1	4
Taco Filling, 2 oz	**105**	9	79%	4	16	230	2	3
Taco Shells, each	**50**	2	36%	0	0	20	1	7

	Cal	Fat	%Fc	S.Fat	Chol	Sod	Pro	Carb
Salads & Toppings								
Prepared Salads: *Per 2 oz*								
Carrot & Raisin	130	10	69%	2	10	105	1	10
Chinese Chicken	55	2	33%	0	10	120	4	6
Mediterranean Minted Fruit	30	0	0%	0	0	10	1	7
Mexican Fiesta	55	1	17%	0	0	100	2	10
Old Fashioned Potato	85	5	53%	1	10	230	1	10
Red Herb Potato	120	9	67%	1	10	270	1	9
Seafood	55	3	48%	1	7	255	3	4
Seafood Louis Pasta	65	2	28%	0	15	140	3	9
Spicy Jicama	15	0	0%	0	0	30	0	4
Teriyaki Beef	50	2	37%	1	7	135	4	5
Tuna Pasta	135	10	68%	1	10	190	6	6
Sides								
Cottage Cheese, 2 oz	50	1	18%	1	5	230	8	2
Eggs, 1 oz	45	3	61%	1	120	35	4	0
Garbanzo Beans, 1/4 cup	65	1	14%	0	0	255	3	11
Turkey Ham, 1 oz	60	5	73%	2	19	375	4	0
Kidney Beans, 1/4 cup	50	0	0%	0	0	220	3	10
Olives, 1 oz	60	6	87%	1	0	180	1	1
Peas, 1/4 cup	30	0	0%	0	0	35	2	6
Peaches, 1/4 cup	35	0	0%	0	0	5	0	9
Real Bacon Bits, 1 Tbsp	30	2	67%	0	0	165	2	2
Dressings & Condiments: Per 1 oz								
Dressing: Blue Cheese	110	12	98%	4	8	170	1	1
Honey Mustard	160	16	90%	2	10	110	0	4
Italian, Lite	15	0	0%	0	0	350	0	2
Japanese Rice Vinegar, Fat Free	10	0	0%	0	0	180	0	2
Parmesan Italian	100	10	90%	2	0	450	0	2
Ranch	120	12	90%	2	10	240	0	2
Ranch, Reduced-Calorie	90	8	80%	2	10	270	0	4
Thousand Island	145	15	94%	2	10	125	0	3
Guacamole	40	4	86%	1	0	425	0	2
Salsa	10	0	0%	0	0	155	0	2
Sour Dressing, 2 Tbsp	60	6	90%	5	0	30	0	0
Dessert Bar								
Choc/Van. Soft Serve, 4 oz	135	4	26%	4	0	100	1	24
Chocolate Syrup, 1 oz	90	0	0%	0	0	15	0	21
Strawberry Topping, 1 oz	70	0	0%	0	0	5	0	18
Whipped Topping, 1 Tbsp	10	1	75%	1	0	0	0	1

	Cal	Fat	%Fc	S.Fat	Chol	Sod	Pro	Carb
Soups: Per 1 Cup								
Low Fat: Soup: Chicken Tortilla	100	3	27%	1	20	990	12	5
Chicken/Turkey Noodle	160	3	17%	2	20	480	15	17
Sweet Tomato Onion	110	3	25%	1	0	450	2	12
Vegetable Medley	90	1	10%	0	0	520	2	14
Regular Soup: Albondigas Buenas	190	9	43%	4	15	720	12	17
Chesapeake Corn Chowder	310	13	38%	5	20	720	12	43
Chicken Fajitas & Black Bean	280	7	23%	2	20	980	22	33
Chicken Jambalaya	160	7	39%	2	30	980	12	13
Chunky Potato Cheese	210	10	43%	6	30	480	10	19
Cream of Broccoli/Chicken	250	15	54%	6	40	350	11	14
Cream of Mushroom	290	21	65%	8	30	820	10	15
Irish Potato Leek	260	16	55%	8	35	680	5	23
Minestrone w.Italian Sausage	210	11	47%	4	20	890	13	14
Navy Bean w.Ham	340	10	26%	4	40	980	35	30
New England Clam Chowder	330	20	55%	10	80	630	18	21
New Orleans Style Jambalaya	160	8	45%	3	30	900	8	14
Shrimp Bisque	300	19	57%	8	70	880	11	20
Split Pea Ham; Turk. Cassoulet	350	10	26%	4	40	980	36	32
Turkey Vegetable	270	12	40%	4	40	990	22	16
Vegetarian Harvest	190	8	38%	2	0	990	5	23
Chili: Arizona /Texas Red	230	8	31%	4	20	680	14	30
Yucatan Chili	280	10	32%	4	40	890	28	31
House Chili	230	3	12%	2	15	560	15	26
Santa Fe Black Bean Chili	190	3	14%	0	0	580	9	26
Fresh Tossed Salads: Per 1 Cup								
Antipasto Salad; BBQ Aver.	140	10	64%	3	15	350	5	6
Caribbean Krab Salad	120	7	68%	1	110	180	5	10
Classic Caesar Salad	190	14	66%	2	10	280	5	10
Ensalada Azteca	130	9	62%	3	15	230	6	7
Greek Salad	120	9	68%	3	10	320	3	4
Mandarin Spinach w.Walnuts	170	11	58%	1	0	150	3	14
Roma Tomato, Mozzarella & Basil	120	9	68%	2	10	180	4	7
Shrimp & Krab Louis; Spinach	180	12	60%	4	190	340	10	6
Sonoma w. Artichokes	160	12	68%	2	0	640	2	8
Spinach & Pasta w.Raspb. Vin.	180	6	40%	0	0	620	6	22
Won Ton Chicken Salad	150	8	48%	1	10	220	6	12
Prepared Salads: Per 1/2 Cup								
Artichoke Rice	160	8	45%	1	3	780	3	21
Aunt Doris' Red Pepper Slaw	70	0	0%	0	0	480	18	18
Baja Bean & Cilantro	180	3	15%	0	0	190	9	29
BBQ Potato	160	8	45%	1	5	270	2	20
Carrot Raisin	90	3	30%	0	5	80	1	17
Chinese Krab	160	8	45%	1	3	260	5	19
Confetti Pasta w. Cheddar & Dill	160	9	45%	2	10	380	5	16
Cucumber Tomato w.Chile Lime	20	0	0%	0	0	20	1	4
Dijon Potato w. Garlic Dill Vin.	140	7	51%	1	0	260	3	16

	Cal	Fat	%Fc	S.Fat	Chol	Sod	Pro	Carb
Salads (Cont): Per 1/2 Cup								
German Potato; Gemeilli Pasta	130	3	21%	0	5	380	5	20
Greek Couscous w. Feta Cheese	170	9	42%	1	4	480	6	19
Mazatian Krab & Pasta	160	9	45%	1	2	480	4	15
Mandarin Krab Salad	150	3	18%	0	2	280	5	26
Mandarin w. Broccoli/Almonds	120	3	23%	0	0	380	3	19
Marinated Summer Vegetables	80	0	0%	0	0	210	1	19
Mediterranean Harvest	120	3	23%	1	2	180	3	17
Mediterranean Krab & Rotini	170	10	53%	1	2	380	4	15
Moroccan Marinated Vegetables	90	3	30%	0	0	230	2	9
Old Fashioned Macaroni w. Ham	180	11	55%	2	10	360	4	15
Oriental Ginger Slaw w. Krab	70	3	39%	0	2	80	2	8
Pesto Pasta; Picnic Potato	160	7	39%	1	2	320	4	18
Pineapple Coconut Slaw	150	10	60%	3	15	190	1	14
Poppyseed Coleslaw	120	9	68%	1	10	130	1	9
Rst. Potato w. Chipotle Chile	140	6	39%	1	0	250	3	18
Southern Dill Potato	120	3	23%	2	5	300	4	20
Spicy Southwestern Pasta	130	3	21%	0	0	350	5	21
Spinach Krab	230	12	47%	2	15	550	5	25
Summer Barley w. Black Beans	110	3	25%	0	0	280	4	19
Thai Noodle w. Peanut Sce	170	8	42%	1	0	310	5	17
Three Bean Marinade	170	6	32%	1	0	320	4	27
Tortellini Salad w. Basil	170	10	53%	2	2	260	4	14
Tumbleweed Tortellini	140	9	58%	1	2	330	4	11
Tuna Tarragon	240	14	53%	2	10	480	6	21
Turkey Chutney Pasta	230	9	35%	2	30	310	14	21
Zesty Tortellini	190	15	71%	2	10	460	4	18
Dressing & Croutons: Per 2 Tbsp								
Garlic Parmesan w. Croutons (10)	40	3	68%	1	2	160	2	2
Blue Cheese Dressing	140	14	90%	2.5	10	230	1	3
Blush Vinaigrette	120	12	90%	2	0	320	0	3
Creamy Cucumber Dressing	80	7	79%	1	0	290	0	4
Garden French Tomato	40	1.5	34%	0	0	270	0	7
Honey Mustard Dressing	150	13	78%	2	10	230	0	8
Fat Free	45	0	0%	0	10	160	0	10
Parmesan Pepper Cream	160	17	97%	2.5	5	330	1	2
Ranch House Dressing	130	13	90%	2	10	180	1	1
Fat Free	50	0	0%	0	0	180	1	2
Raspberry Vinaigrette	120	13	98%	2	0	150	0	3
Thousand Island Dressing	110	11	90%	1.5	5	250	0	3
Zesty Italian Dressing	160	18	100%	2.5	0	280	0	1
Fat Free	20	0	0%	0	0	340	0	5
Hot Tossed Pastas: Per Cup								
Bruschetta	260	4	(14%)	2	10	450	10	41
Creamy	360	16	(40%)	8	45	510	12	43
Chipotle Chicken w. Cilantro	390	16	(37%)	9	50	560	22	42
Creamy Pesto w. Sundried Tomatoes	430	21	(34%)	9	45	410	14	44

	Cal	Fat	%FC	S.Fat	Chol	Sod	Pro	Carb
Tossed Pastas (continued)								
Fettucine Alfredo	390	18	42%	10	50	580	15	41
Garden Vegetable: w. Meatballs	270	7	23%	3	10	460	11	42
w. Italian Sausage	300	10	30%	3	20	540	12	42
Italian Vegetable Beef	270	6	20%	2	10	470	10	43
Jalapeno Salsa	240	4	42%	2	10	430	10	41
Nutty Mushroom	390	20	46%	9	45	410	12	42
Smoked Salmon & Dill	360	16	40%	8	45	390	13	41
Vegetarian Marinara w. Basil	260	4	14%	2	10	750	10	44
Muffins: *Per Muffin*								
96% Fat Free: All types	80	0.5	5%	0	0	110	2	17
Regular: Apple Raisin	150	7	42%	1	10	190	2	22
Apricot/Banana/Cherry Nut	150	7	42%	1	10	190	2	22
Carrot Pineapple w. Oat Bran	150	6	36%	1	10	230	3	23
Chili Corn	140	3	19%	1	10	320	3	27
Chocolate Varieties	170	8	42%	2	10	190	3	22
Georgia Peach Poppyseed	150	6	36%	1	10	210	2	20
Lemon	140	4	35%	1	10	190	2	19
Mandarin Almond w. Oat Bran	140	7	45%	1	10	210	3	20
Nutty Peanut Butter	170	8	42%	1	10	210	4	21
Peanut Butter Choc. Chip	190	9	43%	2	10	230	5	23
Pumpkin Raisin	150	6	36%	1	10	210	2	25
Strawberry Buttermilk	140	6	39%	1	10	210	2	21
Wild Maine Blueberry	140	5	32%	1	10	180	2	22
Large	310	12	35%	2	20	380	5	40
Zucchini Nut	150	7	42%	1	10	190	2	22
Breads: Buttermilk Corn	140	2	13%	0	10	270	3	27
Indian Grain	200	1.5	7%	0	15	260	11	35
Sourdough	150	0.5	3%	0	0	240	9	27
Focaccia: Garlic Parmesan	100	3	27%	0	0	170	2	15
Pizza /Tomarillo	140	6	39%	2	10	270	5	16
Desserts: *Per 1/2 Cup*								
Apple Medley	70	0	0%	0	0	5	1	18
Banana Royale	80	0	0%	0	0	5	1	20
Chocolate Chip Cookie, small	70	3	39%	1	5	90	1	10
Chocolate Pudding	140	4	26%	0	10	220	4	23
Ghirardelli Chocolate Frozen	95	0	0%	0	0	80	3	21
Jello, flavored	80	0	0%	0	0	40	1	20
Rice Pudding	110	2	16%	1	10	50	3	20
Tapioca Pudding	140	3	19%	0	10	160	4	24
Tropical Fruit Salad	75	0	0%	0	0	5	1	19
Vanilla Pudding	140	3	19%	0	10	160	4	24
Vanilla Soft Serving	140	4	26%	3	20	70	3	22
Choc. Syrup, 2 Tbsp	70	0	0%	0	10	15	0	18
Candy Sprinkles, 1 Tbsp	70	2	26%	0	0	0	0	11
Granola Topping, 2 Tbsp	110	4	33%	2	0	14	2	16

Sonic® Drive-In

	Cal	Fat	%Fc	S.Fat	Chol	Sod	Pro	Carb
Hamburgers: #1. Hamburger	410	27	59%	10	58	445	20	23
with Cheese	480	32	60%	15	76	710	24	24
#2. Hamburger	325	16	44%	5	50	550	20	23
with Cheese	395	21	48%	10	67	815	24	24
Bacon Cheeseburger	550	39	64%	18	87	840	28	23
Hickory Burger	315	16	46%	6	50	460	20	23
Jalapeno Burger	640	41	58%	12	136	1360	44	22
Super Sonic w. Mayonnaise	730	52	64%	14	144	1025	44	24
with Mustard	645	41	57%	12	136	1130	44	24
Mini Burger	245	12	44%	4	36	510	14	20
Mini Cheeseburger	280	14	45%	6	45	645	17	20
Sandwiches: B-L-T	325	19	52%	7	9	600	8	27
Chicken (breaded)	455	25	49%	9	42	755	23	36
Fish	280	7	23%	2	6	655	17	38
Grilled Cheese	290	17	53%	8	36	840	12	25
Grilled Chicken, no dressing	215	4	17%	1	63	715	21	23
Steak (breaded)	630	42	60%	14	50	1050	19	46
Coneys/Local Flavors: Chili Pie	330	23	63%	8	28	315	12	20
Regular Hot Dog	260	15	52%	6	23	240	8	21
Regular Cheese Coney	360	23	58%	10	40	340	14	23
Extra-Long Cheese Coney	635	39	55%	18	65	630	24	45
Corn Dog	280	15	48%	7	35	700	7	30
Sides: French Fries; regular	235	8	31%	3	8	50	3	37
Large	315	11	31%	4	11	70	5	50
w. Cheese, large	420	20	43%	10	38	470	11	51
Onion Rings: Regular	405	27	60%	13	na	370	5	38
Tater Tots	150	7	42%	3	10	330	2	19
Tater Tots w. Cheese	220	13	53%	6	28	570	6	19

Spaghetti Warehouse®

	Cal	Fat	%Fc	S.Fat	Chol	Sod	Pro	Carb
Lunch: Minestrone Soup	80	1.5	17%	0.5	2	1040	4	12
Grilled Chicken Marinara	530	8	14%	1.5	96	400	46	65
Seafood Marinara	385	5	12%	1	48	400	19	65
Spaghetti: w. Tomato Sauce	425	5	10%	0.5	0	490	13	82
w. Marinara Sauce #12	440	5	10%	1	0	400	14	84
Spicy Marinara Sce Spaghetti	280	4	13%	1	2	280	9	52
Vegetable Primavera	340	4	10%	0.5	0	345	12	65
Dinner: Minestrone, 1 bowl	110	2	16%	1	3	1495	6	18
Grilled Chicken Marinara	640	10	14%	2	96	550	50	85
Grilled Halibut	880	14	14%	2	93	780	78	106
Grilled Marinated Chicken Breast	910	17	17%	3	145	825	74	116
Marinara Sauce #12	520	6	16%	1	0	390	17	99
Seafood Marinara	520	8	14%	1	77	605	27	86
Spaghetti w. Tomato Sauce	525	6	10%	1	0	650	17	101
Spicy Marinara Sce Spaghetti	330	6	16%	1.5	3	410	10	60
Vegetable Primavera	610	8	12%	1	0	660	21	116

Steak 'n' Shake®

	Cal	Fat	%Fc	S.Fat	Chol	Sod	Pro	Carb
Steakburgers & Sandwiches								
Steakburger	275	7	23%)	2	60	425	18	33
with Cheese	355	13	33%	6	80	660	23	33
Super	375	12	29%	4	100	445	30	33
Super with Cheese	450	18	36%	8	120	680	35	33
Triple	475	17	32%	8	160	470	43	33
Triple with Cheese	625	30	43%	15	180	935	52	34
Ham Sandwich	450	22	44%	7	na	1860	29	37
Grilled Cheese Sandwich	250	13	47%	6	20	610	9	24
Grilled Chicken Sandwich	510	22	39%	5	85	1150	26	53
Other Items: Baked Beans	175	4	21%	1	0	655	9	27
Chef Salad	315	18	51%	5	120	1580	41	6
Chili & Oyster Crackers	335	14	38%	4	na	1160	16	37
Chili Mac & 4 Saltines	310	12	35%	3	na	1300	15	34
Chili 3 Ways & 4 Saltines	410	16	35%	4	na	1730	19	45
Cottage Cheese, 1/2 cup	95	4	38%	1	20	200	12	3
French Fries	210	10	43%	3	10	300	3	28
Lett./Tom/ Salad/1oz 1000 Island	170	15	79%	3	15	225	1	7
Desserts: Apple Danish	390	24	55%	6	30	350	6	35
Brownie	260	12	42%	4	10	165	3	39
Cheesecake	370	11	27%	5	60	295	7	61
with Strawberries	385	11	26%	5	60	295	7	65
Pies: Apple	405	18	40%	5	40	480	4	61
Cherry	335	14	38%	4	30	270	6	48
Apple, A La Mode	550	25	41%	9	80	525	4	76
Cherry, A La Mode	475	22	42%	7	70	315	6	63
Sundaes: Brownie Fudge	645	35	49%	15	30	260	7	81
Hot Fudge Nut	530	34	58%	14	60	120	5	51
Strawberry	330	22	60%	8	50	80	2	29
Vanilla Ice Cream	215	12	50%	6	40	70	1	23
Shakes & Drinks: Hot Chocolate	685	19	25%	6	50	670	17	129
Floats: Coca-Cola	515	17	30%	8	0	230	16	76
Orange	500	17	31%	8	0	225	16	74
Lemon	555	19	31%	9	0	250	18	82
Root Beer	530	17	29%	8	0	240	17	78
Freezes: Lemon	550	25	41%	10	0	215	15	69
Orange	515	24	42%	10	0	200	14	63
Shakes: Chocolate/Vanilla	610	38	56%	10	100	180	13	57
Strawberry	650	40	55%	11	100	190	16	62

(Cholesterol & Saturated Fat Figures - Estimates only)

Sub Station®

	Cal	Fat	%Fc	S.Fat	Chol	Sod	Pro	Carb
Sandwiches: Ham/Turkey & Cheese	510	30	53%	na	na	1160	18	40
Roast Beef/Turkey & Cheese	525	31	54%	na	na	1045	24	39
Salami, Pepperoni, Turkey Bologna, Ham, Cheese	635	42	60%	na	na	1590	23	40

	Cal	Fat	%Fc	S.Fat	Chol	Sod	Pro	Carb
6" Cold Subs: Cheese & Condiments Not Included								
Classic Italian BMT	450	21	44%	8	52	1580	21	45
Cold Cut Trio	375	14	33%	5	47	1435	19	45
Ham	295	5	15%	2	25	1340	18	45
Roast Beef	295	5	15%	2	20	930	19	45
Subway Club	305	5	16%	2	26	1240	21	46
Subway Seafood & Crab w. Light Mayo.	340	9	24%	2	14	1035	14	51
Tuna w. Light Mayonnaise	380	14	33%	3	32	940	18	45
Turkey Breast	280	4	13%	1	20	1170	17	45
& Ham	290	4	14%	2	23	1255	18	45
Veggie Delite	230	3	11%	1	0	580	9	43
6" Hot Subs: Cheese & Condiments Not Included Unless Indicated								
Meatball	415	15	33%	6	35	1025	19	50
Roasted Chicken Breast	340	6	16%	2	48	965	26	46
Steak & Cheese	365	10	24%	4	37	1160	24	47
Subway Melt (w. cheese)	370	11	27%	5	41	1620	23	46
Super Subs: Cheese & Condiments Not Included								
Classic Italian BMT	670	39	52%	14	104	2575	33	47
Cold Cut Trio	520	24	42%	8	93	2290	29	47
Subway Club	380	7	16%	2	52	1895	32	48
Wraps: Condiments Not Included								
Chicken Parmesan Ranch	335	5	96%	2	45	1395	17	56
Steak & Cheese	355	9	0%	4	37	1450	16	53
Turkey Breast & Bacon	355	10	0%	4	39	1825	14	52
Deli Style Sandwiches: Cheese & Condiments Not Included Unless Indicated								
Bologna	285	10	32%	3	19	785	11	37
Ham	225	3	12%	0	12	830	12	37
Roast Beef	235	4	15%	0	13	680	14	37
Tuna w. Light Mayonnaise	270	8	26%	1	16	630	12	37
Turkey Breast	230	3	12%	0	13	840	13	37
Salads: Cheese & Condiments Not Included Unless Indicated								
Classic Italian BMT	270	19	63%	7	52	1305	14	11
Cold Cut Trio	195	12	55%	4	47	1160	12	12
Ham	110	3	24%	1	25	1070	12	11
Meatball	230	13	51%	5	35	750	13	17
Pizza (w. cheese)	280	20	65%	10	50	1335	12	12
Roast Beef	115	3	23%	1	20	655	12	11
Roasted Chicken Breast	160	4	23%	1	48	695	20	13
Steak and Cheese	180	8	40%	4	37	890	17	13
Subway Club	125	3	22%	1	26	965	14	12
Subway Melt (w. cheese)	190	9	42%	4	41	1345	16	12
Subway Seafood & Crab w. Light Mayo	160	7	39%	1	14	760	7	17
Tuna Salad w. Light Mayonnaise	200	12	54%	2	32	670	11	11
Turkey Breast and Ham	105	2	17%	1	23	980	11	11
Turkey Breast Salad	100	2	18%	0	20	895	11	12
Veggie Delite Salad	50	1	18%	0	0	310	2	10

Subway® (Cont)

	Cal	Fat	%FC	S.Fat	Chol	Sod	Pro	Carb
Breads/Wraps								
6" White Bread	190	1	5%	1	0	420	7	38
6" Wheat Bread	210	3	13%	1	0	430	8	39
Deli Style Roll	170	2	10%	1	0	350	6	31
10 1/2" Tortilla	200	2	10%	1	0	720	0	45
Condiments & Extras								
Bacon, 2 strips	40	3	64%	1	9	160	3	0
Cheese, 2 triangles	40	3	67%	2	10	205	2	0
Mayonnaise, 1 tsp	40	4	90%	1	3	30	0	0
Light Mayonnaise, 1 tsp	15	2	100%	0	2	35	0	0
Mustard, 2 tsp	10	1	90%	0	0	115	0	0
Olive Oil Blend, 1 tsp	45	5	100%	1	0	0	0	0
Vinegar, 1 Tbsp	1	0	0%	0	0	0	0	0
Salad Dressings: Per 2 oz Packet								
Creamy Italian, 1 pkt	260	28	97%	4	16	530	0	12
Fat-Free Italian, 1 pkt	20	0	0%	0	0	610	0	4
French, 1 pkt	280	24	85%	4	0	400	0	20
Fat-Free, 1 pkt	70	0	0%	0	0	390	0	16
Thousand Island, 1 pkt	260	28	97%	4	32	620	0	12
Ranch, 1 pkt	350	40	73%	8	24	470	0	8
Fat-Free, 1 pkt	60	0	0%	0	0	710	0	16
Cookies: Per Cookie								
Dbl Choc Brazil Nut	215	10	42%	3	14	155	2	29
Chocolate Chip/Chunk; M & M	215	10	42%	3	15	145	2	29
White Choc Macadamia Nut	220	11	45%	2	12	145	2	28
Oatmeal Raisin	200	8	36%	2	14	160	3	29
Low Fat Oatmeal Raisin	170	3	16%	1	15	170	3	33
Peanut Butter	225	12	48%	2	0	215	3	27
Sugar Cookie	225	12	48%	3	18	180	2	28

Sweet Tomatoes®

~ Same Menu & Data as Souplantation (Page 232) ~

	Cal	Fat	%Fc	S.Fat	Chol	Sod	Pro	Carb
Tacos: Taco, regular	170	10	53%	4	30	330	9	12
Taco Supreme®	210	14	60%	6	40	350	9	14
Soft Taco - Beef	210	10	43%	4	30	570	11	20
Soft Taco - Chicken	190	7	33%	2.5	35	480	13	19
Soft Taco - Steak	190	7	33%	3	25	490	14	18
Soft Taco Supreme® - Beef	260	13	45%	6	40	590	11	22
Soft Taco Supreme® - Chicken; Steak	240	11	41%	5	45	490	14	21
Double Decker® Taco	330	15	40%	5	30	740	14	37
Double Decker® Taco Supreme	380	18	42%	7	40	760	15	39
Gorditas								
Gordita Baja™ - Beef	360	21	52%	5	35	810	13	29
Gordita Baja™ - Chicken; Steak	340	18	47%	4	35	725	17	28
Gordita Santa Fe™ Beef	380	23	54%	5	35	700	14	31
Gordita Santa Fe™ Chicken; Steak	370	20	48%	4	40	610	17	30
Gordita Supreme® - Beef; Steak	300	14	42%	5	35	550	17	27
Gordita Supreme® - Chicken	300	13	40%	5	45	530	16	28
Gordita Nacho Cheese - Beef	310	15	53%	4	25	780	13	30
Gordita Nacho Cheese - Chkn; Steak	290	13	49%	3	20	695	16	29
Chalupas: Chalupa Baja® - Beef	420	27	58%	7	35	760	14	28
Chalupa Baja® - Chicken; Steak	400	24	54%	6	40	670	17	27
Chalupa Santa Fe™ - Beef	440	29	60%	7	35	650	14	31
Chalupa Santa Fe™ - Chicken; Steak	420	26	56%	5	40	580	17	30
Supreme® - Beef	380	23	55%	8	40	580	14	29
Chalupa Supreme® - Chicken	360	20	50%	7	45	490	17	28
Chalupa Supreme® - Steak	360	20	50%	7	35	500	17	27
Chalupa Nacho Cheese - Beef	370	22	53%	6	25	740	13	30
Chalupa Nacho Cheese - Chkn; Steak	350	19	49%	4.5	20	650	16	29
Burritos: Bean Burrito	370	12	30%	3.5	10	1080	13	54
Burrito Supreme® - Beef	430	18	37%	7	40	1210	17	50
Burrito Supreme® - Chicken	410	16	35%	6	45	1120	20	49
Burrito Supreme® - Steak	420	16	34%	6	35	1140	21	48
Double Burrito Supreme® - Beef	510	23	40%	9	60	1500	23	52
Double Burrito Supreme® - Chicken	460	17	33%	6	70	1200	27	50
Double Burrito Supreme® - Steak	470	18	34%	7	65	1230	28	48
Fiesta Burrito - Beef	380	15	38%	5	30	1100	14	49
Fiesta Burrito - Chicken; Steak	370	12	29%	4	35	1000	17	48
Chili Cheese Burrito	330	13	35%	5	25	900	13	40
7-Layer Burrito	520	22	38%	7	25	1270	16	65
Specialities: Tostada	250	12	43%	4.5	15	640	10	27
Cheese Quesadilla	350	18	46%	9	50	860	16	31
Chicken Quesadilla	400	19	43%	9	75	1050	25	33
Enchirito® - Beef	370	19	46%	9	50	1300	18	33
Enchirito® - Chicken; Steak	350	16	41%	8	50	1215	22	31
Meximelt®	290	15	46%	7	45	830	15	22
Mexican Pizza	390	25	58%	8	45	930	18	28
Taco Salad w. Salsa & Shell	850	52	55%	14	70	2250	30	69
Taco Salad w. Salsa, w/out Shell	400	22	50%	10	70	1510	24	31

Taco Bell® (Cont)

	Cal	Fat	%Fc	S.Fat	Chol	Sod	Pro	Carb
Nachos and Sides: Nachos, 3.5 oz	**320**	18	50%	4	4	560	5	34
Nachos Supreme®	**440**	24	49%	7	35	800	14	44
Nachos BellGrande®	**760**	39	46%	11	35	1300	20	83
Mucho Grande Nachos	**1320**	82	56%	25	75	2670	31	116
Pintos 'n Cheese, 4.5 oz	**180**	8	40%	4	15	640	9	18
Mexican Rice, 4.75 oz	**190**	9	42%	3.5	15	750	5	23
Cinnamon Twists, 1.25 oz	**150**	4.5	27%	1	0	190	1	27
Side Items/Condiments: Per Serving								
Average other Sauces	**15**	0	0%	0	0	90	0	1
Guacamole, 3/4 oz	**35**	3	77%	0	0	80	0	1
Nacho Cheese Sauce, 2 oz	**120**	10	75%	2.5	5	470	2	5
Pepper Jack Cheese Sauce, 1/2 oz	**70**	7	70%	1	5	120	0	1
Sour Cream, 3/4 oz	**40**	4	90%	3	10	10	1	1
Three Cheese Blend, 1/4 oz	**25**	2	1%	1	5	60	2	0

Taco Time®

	Cal	Fat	%Fc	S.Fat	Chol	Sod	Pro	Carb
Burritos								
Casita Burrito®, Meat	**645**	31	43%	15	90	1235	40	54
Crisp Burrito: Bean	**430**	18	37%	5	12	455	15	53
Chicken	**420**	25	53%	8	54	795	17	32
Meat	**550**	30	49%	10	58	1000	34	39
Double Soft Bean Burrito	**505**	12	22%	6	22	860	23	77
Double Soft Combination Burrito	**615**	23	34%	10	63	1345	10	39
Double Soft Meat Burrito	**725**	33	41%	14	100	1810	57	55
Value Soft Bean Burrito, Single	**380**	10	24%	4	15	715	16	58
Value Soft Meat Burrito, Single	**490**	21	38%	8	56	1200	31	48
Veggie Burrito	**490**	16	30%	6	24	645	21	70
Taco: Chicken Soft Taco	**390**	16	37%	6	48	935	21	41
Crisp Taco	**295**	17	52%	7	48	610	22	16
Natural Super Taco, Meat	**630**	27	38%	13	82	915	41	60
Rolled Soft Flour Taco	**510**	23	40%	10	63	1110	33	46
Super Shredded Beef Soft Taco	**370**	11	28%	6	22	555	12	38
Taco Cheeseburger, Meat	**635**	36	51%	10	66	1290	31	48
Value Soft Taco	**315**	15	43%	7	48	600	24	23
Specialties: Crustos®	**375**	15	36%	na	0	85	9	47
Empanada, Cherry	**250**	9	32%	na	9	45	5	37
Mexi Fries®: Regular, 4 oz	**265**	17	58%	na	0	800	3	27
Mexican Rice, 4 oz	**160**	2	11%	1	0	530	3	30
Nachos: Regular, 10.5 oz	**680**	38	50%	19	78	1250	26	61
Deluxe, 15.25 oz	**1050**	57	49%	23	109	2250	46	91
Quesadilla, Cheese	**205**	11	48%	6	30	255	11	17
Refritos	**325**	10	27%	5	22	525	18	44
Salads: Taco Salad (no dressing)	**480**	28	52%	11	63	895	30	30
Chicken Taco Salad (no dressing)	**370**	21	51%	7	48	860	19	27
Tostada Delight® Salad, Meat	**630**	33	47%	14	82	1005	36	48
Sauce: Enchilada/Hot Sauce, 1 oz	**12**	0	0%	0	0	135	0	3

	Cal	Fat	%FC	S.Fat	Chol	Sod	Pro	Carb
Tacos								
Bravo	355	15	38%	5	26	655	15	39
Burger	280	11	35%	5	35	580	14	29
Crispy	195	12	55%	4	26	255	9	13
El Grande	480	29	54%	10	67	765	24	30
El Grande Chicken	330	18	49%	5	41	735	17	24
Softshell	230	10	39%	4	26	505	11	23
Softshell Chicken	175	5	25%	2	21	615	11	22
Burritos								
Bean Burrito	380	12	28%	5	15	810	15	54
Beefy Burrito	440	20	41%	9	53	860	22	44
Chicken and Potato Burrito	455	19	37%	5	19	1345	15	56
Meat and Potato Burrito	510	23	40%	7	23	1235	15	58
Super Burrito	455	19	37%	7	34	910	19	51
Specialities								
Chicken Festiva Burrito	545	28	46%	7	37	1150	17	56
Chicken Festiva Salad (w. dressing)	685	50	65%	11	70	1425	21	39
Chicken Festiva Salad (no dressing)	360	19	47%	6	49	660	21	27
Potato Olés Bravo	585	36	55%	10	13	1810	9	55
Sierra Chicken Sandwich	510	28	49%	6	70	930	27	40
Super Nachos	925	62	60%	15	47	1450	24	70
Super Potato Olés	990	63	57%	19	47	3025	23	83
Taco Salad (with dressing)	715	45	56%	12	40	1795	21	55
Taco Salad (no dressing)	545	28	46%	9	40	880	20	50
Platters								
Beef and Bean Chimi	745	34	41%	9	41	1770	26	82
Beef Enchilada	850	43	45%	15	71	2255	34	80
Chicken Enchilada	710	33	42%	11	48	2310	28	72
Cheese and Chiles Chimi	800	43	48%	14	50	1915	27	74
Sides								
Green Chili	225	12	48%	5	15	1235	10	20
Mexican Rice	250	5	18%	1	0	855	6	44
Nachos	455	32	63%	8	14	850	8	36
Potato Olés: Small (Kid's Meal)	305	18	53%	4	0	880	3	33
Regular	415	24	52%	6	0	1195	4	45
Large	545	32	53%	8	0	1570	5	60
Refried Beans	375	13	31%	5	15	990	20	46
Side Salad	290	24	74%	5	20	555	3	15
Texas Style Chili	375	22	52%	10	56	945	21	23
Desserts								
Apple Grande	260	9	31%	3	7	240	5	40
Choco Taco	310	17	49%	10	20	100	3	37
Churros	160	11	63%	2	10	115	2	13
Dichos Cookies, 2	70	4	53%	0	0	10	2	6
Taco John's Cinnamon Mint Swirl	60	0	0%	0	0	5	1	14
Teddy Graham Cubs	60	2	30%	0	0	80	1	10

Taco John's® (Cont)

	Cal	Fat	%FC	S.Fat	Chol	Sod	Pro	Carb
Local Favourites								
Bean Tostada	165	8	43%	2	7	230	6	18
Cheese Crisp	220	16	65%	8	37	250	10	10
Chicken Fajita	320	10	28%	4	34	890	18	41
Chicken Fajita Salad	645	39	54%	9	34	1945	20	53
Chilito	445	22	44%	12	58	1065	21	41
Chicken Quesadilla	440	20	41%	7	44	1140	20	42
Chimichanga	590	29	44%	8	34	1140	20	57
Combination Burrito	410	16	35%	7	34	835	18	50
Double Enchilada	545	32	53%	12	79	860	28	34
Mexi Rolls	670	41	53%	13	75	1345	29	53
Potato Olés w. Cheese	550	35	57%	11	14	2045	8	51
Quesadilla	465	24	46%	10	45	940	18	41
Ranch Burrito	435	22	45%	8	45	830	16	43
Smothered Burrito	580	27	42%	9	48	1125	25	48
Taco John's Mexican Pizza	585	32	49%	8	50	720	23	50
Tostada	195	12	55%	4	26	255	9	13

TCBY® Frozen Yogurt

	Cal	Fat	%FC	S.Fat	Chol	Sod	Pro	Carb
Hand-Dipped Ice Cream:								
Small	320	19	53%	11	56	115	6	37
Medium	440	26	53%	15	77	160	9	50
Large	560	34	53%	20	98	200	11	64
Frozen Yogurt: Nonfat: Medium	240	0	0%	0	99	130	9	51
Large	310	0	0%	0	126	170	11	64
Regular, all flavors: Medium	285	6.5	21%	4.5	33	135	9	51
Large	365	8.5	21%	5.5	42	170	11	64
Hand-Dipped: Medium	310	6.5	20%	4.5	11	175	6.5	57
Large	390	8.5	20%	5.5	14	225	9	73
No Sugar Added Nonfat: Medium	175	0	0%	0	6	77	9	44
Large	225	0	0%	0	8	98	11	56
Sorbet: Medium	220	0	0%	0	0	65	0	53
Large	280	0	0%	0	0	85	0	67
Paradise Ice: Medium	430	0	0%	0	0	0	0	110
Large	550	0	0%	0	0	0	0	140

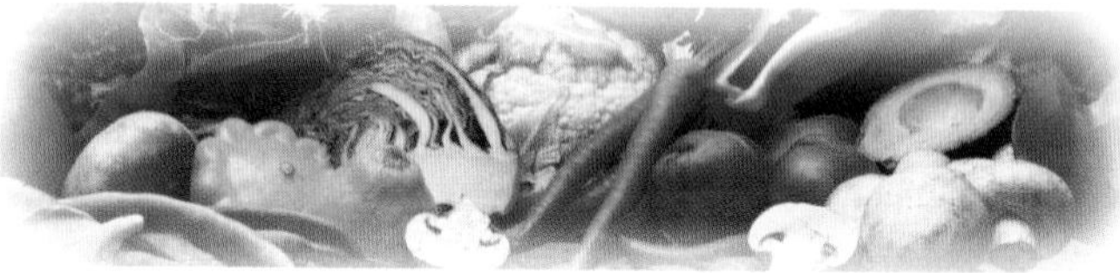

	Cal	Fat	%FC	S.Fat	Chol	Sod	Pro	Carb
Salads								
Caesar Salad	470	30	57%	na	72	1190	30	22
Chef's Salad	385	19	44%	na	65	1585	26	26
Chicken Caesar	300	4.5	14%	na	65	490	30	35
Cobb Salad	485	24	44%	na	294	985	40	29
Farmers Market	160	4.5	25%	na	0	510	6	24
Garden Salad	255	10	32%	na	214	580	11.5	31
Mandarin Orange Chicken	300	10	30%	na	60	210	27	25
Oriental Chicken	320	14	40%	na	60	290	30	18
Taco Salad	945	59	56%	na	70	1625	29	76
Sandwiches: *Per 6" sandwich on white roll*								
Albacore Tuna	700	30	38%	na	67	1655	32	78
Avocado & Cheese	715	37	47%	na	28	1545	18	81
Avocado & Turkey	675	28	37%	na	35	1605	27	80
Avocado, Cucumber & Alfalfa Sprout	635	28	40%	na	6	1150	16	85
BBQ Beef	725	22	27%	na	88	2120	39	94
BBQ Chicken	560	8	13%	na	95	1540	48	74
California Roasted Chicken	510	15	26%	na	65	1770	36	73
Cheese (Swiss, Amer., Provolone)	860	46	48%	na	107	2196	42	77
Chunky Chicken Salad	635	26	37%	na	42	1560	40	72
Egg Salad w. Cheese	730	35	43%	na	456	1765	29	76
Ham & Cheese	660	26	34%	na	68	2900	33	76
Hot Pastrami	705	26	33%	na	72	2260	34	85
Hummus	665	21	28%	na	9	1510	20	102
Italian Dry Salami & Cheese	770	33	38%	na	118	3290	42	78
Italian Dry Salami, Capicolla, Mortadella, Cotto & Provolone	735	32	39%	na	85	2190	31	74
Meatballs w. Pizza Sauce	710	28	35%	na	97	1605	36	78
Mort., Provolone & Dry Salami/Cotto	785	39	45%	na	84	2300	36	74
Roast Beef (Hot or Cold)	550	11	18%	na	84	1535	42	73
Roast Beef & Avocado	615	20	29%	na	64	1440	44	85
Roasted Bell Pepper & Provolone	580	22	34%	na	33	1755	21	79
Seafood Salad	610	21	30%	na	105	2010	31	74
Sicilian Chicken	560	10	16%	na	33	1690	50	67
Smoked Turkey	725	19	24%	na	96	2545	46	94
Spicy Chkn w. Jamaican seasoning	560	14	22%	na	85	1190	32	78
Turkey & Bacon Club	665	26	35%	na	80	2110	37	73
Turkey & Cheese	640	23	32%	na	70	2275	34	75
Turkey & Cranberry	625	13	19%	na	50	1905	30	96
Turkey, Ham & Cheese	670	25	33%	na	76	2770	37	76
Turkey, Ham, Salami & Cheese	700	26	34%	na	88	2975	40	77
Turkey, Roast Beef & Cheese	680	23	30%	na	97	2225	43	75
Turkey, Salami & Cheese	715	28	35%	na	98	2800	40	76

	Cal	Fat	%Fc	S.Fat	Chol	Sod	Pro	Carb
Sandwiches								
Plain Single	360	16	40%	6	65	580	24	31
Single with Everything	420	20	43%	7	70	920	25	37
Big Bacon Classic	580	30	46%	12	100	1460	34	46
Jr. Hamburger	270	10	33%	3.5	30	610	15	34
Jr. Cheeseburger	320	13	37%	6	45	830	17	34
Deluxe	360	17	42%	6	50	890	18	36
Jr. Bacon Cheeseburger	380	19	45%	7	60	850	20	34
Kids' Meal: Hamburger	270	10	33%	3.5	30	610	15	33
Cheeseburger	320	13	37%	6	45	830	17	33
Grilled Chicken	310	8	23%	1.5	65	790	27	35
Breaded Chicken	440	18	37%	3.5	60	840	28	44
Chicken Club	470	20	38%	4	70	970	31	44
Spicy Chicken	410	15	33%	2.5	65	1280	28	43
Fresh Stuffed Pitas (w. dress.): Greek	440	20	41%	8	35	1050	15	50
Caesar/ Garden Chicken	490	18	33%	5	65	1320	34	48
Garden Veggie	400	17	38%	3.5	20	760	11	52
French Fries								
Small	270	13	43%	2	0	85	4	35
Medium	390	19	44%	3	0	120	5	50
Biggie	470	23	44%	3.5	0	150	7	61
Great Biggie	570	27	43%	4	0	180	8	73
Garden Spot Salad Bar								
Applesauce, 2 Tbsp	30	0	0%	0	0	0	0	7
Bacon Bits, 2 Tbsp	45	2	40%	1	10	550	6	0
Bananas & Strawb. Glaze, 1/4 cup	30	0	0%	0	0	0	0	8
Broccoli/Carrot/Cauliflower, 1/4 c.	5	0	0%	0	0	0	0	1
Cantaloupe, 1 slice	15	0	0%	0	0	0	0	4
Cheese, shred. (imitation), 2 T.	50	4	72%	0.5	0	260	3	1
Chicken Salad. 2 Tbsp	70	5	64%	1	0	135	4	2
Cole Slaw, 2 Tbsp	45	3	60%	0	5	65	0	5
Cottage Cheese, 2 Tbsp	30	1.5	45%	1	5	125	4	1
Croutons, 2 Tbsp	25	1	36%	0	0	65	1	4
Eggs, hard, 2 Tbsp	40	3	68%	1	110	30	3	0
Parmesan Blend, grated, 2 T.	70	4	51%	2	10	290	4	5
Pasta Salad, 2 Tbsp	35	1.5	39%	0	0	180	1	4
Peaches, 1 slice	15	0	0%	0	0	0	0	4
Pepperoni, 6 slices	30	3	90%	1	5	70	1	0
Potato Salad, 2 Tbsp	80	7	79%	2.5	5	180	0	5
Pudding, 1/4 cup: Chocolate	70	3	39%	0.5	0	60	0	10
Red Onions, 3 rings	5	0	0%	0	0	0	0	1
Sesame Breadstick, 1 each	15	0	0%	0	0	20	0	2
Soft Breadsticks	130	3	21%	0.5	5	250	4	23
Strawberries, 1 each	10	0	0%	0	0	0	0	2
Sunflower Seeds & Raisins, 2 T.	80	5	56%	0.5	0	0	0	5
Tomato, wedged, 1 piece	5	0	0%	0	0	0	0	1
Turkey Ham, diced, 2 Tbsp	50	4	72%	1	25	280	3	0

	Cal	Fat	%FC	S.Fat	Chol	Sod	Pro	Carb
Fresh Salads-To-Go: No Dressing								
Caesar Side	**110**	5	41%	2.5	15	650	10	7
Deluxe Garden	110	6	49%	1	0	350	7	9
Grilled Chicken	**200**	8	36%	1.5	50	720	25	9
Side Salad	60	3	45%	0	0	180	4	5
Taco Salad	**380**	19	45%	10	65	1040	26	28
Taco Chips, 15 chips	210	11	47%	1.5	0	180	3	24
Dressings & Sauce								
Barbeque Sauce, 1 pkt	50	0	0%	0	0	160	1	10
Blue Cheese, 2 Tbsp	**180**	19	100%	3.5	15	180	1	0
Caesar Vinaigrette, 1 Tbsp	70	7	70%	1	0	170	0	1
French, 2 Tbsp	**120**	10	75%	1.5	0	330	0	6
French Fat Free, 2 Tbsp	35	0	0%	0	0	150	0	8
Garden Ranch Sauce, 1 Tbsp	**50**	4.5	81%	1	10	125	0	1
Hidden Valley Ranch, 2 Tbsp	100	10	100%	1.5	10	220	1	1
Reduced Fat, 2 Tbsp	**60**	5	75%	1	10	240	1	2
Honey Mustard, 1 pkt	130	12	83%	2	10	220	0	6
Italian Caesar, 2 Tbsp	**150**	16	96%	2.5	20	240	1	1
Italian Red. Fat; 2 Tbsp	40	3	67%	0	0	340	0	2
Salad Oil, 1 Tbsp	**120**	14	97%	2	0	0	0	0
Sweet & Sour Sce, 1 pkt	50	0	0%	0	0	120	0	12
Thousand Island, 2 Tbsp	**90**	8	80%	1.5	10	125	0	2
Baked Potato: Plain	310	0	0%	0	0	25	7	71
Bacon & Cheese	**530**	18	30%	4	20	1390	17	78
Broccoli & Cheese	470	14	27%	2.5	5	470	9	80
Cheese	**570**	23	36%	8	30	640	14	78
Chili & Cheese	630	24	35%	9	40	770	20	83
Sour Cream & Chives	**380**	6	14%	4	15	40	8	74
Sour Cream, 1 pkt	60	6	90%	3.5	10	15	1	1
Whipped Marg., 1 pkt	**60**	7	100%	1.5	0	115	0	0
Chili: Small	210	7	30%	2.5	30	800	15	21
Large	**310**	10	29%	3.5	45	1190	23	32
Cheddar Chse, shred. 2 Tbsp	70	6	77%	3.5	15	110	4	1
Saltine Crackers, 2	**25**	0.5	18%	0	0	80	0	4
Chicken Nuggets:								
Chicken Nuggets, 5 Piece	230	16	63%	3	30	470	11	11
4 Piece Kid's Meal	190	13	62%	2.5	25	380	9	9
Desserts & Drinks								
Choc. Chip Cookie, 1 cookie	270	13	43%	6	30	120	3	36
Frosty Dairy Dessert: Small, 12 oz	**330**	8	22%	5	35	200	8	56
Medium, 16 oz	440	11	22%	7	50	260	11	73
Large, 20 oz	**540**	14	23%	9	60	320	14	91
Cola, small	130	0	0%	0	0	36	0	36
Lemon-Lime, small	**130**	0	0%	0	0	30	0	36
Lemonade, small	130	0	0%	0	0	0	0	37
Milk (2%), 8 oz	**110**	4	33%	2.5	15	115	8	11
Hot Chocolate, 6 oz	80	3	34%	0	0	135	1	15

Weinerschnitzel®

na - figures not available	Cal	Fat	%Fc	S.Fat	Chol	Sod	Pro	Carb
Breakfast Burrito	570	37	58%	13	530	1105	na	na
Breakfast Sando	445	27	55%	10	285	1040	na	na
Chicken Sandwich	540	32	53%	9	48	960	na	na
Chili Burger	625	40	58%	12	96	1350	na	na
Deluxe: Hamburger	580	37	57%	12	90	1145	na	na
Cheeseburger	635	42	59%	14	103	1350	na	na
Bacon Cheeseburger	690	46	60%	16	110	1520	na	na
Hickory Burger	605	37	55%	12	90	1215	na	na
Patty Melt	580	35	54%	16	108	1330	na	na
Dogs: Chili Dog	295	16	50%	5	28	935	na	na
Chili Cheese Dog	350	21	54%	8	41	1140	na	na
Corn Dog	290	23	70%	8	26	460	na	na
Deluxe Dog	275	14	45%	5	21	1620	na	na
Kraut Dog	265	14	46%	5	21	1150	na	na
Mustard Dog	260	14	48%	5	21	795	na	na
Relish Dog	280	14	45%	5	21	900	na	na
Western Dog	380	23	55%	9	43	985	na	na
Fries: Small	175	13	67%	8	19	345	na	na
Medium	270	21	70%	13	30	460	na	na
Large	380	29	69%	17	42	690	na	na
Chili Fries	470	36	69%	19	64	1000	na	na

Whataburger®

Burgers/Sandwiches	Cal	Fat	%Fc	S.Fat	Chol	Sod	Pro	Carb
Justaburger®	300	13	39%	5	42	600	15	30
Whataburger®	600	26	39%	9	84	1095	30	61
Small bun no oil	410	19	42%	7	84	840	25	34
Double Meat Whataburger®	830	46	50%	20	168	1460	50	60
Whataburger Jr.®	320	13	36%	6	42	605	16	35
Grilled Chicken Fajita Taco	335	7	19%	2	66	960	31	37
Beef Fajita Taco	325	12	33%	3	28	670	22	34
Grilled Chicken Sandwich: w. dressing	440	14	28%	3	66	1105	34	48
No dressing	385	9	20%	2	66	990	34	45
No bun oil or dressing	360	6	14%	2	66	990	34	45
Small bun, mustard (no dressing)	300	3	9%	1	66	995	33	35
Whatacatch®	470	25	48%	4	33	635	17	43
Whatachick'n®	500	23	41%	4	40	1120	27	51
Salads: Garden Salad	55	0.5	8%	0	0	30	3	11
Grilled Chicken Salad	180	1.5	7%	1	66	570	30	14
Shakes: Chocolate (Jr. Size)	365	10	24%	5	36	170	9	61
French Fries: Junior	220	12	49%	7	0	140	3.5	25
Regular	330	18	49%	11	0	210	5.5	18
Large	440	24	49%	14	0	230	7	49
Breakfast: Biscuit w. Bacon, Egg, Chse	510	33	58%	14	213	1010	18	38
Breakfast-On-A-Bun™: w. Sausage	455	28	55%	13	232	885	20	30
Egg Omelet Sandwich	290	13	40%	7	200	600	13	30

White Castle®

Hamburgers	Cal	Fat	%Fc	S.Fat	Chol	Sod	Pro	Carb
Hamburger	135	7	47%	3	10	135	6	11
Cheeseburger	160	9	51%	4	15	250	7	11
Sandwiches: Chicken	190	8	38%	2	20	360	8	20
Fish (w/out Tartar), 1 serving	160	6	34%	2	15	210	8	18
Breakfast Sandwich	340	25	66%	10	130	900	14	17
Bacon Cheeseburger	200	13	58%	6	25	400	10	12
French Fries: Small	115	6	47%	1	15	195	2	37
Onion Chips, small	180	9	45%	2	0	580	3	25
Onion Rings, 8 piece	540	26	43%	na	0	1300	8	69

Yoshinoya Beef Bowl®

Bowls	Cal	Fat	%Fc	S.Fat	Chol	Sod	Pro	Carb
Beef Bowl: Regular, 15 oz	840	30	32%	13	75	1120	32	108
Large, 21 oz	1160	41	32%	18	105	1530	44	153
Kids, 9 oz	340	11	29%	5	30	690	13	48
Chicken Bowl: Regular,19 oz	760	15	18%	4.5	80	1280	33	125
Large, 30 oz	1110	22	18%	7	120	2120	49	180
Kids, 10 oz	370	9	22%	3	55	720	20	53
Combo Bowl: Regular, 17 oz	750	19	23%	7	70	1120	29	117
Large, 27 oz	1220	36	26%	14	135	2080	54	171
Vegetable Beef Bowl: Regular,18 oz	770	23	27%	10	55	1240	26	114
Large, 28 oz	1090	32	26%	13	75	1970	37	163
Vegetable Bowl: Regular 19 oz	530	3.5	6%	0.5	0	870	9	116
Large, 32 oz	780	5	6%	1	0	1710	14	169
Tempura: Fish Tempura, 22 oz	990	24	22%	6	80	1720	26	168
Fish & Beef Tempura, 30 oz	1450	45	28%	15	135	2520	47	214
Fish & Chicken Tempura, 31 oz	1450	37	23%	10	160	2560	53	225
Shrimp Tempura, 20 oz	890	19	19%	4.5	55	1840	20	160
Shrimp & Beef Tempura, 28 oz	1350	40	26%	14	110	2450	41	206
Shrimp & Chicken Tempura, 29 oz	1340	32	21%	8	135	2480	48	217
Extras: Beef, 5 1/2 oz	370	28	68%	12	75	1090	25	6
Chicken & Vegetables, 9 1/2 oz	300	12	36%	4	80	1250	26	21
Rice, 10 oz	460	2.5	5%	0.5	0	30	7	104
Vegetable, 9 oz	60	0.5	7%	0	0	840	2	12

Note: Yoshinoya Beef Bowl Restaurants are based in California.

Zantiago®

	Cal	Fat	%Fc	S.Fat	Chol	Sod	Pro	Carb
Burrito: Hot Cheese, Chilito	330	15	41%	7	35	466	14	35
Mild Cheese, Chilito	335	15	41%	7	35	505	14	36
Enchilada: Beef	315	15	43%	5	30	904	18	26
Cheese	390	23	53%	11	40	759	20	26
Taco: Burrito	415	19	41%	8	40	815	21	41
Regular	200	12	55%	4	20	318	10	13

Notes on Cholesterol

- **Cholesterol** is a white waxy substance produced mainly by our liver. It is also found in animal food products. Plant foods have no cholesterol.
- **Cholesterol is essential to life.** It is a structural part of every body cell wall and is the building block for vitamin D, sex hormones, and bile acids which help in the digestion of dietary fats.
- **The body makes sufficient cholesterol** for its needs and does not rely on cholesterol in the diet. Dietary fats have a major influence on blood cholesterol levels - more so than dietary cholesterol.
- **A high blood cholesterol increases** the risk of atherosclerosis - the thickening of arteries that can reduce or block blood flow to the heart muscle, brain, eyes, kidneys, sex organs and other body parts.

  This in turn increases the risk of heart attack, stroke, blindness, kidney failure, impotence and other blood circulatory problems.

  Other risk factors which increase the risk of atherosclerosis include high blood pressure, tobacco smoking, obesity and diabetes (uncontrolled).

HEART ATTACK WARNING SIGNALS

Many victims die before reaching hospital by ignoring warning signals and delaying medical help.

Symptoms vary and commonly include:

- **Chest pain,** vice-like squeezing or burning sensation in centre of chest or between shoulder blades, or feeling of severe indigestion.
- **Pain** may spread to shoulders, neck, jaw or arms.
- **Sweating,** nausea, dizziness, shortness of breath, irregular pulse.

If you experience any of the above symptoms seek IMMEDIATE medical attention!

Every minute counts.

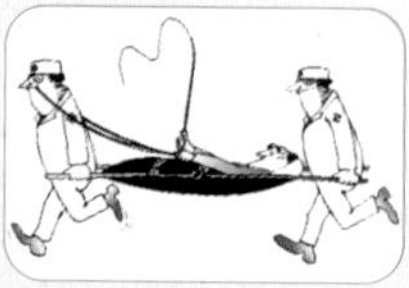

BLOOD CHOLESTEROL

Check Your Risk

Cholesterol Level (mg per deciliter) ▼	Risk of Heart Attack ▼
240 and above	High Risk
200 - 239	Borderline/High
Below 200	Desirable

- **Know your cholesterol level, particularly if there is a family history of heart disease or stroke. If high, see your doctor.**
- **All adults should have their cholesterol, HDL and triglycerides tested at least every 5 years.**

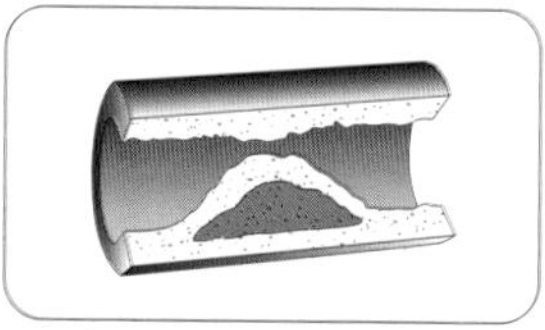

▲ Atherosclerosis can clog arteries and impede blood flow to the heart muscle or other body organs.

▼ A thrombus (blood clot) can form on unstable, festering atherosclerotic plaque and rapidly block blood flow.
A heart attack or stroke can result.

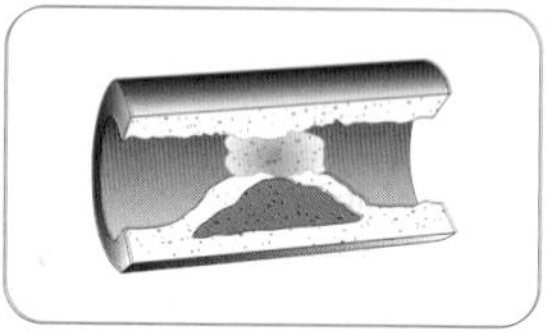

The amount and type of dietary fat has the greatest influence on blood cholesterol levels.

Fats in food are a mixture of 3 basic types: saturated, monounsaturated, and polyunsaturated. Animal fats are mainly saturated while plant oils and fish oils are mainly mono- and polyunsaturated.

Saturated fats have subgroups known as long chain, medium chain, and short chain fats. Most of the long chain fats raise blood cholesterol; and increase the risk of blood clots and thrombosis leading to artery blockage.

Long chain saturated fats are found mainly in full cream milk, cheese, butter, cream, fatty meats and sausages, and processed foods.

Monounsaturated fats tend to more selectively lower 'bad' LDL-cholesterol and maintain the protective 'good' HDL-cholesterol in the bloodstream - but only if they replace saturated fats in the diet.

Foods rich in monounsaturates include canola and olive oils, canola margarine, peanuts, and avocados.

Polyunsaturated fats consist of two main classes. **Omega-6** polyunsaturates tend to lower blood cholesterol. Rich sources include safflower, sunflower and corn oils.

Omega-3 polyunsaturated fats can lower blood cholesterol, and also confer extra benefits by lowering blood triglycerides, and reducing the risk of thrombosis, heart arrhythmias, and artery spasm.

Best practical omega-3 sources include canola oil and margarine, soybean oil and fish. (See adjoining chart)

A balanced intake of the two omega classes is important for optimal health. Increasing slightly omega-3 intake by Americans would help to attain a more ideal balance. Adequate vitamin E intake is also important.

All fats are high in calories and need to be limited for weight control.

DIETARY FATS COMPARISON

■ Saturated Fat ■ Monounsaturated Fat
■ Linoleic (Omega-6) ■ Alpha-Linolenic (Omega-3)

OILS — **PERCENTAGE CONTENT**

Oils	Saturated Fat	Monounsaturated Fat	Linoleic (Omega-6)	Alpha-Linolenic (Omega-3)
CANOLA OIL	7	63	20	10
LINSEED/FLAX OIL	9	19	17	55
SAFFLOWER OIL	9	14	77	
GRAPESEED OIL	10	22	68	
SUNFLOWER OIL	11	23	66	
CORN OIL	14	32	52	2
OLIVE OIL	14	76	10	
SOYBEAN OIL	15	23	54	8
PEANUT OIL	19	45	34	2
COTTONSEED OIL	26	16	58	
PALM OIL	51	39	10	

SPREADS & FATS
Saturated Fat includes 'Trans Fats' ❑ WATER CONTENT

Spreads & Fats	Saturated Fat	Monounsaturated Fat	Linoleic (Omega-6)	Alpha-Linolenic (Omega-3)	Water Content
LIGHT MARGARINE	14	14	21		51
CANOLA MARGARINE	18	45	12	6	19
POLYUNSATURATED MARG.	24	20	36		20
BUTTER	57	18	2		24
LARD	41	47			12
BEEF FAT	44	37	4		15

GOOD SOURCES OF OMEGA-3 FATS

Plant Sources	Omega-3 Fats (Grams)
Canola Oil, 1 Tbsp, 1/2 fl.oz	1.5g
Flaxseed Oil, 1 Tbsp	8g
Soybean Oil, 1 Tbsp	1.2g
Canola Margarine, 1 Tbsp, 1/2 oz	1g
Soybeans, cooked, 1/2 cup, 4 oz	0.5g
Walnuts, 1/2 oz	0.5g

FISH - *Per 4 oz Serving*

High Content: Salmon (Chinook), Tuna,	3g
Trout (Lake), Sardines, Herring, Mackerel	3g
Medium Content:	
Salmon (Pink/Red/Coho), 4 oz	2g
Fair Content: *Per 4 oz Serving*	
Bass, Catfish, Cod, Grouper, Hake, Halibut, Kingfish, Perch, Pollock, Shark, Trout (rainbow), Tuna (Skipjack), Crab, Oysters, Blue Mussel, Shrimp, Squid	0.5-1g

How Much is Needed?

As little as 1-2 grams daily of omega-3 fats may benefit general health. High doses of fish oil supplements should only be taken as directed by your doctor.

Dietary Cholesterol

Cholesterol in food varies in its effect on blood cholesterol level (BCL) from person to person. Much depends on the amount and type of fat, and fiber eaten at the same meal.

Any elevating effect of dietary cholesterol on BCL is more likely to occur when the diet is high in saturated fat. Little elevation, if any, generally occurs when dietary fats are balanced in favour of mono- and polyunsaturated fats (including omega-3 fats).

For example, while fish does contain cholesterol, the omega-3 fats can prevent any increase in BCL. Conversely, a meal containing no cholesterol but rich in saturated fat, may see a significant increase in BCL.

Consequently, the need to be overly concerned about dietary cholesterol is being de-emphasised in favour of a stricter approach to limiting total fats, and saturated fat in particular.

The liver usually cuts back its own cholesterol production in response to cholesterol in the diet. Many people can consume normal amounts of high cholesterol foods without concern.

However, it is difficult to identify just who is at risk - the so-called 'hyper-responders' - and because over 50% of Americans have a BCL above ideal levels, the **American Heart Association** advises all Americans to be prudent and limit their cholesterol intake to less than 300mg daily.

This limitation still allows the inclusion of most foods regularly eaten - even the overly maligned egg.

Note: Eggs contain a modest 5 grams of fat per large egg of which barely 2 grams are saturated, the rest being mono- and polyunsaturated.

By comparison, a cup of whole milk has almost 10g fat of which 6g are saturated.

CHOLESTEROL COUNTER

Cholesterol is found only in foods of animal origin. Plant foods contain no cholesterol. AHA recommends limiting dietary cholesterol to less than 300mg/day.

	Chol mg
Meat - Average all types:	
Lean Meat, cooked, 4 oz	70
Fatty Meat, cooked, 4 oz	105
Fat, thick strip, 2 oz	35
(Note: While lean meat and fat have similar amounts of cholesterol, choose lean meat to limit fat intake.)	
Chicken/Turkey, average, 4 oz	90
Organ Meats: Liver, fried, 4 oz	500
Brains, beef, pan fried, 3 oz	1700
Sausages: Frankfurter, 1.5 oz	25
Salami, 2 slices, 2 oz	40
Bacon: 3 slices, cooked, 1 oz	20
Fish: Fish fillets, average, ckd, 4 oz	70
Tuna/Salmon, canned, 3 oz	30
Scallops, 9 medium, 3 oz	30
Shrimp, 12 large, raw, 3 oz	130
Oysters, raw, 6 medium, 3 oz	45
Lobster, Crab, raw, 3 oz	80
Eggs (Chicken), 1 large	210
1 medium	180
Egg White, *Egg Beaters*	0
Milk/Yogurt: Whole, 1 cup, 8 fl.oz	35
1% Milk, 1 cup	10
Skim/Non-fat, 1 cup	5
Soy Milk	0
Cheese: Natural/Hard/Cream 1 oz	30
Cottage, lowfat, 4 oz	5
Ricotta, part skim, 4 oz	25
Fats: Butter, 2 Tbsp, 1 oz	60
Margarine, Oils (vegetable)	0
Mayonnaise, 1 Tbsp	10
Cream: Heavy, whipping, 2 T, 1 oz	40
Half & Half/Sour, 2 Tbsp, 1 oz	10
Icecream: Regular, 1/3 cup, 4 fl.oz	30
Fruit, Vegetables, Avocados	0
Nuts, Seeds, Grains	0
Coffee, Tea, Soda, Beer, Wine	0

Fast-Foods ~ See Pages 160 - 247

Dietary Hints to Lower Blood Cholesterol

1. **Maintain a healthy weight.**
If overweight, lose weight with lowfat eating and daily exercise.

2. **Reduce saturated fat intake by:**
(a) eating less dairy fat. Choose lowfat or fat-reduced varieties of milk, yogurt, cheese, and icecream. Enjoy soy drinks.
(b) replacing saturated fats with fats and oils rich in mono- and polyunsaturated fats; and carbohydrate-rich foods. Choose vegetable oils such as canola, olive, sunflower and soybean. Avoid solid frying fats.
Note: *Benecol* food products (spreads and dressings) contain plant stanol ester which can lower total and LDL cholesterol.
(c) eating less fat from meat and poultry. Choose lean cuts of meat and skinless chicken. Go easy on luncheon meats, salamis and fatty sausages. Enjoy fish.
(d) eating less saturated fats from baked and fried fast-foods. Avoid deep-fried foods. Avoid donuts, cakes, pastries and cookies unless made with healthier fats and oils.

3. **Increase your 'soluble' fiber intake.**
Foods rich in 'soluble' fiber include dried beans, baked beans, lentils, chick peas, hummus, nuts, seeds, psyllium seed husks and psyllium fiber supplements.
Oat bran, rice bran and barley are also useful, as are fruit, veges and avocados.

4. **Eat more soya bean products** such as: soy drinks, tofu, tempeh (cultured soya beans), soy flour and soy vegetarian foods.
Soy protein in place of animal protein can significantly decrease high blood cholesterol levels - as well as 'bad' LDL-cholesterol and blood triglycerides.
Good' HDL-cholesterol is maintained.
For best results, eat at least 25g of soy protein per day (from 3-4 servings)

5. **Eat more fruit and vegetables in place of high-fat foods.**
Aim for 2 fruits and 5 servings of vegetables per day. They also contain valuable antioxidants.
The fat of avocados is mainly unsaturated and lowers blood cholesterol levels.

6. **Limit cholesterol to 300mg per day.**
(Extra Notes ~ See Previous Page)

7. **Avoid brewed unfiltered coffee** (espresso; plunger-style). It contains oil compounds (diterpenes) which can raise blood cholesterol. American style filtered coffee is fine.

8. **Spread your food intake over the day.**
Have 5-6 small meals per day rather than just 2-3 large meals. Nibbling, versus gorging, favors lower blood cholesterol.

ALCOHOL - WINE

Alcohol is a mixed bag. Moderate amounts of 1-2 drinks daily appear to reduce the risk of heart attack and ischaemic stroke in older persons.

However, larger amounts increase the risk of high blood pressure, obesity, heart failure and hemorrhagic stroke; and can aggravate hypertriglyceridemia - in addition to many other health hazards.
(See Alcohol Guide - p.149)

The over-riding harmful effects of excess alcohol do not allow its recommendation for any aspects of health promotion.

Note:
Red wine (more so than white) contains antioxidants which may help protect cholesterol in the blood from becoming oxidized.

Many fruits, vegetables and tea also contain protective antioxidants.

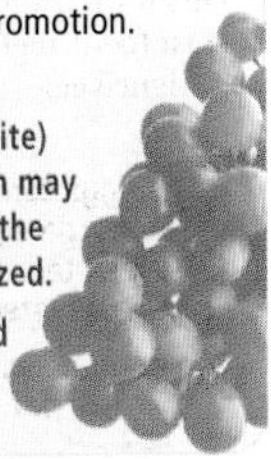

How Fats Affect Blood Flow

Fats in the diet not only affect blood cholesterol levels. They can also strongly influence blood clot formation and thrombosis, as well as blood flow and ultimate oxygen delivery to body parts and organs.

While advanced atherosclerosis can impede blood flow to the heart and other organs, it is thrombosis (complete blockage by blood clots) or arterial spasm which commonly result in a heart attack or stroke.

Plant and fish oils rich in omega-3 fats lessen the risk of blood clots, thrombus formation and artery spasm by reducing platelet stickiness and adhesion to artery walls. This reduces the risk of atherosclerotic plaque becoming unstable and reactive.

Omega-3 fats also improve blood flow by reducing blood viscosity; and increasing the flexibility of red blood cells (RBC) that need to flex and twist on themselves in order to squeeze through tiny narrow capillaries often half their diameter.

A diet high in saturated fats has the opposite effect by stiffening RBC membranes and increasing blood viscosity thereby hindering blood flow. The stiffening of the RBC membrane also reduces its ability to release vital oxygen to body cells and take up carbon dioxide.

Stiff red blood cells may also form aggregates like coin stacks. In narrow blood vessels, this further impedes blood flow and impairs oxygen release through the much lessened surface area of red blood cell membranes exposed to blood. (Smoking, lack of exercise, and stress can have similar adverse effects on thrombosis, red blood cell flexibility and blood flow.)

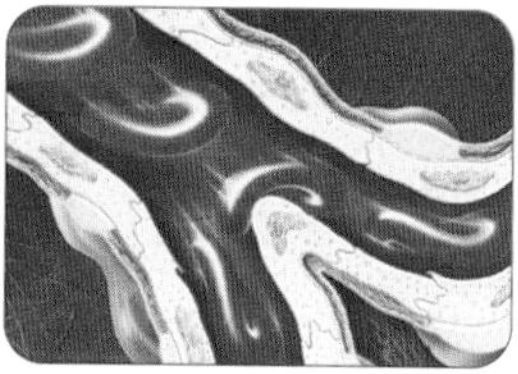

▲ Picture of Healthy Blood Flow

Flexible red blood cells twist and slide through tiny capillaries - often half the diameter of red blood cells.

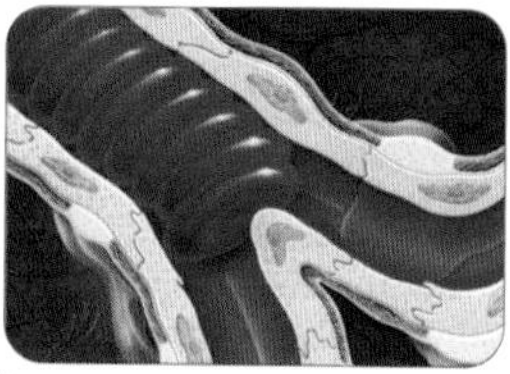

▲ A Not-So-Healthy Picture!

Red blood cells have lost their flexibility and ability to twist and slip through capillaries. They are stacked up thereby impeding blood flow.

A diet high in saturated fats can contribute to this picture - as can smoking, lack of exercise and stress.

Ongoing research suggests that it may be the **oxidation of cholesterol** in the blood that promotes atherosclerosis in artery walls; and that taking steps to prevent this oxidation may well complement the benefits of controlling blood cholesterol levels.

Vitamin E appears to be the major **antioxidant** that defends cholesterol against oxidation. Low blood levels of vitamin E are associated with a greater incidence of heart disease deaths. Vitamin C and beta-carotene also appear to play important support roles (as may other food substances).

This research strengthens the current dietary advice to moderate fat intake, and to eat plenty of antioxidant-rich plant foods such as whole-grain cereals, fresh fruit and vegetables (5 serves daily), legumes, soybeans, nuts, seeds, and garlic.

While future research may prove the value of supplemental antioxidants in persons at high risk of heart attack, such supplements will not replace the current preventive advice to lower the risk of heart disease and stroke by: lowering saturated fat intake, not smoking, losing weight if overweight, exercising regularly, and controlling hypertension.

Extra Notes for High-Risk Persons:

- **Vitamin E supplements** are required to attain the pharmacological doses (400 - 800 IU daily) suggested in some research reports to provide maximum oxidative protection in persons at high coronary risk. Check with your doctor before taking large doses of vitamin E or other supplements.
- **Daily supplemental intake** of beta-carotene and vitamin C may also complement vitamin E.
- **Eat at least 3 different colors of fruit** and vegetables from at least 5 servings daily. There are many non-vitamin antioxidants that cannot be put in vitamin supplements.

LDL PARTICLE - CHOLESTEROL CARRIER

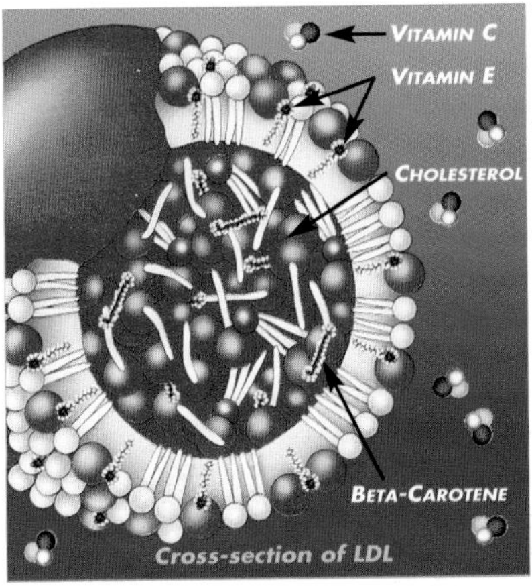

- Low density protein particle (LDL) transports cholesterol in the blood since cholesterol is not soluble in blood (largely water).
- 'Free radical' attack on the LDL particle can oxidise it into a toxic form that may injure artery walls and promote atherosclerosis.
- Vitamin E molecules embedded in LDL shell provides the first line of defence against 'free radical' attack and oxidation.
- Vitamin C may help to directly neutralise 'free radicals' and to also regenerate vitamin E. Beta-carotene in the LDL core provides a second oxidation barrier.
- An antioxidant-rich diet will boost antioxidant blood levels and provide better resistance to LDL oxidation.

- **Moderate caffeine intake** is probably not harmful to healthy adults. However, regular large amounts (over 350mg/day) may cause dependency ('caffeinism') and adversely affect health.
- **Symptoms of excessive caffeine** intake include chronic insomnia, persistent anxiety and depression, restlessness, heart palpitations, stomach upset and increased need to urinate. (It can take 4-6 hours for caffeine's effects to wear off.)
- **Caffeine-withdrawal** headaches, fatigue and irritability are more commonly experienced on weekends when any heavy coffee drinking at work is suddenly reduced. Such headaches are relieved by drinking coffee. As little as 100-200 mg caffeine daily can produce withdrawal effects. (Withdrawal symptoms only last one week or less.) Reduce gradually by mixing with decaffeinated.
- **Sensitivity to caffeine** may increase during pregnancy and with age. To be safe, limit caffeine to 200mg/day.
- **Persons wise to avoid caffeine** entirely include those who get irritable and jittery from just one cup of coffee, pregnant and nursing women, children under eight, people with stomach ulcers or heart arrhythmia.
- **Large amounts of cola drinks** (4-6 cans per day) as well as coffee may also lead to excessive caffeine intake, particularly in children. Caffeine-free colas are available.
- **Coffee alternatives** such as *Postum, Kaffree Roma, Teeccino Caffre* are caffeine-free. Decaffeinated coffee is also suitable.

- **Blood cholesterol can be raised** by several drinks daily of boiled unfiltered coffee (such as espresso and cafetiere/plunger pot style). American-style filtered coffee does not contain the oil compounds (diterpenes) which appear to raise blood cholesterol.
- **Coffee does not sober up** an inebriated person. It simply turns him or her into a wide-awake drunk!

Coffee	Caffeine (mg)
Instant Coffee:	
Weak, 1 level tsp	45
Medium, 1 rounded tsp	60
Strong, 1 heaping tsp	90
Decaffeinated, 1 rnd tsp	2
Bags(*Folgers*), 1 bag (6-8 fl.oz)	115
Decaffeinated, 1 bag	3
Brewed: Percolator, 8 oz cup	120
Drip Method, 8 oz cup	160
Ground, 1 Tbsp, 6g	60
Decaffeinated, 1 Tbsp	2
Bottled (Ready-To-Drink), 9.5 fl.oz	75
Flavoured Coffee Mixes	
Coffee with Chicory, 1 rnd tsp	40
General Foods: Irish Mocha Mint	25
Orange Cappuccino	70
Other flavors, average	50
Coffee Shop Style	
Coffee: Drip-brew, average, 8 fl.oz	160
Percolated, 8 fl.oz	120
Cappuccino, 8 fl.oz	80
Decappuccino (decaffeinated)	5
Espresso: Regular/Solo	80
Double (Doppio) Espresso	160
Latte/Macchiato	80
Iced Coffee, 8 fl.oz	80
Mocha, 8 fl.oz	90
Vienna Coffee, 8 fl.oz	80
Cocoa, 8 fl.oz	10
Starbucks (Franchise Chain)	
Drip Coffee: Short, 8 fl.oz	140
Tall, 12 fl.oz	210
Grande, 16 fl.oz	280
Cappuccino: Short or Tall	70
Grande	100
Caffe Americano: Tall, 14 fl.oz	150
Grande, 16 fl.oz	220
Venti, 20 fl.oz	250
Caffe Latte, Short or Tall	75
Grande	150
Cafe Mocha, Short or Tall	85
Grande	170
Espresso (Reg./Macchiato): Solo	75
Doppio	150
Frappuccino, Reg./Mocha, Tall	75
Grande	100

Coffee Alternatives

	Caffeine (mg)
(Roasted Cereals - Caffeine-Free)	
Kaffree Roma/Postum/Teeccino Caffe	0

Bottled Milk Coffee (Ready-To-Drink):

Starbucks/ Nestle: Average, 9.5 fl.oz	75

Tea

Brewed or Tea Bags: Weak, 1 cup	20
Medium Strength	40
Strong	70
Instant Tea Powder: 1 tsp	30
w. lemon flavor, 1 tsp	25
+ sugar, 3 rnd tsp	30
Decaffeinated Tea (*Kaffree*)	1
Herbal Tea	0
Iced Tea, regular: 8 oz Glass	20
12 oz Glass	30
16 oz Glass	40
Flavored Teas, Ready to drink, Average, 12 fl.oz	25

Cola Soft Drinks: *Per 12 fl.oz*

Coca Cola: Can/Bottle	30
Fountain/Restaurant	38
Diet Coke: Can/Bottle	40
Fountain/Restaurant	45
Pepsi: Can/Bottle	32
Fountain/Restaurant	37
Diet Pepsi: Can/Bottle	30
Fountain/Restaurant	37
Caffeine Free Coke/Pepsi	0

Other Colas: *Per 12 fl.oz*

Cherry Coke	35
Cherry Cola (Shasta)	40
Diet Rite Cola, regular	0
Jolt Cola	55
K-Mart Amer. 1 Can Fare Cola/Diet	12
Kroger Big K Cola	5
Diet Cola	30
Pepsi Kona	55
RC Cola	43
Diet RC Cola	50
Shasta Cola	42
Diet Shasta Cola	37
Slice Cola	10
Slice: Dr. Slice, Cherry Spice, Red	35
Surge	53
TAB	50
Wal-Mart Sam's Choice/Diet	12
Wild Cherry Pepsi	38
Winn-Dixie Chek Cola	8

Non-Cola Soft Drinks

Per 12 fl.oz Can/Bottle	Caffeine (mg)
National: Cherry Spice; Dr Slice	35
Dr Pepper, Reg./Diet	42
Java Juice, all flavors, 20 fl.oz	140
Josta (Pepsi)	60
Kick	55
Mello Yellow	50
Mountain Dew, Reg./Diet	55
Mr PiBB, Reg./Diet	43
Red	35
Sunkist Orange	43
Store Brands - Non- Cola Drinks	
Kroger Big K Citrus Drop, Reg./Diet	26
Kroger Dr K, Reg/Diet	17
Wal-Mart Sam's Choice: Green Lightning	50
Southern Lightning	30
Winn-Dixie: Dr Chek	18
Chek Kountry Mist	53

Caffeinated Waters

Aqua Java; Water Joe 17 fl.oz	60
Java Johnny, 20 fl.oz	70
Krank20, 17 fl.oz	100

Java Juice all flavors, 20 fl.oz — 140

Chocolate/Cocoa

Chocolate: Milk Choc., 2 oz	20
Dark Chocolate/Bakers, 2 oz	35
Choc Chips, 1/4 cup., 1.5 oz	15
Candy Bars, average, 1.5 oz	10
Cocoa, dry, unsw. 1 Tbsp, 5g	12
Cocoa/Hot Choc. Mix, 1 oz pkt	5
Chocolate Milk, 8 fl.oz	8
Chocolate. Cake, 1 pce	10
Choc Chip Cookie, 1 oz	4
Chocolate Icing, 1 serving	5
Chocolate Icecream, 1/2 cup	2
Chocolate Pudding, 1/2 cup	5
Chocolate Syrup, 2 Tbsp	6

Pharmaceuticals & Guarana

Anacin/Empirin/Midol, 2 tabs	65
Aqua-Ban (diuretic), 2 tabs	200
Dexatrim (weight control), 1 tab	200
Excedrin, 2 tablets	130
NoDoz: Regular Strength, 1 tab	100
Maximum Strength, 1 tab	200
Tylenol, 1 tablet	0
Vivarin, 1 tablet	200
Guarana: Powder, 1 tsp, 3 g	120
Tablet/Capsules (800mg), 1	30
Drinks/Soda, average, 12 fl.oz	50

Calcium's Role in the Body

Calcium plays a vital role in nerve and muscle function, clotting of blood, enzyme regulation, insulin secretion and overall bone strength. Bones and teeth store 99% of the body's calcium.

The calcium level in blood is kept at a steady level by the continual exchange of calcium between blood and bone. When insufficient calcium is obtained from food the body draws calcium out of the bones.

This bone loss over a period of years may lead to **osteoporosis** - thinning of the bones (*porous bones*).

The bones become weak, brittle and easy to fracture, particularly the bones of the wrist, hips and spine. Loss of height and curvature of the spine may also result, as may periodontal disease - the deterioration of the jaw bones that support the teeth.

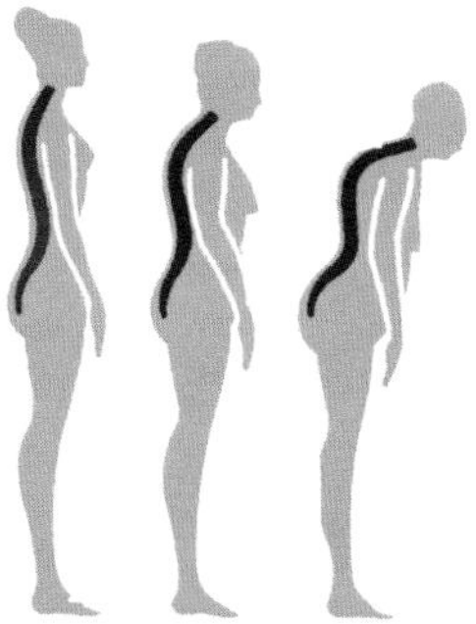

As osteoporosis progresses after menopause, vertebrae may collapse causing the spine to curve and shoulders to hunch.

Osteoporosis - Common in Women

While osteoporosis also occurs in men, women are particularly vulnerable (1 in 4 by age 60). They have about 30% less bone than men, and a greater bone loss at menopause when estrogen levels drop. Slender framed women are at greater risk. (A woman in her eighties can have lost up to two thirds of her skeleton.)

Insufficient dietary calcium during pregnancy and breastfeeding will see bone reserves drawn upon, increasing the risk of osteoporosis.

Causes of Osteoporosis

The major factors associated with the bone loss of osteoporosis appear to be:

- **Hormone changes of menopause.**
- **Insufficient calcium in the diet. (Absorption decreases with age.)**
- **Insufficient exercise (weight bearing - such as walking, cycling.)**
- **Family history of osteoporosis.**
- **Other contributing factors may include**: excess amounts of alcohol, protein and phosphorus (from meats and soft drinks); insufficient vitamin D and magnesium; and cigarette smoking.

RECOMMENDED DAILY INTAKE OF CALCIUM

		Calcium
Infants:		
	0-6 mths	360mg
	6-12 mths	540mg
Children:		
	1-10 yrs	800mg
	10-12 yrs	1200mg
Teenagers:		
	13-18 yrs	1200mg
	16-18 yrs	800mg
Adults:	19+ yrs	800mg
Women:		
Pre-menopausal		1000mg
Menopausal(beginning)		1200mg
Post-menopausal		1500mg
Pregnancy/breastfeeding:		
	10-18 yrs	1600mg
	19+ yrs	1200mg

Early Prevention Important

Gradual loss of bone begins in the thirties after maximum bone mass is reached. The stronger the bones at that time, the less trouble is likely to occur later. The earlier that prevention or treatment begins the greater the benefit. **The key to prevention** is to build strong, dense bones early in life. **By age 16,** some 80% of peak bone mass is reached.

Young women may lessen the risk by eating high-calcium foods, not engaging in excessive dieting that results in period cessation (less estrogen), taking regular exercise and not smoking.

In menopausal women, hormone therapy as well as calcium supplements and exercise, can help retard osteoporosis. Your doctor can advise you.

Dietary Sources of Calcium

Milk, yogurt, calcium-enriched soy drinks and cheese are the richest sources of calcium. (Lowfat and nonfat varieties contain similar calcium.)

Canned fish with edible bones (salmon/sardines) are high in calcium. Tofu (soybean curd), tempeh, broccoli and dried beans are also good sources.

- **Soy drinks (calcium-enriched) may be preferable to cow's milk. Body calcium losses are much greater with animal protein. Soy protein is relatively 'bone-sparing'.**
- **Phytoestrogens in soy foods may also lessen calcium losses at menopause. Soy drinks are suitable for persons with lactose intolerance.**

Extra Notes on Calcium

Persons who have difficulty eating sufficient calcium-rich foods should consider a **calcium supplement.** Prescribed high doses of calcium (1.5-2g/day) may benefit persons with osteoporosis - as well as vitamin D (up to 400 IU), and magnesium (100mg).

Calcium in food reduces iron absorption by up to 60% when eaten with iron-containing foods. Consume calcium-rich foods/supplements at smaller meals and mid-meal snacks.

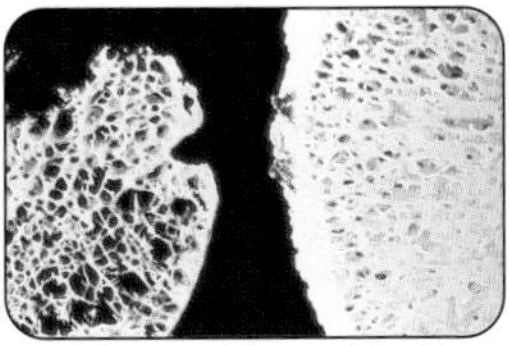

▲ *Osteoporotic Fragile Bone* ▲ *Healthy Dense Bone*

GOOD SOURCES OF CALCIUM (MILLIGRAMS)

Milk & Milk Drinks

	Calcium (mg)
Milk Fluid:	
Whole: 1 cup, 8 fl.oz	300
1 small glass, 6 fl.oz	220
1% or 2%: 1 cup, 8 fl.oz	300
Lowfat/Skim: 1 cup, 8 fl.oz	300
Hi-Calcium *(Borden)*, 1 cup	1000
Viva, w. extra Calcium, 1 cup	500
Condensed Milk, sweet, 1 fl.oz	110
Evaporated Milk: Skim, 1 fl.oz	90
Whole/Lowfat	80
Dry/Powder: Whole, 1/4 cup	290
Skim/Nonfat, 1/4 cup	380
Other Milks & Drinks	
Buttermilk, average, 1 cup	300
Chocolate Milk, average, 1 cup	300
Cocoa/Chocolate w. Milk, 1 cup	300
Goats Milk, 1 cup	320
Malted Milk, 1 cup	350
Milkshakes: Small, 10 fl.oz	280
Medium, 15 fl.oz	450
Milk Drink Powders:	
Malted Milk, dry powder, 1 oz	80
Chocolate, Instant, 3 Tbsp	10
Cocoa Powder: Regular, 1 Tbsp	10
Cocoa Mix: *Hershey*, 1/3 cup	40
Alba High Calcium, 1 envelope	320

Soy & Grain Drinks: *Per 8 fl.oz Cup*

	Calcium (mg)
Soy: Regular, non-fortified	60
Calcium-fortified (*e.g. Edensoy Extra*)	300
Dry Powder, 1 oz	80
Rice/Oat Drinks: Average, 1 cup	10

Yogurt

	Calcium (mg)
Average All Brands	350
Fruit-flavored, 1 cup, 8 oz	250
Small cup, 6 oz	230
4 1/2 oz cup	350
Plain: Average, 1 cup, 8 oz	430
Dannon, Nonfat/Lowfat, 8 oz	200
Custard-style, 6 oz	100
Frozen Yogurt, average, 1/2 cup	100

Fats/Oils

	Calcium (mg)
Butter, Lard, fats	0
Margarine, Regular/Imitation	0
Oils, Salad Dressings	0

Cream

	Calcium (mg)
Average: Unwhipped, 1 Tbsp	15
Whipped, 1 heaping Tbsp	15
Half & Half, 1 Tbsp	15
Non-dairy Creamers, 1 tsp	0

Ice Cream & Ices

	Calcium (mg)
Ice Cream: Regular, 1 scoop	65
1/2 cup	90
Premium, 1 serve, 4 oz	150
Soft Serve, 1/2 cup	120
Ice Milk, average, 1/2 cup	100
Sherbet, average, 1/2 cup	50
Fruit Sorbet	0
Sundae, regular, 6 fl.oz	200
Tofu Ices, average, 1/2 cup	10

Cheese: *Per 1 oz (1 1/2" cube)*

	Calcium (mg)
Natural, Hard: Average, 1 oz	200
Processed Cheese: Average, 1 oz	150
Single-wrapped, 3/4 oz	120
Cheese Substitutes: Average, 1 oz	200
Specific Cheeses:	
Blue, 1 oz	150
Brie	50
Camembert	110
Cheddar	200
Cottage Cheese: 1 round Tbsp, 1 oz	20
1/2 cup, 4 oz	80
Cream Cheese	20
Dorman's Light, average 1 oz	200
Edam, Gouda	200
Feta	140
Goat, semi-soft	85
Gruyere	290
Kraft Light Naturals, average	250
Light-Line (*Borden*), singles	200
Monterey Jack	210
Mozzarella, average	170
Parmesan, grated, 1 Tbsp	70
Processed, average	160
Provolone	210
Ricotta, part skim, 1/2 cup, 4 1/2 oz	330
Swiss	270
Cheese Dishes:	
Souffle, 4 oz	240
Macaroni & Cheese, 1 cup, 8 oz	150
Ham & Cheese Crepes, 8 oz	350
Quiche, 1 serve, 6 oz	200

Eggs	Calcium (mg)
1 large Egg	30
Scrambled, with Milk	50
Omelet w. Cheese ($^1/_2$ oz)	260
Fish & Seafood	
Canned Fish:	
Salmon: with bones, 3 oz	190
without bones, 3 oz	10
Sardines, with bones, 3 oz	90
Tuna, canned, 3 oz	10
Fresh Fish: cooked, average, 4 oz	35
Seafood: Lobster, cooked, 4 oz	60
Mussels/Oysters, (10), 4 oz	95
Crabmeat, cooked, 4 oz	50
Meats & Poultry	
Average all types, cooked, 4 oz	20
Soups	
Average all types:	
No Milk or Cheese added, 1 serve	30
with Milk, $^1/_2$ cup, 1 serve	180
Sauces	
Average all kinds, 1 Tbsp	10
Cheese/White Sauce, 2 Tbsp	40
Spices	
Average all types, 1 tsp	5-20
Bread, Bagels	
Bread: White, 1 slice	30
Wholewheat, Rye, 1 slice	30
Bagels, average	30
Buns/Rolls: Small	40
Large	90
English Muffins, 2 oz	90
Pita, $6^1/_2$ " diameter, 2 oz	50
Tortillas, Corn, 1 oz	40
Breakfast Cereals	
Ready To Eat:	
Average all types, 1 oz	20
with $^3/_4$ cup Milk/Soy (enriched)	250
Total (General Mills), 1 oz	200
Hot Type, cooked	
Corn (Hominy) Grits, 1 cup	5
Cream of Wheat, 1 cup	50
Oatmeal/Rolled Oats:	
Regular, non-fortified, 1 cup	20
Instant, fortified, 1 pkt	100

Note: Breakfast cereals are a good medium for calcium-rich milk or soy drinks (150mg per $^1/_2$ cup).

Flours, Grains	Calcium (mg)
Wheat Flour: All-purpose, 1 cup	20
Self-rising, 1 cup	330
Whole-wheat, 1 cup	50
Carob Flour, 1 cup, $3^1/_2$ oz	360
Corn meal, 1 cup, 4 oz	20
Soybean Flour, 1 cup, 3 oz	170
Grains, Barley, Rice, average:	
Cooked, 1 cup	15
Pasta, Spaghetti	
Average all types, cooked, 1 cup	15
Lasagne, average, 1 serve	300
Macaroni & Cheese, aver., 1 cup	150
Spaghetti w. Meat Sce, 1 serve	20
with 1 Tbsp Parmesan	90
Sugar & Syrups	
Sugar: White	0
Brown, 1 Tbsp	10
Syrups: *Per 2 Tbsp, 1 oz*	
Choc., Thin type, 2 Tbsp	5
Fudge type, 2 Tbsp	40
Molasses: Light, 2 Tbsp	70
Blackstrap, average, 1 Tbsp, $^3/_4$ oz	270
Table Syrup, 2 Tbsp	0
Honey, Jam, Jelly	
Contain negligible calcium.	
Cookies & Cakes	
Cookies: Average all types, 1 only	5
Crackers, average, 1 only	5
Cake: Plain, average, 2 oz	40
Carrot Cake with Icing	45
Cheesecake, 1 piece	80
Fruitcake, 1 piece	40
Croissants, average, 2 oz	20
Danish pastry, average, 2 oz	60
Donuts, average, 2 oz	20
Muffins:	
Regular, average, $1^1/_2$ oz	40
English Muffins, 2 oz	90
Pancakes, 4" diameter, average, 1 oz	40
Pies:	
Apple/Fruit, average, 5 oz	20
Custard Pie, average, 5 oz	140
Pecan Pie, 1 piece, 5 oz	70
Pumpkin Pie, 1 piece, 5 oz	80
Waffles, 7" diameter average	160

Desserts	Calcium (mg)
Custard, average, 1/2 cup	150
Gelatin, plain w. water, 1/2 cup	2
Puddings: Canned, aver., 5 oz	80
Dry Mix, made w. milk, 1/2 cup	150
Rice Pudding, 1/2 cup	120
Snack Can, 5 oz	60
Pancakes, 4" diam., 2	120
Candy, Chocolate	
Chocolate: Milk	50
Plain/Fruit, 1 oz	65
with Almonds, 1 oz	80
Kit Kat Wafer, 1 1/2 oz	80
Mars Bar	80
Milky Way Bar, 2 oz	60
Carob Bar, average, 2 oz	220
Plain candy, uncoated, 1 oz	0
Jelly Beans, Marshmallow, 1 oz	0
Snacks & Bars	
Breakfast Bars (*Carnation*)	20
Corn Chips; Tortilla Chips, 1 oz	40
Granola Bars, average	30
Popcorn, 1 cup	5
Potato Chips, 1 oz	10
Power Bar	300
Tiger's Milk/Sport	350
Nuts & Seeds (Shelled)	
Almonds, 12-15 nuts, 1/2 oz	40
Brazil Nuts, 4 medium, 1/2 oz	30
Cashews, 6-8 nuts, 1/2 oz	5
Coconut, fresh, 1/2 oz	5
Filberts (Hazelnuts), 1/2 oz	40
Macadamias, 6 medium, 1/2 oz	10
Peanuts, raw, 1 oz	25
Walnuts, 1 oz	20
Seeds: Pumpkin, 1 oz	15
Sesame, 1 Tbsp	10
Sunflower, 1 oz	30
Tahini, 1 Tbsp, 1/2 oz	20
Beverages - Alcohol, Soda	
Beer, Cider, Wine, 1 glass	5
Spirits, 1 fl.oz	0
Coffee, Tea, Soda, Fruit Drinks	5
Water: Tap, average, 1 cup	5
Perrier, 1 glass, 6 oz	20

Fruit & Fruit Juice	Calcium (mg)
Fresh Fruit: Average all types, 1 serve	20
Apple, 1 medium	10
Avocado, 1 medium	20
Banana, 1 medium	10
Orange, 1 medium	50
Pear, 1 medium	20
Rhubarb, cooked, 1/2 cup	170
(calcium largely not available to body)	
Dried Fruit: Average, 1 oz	20
Figs, 3 medium, 1 1/2 oz	55
Fruit Juice: Average, 1 cup, 8 fl.oz	25
Orange Juice, calcium fortified:	
Citrus Hill Plus Calcium, Hi-C	300
Minute Maid (Premium Calcium)	300
Jui2ce, 8 fl.oz	200
Tropicana Grapefruit & Calcium	300
Vegetables	
Average all types, 1/2 cup	20
1 cup	40
Higher Calcium Content:	
Beans, dried: cooked, 1/2 cup	50
Baked/Refried Beans, 1/2 cup	60
Broccoli, chopped, 1 cup	100
Chickpeas, boiled, 1/2 cup	40
Collards, cooked, 1 cup	150
Dandelion Greens, cooked, 1 cup	150
Kale, 1 cup	130
Mustard Greens, 1 cup	100
Potato: Plain, 1 large	20
Au Gratin, 1 cup	200
Mashed w. Milk, 1 cup	60
Spinach, cooked, 1/2 cup	120
Soybeans, cooked, 1/2 cup, 3 oz	90
Tofu: *Mori Nu:* Silken, 4 oz	90
Azumaya: Silken, 3 oz	20
Firm/Extra Firm, 3 oz	150
Hinoichi: Regular, 1" slice, 3 oz	100
Firm/Extra Firm, 3 oz	150
Soft, 1" slice, 3 oz	60
Nasoya: Firm, 3 oz	120
Extra Firm, 3 oz	150
Soft, 3 oz	120
Silken, 3 oz	60
Miso: 1/2 cup, 5 oz	100
Tempeh: 4 oz serving	100

Frozen Entrees/Meals	Calcium (mg)
Budget Gourmet Light	
Chicken Parmigiana; Ziti Parmesano	160
Three Cheese Lasagne	360
Lean Cuisine: Cheese Ravioli	160
Cheese Lasagna w. Chicken	360
Chicken Fettucine	160
French Bread Pizza, Deluxe	360
Stouffer's: Cheese Manicotti	320
Chicken Enchilada; Fettucini Alfredo	200
Extra Cheese Pizza	280
Five Cheese Lasagna	400
Turkey Pie/Tetrazzini	80
Weight Watchers	
Bowtie Pasta & Mushroom Marsala	160
Lasagna w. Meat Sauce	320
Tuna Noodle Casserole	160
Frozen Pizzas	
Average All Brands: Cheese, 1/4 pizza	350
Meats (Sausage/Pepperoni), 1/4 pizza	250
Calcium Supplements	
Caltrate 600, 1 tablet	600
Citracal, 1 tablet	200
Ethical Nutrients 'Bone Builder', 1	200
IDN LifePak: Reg./Prime, 2 pkts	500
Women, 2 pkts	1000
Nature's Life 'Super Cal-Mag', 1	500
Os-cal; 1 tablet	500
Posture Calcium, 1 tablet	600
Tums: Regular, 1 tablet	200
Extra Strength, 1 tablet	300

Exercise enhances bone growth, bone density and strength.

Fast-Foods, Restaurants	Calcium (mg)
Chicken:	
Grilled/BBQ, 1/4 chicken	20
Battered & Fried, 2 pieces	80
Nuggets, 6 pack	20
Crispy Chicken Deluxe Sandwich	50
Croissant Sandwich: Plain	40
with Cheese, 1 oz	240
Fish Sandwich: no Cheese	60
with Cheese	140
Fish Filet Deluxe	70
Fish, fried, 2 pieces	20
French Fries: Small Serving	10
Hamburgers: Average all outlets,	
Regular, no Cheese	120
Cheeseburger, regular	120
McDonald's: Big Mac	160
Arch Deluxe w. Bacon	70
Quarter Pounder w. Cheese	120
Egg McMuffin	120
Hot Dog: Plain	60
with Cheese	150
Mexican: Burrito	120
Enchilada	300
Nachos, regular	200
Taco, regular	140
Taco Bell Salad	400
Pizza: Average all types,	
Medium (12"), 2 slices	250
Double Cheese, 2 slices	350
Large (16"), 2 slices	350
Double Cheese, 2 slices	500
Pizza Hut, Medium:	
Cheese, 2 slices	290
Pepperoni, 2 slices	300
Potato: Plain, baked, 8 oz	20
Stuffed w. Cheese Topping	100
with Cheese Filling	300
Sandwiches: Average	
no Cheese	60
with 1 oz Cheese	200
with 2 oz Cheese	460
Subway: 6" Sandwich average	100
Tuna, 6"; Tuna Salad (small)	100
Salads, small, average	100
Salads: Chef, regular	300
Coleslaw, small	20
Shakes, average	330

Introduction

Fiber is the general term for those parts of **plant** food that we cannot digest (although bacteria in the large bowel partly digests fiber through fermentation). It is not found in foods of animal origin (meats, dairy products).

Fiber promotes intestinal health, bowel regularity, can benefit diabetes and blood cholesterol levels, and may help prevent colon cancer. High fiber foods also assist weight control.

Most Americans don't eat enough fiber - less than 20 grams/day - instead of a **healthier 25 to 35 grams/day.**

Types of Fiber

Plant foods contain a mixture of different fibers in varying proportions. Insoluble and soluble fiber categories are based on their solubility in water. All types of fiber are beneficial to the body.

◆ **Insoluble fibers** (cellulose, hemi-celluloses, lignin) make up the structural parts of plant cell walls. The **best sources** are wheat bran, corn bran, rice bran, wholegrain cereals and breads, dried beans and peas, nuts, seeds and the skins of fruits and vegetables.

These fibers absorb many times their own weight in water. They create a soft bulk and hasten the passage of waste products through the intestines.

They promote bowel regularity, and aid in the prevention and treatment of uncomplicated forms of **constipation, diverticulosis and haemorrhoids.**

The risk of colon cancer may also be reduced by fiber's diluting effect of potentially harmful substances.

◆ **Soluble fibers** (pectin, gums, mucilages) are found mainly within plant cells, soy milk (whole bean) and products.

Fiber promotes good health, and better control of diabetes and cholesterol.

'An apple a day keeps the doctor away.'
... it just might!

Types of Fiber (Cont)

Best Sources of Soluble Fiber:

Fruits and vegetables, oat bran, barley, dried beans and peas, psyllium and flax seed.

These fibers form a gel which slows both stomach emptying and the absorption of sugars from the intestines. This helps to control **blood sugar** levels.

Weight control is also aided by the slower emptying of the stomach and the feeling of **fullness provided by soluble fiber.**

Some soluble fibers can lower **blood cholesterol** by binding bile acids and excreting them. More body cholesterol must then be broken down to supply bile acids for emulsification of dietary fats. **Rice bran, while not high in soluble fiber can also lower blood cholesterol.**

◆ **Resistant starch** is that part of starchy foods (approx. 10%) which is tightly bound by fiber and resists normal digestion. Friendly bacteria in the large bowel ferment and change the resistant starch into short-chain fatty acids which are important to bowel health and may protect against colon cancer.

Starchy foods include bread, cereals, rice, pasta, potatoes and legumes.

Fiber & Weight Control

Fiber can assist weight control in several ways. Fiber-rich foods such as fresh fruit and vegetables, potatoes and whole-grain bread contain few calories for their large volume (due to their lowfat, high water content).

Their bulk fills the stomach and satisfies appetite much earlier than fiber-depleted foods. The extra chewing time also contributes to satiety, and gives the stomach time to register a feeling of fullness. Excessive calories are less likely to be consumed.

Fiber-depleted foods and drinks are more concentrated in calories; e.g. fats, sugar, candy, soft drinks, fruit juices, alcohol. They require little or no chewing. Large amounts with excessive calories can be consumed before appetite is satisfied.

Example: Whereas one fresh apple might satisfy our appetite, an apple juice drink with the equivalent sugars and calories of 2-3 apples does little to satisfy appetite. (See illustration below.)

High Fiber Foods fill the stomach. Fewer calories are consumed.

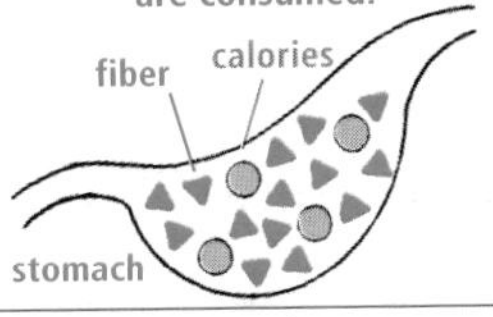

Low Fiber Foods are more concentrated in calories. More food must be eaten to fill the stomach.

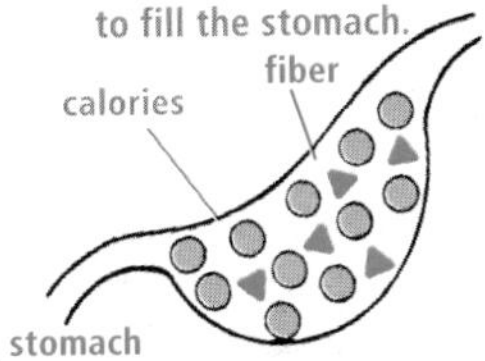

EFFECTS OF REMOVING FIBER FROM FOOD

2-3 pieces of fresh fruit produces 1 glass of fruit juice. The removal of fiber concentrates the sugar and calories.

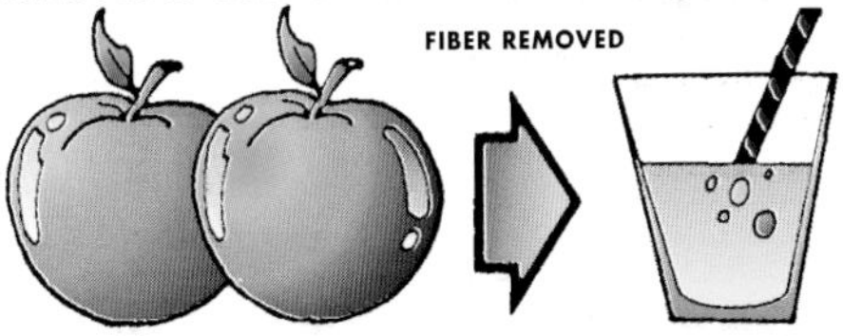

Fresh Fruit	Fruit Juice
High Fiber	Negligible Fiber
Low Calorie Density	High Calorie Density
Long Eating Time	No Eating Time (Drink)
Satisfies Hunger	Does Not Satisfy Hunger
Sugar Slowly Absorbed	Sugar More Quickly Absorbed
Less Insulin Required	More Insulin Required

Constipation

Constipation can reasonably be defined as a failure to have a bowel movement at least every second day - and just as importantly, without straining or pain.

Typically, stools are too hard, too narrow, and too small . . . *sinkers* rather than *floaters*.

The **main cause** is simply a lack of dietary fiber. Other contributing factors include insufficient fluids, too little exercise, emotional stress, gastro-intestinal disease, lack of proper dentition to chew high-fiber foods, and some medications (e.g. some antacids, antidepressants, tranquilizers).

Note: Check with your doctor to rule out any underlying medical problem – especially if you have a change in bowel habits in middle-age or later years.

DESIRABLE FIBER INTAKE

Adults: 25-35gm per day
Children (under 18): Age + 5gm
Example: 6-year old (6 + 5)= 11gm

SAMPLE FOOD QUANTITIES

For 35 Grams of Fiber/Day	Fiber
Breakfast Cereal (higher-fiber)	5g
plus 4 slices whole wheat Bread	6g
plus 3 servings fresh Fruit	9g
plus 1 medium Potato (w. skin) **or** 1 cup Brown Rice **or** 1/2 cup whole-wheat Pasta	4g
plus 3-4 servings Veges/Salad	6g
plus 1 cup Bean Soup **or** 1/4 cup Baked/Soy Beans **or** 1/2 cup Corn/Peas/Lentils **or** 1 1/4 oz Almonds (natural) **or** 3 medium Figs	5g

Hints to Increase Fiber and Avoid Constipation

1. **Breakfast is an important** contributor to daily fiber intake. Eat high-fiber breakfast cereals (bran-based cereals, oatmeal etc.). Add 1-2 tablespoons of unprocessed bran (wheat/ barley/ rice) and wheat germ if required.

Dried fruits, chopped nuts, soy grits, and seeds are also excellent additions to cereals.

Note: A gradual increase in fiber will prevent bloating, gas or pain. Persons intolerant to bran may benefit from psyllium-based fiber supplements and cereals.

2. **Drink 6-8 glasses of water daily.** Fiber works by absorbing many times its own weight of water.

3. **Eat wholegrain breads,** or fiber-enriched breads. One slice of whole-wheat bread has over double the fiber of regular white bread.

4. **Enjoy fruit as fresh fruit** with skins rather than as fruit juice. Enjoy whole-wheat pasta, barley, brown rice, nuts and seeds.

5. **Eat more vegetables,** salads and legumes - especially dried beans, baked beans, lentils, potatoes with skins, avocado, broccoli, brussel sprouts, cabbage, carrots, celery, and peas.

6. **Add bran** (barley/rice/wheat) or soy grits to soups, casseroles, yogurt, desserts, biscuits, cakes. Also use wholemeal flour or soy flour in place of white flour. Use nuts and seeds.

7. **Snack** on fresh or dried fruits, carrot or celery sticks, popcorn, nuts or seeds, wholegrain crackers, high-fiber bars (low-fat). Limit amounts if overweight.

8. **Exercise regularly** to strengthen abdominal muscles and stimulate the gut. Keep up fluids, especially in warm weather.

9. **Avoid** indiscriminate and regular use of harsh laxatives. They can overstimulate the intestinal muscles and may make normal bowel activity impossible. It may take several weeks to restore normal bowel function.

FOODS WITH ZERO FIBER

- **Dairy Products (Milk, Cheese, etc)**
- **Meats, Poultry, Fish, Eggs**
- **Fats/Oils, Sugar/Syrups**

(Only foods of plant origin contain fiber.)

Breakfast Cereals

	Fiber
General Mills: Cheerios, 1 cup, 1 oz	3
Basic 4, 1 cup, 2 oz	3
Crispy Wheaties, 1 cup, 1 oz	3
Fiber One, 1/2 cup, 1 oz	13
Raisin Nut Bran, 3/4 cup, 2 oz	5
Oatmeal Crisp, 1 cup, 2 oz	4
Wheat Chex, 1 cup, 1 3/4 oz	5
Health Valley: Amaranth Flakes, 3/4 cup	4
Banana Gone Nuts! 3/4 c., 2 oz	4
Bran w. Apple & Cinnamon, 3/4 cup	7
Bran w. Raisins, 1 1/4 cup	6
Blue Corn/Bran Flakes, 3/4 cup	4
Fiber 7 Flakes, 3/4 cup	4
Golden Flax, 1/2 cup	6
Granola (Fat Free), 2/3 cup	6
Healthy/Honey Crunches & Flakes, 3/4 cup	4
Healthy Fiber Flakes, 3/4 cup	4
Honey Crunch O's, 3/4 c., 1 oz	3
Oat Bran Flakes, all types, 3/4 cup	4
Real Oat Bran, 1/2 cup	5
Rice Crunch-Ems, 1 1/4 cup, 1 oz	4
10 Bran O's, 3/4 cup	4
Kellogg's:	
All-Bran, 1/2 cup, 1 oz	10
All-Bran w. Extra Fiber, 1/2 cup	13
Bran Buds, 3/4 cup, 2 oz	12
Bran Flakes, 3/4 cup	5
Corn Flakes, Fruit Loops, Smacks, 3/4 cup	1
Cracklin' Oat Bran, 3/4 cup, 2 oz	6
Cocoa/Rice Krispies, 3/4 cup	0
Complete Wheat, 3/4 cup, 1 oz	5
Frosted Mini Wheats, 1 cup, 2 oz	6
Healthy Choice, all types, 1 cup	5
Nutri-Grain (Almond Raisin), 1 1/4 cup	4
Mueslix (Almond. Raisin, Date), 2/3 cup	4
Raisin Bran, 1 cup, 2.2 oz	8
Smart Start, 1 cup	2
Special K; Product 19, 1 cup	1
Nabisco: 100% Bran, 1/2 cup, 1 oz	8
Shredded Wheat, 2 biscuits	5
Shredded Wheat & Bran, 1 1/4 cup, 2 oz	8

Fiber ~ Fiber (grams)

Breakfast Cereals (Cont)

	Fiber
Nature Valley: Average, 1/3 cup, 1 oz	1
Quaker: *Per 1 oz*	
Cap'n Crunch; Cr. Nut Oh's, 3/4 cup	1
Crunchy Bran, 3/4 cup, 1 oz	5
Life Cereal (3/4 cup), Oat Squares (1/2 c.)	2
Oat Bran, 1/3 cup	6
Oatmeal, average, 1 packet	3
100% natural cereals, average, 1/2 cup	3
Puffed Rice, 1 cup	1
Puffed Wheat, 1 cup	2
Toasted Oatmeal; Honey Nut, 1 cup	3
Post: Banana Nut Crunch, 1 cup, 2 oz	4
Blueberry Morning, 1 1/4 cup, 2 oz	2
Bran Flakes (Natural), 3/4 cup, 1 oz	5
Cocoa/Fruity Pebbles, 3/4 cup	0
Cranberry Almond Crunch, 1 cup, 2 oz	3
Frosted Alpha Bits, 1 cup	1
Fruit & Fiber, 1 cup, 1 3/4 oz	5
Grape-Nuts, 1/2 cup, 2 oz	5
Grape-Nuts Flakes, 3/4 cup, 1 oz	3
Great Grains, 2/3 cup, 2 oz	4
Honey Bunches of Oats, 3/4 cup, 1 oz	1
Oat Flakes, 1 cup, 1 oz	2

Brans & Supplements

Oat Bran: 1 Tbsp (level)	0.8
1/3 cup, (5 1/3 Tbsp), 1 oz	4.2
Rice Bran: 1/3 cup, 1 oz	6
Wheat Bran: unprocessed: 1 Tbsp	1.6
2 Tbsp (level), 1/4 oz	3.2
1/4 cup, (4 Tbsp), 1/2 oz	6.4
1/2 cup, 1 oz	13
Corn Germ: 1/4 cup, 1 oz	5
Wheat Germ: 1/4 cup, 1 oz	3
Psyllium Seed Husks, 2 Tbsp	8
Bios Life 2(Rexall), 1 pkt	5
Metamucil, 1 dose	3.4

Hot Cereals, Oatmeal

Bulgur (cracked Wheat), ckd, 1 cup	8
Cream of Wheat, ckd, 2/3 cup	1
Hominy Grits, dry, 3 Tbsp, 1 oz	1.2
Kashi (Breakfast Pilaf), 1/2 cup, cooked	6
Kashi 'Go', all varieties, 1/2 cup	6
'From Kashi to Good Friends', 3/4 cup	8
Puffed Kashi, 1 cup, 0.8 oz	2
Oatmeal, uncooked, 1/3 cup, 1 oz	2.7
cooked, 2/3 cup	2.7

Breads & Crackers

	Fiber
Bread: White, 1 slice, 1 oz	0.7
Whole-wheat, 1 slice, 1 oz	1.5
Whole-grain, 1 slice, 1 oz	2
Rye, Pumpernickel, 1 oz	1.5
Bagel/Roll/Bun, 1 medium, 2 oz	1.5
Pita, whole wheat, 5" pocket	4.5
Crackers: Graham, average, 2	1.4
Saltine, 4 crackers	0.3
Crispbreads (Rye), average, 2	4
Matzo 1 board, 1 oz	1
Rice Cakes: Average, 1 cake	0.3
Tortilla: Regular, 6"	0.5
Whole-wheat, 6"	1.3

Barley, Pasta, Rice & Flours

Barley, pearled, raw, 1/4 cup, 1.7 oz	5
Rice: White, cooked, 1 cup, 7 oz	1.6
Brown, cooked, 1 cup	3.2
Rice-A-Roni, average, 1 cup	1.5
Spaghetti/Noodles: cooked, 1 cup	2
Whole-wheat, cooked, 1 cup	7
Amaranth (Health Valley), 1 cup	9
Flour: Wheat, All-purpose, 1 cup, 4 1/2 oz	3.5
Whole-wheat, 1 cup, 4 1/2 oz	15
Cornmeal, stone ground, 1 cup, 4 1/2 oz	13
Carob Flour, 1 cup, 3 1/2 oz	13
Rye Flour, 1 cup, 3 1/2 oz	15
Soy Flour: Defatted, 1 cup, 3 1/2 oz	17
Full-fat, raw, 1 cup, 3 oz	8
Soy Meal, defatted, 1 cup, 4 1/2 oz	14

Frozen Entrees & Dinners

Average All Brands: *Per Serving*	
Potato/Pasta base, average	4-6
Vegetable base, average	3
Meat/Chicken base, average	2-3
Pizzas, 1/4 large, average	3

Soups

Chicken Noodle, 1 cup	<0.5
Tomato Soup, average, 1 cup	<1
Vegetable Soup, average, 1 cup	3
Health Valley: *Per 1 Cup Serving*	
Black Bean; Minestrone	10
Tomato	4
Organic Split Pea Soup	8
5-Bean Vegetable; Lentil & Carrots	13
Mushroom & Barley; Vegetable	7
Chili:	
w. Beans, average, 1 cup, 8.8 oz	7
without Beans, average, 1 cup, 8.3 oz	3

Fast Foods & Restaurants

	Fiber
Hamburgers: Small, average	1.5
Large/Whopper, average	2.5
Hot Dog, Regular	1.5
French Fries: Small serving, 2 1/2 oz	2.5
Regular/Medium, 3 1/2 oz	3.5
Chicken Nuggets, 6 pack	<0.5
Chicken Sandwich, average	2
Taco, average	4
Sundaes, Shakes, Soft Drinks	0
Arby's: Baked Potato w. Broccoli	9
Roast Beef Sandwich, regular	3
Denny's: Oriental Chicken Salad	7
Dennyburger w. fries	3
Club Sandwich	3
Grilled Chicken Sandwich	1
***Domino's* (Pizza):** Veggie, 2 sl. (12")	4
Pepperoni, 2 slices (12")	2.5
Cheese., Saus/Mushr., 2 slices, (12")	3
McDonald's: Arch Deluxe; Crispy Chicken	4
Big Mac	3
Egg McMuffin	1
Salads: Garden; Grilled Chicken	2
Pizza Hut: *Per 2 slices, Medium*	
Pan Pizza: Cheese, Pepperoni	2
Supreme	4
Thin 'n Crispy: Supreme	4
Hand-Tossed, average	3
Personal Pan Pizza, 1 whole	5
Subway: Sandwich, white roll	2.5
w. honey Wheat Roll	3.2
Footlong, w.Wheat Roll	6.4
Salads, average	2

Cakes, Cookies, Snack Bars

Apple/Fruit Pie, 1 serving	2
Cake, w. plain flour, 1 serving	1
w. whole-wheat flour, 1 serving	3
Carrot Cake, 1 serving	2
Cookies, oatmeal, (3 small/1 large)	3
Donuts	0
Fruit Cake, 1 serving	3
Fi-Bar (Natural Nectar), 1 bar	4
Fig Bars, 2	1.3
Granola Bars, average	1
Health Valley: Fat-Free Fruit Bars	3.7
Oat Bran Jumbo Fruit Bars	7
Fat-Free Cookies, 2	2
Fat-Free Fruit Muffins, 1	5
IDN Fiberry Snack Bar	3
Muffins, Oat Bran (2 small, 1 large)	5

Chocolate, Chips, Popcorn

	Fiber
Cheese Balls/Curls/Twists	0
Chocolate, Hard Candy, Cheese Balls	0
Chocolate with nuts/fruit, 2 oz bar	1
Mars Bar	1
Potato Chips, corn chips, 1 oz	1
Popcorn, 3 cups	2
Pretzels, Twists, 6	1

Nuts, Seeds

Almonds: Natural, 25 kernels, 1 oz	4
Blanched (skins removed), 1 oz	3
Cashews, Filberts, Pecans, 1 oz	1.7
Peanuts, Mixed Nuts, Coconut, 1 oz	2.5
Peanut Butter, 2 Tbsp, 1 oz	1.8
Pistachio Nuts, dried, shelled, 1 oz	3
Walnuts, Black/English, dried, 1 oz	1.5
Seeds: Amaranth, 2 1/2 Tbsp, 1 oz	3.5
Flax Seeds, 3 Tbsp, 1 oz	7
Psyllium Seed Husks, 5 Tbsp, 1 oz	20
Quinoa Seeds, 3 Tbsp, 1 oz	2.7
Sesame Seeds, whole, 1 oz	3
Sesame Butter/Tahini, 2 Tbsp, 1.1 oz	3
Sunflower kernels, 1/4 cup, 1 oz	4.4
Teff Seeds, 1 oz	3.8

Fruit – Fresh

Apples: 1 medium, 6 oz (whole)	
with skin + core	5.5
with skin, no core	4.5
without skin, no core	3.7
Apricots, 2 medium, 4 oz	2
Avocado, average, 1/2 medium	3
Banana, 1 medium, 6 oz (w. skin)	2
Blueberries, raw, 1/2 cup, 5 oz	4.4
Cherries, sweet, raw, 10 fruits, 2 1/2 oz	1.5
Grapefruit, average, 1/2 fruit, 8 1/2 oz	1
Grapes, 1 medium bunch, seedless, 7 oz	3
Kiwifruit, 1 medium, 3 oz	3
Mango, 1 medium, 11 oz (whole)	1.6
Melons, cantaloup, 4 oz (edible)	1
Nectarine, 1 medium, 4 oz	1.8
Olives, average all types, 7 jumbo, 2 oz	1.5
Oranges, 1 medium (7-8 oz w. skin)	
5 1/2 oz (peeled)	3.8
Passionfruit, 2 medium, 2 1/2 oz	5
Peaches, 1 large, 6 oz	2
Pears, raw, 1 medium, 6 oz	4.5
Pineapple, 1 slice, 3 oz	1.8
Plums, 2 medium, 6 oz	2.8
Strawberries, 6 medium/3 large, 2 oz	1.5
Watermelon, 4 oz (edible)	0.5

Fruit – Dried, Juice

	Fiber
Dried Fruit: Apricots, 8 halves, 1 oz	2.2
Dates (3 med); Raisins (2 Tbsp), 1 oz	1.5
Figs, 3 medium, 1 1/2 oz	5
Prunes, 4 medium, 1 oz	2
Fruit Juice: Orange/Apple etc, 1 glass	<0.5
Prune Juice, 5 oz	1.4
Carrot Juice, 8 oz	1.8

Vegetables

Asparagus, 4 spears	2
Bean Sprouts, 1/2 cup, 2 1/4 oz	1.5
Beans: Snap/Green, 1/2 cup, 2 1/2 oz	2
Baked Beans in Tom Sce, 1/2 c, 4 1/2 oz	10
Dried Beans, ckd, average, 1/2 cup	7
Beets, ckd, slices, 1/2 cup, 3 oz	1.5
Broccoli, cooked, 1/2 cup, 3 oz	2.2
Brussels Sprouts, ckd, 1/2 cup, 3 oz	3.5
Cabbage: White, ckd, 1/2 cup, 2 1/2 oz	1
Red, ckd, 1/2 cup, 2 1/2 oz	2
Carrots, 1 medium (7 1/2"), 1/2 cup, 3 oz	2.7
Cauliflower, cooked, 1/2 cup, 3 oz	2.8
Celery, raw, diced, 1/2 cup, 2 1/2 oz	1
Chick Peas (Garbanzos), ckd, 1/2 c., 3 1/2 oz	6
Corn, kernels, ckd, 1/2 cup, 2 1/2 oz	2.5
Cream-style, 1/2 cup, 4 1/2 oz	1.5
Cucumber/Lettuce/Mushrooms, 2 oz	0.5
Eggplant, raw, sliced, 1/2 cup	2.5
Lentils, cooked, 1/2 cup, 3 1/2 oz	4
Onions, 1 medium, 4 oz	2
Spring Onions, chop., 1/4 cup, 1 oz	1.5
Peas: Green, 1/2 cup, 3 oz	3
Cowpeas (Black-eyed), ckd, 1/2 cup	10
Split Peas, ckd, 1/2 cup, 4 1/2 oz	6.5
Peppers, sweet, raw, 1 large, 3 1/2 oz	1.5
Potatoes: 1 medium, with skin, 5 oz	4
without skin	2
1/2 cup mashed, 3 1/2 oz	1.5
French Fries, 3 oz serving	3
Spinach, cooked, 1/2 cup, 3 oz	2
Squash: Summer, cookd, 3 oz	1.2
Winter, cooked, 3 oz	2.4
Tomatoes: 1 medium, 5 oz	2
Tomato Sauce, 1 cup	0.3
Frozen: Mixed Vegetables, ckd, 1/2 cup	3
Soybean Products: Miso, 1/2 c., 5 oz	7.7
Tempeh, 1 piece, 3 oz	2
Tofu, 4 oz	1.4

Salads: Side Salad, average	1
Bean Salad, 1/2 cup	5
Coleslaw, 1/2 cup	1
Potato Salad, 1/2 cup	2

General Notes

- **Protein has many important body functions.** It builds and repairs muscle, and is the basis of our body's organs, hormones, enzymes, and antibodies to fight infection.
- **Protein is also an emergency fuel** in the absence of sufficient carbohydrate and fats. For this reason, weight loss should be gradual so as to preserve protein levels in muscle, the heart and other body organs.
- **It is easy to obtain sufficient protein,** even if vegetarian. **Plant proteins are not inferior to animal proteins.** In fact, eating more soy and other plant proteins, and less animal protein, may help to build stronger bones and prevent osteoporosis; and may help to control blood cholesterol levels.
- **When changing to a vegetarian diet,** include soybeans, and other dried beans, soy milk drinks (calcium-enriched), lentils, tofu, tempeh, nuts, and wholegrain breads and cereals. Milk, yogurt, cheese and eggs may enhance nutrient intake.

Protein & Muscle

- Although muscles are built of protein, protein is not a special fuel for working muscle cells - carbohydrates and fats are.
- In fact, a diet high in protein (and fat) and low in carbohydrate, can significantly reduce the performance of endurance sports athletes. **Carbohydrate** is the best fuel for muscles exercised for long periods.
- Any **extra protein** required by athletes and body-builders, can easily be obtained from the extra food eaten to satisfy hunger and energy needs - even allowing an excessive 120g protein daily for a 170 lb athlete (0.7g/lb body wt; twice the RDI).
- Remember, **excess protein** in food will not build bigger muscles. Any excess is converted and stored as fat. Excess protein can also strain the kidneys which excrete the waste products of protein metabolism.

Elderly people (and dieters) must eat sufficient food to ensure adequate protein intake.

Inadequate protein leads to a drop in immune response with greater susceptibility to illness and infections. Muscle strength and muscle mass also drop.

Protein needs are easily met with sensible eating. Athletes who eat enough food for their energy needs, can obtain sufficient protein.

RECOMMENDED DAILY PROTEIN INTAKE (Grams)

(Figure in brackets - Recommended amount of protein per lb of ideal body weight.)

Infants:	0-6 mths	**13g**	(1g/lb)
	6-12 mths	**14g**	(0.7g/lb)
Children:	1-3 yrs	**16g**	(0.6g/lb)
	4-6 yrs	**24g**	(0.5g/lb)
	7-10	**28g**	(0.5g/lb)
Males:	11-14 yrs	**45g**	(0.45g/lb)
	15-18	**59g**	(0.4g/lb)
	19-24	**58g**	(0.36g/lb)
	25+	**50g**	(0.4g/lb)
Females:	11-14 yrs	**46g**	(0.45g/lb)
	15-18	**44g**	(0.37g/lb)
	19-24	**46g**	(0.36g/lb
	25+	**50g**	(0.36g/lb)
Pregnancy:		**60g**	
Breastfeeding:		**65g**	

Note: Above figures allow for a large safety margin for most persons.

Iron & Anemia Guide

- **Iron deficiency** is one of the most common nutritional deficiencies in women. The risk is increased in dieters who do not eat well-balanced meals. Chronic shortage of iron leads to **anemia**.
- **Women** between 11 and 50 years of age are at greater risk because of the monthly loss of menstrual blood. Pregnancy, growth, and endurance sports also demand extra iron.
- **In red blood cells,** iron combines with protein to form **hemoglobin** - the red pigment which carries oxygen in the blood. A lack of iron limits the production of hemoglobin and hence the amount of vital oxygen delivered to body cells.

Note: A blood test will tell you if your Hb and Iron stores (ferritin) are adequate. (Iron stores can be low even when Hb is normal.)

- **Vitamin C** (in fruits/veges/salads) enhances absorption of 'non-heme' iron in bread, cereals, milk, vegetables, nuts, eggs and iron supplements. Small amounts of meat, fish or poultry also help. (They contain 'heme' iron).
- **Iron absorption is lessened** by up to 60% when high calcium foods are consumed with iron-rich main meals. Tea, coffee, phytates (in bran) and oxalates lessen absorption of non-heme iron.
- **For infants to 1 year,** use iron-fortified milk/soy formula if not breast-feeding. Introduce iron-fortified baby cereals at 4-6 mths.

Note: Iron deficiency in children (even without anemia), can result in lethargy, irritability, repeated infections, and developmental problems.

Iron Supplements

- **Most people** can obtain adequate iron from their diet. **A wide variety** of animal and plant foods contain iron. (See Iron Counter)
- **Iron supplements** are only recommended for women with heavy menstrual blood losses, during pregnancy (if tests show a low-iron status), endurance athletes with low blood ferritin (iron stores) and for persons with diagnosed anemia. Check with your doctor.
- While the 5 mg of iron in multi-vitamin/mineral supplements is safe for most people, large amounts can be toxic, (especially in persons with hemochromatosis iron overload condition).

ANEMIA SYMPTOMS

Anemia reduces the amount of oxygen carried in the blood. The body tissues become starved of oxygen. Symptoms include:

- **Pale skin; brittle finger nails (may turn up into spoon shape).**
- **Excessive tiredness or fatigue**
- **Breathlessness**
- **Feeling of malaise and irritability.**
- **Always feel cold.**
- **Decrease in attention span.**

Note: Other medical conditions may also cause similar symptoms. Check with your doctor.

A nutritious diet with adequate iron is important particularly for women and athletes.

RECOMMENDED DAILY IRON INTAKE (mg)

Infants (0-6 mths):			
	Breastfed	~	0.5mg
	Bottlefed	~	3mg
	6-12 mths	~	9mg
Children:	1-11 yrs	~	6-8mg
Males:	12-18 yrs	~	10-13mg
	19+ yrs	~	7mg
Females:	12-50yrs	~	12-16mg
	51+ yrs	~	5-7mg
	Pregnancy	~	22-36mg
	Breastfeeding	~	12-16mg

Protein & Iron Counter

Pro ~ Protein (grams) **Iron** ~ Iron (mg)

Meat

	Pro	Iron
Steak: Average all cuts, lean (no fat)		
Small (4 oz raw/3 oz ckd)	23	2.3
Medium (6 oz raw/4¼ oz ckd)	34	3.4
Large (10 oz raw/7¼ oz ckd)	57	5.7
Roast Beef: lean, 2 slices, 3 oz	24	2.5
Ground Beef patty, lean, ckd, 3 oz	21	2
Lamb chop, broiled, 3 oz	22	1.5
Liver, cooked, 3 oz	23	5.5
Veal cutlet, 1 medium	23	1
Pork, cooked, lean, 3 oz	24	1
Bacon, 3 medium slices	6	0.3
Ham, roasted, 2 pieces, 3 oz	18	1
Ham, luncheon, 2 slices, 1½ oz	7	0.3
Pastrami (*Oscar Mayer*), 3 sl., 1¾ oz	10	1.3
Sausages: Bologna, 2 sl., 2 oz	7	1
Braunschweiger, 2 sl., 2 oz	8	5.3
Pork link, thick, 2 oz	6	0.4
Frankfurter, 1⅓ oz	5	0.5
Salami, hard, 3 slices, 1 oz	7	0.5

Chicken/Turkey

	Pro	Iron
Chicken, ckd; Breast portion, 3 oz	27	1
Leg/Thigh, lean, 3 oz	24	1
½ Whole Chicken	60	2.5
Drumstick, 1 medium, 3 oz	12	0.6
Turkey, cooked: Light meat, 3 oz	24	2
Dark meat, lean, 3 oz	24	2

Fish

	Pro	Iron
Finfish: *Per 4 oz, cooked*		
Cod, Flounder/Sole, Pollock	28	0.5
Catfish, Haddock, Halibut, M/Mahi	28	1.3
Ocean Perch, Swordf., Orange Roughy	28	1.3
Canned Fish: Tuna, Light, 3 oz	25	1.5
White, 3 oz	23	0.5
Salmon, pink, 3 oz	17	0.7
Salmon, red, 3 oz	17	1
Sardines, 3 whole (3"), 1¼ oz	9	1
Anchovies, 1 can, 1½ oz	13	2
Shellfish: Crabmeat, 3 oz	17.5	0.7
Clams, raw, 4 large/9 sml, 3 oz	11	12
Crayfish, cooked, 3 oz	20	2.7
Lobster, cooked, 3 oz	17	0.5
Oysters, raw, 6 medium, 3 oz	7	5
Scallops, 2 lge/5 small, 1 oz	5	0.1
Shrimp, raw, 6 large, 1½ oz	8.5	1
Fish Products: Fish Sticks, 4 sticks	10	0.5
Fish Portions, in batter, 4 oz	13	0.6
Gefilte Fish, 1 medium ball, 2 oz	8	1

Eggs

	Pro	Iron
1 Large Egg, whole	6	0.7
Egg Yolk	3	0.7
Egg White	3	0
Omelet: Plain, 2 eggs	13	1.7
Ham & Cheese	17	3
Egg Substitutes (liquid):		
Eggbeaters, 1 egg equiv.	4.5	1
Scramblers, ¼ cup, 2 oz	6	0.7

Milk, Yogurt, Ice-Cream

	Pro	Iron
Milk: Whole/Lowfat/Skim, 8 fl.oz cup	8	0.1
Protein Enriched, 1 cup	10	0.1
Chocolate Milk, 1 cup	8	0.6
Thick Shake, Chocolate, 10 oz	9	1
Vanilla, 10 oz	11	0.3
Soymilk (fortified), average, 1 cup	7	1
Yogurt: Plain, 6 oz	10	0.1
Fruit flavors: 6 oz	8	0.3
8 oz	11	0.5
Ice-Cream: Rich, ½ cup	2	0
Regular, Vanilla, ½ cup	2.5	0
Sherbet, ½ cup	1	0
Custard, baked, ½ cup	7	0.5

Cheese

	Pro	Iron
Hard Cheeses, average, 1 oz	7	0.2
4 oz piece	28	0.8
Cottage Cheese, ½ cup	13	0.3
Ricotta, part skim, ½ cup	14	1

Bread, Bagels, Biscuits

	Pro	Iron
Bread (w. enriched flour): 1 slice, 1 oz	2	1
4 slices, 4 oz	8	4
4 thick slices, 6 oz	1.2	6
Bagel, plain 2 oz	6	1.5
Biscuits, 1 oz	2	0.7
Pita Bread, 1 pita, 1½ oz	4	1
Pumpernickel, 1 slice, 1 oz	3	1

Infant/Baby Foods

	Pro	Iron
Infant Formula Milk:		
Enfamil/Gerber/Similac, 5 fl.oz		
Regular/Low Iron	2.2	0.2
With Iron	2.2	1.8
Isomil/Nursoy/ProSobee	3	1.8
Baby Cereals: *Average All Brands*		
Dry, 4 Tbsp, ½ oz	1	7
Jars (w. fruit), 4½ oz	1	7

Breakfast Cereals

	Pro	Iron
Hot Type, cooked:		
Bulgur, cooked, 1 cup, 5 oz	9	2
Oatmeal: Reg., non-fortified., 1 cup	6	1.5
Instant, fortified, average, 1 pkt	4	8
Quaker Extra, all flavors	4	18
Total, all types, 1 pkt	4	18
Corn/Hominy Grits: Reg., 1 cup	3	1.5
Quaker: Reg., 3 Tbsp, 1 oz	2	0.8
Instant White, 1 packet	2	8
Cream of Wheat, 1 cup	4	10
Ready-To-Eat: *Per 1 oz serving*		
Arrowhead, Average, all varieties	3	1
General Mills:		
Basic 4, 1 cup, 2 oz	4	3.8
Cheerios, regular, 1 cup, 1 oz	3	6.8
Cocoa Puffs, 1 cup, 1 oz	1	3.8
Corn Flakes, 1 cup	2	6.8
Fiber One, ½ cup	2	3.8
Kix, 1⅓ cups; Kaboom, 1¼ cup	2	6.8
Total, Raisin Bran, 1 cup, 2 oz	4	15
Wheaties, 1 cup	3	6.8
Health Valley:		
10 Bran O's, ¾ cup	3	0.9
Amaranth Flakes, ¾ cup	3	0.6
Bran Cereal w. Raisins, ¾ cup	5	1.5
98% Fat Free Granola, ⅔ cup	5	1.2
Real Oat Bran, ½ cup	6	0.6
Golden Flax, ¼ cup	6	1.2
Kellogg's: All Bran, ½ cup	4	4.5
Bran Flakes, ¾ cup	3	8.5
Cocoa Krispies, ¾ cup	2	1.8
Corn Flakes, 1 cup	2	8.4
Just Right, 1 cup	4	16
Nutrigrain Almond Raisin, 1¼ cup	4	1.4
Product 19, 1 cup, 2 oz	2	18
Raisin Bran, 1 cup, 2 oz	6	4.5
Raisin Squares, ¾ cup,	4	16
Rice Krispies, 1¼ cup	2	1.8
Special K, 1 cup	6	8.7
Nature Valley: All varieties, ⅓ cup	2	0.7
Post: Raisin Bran, 1 oz	3	4.5
Grape Nuts, 1 oz	3	1
Quaker: Crunchy Bran, ⅔ cup	2	8
Oat Squares, ½ cup, 1 oz	4	6
100% natural cereal, ¼ cup	3	1
Puffed Rice/Wheat, 1 cup, ½ oz	1	0.5
Shredded Wheat, 2 biscuits	4	1

Brans & Wheatgerm

	Pro	Iron
Oat Bran, raw, 1 Tbsp	2	0.5
Rice Bran, raw, 2 Tbsp	1	1
Wheat Bran, unprocessed, 2 Tbsp	1	1
Wheat Germ, 2 Tbsp, ½ oz	4	1.3

Grains & Flours

	Pro	Iron
Amaranth, 1 cup, ½ oz	10	3
Barley, ½ cup, 3½ oz	8	2
Buckwheat Flour, dark, 1 cup	11.5	2.7
light, 1 cup	6	1
Carob Flour, 1 cup	5	3
Corn Flour, 1 cup, 4 oz	9	2
Corn Meal, enriched, 1 cup	11	3.5
Flour: White, enriched, 1 cup, 4½ oz	13	6
Wholegrain, 1 cup, 4¼ oz	16	5
Millet, wholegrain, 1 cup, 3½ oz	10	7
Rye Flour, dark, 1 cup, 4½ oz	21	6
light, 1 cup, 3½ oz	10	1
Soy Flour, full fat, 1 cup, 3 oz	32	5.5
Yeast: Brewer's, dry, 1 Tbsp	3	1.5

Rice, Spaghetti

	Pro	Iron
Rice: brown/white, average		
1 cup cooked, 6½ oz	5	1
Spaghetti/Macaroni/Noodles (enriched):		
Cooked, 1 cup, 4½ oz	7	2
Canned: in Tomato Sauce, ½ cup	2	0.5
w. Meatballs, 1 cup, 8 oz	9	2

Soups

	Pro	Iron
With Noodles/Vegetables, 1 cup	3	0.5
With Meat/Beans/Peas, 1 cup	8	1.5

Fruit

	Pro	Iron
Fresh/Canned: Average, all types, 1 serving		
1 medium/2 small fruit	1	0.5
Avocado, ½ medium	2	1
Dried Fruit: Apricots, 8 halves, 1 oz	1	1.3
Dates, 6 dates, 2 oz	1.5	0.7
Figs, 4 medium figs, 2 oz	2	1.7
Prunes, 5 medium, 1½ oz	1	1
Raisins, 1 oz	1	0.7
Fruit Juice: Average, 1 cup	0.5	0.5
Prune Juice, 6 fl.oz	1	2.5
Tomato Juice, 6 fl.oz	0.5	1

King Kong was a vegetarian

Protein & Iron Counter

Vegetables

	Pro	Iron
Beans: Snap/green, 1/2 cup	1	0.8
Dried: Average all types, cooked, 1/2 cup	7	2.5
Baked Beans, 1/2 cup 4 1/2 oz	5	2
Bean Sprouts, mung, 1 cup	3	1
Broccoli, 3/4 cup pieces, 4 oz	4	1.4
Cabbage; Cauliflower, 1 cup	1	0.6
Corn, 1/2 cup kernels, 3 oz	2.5	0.3
1 ear trimmed to 3 1/2"	2	0.4
Lentils, cooked, 1/2 cup, 3 1/2 oz	9	3.3
Mushrooms, raw, 1/2 cup, sliced	0.5	0.5
Peas: green, 1/2 cup, 3 oz	4	1.2
Split Peas, cooked, 1 cup	16	2.5
Potatoes, cooked:		
1 medium, with skin, 5 oz	3.3	2
without skin, 4 oz	2.3	1
French Fries, 3 oz	3	1
Potato Salad, 1/2 cup	3.5	2.5
Pumpkin, 1/2 cup mashed	1	2.5
Seaweed, kelp, 1 oz	<1	2.5
Spinach, cooked, 1/2 cup, 3 oz	2.7	2.5
Squash, ckd, all types, 1/2 cup	1	0.3
Tomatoes, 1 medium, 4 1/2 oz	1	0.6
Vegetables, mixed, ckd, 1 cup	2.5	0.7
Soybeans, cooked, 1/2 cup, 3 oz	14	4.4

Tofu, Tempeh, Miso

	Pro	Iron
Tofu, raw, firm, 1/2 cup, 4 1/2 oz	10	1.5
Tempeh, 1/2 cup, 3 oz	16	2
Miso, 1/2 cup, 5 oz	16	4
Soybean Protein (TVP), 1 oz	18	3

Cakes, Pastries, Pies

	Pro	Iron
(Made with enriched flour)		
Carrot w. cream cheese frosting, 4 oz	4	1.3
Cheesecake, 1 piece, 3 1/2 oz	5	0.5
Chocolate, 1 piece, 2 oz	2	2
Fruitcake, 1 piece, 1 1/2 oz	2	1.2
Plain, 1 piece, 3 oz	4	1.2
Croissant, plain, 2 oz	5	2
Danish Pastry, 1 pastry, 2 1/4 oz	4	1.3
Donuts, average, 2 oz	4	1.2
Muffins, average, 1 medium, 1 1/2 oz	3	1
Pancakes, 4" diam., two, 2 oz	4	1
Pies: Fruit, 1 piece, 5 1/2 oz	4	1.5
Pecan, 1 piece, 5 oz	7	4.5
Puddings, average, 1/2 cup, 4 1/2 oz	4	0.3
Waffles, 1 large, 2 1/2 oz	7	1.5

Sugar, Honey, Jam

	Pro	Iron
Sugar: White	0	0
Brown, 1 Tbsp	0	0.3
Molasses: Light/Medium, 1 Tbsp	0	1
Blackstrap, 1 Tbsp, 3/4 oz	0	3
Corn Syrup, 1 Tbsp, 3/4 oz	0	1
Honey, Jams, Jelly	0	0.2

Candy, Chocolate, Carob

	Pro	Iron
Candy, sugar-based	0	0
Chocolate: Plain, 2 oz bar	4	0.8
with nuts, 2 oz bar	6	0.8
Carob, plain, 2 oz	6	0.7

Cookies, Crackers, Chips

	Pro	Iron
Cookies, average, 4 cookies	2	1
Crackers: Graham, 2 1/2" sq., 2	1	0
Rice Cakes, average, one	1	0
Corn/Potato Chips, 1 oz	2	0.3

Nuts

	Pro	Iron
Nuts: Almonds, shelled, 20-25 nuts	6	1
Brazil Nuts, 7-8 medium nuts, 1 oz	4	1
Cashews, 12-16 nuts, 1 oz	5	1.5
Coconut, raw, 1 1/2 oz pce (2" x 2 1/2")	1	1
Macadamias, 1 oz	2	0.5
Mixed Nuts, 1 oz	5	1
Peanuts, dry roasted, 40 nuts, 1 oz	6	0.6
Pecans, 24 halves, 1 oz	2	0.5
Walnuts, 15 halves, 1 oz	4	0.7
Peanut Butter, 1 Tbsp	1	0.5

Seeds: *Per 1oz*

	Pro	Iron
Pumpkin Kernels, dry, hulled, 1 oz	7	4.2
Sesame Seeds, dry, 1 Tbsp	2	0.6
Sunflower Seeds, dried, hulled, 1 oz	6	2
Tahini, 1 Tbsp, 1/2 oz	2.5	1.4

Granola & Food/Protein Bars

	Pro	Iron
Granola Bar, average	2	0.5
Peanut Bar (*Planters*), 1 1/2 oz	7	0.7
Bariatrix: Nutra Bars, 1	11	3.6
Proti Bars, 1	15	1.5
Choice dm Bar, 35g	6	3.6
Diet Center Meal Repl. Bar, 65g	14	2
Fi-Protein Nutritional Bar, 1	9.5	0
Genisoy Protein Bar, 2.2 oz	14	4.5
IDN: proGram-16, 65g	16	3.6
MetaForm Bar	30	7.2
Met-Rx Bar, 100g	27	7.2
MightyBite Nutritional Bar, 25g	6	1
Power Bar, 1 bar	10	6.3
Slim-Fast Bar, 34g	6	4.5
Source One Bar, 2.2 oz	15	4.5
Sweet Success Bar, 33g	2	2.7
Tiger Sport, 65g	11	4.5

Nutritional & High Protein Drinks

	Pro	Iron
Bariatrix Shakes, dry, 1 oz	15	3.6
Fruit Drinks, mix, 20g	15	0
Proti-Max Meal Replacement, 67g	35	6.3
Boost Nutrition Energy Drink, 8 oz	10	3.6
Ensure, all flavors, 8 oz	9	2.3
Ensure Plus, 8 oz	13	3
Carnation Instant Breakfast, 10 oz	12	4.5
Diet Center Meal Repl. Powder, 1 pkt	12	6.3
GatorPro, 11 oz can	17	5.5
GemSoy Shake: Pro-Cal 100, 1 pkt	14	3.6
IDN Appeal, 1 pkg, 1 cup	16	2.7
Kindercal, 8 fl.oz	8	2.5
Met-Rx, Drink Mix, 72g	38	9
Nature's Best, Protein Shake, 11 oz	20	3.6
Nutra Start, 11 oz	10	3.6
Resource (Novartis) Standard, 8 fl.oz	9	4.5
Slim Fast, 325 ml can	10	2.7
Sweet Success (Nestle), 10 fl.oz can	10	4.5
Sustacal/Plus, 8 oz	15	4
Ultra Slim Fast, powder, 3 Tbsp, 33g	5	6.3
Walgreens Nutritional Suppl.: Plus, 8 oz	9	4.5
Advanced, 8 oz can	13	2.7
Lite, 8 oz can	10	4.5
Weider: Muscle Builder, 2 scoops	18	9
90% Plus Protein, 3 Tbsp	24	2.7
Coffee, Tea, Soda		
Coffee, Coffee Substitutes, 1 cup	0	0.1
Tea (all types); Soft Drinks/Soda	0	0
Hot Chocolate, 6 fl.oz	2	2.2
Beer, Wine, Spirits		
Beer, 12 fl.oz	1	0
Wines, red/white, 1 glass	0	0.4
Spirits/Liquor	0	0
Fast-Foods/Burgers		
Note: See Fast-Foods Section for comprehensive protein counts.		
Arby's: Roast Beef Sandwich, reg.	23	4
Giant Roast Beef S/wich	35	6
Italian Sub	30	2
Roast Turkey Deluxe	20	3
Burger King: Whopper S/wich	27	2.5
Hamburger	20	1.5
Double Bacon Cheeseburger	44	2.5
Chicken Sandwich; Big Fish Sandwich	26	2
Carl's Jr: Famous Star Hamburger	26	2
Super Star Hamburger	43	3
Chicken Club Sandwich	35	2
Hot & Crispy Sandwich	14	1

Fast Foods/Burgers (Cont)

	Pro	Iron
Domino's Pizza: Deep Dish (12"), 2 sl.		
Cheese, 2 slices	18	4
Pepperoni, Sausage/Pepperoni	21	4
X-tra Cheese & Pepperoni	24	4.5
French Fries: Medium, 3 1/2 oz	4.5	0.7
KFC		
Original, Wing & Breast	38	0.4
3-Pce. Dinner, Original	51	0.4
Kentucky Nuggets, 6	16	0.4
Colonel's Chicken Sandwich	29	1.5
McDonald's: Arch Deluxe	29	2.5
Big Mac	25	2.5
Cheeseburger	15	1.5
Chicken McNuggets (6)	18	0.6
Fish Filet Deluxe	24	1.5
Grilled Crispy Chicken Deluxe	27	1.5
Hamburger	12	1.5
Quarter Pounder	23	2.5
French Fries: Small, 2 1/2 oz	3	0.2
Large, 5 oz	6	0.6
Breakfast: Egg McMuffin	17	1.5
Hotcakes w. Marg/Syrup	9	1.5
Sausage McMuffin w. Egg	19	1.5
Grilled Chicken Salad Deluxe	21	1
Muffin, Lowfat, Apple Bran	6	1
Pancakes: 3 Pancakes	8	2
Pizza Hut: Per Medium, 2 slices		
Pan Pizzas, average	26	4
Thin 'n Crispy: Supreme	28	2
Hand Tossed: Pepperoni	24	3
Supreme; Personal Pan Pizza	32	4.5
Shakes, Chocolate	12	0.4
Subway: 6" Subs, average	22	2
Del Style Sandwiches, average	12	1
Subway Club Salad, reg.	16	2
Sundaes: Average all outlets	7	0.3
Taco Bell: Bean Burrito	13	3.5
Beef Burrito	22	3.7
Tostado	10	1.5
Enchirito; Nachos Bellgrande	20	3
Taco Bellgrande	18	2
Taco Light	19	2.5
Taco Salad w. Shell	35	7
Wendy's: Single w. Everything	26	3
Big Bacon Classic	34	3
Hamburger Kid's Meal	15	2
Grilled Chicken Sandwich	27	1.5
Stuffed Potatoes: Broc. & Cheese	9	2.5
Bacon & Cheese	17	2.5
Taco Salad	29	2.5

High Blood Pressure

Many American adults have hypertension (high blood pressure), and are unaware of it. It is generally symptomless, so **have your blood pressure checked annually** - particularly if there is a family history of hypertension.

Untreated hypertension overworks the heart, damages arteries and promotes atherosclerosis. This in turn greatly increases the risk of heart disease, stroke, blindness, kidney disease and impotence. The earlier hypertension is detected, the sooner it can be brought under control.

Treating Hypertension

If your blood pressure is high, consult your doctor about diet and medication. You may be referred to a dietitian for more detailed dietary advice and meal planning.

High-Normal and Stage 1 hypertension can often be treated by reducing sodium intake, losing weight if overweight, limiting alcohol to 2 drinks or less daily, exercising regularly, and dealing with stress.

Stages 2, 3 and 4 hypertension usually require drug therapy. However, salt restriction, abstaining from alcohol and the above lifestyle changes will improve the success of drug therapy, and enable smaller drug doses to be prescribed.

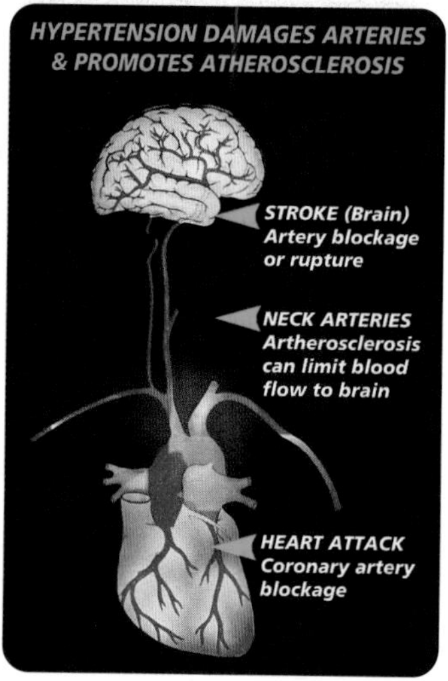

BLOOD PRESSURE CLASSIFICATIONS

National High Blood Pressure Educ. Prog. (1993)

	DIASTOLIC	SYSTOLIC
Normal ►	80-84	120-129
High-Normal ►	85-89	130-139
Stage 1 ►	90-99	140-159
Stage 2 ►	100-109	160-179
Stage 3 ►	110-119	180-209
Stage 4 ►	120 or over	210 or over

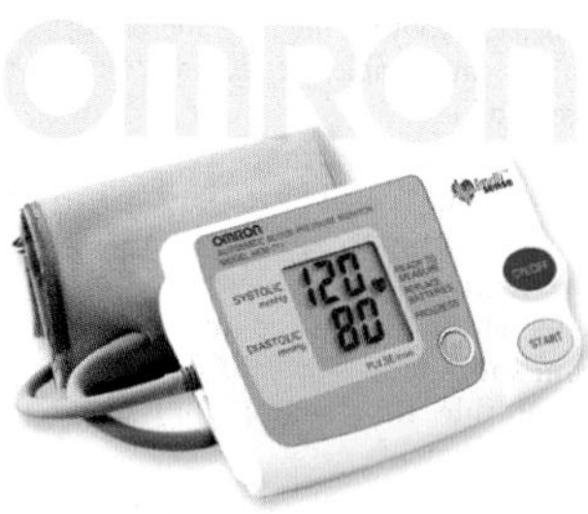

Blood Pressure Monitors aid home management of high blood pressure.

Salt & Sodium

- **Sodium is a mineral element** most commonly found in salt (sodium chloride). It also occurs naturally in much smaller amounts in animal and plant foods, and water - normally sufficient for our needs without having to add salt.
- **Sodium is required** for nerve and muscle function as well as to balance the amount of fluid in our tissues and blood.

  Sodium acts like a sponge to attract and hold fluids in body tissues.
- **Excess sodium** can cause water retention, and increase the risk of developing hypertension. Very high salt intake may also increase the risk of stomach cancer.
- **Too little sodium** may cause low blood pressure (hypotension), and decrease blood flow to the heart, brain and kidneys - especially during exercise. (A certain blood volume is required to sustain the blood pressure needed for adequate blood flow in the capillaries).

Salt - Sensitive Persons

- **Normally, our kidneys** excrete excess dietary sodium. The thirst we feel after a salty meal is the body calling for water to dilute the sodium, and enable the kidneys to flush out excess sodium.
- **However, 'salt sensitive'** persons (perhaps 1 in 2-3 adults) tend to retain excess sodium (above approximately 3000mg daily) instead of excreting it. Such persons are more likely to develop hypertension and would most benefit from sodium restriction. Assume you are susceptible if there is a family history of hypertension.
- **Although not everyone will benefit**, all Americans are being asked to **moderate their salt and sodium intake** as a public health measure - particularly that so many do not know whether or not they have hypertension; and also because we do not know just who is salt-sensitive.

Safe Sodium Levels

The American Heart Association recommends a maximum sodium intake of 2400mg per day for adults with normal blood pressure. Many Americans have double this amount.

Persons with hypertension and kidney ailments are usually restricted to as little as **1000mg sodium per day**. Your doctor will discuss the correct sodium level for you.

Persons engaged in prolonged strenuous work or exercise may lose sodium through heavy sweating - especially in hot, humid weather. Adequate salt (and fluids) is necessary to avoid dehydration. A little extra salt at mealtimes is usually sufficient to satisfy any extra need. Do not take salt tablets.

Finding Hidden Sodium

On average, only one third of our sodium intake comes from the salt shaker. The rest is hidden in processed foods that have salt added during manufacture.

Sodium compounds added to food or medicinals can also contribute significant sodium.

Sodium bicarbonate in particular is widely used in antacid tablets and powders, and saline drink powders (such as *Alka Seltzer*). Sodium bicarbonate contains 27% sodium by weight. Each gram contributes 270mg sodium. Large amounts of sodium can be unwittingly consumed.

Other sodium compounds include monosodium glutamate (MSG), sodium ascorbate, sodium nitrite, and sodium citrate.

ALCOHOL

Excess alcohol causes up to 20% of hypertension in America.

Susceptible persons should abstain to normalize their blood pressure.

Salt-Sodium Guide

Sodium accounts for only 40% of the weight of salt (sodium chloride). Examples:
1 gram (1000mg) Salt has 400mg Sodium

1 teasp. (5g) Salt has 2000mg Sodium

Hints to Reduce Sodium

- **Watch the salt shaker.** Start with an easy 50% cut in sodium by using Lite Salt (*Morton*). Then gradually cut back until you can leave the salt shaker off the table.
- **Taste your food before salting.** Use the pepper shaker (small holes) for more controlled sprinkling of salt.
- **Choose low sodium,** sodium free, and reduced sodium products in place of regular salted products.
- **Check labels for sodium levels.** The following sodium descriptors may appear on labels:

  Reduced Sodium: At least 75% less sodium than the original product.
  Low Sodium: 140 mg or less/serving.
  Very Low Sodium: 35mg or less/serving.
  Sodium Free: Less than 5mg per serving.
- **Use reduced-sodium breads,** butter and margarine. Regular varieties contain up to 2% salt. This is considered high in view of their significant contribution to our diet.
- **Go easy on condiments and sauces** such as tomato ketchup, mustard, soy sauce and spaghetti sauces, plus salad dressings. Use low sodium varieties.
- **Limit pizzas and salty fast-foods.** Check the *Fast-Food Restaurant* Section.
- **Avoid salty snack foods** such as potato chips, corn chips, salted nuts, pretzels and cheesy-flavoured snacks. **Choose unsalted** popcorn, nuts or seeds. Eat more fruit.
- **Don't salt children's food** to your taste.
- **Limit or avoid antacids and saline powders** with sodium bicarbonate (such as *Alka-Seltzer).* They are high in sodium.

FOODS HIGH IN SODIUM

- Cheese, Butter, Margarine
- Pickles, Sauerkraut, Olives
- Condiments, Sauces
- Salad Dressings
- Canned vegetables/salads/beans
- Deli Salads (with dressing)
- Frozen/Packaged Meals/Entrees
- Soups: Canned/dry; bouillon cubes
- Meats: Ham, bacon, sausage, luncheon meats, smoked meats
- Canned Fish (in brine)
- Seasoning Salts (e.g. garlic, celery)
- Snack Foods (potato chips, pretzels)
- Tomato Jce (Canned), V8 Vegetable Juice
- Fast Foods: Pizza, Burgers, Chicken
- *Alka-Seltzer* Antacid

MODERATE SODIUM

- Bread (Reduced Salt)
- Meat, Fish, Poultry - Unprocessed
- Milk, Yogurt, Soy Drinks, Eggs
- Peanut Butter
- Breakfast Cereals (<200mg/serving)
- Chocolate Candy, Fruit/Nut Bars
- *Reduced & Low-Sodium* Products

FOODS LOW IN SODIUM

- Products labelled *Very Low Sodium,* or *Sodium Free*
- Fresh fruits and vegetables
- Canned and Dried Fruits
- Potatoes, Rice, Pasta
- Dried Beans & Lentils, Tofu
- Nuts & Seeds (unsalted)
- Corn & Popcorn (unsalted)
- Pepper, Spices, Herbs
- Jam, Honey, Syrup
- Candy, Gum
- Hard & Jelly Candy
- Coffee, Tea, Alcohol
- Fresh Fruit Juices, Water

The American Heart Association recommends a sodium intake of **less than 2400mg/day**

Sod ~ **Sodium (mg)**

Milk & Dairy Products

	Sod
Milk: Whole/lowfat/skim, average	
1 cup, 8 fl.oz	120
Whole, low sodium, 1 cup	5
Choc Milk (*Hershey's*), 1 cup	130
Human Milk, 8 fl.oz	40
Soy Milk, 8 fl.oz	30
Buttermilk, cultured, 8 fl.oz	250
Dry/Powder, skim, 1/4 cup, 1 oz	110
Yogurt: with fruit aver., 8 oz	130
Cheese:	
Blue, 1 oz	330
Parmesan, 1 oz	450
Kraft: Cheddar, 1 oz	180
Philadelphia Brand Cream Cheese	85
Process Cheese., average, 1 oz	430
Swiss, 1 oz	40
Cottage Cheese, 1/2 cup, 4 oz	450
Ricotta Cheese, 1/2 cup, 4 oz	150

Icecream, Frozen Yogurt

Icecream, average, 1/2 cup	50
Frozen Yogurt, 1/2 cup	50

Fats/Oils

Butter/Margarine:	
Regular, 2 Tbsp, 1 oz	230
Unsalted, reg., 2 Tbsp, 1 oz	5
Mayonnaise, aver., 2 Tbsp, 1 oz	160
Molly McButter, 1 tsp	120
Oils/Lard/Dripping	0
Cream, average, 1 Tbsp	6
Coffee-Mate: Powdered, 1 tsp	2
Liquid, 1 Tbsp	5

Eggs

Whole, 1 large	70
Omelet, 2 egg, plain	220
w. cheese	400
Egg Beaters (*Fleischmann's*), 1/4 cup	80

Meats

Meat, average all types, cooked (Beef/Lamb/Veal/Pork), 4 oz	80
Corned Beef, cooked, 3 oz	800
Bacon, cooked, 2 slices, 1/2 oz	270
Ham, 3 oz	1100

Chicken & Turkey

Chicken/Turkey, cooked, unsalted, 4 oz	80
Stuffing Mixes, average., 1/2 cup	500

Sausages & Meats

	Sod
Bologna, 1 oz	280
Frankfurter, 2 oz	640
Ham, chopped, 3/4 oz slice	290
Liverwurst (Braunschweiger), 1 oz	320
Pepperoni, 5 slices, 1 oz	570
Salami, cooked, 1 oz	350
dry/hard, 1 oz	600
Sausage, 1 oz link	220
Pork, 2 oz patty	260
Turkey Roll, 1 oz	160

Fish: Fresh Fish, average, plain

Cooked, 4 oz (no bone)	60
Broiled w. butter, 4 oz	150
Breaded & fried, 4 oz	320
Fish fillets, bat.-dipped 3 oz	350
Fish sticks, 1 oz stick	160
Gefilte Fish (w. broth), 1 pce, 1 1/2 oz	220
Herring, pickled, 2 pces, 1 oz	260
Lobster, meat only, 4 oz	180
Oysters, fresh, 6 med., 3 oz	95
Salmon, canned, 3 oz	460
No Salt Added, 3 oz	65
Smoked fish, average, 3 oz	650
Tuna, canned, 3 oz	330
No Added Salt, 3 oz	40

Entrees & Meals

Frozen Meals, average	600-900
Lean Cuisine, average	900
Stouffer's, average	580
Dinners, average	900-1200
Side Dishes, average	400-600
Pizza, frozen, 1/4 large, 6 oz	800-1200
Microwave Cup Meals	900-1200
Cup O'Noodles, average	1500

Fast-Foods & Restaurants

(Comprehensive listings in **Fast-Foods Section**)

Cheeseburger	750
Chicken Dinner (3 piece)	2200
Chicken Nuggets w. Sauce	800
Fish/Chicken Sandwich	1000
French Fries, small, 2 1/2 oz	150
Hamburger: Regular	500
Large with cheese	1100
Hot Dog (Frankfurter)	800
Pizza, 2 medium slices	1200
Shake, chocolate	250
Taco	400

Sodium Counter

Sod ~ **Sodium (mg)**

Soups:

	Sod
Condensed, 1 c., 8 oz	800-1000
Low Sodium	70
Chicken Noodle, 1 cup	900
Bouillon Cube, average	950
Cup-A-Soup, average	850
Lite, average	450
Soup Mixes, average, 1 cup	900

Condiments, Sauces, Dressings

	Sod
A-1 Sauce, 1 Tbsp	270
Barbecue Sauce, 1 Tbsp	130
Bragg Liquid Aminos, 1 tsp	220
Chili Sauce, 1 Tbsp	230
Ketchup: tomato, 1 Tbsp	180
Low Sodium, 1 Tbsp	20
Mayonnaise, 1 Tbsp	80
Mustard, 1 tsp	70
Pizza Sauce, 1/2 cup	700
Salad Dressings, 2 Tbsp, 1 oz	160-400
Spaghetti Sauce, 1/2 cup	500
Soy Sauce, 1 Tbsp	900
Lite *(Kikkoman)*, 1 Tbsp	600
Sweet & Sour, 1/2 cup	250
Tabasco, 1 tsp	25
Vinegar, Lemon Juice	0
Worcestershire, 1 Tbsp	200
Tomato: Sauce, 1 cup	1200
Paste/Puree (salted), 1/2 cup	1000
No Salt Added, 1/2 cup	25

Salt & Salt Substitutes

	Sod
Table Salt: 1 tsp, 6g	2400
Single Serve packet, 1 g	400
Lite Salt (*Morton*), 1 tsp, 6g	1200
No Salt Alternative, 1 tsp	5
Garlic/Seasoned Salt 1 tsp, 4g	1300
Sea Salt, 1 tsp, 5g	2250

Seasonings, Herbs & Spices

	Sod
Baking Powder, 1 tsp, 3g	340
Baking Soda (Sodium bicarb), 1 tsp, 3g	810
Accent (Flavor Enhancer), 1 tsp	600
Chili Powder, 1 tsp, 3g	25
Herbs/Spices: Curry Powder	0
Lemon Pepper (*Lawry's*), 1 tsp	340
Meat Tenderizer, 1 tsp, 5g	1750
MSG (Monosodium glutamate), 5g	500
Mrs Dash (Herb/Spice Blend), 1 tsp	0
Pepper, Mustard (dry), 1 tsp	1
Yeast, Nutritional, 1 Tbsp	10

Breakfast Cereals

	Sod
Kellogg's: All-Bran, 1/3 cup, 1 oz	260
Bran Flakes, 2/3 cup, 1 oz	220
Corn Flakes, 1 cup, 1 oz	290
Just Right, 2/3 cup, 1 oz	200
Shredded Wheat Squares, 1/2 cup, 1 oz	5
Health Valley Cereals, 1 serving	5
Quaker: Crunchy Bran, 1 oz	320
100% Natural, 1 oz	15
Puffed Rice/Wheat, 1 oz	1
Total, 1 cup, 1 oz	140
Nature Valley: Average, 1 oz	90
Oatmeal: Regular, 3/4 cup	1
Instant (*Quaker*), 2/3 cup (1 pkt)	270

Breads, Bagels, Crackers

	Sod
Bread: Average all types, 1 oz	140
Low Sodium, 1 oz	10
Bagels, plain, 2 oz	200
Sara Lee, 3 oz	500
Biscuits, average, 1 oz	180
Bun/Roll, 1 medium, 1 1/2 oz	200
Crackers: Saltine, 2 crackers	70
Low Salt (Premium), 2	45
Graham, 2 regular	50
Croissant, average, 2 oz	280
Rice Cakes, average	25
RyKrisp Crispbread, Sesame, 2	100

Cookies, Cakes, Desserts

	Sod
Cookies, average, 2-3 cookies, 1 oz	100
Mrs Fields', average, 2 1/2 oz	180
Baked Custard, 1/2 cup	100
Brownie, 1/4 oz piece	75
Cake, average, 3 oz piece	250
Cinnamon Sweet Roll, 2 oz	250
Danish, Apple	250
Donut, average	150
Muffins, 1 medium, 2 oz	150
Sara Lee, average, 2 1/2 oz	300
Pancakes, 3 x 4"	360
Pie, average 1/6 of 9" pie	300
Pudding, average, 1/2 cup	160
Jell-O (Mix), Instant, 1/2 cup	400
Waffles:	
Home-made, 7", 2 1/2 oz	350
Frozen, average, 1 1/4 oz	260
Aunt Jemima, aver., 2 1/2 oz	630

Fruit & Juices

	Sod
Fresh Fruit, average all types, 1 serving	1
Dried/Canned Fruit, 1/2 cup	1
Fruit Juice: Fresh, sqz'd, 6 fl.oz	1
Commercial, aver., 6 fl.oz	20
Carrot Juice (*Ferraro's*), 8 fl.oz	230
Tomato Juice (*Campbell's*), 6 fl.oz	570
Low Sodium (No Salt Added)	20
V8 Vegetable (*Campbell's*), 6 fl.oz	600
(No Salt Added), 6 fl.oz	45

Vegetables

Fresh/Frozen (No Salt Added), 1/2 cup

Asparagus, Bean Sprouts, Corn	3
Beets, Carrots, Celery, 1/2 cup	40
Broccoli, Cabbage, Cauliflower	10
Cucumber, Green Beans, Mushroom, Okra	3
Onions, Peas, Potato, Pumpkin, Squash	3
Peppers, Hot Chili, raw, each	3
Spinach, Turnips, 1/2 cup, ckd	40
Tomato, 1 medium, 5 oz	10
Canned: Asparagus, 4 spears	300
Beans, baked in tomato sauce	450
Beets, 1/2 cup, 3 oz	240
Corn Kernels, 1/2 cup, 3 oz	190
Creamed, 1/2 cup, 4 1/2 oz	330
Mushrooms w. butter sce, 2oz	550
Peas, 1/2 cup, 3 oz	250
Sauerkraut, 1/2 cup, 4 oz	750

Pickles, Olives

Olives, pickled: Green, 1 large	90
Ripe/black, 1 large	40
Pickles: Bread & Butter, 4 sl., 1 oz	200
Dill, 1 pickle, 2 1/2 oz	900
Sweet, 1 gherkin, 1/2 oz	130

Soybean Products

Miso (Soy Paste), 1/4 c., 2 1/2 oz	2500
Soybean Protein Isolate, 1 oz	280
Tempeh, 1/2 cup, 3 oz	5
Tofu, average, 1/2 cup, 4 oz	5

Jam, Honey, Syrups

Jam/Jelly, 1 Tbsp	2
Honey/Maple Syrup, 1 Tbsp	1
Log Cabin Syrup, 1 fl.oz	35
Lite, 1 fl.oz	90

Peanut Butter

Peanut Butter, regular, 1 Tbsp	70
Unsalted, 1 Tbsp	1

Snacks, Nuts

	Sod
Cheese Balls/Curls, 1 oz	280
Corn/Tortilla Chips, aver., 1 oz	220
Granola bars, aver., 1 bar	80
Nuts: Plain, unsalted, 1 oz	1
Lightly salted, 1 oz	80
Salted or Honey Roasted, 1 oz	160
Popcorn: Plain (unsalted), 1 cup	1
Flavored, average, 1 cup	60
Salt added, 1 cup	180
Potato Chips, plain, 1 oz	160
Flavored, average, 1 oz	250
Pretzels, regular, 3, 1 oz	450

Candy, Chocolate

Chocolate, milk, 1 oz	30
Carob Milk Bar, 1 oz	55
Fudge, chocolate, 1 oz	55
Candy Bars, average, 1 1/2 oz	60
Hard Candy, Jelly Beans, 1 oz	10
Licorice, 1 oz	30

Beverages, Alcohol

Coffee (& Substitutes), Tea, 1 cup	1
Cocoa, dry, plain, 1 Tbsp	0
Mix, average, 1 envelope	120
Quik (*Nestle*), 2 tsp	35
Soft Drinks, average, 8 fl.oz	20
Mineral Water, Perrier, 8 fl.oz	5
Gatorade Thirst Quencher, 8 fl.oz	110
Water, average, 1 cup, 8 fl.oz	5
Drier regions, 1 cup	20+
Alcohol: Beer, average, 12 fl.oz	15
Wines, average, 4 fl.oz	10
Spirits (distilled), 1 1/2 fl.oz	1

Antacids – Alka-Seltzer

	Sod
Alka-Seltzer *(Per Tablet):*	
Alka-Seltzer P.M., 1 tablet	500
Original (Light Blue Box)	570
Extra Strength (Dark Blue Box)	590
Flavored Lemon/Lime & Cherry	500
Antacid (yellow Box)	310
Gelatine Capsule, 1	0
Alka-Mints, chewable	0
Bromo Seltzer, 3/4 capful	760
Rolaids: All types	0
Tums: Regular/Extra Strength	0
Sodium Bicarbonate (27% sodium), 1g	270

FAST-FOODS INDEX ~ PAGE 161

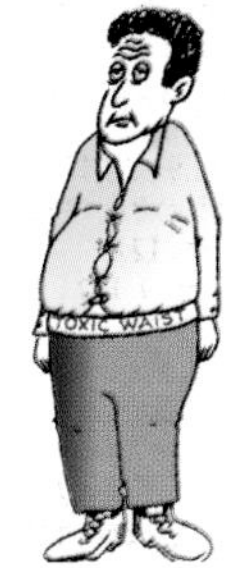
TOXIC WAIST

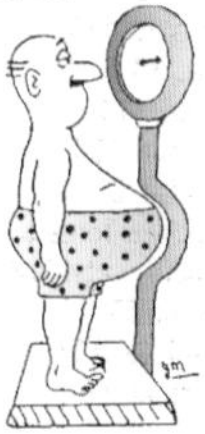

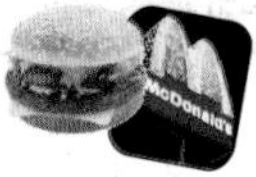

FAST-FOOD RESTAURANTS INDEX
~ SEE PAGE 161 ~

Mail Order Service

- **The Doctor's Pocket CALORIE, FAT & CARBOHYDRATE COUNTER** — **$7.00**
- **The Pocket FOOD & EXERCISE DIARY** — **$4.00**
- **STOP! Fridge Poster (8"x 8" size, with magnet)** — **$3.00**
  Extra Info ~ See Page 49
- **GROOVY GRANNY VIDEO** — **$15.00**
  June McClean's Low Impact AEROBICS FOR SENIORS (Lively fun exercises to music)
- **PEDOMETERS**
  - **Yamax (Clinical Calorie Model) Measures steps, miles, calories** — **$25.00**
  - **Omron Pedometer Measures steps, miles, time** — **$20.00**
    (Phone for Quantity Discounts)
- **BODY FAT SCALES & MONITORS**
  (Phone or see Website)

Shipping & Handling:

Add $3.00 for first item.
and $1.00 for each extra item.
(In California, add 7.75% Sales Tax)

Phone (949) 642-8500

www.calorieking.com

VISA · MasterCard · AMERICAN EXPRESS

OR Mail your order with payment to:

Family Health Publications
PO Box 1616
Costa Mesa, CA 92628

Special Quantity Discounts Available

Health Professionals, Companies, Clubs, Schools, Organizations, Fund-Raisers